INDIA and EUROPE

INDIA and EUROPE

An Essay in Philosophical Understanding

Wilhelm Halbfass

MOTILAL BANARSIDASS
PUBLISHERS PVT. LTD.
DELHI

First Indian Edition: Delhi, 1990

ISBN: 81-208-0736-7

Also available at:

MOTILAL BANARSIDASS
41 U.A., Bungalow Road, Jawahar Nagar, Delhi 110 007
120 Royapettah High Road, Mylapore, Madras 600 004
24 Race Course Road, Bangalore 560 001
Ashok Rajpath, Patna 800 004
Chowk, Varanasi 221 001

Library of Congress Cataloging-in-Publication Data

Halbfass, Wilhelm.
India and Europe: An essay in understanding.

Translation of: Indien und Europa.
Includes index.
1. Philosophy, Indic. 2. Philosophy, European.
3. Europe—Civilization—Oriental influences. I. Title.

PRINTED IN INDIA
BY JAINENDRA PRAKASH JAIN AT SHRI JAINENDRA PRESS, A-45 NARAINA INDUSTRIAL AREA, PHASE I, NEW DELHI 110 028 AND PUBLISHED BY NARENDRA PRAKASH JAIN FOR MOTILAL BANARSIDASS PUBLISHERS PVT. LTD., BUNGALOW ROAD, JAWAHAR NAGAR, DELHI 110 007.

Contents

II. The Indian Tradition and the Presence of Europe

III. Appendices: Illustrations and Reflections

Preface to the Indian Edition

This is a book not only about India, but also for Indians. It is thus very appropriate that it appears in an Indian edition. It is a book which seeks to contribute to the living dialogue between India and the West by clarifying its historical and hermeneutical conditions. Its tone may often be critical and analytical; but such analysis and critique is always motivated by an intense fascination and by the conviction that ancient and classical Indian thought is one of the most significant, still unexplored challenges to the modern Western and westernized world. We cannot expect quick and easy solutions of current problems from ancient India; this is a constant theme of the book. Yet we can and must learn from it; the predicament of modernity leaves us no choice. Indians and Westerners will have to collaborate in this difficult process of learning. They have to speak and listen to each other, and respect one another in their otherness. Mutual respect is not incompatible with mutual critique; indeed, it calls for such critique. We have to avoid the superficial rhetoric of reconciliation, harmony and ultimate identity which has often been a temptation in comparative philosophy and in the East-West dialogue. Such rhetoric cannot do justice to the extraordinary greatness and complexity of the classical Indian tradition of thought and debate, which was, after all, an intensely critical tradition.

This is a book by a European who has spent many years in America, teaching and studying Indian philosophy, and who has also lived, taught and studied in various Asian countries. The prefaces to the different editions of the book reflect this cosmopolitan dimension. The preface to the original German edition was written in America; the preface to the American edition was written in Japan; the preface to the present Indian edition is being written in Germany. However, what is much more important than such geographical diversity is a genuine "fusion of horizons", i.e., a combination and merger of the spiritual and philosophical horizons of India and Europe. It is hoped that this book, in spite of its limited historical perspective, will make at least a modest and preliminary contribution to this goal.

In the preface to the American edition, I announced a companion volume dealing with central issues of traditional Indian thought and self-understanding, including such topics as reason and revelation, ritualism and ethics, karma and rebirth, man, nature, and society. This volume has now been completed and gone to the press. Its title is "Tradition and Reflection. Philosophy in the Light and Shadow of the Veda". In the same preface, I referred to my friend and mentor, Professor J. L. Mehta, my partner-in-dialogue and one of the most subtle, serious and sensitive East-West thinkers. Professor Mehta passed away in 1988, while on a visit to America. I dedicate this edition to his memory.

WILHELM HALBFASS

Berlin
Wissenschaftskolleg/Institute for
Advanced Study
October 1989

Preface

India and Europe: An Essay in Understanding is, indeed, nothing but an essay, a preliminary attempt, an introduction. There is no need to enlarge upon what could or should have been done in order to do justice to the magnitude of the topic. The basic limitations are obvious from the presentation itself: This is *not* a book on the current situation or the most recent developments in the "East-West dialogue," nor is it a comprehensive history of the mutual relations and influences between India and Europe. Instead, it is an attempt to describe and clarify some of the historical presuppositions of their mutual understanding, specifically in such areas as religion, philosophy and science. It is an attempt to show how Indians and Europeans have viewed each other in these areas of encounter, how they have asserted and questioned themselves, what they have expected from each other, how they have articulated their own identity, and how they have dealt with the otherness of the other.

In this sense, the book is an "essay in *understanding*"—an attempt to clarify and "understand" horizons of self-understanding and perspectives of mutual understanding and, perhaps, to articulate some of the basic problems and ambiguities concerning the global process of "Westernization." That ancient and classical Indian thought continues to provide deep, though elusive challenges to our modern Westernized world, and to the global constellation of science and technology, is one of the premises of this presentation. *India and Europe* deals primarily with images, projections, theoretical responses and reflections, as they occurred in the history of encounters between these two great cultural domains. It seems to neglect the "real world" of social, anthropological, economic, political, and military events and conditions. But the sense in which projections, ideas, fundamental "theoretical" orientations and hermeneutic constellations reflect and shape this "real world," and are realities themselves, should not be underestimated.

The German original of this book appeared in 1981 under the title *Indien und Europa: Perspektiven ihrer geistigen Begegnung*. The reception and response, in the form of numerous reviews, private communications, exchanges and discussions with scholars of different disciplines, and from a variety of Western and Eastern countries, have been both gratifying and stimulating. The process of thinking about the questions raised in this book, and the accumulation of relevant information, have continued. As a consequence, *India and Europe* is much more than a translation of *Indien und Europa*. It has been thoroughly revised and updated, although nothing of substance has been withdrawn or fundamentally altered. No effort has been made to conceal the original European background of the book, or the fact that its approach to India is committed to certain Continental European ways of thinking. Even its external appearance and organization reflect, to some extent, its origin and background; the fact that publishers are not mentioned in the bibliographical references is an example. However, much new material has been added to the twenty chapters contained in the original edition; this includes a new section on Schelling. Most significantly, the new edition contains four major appendices (i.e., chapters 21–24) that deal with the history and the intercultural implications of such crucial and exemplary notions as "experience" and "tolerance," as well as with the history and methodology of comparison itself. These four appendices are adaptations of presentations that followed, and were directly related to, the publication of *Indien und Europa*. Chapter 21 is a greatly enlarged English version of an article first published in *Epiphanie des Heils*, edited by G. Oberhammer (Vienna, 1981). Chapter 22 is a revised translation of a contribution to *Inklusivismus. Eine indische Denkform*, also edited by G. Oberhammer (Vienna, 1983). Major parts of chapter 23 are based upon an article published in PEW 25 (1985). Chapter 24 is an abbreviated version of a presentation given at the Papal Summer Residence (Castel Gandolfo, Italy) in August, 1987. The full text will be published in several languages, including Hebrew and German.

A companion volume to *India and Europe*, with the tentative title *In the Light of the Veda*, will discuss related questions concerning traditional and "orthodox" Indian self-understanding from a more technically Indological angle. This collection of previously published and new, unpublished investigations is now close to completion and should follow within a year. Several other recent and forthcoming publications enlarge upon, or were utilized for, different sections of *India and Europe*. Among these, I would like to mention: "Hegel on Meditation and Yoga," *Zen Buddhism Today, Annual Report of the Kyoto Zen Symposium* 3 (1984); "Hegel, Schelling, Schopenhauer und Indien," *Zeitschrift für Kulturaustausch* (Stuttgart) 37/3 (1987); "Schopenhauer im Gespräch mit der indischen Tradition,"

Schopenhauer und das Denken der Gegenwart, edited by V. Spierling (Munich, 1987). "Early Indian References to the Greeks and the First Western References to Buddhism," a contribution to a symposium on the date of the historical Buddha, held in 1988 under the auspices of the Academy of Sciences in Göttingen and to be published in its proceedings, discusses questions raised in chapters 1 and 11 in greater detail.

Finally, it is my pleasant duty to acknowledge the encouragement and support I have received from many sides, from persons as well as from institutions. I cannot give a full account; I have to be selective. Generous financial support was, above all, provided by Inter Nationes (Bonn). This was supplemented by the Department of South Asia Regional Studies and the Research Foundation of the University of Pennsylvania (Philadelphia). Frank Korom and David Purpur, graduate students at the University of Pennsylvania, provided most valuable and competent assistance in producing the final manuscript of the translation. But most of all, I am indebted to John Baker. Without his cheerful and flexible cooperation, and without his experience as a translator, the work would certainly not have been completed by now. He is primarily responsible for chapters 3–5, 7–9, 12–14, and 16–19. Although I revised and sometimes rewrote the drafts he sent to me from Hamburg in a way that he may not find entirely agreeable, he deserves principal credit for these sections. In the remaining sections, I often took the liberty of re-articulating my own thoughts, instead of merely translating my own words. The fact that this translation represents a collaborative effort may help to explain (although it does not excuse) certain stylistic discrepancies, as well as occasional inconsistencies in other areas, including bibliographical conventions.

Harvey Alper, who supported this project in its early stages, did not live to see its completion. In the final stages of proofreading etc., I enjoyed the company and encouragement of friends and colleagues in Japan, in particular Richard F. Young and Minoru Hara. Among those from whom I received intellectual and "hermeneutical" inspiration during my work on both the German and the English versions of this book, I have to mention Jarava Lal Mehta. It would be difficult to imagine a better partner-in-dialogue.

University of Tokyo
February 1988

Extracts from the Preface to the Original German Edition

"There ought to be a philosophizing which is based on an immediate knowledge of Indian *and* European sources."

(P. Hacker, Kl. Schr., p. 38).

The following presentation attempts to contribute to a better understanding of the spiritual and intellectual relations between India and Europe. The exposition leads us only to the threshold of the present era, which is not included in its theme. It deals with the historical and hermeneutical presuppositions of the philosophical "dialogue" between India and Europe. It does, however, not explicitly discuss the current situation and its future possibilities. The course of this dialogue so far and the development of "comparative" philosophizing have shown that a clarification of the historical conditions is indispensable for any discourse between the traditions, if it is not to be philosophically naive.

The chapters of this book investigate first of all the role of India in the philosophical thought of Europe since the days of classical antiquity and then the reception of European philosophy in Indian thought as well as the tension between traditional and modern Indian self-understanding. The book does not aim at exposing and "correcting" prejudices and misunderstandings; it is, however, concerned with historical and hermeneutical critique. This critique may, when it comes to Neo-Hindu thinking and self-understanding, appear very pronounced. It is, nevertheless, based upon the conviction that our European philosophizing has by no means surpassed or superseded the Indian tradition. The final words of chapter 20 may serve as an introductory note: "Modern Indian thought finds itself in a historical context created by Europe, and it has difficulties speaking for itself. Even in its self-representation and self-assertion, it speaks to a large extent in a European idiom. This does not, however, mean that the dialogue and debate between India and Europe has been decided in favor of Europe, or that India has been superseded by Europe. The power of the Indian tradition has not exhausted itself in the self-representation and self-interpretation of modern India. The dialogic situation is still open." Those in particular who are prepared to accept the Indian tradition as a philosophical challenge, or as a challenge to philosophy itself, must be attentive to the historical forms of its transmission and cannot afford to disregard philological and hermeneutical details.

The following chapters aim at a combination and even integration of Indological and historically oriented philosophical work which may appear unusual and problematic to Indologists as well as to philosophers and historians of philosophy. I am fully aware that the result of my efforts is not without idiosyncratic features. It reflects an academic career which from the outset was guided by Indological and philosophical interests, and which subsequently led me to partly Indological, partly philosophical appointments in several North American and European universities. Thus, from different sources and situations much has accumulated which created the necessary momentum to go beyond specialized investigations and to venture upon a comprehensive and synthetic effort such as the present study. Such synthesis is obviously not without risk. But it has to be undertaken if the results and perspectives of specialized research in the different scholarly disciplines are to be joined in a new context of knowledge and understanding, instead of being left to what E. Troeltsch has termed the "bookbinder's synthesis" (ch. 20, §6).

The book summarizes and coordinates materials which have been accumulated in many years of teaching and research. More specifically, it makes use of some of my earlier publications. A first sketch for major parts of the present work is found in my article "Indien und die Geschichtsschreibung der Philosophie" (*Philosophische Rundschau 23,* 1976, 104–131). Two further articles have been incorporated into chapters 6 and 15 respectively: "Hegel on the Philosophy of the Hindus" (*German Scholars on India*, vol. 1, Benares 1973, 107–122) and "Observations on *darśana*" (WZKS 23, 1979, 195–203).

While preparing and writing this book, I received much personal and institutional support. The work with my graduate students, and in particular the supervision of dissertations, was an important part of my own learning process. A number of colleagues in America as well as in Germany have helped me with useful information and advice. In particular, I want to thank Gerhard Böwering and David McAlpin for their advice concerning the Arabic-Persian and Dravidian areas respectively, as well as Lambert Schmithausen for his valuable observations and suggestions, primarily with reference to Buddhist thought. This book, especially its second part, is greatly indebted to the work of Paul Hacker. After his retirement in 1978, I accepted his invitation to represent his chair at the University of Münster until the fall of 1979 and, at the same time, to complete the second part of the book. It is a tragic coincidence that Paul Hacker died during this period, on March 18, 1979. This book is dedicated to his memory.

Notes on Transliteration and the Spelling of Indian Names

Transliterations from Sanskrit (commonly written in the *Devanāgarī* script) are in accordance with the internationally accepted scientific system, with certain adjustments in the treatment of *sandhi*. As far as possible, the same system has been used for transliterations from modern Indian languages written in *Devanāgarī* or related scripts. This means that the mute *a* usually appears in the transcriptions of modern Indian terms and names, and generally in all words with a clearly recognizable Sanskritic background (*tatsama; tadbhava*); it was dropped only in non-Sanskritic, specifically vernacular particles and grammatical forms. Modern Indian names, for which there is a commonly accepted Anglicized or otherwise simplified spelling, usually appear in this form and not in their scientific transliteration. In borderline cases, different spellings may appear in accordance with different contexts, or an alternate spelling is given in parenthesis. The index may be consulted for all ambiguous or questionable cases.

Names of cities, specifically places of publication, are generally given in their Anglicized forms (e.g., *Benares* instead of *Vārāṇasī*). Arabic and Persian terms and names, for which there is no single and universally accepted system of transliteration, have in some cases been simplified. Older and obsolete forms of Romanization have been preserved or used in addition to the scientific transliteration whenever this seemed to be historically informative or required by the context. While the spelling has in general been adjusted to current orthographic norms, certain peculiarities of Indian English (specifically the use of *s* instead of *z* in words like "reali*s*ation") have been preserved.

Because of technical problems beyond the control of the author, Greek words appear without accents.

I

India in the History of European Self-Understanding

1. The Philosophical View of India in Classical Antiquity

1. Looking back at the history of European speculation about and fascination with India G.W.F. Hegel (1770–1831), a contemporary and careful observer of the beginnings of modern Indian studies, characterized India as a land which had exerted its world-historical influence in a passive manner, by being sought: "Without being known too well, it has existed for millenia in the imagination of the Europeans as a wonderland. Its fame, which it has always had with regard to its treasures, both its natural ones, and in particular, its wisdom, has lured men there."[1] In Hegel's view, the beginnings of modern research and European domination over Asia mark the end of this search for India's mythical wisdom and "philosophy". India cannot teach the West; its tradition is a matter of the past; it has never reached the level of philosophy and science which is a genuinely and uniquely European achievement.[2]

Is Hegel's scheme of historical subordination and his association of the idea of philosophy with the historical identity and destiny of Europe entirely obsolete? Does it reflect the attitude of his own time and the earlier history of European interest in India? To what extent has it influenced its subsequent development? Has it finally been superseded by the progress of Indian and "Oriental" studies and by the results of objective historical research? But to what extent is such research itself a European phenomenon and part of European self-affirmation? To what extent does it reflect European perspectives and motivations? How, on the other hand, has the encounter with India, the accumulation of information about it, affected the European self-understanding and sense of identity? Has it affected the meaning of religion and philosophy itself? How and why did Europeans become interested in Indian thought? Which questions and expectations did they have concerning India and themselves? How much "search" for "Indian wisdom" has there been, and what is its significance?

Modern Indological research and the systematic exploration of India's religious and philosophical tradition began in Hegel's own time, with the foundation of the Asiatic Society of Bengal (1784), and the works of W. Jones, Ch. Wilkins and H. Th. Colebrooke. But the encounter between Europe and India, as well as the development of interest in, attitudes towards, and images of Indian life and wisdom began much earlier, and can be traced back to classical antiquity. There is certainly no coherent history of European search for India. Indeed, there are periods of neglect and latency, along with much casual response to casual information and random encounters. Yet, there is an identifiable historical path leading to the situation of modern Indological research and of intercultural communication. It is a process which accompanies and reflects the development of European thought in general—a process in which Europe has defined and questioned itself, and in which misunderstandings and prejudices may be as significant as the accumulation of factual truth and correct information.

2. When the Greek doxographer Diogenes Laërtius, writing in the third century A.D., referred to the question of the beginning of philosophy and tried to determine whether it was of autochthonous, Greek or of foreign, Oriental origin, he summarized and continued a debate which had been going on for centuries.[3] Along with the Persian "Magi," Chaldeans and Egyptians, the Indian "gymnosophists" are among the groups which are usually mentioned in these debates. Such debates are also documented in the works of other ancient authors such as Clement of Alexandria.[4] Diogenes introduces us to the question of the origin of philosophy in the opening sentences of his "Lives and Opinions of Eminent Philosophers." Referring to the *Magikos* by Ps. Aristotle and the *Diadoche* by Sotion of Alexandria,[5] he mentions and subsequently refutes the thesis that philosophy had its origin among the barbarians.

Diogenes' reputation is that of a compiler; he presents and arranges his materials without any deeper understanding, and he does not provide philosophical perspectives of his own. His discussion of the origin and autonomy of Greek philosophy follows mostly older opinions.[6] He also neglects the "latest views" of his contemporaries in this matter. Neoplatonist, Neopythagorean, Jewish and Christian philosophers, who responded to this question with new intensity while presenting the relationship between Greek and Oriental culture in new and different perspectives and contexts, receive only slight attention in Diogenes' discussion. Diogenes is hellenizing and "classicist" in approach. Further, in spite of his "compilatory" style, his personal position in the controversy with which he introduces his work is unambiguous: the origin of philosophy, in his view, is Greek and nothing but Greek. He goes on to state that the term "philosophy" itself defies all attempts at translation into Oriental, "barbaric" languages.[7]

3. The question of the origin and autonomy of philosophy has stayed alive for many centuries, and it has been revived in more recent periods of European thought. It has affected the European approach to Indian and "Oriental" thought in various ways. It has aided the focusing of attention on this thought, but has also contributed to its dismissal and neglect. The renewal of classical studies in the post-medieval period has also revived the Greek concern with the origin of their philosophical traditions. To a considerable extent, the rediscovery and direct influence of Diogenes Laërtius himself, from Walter de Burleigh (fourteenth century) to J. Brucker (1696–1770) and beyond, were instrumental in renewing the doxographic interest, and with it, the question of the potential Oriental roots of Western thought. In the perspective of this question, Indian and Asian thought are significant only insofar as they provide a background and basis for the history of European philosophy.

But even in more recent works on the history of philosophy, which are no longer under the specific influence of Diogenes and the doxographic method in general, the treatment of the Orient and India is often confined to brief remarks concerning the origin or "prehistory" of Greek thought. Moreover, referring to the Orient may just be a device to demarcate and identify the alleged core and essence of Greek philosophy, the step "from myth to *logos*," and the "spontaneous development" of scientific thinking and autonomous reasoning with the Greeks.[8] In a variety of ways, India has also been included in discussions concerning the origin and background of Christianity.[9]

In the present context we are not concerned with the probability and the extent of actual historical influences of the Orient, and in particular of India, on early Occidental thought.[10] Instead, we are focusing on the role of India in the philosophical awareness of the ancients, their ways of viewing India, the development of thought which prompted the interest in India, and the intellectual horizon within which the Greeks themselves asked the question concerning the originality of their way of thinking and the possibility of their own tradition's having Oriental roots.[11]

Before we deal more specifically with the role of India in the philosophical thought and self-understanding of the Greeks, it will be useful to say a few words about the ancient, especially the Greek, view of the Orient and the non-Greek world in general.

4. The entire complex of questions related to this issue has been assessed by E. Zeller in a manner which is still significant today. After a critical presentation of various speculative views concerning actual Oriental sources for the Greek approach to philosophy (especially the theories of E. Röth and A. Gladisch), he remarks on the Greek attitude towards the question of origin:

The Greeks themselves were inclined from early times, as we know, to grant the peoples of the Orient, the only ones whose intellectual culture preceded their own, that they had a share in the origination of their philosophy. In the early days it is only individual doctrines which in this manner are derived from the Orient. The claim that Greek philosophy as a whole stems from there comes, as far as we know, not from the Greeks but from certain Orientals. By making this claim, Greek-educated Jews of the Alexandrian school attempted to explain, with their own position and interest in mind, the supposed agreement of their religious regulations with the doctrines of the Greeks. In a similar manner, the Egyptian priests, having, under the Ptolemaic rule, become acquainted with Greek philosophy, prided themselves on the wisdom which not only prophets and poets but also philosophers had supposedly obtained from them. Some time later the Greeks themselves adopted this view as their own.[12]

Zeller's opinion became widely accepted, explicitly or tacitly. Among the relatively rare cases of criticism we find F. Schäfer's response, in his dissertation *Quid Graeci de origine philosophiae a barbaris ducenda existimaverint, secundum Laertii Diogenis prooemium exponitur* (Leipzig, 1877). His thesis, directed against Zeller, says that the doctrine of the Oriental origin of Greek philosophy could also be found in the thought of the Greeks themselves, independently of the claims of extra-Greek circles.[13]

Certainly, it would be difficult to prove that the view of the "barbaric" origin of Greek philosophy goes back to no other but Egyptian, Jewish or, in later times, Christian sources.[14] On the other hand, neither Schäfer nor any other authors who wrote on this subject have been able to produce unambiguous testimony from classical times which places the origin of philosophy wholly in the Orient, although manifold forms of wisdom as well as the development of important skills and insights may have been attributed to the Orient from the earliest days.[15]

5. The relationship between Greek thought and the world outside of Greece, the Orient, is marked by a particular ambivalence. It is precisely the openness for the possibility of alien sources, the readiness to learn and the awareness of such readiness which sustains the Greek claim of being different from the Orient. In fact, ἱστορια implies "openness for the alien, the other." Claiming such openness is a means of Greek self-identification and self-definition.

ἱστορειν is essentially connected with curiosity, with openness, and with journeys outside of Greece. Not only the "historians," but also the philosophers, are traditionally considered as widely travelled. Regardless of what may be legendary in these traditions, "undeniable in any case is a philosophical atmosphere in which the knowledge of the wide world plays a part."[16]

Ethnography presents itself as an exemplary discipline which also affects philosophical thought in this respect. Here, the antithesis of *nomos* and *physis*, which was so important for the development of Greek thought, for its particular freedom and tension, found its most distinctive and exemplary expression.[17] Greek thinking opens itself to far-reaching possibilities and problems along with its readiness to look upon itself and its indigenous customs and manners as examples among others; it practices a self-detachment and self-objectification which the Sophists push to the level of self-relativization, and prepares itself for "a reflection in foreign eyes."[18]

6. It is symptomatic that the earliest authenticated use of the word "philosophize" occurs in a context where there is mention of travels in foreign lands, and of "travelling for the sake of theory."[19] Also, Pythagoras, the alleged inventor of the word "philosophy," is frequently connected with the idea of travelling and exploring as well as a "purely theoretical" watching and viewing. A report which may have been handed down by Plato's disciple Heracleides Ponticus, has it that he compared the attitude of the philosopher to that of the "mere spectator" at the Olympic Games, who was free of any striving after profit.[20] In addition, Pythagoras is said to have defined philosophy as something strictly human, as a conscious giving-up of the claim of "wisdom," which must be reserved for God.[21] At the same time the idea of "wisdom" is also associated with Greek pre-history and, especially, with the traditions of the Orient.

At a further stage in the development, Pythagoras, supposedly the representative of a specifically Greek concept of philosophy and theory, also ranks increasingly as the recipient and transmitter of Oriental wisdom. He is presented to us for the first time in Isocrates' *Busiris* as a traveller to Egypt.[22] According to the later view, which emerges in Neopythagorean thought, his receptivity towards the Orient exemplifies a dissolution of the Greek sense of autonomy. This interpretation is certainly incompatible with the classical tradition. Here the openness and willingness to learn still appears as an expression of Greek independence and originality. The spirit of theory, of science, of *logos*, is distinguished from whatever may have been received from the Orient, as the Greek's own potential of appropriation and transformation.[23] Herodotus, Plato and Aristotle emphasize the Greek debt to the Orient. However, they equally stress the independence of Greek thought.[24] Plato contrasts the Greeks' desire for pure knowledge with the ultimately pragmatic efforts of the Phoenicians and Egyptians.[25] In a widely influential model, Aristotle presents Thales as the autochthonous Greek founder of philosophizing.[26] The Platonic *Epinomis*, typical of the classical era, says that whatever the Greeks may owe to the "barbarians," they ultimately make it better and ennoble it.[27] This view has frequently been renewed in more recent European thought. For instance, Hegel incorporates it in a very pronounced manner into his scheme of a universal history: "Just as intellectual culture in general, the Greeks, to be sure, have received alien impulses; the very fact that they have transformed these, however, is what constitutes their own intellectual culture. They have received, but also suspended, the Asian principle."[28] In Überweg's *Grundriss* we read: "The main point is that the religious ideas of the Orient, even if they had been transmitted to the Greeks, would not suffice to explain what is essential and typical of Greek philosophy, the free speculation on the nature of things."[29]

7. The consciousness of what is Greek and what is alien, the interpretation of "philosophy" and "wisdom" and the attitude toward the Orient change fundamentally during the final part of classical antiquity. Another kind of receptivity takes the place of the curiosity and openness of the ἱστορεῖν. The external, but by no means merely accidental, event which opens up much vaster dimensions for the Western view of the Orient, and totally new possibilities for the relationship of East and West, is the appearance of the "world conqueror" Alexander. This event overcomes more than external barriers, and represents more than merely a military conquest. The idea of a genuine cultural encounter between East and West, a synthesis as it were, a marriage of Orient and Occident, has been associated with Alexander's conquests from the beginning, and we may assume that this was also a part of his own world-view.

In this connection, the Greek-Persian mass-wedding at Susa, the historicity of which may well be accepted, has symbolic as well as pragmatic significance. The boundaries change; the relationship between Greeks and barbarians, between Orient and Occident, changes; East and West move closer together within the context of a new universality and globality. It is certainly no mere coincidence that the Stoic idea of the "cosmopolitan" is articulated during this era. The whole world is, in the eyes of Marcus Aurelius, "like a city."[30] The sage "dwells" in the world, he places himself within the sphere of a common East/West humanity, of a common νοερον, a common λογος. The Stoic idea of cosmopolitanism is, however, largely an abstract idea, a basic and general recognition of the foreigner, the alien, the "barbarian" in his humanness, without any real recognition of the concrete intercultural problems of access and understanding. Furthermore, the conception of the world as "polis" follows a Grecocentric orientation. Nevertheless, the historical potential of this idea remains considerable.

The diverse tendencies towards identification, "syncretism," and universalism, are among the most familiar, most frequently invoked chacteristics of the religious life of this epoch. The idea of a divine being, appearing in various shapes, under many names and being worshipped differently by different nations and religious traditions, is exemplified on a grand scale by the cult of Isis.[31] Isis is πολυμορφος and πολυωνυμος, has many forms and names. In Apuleius she appears as a universal goddess.[32]

8. The Greeks turn to the Orient with a new attitude. But it is not only their changing attitude, it is also the reception and adaptation of Greek thought by "Orientals," which characterizes the situation of philosophical thought during and after the Hellenistic age. The participation of the Orient in the context of the "encounter" provides a new standard for Greek thinking and self-understanding. It is well-known that thinkers of Oriental descent have a decisive share in the continuation and reinterpretation of Greek philosophical traditions in Hellenism and in late antiquity. Suffice it to recall the names of Zeno, Plotinus, Posidonius, and Porphyry. However, the extent to which originally Oriental religious traditions and movements avail themselves of Greek concepts and theories, as a medium of expressing themselves as well as a contrasting background of self-definition and self-demarcation, is historically more important, and hermeneutically more remarkable. This development is exemplified by Egyptian, Phoenician, and most persistently, Jewish and Christian thinkers. Alexandria, Alexander's Egyptian city, was the center of such efforts. Their goal is, on the one hand, to present their own tradition *as philosophy*, to prove that it is philosophy in accordance with the Greek tradition, and on the other hand, to demonstrate that it represents superior wisdom, that it surpasses and transcends Greek thought. Either mode seeks self-understanding through Greek conceptualization. They utilize Greek thought as a medium and context for reinterpreting and articulating their own religious traditions and convictions. A decisive influence upon the whole development, not only in Judaism but also in Christianity and Islam, came from Philo the Alexandrian, who lived at the beginning of the Christian era.[33] Authors such as Clement of Alexandria and Origen were among the most important Christian representatives of this process of appropriation. Their thought opened new perspectives on the meaning of philosophy, and the Greek tradition of autonomous, rational thinking. It also led to new questions concerning the relationship of philosophy and religion, as well as the relationship between Orient and Occident.

The church father Eusebius relates the tradition, supposedly going back to the Aristotelian Aristoxenus (ca. 300B.C.), that an Indian visited Socrates, the philosopher *par excellence*, in Athens, and asked him about the meaning of his philosophizing. When Socrates replied that he was studying problems of human life, the Indian laughed and explained that it was impossible to study and understand human things without considering the divine.[34] It is the idea of an original wisdom—leaving religion and philosophy, metaphysics and ethics, God and man undivided—which is thus invoked against the concept and project of philosophy as a rational, merely human enterprise.

9. The thesis of the Oriental origin gained increasing significance among Egyptians, Jews and other "Orientals" who claimed the Greek tradition of thought as their own.[35] In the works of some Christian authors, especially Clement of Alexandria,[36] the thesis of the Oriental "barbarian" origin takes a new and peculiar turn: It becomes a means of criticizing the Greek confidence in human reason, the uniqueness of the Hellenic tradition, and their proud proclamation of philosophy and theory. From the point of view of the Christian belief in revelation, this tradition represents nothing unique at all: basically, it remains at the same level as the "heathen" thought of the Orient, to which it owes its origin and direction. In this sense, the entire range of the "natural," "worldly" *logos*, comprising Oriental and Greek thought, may be contrasted with the fulfilling revelation of Christianity. However, radical reinterpretations and far-reaching reductions to Oriental wisdom occur not only in situations where the Greek, "heathen" tradition of philosophy is confronted by revealed religion, but also in purely "pagan" movements of philosophical restoration and renewal. Here, too, a new attitude emerges, a readiness to look for Oriental origins and sources as well as to see the founders of the great movements of Greek thought as being indebted to the Orient, or to present them as mere transmitters or spokesmen of Oriental wisdom. This includes late Platonism and, even more so, Neopythagoreanism. Numenius of Apameia (second century A.D.), both a Platonist and a Pythagorean, refers to Plato as an "atticizing Moses."[37] His younger contemporary Philostratus presents Pythagoras as a recipient and transmitter of Egyptian and, ultimately, Indian wisdom. In general, he attempts to derive Greek philosophy from Oriental manticism.[38] Porphyry reports[39] that Plotinus tried to gain personal access to the sources of Oriental wisdom. Occasionally authors of non-Oriental origin present themselves in Oriental guise, such as the presumably Greek author of the "Chaldean oracles" (probably the theurge Julianus at the time of Marcus Aurelius). The Neoplatonist Iamblichus (ca. 300A.D.) also plays an important and exemplary role.

10. We now find a new readiness for what is most ancient, original, prior and inaccessible to progress and change, and for the continuity and power of traditions not affected by rationality, scepticism and relativity. In the first century A.D., Diodorus cites the spirit of those ancient traditions and nations which despise the philosophy of the Greeks, because it is so new and constantly changing. Around 200 A.D., Claudius Aelianus states that no Indian, Celt or Egyptian ever expressed such doubts concerning the existence of the Gods and divine providence that could be compared with the radical criticism of religion put forth by Euhemerus, Diagoras and Epicurus.[40]

Ancient and original wisdom in this sense is not only a matter of the distant past, and it concerns not only the question of the past origins of the

Greek tradition. Instead, it has become a present and actual challenge; the most ancient seems to surpass what is most modern and advanced. The idea of philosophy as a human, provisional and always unfinished search, is eclipsed by the idea of an integral, primeval wisdom, which is inaccessible to the self-confident curiosity of Hellenic ιστορια (*historia*) and θεωρια (*theoria*). Such curiosity now tends to give way to expectations of hidden wisdom and secret revelation. There is a distinct sense of readiness for changing one's conceptual presuppositions, and for knowledge which amounts to transformation.[41]

The Greek cultural and military expansion itself – Alexander's conquests as well as the application of Greek conceptual thought to Oriental traditions – opens new channels for the influx of foreign, Oriental ideas which threaten the identity and continuity of the Hellenic tradition. The legend of the Egyptian Nektanebo, the alleged father of Alexander, which we find in the *Alexander Romance*, illustrates the ambiguity of the Greek military and intellectual conquests. According to this legend, the great conqueror of the Orient was himself a product of the Orient; in him and with him, the Orient itself created the conditions for its conquest by Greece and Europe. Through this process, it somehow emerged victorious in being conquered.[42]

11. What then is the status of India within the classical image of the Orient? What did Greeks and Romans know about it? Which specific questions did they ask about it? To what extent was India simply included in the general image of Asia, the Orient, the non-Greek, "barbarian" world? To what extent, and since when, was it referred to individually as a country, with special features and an identity of its own?

Homer mentions two Ethiopias, one of which was later identified, or at least associated, with India.[43] However, this association is uncertain, mythical and without any tangible and specific content. In general, we can characterize the entire period prior to the Indian campaign of Alexander the Great (327–325B.C.) as follows: India is viewed as a peripheral phenomenon, a vaguely conceived realm at or beyond the Eastern horizon of the known world. There is no specific concept of Indian cultural achievements, no specific speculation about its potential influence on Greece, no "search" for India.

Egypt plays the most distinctive role as a precursor or cultural partner in this regard, although recent research suggests that the actual historical and cultural impact of the Phoenician, Hurritic and Hittite traditions may have been at least equally significant.[44] In general, India is outside the shared world of cultural interaction by which pre-classical Greece is affected and in which it participates.

The encounter with Asia turns into a confrontation with the expansion of the Persian empire and its assault upon Greece. It is in this confrontation that the idea of Europe and the "myth of the Orient and Occident" takes shape.[45] Nevertheless, the relationship between Hellas and Iran is not merely one of hostility and confrontation. Its complexity and ambiguity finds exemplary expression in the fact that Themistocles, the Greek victor in the battle of Salamis (480B.C.), later joined the Persians and ended his life as their vassal. The Persians employed a large number of Greeks—whom they called *yauna*—in their service. In this way, Persia became a mediator between Greece and India, and also served as a conduit for the transmission of information or speculation about India to the West.[46] Both Scylax of Karyanda and Ctesias of Knidos, authors of the two standard descriptions of India before Alexander the Great, were in Persian service. Scylax, who in the years 519–516 B.C. explored the Indus region for the Persian ruler Darius I, is the first recorded European traveller in India. "The geographical picture of the Indus region which the Scylax expedition had created, remained practically unchanged until the Indian campaign of Alexander the Great."[47] The works of Scylax and, even more so, of Ctesias, whom his contemporaries already accused of uninhibited exaggeration and fiction, became notorious and famous for their broad emphasis on the miraculous, the fabulous and the exotic. Their stories of bizarre creatures and "fabulous races" played their part in the European image of India up to the Middle Ages and beyond. However we assess the reliability of Scylax and Ctesias, some of these fabulous creatures have clearly identifiable counterparts in Indian mythology and literature, for instance the "dog-headed" creatures (κυνοκεφαλοι; Sanskrit *śunāmukha* or *śvamukha*), those with "blanket ears" (ωτολικνοι; Sanskrit *karṇaprāvaraṇa*) or the "one-footed" and "shadow-footed" (*μονοκωλοι, σκιαποδες*; Sanskrit *ekapāda*, etc.).[48]

As far as we can judge from the references in other works and the few extant fragments, the religion and philosophy of India did not yet play a distinctive part in the works of Scylax and Ctesias.[49] However, it appears that some ideas which later generations associated frequently and commonly with Indian religion and the Indian way of life, such as vegetarianism (even though we also find associations with cannibalism) and the contempt for death, already emerged in the pre-Alexandrian image of India.[50]

We have no indication whether Greeks expected to find "treasures of wisdom" in India during that period. Reports on travels to India, or other Indian connections, of Greek philosophers are not found in Greek literature before Alexander. Above all, Egypt continues to be seen as a storehouse of ancient learning, a tradition which precedes that of the Greeks and deserves attention as a possible source of inspiration for them.

12. Alexander's campaign into Northwestern India (327–325B.C.) initiates an entirely new period of encounter. Hellenistic tradition from this time onward connects the military advance with the idea of a genuine religious and

philosophical encounter coupled with explicit dialogue.[51] We learn that several philosophers travelling in Alexander's entourage met Indian sages, specifically Onesicritus, the Alexander historian and Cynic, one of the founders of this literary tradition, as well as Anaxagoras, the Democritean, and Pyrrho, the radical sceptic.[52] Moreover, the ruler himself is presented in conversation or correspondence with the gymnosophists, the "naked sages" of India.[53] In this case, we can once again disregard questions concerning historical truth and accuracy. It is the attitude as such, manifested by these traditions, which is of interest, i.e., the readiness to accept the possibility of a philosophical partnership, of debate and instruction, in what is foreign, specifically Indian.

The literature about Alexander does not question that the concept of philosophy can be applied to the teaching and way of life of the Indian sages. Of course, everything remains vague as far as content is concerned. Basically, the Greeks present the Indian sages as exemplifying a concept or ideal of practical and ethical wisdom, which may be associated with the idea of a an antithesis of Alexander's activism, or even that of antidote for the *hybris* of the world conqueror. In this sense, the "Brahmins" and "naked sages" of the early historians of Alexander[54] became exemplary figures in Greek and Roman literature. According to Strabo,[55] Alexander's admiral Nearchus had already divided the Indian sages into two classes: those who acted as political advisors, and those who investigated nature. However, it is not these two activities of the Indian sages which attracted the interest of the Hellenistic world. It is, rather, their way of life, their immunity against pain and pleasure, their contempt of death and their indifference towards customs and social conventions. The gymnosophist Kalanos (also known as Karanos) is the most famous personification of this attitude. According to the account of the Alexander historians, which is frequently repeated with various embellishments in the literature of the following centuries, Kalanos accompanied the Greeks on their march back from India. Subsequently, in Persia (or Babylonia according to other sources), he mounted a pyre and immolated himself by his own free will in front of the entire army.[56] On the other hand, Kalanos appears less favorable when compared with the senior gymnosophist, known as Dandamis (also Dindimos) or Mandanis, who remains more faithful to his origin, does not leave his native country and is less inclined toward the theatrical. As a matter of fact, we hear that the reactions to Kalanos' self-immolation were rather mixed.[57]

13. Since Cleitarchus, the early Alexander historian, the disregard for pain and the defiance of death, demonstrated by Kalanos, appear as general characteristics of the gymnosophists.[58] In this connection the best known statement comes from Cicero. He says that the Indian sages spend their lives naked, are capable of withstanding the cold of winter and have burnt them-

selves "without a sigh:" "Quae barbaria India vastior aut agrestior? In ea tamen gente primum ei, qui sapientes habentur, nudi aetatem agunt et Caucasi nives hiemalemque vim perferunt sine dolore, cumque ad flammam se adplicaverunt, sine gemitu aduruntur."[59] After this remark, Cicero refers to those women who follow their husbands voluntarily onto the funeral pyre and even fight for the honor of having this privilege. This, too, is a *topos* which is wide-spread in ancient literature and which is already found in the writings of the Alexander historian Aristobulus, and later, among others, in Plutarch, Diodorus, Philo and Seneca.[60] An explicit continuation of the Brahminical-Gymnosophist practice is witnessed in Peregrinus Proteus' self-immolation in 165A.D. Peregrinus received praise from the Cynics, but was portrayed as a theatrical charlatan by Lucian.

Another characteristic theme, which is most conspicuous in the account of Onesicritus, the Cynic, consists in presenting the gymnosophists as advocates of *physis* against *nomos*, i.e. of the ways of nature against social and artificial conventions. In Onesicritus' account, Mandanis/Dandamis first states various correspondences between his own philosophical orientation, and that of the Greeks, specifically Pythagoras, Socrates and Diogenes of Sinope; but then he criticizes the Greeks for replacing *physis*, the "natural" attitude, with *nomos*, i.e., "unnatural" customs and conventions.[61] According to Onesicritus, the nudity of the gymnosophists is a result and expression of their "natural" attitude, their adherence to *physis*; his presentation exemplifies and continues the glorification of the barbarians and the critique of Greek customs, which we find in the Cynic school since the days of Antisthenes, its founder, and Diogenes of Sinope, his most famous follower.

According to Strabo, Onesicritus also left some information concerning the actual procedure and practical difficulties involved in the debates between Greeks and gymnosophists. Three successive interpreters were needed to carry the conversation through several languages, and often a precise understanding of the Indian ideas was virtually impossible.[62]

Several Greek authors state that "Kalanos" was not the real name of the famous gymnosophist. Instead, these writers claim that this name was given to him by the Greeks because he used to greet them with the expression *kale*; as a matter of fact, *kalyāṇam* may be used as a form of salutation in Sanskrit.[63]

14. Several decades after the death of Alexander, a work was completed which in its breadth and density of information went far beyond the reports of the Alexander historians and was to become the culminating statement on India in classical antiquity: the *Indika* of Megasthenes. Megasthenes served as Indian envoy of the Syrian diadoch Seleucus Nicator between 302 and 291B.C. He seems to have spent a considerable amount of time[64] at the

court of the Maurya ruler Candragupta (in Greek: *Sandrakottos*) in Pāṭaliputra (present-day Patna in Bihar). In spite of his extended stay in the country, his open and inquisitive mind and his obviously favorable inclination towards Indian thought and life, Megasthenes did not gain any real access to the peculiarity of Indian thought and to the indigenous context of the Indian religious tradition. It seems that he did not know any Indian language, something that would be in accordance with the general reluctance of the Greeks to learn foreign languages. Invariably, he transferred his observations into his own Greek framework of understanding; only Greek names and concepts are used to describe and interpret Indian cultural and religious phenomena. His practice of retaining Greek proper names and religious concepts seems to presuppose that the foreign, Indian tradition recognizes the Gods and heroes of his own, Greek tradition, worshipping them only under different names and in different guise. This approach was rather common in the ancient world:

> Greek and Roman writers, even in strictly scholarly works, anxiously avoided using 'barbaric' words, preferring to replace them, wherever possible, with expressions from their own language. Above all, this applies to the names of the 'barbaric' deities. The final result of this tendency was a firmly established usage of terminology. Just as Athene was regularly translated as Minerva, Hera as Iuno, and so forth, in the same manner the foreign deities were dealt with. . .[65]

Heracles and Dionysus are the central figures in Megasthenes' presentation and interpretation of Indian religion.[66] In both cases, though more conspicuously in the case of Dionysus, there is evidence for earlier mythical or legendary associations with India upon which Megasthenes could rely.[67] The question to which Indian deities – perhaps Indra and Śiva – the Greek names Heracles and Dionysus refer, and to what extent Megasthenes' description corresponds to the Indian data need not concern us here. It is also not necessary to discuss the intricate and elusive problem of whether Megasthenes was dealing with late Vedic religion or early Hinduism.[68]

15. Megasthenes divides the population of India into seven classes; the most distinguished group being the "sophists" or "philosophers." According to Megasthenes, they rank highest in prestige, but lowest in number. He further divides the "philosophers" into two groups – the "Brahmans" and the "Sarmans"[69] This distinction remains a familiar one in later literature, sometimes with more or less significant variations. In addition to Megasthenes' Brahmans and Sarmans, Clement of Alexandria (ca. 150–220 A.D.) mentions the Bactrian *σαμαναιοι*,[70] whom we may identify as Buddhists. Porphyry simply contrasts *βϱαχμανες* and *σαμαναιοι*.[71] The association of these terms with the Sanskrit words *brāhmaṇa* ("Brahman")

and *śramaṇa* ("renouncer" for both σαϱμανες and σαμαναιοι), is obviously justified.[72]

According to Megasthenes himself, the Brahmans represent a more consistent philosophy as well as a more orderly and civilized way of life, while the Sarmans (probably not Buddhists, but renouncers in a more general sense) appear as radical, uncompromising Stoics or Cynics. Megasthenes also tells us that the Brahmans, just like the Jews, already knew all those doctrines concerning nature which were subsequently taught by the Greeks.[73] Later authors sometimes present the Jews as descendents of Indian philosophers.[74] As examples of such teachings, Megasthenes mentions the theory that water is the ultimate substance of the world and the doctrine of the five elements; but he does not add any details. In general, and in accordance with the attitude of the Stoics and the Cynics, he seems to be more interested in the ethical and practical aspects of the Indian tradition, than in its theoretical teachings. He refers, for instance, to austerities and acts of self-discipline, such as staying in one bodily posture for a whole day, and the special interest which Indians take in preparing themselves for death.[75] As a source book on India, Megasthenes' work remained unsurpassed in Greek and Roman literature. Its extensive use by authors such as Diodorus, Strabo and Arrian, in whose writings it has survived, attests to its significance.

It may seem surprising that the intensive trade connections between the Roman Empire and India in the first centuries A.D.[76] left so few traces in the literary tradition of late antiquity. A certain classicism, which defined and stylized India as "the country Alexander subjugated and Megasthenes lived in" is among the reasons for this neglect: "India's literary dignity entirely depended on Alexander and his campaign, and that is why later information, arising from increasing commercial intercourse and utilized by scientists, was never admitted into the literary tradition."[77] The Buddha and Buddhism were apparently never explicitly mentioned in "Greco-Roman texts of pagan origin and literary pretension"; however, we find them in the works of some Christian authors, most notably Clement of Alexandria, who were less committed to the "classicist" conception of India.[78]

16. While little was added to what we find in the Alexander histories and Megasthenes, the available materials were used in a variety of ways and were interpreted from various religious and philosophical angles. Explicitly or implicitly, the different assessments of the Indian materials also reflect different attitudes towards the Greek tradition; they may express critique as well as affirmation of the Greek-Occidental spirit.

The meaning and purpose of philosophy itself is at stake in the curious story already mentioned earlier, of Socrates and the Indian in Athens. This tale can be traced back to Aristoxenus of Tarent, a contemporary of Alexander. The Indian does not know what philosophy is; he asks Socrates what kind of activity he is pursuing as a philosopher. When Socrates responds that he is studying problems of human life, the Indian laughs and says that it is impossible to understand human affairs while ignoring the divine. It seems likely that the Aristotelian Aristoxenus, who also had Pythagorean connections, introduced the story shortly after Alexander's Indian campaign as a device for criticizing the Socratic idea of philosophy.

The doxographer Aristocles (second century A.D.), from whom the church father Eusebius quotes it, notes that the Indian view is similar to that of Plato, who unlike Socrates recognized the inseparability of the human and the divine. The Pseudo-Platonic *Alcibiades* I had apparently attempted to defend Socrates against Aristoxenus by attributing a similar integrated way of thinking to him also. All this shows how references to "Indian" themes reflect and accompany tensions and debates within the Greek tradition.[79]

In the different versions of the tradition concerning Alexander and the Brahmins, Alexander represents either a positively interpreted worldliness, the *hybris* of the conqueror, or the readiness of the West to learn from the wisdom of the Orient. In the fictitious correspondence between Alexander and Dindimos/Dandamis, the Indians appear as radical advocates of world-denying asceticism and cynical contempt for society, while Alexander represents a this-worldly, life-affirming attitude.[80] In this case, the author favors Alexander; yet, the reverse kind of "moral confrontation of East and West"[81] has become more familiar and frequent, not only under the influence of Stoic thought, but also from the Christian perspective. In St. Ambrose's version of the encounter between the Brahmins and Alexander, the Brahmins say:

> If, then, you want to know the truth, come to India and live naked in the wilderness, renouncing all the honors you love, all the marks of distinction you wear; only then shall we receive you into our midst. You will then learn to love what you saw and wondered at a little while before. Nobody will fight any battle against you, nor will anyone have the power to carry away any of your possessions. You will not live by the sweat and spoliation of others, for you will be rich in everything.[82]

The assessment of the gymnosophists' practice of self-cremation has also been ambivalent. On the one hand, it appears as the fearless fulfillment of true catharsis, the purification of the soul from its body.[83] On the other hand, Christian authors tend to contrast it with "real" martyrdom and to criticize it accordingly.[84]

17. As we have already mentioned, India played an increasingly important and conspicuous role in the speculation on the origin of religion and philosophy when the debate assumed new dimensions in late antiquity. Journeys to India and indebtedness to Brahminical wisdom are now ascrib-

ed to numerous founders and leaders in Greek thought, such as Plato,[85] Democritus,[86] Pherecydes of Syrus[87] and, quite often, Pythagoras. We hear that Pythagoras studied astronomy and astrology with the Chaldeans, and psychological as well as soteriological doctrines with the Indian gymnosophists.[88] It may seem surprising that the idea of a connection between Pythagoras' doctrine of transmigration and that of the Indian tradition, which has been the focus of more recent literature on the question of Indian influences on Greek thought, emerged only at a relatively late date.[89] Earlier writers considered Egypt as the doctrine's country of origin. In the post-Christian era, the Neopythagorean Apollonius of Tyana (ca. 100A.D.) was most closely associated with India. In the legendary biography by Philostratus, Apollonius advocates the wisdom of the Indians against that of the Egyptians. Here, the Egyptians (Philostratus even mentions Egyptian gymnosophists) appear as learners who depend upon, or even corrupt, a much more original sort of wisdom, namely, that of the Brahmins.[90]

According to a tradition which is not as legendary, Plotinus (205–270A.D.) made an unsuccessful attempt to learn more about the wisdom of the Persians and the Indians, by joining the campaign of Gordian III against the Sassanians, which ended with the assassination of the emperor. While Plotinus' basic interest in Eastern wisdom seems easily acceptable, we have no sufficient evidence to support the hypothesis of E. Bréhier and others, that Plotinus owed essential parts of his philosophy to the Indian tradition.[91] We do not even know what kind of information or hearsay attracted Plotinus to Indian thought, and what motivated him to undertake his ill-fated attempt. The structural correspondences between his transspiritual monism and the non-dualistic traditions of India are, of course, intriguing and make us wonder about the effects an actual encounter might have had.[92]

It has been suggested that Plotinus' teacher, the Alexandrian Ammonius Sakkas, might have been a transmitter of Indian ideas and thus responsible for his disciple's interest in India and the East in general, and that the epithet "sakkas" itself ought to be derived from the Sanskrit word *śākya*, "(follower of) the Buddha," instead of meaning "sack-carrier." This would, therefore, indicate a Buddhist affiliation.[93] We need not dismiss this suggestion, but we should always remember that it is nothing more than a hypothesis. What we know about Ammonius' teachings is vague and uncertain and does not contain any recognizable Indian elements.

Equally elusive, but also equally intriguing is the question of possible Indian affiliations with Gnostic thought, and more specifically, the connection with the Buddhist *Prajñāpāramitā* literature; it is a question which has been debated repeatedly since the very beginning of Western studies of Buddhism.[94] At any rate, the Gnostic Carpocratians were among the most ardent advocates of transmigration in the early post-Christian period. And at least for one important Gnostic teacher, Bardesanes of Edessa (ca. 200A.D.), the tradition itself postulates extensive Indian contacts, including a possible journey to India.[95] In the third century A.D., the Persian Gnostic and Neozoroastrian Mani spent some time in India, and various Buddhist elements, including the name of the Buddha himself, found their way into Manichaeism.[96]

Whatever the actual extent of Indian contacts and influences may have been, by the second century A.D. the search for Eastern origins of thought and learning had moved farther and farther to the East. India had nearly replaced Egypt as the land of origins par excellence. Lucian of Samosata, himself of Oriental (Syrian) origin, could caricature this development as follows: In one of Lucian's satires, personified philosophy decides to present herself to the "barbarians" first. She then presents herself to the Greeks. Philosophy personified justifies this decision with the assumption that it would be more difficult and time-consuming to teach and educate the barbarians than the Greeks. Accordingly, she first goes to India, then to Ethiopia, Egypt, and so forth. Finally, she arrives in Greece via Thracia. However, it turns out that it is much easier and less frustrating to convert and educate the Indians than the Greeks.[97]

18. "Syncretism" is among those terms which have been frequently employed to describe the religious atmosphere of late antiquity, its coalescence, amalgamation and mutual adaptation of Eastern and Western ideas. Disregarding the problems and ambiguities inherent in this term, we may say that there is no syncretism of Indian and Greek thought in this sense. Unlike other "Orientals," Indians did not actively participate in the shared culture of late antiquity. Nor is there anything like an ongoing dialogue between India and the Hellenic or hellenized world. Actual contacts were sporadic and limited; linguistic barriers continued to prevent closer intellectual interaction. The Greeks themselves did not give up their reluctance to learn foreign languages; and apart from some Greek and Aramaic edicts of emperor Aśoka (third century B.C.), there are no traces of efforts by the Indians to express and convey their teachings in Western languages.[98]

References to actual encounters and conversations between Indians and representatives of the hellenized world remain rare, and we learn little about the concrete and specific circumstances under which they took place. One of these rare cases is the report concerning a meeting between an Indian delegation in Syria and the Gnostic teacher Bardesanes. For him, this was an occasion for acquiring information about India.[99] There can be no doubt that such encounters and conversations were possible, and that they took place in the cosmopolitan atmosphere of Alexandria in Egypt. In the early years of the Christian era, a small community of Indians were indeed among the inhabitants of this city. However, most of these Indians were obviously merchants without any thorough knowledge of the religious and philosophical traditions of their homeland. There is also no evidence that they transmitted any precise information about Indian religious and philosophical texts to the Mediterranean world.[100]

The *Elenchos* written by the church father Hippolytus (third century A.D.), which was commonly referred to by the title of its first chapter, "Philosophumena," and falsely attributed to Origen, shows an acquaintance with Indian religious and philosophical doctrines which goes beyond the data found in the Alexander histories and the *Indika* by Megasthenes. Hippolytus' work seems to exhibit a certain basic familiarity with Upaniṣadic ideas which may be due to contacts in Alexandria. However, it does not provide sufficient evidence to support the thesis of J. Filliozat that Hipploytus was acquainted with a particular Upaniṣadic text, i.e., the *Maitrī Upaniṣad*.[101]

We might also expect documents of intellectual interaction to appear from another region, Greek-ruled Bactria, with its rich tradition of Greco-Indian art. This area, however, leaves us entirely disappointed as far as religious and philosophical doctrines are concerned: ". . . we know nothing —nothing but a little Greek ivory pendant from Taxila, which bears on each of its faces the head of a philosopher."[102]

In the opposite direction, astrological and astronomical doctrines have found their way from the Mediterranean world into India.[103] Apart from this, however, it remains true that the Indians did not take an active role in the "syncretistic" movements of this epoch and in its processes of adaptation, inclusion and reinterpretation. On the whole, even the period of direct encounters has left very few recognizable traces in Indian literature and in Indian thought. It is characteristic that the story of Alexander, which gained extraordinary popularity in other parts of Asia, found no place in the Indian tradition.[104] As far as traditional Hinduism is concerned, the Greeks, just like other invaders and foreigners (*yavana, mleccha*), were a peripheral and unimportant phenomenon although they enjoyed a certain recognition as craftsmen and soldiers. The situation is somewhat different in the case of Buddhism with its generally more open and universalistic attitude. In the third century B.C. the Greek-Aramaic Aśoka inscription of Kandahar shows that the Buddhist ruler recognized the Greek-speaking population in the northwestern region of the country. The *Milindapañha* , a Pali dialogue between the Greek-Bactrian king Milinda (known as Menander in Greek sources, second century B.C.) and the Buddhist monk Nāgasena, gained great popularity in Buddhism. However, there is little in the text which is Greek, aside from the name of the king.[105]

19. Trying to sum up the main phases, perspectives and motivations in the Greek approach to the Orient in general and India in particular, we can say: Early on, the Greeks began to speculate on Oriental, and subsequently Indian, wisdom and its significance for the initiation and development of their own tradition. In the period of their classical historians and philosophers such as Herodotus, Plato and Aristotle, they did this fully assured of their Hellenic identity and proclaiming the uniqueness of their purely theoretical pursuit of knowledge—"not, as in late antiquity, hoping for secret revelations, but critically, attracted by the foreign aspect."[106] In accordance with their emphasis on ethics, the interest of the Stoics, Cynics and other post-classical schools focuses on practical aspects of Oriental and Indian wisdom: modes of behavior and mental dispositions, such as contempt of death, indifference towards pleasure and pain, self-control, freedom from social conventions. Soteriological themes, such as the catharsis of the soul from its body, became increasingly important. The Hellenic confidence in philosophy, theory and the autonomy of human reasoning gave way to a greater readiness for accepting sacred tradition and divine inspiration. In a sense, the curiosity of the classical period turned into readiness for self-transformation.

Among the traditions of the Orient, India rises to greater significance after the campaign of Alexander. Yet, this does not lead to a systematic exploration. In spite of extensive contacts, the factual knowledge of Indian religion and philosophy remains very limited. A set of rather stereotyped ideas and associations emerges. It seems that no Greek had access to literary documents of the Indian religious and philosophical tradition. An awareness of hermeneutic problems does not develop, and no effort is made to understand Indian ideas in their own context and horizon. The image of India in classical antiquity remains largely a mirror of Hellenic self-affirmation, self-exploration and self-questioning. In its very openness, the Greek attitude towards foreign cultures and traditions is limited and ambiguous; its proclamation of universalism and cosmopolitanism remains, in spite of its programmatic potential, self-centered and abstract. The Greeks of antiquity did not like to learn foreign languages, and they did not favor translating into their own tongue.[107] They never opened themselves to a foreign religious and literary tradition in a manner comparable to the comprehensive acquisition and translation of Indian Buddhist texts by the Chinese or Tibetans.

In spite of its limitations, however, the Greek approach to the foreign world, the Orient and India in particular opens new perspectives and possibilities of human orientation. The curiosity of their classical historians and ethnographers, the relativism of the Sophists, the universalism and cosmopolitanism of the Stoics—all this has far-reaching implications for future developments of Western thought. Further, late antiquity creates an atmosphere of unprecedented "syncretism"—of assimilation and interpenetration of different Eastern and Western religions and philosophies, which anticipates aspects and aspirations of the modern situation of encounter and interpenetration. It is of exemplary significance that hymns of the bishop Synesius of Cyrene (ca. 400A.D.), which invoke the spirit of assimilation and harmonization, appear as a motto at the beginning of Anquetil Duperron's *Oupnek'hat* (1801/02), a work of seminal importance for the modern European understanding of Indian thought.[108] It was, however, the uncompromising message of Christianity which emerged victorious from this "syncretistic" epoch of openness. Its absolutism and exclusivism as well as its missionary zeal created entirely new conditions for European approaches to India.

20. The first phase of the European encounter with India terminates as the result of various, and not merely external, circumstances. Of course, the powerful empires of the Parthians, Sassanians and finally Islam constitute barriers between Europe and India which preclude direct contacts for many centuries. But is is also the closed and self-centered world-view of the Christian Middle Ages, a kind of self-withdrawal or introversion, which restricts Europe to itself. The foreign, non-European world manifests itself primarily in the experience of confrontation with Islam, and it appears as a hostile force, a threat to Christian states and Christianity in general.[109]

Even during this period, some Indian materials reach Europe. The originally Buddhist legend of Barlaam and Josaphat, for instance, or the fables of Bidpai, which derive from the *Pañcatantra* or a related Indian collection received wide-spread recognition and popularity, yet without any knowledge of their Indian origin.[110] Explicit references to and speculations about India are usually based upon a vague and incomplete acquaintance with the Greek and Roman sources. Legendary themes and fantastic stories predominate, such as the tradition of the "fabulous races" and the legendary embellishments of the *Alexander Romance*. We also find "geographical" associations of India with the region of paradise. The presentation and interpretation of Indian themes is rather stereotyped in most cases. Among the works with Indian themes apart from the *Alexander Romance* which enjoyed special popularity in the Middle Ages, we find the *Physiologos* and the *Gesta Romanorum*. Chapter 175 of the latter gives a Christian-symbolic interpretation of the "fabulous races." Ancient knowledge and ideas about India, handed down by Solinus, Orosius and Isidore of Seville, were also included in the encyclopaedic works of the Middle Ages, especially those of Honorius Augustodunensis (twelfth century) and Vincent of Beauvais (thirteenth century. The medieval versions are characterized by frequently portraying Brahmins as positive illustrations of asceticism, self-control and related

Christian ideals.[111] Regarding the gymnosophists, Honorius Augustodunensis, like Augustine and Isidore before him, emphasized that they were not completely naked but kept their private parts covered.[112]

While the image of India, inasmuch as the description of the geographical and natural environment is concerned, had essentially been fixed since the final days of antiquity, being passed on in learned works as 'static' knowledge, as it were, Christian thought itself provided for contemporary references. From time to time the nebulous knowledge of an Indian Christianity received some usually dubious support and new stimuli.[113]

In this connection, the old tradition of the apostle Thomas and a Christian community founded by him has to be first and foremost mentioned. Then, in the twelfth century, the legend of the Indian priest-king John emerged. During the Crusades this hero figure represented the hope to find a Christian power behind the lines of Islam.[114]

21. We can ignore the few, partly legendary, travel reports on India which reached Europe in the centuries before Vasco da Gama's expedition (1497–1498),[115] since they do not contain new themes or additions to the available information in the field of religion or philosophy. The notion of an Indian Christian community did not lose its significance. Together with the growing commercial interests, it strengthened those efforts to rediscover India and to overcome the Islamic barrier which finally led to da Gama's voyage. Even after the Europeans had regained and secured their direct access to India, the ideas inherited from antiquity did not lose their significance. The rediscovery and reevaluation of the Greek and Roman sources accompanied the acquisition of new, direct information. A considerable amount of time passed before a clear separation and coordination of the old and the new materials was achieved, and before old conceptions were replaced by newly acquired knowledge.

The study of Indian religion and philosophy, in particular, continued to follow the Greek patterns. The comprehensive rediscovery of classical antiquity in the Renaissance period also led to a renewed interest in the classical accounts of Indian and Oriental thought. In spite of the obvious limitations of these accounts, they stand as a testimony to the Greek openness and curiosity concerning non-Western, extra-European ways of thinking, an attitude which the Middle Ages had not known. They were further capable of reinforcing the new spirit of discovery which characterizes the Renaissance.

The modern Western doxographic and historiographic tradition of philosophy began with Walter de Burleigh's adaptation of Diogenes Laërtius' doxography in the fourteenth century.[116] Still in P. Bayle's very influential *Dictionnaire historique et critique* (1697), the articles dealing with Indian topics were for the most part derived from Greek and Roman sources. Not only J. Brucker's representative *Historia critica philosophiae* (1742–1744) but even later works on the history of philosophy deal with Oriental and Indian thought in a manner which reflects the continued influence of Greek doxographic literature. Even such pioneers of modern Indian studies as W. Jones, Anquetil Duperron or Chr. Lassen still combined the retrospective study of the Greek and Roman materials with the direct, future-oriented exploration of the original Indian sources. It is characteristic that Lassen published his edition and Latin translation of Īśvarakṛṣṇa's *Sāṃkhyakārikā* under the title *Gymnosophista* (1832). His *Indische Altertumskunde* (1847–1858), an early standard work of modern Indology, continues to be one of the most thorough and comprehensive surveys of the Greek and Roman acquaintance with India to date.

2. Islamic Encounters With Indian Philosophy

1. It is one of the paradoxes of European intellectual history that Islam, while barring the West from any direct access to the Indian tradition for centuries, served as a bridge to its own Greek tradition and origin. The Islamic acquisition of important parts of Greek philosophy and science happened considerably earlier and, in the beginning, on a more comprehensive scale than the Latin-Christian one. Moreover, the transmission of Aristotelian thought through Latin renderings of Arabic translations and commentaries played an important role during the transitional phase from early to high Scholasticism.[1] After the first Islamic campaigns into Western India at the beginning of the eighth century, the translators' interest also turned towards Indian texts, although to a much lesser extent. In response to its encounter with India, Islam developed its own ways of approaching the Indian tradition. The Muslim knowledge about and image of India has influenced Europe in some important cases, resulting in an indirect connection between Europe and India. But even where there is no evidence of such influence, the Islamic approaches are significant in and of themselves, and they supplement and complete our understanding of the Western awareness of India. At this point, it seems appropriate to refer to some of their general developments and culminating achievements.

The translation and reception of Indian works—not necessarily from the original texts, but sometimes from already available versions in Middle Persian—involved primarily medical, astronomical, mathematical, alchemical and astrological works. One of the best-known and most far-reaching consequences of the Arabic encounter with Indian mathematics is the introduction of the decimal system and the zero, i.e., the system of numbers which in the West has become known as "Arabic." Isolated references to it can already be found before the Islamic campaigns in India.[2]

In this connection, religious and philosophical sources were largely ignored. Observations concerning Indian religion are included in different classes of works, especially in writings on the wonders of the world (*ʿajāʾib*), in travel reports and encyclopaedic works. While the first group of texts mentions mainly extraordinary practices of magicians, yogins etc., the travel reports, for instance, that of Idrīsī of the twelfth century, contain many observations on sects, castes and other phenomena pertaining to Indian religious life, but without showing any understanding of the theoretical or philosophical background. Among the authors of encyclopaedic works and compilations which contain material on Indian religion, we may mention Ibn an-Nadīm and al-Maqdisī in the tenth century, as well as Gardīzī and Marvazī in the following century.[3] None of these works are based upon any direct knowledge of Indian sources. We are not concerned with the extent to which Indian themes and ideas may have reached the Muslim world, and influenced Islamic thought indirectly, perhaps without an awareness of their Indian origin, in this presentation. In any case, it would be speculative to assume a really penetrating and comprehensive influence in this regard, as some scholars, such as M. Horten, have suggested.[4]

2. All of the attempts mentioned thus far were totally overshadowed by a work which is one of the greatest achievements not only in the history of Islamic studies of India specifically, but in the study of South Asia in general—the description of India by al-Bīrūnī, commonly referred to as *Taʾrīkh al-Hind* or *Kitāb al-Hind*.[5]

Al-Bīrūnī, who was born in Chwarezm in Central Asia in 973 A.D. and died in Ghaznī (in present-day Afghanistan) in 1048 A.D., ranks as one of the greatest scholars ever, not only of the Islamic or medieval world of his day. At the time when the Turkish conqueror Mahmūd of Ghaznī took him along to his court from the conquered Chwarezm, he was already one of the leading astronomers, mathematicians and geographers of his time. He devoted himself to the study of the Indian world from Ghaznī. This was obviously in connection with Mahmūd's military activities in northern India. However, his own remarks indicate that the compilation of his book on India, which he wrote in Arabic, did not result from a direct order of his ruler. Bīrūnī, who, on the one hand, deplored his lack of freedom, and on the other hand appreciated the favorable external circumstances of his work, referred to a suggestion by Abū Sahl. As he says himself, his goal is, above all, a presentation of the facts, a clear and sober description of a religion and philosophy which has been entirely unknown or misunderstood so far.[6] His enterprise resulted in a pioneering piece of work, equally innovative with regard to its content and methodology. To be sure, the Indian scene had changed considerably since the days of Megasthenes, the representative

Greek "Indologist," but apart from this, it is al-Bīrūnī's radically new approach which is most significant and conspicuous.[7]

Unlike Megasthenes, Bīrūnī studied the Sanskrit language and tried to gain a precise knowledge of Hindu sources. The list of works mentioned or used by him is long and impressive, even though there are numerous problems with regard to textual specification and identification .[8] In the field of "sciences" or "occult sciences," he was able to resort to various earlier works, including some Arabic translations of Indian texts, even though his own work extended far beyond those. There is no comparable precedent or preparation for his research in the religious and philosophical literature of the Hindus. His observations on this subject range from the Vedas to the *Bhagavadgītā* and from various Purāṇas and *Dharmaśāstra* works to texts of the classical philosophical systems.[9] He mentions some of these works only in vague and sometimes inaccurate title references.[10] Elsewhere, he quotes extensively from other texts such as the *Bhagavadgītā*. However, it is difficult to coordinate these quotations with the text as we know it. Indeed, one might ask to what extent he may have incorporated commentarial passages or oral communications of his Hindu informants.[11] Apart from his book on India, Bīrūnī translated, obviously with the help of Indian scholars, Patañjali's *Yogasūtras*, for example, together with parts of a commentary which has not yet been clearly identified. He also translated an equally unidentifiable Sāṃkhya text.[12]

3. Bīrūnī was fully aware of the fact that he had engaged himself in something completely new: religious fanaticism and the claim of exclusiveness on the one hand as well as total ignorance on the other, had, prior to his own work, precluded any serious study of the religion and philosophy of Hinduism. According to Bīrūnī, only a single one of his predecessors, Īrānshahrī, was prepared to study other religions *sine ira et studio*. Īrānshahrī, however, restricted himself to Judaism, Christianity and Manichaeism, and was very unreliable with regard to India.[13] Bīrūnī always speaks as a Muslim believer, while being convinced of his superior scholarly approach. In addition, he develops a positive interest in his Indian studies, an interest which he feels is totally unique for his time.[14] Besides, missionary intentions are totally alien to him. He models his scholarly standards and his ideal of objective research on the Greeks, whom he contrasts, in this respect, with the Indians.[15] Nevertheless, he considers the Greeks to be just as far away from Islamic monotheism as the Indians, and, in this regard, basically comparable to them. This provided him with a framework within which he could compare the Indian tradition in a sober and objective manner with Greek and, above all, Islamic thought at the same time. A clear awareness of his *own* religious horizon as a particular context of thought led him to perceive the "otherness" of the Indian religious

philosophical context and horizon with remarkable clarity, and he understood the difficulties of penetrating it. This clarity of hermeneutic awareness is unparalleled in the world of classical antiquity with its attitude towards the "barbarians" and the Orient. Unlike Megasthenes, Bīrūnī did not "translate" the names of foreign deities; nor did he incorporate them into is own pantheon, and of course he did not possess the amorphous "openness" of syncretism and the search for "common denominators." That is why he could comprehend and appreciate the other, the foreign as such, thematizing and explicating in an essentially new manner the problems of intercultural understanding and the challenge of "objectivity" when shifting from one tradition to another, from one context to another. The fact that the Indians remained basically ethnocentric, in that they experienced all things foreign as marginal, peripheral phenomena relative to their own sphere of identity, or that they simply excluded themselves from these and withdrew within the bounds of their own tradition, was considered an essential criterion of Indian "otherness" by Bīrūnī. Observations of this nature, characterized by a distinctive combination of detail and methodological, hermeneutic, reflection, of factual statements as well as sensitivity concerning self-understanding and self-definition, distinguish Bīrūnī's work from all previous studies of India.[16]

4. At the outset of his work, Bīrūnī states the methodological principles and fundamental difficulties of his undertaking:[17] he points to the fundamental religious, philosophical and social antagonisms which exist between Hinduism and Islam; he discusses problems of translating, of acquiring and processing information, and of penetrating the horizon of self-contained Indian thought. Being aware of these difficulties, aware of the "otherness," the hermeneutic distance, he gains the freedom and the firmness of his claim to objectivity: whatever his Islamic contemporaries considered as strange, "heathen," or unacceptable in Hinduism, Bīrūnī was able to reply that "this is as it is."[18]

Bīrūnī certainly did characterize many of the phenomena which he described as bizarre, repugnant and unacceptable, such as phenomena in the realm of law and morals, religious and social institutions and, above all, the peculiarities of the caste system. However, he thematizes the element of "otherness" and repugnance as such, reflecting critically on it and relating it to the conditions of his own standpoint: he introduces his survey of "strange" customs of the Hindus by defining the strangeness of a phenomenon as a deviation from what is familiar and common within one's own horizon.[19] The willingness and ability to step back in order to see the relativity of one's own standpoint, something implied in this kind of understanding of the alienness of things alien, is of course common in the ancient ethnographic and sophist[20] concept of νομος. However, in Bīrūnī this understanding gains new content and concrete relevance by the very fact that it remains connected with the clear awareness and the conscious acceptance of his own position and horizon. Furthermore, it is interesting to note the manner in which Bīrūnī differentiates within his description of the Indian world. He clearly recognizes historical developments and changes in the thought and self-understanding of India. He notes that the tendency among the Indians of his time to isolate and overestimate themselves has not always been a trademark of the Indian attitude.[21]

5. Throughout his work, just as in the case with the Greeks and Muslims so also when it comes to India, Bīrūnī basically distinguishes between the common views of the people and the opinions of the philosophically learned. Inasmuch as the philosophical dimension of Hinduism is concerned, he actually sees the principle of monotheism, the idea of the one, almighty, non-anthrophomorphic God and of the cosmic Absolute, in the concept of *īśvara*.[22] Bīrūnī is in a position to make many comparisons with the metaphysical thought of the Greeks. Beyond this he finds certain links with the basic principles of Islamic religion and philosophy, though it is never without a hint of reservation. Sūfism, which Bīrūnī views from a distance, serves as a mediating element in this task.[23] As mentioned earlier, from his own knowledge of the sources, he is well acquainted with the doctrines of Sāṃkhya and Yoga in the philosophical realm. He presents extensive and, to a remarkable extent, accurate explanations of the cosmology and soteriology of Sāṃkhya.[24] He knows, though without any details, of the existence of Nyāya and Mīmāṃsā. But he does not refer to the classical Advaita Vedānta of Śaṅkara's school at all, not even in connection with his remarks on Sūfism. Bīrūnī's references to Buddhism are relatively vague and isolated, as is to be expected.

To sum up, Bīrūnī's work on India is based on a systematic study of the sources and a fundamental awareness of the hermeneutic difficulties inherent in the task. It is conceived as a presentation *sine ira et studio*. Although it reflects the spirit and horizon of a particular religion, it exemplifies scholarly distance and objectivity. Bīrūnī neither associates himself with any missionary intentions, nor does he reveal any readiness to learn from the foreign doctrines or to modify his own convictions according to them. Comparisons and contrasts are drawn up from various directions and with different associations, yet their aim is not to detect "common demoninators." The tendency towards syncretism is minimal also.

6. Apparently al-Bīrūnī's book on India did not enjoy a recognition commensurate with its significance and the general fame of its author. Even within the Islamic world, it was never generally acknowledged or used as a standard work. The *Kitāb al-Milal wa'n-niḥal* by Shahrastānī (1086–1153), an influential work on comparative religion relatively well-known in the

West, does not even mention Bīrūnī's book, although it deals in detail with India.[25] According to Shahrastānī, the Indians are one of the four most important peoples in the history of religion and philosophy, along with the Arabs, Persians and Greeks. As regards the level of both information and reflection, Shahrastānī's book on the "Religious Parties and Philosophical Schools" can certainly not be compared with Bīrūnī's work. Apart from a short, but comparatively precise, section on Buddhism, Shahrastānī does not go beyond the contents known from older encyclopaedic works. Rather, with respect to the thoroughness of presentation, he does not seldom lag behind them.[26] What distinguishes him is his tendency towards theological categorization and typification. The Indian background of his classification of sects is generally obscured and often hardly recognizable in his typologies. Characteristic of, although by no means exclusive to Shahrastānī, is the assumption that the philosophy of the Brahmins is genetically dependent on Greek philosophy. His thesis reverses the speculations on the origin of philosophy as known from late antiquity. He claims that Pythagoras sent two of his disciples, one of whom was Qalānūs (Calanus?), to India in order to spread his teaching. An Indian disciple of Qalānūs, named Brahmanan, then became the founder of the tradition of Brahminical philosophy.[27]

A curious aspect of Shahrastānī's description of the Brahmins is that prophets were unknown to them, and that they tended towards a kind of rationalism which does not depend on revelation.[28] With this view of the "Barāhima" he follows a tradition already centuries old during his time and found not only in Islamic authors, but also, for instance, in the work of Sa'adia Gaon, the Jewish religious thinker who lived around 900 A.D.[29] The identification of the Barāhima with the Indian Brahmins has been questioned and the attempt has been made to show that "all sources are dependent on Ibn al-Rāwandī's *Kitāb al-Zumurrud*, and that it was Ibn al-Rāwandī himself who invented the Barāhima as a cover for his own views."[30] However, recent research leaves no doubt that the tradition is older than Ibn al-Rāwandī, and that it may indeed reflect—although through misunderstandings—"the reality of Indian-Moslem debates, and the lasting impression those debates made on Islam.."[31]

7. The religious and philosophical traditions of India are also included in the grand and comprehensive framework of Rashīd ad-Dīn's history of the world, which, unlike Shahrastānī's work, gives full consideration to Bīrūnī's investigations. In 1300, Rashid ad-Dīn, a physician of Jewish-Persian descent (1247–1381), was commissioned by the Mongol ruler Ghāzān Mahmūd (d.1304), a Muslim convert, to compile a history of the Mongols and Turks since Genghis Khan. After Ghāzān's death, his brother Oljāitu (d.1316), became the patron of this enterprise and expanded it into

the project of a universal history. This meant, above all, a history of those peoples who somehow came into contact with the Mongols in the course of their military campaigns. According to K. Jahn, the work, written in Persian and known under the title *Jāmi' at-tawārīkh* ("Gatherer of the Stories"), presents the first real universal history of the Orient and the Occident.[32] Its contents extend from China to Europe, and it deals with India in considerable detail, especially its religious and philosophical traditions. As mentioned, it makes full use of Bīrūnī's work, along with adding much new material, such as the doctrine of the four world ages (*yuga*) and, more significantly, information on Buddhism, which Bīrūnī had hardly touched on, and for which Rashīd could rely on the expertise of a Buddhist scholar from Kashmir. The presentation is chiefly "biographical" and anecdotal: stories of the type found in the *Jātaka* literature, stations in the process of reincarnation, a biography of the Buddha and an outline of his doctrine, generally with a tendency towards syncretism and popularization.[33] In its breadth and accuracy, Rashīd's account of Buddhism is without precedent and unsurpassed in traditional Islamic literature, where references to Buddhism are usually vague and elusive.[34]

Rashīd ad-Dīn's presentation of India demonstrates nothing of the independent spirit of philosophical and hermeneutical reflection which were found in Bīrūnī's work. Nonetheless, it is an impressive and significant document. Although it was later translated into Arabic, its historical impact remained rather limited; however, it was used and excerpted by later historical compilers, especially Banākatī and Hāfiẓ-i Abrū.[35] These authors do not provide us with new information or original perspectives on Indian thought and life; and their works exemplify F. Rosenthal's observation:

> The Muslim approach to the writing of universal history always offered many inducements to historians to be superficial, to copy their sources mechanically, to prefer quantity to quality. But it represented a kind of historic consciousness which is one of the first necessary stages on the road toward a truly human concept of the world.[36]

8. From both al-Bīrūnī's and Rashīd ad-Din's point of view, India was a strange and exotic land. In more than one sense their interest came from outside, from a distance. However, as we know, Islam itself penetrated India, established itself there, and developed peculiar traditions of confrontation and disregard, but also coexistence and occasionally symbiosis with Hinduism. A detailed discussion would exceed the limits of this presentation. We can only provide a few brief hints. We will focus on such references to Hinduism which have philosophical implications, and which reflect the diversity and coexistence of the two traditions on an explicitly theoretical level.[37]

After the first contacts through merchants on the Malabar coast in the eighth century, and after the occupation of Sindh by Muhammad ibn Qāsim, which also occurred in the same century, it is the raids and annexations of the Ghaznavids since the beginning of the eleventh century which inaugurated the spread of Islam in India, first in the Punjab, Kashmir and Gujarat. Since 1193, Delhi was the seat of the Ghor dynasty as well as the center of Islam in India. Numerous more or less short-lived dynasties followed. Indian Islam entered its golden age with the establishment of the Mogul empire in 1526. This was especially the case under the four Mogul emperors, Akbar, Jahāngīr, Shāh Jahān, and Aurangzeb (the period of their reign extending from 1556 till 1707).

Basically we can say: "The Muslims, whose religious beliefs and social institutions sharply contrast with those of the Hindus, resisted the process of absorption, without in turn being able to leave their own imprint on India."[38] There was not much common ground between Islam, which was "iconoclastic, priestless and militant-democratic,"[39] and Hinduism, which divided society into hereditary groups, accepted many forms of image worship, and tended to isolate itself from non-Indian traditions. Over the centuries, the relationship seems to have been characterized by fundamental and unreconciled opposition along with mutual disregard. However, the actual development is somewhat more complex and differentiated. Periods of radical Muslim iconoclasm and proselytizing zeal were followed by extended periods of quiet coexistence; and against numerous expressions of disregard, misunderstanding and mutual isolation, we find occasional statements of openness also. This is coupled by a search for common denominators, as well as various forms of practical, though tacit symbiosis and interaction.

The great Indo-Persian poet Amīr Khusrau (1253–1325) describes on the one hand "in poetical metaphors the destruction of Hindu temples for the sake of transformation into mosques."[40] But on the other hand, he celebrates the unequalled learning of the Brahmins, recognizes a deep and pervasive monotheism in Hindu thought, and glorifies the Sanskrit language (which he did not master himself). In particular, he points out that the world owes the zero and the decimal system to the Indians.[41]

9. In the following centuries, it was above all the monotheistic devotion of the Vaiṣṇavite sects which provided a basis for contacts, rivalries and attempted reconciliations with Islam. One of the most representative figures was Kabīr (ca. 1440–1458). According to tradition, he was the son of a widowed Brahmin woman, who abandoned him; he was then raised and educated by a Muslim weaver and finally became the disciple of the *Vaiṣṇava bhakti* teacher Rāmānanda.

We need not discuss the attempts of Hindu-Muslim syncretism and universalism, which are associated with such names as Nāmdev or Lallā and, later, Dādū Dayāl, in detail here.[42] It may suffice to mention that the generally most important and influential of these movements, Sikhism, which was founded by Guru Nānak (1469–1539), included poems of Kabīr in its collection of sacred texts, the *Ādi Granth*, but subsequently turned into a militant anti-Islamic movement.[43]

On the Muslim side, the Sūfīs became the most important religious and philosophical mediators. It is difficult to decide to what extent Indian, specifically Vedāntic, influences may have affected Muslim mysticism even before the Sūfī tradition extablished itself in India. According to R.C. Zaehner's controversial thesis, Abū Yazīd al-Bisṭāmi, who lived in the ninth century, had access to non-dualistic Vedānta, possibly through his teacher, Abū 'Alī al-Sindī.[44] At any rate, the Sūfīs were more willing than others to tolerate a variety of religious manifestations, i.e., of cults and practices, and to consider the possibility of one and the same divine reality being the implicit goal of the different approaches. Al-Bīrūnī had already noticed that their views could be compared and associated with certain Hindu ideas.[45] On the one hand, the Sūfīs gained influence as popular saints, who were in some cases even accepted by Hindus. On the other hand, they reached an intellectual level which qualified them for an important role in a process which represents a climax in the history of Hindu-Muslim reconciliations—the universalistic effort of the Mogul emperor Akbar and, above all, his great-grandson Dārā Shukōh.[46]

> Emperor Akbar (1542–1605), who was inclined towards mysticism and unorthodox speculation, was following a mixture of religious and political motives when he tried to create a monotheistic Indian national religion (1582), which, free of idols, composed of Islamic, Indian and Christian elements, was to assure proper reverence for God and peace and unity for the empire.[47]

The motive of religious agreement and unity was fused with the aim of political unity and consolidation; the bridging of the fundamental religious-philosophical gap between Islam and Hinduism was seen as the basis for the stability of the empire.[48] In a systematic and methodic manner, Akbar attempted to create some of the prerequisites for a better understanding of the Hindu tradition and for mutual accommodation; a comprehensive library with works in many languages was founded, and Sanskrit literature was systematically explored and translated with the help of Hindu scholars.[49]

10. Leading men of the empire took an active part in this work, in particular, the prime minister Abu'l-Faḍl, and his brother, Faiḍī. However, the leading translator, Badaunī, carried out his work without showing any sign of appreciation for Hinduism or Akbar's religious program.

Among Sanskrit works which were partly or wholly translated into Persian we find the great epics, *Rāmāyaṇa* and *Mahābhārata* (from this, the *Bhagavadgītā* in particular), the *Yogavāsiṣṭha*, and Kalhaṇa's *Rājataraṅginī*. The authoritative compilation of Islamic knowledge on Hinduism can be found in Abu'l-Faḍl's *A'īn-i Akbarī*.[50] Among other things, it contains a very detailed presentation of the traditional sciences and, especially, the philosophical systems of the Indians. Apart from the six "orthodox" systems of Nyāya, Vaiśeṣika, Vedānta, Mīmāṃsā, Sāṃkhya and Yoga, it also includes the doctrines of the Jainas, Buddhists and materialists.

The way in which the material is arranged and presented corresponds largely with the traditional Hindu classification of sciences and, as far as the philosophical systems are concerned, with the level of the later doxographies and compendia. The synopsis of the "eighteen sciences" of the Hindus, which Abu'l-Faḍl provides, follows the patterns which we find, for instance, in the *Prasthānabheda* by Madhusūdana Sarasvatī.[51] The information offered in the *A'īn-i Akbarī* is by far more detailed and precise than what we have from Bīrūnī, especially when it comes to the philosophical systems. However, the spirit of searching, questioning and the critical study of the sources, which we find in Bīrūnī's work, is as absent as Bīrūnī's methodological and hermeneutic awareness. Abu'l-Faḍl himself had no command of Sanskrit. He was satisfied with compiling, though carefully organizing, the material which his experts, Hindu scholars in Akbar's service, had prepared for him. He succeeded in producing a rich, well-organized body of information which provides, however, very few perspectives for critical debate or philosophical and religious evaluation.[52] The religious reconciliation attempted by Akbar largely remained an abstract program. The universalistic-syncretistic religion founded by him died with its founder. While Akbar's son Jahāngīr was still tolerant in matters of religion, Shāh Jahān's reign mandated orthodoxy and intolerance once agian. Under Shāh Jahān's sons, Aurangzeb and Dārā Shukōh, the contrast between the two attitudes erupted into bitter and ultimately deadly hostility.

11. Dārā Shukōh's most important legacy is the translation of fifty Upaniṣads, known under the title of *Sirr-i Akbar* ("The Great Secret"). It was completed in 1657, together with paraphrases and excerpts from commentaries which in various cases, though by no means throughout, can be traced back to Śaṅkara.[53] The question whether or to what extent Dārā Shukōh participated in the project as a translator or redactor himself, or whether he left the actual work to Indian scholars, has not yet been answered and need not concern us here.[54] It is certain that he took a strong personal interest in the meaning of Indian concepts and terms, studying not

only the Upaniṣads, but also other Indian texts, especially the *Bhagavadgītā*. He repeatedly engaged in debates on religious and philosophical questions with Hindu scholars. We have records of seven dialogues with Bābā Lāl, who was prepared for such an encounter by his familiarity with Kabīr's tradition.[55] A contemporary of Dārā Shukōh, who has not yet been identified, wrote the *Dabistān*, a work on comparative religion which also deals with Hindu sects and systems. This work was used by scholars such as W. Jones and others during the early days of modern Indology.[56]

From Dārā Shukōh's own pen, we have an attempt to compare and harmonize Hinduism and Islam under the title *Majma' al-baḥrain* ("Mingling of the Oceans").[57] Among the topics discussed in this work, we find the cosmic cycles of Hindu mythology, other cosmological ideas, the concepts of God and an absolute Being, resurrection and final release as absorption in the Absolute, although without much attention to details or to questions of intercultural hermeneutics. Again and again, Dārā Shukōh tries to defend the legitimacy of Indian ideas and theories by referring to often allegorically interpreted passages from the Koran.[58] Dārā Shukōh takes it for granted that Hinduism is basically monotheistic; he considers the monistic-monotheistic source books of Hinduism, the Upaniṣads, as sources of monotheism *per se*, antecedent to the Koran, and he is convinced that the Koran itself refers to this "first heavenly Book, and the fountain-head of the ocean of monotheism."[59] True and original monotheism is not confined to the Koran. Prophets have appeared in many countries, and many traditions know of the true God. In his introduction to the *Sirr-i Akbar* Dārā Shukōh describes how he tried to discover the idea of the oneness of God and the monotheistic creed in its different expressions and manifestations. "The Holy Qur'ān being mostly allegorical, and those who understand these allegories being small (in number), he desired to inspect all heavenly books."[60] He studies the Torah, the Gospels and the Psalms,[61] but it is the "Great Secret" (*Sirr-i Akbar*) of the Upaniṣads which, in his view, represents the most original testimony of the oneness of God or the Absolute.

Dārā Shukōh's personal fate is well-known: in 1659, two years after the completion of the *Sirr-i Akbar*, he was executed by order of his brother, Aurangzeb, and with the consent of the Islamic orthodox community (*Ulamā*), who claimed that he was a heretic and a danger to the state, the faith and the public order.[62]

12. Essential theoretical prerequisites for the strengthening of orthodoxy and for the controversy with syncretistic and monistic developments were already created by Akbar's younger contemporary Ahmad Sirhindī (1564–1624), a declared enemy of Hinduism and of syncretism, who had nevertheless a deep and subtle understanding of Sūfism. According to his own words, he himself went through a monistic phase during which he was

convinced of the "oneness of Being", and he became perfectly familiar with the Sūfī, and implicitly, the Vedāntic notion of supreme unity. However, he discovered that such unity is only a state of mind, an experience and appearance.[63] "Unity of vision" (*waḥdat ash-shuhūd*), i.e., testimonial unity or the personal experience of unity, should not be confused with "unity of being" (*waḥdat al-wujūd*), i.e., objective existential unity.[64] Interpreted in this manner, the monistic temptation has been neutralized: the idea of absolute oneness, which Dārā Shukōh later tried to find in the Upaniṣads, does not represent a possible completion or fulfillment of Islam, but it is itself nothing but a preliminary and transitional phase.

Dārā Shukōh's impact on Indian Islam was rather limited, although his attitude towards Hinduism was certainly not entirely isolated. For instance, in the eighteenth century, Jānjānān Maẓhar insisted that one should be cautious in applying the expression "infidels" (*kāfir*) to the Hindus, since at the beginning of the creation of mankind true and divine revelation had been bestowed on them through the Vedas.[65]

It is particularly important for the development of the European philosophical interest in India that a long time after the re-discovery of the route to India, and after the discovery of many original Indian sources, it was Dārā Shukōh's Persian translation which, through Anquetil Duperron's Latin translation (*Oupnek'hat*, 1801–1802), introduced Western readers to the Upaniṣads.[66] Schopenhauer's reaction to it is well-known. In 1882, Mischel's German translation of Anquetil's Latin text was published in Dresden. In 1808, Th. A. Rixner had presented a sample from the *Oupnek'hat*, i.e., a section from the *Chāndogya Upaniṣad*, in German translation. Still in 1897, several texts in P. Deussen's pioneering *Sechzig Upanishad's des Veda* appeared in a version based on the *Sirr-i Akbar*.[67] Thus, the reception of the *Sirr-i Akbar*, and its Latin version, the *Oupnek'hat*, represents the culmination and at the same time the end of the Islamic mediation of Indian thought to the Occident. Generally, we should also remember the important role which Persian played during the early days of modern Indology, for instance, in the case of W. Jones. The Persian language and Islam are also of significance for the work of Rammohan Roy, the Bengali pioneer of Hindu revivalism at the beginning of the nineteenth century.[68]

3. The Missionary Approach to Indian Thought

1. The interests of Vasco da Gama and his contemporaries, who reopened the seaway to India around 1500, were not directed towards documents of pristine wisdom, but rather towards "Christians and spices."[1] The spice trade was the main objective of the Portuguese expeditions to India. "Most of what Europe in general learned about the East during the first half of the sixteenth century related to the spice trade."[2] In addition, the desire to search for Christians behind the backs of the Islamic powers, a desire that was a legacy of the Middle Ages, also played a role. In 1498, Vasco da Gama arrived in the South Indian port city of Calicut. In 1500, Pedro Cabral led the second Portuguese expedition to Cochin, established contacts with Indian, i.e. Syrian-Malabarian, Christians and took one of them, "Joseph the Indian," to Europe. During the second voyage of Vasco da Gama, in 1502, an official delegation of Christians greeted him in Cochin and presented him with a "rod of justice."[3] Regardless of such curiosities, however, it soon became obvious that the primary concern in India was not in locating old Christians but instead in winning over new ones, and that, apart from the Muslim population and approximately 30,000 "Thomas Christians" of questionable orthodoxy, India was mostly inhabited by Hindus, followers of a religion about which virtually nothing was known. Nevertheless, the motive of searching for Christian elements remained alive in various forms and played a considerable role in shaping the early interest in Hinduism; there was hope to find within Hinduism remnants of a lost Christianity which was thought to have been supplanted and suppressed by Islam.[4] It was felt that analogies to the ideas of the Holy Trinity, the worship of the Virgin Mary, etc. could be both seen among and explained with respect to the Hindus.[5] D.F. Lach says about the general picture of India during the Portuguese pioneer period: "The Europeans also persist in believing that the Hindus adhere to some early form of Christianity which

they were forced to give up or modify under pressure from the Muslims. Consequently, they seek to associate Hindu practices with Christian beliefs rather than trying to understand Hinduism for itself."[6] Various speculations about ancient and forgotten influences of Christianity or Judaism upon the Indians continued during the centuries that followed.[7]

2. The first reports of the conquerors and spice traders, for example those of Albuquerque, Duarte Barbosa, and Castanheda, contributed little towards the understanding of the Indian tradition, in particular in the religious-philosophical domain. This fact notwithstanding, Albuquerque did confirm the existence of a Brahmanic "scientific" language analogous to Latin, viz., Sanskrit; later, during the sixteenth century, the merchant and humanist F. Sassetti (in India from 1583 to 1588) expressed detailed opinions about the uniqueness of this language and about its age and linguistic affiliations.[8] Among the missonaries who went to India (the first of whom were chiefly members of the Franciscan and Dominican orders but who were later primarily Jesuits) there was also little initial penchant towards learning and intellectual debate. To be sure, the pioneer of the Jesuit mission to Asia, Francisco Xavier, helped to awaken interest in and missionary hopes for India as well, yet his attention ultimately shifted more strongly towards the East Asian countries of China and Japan. And while A. Valignano, the thoroughly studious and highly educated Jesuit principal of India (in which function he was responsible for the area ranging from Mozambique to Kyushu) also showed himself to be open-minded towards Eastern Asia, he nevertheless remained very reserved about Hinduism, which he primarily considered to be an example of superstition and "idolatry."[9]

Doubtlessly, it was the desire of the missionaries to preach the Christian gospel. They wanted to teach; this required that they could make themselves understood. The key to such understanding lies in the language of a region, a fact which the Jesuits in particular accepted with great determination and carried out assiduously, making it one of the principles of their missionary activity. Around the middle of the sixteenth century, the first attempts were already being made out of Goa to gain access to Hindu texts. An Indian convert, Manoel d'Oliveira, translated several samples of Marathi translations or adaptations of Sanskrit texts, specifically sections of the *Jñāneśvarī*, the great Marathi paraphrase of the *Bhagavadgītā* by Jñāneśvara, into Portuguese.[10] In 1579, the British Jesuit Thomas Stephens (or Stevens, 1549–1619) arrived in Goa, and he became "one of the first Europeans to master an Indian language so well as to be able to write in it idiomatically."[11] In addition to a grammar of the Konkani language of Goa and a Konkani manual of Christian instruction, he produced the unsurpassed masterpiece of Christian missionary literature in an Indian vernacular, the so-called *Christian Purāṇa*, or *Purāṇa of Biblical History*, in Marathi. This work in 11,000 verses was written at the request of a Brahmin convert and published in 1616.[12]

Even earlier, important linguistic advances were made in the South Indian Tamil country. The Jesuits Antonio Criminali (d. 1549) and Henrique Henriques (d. 1600) were able to express themselves in Tamil. A Tamil-Portuguese Christian manual appeared in Lisbon in 1554, apparently "the first book ever to be printed in any Indian language."[13] Henriques' Tamil translation of the Catechism of Francisco Xavier was published in India in 1576; however, his grammar of the Tamil language remained unpublished. Protestant missionaries later on continued the pioneering work of the Jesuits in this area of India.[14]

The works of Henriques, Stephens and other early pioneers were meant to be practical tools for the propagation of the Christian teachings; they did not indicate any theoretical interest in Hinduism *per se*, nor did they provide perspectives for hermeneutic reflection. It was the great Italian Jesuit Roberto Nobili (usually called de' Nobili[15]) who led the missionary efforts to an entirely new level of theoretical and hermeneutic awareness.

3. Roberto Nobili (1577–1656) is one of the most famous and at the same time controversial figures in the history of the missions. Like few others, he exemplifies the idea and the problematic nature of the encounter between Christianity and Hinduism and, more generally, the hermeneutic ambivalence and dialectic of missionary teaching and scholarship. His surprising success at the mission in Madurai aroused both astonishment and suspicion among his contemporaries and led to some fundamental thinking about the methods involved in missionary work. His great aptitude and energy in learning Indian languages has been much admired among posterity, although it has also been greeted with scepticism. For while he has indeed been called "the father of Tamil prose," "the first European Sanskrit scholar," etc., he has also been suspected of incompetence, forgery, and charlatanry and been attacked from both the Christian and the Brahminic sides.[16]

That uncertainties and doubts as to the character and extent of Nobili's achievements could exist for so long may be at least partially explained by the fact that most of his writings remained unpublished—although by no means entirely without effect. Actually, most were considered irretrievable or lost until recently. In the meantime, a number of his works have appeared, primarily in Tamil and Latin. These editions and several recent studies have led to the emergence of a clearer and more reliable picture of a man whose life and work represents one of the exemplary milestones in the intellectual encounter of Europe and India.

Nobili's Tamil writings, among them a Catechism (*Jñānopadesam*) and a "Disquisition on the Soul" (*Āttuma-nirṇayam*), demonstrate the practices of one who wrestles with the "word" and the attempt to be understood; they also illustrate the basic problems involved in the transmission or transplantation of Christian ideas and concepts into the complex context of Indian religious-philosophical terminology, with its rich associations. In this regard, it will suffice to recall such terms as *āttumam* (Sanskrit *ātman*, as the translation for "soul"), *mokṣam* (*mokṣa*, for "heaven"), or *putti* (*buddhi*, for "intellect")[17] With full lucidity and resolve, Nobili set himself the task of fathoming the associational context and the associational horizon of the Hindus. He saw the possibility of making the Christian message understood as lying therein; therein, to be sure, also lies a great potential for false interpretation and misunderstanding.

Two of Nobili's Latin treatises are of fundamental theoretical and methodological interest: *Informatio de quibusdam moribus nationis indicae* (written in 1613, published in 1972) and *Narratio fundamentorum quibus Madurensis Missionis institutum caeptum est et hucusque consistit* (written in 1618–19, published in 1971). Of the two, the *Informatio* is the more scholarly work, while the *Narratio* is the methodologically more acute.[18]

4. Let us first turn our attention to the *Informatio*. In eleven chapters, this work deals with the social order (caste system), the position and functions of the Brahmins, the traditional Indian sciences, some of the sects, the priesthood, and such Brahminic manners and customs as the wearing of the "sacred thread" and the "tuft of hair." It is Nobili's argument that such customs should be seen simply as traits typical of the country, devoid of religious implication, and containing no meaning contradicting the spirit of Christianity. There is thus no reason for any attempts to abolish them.[19] He also lays particular emphasis upon the fact that the role of the Brahmin caste is primarily social and not religious in nature and is thus not offensive in a Christian sense.

The third chapter, "De scientiis quas Brahmanes tractant," is of especial interest when considering the history of the Western approach to Indian philosophy. In this chapter, Nobili provides a survey of the following traditional Indian sciences; 1) Grammar ("Siabda Siastram," i.e., *śabdaśāstra*); 2) Poetics ("*Cavviam*," i.e., *kāvya*, with *vṛtta* and *alaṃkāra*); 3) Astronomy and Astrology ("Giodi Siastram," i.e., *jyotiṣa*); 4) *Nyāya* ("Gnaiana," "Tarca," "scientia disputativa;" here, a list of the 16 "categories," *padārtha*, is given, which are the subject matter of the classical *Nyāya* system); 5) "Natural Philosophy ("philosophia naturalis," "Cintamani," i.e., *cintāmaṇi*, a survey of the Navyanyāya, whose title refers to the title of the basic work of this philosophical school, the *Tattvacintāmaṇi* by Gaṅgeśa, and which also contains noteworthy references to some of the less well-known contemporaries and successors of Gaṅgeśa); 6) "Theology ("Adiatmicam," i.e., *ādhyātmika*, paraphrased by Nobili as "scientia de Deo seu theologia"; with references to Buddhism and Vedānta); 7) a "science of law" ("scientia legum") not referred to by any Sanskrit term (these are the basic rules of the "sects" discussed in ch.4); 8) *Dharmaśāstra* ("darmasiastram," with the *Nītiśāstra*); finally, reference is made to the medical system ("Aiur vedam," i.e., *āyurveda*). In addition, mention is also made of the traditional scheme of the 18 "sciences" (or "artes").[20]

The fourth chapter, "De sectis Brahmanum quantum attinet ad religionem," presents the main Indian "sects:" 1) "De Buddheris sive Atheis," in which the Buddhists and the Jainas are encompassed under the heading of *one single* sect; 2) "De Gnanis," which deals with spiritual purists who place their faith in knowledge alone (i.e., *jñānin*); 3) "De idolatris"; in this section, mention is made of the *Śaivas, Vaiṣṇavas,* and *Śāktas* ("Siacti") along with the materialists ("Logaides," i.e., *lokāyatika*, "qui dicunt elementa ipsa Deum esse," "who say that God is nothing but the elements"). We find here what is probably the oldest, albeit somewhat confused, reference in European literature to Śaṅkara ("Ciancaraciarien," i.e., Śaṅkarācārya, as the head of the "*maiavadae*," i.e., *māyāvādin*); Rāmānuja ("Ramanugen") and Madhva ("Madhven") are also named. Within the same context, a survey of the four Vedas and the Vedic literature is provided. Here, Nobili also discusses the Upaniṣads ("Upanisiat") as well as the term *brahman*, which he considers to be the "most general name for God",[21] giving several Sanskrit citations. He even finds intimations of the "recondite mystery of the most sacred trinity" ("misterium reconditum Sanctissimae Trinitatis") in the Upaniṣads.[22]

5. One of the most important aspects of Nobili's treatment of the Upaniṣads and of the literature and sciences of the Brahmins in general is his search for expressions of a pristine, natural, monotheistic, and non-"idolatrous" sense of God. As mentioned above, he found this in particular in the concept of Brahman: for him, the word *brahman*, when used in the neuter ("vox Brahma ultima brevi"), did not denote a "specific and false god," but rather "God in general" ("non significat deum aliquem determinatum et falsum, sed Deum in communi"); it was used to designate the one, true, immaterial God, at least as far as it was possible for him to be known through the natural light of reason ("qui lumine naturae cognosci potest").[23] In general, he defended the Brahminic sciences against the argument that since they had been cultivated by heathens, they should be condemned as superstition one and all—"as if the heathen sages were not also capable of bringing forth valuable teachings which could likewise be of use to Christians." In making such a statement, Nobili was able to adduce the

liberal positions of such church fathers as Gregory of Nazianzus, Ambrose, Hieronymus, and Augustine concerning non-Christian wisdom.[24] In his view, the Brahminic teachings were a primarily secular, natural wisdom; the role of the Brahmins and their function, as well as their customs and insignia, were mundane and social in nature, not religious; they were "wise men," not idolators or temple priests.[25] He paid special attention to questions concerning the meaning and permissibility of the Brahminic thread, an issue which was to become a test case in the discussions of the time;[26] since the wearing of the thread was merely a sign of a worldly custom, and not an idolatrous superstition, there was no reason for it to be forbidden among the converts to Christianity.[27] — In the context of both this and other matters, Nobili also makes sweeping references to such writers of antiquity as Megasthenes, Clearchus, and Strabo, all of whom had consistently referred to the Brahmins as philosophers and not as priests.[28]

In the two closing chapters, the author recapitulates that a clear distinction should be made between social customs ("mores civiles") and religious ceremonies; that not only could and should the former be tolerated, but that the missionary must actually adapt himself to them so that he might be met with an attentive ear in religious matters and be able to present himself and his teachings within the horizon of understanding of those who were to be taught and converted. In other words, that which is human in nature should be learned and adopted so that that which is divine could be transmitted and consolidated.[29] In contrast, there was no room for compromise and no possibility of accommodation as far as fundamental questions of the Christian faith and dogma were concerned; Nobili thus, for example, found the doctrine of metempsychosis to be completely unacceptable.[30]

6. The conclusions Nobili reached in the *Informatio* (1613) were presented with a much greater eye towards their practical missionary application in the *Narratio* , which was submitted to the council of Goa in 1619: The basic missionary principle is that those conditions must be fulfilled which make it possible for the persons addressed to listen to those proclaiming the Christian gospel. To achieve this, it was not enough to merely learn the language of the intended listeners, it was also necessary to penetrate into their way of life, to gain their "pia affectio" and their esteem in a human and social sense: "Evangelicus concionator illam instituere debet vivendi rationem, qua dignus iudicetur ab iis, inter quos versatur, qui audiatur."[31] The upshot was that the proclaimer of the Gospel must be prepared "to set aside the customs of his homeland and to be an Indian among Indians" ("patrios abnegare mores, et inter Indos Indum esse").[32]

Nobili defended such hermeneutic and pedagogic pragmatism, which finds parallels in the Jesuit missions of the Far East, by referring to the "adaptive" tradition of the church. He cited the Apostle Paul's appearance before the Athenians as being analogous in a certain sense, for Paul had addressed the Athenians as "learned" and "wise," just as the Brahmins should be addressed as learned and wise and treated with respect. Paul had taken notice of the educational background and expectational horizon of the Athenians, even making reference to their "unknown God." In this way, he tried "to appear not as the inventor of a new religion, but rather as an advocate and proclaimer of their own primal worship of God" ("ne novi numinis videretur inventor, sed potius antiqui illorum cultus assertor ac praedicator.")[33]

As a matter of fact, Nobili himself became known in Madurai as the "Guru of the lost law." He called upon the Brahmins "to become his pupils in order to learn about the 'lost Veda";[34] the Indians should be shown that it was possible for them to accept the alien religion as a rediscovery and fulfilment of the original substance of their own tradition. Suspicions, doubtlessly wrong, even grew that Nobili had written a syncretic "Veda."[35] At any rate, it seems certain that he was not the author of the *Ezourvedam*, which Voltaire received in manuscript form in 1760 and which gained some notoriety in eighteenth-century Europe.[36]

The following brief summary characterizes the reaction to Nobili's efforts: While the Papal Bull *Cum sicut fraternitatis* of Paul V (1616) may indeed have evinced a certain esteem for his methods, the predominant reactions were rejection and hostility, both among the Portuguese, who had the say in India, and in the Vatican. This reaction was similar to that reaped by the Jesuit mission in China, in particular as represented by Matteo Ricci. In the North, where the Moguls had control of India, another Jesuit missionary followed Nobili's example several decades after the latter first began his work in South India. Heinrich Roth (1620–1668) devoted himself with comparable energy, but more strongly developed philological interests, to the study of Sanskrit and the literature of India, including works of a philosophical nature. Yet his writings, which include the first European Sanskrit grammar as well as a copy of the *Vedāntasāra* by Sadānanda, also remained unpublished and have only recently been rediscovered in handwritten form.[37]

7. The contrast between al-Bīrūnī and de'Nobili is conspicuous and instructive: While Bīrūnī also possessed a well-defined religious and hermeneutic awareness, he was essentially a scholar and not driven to preach. In contrast, Nobili learned in order to teach and be understood. We may say that he represents an active, transitive form of hermeneutics in which, in so far as he was interested in introducing his own Christian message into the horizon and context of a foreign cultural tradition, pedagogic and strategic points of view were of primary concern. His readiness to learn and to adapt was motivated by the principle of soteriological

efficacy; his idea was to make as many accommodations as possible to the people to be addressed and taught and to limit the contents of the message to the essentials, freeing it of all unnecessary ballast. For Nobili, there was as little reason to doubt that the Christian gospel as such, freed of all its social and poetic trappings, could be transplanted without damage into an alien social context and into alien ways of thinking, as there was to doubt the truth of the gospel itself.[38] He had no fundamental questions as to the intercultural communicability of his message, indeed, he could not have them if he was to take his mission seriously, and thus, as much as he was willing to make concessions with respect to ways of life, so little was he able to allow Hindu thought to affect the dogmatic substance of his own Christian convictions.[39] Moreover, in the debate with his fellow Christians, it was also important for Nobili to let as wide as possible a foundation of "natural light" and basic human reason appear as a bridge and basis for potential receptivity to the Christian revelation. Just as the church fathers had accepted the "natural light" of Greek learning, so too did he decide to accept the "natural light" of Brahminic learning and pursue the study of Indian philosophy, for this was the common denominator, the precondition for the possibility of understanding and being understood. The concept of *brahman*, as a natural conception of God, exemplifies the common denominator and the receptiveness for the revelation which he had postulated.

Nobili is evidently not satisfied with a simple "retrieval" of fundamental, generally acceptable religious and philosophical ideas in the Indian tradition. He is a missionary and not a theorizing universalist. Yet his far-reaching readiness to find a common basis of "natural religion" in India, and to separate the pure essence of Christianity from all social and cultural paraphernalia, appears as a potential threat to the missionary impetus itself. Could it not, if pursued to its radical consequences, turn into a merely theoretical interest in recovering religion as such from underneath its social and historical manifestations, an abstract deistic recognition of what has always been there?

The mistrust which often greeted Nobili within the church was not due to the shortcomings of his opponents alone. Moreover, it is certainly no coincidence that the deists and Enlightenment figures of the eighteenth century drew some of the concrete support for their criticism of Christianity from the reports of the Jesuit missionaries in Asia. What is more, the persons addressed by these missionary methods also found leads to their own religious and philosophical self-defense and self-representation therein and, for their own part, began to measure the alien religion against the standards of "natural theology," reason and ethics which the missionaries applied to them.[40]

8. Our concern here cannot be with offering an even somewhat complete or representative look at other missionary contributions to the understanding or the criticism of Indian thought. We can only cite a few exemplary cases that were significant not just within the context of missionary history. During the eighteenth century, a number of Jesuit reports with philosophical contents appeared in print, in particular in the series *Lettres édifiantes et curieuses*. This was part of a greater tradition of publishing the letters of missionaries from India and other parts of the world which had begun as early as the sixteenth century. From a philosophical point of view, one letter which is especially remarkable is that from J.F. Pons to J.B. du Halde dating from 1740.[41] This letter provides a concise but knowledgeable overview of the scientific and philosophical literature of the Indians. In addition to remarks about their achievements in the domain of grammar, there are also brief accounts of the doctrines of the classical systems of philosophy, in particular those of the Nyāya ("Oudayanacarya," i.e., Udayana, is named), Vedānta (with a reference to "Sankrachary," i.e., Śaṅkara), and Sāṃkhya (Kapila). Father Pons' criticism and aversion is directed especially against Advaita Vedānta. He considers the identification of the self with the absolute to be a sign of a Luciferian hybris. The missionaries are warned against accepting the Vedāntic emphasis upon the unity of God—"l'unité de Dieu (addvitam)."[42] Pons did not attempt to view the concept of *brahman* as a concept of God formulated by a natural theology, as did Nobili, to whom Pons refers with great respect as a Sanskrit scholar. Another remarkable thing about this letter, which, by the way, also refers to Buddhism ("bauddamatham") as a heresy,[43] is its repeated mentions of the gymnosophists and of Pythagoras as a traveler to India who learned the Brahminic sciences.[44] The Jesuit J. Bouchet compared the beliefs of the Indians with those of the Hebrews ("Croyances des Indiens comparées à celles des Hébreux").[45] In a remarkable adaptation of Numenius' reference to Plato as "atticizing Moses," he characterized the Veda as Moses using the medium of Sanskrit ("quid est Veda nisi Moses sanskritisans?")[46] Father J. Calmette, one of the most active and productive members of this group of French missionaries, rearticulated the method of appealing to certain "reasonable" premises which the Indians themselves employed in their philosophical teachings: "The method which we observe with the Brahmins is to let them at first acknowledge certain principles which reasoning has spread abroad in their philosophy; and by the conclusions which we draw from them, we then demonstrate to them without difficulty the falsity of the views which they commonly accept." ("La méthode que nous observons avec les brames est de les faire convenir d'abord de certains principes que le raisonnement a répandu dans leur philosophie; et par les conséquences que nous en tirons, nous leur démonstrons sans peine la fausseté des opinions

qu'ils reçoivent communément").[47] In a letter to Tournemine dating from 1737, Calmette also emphasized the rich presence of "natural light" in India and expressed his amazement that the Indians were nevertheless able to become involved in such superstitions.[48] In the eighteenth century, several other authors from the Catholic, and in particular Jesuit, missions made contributions to the knowledge of Sanskrit and Indian culture and influenced the picture of India in general. Among these were the Jesuits J.E. Hanxleden and J. Tieffenthaler and, in particular, the Carmelite Paulinus a S. Bartholomaeo (i.e., J. Ph. Wessdin, or Vesdin). The youngest and most productive of this group, Paulinus (1749–1806) also marks the close of this epoch of pioneering missionary work and, in his polemic disputes with Anquetil Duperron and the British Orientalists, the transition to a new stage in the understanding of India.[49]

Missionaries, most of them working outside of India, were also responsible for bringing the first accounts of Buddhism to Europe. However, they rarely recognized the original ties between Buddhism and India.[50]

9. The contributions of the Jesuits and other missionaries in the seventeenth and eighteenth centuries are intricately related with the religious, intellectual and political movements in Europe. They reflect the contemporary debate on such topics as faith and reason, religion and science, church and state, and they have an ambiguous, yet significant impact upon the thought of the Age of Enlightenment. Apart from this, it is the sheer accumulation of new information on India, and the preparation of tools and materials of research, which makes the work of these missionaries important. In several areas, their achievements are unequalled before the beginning of modern Indological research, which is usually associated with the foundation of the Asiatic Society of Bengal in 1784 and the work of the British pioneers W. Jones, Ch. Wilkins and H. Th. Colebrooke.

As a matter of fact, the claim has been made that French missionaries of the eighteenth century, together with their Indian collaborators, are the true founders of modern Indology. "The birth of Indology as a real science is the result of a collaboration between Indian traditional scholars and French missionaries. The first work that can be recognized as a scientific achievement is a grammar of Sanskrit written in Latin, at about 1733. It is probably the work of J.F. Pons, a Jesuit, who resided in India, especially at Chandranagore, Karaikal and Pondicherry, in the first dęcades of the eighteenth century."[51]

However we assess this claim, it is certain that Father Pons and others took an important step even beyond Nobili's achievements. They collected Indian manuscripts and sent them to Europe.[52] They developed tools of research. They devised methods of collaboration with native Indian scholars. Among these Indians, Maridas Poullé (Mariyadās Pillai, born

1721), a baptized Tamil scholar, became the most famous. He learned French and Latin, became "Indian Interpreter of the French Company," and translated a Tamil version of the *Bhāgavatapurāṇa* into French.[53]

Yet, for a variety of reasons these remarkable efforts did not inaugurate the tradition of modern Indological research as such. Within the Jesuit order and the Catholic church, room for research and, even more so, the dissemination of its results was limited. As was the case with Nobili in the seventeenth century, many important works of the eighteenth century were never published. Others were censored and truncated. The *Lettres édifiantes et curieuses* were not normally the originals as they had been written in India or elsewhere, but they were edited and revised in Paris. The great work of G.L. Coeurdoux on the "Manners and Customs of the Indians" (*Moeurs et coutumes des Indiens*), a systematic continuation and summary of earlier Jesuit efforts in India, remained unpublished, although it was utilized by the Abbé J.A. Dubois and others.[54] In general, we have to recall the precarious situation of the Jesuit order in the eighteenth century, and the military and political defeat of the French in India.

Towards the end of the eighteenth century, the Jesuits were more commonly associated with the scandalous *Ezourvedam* than with sober research. The French text of this false Veda, which had probably been conceived (though never employed) as a device for the Christianization of the Hindus, was cited as a document on ancient Indian religion by Voltaire and others. It was finally published in 1778 and translated into German in 1779. But with its growing popularity came increased criticism. In 1782, P. Sonnerat declared that it was a forgery, and few were left who were willing to defend its authenticity. In 1822, it became known that the *Ezourvedam* was only one of a group of "Pseudo-Vedas" which had either been produced or solicited by the Jesuits in India.[55]

10. In addition to the Catholics, Protestants have also been active in missionary work in India since the seventeenth century. In the beginning, they too were primarily found in South India. The Dutch Calvinist missionary Abraham Roger made an especially important and influential contribution to the European understanding of Indian religion and literature. Based upon his experiences in South India, he wrote a book entitled *De Open-Deure tot het verborgen Heydendom* which, in an appendix, included a translation of the poems of Bhartṛhari as explained to him by a native pandit—the first example of a Sanskrit text having been translated into and published in a European language.[56] Roger's "Open Door" soon appeared in German (Nuremburg, 1663), and French (Amsterdam, 1670). The French translator, Thomas La Grue, gave special emphasis in his introduction to what was also clearly a motif with Roger himself: that the Indians did indeed possess a pristine and natural knowledge of God, but that it had

decayed almost completely into superstition as a result of moral lapses.[57] Another Dutch missionary, Philippus Baldaeus, published his work on the *Afgoderye der oost-indische Heydenen* in Amsterdam in 1672. Like several other familiar and influential works on India, the "Idolatry of the East-Indian Heathens" is not a very original work; it is largely based upon an older, anonymous manuscript.[58]

Since the beginning of the eighteenth century, Moravian missionaries were active with great engagement in South India, using Tranquebar (Tarangambādi, south of Madras) as the center and base of their activity. Most of them German, they worked under Danish commission and made a name for themselves through their pioneering work in the area of South Indian lexicography and the translation of Christian literature into Indian tongues.[59] The actual founder and most prominent exponent of this Lutheran missionary tradition in South India was Bartholomäus Ziegenbalg (1682–1719). Like that of Nobili, Ziegenbalg's influence was rather limited during his own lifetime, and his major works were not published until many years after his death. A.H. Francke categorically refused to allow publication of one of Ziegenbalg's two main works, the *Genealogie der malabarischen Götter* (written 1713), because "the missionaries were sent out to exterminate heathendom in India, and not to spread heathen nonsense throughout Europe."[60] It was not until 1867 that this work was "officially" published in an essentially unabridged, though not very reliable edition. Its editor, W. Germann, obviously failed to notice that a partially reworked edition of the book had appeared in Berlin in 1791 under the title *Beschreibung der Religion und heiligen Gebräuche der malabarischen Hindous* ("Description of the Religion and Sacred Customs of the Malabarian Hindus"); in this edition, Ziegenbalg's name was not given on the title page, but mentioned only in a short "Postscript." Ziegenbalg's other main work, the *Ausführliche Beschreibung des malabarischen Heidentums* ("Detailed Description of the Malabarian Heathendom") was first published in Amsterdam in 1926, with W. Caland as editor. Special attention is also due to the detailed letters and reports by Ziegenbalg and his associates in Tranquebar describing conversations with Hindus and their positions vis-à-vis Christianity. Unlike Ziegenbalg's major works, these reports became known in Europe during his own lifetime.[61]

11. In contrast to Nobili, Ziegenbalg had no knowledge of Sanskrit, although he was familiar with Tamil. His penetration into the Brahminic literary tradition, like his methodological and hermeneutic thinking, cannot be compared with that of his Jesuit predecessor. And yet the way in which he deals with one great and central theme is exemplary and impressive. This is the idea of the unity of God lying in and behind the multitude of "heathen" gods, of a pristine and natural knowledge of the true God as the

background to the current "superstition": "These heathens recognize from the light of nature that there is a God, a truth which they did not need the Christians to teach them."[62] Ziegenbalg referred to this *one* highest being which he found implied in the Hindu doctrines by using the term "Barába-rawastu" (i.e., *parāparavastu*), making a distinction between it and the many *deva*. To be sure, he also noted: "In spite of the knowledge that there is only one single divine being, these heathens have nevertheless allowed themselves to be seduced by the devil and their ancient poets into believing in a multitude of gods, whereby they have strayed so far away from the signs of the one God that they do not know how to find their way back."[63] The Indians no longer understood the true, lost origins of their own religion; this is why they needed to be reawakened by Christianity. Ziegenbalg found the potential for such a reawakening lying in the forgotten depths of their own traditional wisdom; indeed, he even found a certain implicit anticipation of true monotheism therein. He relates that the father of one Indian convert to Christianity wrote the following lines to his son: "You do not yet know the secrets of our religion, for we do not worship many gods in the preposterous fashion you think we do, but instead just worship one divine being among all. There are wise persons among us, and if you would speak with them, then they would explain this to you and remove your doubts. A person who understands our religion correctly is certainly able to attain salvation through it, and there are many instances of this among us to whom God has given salvation in an obvious manner."[64]

12. In various ways, the understanding of India was drawn into the polemics between the Protestants and the Catholics, as, for example, when it was claimed that the ritualism of the Roman Church exhibited Hindu influences.[65] In one important point, however, there was agreement among numerous statements made on both the Protestant and the Catholic sides: "Running like a thread through the reports of the missionaries is the thought that the Indians, 'nonobstant la plus grossière idolatrie,' nevertheless possessed a monotheistic belief in one highest, most perfect being from the very beginning."[66]

This is a theme which also occurs often in some of the travel accounts which are not part of the missionary literature, particularly in the widely read works of F. Bernier and J.B. Tavernier from the seventeenth century and of P. Sonnerat from the eighteenth century.[67] Two main reasons were given in order to explain this essential agreement with Christian monotheism. Firstly, as the previous discussions have already shown, references were made to a "natural light" that was also accessible to the Indians, as well as to a pristine or natural revelation. Secondly, Christian or Jewish influences or the lost memories of a unified tradition dating from before the Tower of Babel that had been held in common with the people of the Bible were assumed.[68] The influence of sin and evil and the wrath of God were cited as reasons why the Indians fell from such pristine knowledge into superstition and darkness, and now and again the hope was uttered in this connection that God would spare the Occident such a deprivation of his mercy and the light of his truth.[69] From time to time, more recent Christian theologians and missionaries, e.g. W. Koppers, have also advocated this conception of an originally pure monotheism among the Indians, as among other "heathen" peoples;[70] some authors still refer to an Indian "fall from the true God."[71]

During the further course of development, it has turned out that the observations or assumptions which missionaries made about the monotheistic origins and bases of Hinduism could be easily reinterpreted and used in other lines of reasoning, both deistic and anti-Christian.[72] Thus, Hinduism and Christianity have been juxtaposed as being of equal value or, alternately, a greater originality and historical priority has been claimed for Hinduism. In this context, we may recall the edition of Ziegenbalg's *Genealogie der malabarischen Götter*, which appeared in Berlin in 1791. Through a few counterproductive measures—in this edition, for example, Ziegenbalg's word "heathen" was usually replaced by the word "Indian," while the summons to missionary work at the end of the book was omitted completely—a piece of missionary literature was transformed into a work of the Enlightenment. And the *Ezourvedam*, which owed its existence to Christian missionary zeal, became a source of inspiration for Voltaire's anti-Christian ideology.

13. Until well into the nineteenth century, the "active hermeneutics" (which by then enjoyed the decisive support of the British Missionary Societies) of the missionaries remained one of the most important channels of European access to Indian thought. Up to the turn of the nineteenth century, it had been the policy of the British East India Company to avoid or even prohibit missionary activities. Baptist missionaries had nevertheless been active in Bengal since the end of the eighteenth century, using the Danish enclave of Serampore as their basis. Their leading exponents, W. Carey, J. Marshman, and W. Ward,[73] began to study Sanskrit and Bengali at once, as well as Indian literature, with great energy. Even back in England, the study of Sanskrit and the vernacular languages as well as the production of dictionaries and other resources was often explicitly placed in the service of the proclamation of the Christian gospel. This, for example, was the case with the Sanskrit dictionaries of M. Monier-Williams, which are still in wide use today.[74]

Despite the intolerant attitude which often prevailed among the missionaries, their goals of teaching and of translating the Bible into the languages of India resulted in an ever more systematic and thorough inquiry into the contexts of Indian thought which was carrried out with the cooperation of native pandits. Thus the work of W. Ward includes a remarkable presentation of Indian philosophy (which is admittedly indebted to Colebrooke's research), while W. Carey, in his position at the College of Fort William (founded in 1800), displayed an enthusiasm for teaching and learning which went far beyond mere "missionary work."[75] The exegesis and appropriation of traditional Indian concepts as a means for proclaiming Christianity which we have already observed in South India was now taken up once more, this time within an expanded framework, by practitioners and theoreticians among both the missionaries and the colonialists. The impact which this process had not just upon the Western understanding of India, but in particular upon the Indian answer to the Western challenge, shall be dealt with in greater detail at a later point.[76]

Even J.R. Ballantyne, one of the nineteenth century's most dedicated sponsors and organizers of the study of Indian philosophy and the cooperation with pandits, stressed that he did not recommend such a study because of the "intrinsic value" of Indian philosophy, but rather to be able to approach the learned among the Indians and have them listen, as well as to avoid having the Christian doctrine misunderstood as a result of an insufficient consideration of the Indian context.[77] In this connection, Ballantyne criticized the use of such Sanskrit terms as *ākāśa* and *pṛthivī* (as renderings of "heaven" and "earth) in the translation of Genesis made by the Baptists at Serampore because these expressions had been compromised through their frequent usage in Indian natural philosophy and the theory of the elements and were therefore liable to be misconceived. He recommended the expression *diva* and *bhūmi* instead.[78] It is, of course, obvious that Ballantyne's sympathy for Indian philosophy went far beyond a merely instrumental interest, and the intolerant polemics found among many of the missionaries and Christian authors are completely foreign to him.[79]

14. J. Muir was of equal importance as an Indologist and as a theoretician of the Christian missions. In accordance with the example set by W. Carey and W.H. Mill, he was deeply committed to the principles of "conciliation" and "adaptation." Like Roberto Nobili in the seventeenth century, he invoked the Apostle Paul as a "model for the missionary."[80] Even his Indological investigations, above all the five volumes of his *Original Sanskrit Texts on the Origin and History of the Indian People* (1858–1872) were at least as much addressed to the Indians as to the Europeans. His Sanskrit treatise *Mataparīkṣā* (Calcutta, 1839), which offers a critique of the religious and philosophical teachings of Hinduism from a Christian point of view, is an important piece of missionary literature. It provoked a series of responses from Hindu scholars.[81] The activities of learned Indian converts, such as N. Nīlakaṇṭha Śāstrī Gore—who had argued against the

Mataparīkṣā while still a Hindu—and K.M. Banerjea, also merit mention in this context. From the angle of their newly acquired Christian convictions, they reexamined and reinterpreted their own tradition for both Indian and Western audiences.[82]

One model for the encounter of the Christian missionaries with Indian religious life and thought which gained increasing significance during the nineteenth century was the idea of fulfilment, which Nobili had already alluded to. This idea held that Indian religious concepts and convictions were not to be refuted and dismissed, but instead ought to be led beyond their own limitations to a perfection and fulfilment which the Indians themselves were incapable of seeing without being awakened to it by the Christian missionaries.

M. Müller and, more specifically, M. Monier-Williams contributed to the popularity of this idea, although the latter subsequently denounced it as reflecting "a limp, flabby, jelly-fish kind of tolerance."[83] About his earlier usage of the term, E. Sharpe says: "By 'fulfilment,' Monier-Williams meant two distinct things: first that 'lower' religions are 'fulfilled' by 'higher' religions in the process of evolution, and that Christianity is the fulfilment of Hinduism since it exists on the highest possible evolutionary plane of development; and secondly, that Christianity is that form of religion which satisfies or 'fulfils' the religious instincts and desires in the heart of every man, of whatever religion he may be."[84] The missionary T.E. Slater declares: "All religions wait for their fulfillment in Christianity."[85] And J.N. Farquhar, missionary, Indological scholar and the most famous advocate of the idea of fulfilment, adds: "This is the attitude of Jesus to all other religions also. Each contains a partial revelation of God's will, but each is incomplete; and He comes to fulfil them all. In each case Christianity seeks not to destroy but to take all that is right and raise it to perfection."[86]

15. In particular, the Upaniṣads and the Vedānta were presented as the highpoint of Indian religious thought, as a transitional stage and as a signpost on the way to Christianitry, and as the basis for the latter's proclamation. The Vedānta should be envisaged as a "presentiment of Christian truth,"[87] as an allusion to the life and passion of Christ and as a preparation for Christianity. "The Vedānta is not Christianity, and never will be—simply as the Vedānta; but it is a very definite preparation for it . . . It is our belief that the living Christ will sanctify and make complete the religious thought of India. For centuries . . . her saints have been longing for him, and her thinkers, not at least the thinkers of the Vedānta have been thinking his thought."[88] Even the title of J.N. Farquhar's famous work, *The Crown of Hinduism* (London, 1913; reprinted in Delhi, 1971), is exemplary in this regard. In a sequence of chapters, Farquhar presents both Christ and Christianity as the "crowning" and the inner fulfilment of the

deepest aspirations of Hinduism. An Indian Christian version of the idea of fulfilment is found in the writings of the great Bengali convert K.M. Banerjea.[89]

R.G. Milburn invokes the analogy of the Old Testament: "A very useful step would be the recognition of certain books or passages in the literature of the Vedānta as constituting what might be called an Ethnic Old Testament . . . " According to Milburn, the Vedānta is not only important as an "introduction" to Christianity; it can also help the missionary to understand his own religion better, to move it in more "freely and joyfully," since it provides him with "terms and models of expression" which can help him to appreciate and articulate "the more immanental aspects of Christianity."[90] Several more recent authors have pursued and radicalized the idea of a "Christian Vedānta," or even turned it into the idea of a "Vedāntic Christianity."[91]

It is no surprise that the idea of fulfilment was also taken up from the side of Hinduism, where it was placed into the service of Hindu self-assertion and turned against Christianity. To be sure, this did not normally lead to calls for a counter-mission or concrete acts of conversion; nor was it associated with a *historical* subordination of Christianity to Hinduism. Rather, it was claimed that the relative truth of Christianity as such was fulfilled through and included in the absolute and timeless truth of the Vedānta, and that the Vedānta provided the encompassing context within which Christianity, like all other religions, was contained and *a priori* superseded. We may even suspect that the development of the idea of fulfilment among the Christian missionaries is, in part at least, a response to the Neo-Hindu inclusivism, as we find it exemplified by Ramakrishna, Keshab Chandra Sen and Vivekananda. M. Müller, J.N. Farquhar and other proponents of fulfilment were certainly fully aware of the religious and philosophical movements in Neo-Hinduism.

More recently, a somewhat defensive posture appears to have gained ground among Christian writers; and the possibility of a reverse proselytization, as well as the claim of an *a priori* inclusion of Christianity in Vedānta, seems to be a matter of concern.[92]

16. In general, it may be said that as opposed to the early period of Indology, the more recent period has seen little exceptional pioneering Indological work by missionaries. Moreover, the intensity of their "active hermeneutics" has clearly subsided, even though such authors as H.W. Schomerus, C. Bulcke, R. Antoine or R.V. de Smet have made very significant contributions in the twentieth century. The work of R. Otto (1869–1937) is still probably the best-known theological contribution to Indian studies made in this century; Otto, who advocated the foundation of an "Inter-Religious League" ("Religiöser Menschheitsbund"), was fully willing to acknowledge the uniqueness of Hinduism, although he nevertheless

credited Christianity with a "special spirit" of superior quality.[93] Besides this, the idea of the neutralization and fulfilment of Hinduism in Christianity retained its importance in the theoretical debate; and further attempts were made to construe the relation of the New Testament to the Old Testament as being paradigmatic for the position of Christianity vis-à-vis Hinduism and other non-Christian religions.[94] For the rest, it is not necessary to concern ourselves in any more detail with the question as to how far the efforts of more recent theologians, both Catholic and Protestant, and especially of Indian Christian theologians, have led to new and autonomous models for the encounter with Hinduism.[95]

When measured by the extent to which Christianity has spread throughout India, the missionary efforts in this country can hardly be described as having been successful, and dogmatism and intolerance have frequently played a dominating role in the approach of the missionaries to Indian thought. This notwithstanding, the achievements of the missionaries comprise a very important chapter in the history of the Western encounter with Indian thought, a chapter that is exemplary from a hermeneutic standpoint and which, moreover, has also had historical consequences. The missionaries have performed pioneering, detailed work in several areas. But primarily, in spite of or perhaps precisely because of their "prejudice" and dogmatic limitations, they have also helped to define and clarify the central problems involved in approaching and understanding that which is alien: They, or at least their outstanding exponents, embody a desire to understand whose singular power and problematic nature arise from their deep and uncompromising *desire to be understood.*

4. Deism, the Enlightenment, and the Early History of Indology

1. The reports of the missionaries, while never published in their entirety, were the most important sources of the European notions about Indian thought during the seventeenth century and remained as one of the most important in the eighteenth. To be sure, the interest which greeted these reports was by no means limited to an interest in the advance of Christianity or in the problems associated with its diffusion. For the knowledge and observations which the missionaries themselves saw as the means and prerequisites for proclaiming the Christian gospel could also attain an independent status and be applied to other ends as well. As indicated above, they could be used to oppose the very intentions that they were originally designed to serve. The reference to a "natural light" and the discovery of a natural conception of God and a natural theology and *philosophia perennis* were, particularly for the Jesuits, the prerequisite and the stimulus for doing missionary work in India. The same principle which served in the realization of these efforts, namely that of isolating the pure and, moreover, rationally understandable origins and bases from the overlying ritual trappings and superstitious distortions, could also be applied to Christianity itself. And it was in this way that the reports about India and the other non-European traditions, in particular China, which the Jesuits passed on fit those religious and philosophical tendencies of Rationalism and the Enlightenment that are subsumed under the term *Deism.*[1]

In 1624, Herbert of Cherbury, a contemporary of Roberto Nobili, published *De veritate* ("On Truth"), his main work. It goes into as little detail about India as its supplement, *De religione gentilium* ("On the Religion of the Heathens," written between 1642 and 1645, published in 1663). Yet it offered a framework in which many of the reports about the religion and philosophy of India were to find a place. In these works,

Herbert set forth the idea of a "religion of pure reason and suprahistorical catholicity." "The five constituent articles of faith of this new and oldest religion are the following: the belief in one God; the duty to honor him; his moral worship in the form of pious attitudes and virtuous conduct (virtus cum pietate coniuncta), the pain of sin, and the belief in an afterlife in which good and evil are rewarded." It was this—and only this—which was ultimately of importance in Christianity and the other religions. Christianity was one of a number of religions which had been nurtured at the fountainhead of the universal, pan-human revelation of reason. "There are no fully neglected religions: nulla umquam fuit tam barbara sive religio sive philosophia, cui sua non stetit veritas. In every historical religion, a precise distinction must be made between their rational origins and their non-rational development."[2]

2. Herbert used the expressions *notitia communis* and *consensus gentium* to characterize and justify his basic religious truths, expressions which refer to Stoic philosophy and the universalism it posited, and especially to the doctrine of *κοιναι εννοιαι* developed by Chrysippus. Stoic philosophy is known to have experienced a decisive revival in the sixteenth century, e.g., through J. Lipsius. In this context, we may recall the idea of a "natural theology," which found expression as early as the fifteenth century through Raymond of Sabunde as well as Thomas More's concept of a rational religion (*Utopia*, 1516) and the work of Augustinus Steuchus on the *philosophia perennis.*[3] In general, an interest in the diversity of humanity answering to the Age of Discovery worked its way into the literature of the sixteenth century, e.g., in J. Böhm's *Omnium gentium mores* (1520) and S. Franck's *Cosmographia, Weltbuch* (1534), which followed through on Böhm's ideas. An impressive example of this trend was provided by Montaigne (1553–1592), who, in his openness towards the variety of human viewpoints and foreign, unfamiliar patterns of behavior, tended towards scepticism and relativism while nevertheless clinging to the idea of the universality of basic moral principles. G. Postel (1501–1581) was an advocate of a Christian cosmopolitanism oriented around the Orient in the larger sense, as best expressed in his *Des merveilles du monde*, first published in 1552.[4] The *Colloquium heptaplomeres* of J. Bodin (1530–1596) represents a new and revolutionary approach to the comparison of religions and interreligious dialogue. The first published edition of this work appeared in 1841, but its existence was widely known since the end of the seventeenth century. The pamphlet *De tribus impostoribus* ("On the Three Imposters," i.e. Moses, Jesus and Mohammed), which was allegedly published in 1598 and contains "comparative" references to the Veda and the Brahmins, is probably (at least in its extant form) a falsification produced in the eighteenth century.

A number of works, including those by J. Toland, A. Collins, and M. Tindal (*Christianity as Old as the Creation; or the Gospel a Republication of the Religion of Nature*, 1730), continued the "deistic" discussion, brought it to a head, and created an intellectual atmosphere which came to be of considerable importance for the late eighteenth-century understanding of India. The deistic motif may also be clearly seen among many of the eighteenth-century English pioneers of Indian studies, namely in A. Dow and J.Z. Holwell, and to a lesser extent with Ch. Wilkins. As Dow explained in an apparent adaptation of the opening statement from Descartes' *Discours de la méthode*: ". . . common sense, upon the affairs of religion, is pretty equally divided among all nations."[5] He formulated the principle for understanding foreign religions, both Indian and otherwise, as follows: "Whatever the external ceremonies of religion may be, the self-same infinite being is the object of universal adoration."[6] Holwell, who, like Dow, emphasized the extraordinary age of the Indian tradition, contrasted the contemporary, degenerated customs of the Hindus ("their modern ceremonials, and complicated modes of worship") to their originally monotheistic tenets, which he described as "short, pure, simple and uniform." In his *Dissertation on the Metempsychosis*, which he appended to his account of *Interesting Historical Events relative to the Provinces of Bengal and the Empire of Indostan* (first published in 1765–1767) in 1771, he declared that all of the world's religions were founded upon the same pristine truth, revealed to mankind by a gracious God. "This was orthodox deism, but his list of 'primitive truths' was far from orthodox, including belief in fallen angels and metempsychosis."[7] Neither Dow nor Holwell knew Sanskrit, yet the contributions which they made to the knowledge of the Indian religious and philosophical literature were quite remarkable for their time. Dow, for example, made a survey of the various categories of the Vaiśeṣika and the Nyāya in which he introduced the Nyāya of Gautama under the name "neadirsen" (i.e., *Nyāyadarśana*).[8]

3. Although they cannot actually be described as deists, such figures as N.B. Halhed and W. Jones (who founded the Asiatic Society of Bengal in 1784) nevertheless came close to deistic thinking, and their works reveal its influence. The universalistic and deistic foreword by the Pandits who compiled the Sanskrit material for the *Code of Gentoo Laws* (1776) which Halhed then translated from an intermediate Persian version seems to reflect the views which Halhed himself held at that time—if it was not actually inspired by him. Later in his life, Halhed turned to millenarianism.[9] J. Shore (Baron Teignmouth) described the religious-philosophical thought of the Hindus quite simply as "pure deism."[10] Similarly, one of the Baptist missionaries from Serampore, W. Carey, complained about the influence and prevalence of deism in India, remarking that "India swarms with Deists . . . "[11]

Voltaire numbered among the readers of Dow and Holwell. Along with the still influential reports of the missionaries, the works of these two played a significant role in shifting India more clearly into the awareness of the Age of Enlightenment.[12] For the Rationalists and the early followers of the Enlightenment, China was the initial focal point of interest in the non-European world. Leibniz concerned himself minutely with the reports on China, which not infrequently tended to idealize the country.[13] In Halle, Christian Wolff held a famous lecture on the "practical philosophy" of the Chinese (*De Sinarum philosophia practica*, 1721) that was at least partially responsible for his losing his professorship for a number of years. Chinese religion and philosophy, and especially Confucianism, was considered an example of a basically ethical, human, and secular orientation which was relatively uncluttered with abstruse, abstract, and other-worldly considerations. The "practical philosophy" of the Chinese was recommended to Europeans as a corrective and complement to their own tradition. Leibniz even toyed with the idea of sending Chinese missionaries to Europe in order to instruct Westerners about questions of "natural theology" (and, more generally, common sense).[14] Similarly, China at first appeared much more attractive and important than India in Voltaire's eyes, and he played an active role in helping to idealize the "practical philosophy" and civic institutions of the Chinese. However, after studying the manuscript of the *Ezourvedam* which the Chevalier de Maudave had given him in 1760, he became convinced that the world's oldest culture and most pristine religious thought was to be found in India and not in China,[15] and as a result he became embroiled in a controversy which had far-reaching consequences in his time. This was the discussion about the chronology of the Bible as well as the priority and primacy of the Biblical revelation. In his polemics against Christianity, it was vitally important for Voltaire to have chronological arguments at hand which he could use to counter the arguments of the orthodox believers, who clung to the Biblical chronology and, moreover, felt that if there was anything at all acceptable or of value in Indian religious thought (or that of other Asian peoples), then this must surely be some kind of forgotten or overgrown by-product of the Mosaic-Christian revelation. In any case, however, the fundamental priority of the Bible was to be presupposed. Among others, A. Dacier, J. Bouchet, and Th. La Grue argued along these lines for the priority of the Biblical revelation. Even the great Newton became involved in the controversy and tried to defend the Biblical chronology.[16]

4. In this debate, Voltaire took a clear, even radical stand: India is the homeland of religion in its oldest and purest form; it is also the cradle of worldly civilization. In a section added to his *Essai sur les moeurs* in 1761 and under the immediate impression of his study of the *Ezourvedam*, he describes India as the country on which all other countries had to rely, but

which did not rely on anybody else, and which consequently had the most ancient civilization, as well as the most ancient form of religion ("la plus ancienne forme de religion"). He claims: "The first Brahmins, who were kings and pontiffs all at once, could establish religion only on the basis of universal reason" ("Les premiers brachmanes, étants donc à la fois rois et pontifes, ne pouvaient guère établir la religion que sur la reason universelle").[17]

Until 1767, the *Ezourvedam* was Voltaire's main source on India; after that, the works of Holwell, Dow and others supplemented his understanding, but without really changing it. What did Voltaire find in the *Ezourvedam*, this fictitious conversation between "Biach" (i.e., Vyāsa) and "Chumantou" (i.e., Sumantu)? It was, above all, the contrast between Chumantou's pure "Vedic" monotheism or deism, i.e., a kind of primeval religion of reason, and the degenerate and idolatrous religion represented by Biach, the Vyāsa of the Purāṇic tradition. He could easily translate the criticism which Chumantou directed against the superstitious beliefs and practices of popular Hinduism into his own polemics against contempoary Christianity.[18]

Religion in general is derived, and has degenerated from, the pure natural revelation of which the Indians were the first possessors. In a letter to Frederick the Great of Prussia, Voltaire assures the monarch "that our holy Christian religion is solely based upon the ancient religion of Brahma" ("que notre sainte religion chrétienne est uniquement fondeé sur l'ancienne religion de Brama").[19]

D.S. Hawley states correctly that what Voltaire read about India was of great importance for the articulation of his ideas about the origin and development of religion, and that, after 1760, India occupied a special place in his thought. In 1767, he even mentioned his intention to travel to India.[20] Yet, it is also true that he was not interested in India, or Indian religion, *per se*. In the words of Hawley, he "made use of India, rather than studying it."[21]

5. Even during the French revolution (which Voltaire did not live to see), India was played in this manner against the claims of primacy and exclusivity of the Christian revelation, for example by L. Langlès.[22] In different garb and in numerous more or less speculative variations, the thesis of the Indian origin of Christianity survived into the nineteenth and twentieth centuries. It became a favorite topic of mystics and occultists, such as the followers of the Marquis Claude de Saint-Martin. We find it associated with such groups as the Rosicrucians and, later on, the Theosophists. It was frequently referred to by A. Schopenhauer and propagated and popularized in the highly speculative works of L. Jacolliot, A. Lillie and F. Nork.[23] More cautiously, R. Seydel argued for Indian influences; and around 1900, this issue was a topic of intense scholarly debate.[24]

Questions of priority and dependence were also raised in the domains of secular learning and science. The debate on these questions began early in the eighteenth century. In 1716, Polycarp Lyserus (i.e., Michael Kusche) presented a thesis to the University of Wittenberg, in which he argued for the Indians, and against the Hebrews, as originators of culture and "erudition" (*De origine eruditionis non ad Iudaeos, sed ad Indos referenda*). In 1719, N. Fréret argued for the Indian origin of the game of chess; his article inaugurated a series of similar specific studies.[25] J.S. Bailly considered Indian astronomy extremely old; Laplace initially accepted Bailly's conclusions, but criticized them later on.[26]

Voltaire himself was obviously convinced of the priority of the Indian achievements in the area of secular learning and worldly culture. In a letter to the Marquise du Deffand, written in 1773, he described the Indians as the people "to whom we owe our numbers, our backgammon, our chess, our first principles of geometry, and the fables which have become our own."[27]

In general, the thesis of the great antiquity and autonomy of Indian culture contradicted the theory of an enduring Greek influence transmitted especially by Alexander and the Bactrian Greeks.[28]

6. Seen as a whole, the Age of Enlightenment approached India in a manner that tended towards ambivalence and was often superficial or speculative in nature. A marked interest in India was by no means the rule. India had little to do with the idealization of the "primal state" and the "noble savage" that can be found, for example, in Rousseau's thought. Diderot, whose *Supplément au voyage de Bougainville* is an important and impressive tribute to the exoticism of the Enlightenment, also published articles pertaining to India in the *Encyclopédie* which were quite deprecating and, considering the knowledge available at the time, very inadequate.[29] In the article "Brachmanes," Diderot discusses what he calls "extravagances tout-à-fait incroyables," stating that the persons who had referred to the Brahmins as "sages" must have been even crazier than the Brahmins themselves. The article entitled "Bramines" is essentially a summary and in part literal paraphrase of the article "Brachmanes" contained in Bayle's *Dictionnaire historique et critique*; it also reproduces a mixup of Buddhism and Brahminism occurring in the original: citing the Jesuit Ch. Le Gobien, Bayle described a Brahminic sect thought to be living in China as worshippers of the "God Fo."[30]

Based upon Bayle's and Le Gobien's portrayal of the Chinese "Brahmins" and Buddhists, a vision was conjured up of "quietism" and love of "nothingness" among the Indians, and of their desire to stupefy and mortify themselves:

> They assert that the world is nothing but an illusion, a dream, a magic spell, and that the bodies, in order to be truly existent, have to cease existing in themselves, and to merge into nothingness, which due to its simplicity amounts to the perfection of all beings. They claim that saintliness consists in willing nothing, thinking nothing, feel-

ing nothing . . . This state is so much like a dream that it seems that a few grains of opium would sanctify a brahmin more surely than all his efforts.

(Ils assurent que le monde n'est qu'une illusion, un songe, un prestige, et que les corps pour exister véritablement doivent cesser d'être en eux-mêmes, et se confondre avec le néant, qui par sa simplicité fait la perfection de tous les êtres. Ils font consister la sainteté à ne rien vouloir, à ne rien penser, à ne rien sentir . . . Cet état resemble si fort au sommeil, qu'il paraît que quelques grains d'opium sanctifieraient un bramine bien plus sûrement que tous ses efforts.)

Despite the inaccuracy and lack of originality inherent in Diderot's paraphrase of Bayle (which merely added the reference to "opium"), it nevertheless illustrates an important motif through the emphasis it lays upon the "quietism" of the Brahmins. It is a motif which we find also in the *Essais de théodicée*, which Leibniz published in 1710.[31] It will reappear later among Hegel and other critics of Indian thought. Hegel also made use of the opium metaphor (which Marx was to make famous) in his depiction of the Indian world, speaking of persons who "could only attain a dream-world and the happiness of insanity through opium."[32] On the other hand, Schopenhauer invoked the notion of "quietism" to express his appreciation of Indian thought; Bayle himself referred to the Western "quietists" Molinos and Mme. Guyon in this context.[33]

7. Very often, references to India were made to serve polemic ends; they seldom led to an immersion in matters of substance. Of course, India was often viewed as the seat of an extraordinarily old and pristine culture and tradition, yet it also served as an example of degeneration and decay, as an example of a tradition that had been unable to safeguard its original purity against superstition and priestly fraud: "What a difference between that (ancient) philosophy and the one which one professes today in India!" A Christian, as the *Encyclopédie* added,[34] could not fail to see the "effects of divine wrath" in such decay and deprivation, a remark which clearly refers to a quote from Th. Burnet's *Archaeologiae philosophicae* (1692) that was cited by Bayle. Burnet, following the lead of the missionary literature, hoped that the Occident would be spared such heavenly rage. He expressed his sympathy for the fact that the Orient, the seat of such pristine wisdom and culture, should have fallen into such disgusting barbarism.[35] Burnet also associated the motif of pantheism with India in a remarkable statement about the Indian idea of the "world spider"; Bayle makes this association in the context of his presentation of Spinoza.[36]

India thus illustrates the theme of the eclipse and suppression of the "natural light" through superstition and ritualism, a theme that enjoyed great popularity among thinkers of the Enlightenment. It was in connection with this that Kant made the following statements about the Indians: "Their religion had a great purity. A couple of centuries before the birth of Christ, however, it became adulterated with many superstitious things . . . Still, one can find traces of a pure concept of divinity which cannot easily be found elsewhere." He also declared that Indian religious thought was free of dogmatism and intolerance: "It is a principle of the Indians (i.e., the Hindus), that every nation has its own religion. For this reason, they do not force anyone to accept theirs."[37]

8. Here, the idea of religious decay is linked with the motif of tolerance, another characteristic of the Enlightenment. We encounter this same linkage in a remarkable and somewhat idiosyncratic exposition by Moses Mendelssohn, embedded in the context of a theory of religious signs and symbols which makes explicit reference to Indian mythology and is equally committed to the Enlightenment and to Jewish apologetics. In Mendelssohn's eyes, religious decay essentially involves a fall from the use of symbols into polytheism and idolatry, a loss of the distinction between the signs and what they are intended to designate, a misunderstanding of the original sense and function of "metaphors and allegories," and thus, a misunderstanding of the original meaning of one's own tradition.[38] "The pictures had lost their value as signs. The spirit of truth, which should have been preserved therein, had evaporated, and the dull vehicle that remained had been reduced to pernicious poison." This danger of misunderstanding, however, does not just exist *within* a tradition, it also exists to the extent that outsiders are often unable to understand the "scriptural character," i.e., the ultimately symbolic meaning of alien religious customs. "When evaluating the religious concepts of what is otherwise an unknown nation, one has to be . . . careful not to view everything through one's own domestic eyes so as not to call idolatry what is perhaps really only script (i.e., symbolism). . . . Our travelers probably make similar mistakes quite often when telling us about the religions of faraway peoples. They must become very precisely acquainted with the thoughts and opinions of a nation before they can reliably say whether the pictures which they possess still contain the 'spirit of script' or whether they have already degenerated into idolatry." He drew explicit parallels between those misunderstandings which the Jews had been subjected to "by the conquerors of Jerusalem" and the erroneous interpretations of Indian mythology and religion which the Europeans had made with respect to, for example, the "world snake." Here, Mendelssohn referred to the work of J.Z. Holwell, who was supposedly able "to see with the eyes of a native Brahmin" ("mit den Augen eines eingeborenen Braminen zu sehen"); and he defended the Indians against philosophers like Locke, Shaftesbury and Hume, who had ridiculed their mythological ideas of a cosmic elephant, tortoise, etc.[39]

9. A basic willingness to see religious, philosophical and cultural traditions, including the European tradition itself, no longer solely "through one's own domestic eyes" was often postulated in the eighteenth century. As a matter of fact, there was a whole literary genre of works following the scheme of Montesquieu's *Lettres persanes* ("Persian letters," 1721) and pretending to present foreign, exotic views of Europe.[40] However, this program of seeing oneself and others with "foreign eyes" remained usually quite abstract and stereotypical in practice, specifically with regard to India, or it was simply a stylistic device. Even the influential works of A. Dow and J.Z. Holwell, whom Mendelssohn singled out as an open-minded, non-Eurocentric observer, did not establish a tradition of exploring Indian thought in its original sources and contexts of understanding. This was first achieved towards the end of the Age of Enlightenment, through the scholarly works and programmatic activities of the British "Orientalists" in Bengal: above all W. Jones (1746–1794), Ch. Wilkins (1749-1836), and H. Th. Colebrooke (1765–1837). These scholars turned to the original Sanskrit texts, and the use of Persian and other intermediary languages became obsolete.[41] No longer isolated achievements, their effort led to the establishment and institutionalization of a research tradition—the tradition of modern Indology. W. Jones' founding of the Asiatic Society of Bengal in 1784 is exemplary in this respect and points in the direction which later developments were to take. The economic and political presence of the British in India, of course, loomed in the background of these events. As Warren Hastings, the governor-general of Bengal, explicitly formulated it, the study of the Indian tradition and conceptual world simultaneously aided in steering and controlling the Indians within the framework of their own ways of thought.[42] Nevertheless, this does not change the fact that scholarly work now embarked on a sustained development of its own, one, moreover, that was fundamentally oriented around detailed work with the original material. "The birth of the Asiatic Society is a milestone in the history of Oriental Studies. By establishing it Jones helped to usher in the age of scientific specialization, by forming a society which would study the Asians at close quarters . . . ."[43] An imposing number of original translations appeared in the years directly following the founding of the Asiatic Society, which soon became known throughout Europe. They included Wilkins' *Bhagavadgītā* (1785, with a foreword by W. Hastings) and *Hitopadeśa* (1787) and Jones' *Śakuntalā* (1789) and *Manusmṛti* (*Ordinances of Menu*, 1796). These were followed by Colebrooke's pioneering works, especially in the fields of astronomy, mathematics, and philosophy.[44]

10. In some ways, Jones, Wilkins, and, to a lesser degree, Colebrooke were pursuing questions and lines of thought typical of deism and the Age of Enlightenment. They too were advocates of the view that the mytho-

logical, religious, and philosophical tradition of India was especially ancient and pristine. Beyond this, however, they also exhibited a certain openness and tolerance with respect to contemporary Hindu customs. Admittedly, Jones' views were dominated by the idea that India itself was not the original home of the religious and philosophical tradition of the West, but rather represented an old offshoot of an original source common to both East and West: ". . . Pythagoras and Plato derived their sublime theories from the same fountain with the sages of India."[45] This hypothesis of common origins was also applied to other fields, e.g., to Greek and Indian astronomy as well as to numerous alphabets in the East and West.[46] Yet it is in the domain of linguistics that its influence has been felt most deeply and has become most well-known. After Jones had praised the uniqe qualities of Sanskrit vis-à-vis Greek and Latin while emphasizing the basic similarities between all of them, he declared that "no philologer could examine them all three, without believing them to have sprung from some common source, which perhaps no longer exists."[47] Since F. Sassetti's observations in the second half of the sixteenth century, it had been repeatedly conjectured or claimed that Sanskrit and the languages of classical antiquity were in some way related;[48] it was through Jones' work, however, that this theme became more refined and, most importantly, made a wider and deeper impression upon tlhe scientific thought of Europe. Jones was fully aware of the fact that his efforts, together with those of his countrymen working in Bengal, in particular Wilkins, had raised Indian studies to an entirely new level. He considered the publication of Wilkins' *Bhagavadgītā* a major turning-point. Speaking of the Europeans, Jones stated: " . . . if they wish to form a correct idea of Indian religion and literature, let them begin with forgetting all that has been written on the subject, by ancients or moderns, before the publication of the Gita."[49]

11. Among Jones' lesser-known achievements was the first direct translation of an Upaniṣadic text into a Western language—his English translation and paraphrase of the *Īśā-Upaniṣad* (first published in 1799, i.e. five years after Jones' death, in an edition of his collected works).[50] In Jones' mind, the Vedānta school (which follows the teachings of the Upaniṣads) was the most important school of Hindu philosophical thought, and Śaṅkara its most important commentator. He expected that a full treatment of the *Vedāntasūtras* would yield an important contribution to the general history of philosophy. He translated a short didactic poem attributed to Śaṅkara, the *Mohamudgara*, for the first volume of the *Asiatic Researches*. Still, he never attained a real knowledge of the Vedānta literature.

Jones, like several other British "Orientalists," was familiar with the *Sirr-i Akbar*, Dārā Shukōh's Persian translation of fifty Upaniṣads. His opinion of the quality of this work, however, was very reserved: ". . . though sublime and majestic features of the original were discernible, in parts, through folds of the Persian drapery, yet the Sanskrit names were so barbarously written, and the additions of the translator have made the work so deformed, that I resolved to postpone a regular perusal of it till I could compare it with the Sanskrit original."[51] N.B. Halhed, the translator of the *Code of Gentoo Laws* (1776) and one of the main exponents of the "Persian" interlude of early Indology, even completed an English translation of the *Sirr-i Akbar* (1787), although it was never published. Its introduction, which was recently edited by R. Rocher, provides us with testimony of an exemplary sort. It discusses the great age of the Upaniṣads and points out the differences between them and modern Hinduism. It also considers the possibility that Pythagoras, Mani, and Thales were dependent upon Indian sources.[52] In actuality, the great advances in making the original Indian texts available soon made the publication of such secondary translations seem obsolete. And thus, it was all the more remarkable when a Latin secondary translation of the Upaniṣads appeared in 1801/1802, viz., Anquetil Duperron's aforementioned two-volume work *Oupnek'hat*. Considering the idiosyncratic nature and style of this work, it is hardly surprising that it was not very favorably received by the British Orientalists. A. Hamilton, for example, wrote:

> . . . nothing less than the beatitude promised by Dara Shecuh, at the conclusion of his preface, to those who shall read and understand it, could induce any one to persevere in such an attempt, through the medium of M. Anquetil's version . . . We are of the opinion, that a translation of an Upanisad, from the Sanscrit into English, would prove a performance of some interest; but that the value of the work before us is considerably diminished, by coming through the medium of a Persic translation.[53]

12. In some ways, A.H. Anquetil Duperron (1731–1805) was the antipode of the British "Orientalists" surrounding Jones. His proper place is more in the prehistory of Indology, yet at the same time, his influence was felt until well into the nineteenth century. His *Oupnek'hat* is an anachronism; yet it did more to awaken the modern interest in Indian philosophy and made a greater contribution to the philosophical debate about India than Jones' works. The fact that Anquetil's name remains known is chiefly due to Schopenhauer and the enthusiastic reaction with which he greeted the *Oupnek'hat*.[54] For all this, Anquetil's importance is by no means merely limited to his role as a translator or the fact that others have received important stimuli from the texts which he translated. His "comparative" method, his philosophical and hermeneutic reflection, and his peculiar position between the Enlightenment, Romanticism, and scientific Indology all earn him a more direct and primary interest than that he is normally accorded. There is no doubt that he is one of the more impressive and decisive figures in the history of European approaches to Indian and Oriental thought, and

in the preparation of a philosophical "dialogue" between India and the West.

Anquetil Duperron had published another basic and pioneering work in the field of European Oriental studies some thirty years before the appearance of the *Oupnek'hat*. This was his French translation of the Old Persian Zend Avesta (*Zend-Avesta, ouvrage de Zoroastre*, 3vols., Paris 1771), a work that unleashed an extended controversy as to its authenticity. In Germany, its fame was primarily due to J.F. Kleuker, who translated the work and, at the same time, defended it against the doubts and criticism it encountered, in particular from the British.[55] — Anquetil's working procedure was such that the Enlightenment motif of origins led to a methodical search, conducted with a great sense of purpose, for the original, primal sources of the religions of the Orient as well as systematic preparations for their study. He visited India between 1754 and 1761 in the hope of finding such sources. He gained a knowledge of Persian, but his attempts to learn Sanskrit as well did not meet with success. In the "Discours préliminaire" to his *Zend-Avesta*,[56] he wrote: "Convinced that the modern customs of Asia owe their origin to the peoples and religions that subjugated it, I proposed to myself to study in its sources the ancient theology of those nations which are at home in the immense countries located East of the Euphrates, and to consult the original books on their history." ("Persuadé que les usages modernes de l'Asie doivent leur origine aux peuples et aux religions qui l'ont subjuguée, je me suis proposé d'étudier dans les sources l'ancienne théologie des nations habituées dans les contrées immenses qui sont a l'Est de l'Euphrate, et de consulter sur leur histoire les livres originaux.").

13. Anquetil's translation of the *Sirr-i Akbar* did not directly result from his voyage to India; not even the manuscripts of the text upon which his work was based were obtained there. These he first received at a much later date, from his friend Le Gentil, the French Envoy at Oudh. He gave an initial description of the text, along with a promise to translate it, in 1778.[57] The first sample of the translation — four Upaniṣads in French — appeared in 1787;[58] the remainder of the complete French translation, which he claimed to have finished, has, however, never been published. Instead, he followed up these initial efforts with a Latin translation (finished in 1795, published in 1801/1802). Anquetil's attempts to locate and study the oldest sources of Indian religion in Sanskrit were indeed unsuccessful;[59] yet the decisiveness of his approach was important and indicated the direction which later Indological research was to take. His basic position as well as his methodological principles set him distinctly apart from the procedures normally applied by Indian travelers of his time:

The majority of travelers content themselves with asking the Brahmins about the essence of their teachings, or what they believe concerning this or that subject-matter. Some go so far as to get for themselves extracts of their theological books. The answers and the extracts may be accurate; but they may also correspond to the circumstances, the spirit, the views of the person who asks the questions. The only way to know the truth is to learn the languages well, to translate oneself the fundamental works, and to confer subsequently with the scholars of the country on the subject-matters treated therein, the books in hand.

(La plupart des voyageurs se contentent de demander aux Brahmes . . . le fond de leurs dogmes, ce qu'ils croient sur tel ou tel objet; quelques-un vont jusqu'à se procurer des extraits de leur livres théologiques. Les réponses, les extraits peuvent être exacts; ils peuvent être analogues aux circonstances, à l'esprit, aux vues de celui qui interroge. Le seul moyen de connaître la vérité est de bien apprendre les langues, de traduire soi-même les ouvrages fondamentaux et de conférer ensuite avec les savants du pays sur les matières qui y soint traitées, les livres en main.)[60]

And he demanded: "Let us study the Indians as we study the Greeks and Romans" ("Étudions les Indiens, comme nous faisons les Grecs et les Latins")—critically, but respectfully, and without ridiculing them.[61]

Anquetil remained a faithful Christian; yet he developed an openness for extra-European and non-Christian achievements of thought, and a readiness for comprehensive comparisons which not only transcended the limits of "orthodoxy," but also surpassed the abstract openness of deism and the Enlightenment. Even if he himself was unable to fulfil his own programmatic ideas, his postulate to study the Indians "like the Greeks and Romans" and to inquire systematically into the sources and backgrounds of their thought is suggestive of the line of development which A.W. Schlegel and other pioneers of Indian philology would promote and exemplify.

14. In spite of Anquetil's pioneering methodological suggestions, his *Oupnek'hat* does not belong among the founding achievements of Indian philology, or of scientific Indology. In general, its importance lies not so much within the history of Indology as within the history of philosophy. It is there that it has its specific significance, and that its historical impact has been primarily felt.[62] Anquetil himself left no room for doubts as to the primarily philosophical aims of his work. His appeal to a philosophical audience was explicit. He called upon the philosophers of many countries, and in particular the representatives of German Idealism—the "followers and opponents of the profound Kant"—to study the teachings of the *Oupnek'hat* from a philosophical angle, not just seeing them as testimony about ancient India, but also to consider them as a serious philosophical challenge: "Interim ad scrutandạ, rimanda ea qua valent mentis acie τοῦ Oupnek'hat secreta Germanos philosophos, asseclas vel adversarios profundi Kant, videlicet Goethe, Schiller, Humboldt, Jacobi, Maimon, Fichte, Bouterweck, Reinhold, Bardili, Koeppen . . . invitare liceat."[63] He in-

cluded many comparisons with Western philosophical teachings, e.g., with Plotinus and the Gnostics, especially in the comprehensive and scholarly "Emendationes et annotationes."[64]

The introduction to the first volume offers a very detailed attempt to establish the concordance or correspondence of Indian and Judaeo-Christian ideas ("Dissertatio in qua e Judaeorum, Ecclesiae Doctorum, et tam catholicorum quam acatholicorum theologicorum scriptis summa orientalis systematis inquiritur").[65] He cites at length from the hymns of the "syncretic" Bishop Synesius of Cyrene[66] in order to illustrate the fundamental agreement between Christian and Indian thought with respect to such themes as the creation of the world, etc. He generally portrays Indians and Christians side-by-side, and does not insist upon relationships of dependence or qualitative gradations. The two, so to speak, enjoy equal rights as members of the same family. Anquetil also finds "true Spinozism" existing in Indian thought.[67] He was particularly interested in establishing connections with the latest philosophical developments of his own time —above all with Kantian Transcendental Philosophy, which he knew primarily through Ch. Villers' presentation:[68] Anyone who carefully examines the lines of Immanuel Kant's thought, its principles as well as its results, will recognize that it does not deviate very far from the teachings of the Brahmins, which lead man back to himself and comprise and focus him within himself (". . . eum a Brahmanum doctrina, quae hominem ad seipsum revocat, intra se coercet, non multum discedere forsan reperite."[69]

15. Here, Anquetil anticipated developments that would be especially promoted by the most enthusiastic reader of the *Oupnek'hat*, A. Schopenhauer, Schopenhauer's admirer P. Deussen, and the representatives of a "comparative philosophy" which has established itself especially in India. Prior to this, the historian of philosophy Th. A. Rixner declared that "the truth which—through the insightful research of the most recent German students of God and the World— . . . has so happily been brought back to the bright light of the philosophical day" completely corresponds to the "all-is-one-doctrine" of the *Oupnek'hat*. Rixner himself produced a German translation of a section of the *Oupnek'hat* in 1808 and described Anquetil as "the only metaphysician which the French nation can boast of since perhaps the time of Malebranche."[70] Rixner was under the influence of Schelling, who was also among the readers of the *Oupnek'hat*.[71]

Anquetil viewed the demonstration and study of such correspondences as a contribution to the moral regeneration of his time, to the "cause of humanity" ("humanitatis causam agere est"), and as an "incentive to general concord and love" ("generalis concordiae, dilectionis incitamentum.")[72] And thus, through this recourse to ancient Indian wisdom, as well as by uncovering the common sources of religion and humanity, he also felt that he had found a way out of what he referred to as the "malaise européen."[73]

As noted above, the foundations for the modern study of India were not laid by Anquetil Duperron, but by the British Orientalists Jones, Wilkins, and Colebrooke. Back in England, however, a palpable reaction against what was seen as a too benevolent study of Hinduism occurred in the first decades of the nineteenth century.[74] This did not come from the Christian missionaries alone, but also from such historians and politicians as James Mill and Th. Macaulay. Macaulay spoke of the "monstrous superstitions" and of the "false history" and "false religion" of the Hindu texts and asserted that all of the works that had ever been written in Sanskrit (and Arabic as well) were "less valuable than what may be found in the most paltry abridgements used at preparatory schools in England." For the educational system in India, he set a goal of enlisting a class of English-educated Indians "who may be interpreters between us and the millions whom we govern."[75] He saw no reason to study Indian things as such or for their own sake.

Both Indology as an academic discipline, as well as a more far-reaching enthusiasm for India, first developed on the Continent, in particular in Germany. This took place in close association with a movement which seems to be diametrically opposed to the Enlightenment—Romanticism.

5. India and the Romantic Critique of the Present

1. Several recent studies have emphasized the fact that the commonly-held idea of an irreconcilable antagonism between the Enlightenment and the Romantic movement is in need of some modification; there are shadings and transitions between the two.[1] The same holds true with respect to the opinions of the time about the Orient in general and India in particular. As we have already seen, the Age of Enlightenment was characterized by a very distinct association between a general interest in non-European traditions and the motif of criticizing contemporary Christianity and Europe. One shape which the criticism of Christianity took was the attempt to trace it back to older, more original traditions, or the view that a more pristine religious consciousness could be found in Asia, and specifically in India.

Both this motivation towards self-criticism and the theme of origins were assimilated into the Romantic awareness of India and the Orient. To be sure, they here entered a new context of self-awareness, specifically, a more concrete and organic awareness of culture and history that was not determined by abstract categories of progress and degeneration. J.G. Herder (1744-1803) was particularly responsible for shaping this new relationship to history. Herder did not just pioneer the Romantic movement in general, but also broke ground precisely in terms of its awareness of India.[2] In his eyes, nations and their traditions were living wholes existing in organic cohesion and yet, simultaneously, individuals whose uniqueness should be recognized. He saw history as the natural history of "living human force," as a process in which *one* mankind presented itself in multiple forms and expressions while, at the same time, the very idea of humanity acted as a regulatory force.[3] "Because *one* form of humanity and *one* region of the earth were unable to contain it, it spread out in a thousand forms, it journeyed—an eternal Proteus—through all of the areas of the earth and down through all the centuries . . . ."[4] Metaphors of organic growth and development are typical of Herder's thought. For example, the development of mankind "from the Orient to Rome" is likened to the trunk of a tree, out of which branches and shoots grow: "how shot the one, old, simple trunk of humanity into boughs and twigs."[5] The Orient was the infant state, and thus innocent, pure, and with unexhausted potential. Hellenism was adolescence, Rome adulthood. The Orient represents Europe's own childhood. "All the peoples of Europe, where are they from? From Asia."[6] In other words, we find here a new willingness to acknowledge the cultures of the Orient as autonomous structures in their own right. And yet they are also simultaneously viewed as the cultures of our own origins, the sources of our own historical being.

2. Herder had a lasting fascination with Biblical antiquity, with the "Spirit of Ebraic Poesy": "Then come here, poets and artists! Here is the greatest ideal and paragon for your art . . . "[7] Yet he soon became aware of India as well, through contact with such travelers' accounts as that of Sonnerat, through the works of Roger, Dow, and Holwell, and also through the original translations which became increasingly available after 1785, especially Wilkins' *Bhagavadgītā* and *Hitopadeśa* and Jones' *Śakuntalā*.

The most important of the original works and translations which, during Herder's lifetime, first appeared in English, French, or even Latin, were rapidly translated into German or treated in German by such writers as G. Forster, F. Majer, and J.F. Kleuker, who was especially productive in this area.[8] Herder himself was personally involved in some of the works by these authors. He wrote the foreword to Majer's *Kulturgeschichte der Völker* (published in 1798) as well as the foreword to the second edition of Forster's secondary (German) translation of the *Śakuntalā*, which appeared in 1803, the year of Herder's death. In general, Herder was a careful observer of and active participant in the nascent discipline of modern Indology. His sympathy for the people of India became ever more apparent in his friendly and glorifying view of the "childlike Indians."[9] "The Hindus are the gentlest branch of humanity. They do not with pleasure offend anything that lives; they honor that which gives life and nourish themselves with the most innocent of foods, milk, rice, the fruits of the trees, the healthy herbs which their motherland dispenses . . . Moderation and calm, a soft feeling and a silent depth of the soul characterize their work and their pleasure, their morals and mythology, their arts and even their endurance under the most extreme yoke of humanity."[10]

3. With friendly empathy, Herder described the thoughts which he considered to be the core and basis of Hindu thought: the idea of *one* Being in and behind all that there is, and the idea of the unity of all things in the absolute, in God.

Vishnu is in you, in me, in all beings;

It is foolish to ever feel offense.

See all souls in your own,

and banish the delusion of being different.[11]

The theme of "pantheism" which may be seen here in Herder's paraphrase of the *Mohamudgara*, a Vedāntic didactic poem, has long been one of the central themes in the discussion about India.[12]

Yet in spite of all the sympathy which greeted India, it was not glorified as a lost home or a place of refuge and retreat from the aberrations of modern Europe. Herder did not accept the degeneration theory of the Enlightenment without question, but he found much of what had been originally pure in India to have become sullied. He viewed some of the exemplary institutions and convictions of the Hindus in a manner that was both differentiating and ambivalent. For example, he considered the Brahmanic influence upon the people of India as having been essentially salutary. He found their concept of God "great and beautiful," their morals "pure and noble." But he also saw another result: "Manifold fraud and superstition, which had already become unavoidable because astronomy and chronology and the art of healing and religion, transmitted as they were through an oral tradition, had turned into the secret science of one clan." As a result, the populace had been ripe for subjugation. The "distribution of the ways of life among hereditary clans"—i.e., the caste system—had excluded "all free improvement and perfection of the arts almost completely."[13] Herder also considered the Indian doctrine of metempsychosis as having produced disastrous results: "Since it awakens a false sense of compassion for all living things, it simultaneously lessens the true sympathy with the wretched members of our own race, for these unfortunates are held to be wrongdoers suffering under the burden of prior crimes or being tried by the hand of fate, while their virtuousness will be rewarded in a future state." The doctrine of metempsychosis is a "delusion transgressing humanity" ("Wahn, der über die Menschheit hinausreicht").[14] It is incompatible with the idea of mankind, which Herder saw as the greatest regulative idea in the history of the world. The pre-eminence of Christianity over India and the Orient was due to the fact that it is the religion of "purest humanity."[15] And while the Indian "infancy" of mankind may have been glorified and idealized in Herder's writings, he did not believe that it was desirable or possible to return to it. While mankind may have been born in Asia, it reached adulthoood only in the mediterranean world, in classical Greece.[16]

4. Herder was and remained a Christian and a European. Considering this, he exhibited a very remarkable willingness to accept Indian thought and Indian ways of life in their own right, to accede to what he understood

as being the Hindu viewpoint, and to look critically at himself as a Christian and European through, so to speak, Indian eyes. What is more, he was especially willing to reflect on European and Christian assumptions and biases vis-à-vis India. He saw little sense in the missionary activity in India. Shortly before his death, his *Gespräche über die Bekehrung der Indier durch unsere europäischen Christen* ("Conversations on the Conversion of the Indians by our European Christians")[17] appeared in 1802. In this work, he presented an Indian complaining about the ignorance of the missionaries, their arrogance in wishing to show the Indians (whose own characteristic ways they did not recognize at all) the "path to salvation" using "alien formulas." The picture Herder painted of India was essentially positive and occasionally glorifying, and anticipated in some ways the Romantic understanding of India. His programmatic pluralism and his openness to the diversity of human nature and human cultures did not, however, permit him to accord the Indians any kind of privileged position or meet them with an exclusive interest.

In the 116th *Brief zur Beförderung der Humanität* ("Letter for the Advancement of Humanity"), which appeared in Riga in 1797 as part of the tenth collection of such letters, Herder formulated a number of principles for a "natural history of mankind." These were also significant for his relationship with India. He stressed that the author of such a "natural history" was not permitted to have a "favorite tribe" or "chosen people" ("*Lieblingsstamm*," "*Favoritenvolk*"), or to presuppose a hierarchy of nations. Herder also demanded that each nation be considered in its own natural environment, in the context of its entire culture, and without any "arbitrary divisions" being made. By no means, moreover, could European culture serve as the general standard for comparison: "The genius of human natural history lies in and with each nation, as if it were the only one on earth."[18]

5. It is generally known that India became the focal point of an enthusiastic interest, occasionally bordering on fanaticism, within the German Romantic movement. Here, the motif of origins and unspoiled pristineness shared by the Enlightenment became effective in a different, more exalted way. The very idea of India assumed mythical proportions; the turn towards India became the quest for the true depths of our own being, a search for the original, infant state of the human race, for the lost paradise of all religions and philosophies. "The 'eternal Orient' was waiting to be rediscovered within ourselves; India was the 'cradle of humanity' and our eternal home;"[19] it was the "home and youth of the soul."[20] It represented the "spirit of infancy" which Schelling evoked in his early programmatic work *Über Mythen, historische Sagen und Philosopheme der ältesten Welt* ("On Myths, Historical Legends and Philosophemes of the Most Ancient World," 1793). For something was missing from the European present — the

sense of unity and wholeness—and this was mourned as the affliction of the time. There was hope that a return to the Indian sources would bring about a change for the better.

What exactly was the *present* to which the Romantics referred? It was the culmination and termination of the Age of Enlightenment, of its faith in reason and progress, and the secular world of the consequences of the Reformation and the French Revolution. It involved, moreover, a fall into a quantifying, mechanical, merely rational way of viewing the universe. It was a time in which the sense of wonder and the awareness of the unity and wholeness of life had become lost. It was a present which called for transformation and regeneration; in the Romantic understanding, this meant a spiritual return to a superior past, to its own forgotten origins.

In the present context, our interest cannot lie with the diverse views of India which the leading authors of the Romantic movement conceived, the knowledge they obtained about India, or how each of them varied on or even criticized the motif of yearning for the origins. Many authors developed detailed opinions about Indian thought more or less independently of one another and contributed to the Romantic understanding of India, including Schelling, Novalis, Görres, Creuzer, Goethe, M. Claudius, and, more than any of the others, the Schlegel brothers.[21] F. Majer (1771-1818) served as a kind of catalyst through the translations he made as well as his own writings and his many personal acquaintanceships. He also helped in shaping Schopenhauer's interest in India.[22] Like Creuzer, Görres, and many other mythologists, Majer was captivated by the idea of an "original monotheism" thought to be present in the most ancient Indian documents, and in this context he also referred to Anquetil's *Oupnek'hat*. It was his conviction that the religious and philosophical situation in Europe could only be clarified and rectified through a return to the Indian origins, and that the sources of the Western tradition found their integrating context and background in Indian thought: "It will no longer remain to be doubted that the priests of Egypt and the sages of Greece have drawn directly from the original well of India; that only Brahmanism can provide those fragments of their teaching which have come down to us with the clarity which they do not possess."[23]

6. And do you know the land where infant mankind lived its happy childhood years, where stood the pillars of fire in which the gods descended to their darlings and mingled in their spirited play? . . . Towards the Orient, to the banks of the Ganges and the Indus, it is there that our hearts feel being drawn by some hidden urge,—it is there that all the dark presentiments point which lie in the depths of our hearts, and it is there that we go when we follow the silent river which flows through time in legends and sacred songs to its source. In the Orient, the heavens poured forth into the Earth . . . In the primitive cultures of this earth, the original force

must still appear undivided; in them, everything must be contained in the same homogeneity which would later become separated into the various camps . . . [24]

With these words, and in a number of other equally impassioned variations on the same theme, J. Görres (1776–1848) depicted the Romantic myths of infancy and unity. The often overlooked Jacobine and Romantic, N. Müller (1770–1851), used similarly ecstatic phrases in his search for the "unity of primeval faith and knowledge" and the "innocent world of mankind" in India. Müller's desire was to evoke the "Spirit of Brahmanism" from the "buried ruins of temples . . . in order to introduce a new, radiant life into the present with its awakening."[25] Like Görres, Müller also referred to the *Oupnek'hat* of Anquetil Duperron.

In his *Die Christenheit oder Europa* ("Christendom or Europe," 1799), Novalis (1772–1801), the greatest of the early Romantics, primarily spoke of an idealized medieval world, of a time in which God, man, and the world were united in harmony and mankind was filled with a "childlike trust." This was the standard against which he measured his criticism of the present. Because of Herder's influence, however, the Orient and especially an idealized India also became associated with the idea of an original state of harmony and a childlike, unbroken wholeness. Poesy-garbed India, where the people were still "dozing" and dreaming, appeared to be the antithesis of the cold, prosaic Europe of the Age of Enlightenment; it stood "in contrast to the cold, dead Spitsbergen of that sitting-room reason" (". . . dem kalten, toten Spitzbergen jenes Stubenverstandes").[26] The poesy sought in India was at once religion. "Religion is the great Orient in us, which is seldom obscured."[27] Still, for Novalis India never attained the central importance that would have led him to strive after a more detailed knowledge.[28] His friend Friedrich Schlegel (1772–1829), however, did have such a relationship with India, at least for *one* very momentous decade of his life.

7. F. Schlegel's thought was initially at home in what could be called the outskirts of the Enlightenment. Yet his criticism of the European present became ever sharper and more decisive, while the Orient, and especially India, increasingly became a synonym for pristine religiousness and the lost wholeness of human existence. In his eyes, the West had lost its sense of unity and harmony as well as its capacity for religion. "Man cannot sink any deeper; it is impossible. Man has indeed come very far in the art of arbitrary division or, what amounts to the same thing, in mechanism, and thus man himself has almost become a machine . . . "[29] In the same article in his journal, Schlegel then complained about an "abstract unfamiliarity with one's own destiny," ("abstrakte Unbekanntschaft mit der eigenen Bestimmung"), a "non-feeling for everything great that has already existed on

earth" ("Nichtgefühl für alles Grosse, was schon wirklich auf Erden war"). As a way out of this impoverishment, he recommended turning back to the Oriental, and especially the Indian sources, "from where every religion and mythology up till now has come," where the "possibility of enthusiasm" could never be completely obliterated.[30] As early as 1800, he wrote that "we must look for the pinnacle of Romanticism" ("das höchste Romantische") in the East, primarily in India.[31] On September 15, 1803, he wrote to L. Tieck: "Here is the actual source of all languages, all the thoughts and poems of the human spirit; everything, everything without exception comes from India."[32] In his *Vorlesungen über Universalgeschichte* ("Lectures on Universal History," 1805/1806), he stated: ". . . the Persian and German languages and cultures, as well as the Greek and old Roman, may all be traced back to the Indian."[33]

Around the time he was writing these words, and in particular when he wrote the letter to Tieck, Schlegel was intensely busy studying Sanskrit and ancient Indian literature. Arriving in Paris in 1802, he first commenced learning Persian under A.L. de Chézy. Chance then provided him with the desired access to Sanskrit, for an expert in the language, A. Hamilton, had just returned from India.[34] He was detained in Paris in 1803 and thus became available as a teacher for Schlegel, whose mythicizing enthusiasm was now leading to more exact and disciplined linguistic and philological work. Schlegel began to translate original works;[35] he worked on a chrestomathy of Sanskrit and published his book *Über die Sprache und Weisheit der Indier* ("On the Language and Wisdom of the Indians")[36] in 1808, the same year he converted to Catholicism. This book is one of the key works of European Indology, "the first work in the German language in which the Indian language, literature, and history are presented upon the basis of a study of original sources."[37] At the same time, this book also documents the end of his enthusiasm for India and of the period of his really original and intensive study of India. After it appeared, the author occasionally contemplated a new edition, although it was never completed. He no longer worked with original Indian sources, but was content with secondary literature. In his later works, we find only more or less casual remarks on India, which do not indicate much fascination or reflection. Thus, for example, his *Vorlesungen zur Philosophie der Geschichte* ("Lectures on the Philosophy of History," 1828) offers only relatively dry comments about the status of the Brahmins, metempsychosis, etc. as well as a sketchy survey (indebted to Colebrooke) of the Indian philosophical systems.[38] Meanwhile, Schlegel had relocated the "cradle of mankind" to biblical Mesopotamia.[39]

8. *Über die Sprache und Weisheit der Indier* is not just a testimony to Schlegel's scholarship, it is primarily a philosophical statement. Schlegel saw no reason to doubt that there was a fundamental and profound affinity

between Indian studies and philosophy: "For investigating the Orient in general, and India in particular, a knowledge of philosophy is very essential and can therefore hardly be dispensed with."[40]

The work has three parts: I. On Language (treating language families, etc.); II. On Philosophy (the types of systems in Indian thought—the doctrine of emanation, naturalism, dualism, pantheism); III. Historical Ideas (in which the concept of a world literature based upon comparative studies is developed). In this work, Schlegel was still glorifying the religion and philosophy of the "most cultivated and wisest people of antiquity."[41] Yet he no longer viewed the oldest religious and philosophical texts of the Indians as providing evidence of an undistorted pristineness, but instead considered them already to contain distortions and misinterpretations of the true pristine teachings. The original revelation could not be found in an unsullied state even in the thought and tradition of the Indians—an idea that was advanced at the beginning of the work as its very premise.[42] And while the Indian material held the continuing fascination of being old and original, it now appeared, as it were, to illustrate the origins of error, and to provide an opportunity to observe how the processes of obscuration and decay had affected the initially god-given clarity in even its oldest and most original phases. He still adhered to the priority of the Indian sources and to the idea that, in certain particular contexts, viz., in the domains of linguistics, mythology, and philosophy, the developments in the West had depended upon these sources.[43] Nevertheless, India was no longer depicted as the country of origin or the home country. Certainly, it still exhibited numerous traces of pristine truth and clarity; yet only Christianity could teach the "context of the whole" ("Zusammenhang des Ganzen"), and the "sure separation of admixed error" ("sichere Absonderung des beigemischten Irrtums").[44]

9. India no longer appeared as the lost paradise of human totality, purity, and proximity to God, but merely offered "curious and unexpected sidelights about the ways of human thinking in the most ancient times," sidelights about "the rise of error" and "the first monstrosities" which followed the loss of the "simplicity of divine knowledge."[45] In the second part of his work ("On Philosophy"), Schlegel attempted to make the Indian "system of metempsychosis and emanation" understandable in the light of his own concept of "original revelation" ("ursprüngliche Offenbarung," "Uroffenbarung"). In this doctrine, which, in his opinion, found its most exemplary and telling expression in the law book of Manu, he saw "high wisdom compounded with an abundance of error." From this, he concluded: ". . . considered as natural development of reason, the Indian system of emanation is not at all explainable; seen as a revelation that was misunderstood, everything in it is entirely comprehensible."[46]

And it is precisely this most ancient error, which arose from the misuse of the divine gift, from the obscuration and misinterpretation of divine wisdom which we find in the Indian documents, and we shall find even more clear and instructive examples of it the more we become acquainted with the most cultivated and wisest people of antiquity. It is the first system to have occupied the place of truth; wild fabrications and crude errors, yet everywhere still the traces of divine truth and the expression of that shock and sorrow which must have resulted from the first fall from God.[47]

Schlegel emphasized that the doctrine of emanation is not to be confused with pantheism. He considered pantheism (which he discussed in the fifth chapter of the second book and found present especially in the Vedānta and, in other ways, in Buddhism) to be the most recent and degenerate of all the teachings of India:

The most important epochs of Indian and Oriental philosophy and religion in general are the following: first, the system of emanation, which eventually degenerated into astrological superstition and fanatical materialism; the doctrine of the two principles, whose dualistic system eventually changed into pantheism. The human spirit has not sunk deeper in Oriental philosophy than into pantheism, which is just as pernicious for morals as materialism and, moreover, destroys the imagination as well.[48]

10. For Schlegel, the core and basis of pantheism was an abstract, negative concept of the infinite devoid of content, a false concept which leads to indifference, leaves no room for living individuality and moral discernment, and which thus has a "destructive influence upon life." It is the polar opposite of the true concept of the divine omnipotence: ". . . here, we merely notice that the deep living feeling of infinity and the abundance of omnipotence must have already become very weakened and attenuated before it would dissolve itself in this shadow and false concept of the one and all, so difficult as it is to distinguish from nothing."[49] Buddhism, as understood by Schlegel, had as its "actual, most essential, and esoteric doctrine" the teaching "that everything is nothing." He thus viewed it as being naturally close to the Vedānta, indeed, as its very consequence.

When everything else has first been obliterated and has disappeared before the merely abstract and negative concept of infinity, then it ultimately escapes itself and dissipates into nothingness, since it was empty and void of meaning in the first place . . . Once this great disclosure has been made, and this all-encompassing, all-destroying, and yet so easy science and reason-wisdom that all is one has been discovered, then no further search or research is necessary; all that which others know or believe in other ways is simply error, deception, and weak-mindedness, just as all change and all life is mere illusion.[50]

Schlegel considered pantheism "the system of pure reason" and, at the same time, the most profound and most extreme aberration and failure in the history of human thought. Through it, thinking man comes to rely upon himself alone, closing himself to faith and revelation. "It appeals to man's self-conceit just as much as to his indolence." Here, Schlegel felt he had found the point of transition from Oriental to European philosophy, with its aberrations and its hybris.[51]

The critique of pantheism brings us to the philosophical (and religious) heart of the work. Moreover, it provides testimony of Schlegel's own position in the philosophical debate of the time, while simultaneously introducing an important theme in Schlegel's attempts to come to grips with his own earlier thought. For not only had he himself flirted with a Romantically-glorified conception of pantheism during his younger years; this concept was certainly one of the original motivations behind his interest in India. It is symptomatic of Schlegel's development that the motif of pantheism was now cast in a new light and became the keynote of his criticism of India, and it reflects a deeper, not merely chronological, connection between this book and his conversion to Catholicism. It was this shift which was to lead some of his contemporaries, e.g., Schelling, to criticize the basic philosophical position of the work.

11. Schelling provided a defense of pantheism in his *Philosophische Untersuchungen über das Wesen der menschlichen Freiheit* ("Philosophical Investigations on the Essence of Human Freedom", 1809). Following Baader's lead, he accused Schlegel of advocating a subordinate "governess philosophy."[52] Schelling's own philosophy has been characterized by Feuerbach as "an exotic growth" which, so to speak, transplanted "the old Oriental identity onto Germanic soil."[53] During the earlier phases of his philosophical development, Schelling did indeed exhibit an intense yearning for the origins and for unity, which his opponents as well as his followers associated with India.[54] Already the speculations on the mythical and traditional sources of human thought and existence, which he presented in his early work *Über Mythen, historische Sagen und Philosopheme der ältesten Welt* (1793), were obviously applicable to non-European, especially Oriental traditions. As a matter of fact, several "Schellingians" among the historians of philosophy, for instance Th. A. Rixner, C.J.H. Windischmann, and E. Röth, showed an often speculative openness towards India and the Orient.[55] Yet in his earlier years, Schelling's own explicit interest in India was less developed, and his position vis-à-vis the Indian "origins" more reserved than was the case with some of his contemporaries. His later, more explicit and detailed statements on India, specifically those in his *Philosophie der Mythologie* ("Philosophy of Mythology"), are often critical and anti-Romantic.

Hegel's essentially negative attitude towards F. Schlegel and Schlegel's picture of India is well-known. To be sure, it is precisely Schlegel's remarks about pantheism, criticizing as they do an abstract infinite which coincides with nothingness and leads to indifference, that tell us to exert more caution and differentiate more carefully than Hegel himself or some more recent critics of Schlegel. The motif of the abstract "One," that empty substantiality which is not "mediated" and reconciled with the particularities of the world, played a key role in Hegel's own critique of India—even if an entirely different philosophy of history was involved.[56] Schegel's repeated warnings against abstractly comparing Indian and European phenomena, without taking their particular concrete contexts and contents into consideration, are also occasionally reminiscent of Hegel.[57] The decisive difference between the two lies in the fact that Hegel simply could not accept the ideas of an original revelation, a "primitive people," or a perfect and unified state of mankind standing at the dawn of history;[58] he considered these views as representing a totally inverted and perverted sense of the true direction of history.

12. In the closing chapter, "On Oriental and Indian Studies in general, and on their Value and Purpose," Schlegel took what may be called historical and philosophical stock, delineating what he saw as a possible practical application of his book on India. He attempted to place Indian and Oriental thought in general into one basic historical and systematic context together with European thought and thus to sketch out the possible repercussions which the study of India and a synoptic view of culture could have upon the thinking of his European present. As noted above,[59] Schlegel had previously characterized pantheism, which he saw as both the "system of pure reason" and the low point of Indian thought, as the "transition from Oriental to European philosophy." Although he insisted that the complete truth was to be found only in the Christian revelation and not in any of the documents of ancient India, within the domain of philosophy, he nevertheless adhered to his view that the wisdom developed in India was superior to that of European philosophy, and remained a source of spiritual force and orientation untouched by the hybris of critical and autonomous reason. In his eyes, European philosophy depended on the impulses, admittedly often indirect and obscured, which it periodically received from Eastern thought, on an "alien ferment" which was passed on to it from time to time. "Without the continually renewed stimulus of this enlivening principle, the European spirit would probably never have raised itself so high, or it would have fallen back earlier." Moreover, that most sublime philosophy of Europe, the idealism of reason, "as advanced by the Greek thinkers, would, when held against the wealth of power and light in the Oriental idealism of religion, probably appear only as some weak Promethean spark would appear before the full heavenly glow of the sun, as something merely stolen and continually threatening to expire; yet the less there was of substance, the

more elaborate became the form."[60] Of course, Schlegel considered the "merely empirical way of thinking" which dominated his time to be even more deficient, for it was characterized by its "limitation of experience to the domain of the merely useful." This led to the destruction of the "higher spirit" – a situation which, however, provided a reason to "search for a way back to the older and better philosophy" precisely because of its utter desolation.[61]

13. *Über die Sprache und Weisheit der Indier* has often been described as a pioneering work of Indology that indicated the path of the future. Yet is was also a restorative philosophical work firmly committed to the past. Because of this, it is not surprising that Schlegel's work was enlisted by partisans of the political restoration and ultramontanism and generally associated with a specifically Catholic interest in India, in particular in France.[62] In this context, we may mention the name of Baron F. von Eckstein (1790–1861), who served as historiographer of the French Ministry of Foreign Affairs and was an avid amateur Indologist.[63] Using a critical, even polemical tone, Hegel laid stress upon the associations between Schlegel and the French advocates of a "primitive Catholicism," naming Lamennais, Abel Rémusat, and Saint Martin as well as von Eckstein.[64] The doctrine of a decline in the divine light that had originally been given to the Indians and other Oriental peoples, by the way, concurs in a natural way with basic assumptions of many missionaries and Christian authors in the preceding centuries.

We do not need to concern ourselves with the question as to how far Schlegel's conversion to Catholicism represented a break in his development or may have been a logical fulfillment of earlier motives,[65] or whether his book is a document of "disillusionment" or a recantation of his earlier enthusiasm.[66] Apart from this, it does remain to be noted that Schlegel's book on India ultimately achieved a certain kind of academic neutrality above and beyond the fundamental philosophical and religious conflicts of its time,[67] and that it opened up new methodological perspectives as well as the prospect for a new context of research. Schlegel evokes the ideal of the Renaissance scholar who combined solid linguistic knowledge with philosophical training in his studies of classical antiquity; he hopes that it will inspire a methodical and yet not exclusively philological treatment of the Indian material.[68] His book closes with a summons that remains impressive even today, a plea for synoptic, contextual understanding, and for a cross-fertilization of the results obtained from the study of different literatures and cultures: " . . . just as in the history of nations, the Asians and the Europeans form just one large family and Asia and Europe constitute an inseparable whole, so should we exert ourselves even more to view the literature of all educated peoples as a continuous development and one single, intimately connected structure and framework, as *one* large whole. Then, many of those one-sided and limited views would disappear of their own accord, much would become understandable in this context, and everything would appear new in this light" (" . . . so wie nun in der Völkergeschichte die Asiaten und Europäer nur eine grosse Familie, Asien und Europa ein untrennbares Ganzes bilden, so sollte man sich immer mehr bemühen, auch die Literatur aller gebildeten Völker als eine fortgehende Entwicklung und ein einziges innig verbundenes Gebäude und Gebilde, als *ein* grosses Ganzes zu betrachten, wo denn manche einseitige und beschränkte Ansicht von selbst verschwinden, vieles im Zusammenhange erst verständlich, alles aber in diesem Lichte neu erscheinen würde.").[69]

14. While Friedrich Schlegel's brother August Wilhelm (1767–1845) was equally important for the West's awareness and knowledge of India, he was more straightforward and less ambivalent in his attitudes. He also began by criticizing his own European present, i.e., Western culture around the Age of the Enlightenment. His lectures *Über Literatur, Kunst und Geist des Zeitalters* ("On the Literature, Art and Spirit of the [Current] Era") are most exemplary in this regard.[70] In them, he deplored the utilitarian thinking, the pragmatism, and the spirit of modern Europe, directed as it was entirely around economics and the "promotion of the civic good." Faced with this situation, it was his hope that an impetus towards re-orientation might be gained through the Indian sources.[71] India and the Orient, the realm of the lost unity and totality, as the starting point of a possible regeneration, as the field in which the search for the original revelation was to be conducted—these were ideas and motifs which affected August Wilhelm as well, although they touched him more gently, more steadily, less exaltedly, and more continuously than they did his brother Friedrich.[72]

August Wilhelm Schlegel eventually became a professional Indologist. He was the first occupant of a German chair for Indology (Bonn, 1818).[73] He edited Indian texts according to the principles of classical philology and tried to make them available in translations that were understandable. He was succeeded by Chr. Lassen, who presented a comprehensive, scholarly assessment of the classical and modern knowledge of India in his *Indische Altertumskunde*. The speculations about India and the "Indomania" had finally been transformed into institutionalized Indology.

Some of the leading figures of the time, most conspicuously W. von Humboldt, played an active, personally committed role in this transformation. Humboldt himself studied Sanskrit and published important articles on the *Bhagavadgītā*, to which Hegel responded in his even more important review articles.[74]

F. Max Müller was the son of the poet who wrote the poems for Schubert's *Winterreise* and *Schöne Müllerin*, and one of the classic figures of nineteenth-century Indology. When he was older, long after his naturalization in England, Müller still spoke of the stimulus which the Romantic movement had provided for his Indological career. Referring to the opening up of Sanskrit and the culture of India, he said: "It has added a new period to our historical consciousness, and revived the recollections of our childhood, which seemed to have vanished forever . . . We all come from the East—all that we value most has come to us from the East, and in going to the East . . . everybody ought to feel that he is going to his 'old home,' full of memories, if only he can read them."[75]

15. Müller saw an analogy between the Europeans who rediscovered the documents of the Indian past and the hypothetical situation of Americans who had been unaware of the origins of their language and literature in England, and who then suddenly rediscovered these English origins and were led to completely new dimensions of historical self-understanding.[76] The formula of the Indian childhood of our own being and consciousness appears repeatedly throughout Müller's work; the author asserts that for the "true anthropologist" who is concerned with gaining an adequate historical self-awareness of mankind, nothing is as important as that oldest record of Indian thought, the *Ṛgveda*.[77] Nevertheless, Müller, like his friend and patron Chr. C.J. Freiherr von Bunsen, remained committed to a Christian standpoint, although he did become more receptive towards the Vedānta—to the idea of a "Christian Vedānta"—in his later years.[78]

The motif of origins so emphasized by Max Müller may also be found among some of the other leading Indologists of the nineteenth century, although usually in less exuberant form. Even Müller's Parisian teacher E. Burnouf, a highly dedicated philologist, exhitibed its influence, for he considered his Indological work as simultaneously being a pursuit of the history of the origins of the human spirit.[79] More generally, the continuing fascination with the "origins" is indicated, at least implicitly, by the central role of *Ṛgveda* studies in nineteenth-century Indology. To be sure, Indological research developed its own tradition of correcting and neutralizing the cultural and ideological presumptions and prejudices to which it owed its impetus, if not its very existence; the criticism of its own motivations and points of departure became a kind of motivation in itself as the scholarly exploration of the textual sources advanced.

Romantic ideas and aspirations concerning India survived in various transformations, primarily in non-academic movements. The nostalgic fascination with the Indian "origins," the association of India with a critique of quantifying and calculating thought, and the reaction against pragmatism, rationalism and materialism were more than an ephemeral phenomenon. Here it is sufficient to recall New England Transcendentalism, especially R.W. Emerson and H.D. Thoreau,[80] as well as

Theosophy, Anthroposophy and various cults and movements in the twentieth century. In addition, we may refer to the type of "traditionalism" and "cultural criticism" which we find exemplified in the writings of R. Guénon (1886–1951) and his associates.[81]

16. In the life and work of the Schlegel brothers and some of their contemporaries, the Romantic fascination with India merges into academic Indology; the yearning for alternatives and self-transformation leads to the systematic exploration of the sources, and the methodical accumulation of "objective" knowledge about India. The dialectic irony in this development is obvious.

As we have seen, the Romantic interest in India was inseparable from a radical critique of the European present. The preoccupation with the merely useful, the calculable, rational, precisely determinable, the loss of faith, enthusiasm, and the sense of unity and wholeness, were seen as symptomatic deficiencies of this present. As a remedy for such spiritual impoverishment, Friedrich Schlegel proposed a return to the sources of Indian wisdom. Yet in order to bring about such a return, he felt that linguistic studies alone would not suffice; they had to be supplemented by "research," by the historical and philological methods of his time. The types and methods of Indological research which Friedrich and August Wilhelm Schlegel eventually applied proved to be aspects and symptoms of precisely that present, which the *yearning* for India had initially sought to overcome. There is no way which leads out of the present: what had appeared as a promise of retreat and return, as a possible escape from the present, itself became the object and goal of a program of historical and critical research that was committed to the spirit of that present and oriented around classical philology and the ideal of "objectivity." Instead of the desired ascent from the cold and prosaic world of "numbers and figures" (Novalis) to the world of "fairy tales and poems," a process of "objective" research, of scientific and very prosaic exploration of such "fairy tales and poems" was inaugurated.

In the following chapters, we will not trace the course of Indological research any further, nor describe the motivations and presumptions of leading Indologists. Instead, our primary concern will be with the ways in which the newly discovered materials affected the European understanding of philosophy and the history of philosophy. For Indology was in its formative stage at the same time in which the history and historiography of philosophy were, so to speak, changing and acquiring new forms, in particular in the work of Hegel. He and his antipode Schopenhauer provided two exemplary and influential models for approaching Indian thought, and for including it in the horizon of Western philosophical and historical self-understanding.

6. Hegel

1. The first results of modern Indological research became available during one of the most creative and dynamic periods in the history of European philosophy—a period of unprecedented globalization of European thought and science. New standards for the exploration of Indian philosophy and science were set by the works of H. Th. Colebrooke (1765–1837). His presentation of the classical systems of Indian philosophy remained unsurpassed for the better part of the nineteenth century.[1] G.W.F. Hegel (1770–1831), one of the quintessential European thinkers, was not only Colebrooke's contemporary; he was also one of his readers—and his response to Indian thought illustrates some of the most fundamental problems of the encounter and "dialogue" between India and Europe.[2]

Hegel's presentation and interpretation of Indian thought has not met with much interest, not to mention approval, from the side of Indological scholars. According to H. von Glasenapp, Hegel was a "bookman," living in a world of abstractions and speculations, unwilling and unable to adjust his conceptual schemes to empirical evidence. Moreover, he was the "prototype of a Westerner," who saw Western thought as the measure of all things: "Therefore, whatever he knew to say about the Indian world, turned out to be very insufficient; and the result was a caricature which shows—regardless of the fact that he had a correct understanding of certain details—that he ventured on a task for which he was not qualified . . ."[3]

Hegel's statements about India are indeed insufficient in various respects. As far as historical and philological accuracy and objectivity are concerned, they leave much to be desired. But they cannot be measured by the standards of scholarly objectivity alone. Hegel deals with India as a European philosopher whose philosophy commits him to not being neutral.[4] He is not just part of the European philosophical tradition, but makes a conscious effort to comprehend and fulfill it in his own thought. He is one-sided, but his one-sidedness is not a simple bias: It is a matter of intense historical and systematic reflection, and a challenge to the very idea of objective intercultural "understanding."

2. Hegel's interest in India is inseparable from that of the Romantics: He was one of the heirs, but also the most rigorous critic of the Romantic conception of India. What distinguishes his approach above all from that of the Romantics is his commitment to the present, and his sense of an irreversible direction of history. He does not glorify origins and early stages. The spirit of world history progresses to greater richness and complexity. What has been in the beginning cannot be richer and more perfect. It may be true that India, as part of the Orient, is a land of "sunrise," of early origins and "childhood." But this does not justify nostalgia and contempt of the European present. We cannot and need not return to the Orient: It is a matter of the past.[5] Unlike the Schlegel brothers, Hegel was not an Indologist, and he made no attempt to learn Sanskrit or another Indian language. Yet, his judgements on India are not as unfounded and irresponsible as it appears in von Glasenapp's presentation. Hegel made full use of the translations, reports and investigations concerning India which were available to him. His knowledge of Asian, specifically Indian matters was as broad and comprehensive as one could expect in his days. In this respect, he can certainly bear comparison with A. Schopenhauer, who survived him, however, by almost thirty years and gained access to materials on India, especially Buddhism, which were not available to Hegel.[6]

In Hegel's early writings and lectures, India and China play no significant role whatsoever. Only the Near East, Turkey in particular, was always within his historical horizon.[7] Occasional references to India do not demonstrate any specific interest, nor a level of information which would be in any sense remarkable. However, from an early time on, we notice a negative attitude to Romanticism, and this includes a negative response to the Romantic glorification and mystification of the Orient. The anti-Romantic perspective provides the background and an important point of departure for Hegel's approach to India.[8] His initial response to the Indian tradition is an expression and continuation of his response to the contemporary Western phenomena of Romanticism and "Orientalism."

However, with the growth of his knowledge, and with the publication of new and more reliable sources, his understanding and evaluation became more differentiated and balanced—though never really impartial. A period of very intense study of the traditions of China and India began in 1822.[9]

3. In 1818, the year when the University of Bonn established the first chair for Indology in Germany, Hegel assumed his responsibilities as professor of philosophy at the University of Berlin. This was the beginning of a period of very successful and influential teaching; it lasted up to his death in 1831.

During these culminating years of his academic life, he kept studying new publications on India, and he sought advice and information from his colleague at the University of Berlin, the pioneer Sanskritist and linguist F. Bopp.[10] He incorporated the results of his studies into his great lectures on the history of philosophy, the philosophy of world history, aesthetics and the philosophy of religion. The presentation of India became more and more detailed and comprehensive in the later versions of these periodically repeated lectures.[11] The fact that he did not publish his lectures, and that they have to be reconstructed from his own sketches and the notes taken by his students, leads to complex philological and editorial problems.

In 1824, H. Th. Colebrooke's first two essays "On the Philosophy of the Hindus" were published in the *Transactions of the Royal Asiatic Society.*[12] Hegel welcomed these essays, which deal with the systems of Sāṃkhya and Nyāya-Vaiśeṣika, as a new basis for the Western understanding of Indian thought. In his view, they exemplified that type of thorough, sober and sensitive research which he regarded as an indispensable prerequisite of philosophical interpretation and evaluation.[13] He referred to them extensively in his lectures on the history of philosophy. However, he did not utilize Colebrooke's later studies of Indian philosophy, specifically those on Vedānta and the "sectarian" philosophies (including Buddhism and *Cārvāka*), which were also published in the *Transactions of the Royal Asiatic Society.*

Hegel's basis for Buddhism was in general rather narrow. To a considerable extent, he had to rely on older missionary reports from East Asia. For Theravāda Buddhism, F. Buchanan's long article "On the Religion and Literature of the Burmas" was one of the major sources.[14] The pioneering contributions of E. Burnouf (1801–1852) came too late to be utilized for his lectures.[15]

Hegel also praised and studied W. von Humboldt's essays on the *Bhagavadgītā*, and he responded to them in 1827 in an extensive review article. Its two parts fill almost a hundred pages in the *Jahrbücher für wissenschaftliche Kritik*. In his review, Hegel deals not just with von Humboldt's interpretation, but much more with the world-view of the *Bhagavadgītā* itself and with what he sees as the role of Yoga and meditation in the Indian tradition. In a sense, this is Hegel's testament, as far as his understanding of India is concerned.[16]

Although von Glasenapp's statement that Hegel does not mention Anquetil Duperron's *Oupnek'hat* is not correct, references to it are, indeed, casual and perhaps indirect.[17] Unlike Schopenhauer, Hegel did not fulfill Anquetil's explicit hope that German philosophers, specifically followers of Kant, would read and respond to his translation. However, Anquetil receives more attention as pioneer investigator of the *Zend Avesta*.[18]

The Abbé J.A. Dubois, whose influential *Hindu Manners, Customs and Ceremonies* would seem to be more commensurate with Hegel's own critical attitude, appears only in casual and inconspicuous references.[19] In general, British sources, including the writings of W. Jones, F. Wilford and J. Mill, were most important for Hegel.

4. Before we discuss in greater detail Hegel's interpretation of Indian thought, we have to refer briefly to the systematic context of his philosophy, in which his observations on India have their peculiar role and meaning.

In Hegel's thought, system and history are combined, even integrated, in an unprecedented manner. The history of philosophy is the unfolding of philosophy itself, and Hegel's own system is designed as the consummation of the historical development of philosophy. System and history are the two sides of the self-manifestation of the spirit. We are what we have become in and through history. History shows us the genesis and evolution of our present state of being and knowing: " . . . it is the course of history which shows us not the genesis of alien things, but our very own genesis or becoming, the genesis of our science."[20] Historical understanding explicates and objectifies what is implicit in, and presupposed by, the current conditions of our existence. In particular, the history of philosophy aims at comprehending the fundamental constituents and the inner structure of our present existence and self-awareness.

In and by the process and progress of historical development, what is prior is integrated in what is posterior. It is—in Hegel's suggestive and ambiguous terminology—"aufgehoben," i.e., cancelled, suspended, preserved and moved upward all at once. According to one of the central and most controversial principles of Hegel's philosophy and historiography, this implies "that the sequence of the systems of philosophy in history is the same as the sequence in the logical deduction of the conceptual determination of the idea," and that consequently "the study of the history of philosophy is a study of philosophy itself."[21] —"Just as in the logical system of thought each of its formations has its position, at which alone it has its validity . . . , so every philosophy is a particular stage of development in the whole process, and it has its specified position at which it has its true value and meaning."[22]

The philosophy of the present comprehends the philosophy of the past, which is contained in it, by recollecting it. It cannot return to it; there is no way back in history. "Therefore, there cannot be Platonists, Aristotelians, Stoics, Epicureans in our days."[23] The superior "height" of the present which gives us the freedom of viewing and comprehending the past also prevents us from returning to it and from thinking the thought of the past in the same way in which it was thought in the past. The fact itself that we reflect and look back upon the thought of the past, that we comprehend it as something prior to, and presupposed by, our own thought, shows that it is no longer what it was at its own stage: It is now included in and superseded by a new, more developed and comprehensive context. Insofar, it does not provide a real, actual alternative for us, nor should we expect from it solutions to problems which have emerged only with our own, richer and more complex, stage of development. The "reassignment of the developed, enriched spirit to such simplicity" would be nothing but "the refuge of impotence," an attempted, but futile withdrawal from "the rich material of development" into sheer "indigence."[24]

5. Hegel's scheme of the history of philosophy is primarily designed to deal with the history of European thought from Thales to Kant and Hegel himself. However, this is not just one line of development among others. Hegel's conception of "Weltgeist" ("world spirit"), and the corresponding unity of the world-historical process, leaves no room for the assumption of other, independent or parallel streams of historical development.[25] Where in this scheme does Asia, and India in particular, have its place?

According to Hegel, the Orient is essentially beginning, introduction, preparation. The way of the "Weltgeist" leads from the East to the West. The Occident supersedes the Orient, and in dealing with the Oriental traditions, it faces, in a sense, its own petrified past. Compared to Europe, Asia, and India in particular, is "static," i.e., without the dynamics of progress which characterizes European history. Those tensions and dynamic forces which have driven European thought from its Greek beginnings through the unfolding of the ideas of the subject, of human freedom, and of "being-for-itself" to the social and political ideologies of the period of the French Revolution have been absent in India. Although the exploration of India is part of the Western historical self-exploration, it is thus also reflection upon a level of existence and awareness which is essentially different from, and incompatible with, the modern Western level.

The inherent and distinctive principle of the Oriental, and specifically the Indian, stage of thought is, according to Hegel, the principle of "substantiality" or "substanceness" ("Substantialität"), i.e., of the unity and ultimacy of one underlying "substance." The religions of India are basically "religions of substance." They see God as ultimate "substance," pure, abstract being-in-itself, which contains all finite and particular beings as non-essential modifications, leaving them without any identity and dignity of their own.[26]

6. In his *Lectures on the Philosophy of Religion*, Hegel discusses Hinduism – referring also to what he considers as Buddhism – in accordance with his conception of "religion of substance." We may even say that Hinduism appears as the prototype of a "religion of substance."[27] In this discussion, Hegel refers to phenomena in which he sees the potential for further

developments, but no actual transcendence of the underlying "substantiality" of Hinduism. In particular, he deals with the idea of *trimūrti*, the trinity of Śiva, Viṣṇu and Brahman,[28] with the "superficial personification" of the neutral *brahman* (nominative: *brahma*) through the corresponding masculine form *brahmā*[29], and with the interpenetration of polytheism and underlying pantheism. We cannot enlarge on these speculative and idiosyncratic, yet challenging comments. Instead, we will focus on what Hegel himself presents as the philosophical quintessence of Hinduism and the central target of his response as a philosopher.

In Hegel's view, Indian philosophy is inseparable from religion,[30] and the fundamental role of "substantiality" applies to philosophy as well as religion. Pure "substance" means indeterminate being-in-itself. It has no differentiation either within or outside of itself. It is the One out of which everything arises, and in which it vanishes again; and it is ultimately nothing but abstract unity. And exactly this is what Hegel finds in the Indian conception of *brahman* ("Brahm"): It is formless and indeterminate, unspeakable and unthinkable. Any attempt to describe or think it would lead away from it to the particular and non-essential. *Brahman* as such is "abstract unity without determination" ("abstrakte Einheit ohne Bestimmung"), "unity as nothing but abstract universality, as indeterminate substance" ("die Einheit nur als die abstrakte Allgemeinheit, als bestimmungslose Substanz"), "substance without subjectivity" ("Substanz ohne Subjektivität"), "pure being, without any concrete determination in itself" ("das reine Sein, ohne alle konkrete Bestimmung in sich"),[31] "eternal rest of being-in-itself" ("die ewige Ruhe des Insichseins"),[32] "spiritless substance" ("geistlose Substanz").[33]

7. The Indian mind has thus found its way to the One and the Universal which Hegel, too, sees as the true ground of religion and philosophy. But it has not found its way back to the concrete particularity of the world. It has not brought about a mediation and reconcilation of the universal and the particular, the one and the many. The finite is lost in the infinite; the world is lost in *brahman* which is the "naught of all that is finite" ("das Nichts alles Endlichen").[34] The undivided unity of *brahman* and the multiplicity of the world do not and cannot affect or permeate each other. Regardless of all abstract assertions to the contrary, they are related to one another in unreconciled negation and exclusion: " . . . the One, just because it is entirely contentless and abstract, because it has not its particularizations in itself, lets them fall outside it, lets them escape in uncontrolled confusion."[35] This leads to the other extreme of Indian thought – its "wild excesses of fantasy" ("wilde Ausschweifung der Phantasie"), an "unrestrained frenzy" ("haltungsloser Taumel") of particulars,[36] a rampant chaos of mythological and iconographic details. The Indian religion is not only

"religion of substance," it is also "religion of fantasy" ("Religion der Phantasie").[37]

According to Hegel, such constant oscillation between the "supersensuous" and "wildest sensuality" finds its most visible and striking expression in Indian art, and he refers to it repeatedly in his *Lectures on Aesthetics.*[38] In this work, he also proposes his curious yet challenging thesis that the Indian way of thinking leaves no room for "symbols" in the true and full sense of the word.[39]

Hegel reiterates and illustrates his interpretation in his critique of the concept of *māyā* and above all, the role of Kṛṣṇa in the *Bhagavadgītā.* The Indian absolute, regardless whether it is called Brahman or Kṛṣṇa, is either principle of an abstract negation of the finite or—as in the Gītā—principle of an abstract combination of negation and identification. The divine being of the *Bhagavadgītā* is discovered in all finite beings. It permeates them—but only as their abstract indeterminate self-identity, as the "being of their existence" ("Sein ihres Daseins").[40] It does not secure them in their finite individuality, nor is the finite a real factor in or for the infinite. On the contrary, the abstract self-identity of the finite existences, which identifies them with the abstract absolute, is incompatible with their concrete individual identity. Absolute abstract identity of God and the world thus coincides with unreconciled and equally abstract difference and mutual exclusion.[41]

There is, in short, a lack of dialectical mediation: The absolute and infinite is not put to work in and for the finite and relative; and the relative and finite does not affect the infinite. Accordingly, there is no historical progress towards the enhancement of man and the world.

8. What appears as the ultimate depth of Indian thought, is at the same time its essential defect: The finite and particular has not been transcended; rather, it has not been discovered and posited as such. According to Hegel, this discovery has been accomplished only by the "hard European intellect."[42]

The full scope and concrete relevance of these observations becomes manifest in thier application to the themes of human individuality and freedom. "World history . . . shows the development of the spirit's consciousness of its freedom, and of the actualization which is brought about by such consciousness."[43] Philosophy reflects this development. It is inseparable from the unfolding of the idea of human freedom, as well as from its social and political actualizations. Human freedom is autonomy of the person. In order for it to be real, the individual subject, the concrete ego, has to accept its particularity and to affirm itself, its "being-*for*-itself" ("Fürsichsein"), against the "being-*in*-itself" ("Ansichsein") of the ultimate substance.

Hegel does not find such self-affirmation of the free and unique individual in India. Here, the individual in its subjective freedom "has no value in itself." It is part of a world which is a "transitory manifestation of the One. . . . Man has not been posited."[44] Instead of affirming and unfolding its individuality and particularity, the individual tries to subdue and suspend it. The aim of philosophical thought and religious practice is self-identification with *brahman*, return to "substantiality" and "being-in-itself." This requires extinguishing all contents of awareness, creating an "emotionless, will-less, deedless pure abstraction of mind, in which all positive content of consciousness is superseded."[45] "The ascent to Brahman is brought about by utter stupefaction and insensibility."[46] "The abstract unity with God is brought into being in this abstraction of man."[47] "Pure egoity" ("reine Ichheit")[48], i.e., pure, abstract subjectivity, coincides with pure, abstract substanceness. Contrary to what we might expect, Hegel does not cite the correlation and identification of *ātman* and *brahman* in this connection; in general, the concept of *ātman* is conspicuously absent in his presentation.

9. Just like W. von Humboldt, Hegel sees the *Bhagavadgītā* as a most representative, quintessential Indian religious poem; and he believes that Yoga is its central teaching. He thanks von Humboldt for his rich background of scholarly information and analysis concerning the Yoga tradition in general. He also refers to other studies and translations, such as A.W. Schlegel's Latin translation and H. Th. Colebrooke's survey of Sāṃkhya and Yoga. Supplementing his observations on the Gītā with references to other texts and traditions, he concludes: "Therefore we may legitimately consider what is called Yoga as the general center of Indian religion and philosophy."[49] Hegel discusses various attempts to translate the word *yoga* into European languages, primarily Latin, English, German, and he finds von Humboldt's expression "Vertiefung" ("absorption," "immersion") most appropriate. However, he adds that this yogic absorption is neither immersion into an object, such as a piece of art or an object of scholarly investigation, nor immersion into one's own concrete personal subjectivity. Rather, it is absorption, immersion without content or object. Hegel suggests that it could be called "abstract devotion," and he says that it aims at complete contentlessness of the subject as well as the object.[50] Its ultimate goal is isolation from the world and withdrawal into the empty unity of *brahman*.

Yoga exemplifies a "negative attitude" of the mind[51] and the "negative nature of what is the highest in Indian religion."[52] It negates what Hegel calls "mediation" ("Vermittlung"), the dialectical interplay of subject and object, and the creative self-explication of man in history. It aims at immediacy, "pure unity of thought in itself,"[53] involution instead of evolution, return to pure indefinite being which is identical with pure nothingness. It represents "quietism," "mysticism" and "meditative" withdrawal in a sense which is diametrically opposed to Hegel's orientation.

Hegel refers to "contemplation" and "meditation" in his *Bhagavadgītā* review.[54] He also uses the word "meditation" in two sections of his *Lectures on the Philosophy of World History*, of which he delivered five versions between 1822/23 and 1830/31. In a somewhat casual usage, we find the expression "silent meditation" ("schweigende Meditation") in a section which summarizes and paraphrases a report by Col. F. Wilford and which has parallels in the *Lectures on the Philosophy of Religion*.[55] The more significant usages occur in the chapter on "The Mongolian Principle" ("Das mongolische Prinzip"), which precedes the chapter on India. Hegel first introduced this chapter, which replaces a similar, though much shorter appendix to the chapter on India in the version of 1822/23, in the second version of his *Lectures on the Philosophy of World History* (1824/25). He presented it again, with additions and revisions, in 1826/27 and 1828/29, i.e., approximately at the time of the composition and publication of the *Bhagavadgītā* review, which contains a number of literal parallels. However, he did not include it in the last presentation of these *Lectures* before his death, i.e., the winter of 1830/31.[56]

In this chapter, Hegel speaks about Buddhism, which represents for him, perhaps in an even more radical manner, the same basic orientation as the Yogic tradition of Hinduism. In Buddhism, or the "religion of Fo," nothingness—which he finds in the notion of *nirvāṇa*—is the principle, "the ultimate goal, the highest point."[57] Man should try deliberately and methodically to identify himself with it, to produce such emptiness within himself through "constant meditation" ("beständige Meditation"); and that means, according to Hegel, "mental abstraction" ("Abstraktion des Geistes"), getting used to "being nothing, feeling nothing, desiring nothing."[58]

In making these statements about Buddhism and Yoga, Hegel continues and summarizes a tradition of European speculation about and criticism of Eastern "quietism" and obsession with voidness and nothingness, which had its origins in seventeenth-century missionary reports from China and received wide publicity through P. Bayle's *Dictionnaire historique et critique* and the *Encyclopédie* of Diderot and d'Alembert.[59]

10. What the Indians call *mokṣa* is, according to Hegel, only an abstract and negative liberation. It precludes that very context of "mediation" which is the condition of the possibility of concrete human, i.e., personal freedom. And without the explicit recognition of the subject as person, there is, in Hegel's view, no real basis for philosophy in its full sense. "The real philosophy begins only in the Occident. Here the spirit goes down into

itself, immerses itself into itself, posits itself as free, is free for itself. Philosophy can exist only here; and hence we have free constitutions only in the Occident."[60] Philosophical thought and social and political reality are inseparable; again and again, Hegel refers to those features of Indian society which he considers to be incompatible with the spirit of philosophy.

The development of Occidental history, from the Greek and early Christian world to the age of the French Revolution, is the development and self-organization of the substance as *subject*, descent and unfolding of the absolute and divine into the finite and human world, self-discovery and self-affirmation of the autonomous person. The "phenomenology" or self-manifestation of the absolute merges into man's work in history, into human self-fulfillment. Man becomes "present God" ("präsenter Gott")[61] and continues the divine process in his own worldly presence, in taking charge of his world and discovering the dignity of the absolute *in* it. Philosophy has to deal with the present, with *this* world. "Hic Rhodus, hic saltus . . ." ("Here is Rhodes, here is your jump").[62] Philosophy cannot escape from the historical process; it is its mirror as well as its motor.

11. Consciousness of individual freedom, concrete evolution of human autonomy—this is the fundamental criterion which distinguishes the Occident from the Orient and accounts for the fact that the Orient has been "superseded." If we apply this standard, some apparent parallels between Eastern and Western thought turn out to be utterly superficial and irrelevant. But if we neglect "the difference which is related to the self-awareness of freedom" and refer to such "abstract categories" as unity, universality and substance, it is easy to find similarities everywhere. Indeed, "Chinese and Indian philosophy, as well as Eleatic, Pythagorean, Spinozistic and even all modern metaphysics can be paralleled insofar as all of them are based upon the one or unity, upon abstract universality . . . However, such equating proves that it knows only of abstract unity, and in so judging of philosophies is ignorant of what constitutes the interest of philosophy."[63]—"Regarding what is entirely abstract one can find similarities everywhere. But since this is so, such comparison is superficial; it disregards what is peculiar, for instance the peculiarity of what is Greek against what is Oriental, to which it owes its value."[64] In general, Hegel characterizes comparison as a superficial and abstract intellectual activity:[65] It is a co-ordinating procedure, and as such, it is inappropriate for historical understanding, which is guided by the notions of dialectical progression and subordination.

The relationship between Orient and Occident is a relationship of subordination; the Orient has been superseded by the Occident. Yet, it is not simply an obsolete matter of the past. Hegel's view is more ambiguous and complex than we might conclude from some of his explicit statements. The Orient, India is a preliminary stage—yet it can function as a corrective and antidote. It can remind us of aberrations in the modern Western orientation; it can help to supplement and rectify deficiencies and one-sided developments. According to Hegel, a major aberration of modern Western thought is its excessive subjectivism and anthropocentrism, its tendency to isolate itself from any firm ground and context, to display its own peculiarity to itself, and to lose itself in sheer narcissism. "The extreme, the one-sidedness of European thought comprises all the fortuitousness of will, imagination and thought. Insofar, it is the extreme of vanity. Contrary to this vanity, this one-sided subjectivity, solid unity prevails in the Orient. In it, there is no vanity. It is the ground in which all vanity is consumed."[66] It is important for us to know of this unitary ground, of which the Indian tradition keeps reminding us, to "bathe the spirit in this unity which is eternal and restful," "to assert the substantiality of the Orientals, and to drown in it that vanity with all its cleverness."[67] To be sure, the Indian past has been superseded by the European present; nevertheless, or rather therefore, it is to be preserved and recalled.

12. Hegel finds prime examples of bad and abstract subjectivity in the thought of F. Schlegel and his Romantic contemporaries, and specifically in the notion of Romantic irony. Here he sees "infinite absolute negativity" ("unendliche absolute Negativität"), "vanity" ("Eitelkeit"), "shallow arbitrariness" ("hohle Willkür"), and even "what is quite generally evil in itself" ("das in sich ganz allgemeine Böse").[68] Hegel's recommendation to "drown" the vanity of European subjectivity in the Oriental unity may certainly be associated with the Romantics. On the other hand, he is sharply critical of the Romantic fascination with ancient India, and with the "Oriental principle" in general. Does this mean that he criticizes the Romantics for something which he also recommends to them? We may indeed assume that Hegel's argumentation is to a certain extent *ad hominem* and not entirely consistent. Yet, we may also find a peculiar dialectical turn in this apparent inconsistency: It suggests that the "Orientalizing" attitude, which seems to be a potential remedy for the Romantic disease of "subjectivism," only aggravates the condition. In Hegel's view, Romantic subjectivity, this "yearning of the heart" ("Sehnsüchtigkeit des Gemüts") and "consumption of the spirit" ("Schwindsucht des Geistes"),[69] does not really "bathe" or "drown" itself in the Orient; rather, it finds itself reflected in, and confirmed by it. The Romantic correlation of European "subjectivism" and Oriental "substantialism" does not bring about a concrete mediation and reconciliation: An empty and abstract subjectivity relates itself to an empty and abstract substantiality; and instead of finding fulfilment it rediscovers its voidness. More than once, Hegel associates the modern European "vanity" of subjective reflection with the "abstractness" of the Indian absolute, most explicitly in his *Lectures on the Philosophy of Religion*: here he parallels the

modern "faith in reflection" ("Reflexionsglaube"), which recognizes the ego alone as a positive and universal element, as "the exclusive affirmative point" ("der ausschliessende affirmative Punkt"), with the Indian self-identification with the absolute *brahman*.[70]

13. As we have indicated, Hegel's interest in India is inseparable from his anti-Romantic attitude and his criticism of the Romantic glorification of India. However, F. Schlegel himself subsequently revised and modified his evaluation of the Indian tradition, and he distanced himself from the unqualified enthusiasm of his earlier statements.[71] As a matter of fact, his critique of the abstract One and absolute of Indian "pantheism," which in his view leaves no room for the individual and its particularity, seems to concur with Hegel's characterization of the "substantiality" of Indian thought. Furthermore, Schlegel's criticism of Hegel sometimes reminds us of, and even seems to echo, Hegel's own polemics against Schlegel. While Hegel finds "infinite absolute negativity" in Schlegel's thought, Schlegel in turn finds "the evil spirit of negation and contradiction" in Hegel; both accuse each other of abstractness.[72] – Yet, in spite of all parallels, Hegel's and Schlegel's approaches are fundamentally different; Hegel's sense of legitimacy of the present, his belief in the irreversibility of history and the self-perfection of reason in history are incompatible with Schlegel's philosophy.

At this point, we may also recall the name of Schelling, whom we mentioned as an advocate of pantheism against Schlegel. Schelling's philosophy, too, is included in Hegel's criticism of India, although in a different sense than that of Schlegel. It seems that key terms of Hegel's interpretation of India, such as "substantiality," the abstract "One," the empty absolute, were first developed or employed in Hegel's critique of Schelling. In his *Phenomenology of the Spirit* (1807), i.e., at a time when he had no particular interest in India, Hegel says, with an apparent implicit reference to Schelling: "To pit this single assertion, that 'in the Absolute all is one,' against the organized whole of determinate and complex knowledge, or of knowledge which at least aims at and demands complete development – to give out its absolute as the night in which, as we say, all cows are black – that is the very *naiveté* of emptiness of knowledge."[73]

14. Hegel's critique of the "extreme of vanity" and other aberrations of modern European thought does not imply any basic doubts concerning the direction of the Occidental development and the destiny of Western philosophy in general. Hegel never loses his Occidental and anthropocentric self-confidence. Such self-confidence reflects Europe's historical position at the beginning of the nineteenth century. Europe appears as the peak of progress. It claims intellectual, moral and religious superiority over the rest of the world, and it attempts to demonstrate and establish its superiority in its colonial expansion. Hegel himself is a philosophical advocate and herald of

this European self-presentation; and occasionally, he even tries to justify the historical necessity of Europe's colonial activities.[74]

Hegel is a fully conscious European of the early nineteenth century; and his motto that everybody is a "son of his time"[75] has to be applied to him, too. In all his statements about India, he presents himself as a European and a "son of his time." He sees Indian thought from the peak of his own time and his philosophical system, which is meant to summarize and consummate the history of European thought. Hegel is fully aware of his position and the historical conditions of his thought. But this clear and explicit awareness of his historical position and his European identity appears itself as a manifestation of superior reflexivity; and it adds to his historical and cultural self-assurance and the confidence in the hermeneutic potential of his level and context of thought. In his view, his European horizon transcends all Asian horizons. Asian thought is comprehensible and interpretable within European thought, but not vice versa. The question of an adequate standpoint for the evaluation and comparison of different cultural traditions has been decided by the course of history itself, and it has been decided in favor of Europe. European thought has to provide the context and categories for the exploration of all traditions of thought.

15. That Hegel was a "son of his time" has the obvious implication that he had to depend on the amount of information concerning India which was available to him in his time. This information was not sufficient. Hegel had no adequate knowledge of the systematic complexity and historical variability of classical Indian thought. He was not sufficiently aware of its high level of argumentation and reflection, of its deep and pervasive tensions and antagonisms. He knew virtually nothing about the great debates between Hindu and Buddhist philosophy. He tended to reduce what he found in his sources to a few basic ideas, to elements of a "prehistory" of philosophy, to abstract patterns of thinking which occur again and again in more or less insignificant variations.

However, Colebrooke's articles on Sāṃkhya and Nyāya-Vaiśeṣika introduced him at least to some of the technical details of Indian philosophy, and he referred to them in his *Lectures on the History of Philosophy* since 1825/26. He appreciates the "high standard of intellectuality" in these systems, emphasizes the explicit development of "logical forms" in Nyāya and discusses the significance of the Sāṃkhya theory of three *guṇas*.[76] More than once, specifically in his *Bhagavadgītā* review, he cautions against unwarranted generalizations and comparisons, and against an uncritical "application of the next best categories of our culture on the one hand, and of a European philosophy, which is itself often confused, on the other hand," and he advocates an impartial documentation of the "peculiarity of the Indian spirit."[77] There are signs of change, of a process of learning in Hegel's later and latest statements on Indian thought; there is an increasing readiness to differentiate, to await the results of further research, and perhaps even to reconsider some of his own earlier generalizations.[78]

16. As a result of his study of Colebrooke's essays, Hegel seems to be less reluctant to treat Indian philosophy as philosophy. In his earlier statements, he takes it for granted that India and the Orient in general have to be "excluded from the history of philosophy," and that "real philosophy" begins only in Europe.[79] However, Colebrooke's account leads him to the explicit conclusion that there is "real philosophy" ("eigentliche Philosophie"), and "truly philosophical systems" ("wirklich philosophische Systeme"), in India; he adds that these systems were previously unknown in Europe, and that they had been confused with "religious ideas." The "real philosophy" of the Indians is to be distinguished from their cults, their tradition of Yoga, and so forth. It is "the way, the movement through the developed and determinate thought. Of this (real philosophy), little was known to us so far."[80] While the "ultimate goal" of Indian philosophy is the same as that of religion, its form and method have been developed in such a manner, that it is clearly distinguishable from the "religious form," and "that it deserves indeed the name of philosophy" (". . . dass sie sehr wohl den Namen der Philosophie verdient").[81] Even in Hegel's own thought, the ultimate goal and essence of philosophy is the same as that of religion. Philosophy itself is "worship of God" ("Gottesdienst")[82] or cultivation of the absolute. What distinguishes it from religion is its intellectual and conceptual development and "form."

Hegel's oral and written statements are quite unambiguous: He does find philosophy in the true and proper sense in India. Yet, he returns again and again to his assumption that the Indian orientation was basically incompatible with philosophy as a concrete historical process. It is and remains dominated by the principle of "substance"; it has failed to unfold the idea of the person, the autonomous individual subject. In this connection, he takes notice of the doctrine of the plurality of "souls" (*ātman, puruṣa*) in Nyāya-Vaiśeṣika and Sāṃkhya; but in his view, this should not be confused with the true concept of the person or the free, self-affirming individual. Such plurality is ultimately nothing more than a particular application, a multiplication as it were, of the principle of substance.[83] The following passage, which Hegel added to his *Lectures on the History of Philosophy* in the version of 1829/30, may be taken as his final, somewhat ambiguous word: "First of all, we meet with Oriental philosophy. We may regard it as the first part, thus as real philosophy; but we may also see it as preliminary, as a presupposition of philosophy, and we begin only with Greek philosophy . . . In the formation of the Oriental world, we do find philosophizing, too—indeed, the most profound philosophizing. . . . But insofar as it remains the most profound, it remains also abstract . . . For us, the real philosophy begins only in Greece. Measure and clarity begin here."[84]

17. Already in his earliest philosophical publication, *Differenz des Fichteschen und Schellingschen Systems der Philosophie* ("Difference between Fichte's and Schelling's Systems of Philosophy," 1801), Hegel refers to some fundamental problems of his own historical period, which has "such a multitude of philosophical systems as its past" and is thus led towards "indifference." While it accumulates information, the "living spirit" of philosophy "slips from its hands," and it cannot find any other meaning in philosophical systems, "than that they are opinions" ("Meinungen"): "The urge towards totality manifests itself only as urge towards the completeness of information, once the ossified individuality no longer ventures into life. By the variety of what it has, it tries to give an appearance of what it is not."[85] At the time of this statement, Hegel was referring only to the multitude of European systems; he was not thinking of the wider multitude of non-European systems of which he caught a glimpse in his later years. But the problem remains relevant in this wider application.

While it is true that Hegel did not do justice to Indian philosophy, he certainly did not treat what he knew about it as mere "information" or "opinions." He dealt with it in a subordinating and, at times, pejorative manner, but he did not forget that "it has an impact upon the highest notions of our understanding."[86] Hegel was not a neutral scholar and expert. He was a philosopher par excellence, representing like few others the glory and greatness as well as the futility and arrogance of philosophy. His system is one of the most intense and spectacular efforts to think reality, to comprehend it, to subdue it to the power of the concept, and it is instructive even in its failures and excesses. And while Hegel was one of the greatest systematizers and universalizers, he was also one of the most deliberately European thinkers. He tried to demonstrate in concrete terms the universalistic potential of European thought, its conceptual power to cope with all other traditions, and to show that these traditions are in fact superseded by it. His approach exemplifies once and for all one basic possibility of dealing with a foreign tradition.[87]

18. Hegel's influence in the history and historiography of philosophy has been far-reaching and complex. However, his reception has often been one-sided and selective. Among the historians of philosophy in the nineteenth century, Hegel's negative statements on India and the Orient in general, and his pronouncement that "real philosophy" begins only in Greece, found wide acceptance, and they were taken as a justification to dismiss Indian thought entirely from the historiography of philosophy, or to relegate it to a preliminary stage.[88] The later statements that there is

philosophy in the true and proper sense in India had virtually no impact; they were hardly ever noticed.[89]

In spite of his negative and condescending attitude, and regardless of his basic scheme of historical subordination, Hegel was genuinely fascinated by Asian, specifically Indian thought. As a European philosopher of the early nineteenth century, he considered it an essential responsibility to deal with the newly discovered non-European traditions of thought. As we have seen, he was a careful observer of the beginnings of Indological research, and he continued to refer to it in his lectures on the history of philosophy, the philosophy of world history, aesthetics and the philosophy of religion. This puts him apart from most of his academic followers in the nineteenth century, who secluded themselves in the tradition of Western thought.

Hegel tries to comprehend Indian thought as something that is superseded by, and contained in, modern Western thought. This is obviously incompatible with the neutrality and openness which the advocates of the "comparative method"—Comparative Religion, Comparative Philosophy, and so forth—postulate. However, it is also a challenge to some of the unquestioned hermeneutic assumptions of the "comparative" and "coordinating" disciplines: It challenges the very ideas of "comparison" and neutral "understanding."

Hegel's influence is not confined to Europe. There is also a significant tradition of "Hegelianism," "Neo-Hegelianism" and "Anti-Hegelianism"[90] in India, i.e., reception of, critical response to, and comparison with, Hegel's philosophy in general. There has, however, been much less response to his specific arguments concerning Indian philosophy and religion.

7. Schelling and Schopenhauer

1. F.W.J. Schelling (1775–1854) and A. Schopenhauer (1788–1860), Hegel's younger contemporaries, exemplify perspectives on Indian thought which are significantly different from, yet complementary to the Hegelian perspective. Together, Hegel, Schelling and Schopenhauer represent what is still the most memorable episode in the history of European philosophical responses to India.

Hegel and Schelling were fellow-students and roommates at the University of Tübingen,[1] and for a number of years, they remained close to each other. In his first philosophical publication, *Differenz des Fichteschen und Schellingschen Systems der Philosophie* ("Difference between Fichte's and Schelling's Systems of Philosophy," 1801), Hegel dealt with the achievements of his prodigious younger friend. But when his masterpiece, *Phänomenologie des Geistes* ("Phenomenology of the Spirit") was completed in 1806, a process of personal and doctrinal estrangement had begun which turned out to be irreversible. In 1841, ten years after Hegel's death, Friedrich Wilhelm IV of Prussia called Schelling to the University of Berlin, to "eradicate the dragon seed of Hegelianism." However, after a few years, Schelling resigned from this prestigious position.

Among his last academic presentations, the lectures on the "Philosophy of Mythology" (*Philosophie der Mythologie*) deserve special attention. Schelling had been lecturing on this topic since 1828; a final version was delivered in 1845/46. These lectures, which were published after Schelling's death, contain elaborate sections on India and other Eastern traditions, though in a distinctly critical perspective and with a clear commitment to the Christian revelation.[2]

2. Already in Schelling's earlier works and letters, we find expressions of interest in and support for Indian and Oriental Studies, specifically in his correspondence with A.W. Schegel.[3] A general openness for non-European

and Indian thought is indicated by various statements, for instance in the *Vorlesungen über die Methode des akademischen Studiums* ("Lectures on the Method of Academic Studies," 1802). In these lectures, Schelling praises the "sacred texts of the Indians" and suggests that they are superior to the Bible.[4]

However, specific references to Indian teachings are rare in Schelling's early works, and he did not take an active part in the Romantic glorification and exploration of India. In particular, his assessment of F. Schlegel's interpretations was very critical.[5] In his *Philosophy of Mythology*, Schelling notes that his criticism of the Romantic speculation on Indian origins of European developments started at a time when the polemical expression "Indomania" ("Indomanie") had not yet been invented. As a documentation of his early critique, he mentions his work *Über die Gottheiten von Samothrake* ("On the Deities of Samothrake"), which was published in 1815.[6]

But regardless of what Schelling said or knew about India in his earlier years, his way of thinking suggested a certain affinity with Indian ideas, an element of "Orientalism" which became a target of criticism as well as a source of inspiration for others.[7] In particular, Schelling's persistent fascination with ultimate identity and indifference, with a return to the Absolute, with pantheism and the "world-soul," his readiness for a self-transcendence of philosophy, his references to "intellectual intuition," etc. seemed to imply potential associations with India. As a further illustration, we may also quote the following definition of philosophy: "Philosophy is the science which has for its subject, subjectively, the absolute harmony of mind with itself, objectively, the return of everything real to a common identity."[8]

3. Schelling develops his idea of a "system of absolute identity" ("absolutes Identitätssystem") in his programmatic *Darstellung meines Systems der Philosophie* ("Presentation of My System of Philosophy," 1801), and as the ultimate goal of philosophy, he proclaims that "point of indifference" which makes the absolute accessible as "undivided" or "absolute identity" ("ungeschiedene," "absolute Identität").[9] "This identity . . . is not what is produced but what is original . . . It is therefore already in everything which is. The power which flows forth in the mass of nature is essentially the same as that represented in the mental world."[10] In another work, Schelling refers to such unity and identity as "the holy abyss from which everything proceeds and into which everything returns.[11]

Hegel criticized Schelling's notion of identity repeatedly. In the preface to his *Phenomenology of the Spirit*, he referred to "the night in which all cows are black."[12] Although Hegel tried to assure Schelling that this was a criticism directed against some of his followers, it was generally taken as a reference to Schelling himself.[13] Hegel also criticized Schelling's idea of the world as a "falling off" or "secession" ("Abfall") from the absolute, as presented, e.g., in the essay *Philosophie und Religion* ("Philosophy and Religion," 1804): "The absolute is the only reality, the finite things are not real; therefore, their ground cannot be a transfer of reality ("Mitteilung von Realität") to them or their substrate—a transfer which would have proceeded from the absolute; it can only be a removal ("Entfernung"), a falling off ("Abfall") from the absolute. . . ."[14]

4. When Schelling presented the final version of his *Philosophy of Mythology* at the University of Berlin in 1845/46, he still praised the theory of the illusory nature of the finite world, and of a "falling off" from the absolute, as a superior idea. He now found it exemplified in the Vedānta system. Vedānta is "nothing but the most exalted idealism or spiritualism."[15] It sees the world as *māyā*, illusory being. In accordance with A.W. Schlegel and W. von Humboldt, Schelling postulates an etymological connection between *māyā* and *magia*, "magic"; he also associates it with the German *Macht* ("power" and *Möglichkeit* ("potentiality"), and he explains it as "the possibility of other-being, and thus of creating the world, as it presents itself to the creator" ("die dem Schöpfer sich selbst darstellende Möglichkeit des anders-Seins, und demnach der Welthervorbringung") and as "the whole essence of that capability which still rests in volition" ("das ganze Wesen jenes noch im Willen ruhenden Könnens"), i.e., the freedom of the absolute to transcend, even forget itself.[16] As "primeval potentiality" ("Urmöglichkeit"), *māyā* is also a seductive principle, which may distract the absolute from its own timeless identity. "The world comes into being because of a momentary self-forgetfulness ("augenblickliche Selbstvergessenheit"), some sort of mere distraction on the part of the creator—unquestionably the highest point to which idealism, or the belief in the merely transitory and illusory reality of this world could rise without revelation in the proper sense."[17]

However, the Upaniṣads, the authoritative basis of the Vedānta system, provide, in Schelling's words, only "a very unsatisfactory reading." There is, in his view, not enough theoretical clarification in these predominantly practical texts; their presentation of the unity of all reality in *brahman* is abstract. "A positive explanation of the supreme unity is not found anywhere."[18]

5. Critical remarks, idiosyncratic evaluations and speculative interpretations are frequent in the more than one hundred pages of the *Philosophy of Mythology* which deal with India. But just as Hegel, Schelling does not claim to be a neutral scholar and "expert." His response to Indian thought and mythology is a philosophically and theologically committed response, and it cannot be measured in terms of factual accuracy alone. The *Philosophy of Mythology* is certainly not a reliable source of information about India, but an event in the history of intercultural and interreligious

encounters. Whatever its shortcomings may be, it is one of the great constructive attempts to deal with the spiritual history of mankind, and India holds an important position in its scheme.[19] This scheme is dominated by the idea that mythology is estranged, pagan,. natural religion, yet a necessary prerequisite for true revelation. The gods of mythology are false gods: nevertheless, they express a genuine relationship to God. "Mythology is natural religion, revelation is supernatural religion; the supernatural is not the negation of the natural, not the unnatural, but the correlate of the natural. In revelation, God is revealed to consciousness in the unity of his potencies, in the fullness of his being and in his freedom from it."[20]

In Schelling's presentation, India (together with China) has its place between Egypt and Greece. This, however, does not imply any historical sequence or transition from one culture to the other.[21] As a profoundly mythological tradition, India is contrasted with Zoroastrian Persia, which Schelling sees as a basically unmythological tradition.[22]

The Indian mythological tradition reflects deep tensions, a process of decomposition, a yearning for unity, an initial loss of the "truly religious principle" of monotheism.[23] Unlike many of his contemporaries, Schelling does not believe in an original monotheism, an originally pure notion of divine unity in ancient India. That tradition which is in a specific sense Indian or Hindu, was always dominated by the separation and tension of three principles or potencies, which find their expression in the *trimūrti* of Brahman (in the masculine form *brahmā*), Śiva and Viṣṇu.[24] Brahmā, the "real God," is a God of the past, a lost and forgotten God without images and temples. Śiva dominates the Indian awareness. "He is the destructive principle, but not in an evil sense: he destroys Brahma, who is the power of the real principle that keeps man in bondage."[25] Viṣṇu seems to restore the lost and destroyed unity, but his concept and worship cannot recover the true sense of monotheism: Viṣṇu excludes Śiva and functions as a basically sectarian and divisive principle.

6. Schelling discusses and rejects a view which was widely accepted in his days and had the support of authorities such as A.W. Schlegel—the theory that the neuter *brahman*, as found in the Upaniṣads and other ancient texts, represents the "pure worship of the divine being." According to Schelling, this abstract divine principle is not the God of monotheism, but a philosophical afterthought, a secondary, derivative phenomenon.[26] In this connection, he also criticizes the attempt of Rammohan Roy to uncover a "pure theism" and a "religion of reason" as the most ancient and original Indian religious teaching. In a sarcastic passage, he associates him with the rationalistic ministers of the Protestant Church who in his opinion were trying to do with the Bible what Rammohan did with the Veda and who "would have given him a truly brotherly reception" if he had visited Germany.[27]

In general, Schelling deplores that "the concept of monotheism has not yet been properly defined"[28] and that it is commonly misunderstood and misused. As an example of such misuse, he cites Hegel's application of this concept to Spinoza's system.[29] According to Schelling, pantheism, abstract unitarian theism and other systems of "rational religion" fail to recognize what is essential to monotheism: the "factual uniqueness" ("faktische Einzigkeit") of God; such uniqueness is not a matter of abstract, ahistorical and ultimately "negative" reasoning, but it has to be accepted as a "positive" historical fact.[30]

7. Against the background of Indian mythology, Schelling sees the mystical tendencies towards reunification with God, towards inclusion and extinction of the human individual as "a natural phenomenon" ("eine natürliche Erscheinung"). "Everything tends towards this reunification . . . in which all striving, including all science is extinguished."[31] Yoga, too, reflects this fascination with unity and union.[32] But such mystical yearning for absorption in absolute identity is itself a symptom of alienation from the God of monotheism, a response to the pervasive tension and disintegration which Schelling sees in the Indian mythological tradition. In spite of his persistent efforts to subsume the Indian phenomena under his systematic and fundamentally Christian scheme of a world history of mythology, Schelling is fully aware of the complexity of the Indian situation, as well as of uncertainties resulting from the state of research and the nature of the available sources. He refers to the fact that we know about the Indian religious and mythological ideas mainly from works produced "by the higher, more educated castes of India."[33] He discusses the tensions between Hinduism and Buddhism, which he calls "the greatest riddle in the history of Indian culture;"[34] but he also considers the possibility of deep and pervasive Buddhist influences on the Hindu tradition. Unlike Hegel, he is able to refer to E. Burnouf's pioneering *Introduction à l'histoire du buddhisme indien* ("Introduction to the History of Indian Buddhism," 1844).[35]

But it is not only the presence of Buddhism which accounts for the diversity of the Indian tradition: Hinduism itself, with its social stratification and its sectarian divisions, has its own inner differentiation and multiplicity. According to Schelling, one could say that "there is not one single religion, or one single mythology in India, but rather really different religions and different mythologies."[36] What is elsewhere divided among different nations and traditions, is in India only divided among different parts or "organs" of one nation, one comprehensive tradition.

8. Does Schelling's critique of the Indian tradition in the "Philosophy of Mythology" amount to a critique or reversal of the implicitly "orientalizing" tendencies of his own earlier thought? As we have seen, he is still fascinated with the Indian "system of absolute identity," *Advaita Vedānta*. He calls it

the "highest point" to which idealism could rise "without proper revelation," and we may assume that it exemplifies for him a "higher" type of idealism than the system of his erstwhile friend Hegel.

According to Schelling, neither the Indians nor Hegel were able to grasp the truly "positive," i.e., existence in its concreteness, the "factuality" of the one God and of revelation.[37] Just like the Indians, Hegel was unable to comprehend the meaning of monotheism; and that his philosophy is historically more developed, more advanced in terms of reflexivity, does not mean that it is truly "higher" than that of the Indians. On the contrary, that it is more developed means, in a sense, that it has fallen deeper into the arrogance of conceptuality and the negativity of mere reflection. Hegel's thought leaves itself to mere concepts, to thinking about thought; it posits itself as reflexivity. It is fundamentally negative, narcissistic, without "true life:"[38] "Hegel and his followers call only that thought 'pure thought' which has mere concepts as it content. This, however, one cannot call real thinking. Real thinking is such that it overcomes something that is opposed to thought."[39]

The thinking of thinking, the unfolding of reflexivity, the attempt to supersede all presuppositions both historically and systematically—this is, in Hegel's view, the essence and direction of philosophy in the true sense, i.e., philosophy which is inseparable from the destiny of Europe. Schelling's critique of the Hegelian apotheosis of reflection is, implicitly at least, also a critique of fundamental premises of his Eurocentric universalism, or of his apotheosis of Europe.

In a curious, yet intriguing illustration of his critique, Schelling compares Hegel's conceptualism to Viṣṇu's incarnation as Vāmana, the dwarf.[40] This inconspicuous creature requests nothing more than a piece of land to be measured by three steps (Schelling says: "feet"). Bali ("Mahabala"), the powerful demon king, grants the apparently innocent wish, and immediately finds himself deprived of his supremacy over the universe. Vāmana's "three steps" (or "feet")—that is Hegel's trinity of fundamental concepts "being, nothing, becoming" ("Sein, Nichts, Werden"). Once a supposedly autonomous human reflection is allowed to claim these fundamental notions as its own categories, it will soon claim unlimited jurisdiction over the entire universe and, in a sense, devour heaven and earth.

9. A. Schopenhauer's name is much more commonly associated with India than those of Hegel and Schelling. Indeed, it may even be said that no other Western philosopher so signalizes the turn towards India as does Schopenhauer. Within the history of philosophy, Hegel and Schopenhauer are among the notoriously contrastive figures, and this contrast, as will be demonstrated below, is quite clearly reflected in the relations between the two and India.

Whereas Hegel generally refrained from commenting on the eighteen-year younger Schopenhauer (1788–1860), Schopenhauer for his part treated his antipode Hegel to some of the sharpest invective that has been recorded in the annals of philosophy; his opposition to Schelling was equally intransigent, but more restrained.[41] He considered Hegel as having a "completely worthless, indeed, thoroughly pernicious mind," as being a "crude and disgusting charlatan," a "scribbler of rubbish and a corrupter of minds"; his philosophy was "confused, empty verbiage," a "philosophy of absolute nonsense."[42] He did, however, not comment explicitly on Hegel's interpretation of Indian thought. It is obvious that personal elements were involved in Schopenhauer's criticism of Hegel. Nevertheless, there was also strain enough in the factual department; and in both what they shared and what kept them apart, and specifically in their relationships to India and the non-European world in general, the two reflect the ambivalence which typified nineteenth-century Europe. Both simultaneously stood in a peculiar and ambiguous relationship to the Romantic movement.

Yet it is not our intention to present a comprehensive comparison of Schopenhauer and Hegel, nor of Schopenhauer and Indian philosophy, nor shall we attempt to reconstruct an accurate developmental history of Schopenhauer's personal relationship to India.[43] Instead, we shall primarily concern ourselves with Schopenhauer's basic hermeneutical position vis-à-vis India and the role which Indian ideas played in his own philosophical thinking and self-understanding.

10. Schopenhauer's interest in India was awakened early by the Orientalist F. Majer,[44] who was effective as a recruiter for India among the Romantics and was himself influenced by Herder. During the almost three decades in which Schopenhauer outlived Hegel, he became aware of material, especially in the area of Buddhism, to which Hegel could never have had access. Yet like Hegel, and unlike the Schlegel brothers or W. von Humboldt, Schopenhauer never made an effort ot learn Sanskrit, although he repeatedly glorified the excellence of this language and the rewards of mastering it.[45] As noted above, he became acquainted with the Upaniṣads through Anquetil Duperron's Latin translation (*Oupnek'hat*, 1801/1802) of the Persian version made under Dārā Shukōh.[46] Throughout his life, he clung to the belief that this was a definitive achievement and the key to a philosophical understanding of the Upaniṣads; it was "the most rewarding and edifying reading (with the exception of the original text) that could be possible in this world; it has been the solace of my life and will be the solace of my death."[47] He greeted the subsequent direct translations by H. Th. Colebrooke and H.E. Röer, and especially those of Rammohan Roy, with suspicion and dismissal.[48] He found theistic and Europeanizing corruptions in these works, and was not ready to accept them as a basis for reexamining or revis-

ing his own opinion of the Upaniṣads. In general, the Upaniṣads, together with the knowledge of Buddhism he later acquired, remained decisive for his views on the nature and value of the Indian tradition. While he did indeed make note of those works that appeared in European languages and which did not necessarily suit his enthusiasm, his interest and his esteem were nevertheless quite selective and generally limited to the literature on religion and philosophy, insofar as he was able to apply them to his own basic metaphysical doctrines.

11. Schopenhauer exhibited little interest in Indian art, *belles-lettres*, and so on.[49] He described the portions of the *Ṛgveda* and *Sāmaveda* which he knew from the translations by F. Rosen and J. Stevenson as "completely insipid reading."[50] While he generally noted attentively all publications on Indian philosophy, and was also acquainted with Colebrooke's treatises, such systems as the Nyāya and the Vaiśeṣika remained outside the circle of his interests, and he did not treat them in his writings.[51] Among the works on Buddhism with which he worked, those of I.J. Schmidt, Spence Hardy, C.F. Koeppen, and E. Burnouf should be mentioned.[52]

How his knowledge of the Indian material was related to the genesis of Schopenhauer's own system is a question which cannot be answered with complete clarity and certainty; his own explicit remarks, in any case, do not provide a sufficient basis for answering it. Yet one contradiction which he is often accused of in this regard vanishes when a distinction is made between the references Schopenhauer made to Buddhism and those he made to Hinduism. In 1856, referring to Spence Hardy's *Eastern Monachism* and *Manual of Buddhism*, he remarked to his disciple A. von Doss in the following fashion about the relationship of his philosophy to Buddhism: "On the whole, the harmony with my teachings is wonderful, all the more so because I wrote the first volume (of *Die Welt als Wille und Vorstellung*) between 1814 and 1818 and did not, nor could not, have known of all that."[53] Yet he did have contact with F. Majer and had been exposed to the impression of Indian thought since the turn of the year 1813–1814. In 1816, in fact, he wrote during the production of the first volume of his main work: "By the way, I admit that I do not believe that my doctrine could have ever been formulated before the Upaniṣads, Plato, and Kant were able to all cast their light simultaneously onto a human mind."[54] Naturally, the second edition of *The World as Will and Representation*, published in 1844 in two volumes, contains numerous Indological additions and emendations. Schopenhauer notes the great advances of Buddhist studies between the two editions of his work. He is now aware that his original references to *nirvāṇa* (or "nieban," according to Burmese sources) were inadequate, and he presents the following more differentiated statement on the "denial" of the will and its correspondence with *nirvāṇa*: "The Buddhists with complete frankness describe the matter negatively as *nirvāṇa*, which is the negation of this world or of *saṃsāra*. If *nirvāṇa* is defined as nothing, this means only that *saṃsāra* contains no single element that could serve to define or to construct *nirvāṇa*."[55]

12. Schopenhauer's concern with ancient Indian wisdom was also a concern with something incipient and pristine. This did not, to be sure, conform with the Romantic glorification of childhood and yearning for a lost home; even less did it have to do with the Hegelian retrospective attitude towards a supposedly undeveloped and static phase of historical inchoation. For Schopenhauer, there was no such thing as a lost paradise, nor did he recognize a Hegelian sense of direction in history. He saw no pure primal cause, and no lost or decayed totality or harmony. On the other hand, history could not be conceived of as an unfolding system exhibiting progress and structure, nor was there any teleology of ascending and self-surpassing phases in the phenomenology of the spirit. For Schopenhauer, history was ultimately meaningless, a "farce" without aim or direction. Hegel's attempt "to understand world history as a systematic whole" was, in Schopenhauer's eyes, the symptom of a naive and "trivial" realism that was unable to see beyond the "farce" of historical events and the coming and going of historical individuals, and unable to distinguish appearances or ideas from the true nature of the world, since it "believed that history, its configurations and occurrences, were what counted."[56]

In contrast to the Christian doctrine of salvation and, more generally, as opposed to linear views of time and history, he extolled the recurrent periods of the world which he found in the Buddhist teachings, the "thousand Buddhas," and the possibility of a redemption that was not tied to a unique and non-recurrent event.[57] The world does indeed unfold, yet this unfolding has neither a determinable beginning nor a direction nor a purpose. Schopenhauer's central concept was that of the will, which evolves blindly and leaves thought no other goal than to deny and undo this evolution.

Whatever may come to pass in the world, its true cause is blind, its purpose merely a projection of this blindness, and its meaning and substance remain within the realm of appearance or representation. "'The world is my idea.' . . . Thus, no truth is more certain and more independent of all the others and less in need of proof than this: that all that is available to knowledge, i.e., the entire world, is simply object in relation to subject . . . Everything that does and can belong to the world in any way is inescapably tied to this conditionality through the subject and is therefore only for the subject. The world is idea."[58] It is an idea for a subject which, for its part, is not objectifiable, i.e., is not in space and time and cannot be defined through such categories as unity, multiplicity, etc.

13. As an idea, the world is subject to certain conditions which

Schopenhauer found to have been fundamentally revealed in Kant's Transcendental Philosophy and which he traced back to the four-fold figure of the principle of sufficient reason.[59] This principle has a four-fold figure or "root" insofar as it refers to four fundamental types of necessary relationships: 1. As the principle of sufficient reason for being, it is concerned with the perceptual forms of space and time. 2. As the principle of sufficient reason for becoming, it refers to the domain of physical causality. 3. As the principle of sufficient reason for knowledge, it has to do with the domains of the truth and falsity of propositions, with the connection between propositions and facts. 4. As the principle of sufficient reason for action, it refers to causality in the form of motivation. As a whole, the principle of sufficient reason describes the fundamental structure of our world as well as our cognitive abilities, and encompasses the domain of "the context of experience," which, in the terms of Kant's Transcendental Philosophy, is determined *a priori* by forms of perception and categories, in other words, the domain of the possible objects of our empirical knowledge and our practical life.

As noted above, the world of objects, at least to the extent that they are subjected to this ordering principle, is mere appearance: it is a projection of the "thing in itself," the metaphysical basis of the world, which Schopenhauer identified as blind will. The manner in which this absolute will, lying as it does beyond the jurisdiction of the principle of sufficient reason, objectifies itself in the forms of appearance of our world, receives its most thorough treatment in the second book of *Die Welt als Wille und Vorstellung*. The *one* will produces its effects through a succession or hierarchy of objectifications, of forms of spatiotemporal existence. Devoid of any kind of historical teleology, this hierarchy leads from the realm of the inorganic to the higher and more complex forms of organic conscious life, i.e., to increasingly higher and more complex forms of self-assertion and the struggle against others. Within this hierarchy, thought, "the mental," retains an essentially instrumental role; whether implicitly or explicitly, it stands in the service of self-assertion, of the will to live.

14. The will itself knows no purpose and no direction. Once the emptiness and aimlessness of its objectifications has been understood, there is no other meaningful and legitimate goal than to achieve their cancellation, and to destroy all forms of attachment to them. The drive of the will to live and to assert and preserve oneself has to be discontinued, so that it may withdraw itself, and its projections and objectifications collapse within themselves. In Schopenhauer's eyes, art and the aesthetic experience represent a temporary repose in this blind, egoistic drive. Moreover, the projections of egoism are also pierced by the phenomenon of compassion, which is in itself the key to ethics: through compassion, the multiplicity and varie-

ty of individuals becomes visible and transparent as being merely apparent, and the power of egoism wanes. The unity at the world's foundations reveals itself without, however, being understood and clearly seen as such. According to Schopenhauer, it is the task of philosophic thought, and especially his own definitive achievement, to clarify theoretically and explain metaphysically the actual phenomena of aesthetics and ethics, while simultaneously creating a comprehensive theoretical basis for soteriological praxis.

Schopenhauer saw his own philosophy as the perfection of Kantian thought. From its heights, one could survey, ponder, and assess what his predecessors as well as his contemporaries had brought to philosophy. Yet he rejected the Hegelian integration of the system and history of philosophy, and saw no scheme of reflection according to which a succession of cultural traditions and philosophical theories could be construed and following which Indian and European thought could legitimately be coordinated with or subordinated to one another. His approach to Indian philosophy was, so to speak, that of a "recognitive historiography of philosophy" ("wiedererkennende Philosophiegeschichte")[60] which remained open to the possibility of finding the same insights in the most diverse historical contexts. Schopenhauer felt that the basic ideas of his philosophy, viz., the doctrine of the "world as will and representation," of a fundamental unity of reality and an apparent projection into spatiotemporal multiplicity, could be found among the Indians, and not just in the form of historical antecedents, but in a sense of truth which knows no historical and geographical restrictions.

15. Schopenhauer's notion of philosophy is utterly incompatible with the characterization which Hegel presents in the introduction of his "Philosophy of Right" (*Philosophie des Rechts*), i.e., "its time comprised in thought" ("ihre Zeit in Gedanken erfasst"). The "metaphysical urge" makes no reference to time, and its essential aim is everywhere the same: to pierce the veil of spatiotemporal multiplicity and to provide liberation from the cycle of life and suffering. The same motif is able to nourish religious aspirations for salvation just as it can affect philosophical thought; in Christianity,too, it played an important role, although often obscured and suppressed.

Schopenhauer found exemplary expressions of this motif in the Indian concept of *māyā*, in the *tat tvam asi* ("that art thou") of the Upaniṣads, and in the Buddhist goal of *nirvāṇa*—of peace without rebirth, a return into the state of non-becoming. He made repeated use of these concepts and formulas in order to illustrate and even to express his own thoughts. He considered the concept of *māyā* to be the equivalent of his notion of *principium individuationis*,[61] the "principle of individuation." In his view, "the *māyā* of the Vedas . . . and the 'appearance' of Kant" were identical; they were "the world in which we live," or "we ourselves, to the extent that we belong to this world."[62] He was convinced that both the Indian concept of *māyā* and Kant's "appearance" were included in his own concept of the objectification of the will, i.e., the realm of validity of the principle of sufficient reason, and that it was here that their true meaning and identity was made manifest.[63]

Schopenhauer often invoked Indian thought when he wished to illustrate what he saw as the central relationship between ethics and metaphysics. As early as 1813, while working on his doctoral dissertation, he formulated his principle of a "philosophy which should be at once ethics and metaphysics."[64] He attempted to achieve such a unified system of thought by anchoring the fundamental ethical phenomenon of compassion in a metaphysics of identity which he found exemplified in the Vedānta. He repeatedly explained that for him, "the foundation of morals ultimately rests upon that truth" which was expressed in the Upaniṣadic formula *tat tvam asi* ("that art thou").[65]

16. Schopenhauer also repeatedly referred to the Buddhist concept of *nirvāṇa*, which he considered to be mainly a negative idea that agreed in essence with his own goal of liberation from the blind forces of will. Since *nirvāṇa*, the transcendence and denial of all worldly experience (*saṃsāra*), expresses a more radical sense of freedom and negation, he tended to prefer this concept to the metaphysical and soteriological terminology of Hinduism.[66] He found too much unnecessary mythological fiction in the Hindu concepts of *brahman, jīvātman, paramātman*, etc., and the doctrine of the reunion of the individual soul with *brahman* (which when referring to the neuter, he generally rendered as "Brahm").[67] Still, he saw no reason to doubt that the Vedāntic idea of *brahman* also fundamentally corresponded to the theory of the cosmic will which he himself expounded, and he made repeated attempts to find a meaning for the word *brahman* that would approximate his own "will." In doing so, he referred to Max Müller's statement that *brahman* originally meant "force, will, wish, and the propulsive power of creation."[68] He greeted the translations of Tamil Vedāntic works published in K. Graul's "Bibliotheca tamulica" with "great joy and edification" because he saw his own teachings reflected in them "as in a mirror."[69] Time and again, he interpreted Buddhist concepts as precise analogies of his own teachings. Referring to Spence Hardy, for example, he declared that *upādāna* could be understood as the "will to live," and *karman* as "empirical character."[70]

Schopenhauer's basic position was: "in general, the sages of all times have always said the same."[71] Making explicit reference to his own thought, he stated that "Buddha, Eckhardt, and I all teach essentially the same."[72] And speaking of the results of his own thought, he explained that they corresponded "with the most ancient of all world views, namely, the Vedas."[73] In like manner, he found himself in agreement with what he called the "majority" of religious humanity, i.e., the Buddhists; occasionally, he even referred to himself as a Buddhist.[74] In claiming these and other correspondences, he was not concerned with the external forms and specific historical manifestations of such teachings, but rather with their "inner sense and spirit."[75] Here again, Schopenhauer proved himself to be the antipode of Hegel, for Hegel, as we have already seen, considered any comparisons and parallelizations which disregarded historical particularities to be abstract and void. Yet even prior to this, I. Kant, whom Schopenhauer claimed as his own great predecessor, had stated that "since human reason has been enraptured by innumerable objects in various ways for many centuries, it cannot easily fail that for everything new, something old can be found which has some kind of similarity to it."[76]

17. In spite of his penchant for fundamental parallelizations and for rediscovering his own philosophical convictions in ancient Indian thought, the manner in which Schopenhauer related his own philosophy and his own position as a nineteenth-century European to the Indian tradition remained ambivalent in many respects.

On the one hand, he found correspondences and parallels within what was essentially a timeless and non-historical frame and outside all questions concerning genesis and historical derivation. Ideas of progress or regress had no place here; for Schopenhauer, history was metaphysically irrelevant and without purpose. He could not concern himself with discovering an order or sense of direction while gathering together the metaphysical insights and the expressions of a "metaphysical urge" that were scattered throughout the various cultures and historical epochs. On the other hand, Schopenhauer also viewed India in accordance with the Romantic speculations, as the land of the most ancient and most pristine wisdom, the place from which Europeans could trace their descent and the tradition by which they had been influenced in so many decisive ways, and yet behind which they had also fallen. He was convinced that Christianity had "Indian blood in its veins,"[77] especially insofar as it distinguished itself from the world-affirming tradition of Judaism, i.e., in its tendencies to denounce the world, in its asceticism and pessimism. "In contrast, the New Testament (i.e., as compared to the Old Testament) must somehow be of Indian origin: this is attested to by its completely Indian ethics, which transforms morals into asceticism, its pessimism, and its *avatār* (i.e., the person of Christ)."[78]

Occasionally and somewhat ironically, Schopenhauer even claimed that his own philosophy could be called "the truly Christian philosophy" ("die eigentliche christliche Philosophie").[79] Just as Sanskrit opens up a more basic understanding of Greek and Latin, in like manner is a knowledge of Brahmanism and Buddhism the prerequisite for any real understanding of Christianity. Schopenhauer also thought to have found Indian elements in Egyptian religion, in Neoplatonism, etc.[80] In accordance with the Romantic view of India, he characterized the Indians as the "most noble and ancient people" and their wisdom as the "original wisdom of the human race" ("Urweisheit des Menschengeschlechts").[81] He also spoke of the "original religion of our race" ("Urreligion unseres Geschlechts") and "the oldest of all world views"[82] as being native to India, and of India itself as the "fatherland of mankind." ("Vaterland des Menschengeschlechts").[83] Moreover, it was his hope that the European "peoples who stemmed from Asia . . . would also reattain the holy religions of their home."[84]

The signs of downfall and degeneration which he saw in the later Indian developments were, fully in accordance with Anquetil Duperron, blamed primarily upon the predominance of Islam.[85]

18. Along with this historical assessment of the Indian tradition, certain problems and ambiguities arise with respect to the manner in which Schopenhauer assessed his own thought and his own philosophical achievements in relation to the wisdom of ancient India. On the one hand, he took the great age of Upaniṣadic thought (an age which he overestimated) as a sign of its special venerability, as justification of a superior claim to truth, and as indication of an immediacy and originality that was later lost. The Vedas—whereby he was, of course, primarily referring to the Upaniṣads—were the "fruit of the most sublime human knowledge and wisdom" and documents of "almost superhuman conception." Their authors could "hardly be thought of as mere mortals."[86]

Instead, "this direct enlightenment of their spirit" should perhaps "be attributed to the fact . . . that these sages, standing as they did closer to the time of the origin of our race, comprehended the essence of things more clearly and profoundly than the already weakened stock, *οιοι νυν βροτοι εισιν*, was able to."[87] The best that we, the later generations, could hope for was as complete a rediscovery of these origins as possible. Indeed, this seems to be implied in Schopenhauer's prediction that a new Renaissance would be inaugurated by the study of the Indian tradition. He expected the influx of Indian wisdom into Europe to bring about "a fundamental change and reorientation of our thought"; the "influence of Sanskrit literature" would, so he felt, impinge upon our lives in a way no less significant than the "resuscitation of the Greek language during the fifteenth century."[88] As a measure of the quality of his own philosophical work, he invoked, as we have seen, its special closeness to the age-old wisdom of the Indians.

19. On the other hand, Schopenhauer also claimed to have made considerable progress with respect to the systematic coherence of his thought

and the clarity of its presentation. Indeed, he was convinced that he had discovered and systematically unfolded the metaphysical principle that had remained hidden to the Vedic "patriarchs" ("Urväter"), although it was implied in their teachings: "the Vedas, or rather the Upaniṣads, . . . have no scientific form, no presentation that is systematic in any way . . . Yet when one has grasped the teachings which I have advanced, one may afterwards derive all of those most ancient Indian statements as conclusions and then recognize their truth, so that it must be assumed that what I have recognized to be the truth had also been grasped by those sages at the beginning of earthly time and uttered according to their fashion, even if it did not become clear to them in its unity."[89] In the Upaniṣads we are faced with "solitary and abstract statements," which may be explained through recourse to the basic concepts of *The World as Will and Representation*, "although the reverse, that these could already be found there, by no means holds."[90] He repeatedly accused the thinkers of ancient India of having deviated into "myths and meaningless words."[91] Thus, Schopenhauer did not try to validate his teachings by referring to the authority of the Indian sources; instead, he presented his own thought as the standard and fulfilment of the Indian teachings. Schopenhauer, too, saw himself as standing on a pinnacle of knowledge, albeit a different peak from Hegel's. From there, he tried to bring "sense into the matter" ("Verstand in die Sache") of Indian thought[92] and uncover its true meaning and implications, which had been hidden to the Indians themselves. Accordingly, Indian philosophy appears not so much as a source of inspiration or revelation, but rather as a mirror and medium of self-representation and self-confirmation. In another context, Schopenhauer called it a general rule that anybody who establishes a "new philosophical system," declares "all previous attempts to have failed."[93] Nevertheless, even if it did not attain complete clarity and perfect systematization, Indian thought, and especially Buddhism, was still superior to all that was possible within the framework of Christian religiousness. "Buddha, Eckhardt, and I all teach essentially the same." To this sentence, which we have already quoted above, Schopenhauer added the following words: "Eckhardt within the bonds of his Christian mythology. In Buddhism, these ideas are not encumbered by any such mythology, and are thus simple and clear, to the extent that a religion can be clear. Complete clarity lies with me."[94]

20. Schopenhauer was deeply convinced of the originality and unprecedented explanatory power of his philosophical system: "My work is a new philosophical system; but new in the full sense of the word: not a new presentation of something already existing, but rather a series of thoughts that are coherent to the highest degree and that have not entered any human head until now."[95] Schopenhauer claimed that his philosophy did not merely

explain natural phenomena by referring to *one* underlying principle, but also put the ideas of the past into place with respect to just *one* interpretive point of view. He was convinced that it provided what may be termed a metaphysical key to the full understanding of these ideas, moreover, an understanding which fulfilled their own intentions. Of course, this was not an Hegelian scheme of historical inclusion and subordination, yet it nonetheless provided a framework and context for exegesis and appropriation which countered the Hegelian procedure with a universalism of a different kind.

But in contrast to Hegel, and in spite of all the claims to originality which he made for himself, Schopenhauer did not consign Indian thought to an antecedent and subordinate position with respect to our own. Even when, as he was convinced, his own thought had given that of India its definitive clarification and completion (an achievement which Kant had helped prepare), in his mind, Indian thought did not merely belong to the prehistory of Christian-European thought. For he saw it as a corrective and alternative that was in many ways superior to the one-sidedness and aberrations of the Western, i.e., primarily Judaeo-Christian tradition and its theistic and personalistic orientation. As an encouragement and stimulus for his own thought, which was incompatible with the spirit of his time and opposed to the ideas of the person and the personal God, Indian thought certainly had a significant impact upon Schopenhauer's personal development. In this sense, Indian thought was obviously "more important" for him than for Hegel.

21. Although it could not have brought Schopenhauer on to the path which was to lead him to his metaphysics of the *will*, and even though the essential points of his own thinking had probably been taking shape before he had ever even heard of the work, the *Oupnek'hat* nevertheless had an enduring and far-reaching effect upon Schopenhauer's life and thought. Yet all too frequently, the fact is overlooked that his encounter with the *Oupnek'hat* was by no means a purely "Indian" encounter. It was also an encounter with Anquetil Duperron's own ways of thinking and interpreting, with his methods of comparing and parallelizing, and with the manner in which he incorporated the Upaniṣads into the context of contemporary European philosophy. Anquetil himself had repeatedly asserted and attempted to demonstrate that the sages of all countries and all times have basically "always said the same" or at least meant the same, and that the Upaniṣads in particular have parallels in European doctrines. It is especially remarkable that Kant was very explicitly cited in these comparisons, indeed, an entire "Parergon" of the first volume was devoted to the relationship between Kantianism and the Upaniṣads.[96] There, Anquetil claimed that the two do not greatly differ with respect to their emphasis upon man's self-

discovery and return to his own inner reality. This postulated affinity was significant not just for Schopenhauer alone, but also far beyond; we notice its echoes even in modern Indian thought. Of course, Anquetil could not have known of Schopenhauer when he drew up his list of German philosophers whom he hoped to see as students and interpreters of the *Oupnek'hat*. Schopenhauer's stubborn adherence to the *Oupnek'hat* in the face of all the European translations of the Upaniṣads which he subsequently became aware of is certainly also an expression of approval for the very personal and explicitly philosophical approach of Anquetil.

While Schopenhauer proclaimed the concordance of his philosophy with the teachings of Vedānta and Buddhism, he also recognized, although less conspicuously, its factual inseparability from the history of European philosophy: "What I have to present agrees very precisely with the ancient Indian utterances. Yet it is also connected with the entire development of philosophy in the Occident; it is a continuation of its history; in a sense, it follows from it as its result."[97] Indeed, Schopenhauer no less than Hegel is a European thinker of the nineteenth century. His critique of the European tradition, of the ideas of history and progress shows us the other side of the nineteenth century. It negates, but also supplements the Hegelian consummation of European thought. Schopenhauer, too, is "a son of his time."

22. Is it true that Schopenhauer's thought, as has been claimed, represents an entirely new synthesis between East and West? Is it true that with him "the stream of Indian thought flows into the spirit of Europe with an unprecedented force and depth?" Did he really show the way to the "unfolding of a new Europe?"[98] And were the Orient and the Occident truly united in his thought?[99] Or was he in the end nothing but a "crank" ("Querkopf") and "querulous pessimist" ("Entrüstungspessimist")?[100] Is his alliance with the ancient Vedic past and with the Buddhist "majority" of religous mankind a reflection of an anti-European, anti-Hegelian resentment and indignation? Does he use the Indian tradition as a mirror of his own, though negative, Eurocentrism? In what sense is his usage and interpretation of Indian concepts different from the abstract and evasive "comparison" and "equalization" of generalities which Hegel criticized?

In order to clarify these questions and to assess Schopenhauer's significance for the encounter between India and Europe, it is not sufficient to examine the philological "correctness" of his usage of Indian terms, or to balance the "Indian" against the "non-Indian" elements of his thought. More or less successful attempts of this kind have been made by H. von Glasenapp, I. Vecchiotti and J.W. Sedlar.[101] Whatever the merits of these attempts may be, they cannot do justice to the philosophical and hermeneutical dimensions of Schopenhauer's response to India. Moreover, we should not only rely on Schopenhauer's own programmatic claims and statements, or on his explicit self-interpretation. In order to do justice to his historical and philosophical potential, it may occassionally be necessary to defend him not only against his successors and devotees, but also against his own idiosyncratic self-presentation.

23. The concepts of *māyā, brahman* and *jīva, parkṛti* and *puruṣa, karman* and *upādāna, saṃsāra* and *nirvāṇa* are familiar to all serious students of Schopenhauer. Does his usage of these concepts contribute to a better understanding of their original Indian meaning? Does it, on the other hand, contribute to the clarification and better understanding of his own philosophy? What is the significance of these concepts for Schopenhauer's self-understanding and for the articulation of his metaphysical thinking?

Schopenhauer seems convinced that his own concepts and insights provide the definitive tools to explicate and clarify the true implications of the Indian teachings. For himself he claims that systematic clarity which he finds missing in the ancient Indian teachings. Does this mean that he always uses his own European concepts as measures of truth, clarity and validity, and never considers the possibility of re-examining their meaning and validity in the light of Indian ideas? Numerous statements suggest a positive answer to this question; yet his approach is more ambiguous than his explicit self-representation seems to indicate. There is more openness; there is a certain cautious and implicit readiness to re-examine and re-articulate his own ideas, and perhaps even to "bring sense into the matter" of his own thought, by referring to Indian concepts. Schopenhauer's central notion of the "will," and his varying attempts to associate it with Indian ideas, may help us to illustrate this point.

24. The problems inherent in this notion, in the relationship between "will" and "knowledge," and in the enigmatic possibility of a "negation," i.e., self-negation of the will, have often been emphasized. To some extent, Schopenhauer's own statements have been conducive to misunderstandings and confusions, in particular to the familiar, yet inappropriate metaphysical equation of "will" and "absolute."[102] Schopenhauer himself frequently characterizes the will as "thing in itself"; he seems to claim that he has discovered the "ultimate reality" behind all appearances, the unknown absolute which Kant failed to identify, the transcendent cause of the world. On several occasions, however, he sharply rejects this interpretation which his own formulations seem to suggest. He insists that his philosophy is immanent, not transcendent: "It teaches what appearance is, and what the thing in itself is. But this is thing in itself only in a relative sense, i.e., in its relation to appearances . . . but I have never said what the thing in itself is apart from that relation, since I do not know it; but in it, it is the will to life."[103]

In this sense, the "will" is not a transcendent absolute, but the immanent principle of the world of objects and representations, its inner essence and most fundamental condition which we can experience in ourselves. We may even say that it is a new interpretation of the Kantian idea of the conditions of the possibility of experience. "Everybody finds himself as this will, in which consists the inner essence of the world."[104] The world is a constellation of causally interrelated representations, of means and ends, of more or less complex forms of power and domination. In it, the will is "the most real entity which we know" ("das Allerrealste, was wir kennen").[105] It upholds and perpetuates this world of appearances by accepting and affirming it. It is not its absolute cause (which would be a contradiction in terms). Schopenhauer consistently uses the term "absolute" in a pejorative sense.[106]

25. The "negation of the will" ("Verneinung des Willens") is not "destruction of a substance" ("Vernichtung einer Substanz") but a subjective act, an event of self-transformation and of withdrawal from the world of experience and cognition: " . . . the same entity which has willed so far wills no more. Since we know this entity, the will, as thing in itself only in and through the act of willing, we are not able to say or grasp what it is and does after it has relinquished this act."[107] "The essence in itself which may or may not, at its own discretion, express itself as will and thereby as world – this essence in itself, seen in isolation (i.e., in an absolute sense; "dieses Wesen an sich ausserdem betrachtet"), is not accessible to any possible cognition . . . since cognition is only in the world, just as the world is only in cognition."[108]

We can transcend the world by withdrawing the will from it, i.e., in radical soteriological self-transformation. However, we cannot objectify or explain theoretically this practical, soteriological step. The will exists, insofar as we are attached to, and engaged in, the world of representations which is its projection. It is released from existence, insofar as we are no longer committed to the world, and disengage ourselves from the network of means and ends, as well as from all claims of theoretical, representational mastery and domination.

26. "I have named the thing in itself, the inner essence of the world, in accordance with what we know best: as will. This, however, is an expression which has been chosen subjectively, i.e., with reference to the subject of cognition. But since we are dealing with cognition, this reference is essential. Thus it is infinitely better than calling it Brahm or Brahmā or world soul or whatever."[109] In this statement, Schopenhauer counts *brahman* among those dogmatic and mythological conceptions of a first cause and absolute principle with which he contrasts his immanent will. Elsewhere, however, he states that "Brahmaism and Buddhism" are free from the Jewish-Christian "recourse to an unconditional cause."[110] In general, he does not simply relegate the numerous Indian concepts with which he associates his doctrine of the will to a lower or more mythological level of understanding.

Among these concepts, we find the Vedic *asu* as well as the Nyāya-Vaiśeṣika notion of (*pra*) *yatna*, i.e., "effort," "initiative,"[111] In both concepts, he seeks support for his idea of a "will" which expresses itself not only in deliberate actions, but also in unconscious physiological or biological processes. He sees the Buddhist concept of *upādāna*, i.e., attachment to the world and self-identification with worldly objects, as a precise equivalent of his "will to life." *Karman* is the "individual will without the intellect, that which appears as empirical character."[112] He is convinced that his "will" corresponds to the true meaning of the Sāṃkhya concept of *prakṛti*, "nature," i.e., the blind cosmic energy which is contrasted with *puruṣa*, the pure spirit and "witness."[113] Occasionally, Schopenhauer also mentions the Vedānta concept of *māyā* as an equivalent of his will; later on he specifies that it is not so much the will itself, but rather its "objectness" ("Objektität).[114]

27. The concept of *brahman*, for which he postulates an etymological meaning "force, will, wish,"[115] is Schopenhauer's most important Indian point of reference. In particular, it illustrates the deeply problematic relationship between affirmation and negation of the will, and it plays a paradigmatic role in Schopenhauer's understanding of India. Just as we are the will, so *brahman* is ultimately identical with ourselves. The creation of the world, "a sinful act of brahman," is ultimately nothing but our own worldly attitude, our commitment to the network of representations, causes, means and ends, which the Vedāntins associate with the concepts of *māyā* and *avidyā*.[116] However, the *brahman* which unfolds itself into the world is not the true and complete *brahman*. "According to the doctrine of the Veda, only one quarter of *brahman* is incarnated in the world, and three quarters remain free from it, as blissful *brahman* ("seliges Brahm"). The visual representative of this latter *brahman*, or more properly speaking, of the negation of the will to life against its affirmation, is the infinite space against the finite world in which the affirmation objectifies itself, and which in spite of its dizzying size is infinitely small."[117]

The variety of Indian concepts with which Schopenhauer associates his concept of will exemplifies not only the extent and limits of his understanding of Indian materials, specifically of Buddhism and Vedānta, but also the ambivalence and problematic nature of his concept of will itself. Insofar, it illustrates not only his awareness of India, but can also help to clarify his own philosophy. Schopenhauer's invocation of Vedānta and Buddhism is most genuine and significant in connection with his doctrine of the negation of the will, which even his devoted follower J. Frauenstädt called the "Achilles heel" of the system.[118] More than other traditions the Indian tradition provides him with documents of an "immediate experience" ("unmittelbare Erfahrung") of true resignation and "releasement" ("Gelassenheit") to which he does not and cannot add any attempts of theoretical explanation. His own philosophical and theoretical approach to the "negation of the will" is inevitably "abstract," "general" and "cold."[119] Those who understand its true and concrete meaning are the practitioners of detachment and self-liberation, i.e., the yogins and sannyāsins who forget the entire world "and themselves with it." What remains in their state of awareness or being is the "primal essence" ("Urwesen") itself.[120]

28. Regardless of the adequacy of Schopenhauer's interpretations and conceptual equations, he showed an unprecedented readiness to integrate Indian ideas into his own, European thinking and self-understanding, and to utilize them for the illustration, articulation and clarification of his own teachings and problems. With this, he combined a radical critique of some of the most fundamental presuppositions of the Judaeo-Christian tradition, such as the notions of a personal God, the uniqueness of the human individual and the meaning of history, as well as the modern Western belief in the powers of the intellect, rationality, planning and progress. The intellect is in the service of the will; rationality itself is blind. The intellect is committed to the world as representation. It functions in the context of means and ends, but it has no ultimate goal or direction. Schopenhauer's doctrine of the will implies a critique of the European tradition of representational and rational thinking, of calculation and planning, science and technology which foreshadows much more recent developments. In spite of Heidegger's emphatic dissociation from Schopenhauer, it may even remind us of the Heideggerian critique of European metaphysics.[121]

The familiar association of Schopenhauer's thought with "pessimism" and "irrationalism" has not been conducive to an appreciation of the more subtle and ambivalent elements of his approach to the Indian tradition. It is also one of the reasons why the response from the Indian side has in general been rather reserved and superficial. Modern Indian thinkers, such as Vivekananda and Radhakrishnan, have tried to free the Indian tradition from the "stigma" of pessimism and escapism. Radhakrishnan defended the Upaniṣads and the Vedānta against the pessimistic and other-worldly interpretation which he associated with Schopenhauer. In his view, modern European pessimism, as exemplified by Schopenhauer and E. von Hartmann, is nothing but a vulgarized Buddhism.[122] An Indian scholar of the nineteenth century, the great Indologist Rajendralal Mitra, thought that Schopenhauer's doctrine of the will and Hartmann's concept of the unconscious had been anticipated by the classical Yoga system.[123]

Schopenhauer's influence on the development of "comparative philosophy" has, at least indirectly, been considerable. However, the Indian advocates of this approach have generally paid much less attention to Schopenhauer than to Hegel, the great critic of transhistorical and cross-cultural comparison and equalization.

8. Developments in the Interpretation of India Following Hegel and Schopenhauer

1. The European discovery of Indian thought did not bring about the new and greater Renaissance which Schopenhauer and others had anticipated. Nevertheless, an interest in and a tradition of studying Indian philosophy did result which slowly worked its way into the philosophical awareness of the West and its understanding of life. Schopenhauer himself has entered history as one of the pioneers of this process. His example has had remarkable effects, especially in the second half of the nineteenth century. However, we should not forget that Schopenhauer's role in European philosophy has been somewhat ambivalent and precarious, despite the great and enduring fame he met with towards the end of his life. As much as various artistic and ideological movements have made reference to him, and as secure as his doxographic position may be, he still remains an outsider and, in a sense, a curiosity in the history of European philosophy, specifically of academic philosophy. The fact that such an influential "outsider" could become associated with India to such an exemplary degree has in its own way contributed to the exclusion of Indian thought from "official" recognition by academic philosophers, and to its association with a non-academic sectarianism.

In this context, we may recall the movement of "Ideological Pessimism" ("Weltanschaulicher Pessimismus") in nineteenth-century Germany,[1] specifically its best known representatives E. von Hartmann (1842–1906) and Ph. Mainländer (alias Ph. Batz, 1841–1876). These two men both stood outside of the academic tradition, and their work, which was widely read for a time, idiosyncratically combined Schopenhauer's "pessimism"[2] with Hegelian and other ideas, while simultaneously providing detailed references to Indian thought, in particular Buddhism.

2. Mainländer found a welcome illustration of his doctrine of the "will to death" in Buddhism. His *Philosophie der Erlösung* ("Philosophy of Salva-

tion," 1876) explained the world as a divine process of dissolution and construed Schopenhauer's thought as a kind of inverted Hegelianism, a teleology of decay.[3] E. von Hartmann, who was more conservative, less radical, and literarily more attractive than Mainländer, also paid great consideration to Buddhism as well as Hinduism. He attempted to allot both a place within a schema of the philosophy of religion that was opposed to that of Hegel but was nevertheless quite clearly and explicitly oriented around Hegel. Hinduism and Buddhism were construed as examples of "abstract monism" or "idealistic religions of salvation" and assigned a position alongside Judaeo-Christian theism: all three were subsumed under the heading "Supranaturalism," and placed above the more primitive "Naturalism," which also encompassed the religions of Greece and Rome.[4] Hartmann's program, as the title of one of his early publications indicates,[5] is a synthesis of Hegel and Schopenhauer in accordance with the spirit of Schelling. In the foreword to a later edition of his most popular and successful work, the *Philosophie des Unbewussten* ("Philosophy of the Unconscious," 1869), he assigned Hegel the "preponderance" within this synthesis and added "Leibnizian individualism" and "modern natural scientific realism" as further elements.[6] Hartmann's ample willingness to synthesize and compromise between the extremes of Hegel and Schopenhauer is demonstrated in an exemplary fashion in his interpretation of the Indian tradition and its relationship to the Christian-European tradition:

> The development of religion in the West will automatically approach that of the Indian religions as well; it will become capable of directing this ancient Aryan intellectual current into its own stream of development – something the Christian missionary activity has proven itself to be incapable of over an adequately long period of trial. Unlike Schopenhauer's followers, I do not consider the Indian religion to be the absolute religion, nor do I find the Christian religion to be such, as do Hegel and the Christian philosophers of religion. I believe that both are guided by providence and are parallel stages of development in the religious awareness of humanity, but that the Christian branch has continued to grow while that of India has stagnated and thus become stunted and degenerate. It is for this reason that I also expect the next, higher stage to come only from the Christian world and not from the Indian, and believe that the key provisions of the doctrine of faith of the future will be taken from the Christian and not Indian dogmas, although it will also exhibit a greater overall degree of synthesis between the Christian conceptual complex and the Indian.[7]

3. Though not very original, this line of thinking has a certain exemplary significance: Christian thought cannot simply preserve Indian thought or assign it a subordinate position within its own framework. Indian thought merits recognition as a different type of thought essentially equal in its otherness. At the same time, however, it lags historically behind Christianity, not having developed into the present in the same manner.[8] Only Christian-

European thought now possesses the vitality that is needed to pull the potentiality of Indian thought out of its past and shake it from its torpor, to grasp it and bring about the dialogue and prospective synthesis. At the same time, however, Hartmann expects such a "synthesis" to result in a self-transformation of Christianity.

In his *Religionsphilosophie* ("Philosophy of Religion"), first published in 1881-82, Hartmann designated "concrete monism" to be the "synthetic station of reform for all directions of development of religious awareness" in the future. This would supervene upon the parallel developments of Indian and Judaeo-Christian religiousness as a higher stage of development, as the "higher third" in which the other two would be reconciled and superseded.[9] It is a fact worth noting that Hartmann did not concede the Indians any place at all within the actual history of philosophy: "A scientific treatment of metaphysics is first found among the Greeks."[10]

L. Ziegler (1881-1958), an exemplary twentieth-century exponent of an "ideological," non-academic interest in India, was originally attracted by Schopenhauer's and Hartmann's ways of thinking.[11] For him, and in general for the "ideological" interest in India at the beginning of the twentieth century, the translations from the Buddhist Pali canon made by K.E. Neumann (himself a follower of Schopenhauer and son of the Wagner impresario Angelo Neumann) were of central importance. Neumann was convinced that Schopenhauer had "proven once and for all" the truth proclaimed by the Buddha.[12] Among his friends, Neumann counted G. Grimm (1868-1945). Grimm, along with P. Dahlke (1865-1928), was one of the leading German "Neo-Buddhists," and he provides us with another example of the distinct connection between the study of Schopenhauer's work and the shift towards Buddhism.[13] In some ways, even the anthropology of M. Scheler (1874-1928), which contrasts the "blind drive" ("blinder Drang") with the spirit ("Geist"), may be associated with Schopenhauer's thought. Schopenhauer's self-negation of the will to live, the Buddha's doctrine of final liberation, and the later teachings of S. Freud (from *Jenseits des Lustprinzips*) are juxtaposed by Scheler as basic examples of a "negative theory" of man; yet since in his opinion they do not do justice to the concept of the spirit, he is unable to accept them. Compared to the compassionate Buddha himself, Scheler sees Schopenhauer as a mere "crank" and "querulous pessimist."[14] In other contexts as well, Scheler repeatedly refers to Indian thought, in particular Buddhism, and he projects the idea of a "truly cosmopolitan world philosophy" ("wahrhaft kosmopolitische Weltphilosophie").[15]

4. The present context is not the place to go into the multitude of traces which Schopenhauer, the turn towards Indian thought which he represents, or the tension which existed between Hegel and Schopenhauer have left

behind in the field of artistic endeavors. Here, the most prominent example is provided by R. Wagner,[16] who, following Schopenhauer, concerned himself closely with Buddhism for a time and even planned a Buddhist opera (*Die Sieger,* "The Victors"), based on the *Śārdūlakarṇāvadāna.*[17] Although Wagner never completed this work, Buddhist ideas are as obvious in *Tristan und Isolde* as in *Parsifal*, the Christian transformation of *Die Sieger*. No doubt, this was merely *one* phase and *one* element in his thought, and quite different motifs, some of which even came close to the ideas of Hegel and the "Hegelian left," were also of importance to him at other times and in other situations.

This notwithstanding, Schopenhauer was the only philosopher whom Wagner really recognized. In Schopenhauer's thought, Wagner found a metaphysical key to his own artistic endeavors. His interest in India bears the stamp of Schopenhauer, and Schopenhauer is also one of the focal points of Wagner's close and ambiguous relationship with F. Nietzsche (1844–1900), his friend and antipode. Nietzsche himself left a description of how Wagner, during their first encounter, proclaimed Schopenhauer to be "the only philosopher who has recognized the nature of music."[18] It is a symptomatic coincidence that this meeting took place in the house of the Indologist H. Brockhaus, Wagner's brother-in-law, having been arranged by another Indologist who had studied with Nietzsche, E. Windisch.[19] Nietzsche's personal relationship to Indology is made even more obvious through his long friendship with P. Deussen, a relationship which went back to their school days in Schulpforta. Beyond these personal connections, Nietzsche took a serious and philosophically significant interest in the Indological discoveries of his day, assimilating them in the passionate manner that so distinguished his thought. Symptomatic references to Buddhism may be found in his work as early as 1872, in *Die Geburt der Tragödie* ("The Birth of Tragedy"). These references came to play a curious role in the controversy surrounding this work that was initiated by U. von Wilamowitz-Moellendorf in his pamphlet *Zukunftsphilologie!*, which appeared in the same year.[20] Wilamowitz (1848–1931), who later on became the master classicist of his generation, was another alumnus of Schulpforta. In *Schopenhauer als Erzieher* ("Schopenhauer as Educator," 1874), the second piece of his *Unzeitgemässe Betrachtungen*, Nietzsche deplored that the experts in the field of Indian studies, the professional Indologists, had an attitude to the "immortal works of the Indians" which was hardly different from that "of an animal to the lyre."[21] In spite of all this, Nietzsche's Indian studies seem to have been less extensive and systematic than those of Schopenhauer and Hegel. Suggestions that he knew Sanskrit are unfounded; among his sources, we find the speculations of L. Jacolliot.

5. In the vast literature on Nietzsche and Nietzschean topics, this subject has received relatively little strictly biographical and philological attention.

However, there have been persistent conjectures concerning an implicit correspondence, or even concordance, of Indian, specifically Buddhist, and Nietzschean ideas. Nietzsche's friend Lou von Salomé (married Andreas-Salomé) suggested strong Vedāntic influences on his later works.[22] His critic A. Riehl charged that he had "consistently viewed" Christian morals "through a Buddhist fog and veil."[23] Such ideas as the "superman" and "external recurrence" have been associated with Buddhist and other Indian teachings; and the claim has been made that there is an affinity between Nietzsche and Buddhism which is deeper and more significant than their apparent and commonly assumed antagonism. The most sustained effort of this kind has recently been made by F. Mistry.[24]

Sometimes, these associations are not so much attempts to clarify and explain Nietzsche's thought, but speculative and provocative claims as to the true meaning of Buddhist ideas. For instance, the suggestion that Nietzsche's "philosophy of overcoming" is "intrinsically affiliated with Buddhist nirvāṇa" implies the unwarranted assumption that "triumph and creativity in this world" are "components of the authentic Buddhist nirvāṇa."[25] Similar connections have been postulated between Nietzsche's Zarathustra and the *tathāgata* of Buddhism.

Whatever the ultimate potential of Nietzsche's thought for the expansion of the horizon of Western philosophy and for a future dialogue between Indian and Western thought may be, our first responsibility within the historical and hermeneutical account attempted in this study must be the following one: We have to pay attention to the way Nietzsche himself articulated his understanding of Indian and Buddhist thought, how he reflected his own ideas and orientations in this mirror, and how he assessed the potential impact of Indian teachings upon Europe. This does, of course, not preclude us from questioning his self-assessment, or from searching for dimensions of his thought which are not revealed by his explicit assertions.

As to the factual basis of Nietzsche's assessment of Buddhism, we have to keep in mind that he had no knowledge of Nāgārjuna's enigmatic equation of *saṃsāra* and *nirvāṇa*, of related forms of Mahāyāna and Tantrism, or of more recent East Asian, specifically Japanese reinterpretations of Buddhism, which tend to present *nirvāṇa* as freedom *for* this world.

6. Nietzsche's style is intensely personal, aphoristic, and at times erratic. It is thus no surprise that his works do not contain a systematic or even fully coherent presentation of his ideas about India. What he says about Hinduism and Buddhism is inseparable from his thinking and writing in general. It reflects its complexities and idiosyncrasies, but also his deep and passionate concern about modern man and the destiny of Europe.

In a somewhat simplifying fashion, we may say that there are basically two perspectives in which Indian thought and culture became significant for Nietzsche. On the one hand, it provides him with examples of a superior "yea-saying," a degree of commitment to, and acceptance of this world which is higher than what is found in the Christian tradition; on the other hand, it provides him with expressions of a more advanced and refined denial of the world, a more mature pessimism and nihilism.

Nietzsche considers the Law Book of Manu to be an expression of a "yea-saying, affirmative Aryan religion" ("jasagende arische Religion"),[26] a proud and realistic acceptance of life and an undisguised appreciation of power by a non-moralizing elite superior by virtue of its inner spirit and freedom. "Not to forget the main thing, the basic difference from every type of Bible: with this book, the noble classes, the philosophers, and the warriors hold their hands over the throng; noble words everywhere, a feeling of completion, an affirmation of life, a triumphant, pleasant feeling about oneself and about life,—the sun shines upon the entire book."[27] The caste system described by Manu, which rigorously segregates the "excrement" of society,[28] is here seen in a thoroughly positive fashion. Admittedly, "the entire book rests upon the holy lie," and the social system which it advocates is a priestly system of deception and suppression.[29]

7. Nietzsche's references to the "nay-saying," the negative dimension of Indian religiousness, specifically in Buddhism, are more numerous, carry more weight, and offer deeper insights into his own thought. This was, in his view, a pessimism and repudiation of the world, which was more mature, more cultivated, more consistent, and more aristocratic than that of Christianity. It was a higher form of that nihilism which he opposed and yet sought to perfect, a more refined counterpart of the great affirmation of the world and mankind which he anticipated for the future. Buddhism and Christianity belong together to the extent that they are "the two great nihilistic movements" as well as "decadence religions"; both are rooted "in a monstrous disease of the will"[30] and regard man as a "principle of world-negation." At the same time, "among the nihilistic religions, the Christian and the Buddhist may be clearly distinguished from one another." Buddhism is an expression of "a lovely evening, a perfect sweetness and mildness . . ." without bitterness or resentment, a religion for "late men" who have become "over-spiritual and excessively susceptible to pain."[31] It is a "consistent type" of pessimism as compared to the "inconsistent type" of Christianity,[32] a nihilism that is freer, more aristocratic, and more cultivated than the vulgar and unfree nihilism of the Christian "Caṇḍāla religion" ("Tschandala-Religion"), the "religion of the herd" (Herden-religion").[33]

Although Buddhism and Christianity belong together in one sense, they are nevertheless also "separated from one another in the most extraordinary way. The critic of Christianity is deeply grateful to the Indian scholars for the fact that they may now be compared. Buddhism is a hundred times more realistic than Christianity—it possesses a heritage of posing problems objectively and without emotion, it follows a philosophical movement that has endured for hundreds of years; the concept of 'God' had already been disposed of by the time it was born."[34] Buddhism is the "religion of self-salvation"—"how far away from this stage of culture is Europe even now!" Europe must catch up with "what had already been achieved several millenia ago in India, among the people of thinkers, as a precept of thought!"[35]

Indeed, Nietzsche claimed that "Buddhism was making silent progress throughout Europe" and might become capable of replacing an exhausted, "opiatic" Christianity. Moreover, "a European Buddhism may prove indispensable."[36]

8. However, the arrival of such a "European Buddhism" was not conceived of as a historical goal, but rather as an intermediate stage and a means. For Nietzsche, Buddhism is and remains the highest manifestation of what he opposes, i.e., the repudiation of the world. Yet in its inner maturity and frankness, this form of repudiation is much closer to what he tries to bring about: the great affirmation, the apotheosis of this world, and the "humanization" of man and the world.[37]

The new "European Buddhism," as pessimism perfected, is the herald of true nihilism, of the "nihilistic catastrophe," which Nietzsche considers an essentially European phenomenon. This nihilism, in its turn, appears as an "intermediate period," "before the power is there to transvalue the values and to deify and approve the realm of becoming, the apparent world alone."[38]

Nietzsche never suggests that he found the potential for such a "nihilistic catastrophe" and the subsequent "deification" of the world in Buddhism as such or in its Asian form. Buddhism per se is a "tired" and "passive" nihilism; and he never expected the "enhanced power of the spirit," that "violent force of destruction" needed for the "transvaluation of all values," to emanate from Buddhism.[39]

Nietzsche regarded himself as "the first perfect European nihilist," yet one who had already left nihilism "behind him, under him, outside of him."[40] In this way, Buddhism, like the teachings of Schopenhauer, is something he could look back and down upon.

> . . . whosoever has really once looked with an Asian and a supra-Asian eye into and down upon the most world-repudiating of all the possible ways of thought—beyond good and evil, and no longer, like Buddha and Schopenhauer, in the thrall and delusion of morals,—he has, perhaps, without really wanting to, opened an eye to the inverse ideal: to the ideal of the most frolicsome, most alive, and most world-affirming man who has not merely learned to be satisfied with and tolerate that which has been

and which is, but also wishes to have it again, as it has been and as it is, insatiably screaming 'encore' throughout eternity. . .[41]

According to Nietzsche, his own doctrine of "eternal recurrence" affirms what the Buddha denies. The special affinity which he finds between Buddhism and his own thought, is the closeness and affinity of extremes. Nietzsche suggests that he himself "could be the Buddha of Europe: though admittedly an antipode to the Indian Buddha."[42]

9. For Nietzsche, Buddhism is important as a counterpart and steppingstone to the great future affirmation. He never attempts to view Buddhism itself in the sense of this affirmation of, and liberation for, the world. Buddhism does point to the transformation of "perfect nihilism" into world-affirmation, but only to the extent that it, when transplanted to European soil, will contribute to the self-destruction of Christianity and reinforce the European potential for an active "transvaluation." Just like Buddhism, Nietzsche saw the Vedānta essentially on the side of "nay-saying" or world-negation. He characterized this system on which his friend Deussen did pioneering research as "metaphysical pessimism."[43] Generally, however, Nietzsche had much less to say about the Vedānta than about Buddhism. In 1883, he wrote to Deussen, who had sent him a copy of his new book on Śaṅkara's Advaita Vedānta (*Das System des Vedānta*): "It gives me great pleasure to become acquainted with the classical expression of the way of thought that is most foreign to me: your book does this for me." He then added: "Chance wills it that a manifesto of mine is just now in print which says Yes! with more or less the same eloquence as your book says No!" It appears, however, that Nietzsche did not study the work of his friend very thoroughly.[44] In his eyes, the Vedānta did not possess the same meaning or rank as Buddhism.

For Nietzsche, as for Deussen, the interest in Indian thought was tied to the experience of Schopenhauer. Nietzsche's break with Schopenhauer cast his opinion of Indian thought, and Buddhism in particular, in a new light: it also resulted in an estrangement from the way in which his friend Deussen viewed India. "It is clear that they had to part ways, for between the two of them came—Schopenhauer. Nietzsche first arrived at himself by overcoming Schopenhauer; Deussen did the same by becoming Schopenhauer's disciple."[45] Indeed, it was primarily through the work of P. Deussen that Schopenhauer came to have an impact upon the academic study of Indian philosophy.

10. Deussen (1845–1919) dedicated his great translation of sixty Upaniṣads (1897) "to the manes of Arthur Schopenhauer." He also initiated the critical edition of Schopenhauer's works that began appearing in 1911, and was the editor of the yearbook of the Schopenhauer Society. He was "the recognized head, one may even say, the hierophant of the German

Schopenhauer-community."[46] What is more, Deussen has been the only holder of a German chair for philosophy (in Kiel after 1889) up till now who was also an outstanding Sanskritist and who devoted his time and energy primarily to Indian philosophy.

Of course, there have been other nineteenth-century scholars with combined interests in Indology and philosophy. Among Deussen's predecessors, the Iranist and Sanskritist O. Frank (1770–1840) comes especially to mind. Frank was active as a professor of philosophy and Oriental philology in Bamberg, Würzburg, and Munich and espoused the study of Indian philosophy.[47] H.E.E. Röer (1805–1866) began his career in Western philosophy (temporarily serving as a lecturer at the University of Berlin) and later became one of the pioneers in the philological study of Indian philosophy in the service of the Asiatic Society in Calcutta.[48] Max Müller (1823–1900) made a name for himself not just through his Indological work, but also with an English translation of Kant's *Kritik der reinen Vernunft*. Like Deussen, who wrote his doctoral dissertation on Plato's *Sophist*, many other Indologists also first worked on classical philology and, specifically, on Greek philosophy. Yet, Deussen's intense and deliberate integration of Indological and philosophical work remains unique among scholars of the nineteenth century.

As Deussen himself stated, he vacillated for a time "between philosophy and Sanskrit, back and forth as if between two lovers," until, in 1873, "suddenly, as if through inspiration from above, the thought came" to build "his life's house" where the lines of Indology and philosophy met.[49] He adhered to this decision with a systematic consistency and an unusual dedication until the end of his life. Nietzsche claimed to have had an important part in Deussen's "conversion" to Schopenhauer, the crucial event which sparked his interest in India. In 1887, after receiving Deussen's German translation of Śaṅkara's *Brahmasūtrabhāṣya*, he wrote:

> I am responsible for the fact that Deussen is Schopenhauer's most glowing admirer and spokesman (and an eminently rational one at that); he has thanked me emphatically for this main turn in his life. What is more essential (in my eyes) is that he is the first European who has approached Indian philosophy from within; he brought me his freshly published Sūtras of the Vedānta, a book of exquisite scholasticism of Indian thought . . . He is special; even the most learned linguists among the English (like Max Müller), who pursue similar goals, are but asses compared to Deussen, for they 'lack the faith'—they do not come from Schopenhauerian-Kantian premises. He is currently translating the Upaniṣads; what joy would Schopenhauer have known!![50]

11. Although it was soon to be followed, and to some extent superseded, by G. Thibaut's English translation of the same text, and although it had been preceded by the fragmentary attempts of K.M. Banerjea (1870) and others, Deus-

sen's German translation of Śaṅkara's *Brahmasūtra* commentary, just like his translation of *Sixty Upaniṣads* (*Sechzig Upanishads des Veda*, 1897), remains a pioneering and highly significant contribution to Indian studies. Unlike Thibaut, Deussen did not have the collaboration of Indian pandits. The six volumes of Deussen's *Allgemeine Geschichte der Philosophie* (1894–1917), which are devoted equally to the history of Indian and European thought, may appear somewhat uneven and idiosyncratic. Yet, the volumes dealing with India represent an achievement which was unequalled in its time, notwithstanding the fact that the presentation of the philosophical systems was to a considerable extent not based upon their own basic and original texts, but upon a fourteenth-century doxography, Mādhava's *Sarvadarśanasaṃgraha*. As far as the older, "presystematic" literature is concerned, Deussen's exploration of details is noteworthy even today. Regardless of his philosophical premises, he was led by a remarkable "philological instinct."[51] And while the "right faith" of Schopenhauerianism may have led to one-sided and questionable interpretations, it was also his prime motivation in pursuing his indefatigable linguistic and philological work. Deussen became a pioneer of European Indology not in spite of his philosophical preconceptions, but rather because of them. His position as a philosophizing historian of philosophy has, however, remained ambivalent. His commitment to Schopenhauer and his untiring and sometimes naive search for approximations or anticipations of Schopenhauer's philosophy, in particular the idea of the phenomenality of time and space, in Indian and European thought have contributed to his general recognition, but also to his isolation among the academic historians of philosophy.

12. Deussen, who took it for granted that there is no "common name" for the discipline of philosophy in India, tried to anchor his *Allgemeine Geschichte der Philosophie* in an "ideal definition" of philosophy[52] intended to "indicate the goal towards which all of the philosophical efforts of all times and all countries had been directed." For him, this goal is knowledge of the "principle" of the world, of the "thing-in-itself"; all philosophy is thus essentially metaphysics. Consequently, a general history of philosophy should include "all thoughts of importance" in which this goal is manifest, "whether they have appeared in the garb of philosophy or of religion,"—the Upaniṣads as much as Plato and Śaṅkara, the New Testament as much as Kant and Schopenhauer.[53]

"In all countries and at all times, both near at hand and far away, it is one and the same nature of things which is contemplated by one and the same spirit."[54] There is no "final form"[55] of metaphysics, no latest state of research which would sum up and supesede all previous achievements. According to Deussen, philosophy should not be compared to a pyramid "which has been or still remains to be built up gradually during the course of the centuries through the collection and stacking of building blocks," but rather to a pyramid which was complete from its inception, "which is as old as the world itself," and which has been perceived from both far and near, until finally "somebody reached its summit."[56] Thus, nothing needs to be added to the *philosophia perennis*, it remains only to be grasped in a more or less lucid fashion, and to be rediscovered in documents from different times and cultures.

Philosophy may be studied in the history of philosophy "if we know how to remove the shell of tradition," "if we make it a principle to pursue all thoughts back to their point of origin, from which they sprang out of the same nature of things that we are faced with."[57] And when we find the same "inner points of unity" being shared by such spatially and temporally diverse thinkers as Śaṅkara, Plato and Kant, then this agreement offers "not a little guarantee that in all three, we perceive the voice of the one nature in accord with itself, and thus the voice of eternal truth."[58]

13. The "nature of things" is to be clarified and secured by recognizing what is common in the metaphysical efforts of the various cultures. Yet at the same time, the very decision as to which historical material is to be used in this process is dependent upon an "ideal definition" of philosophy and a corresponding conviction about the "nature of things:" they provide the historian of philosophy with the indispensable standards of selection and evaluation, and allow him to play the role of "umpire" which Deussen postulates for him.[59] The circularity of the argument is obvious; yet it has never been fully reflected, or clearly recognized as a problem, in Deussen's works.

In the preface to his translation of Śaṅkara (1887), Deussen presents a line of reasoning which he reproduces in the first volume of his *Allgemeine Geschichte der Philosophie* (1894) in a section entitled "Preliminary Remarks about the Value of Indian Philosophy:" "Let us assume that—as is certainly possible—there are humans or humanoid beings on one of the other planets in our solar system, perhaps on Mars or Venus, and that these, like us, have attained a culture and, as its highest expression, a philosophy, and that we would be given the opportunity to . . . become acquainted with this philosophy, then we would undoubtedly bestow a great interest upon the products of the same . . . The hopes which we would pin upon such a philosophy 'which fell from the skies' are not completely, although nearly, fulfilled by that which the philosophy of the Indians does in fact offer us."[60] Unlike Max Müller's reference to the hypothetical situation of Americans who rediscover the English origins of their language and literature,[61] these lines show a fundamentally unhistorical orientation, a commitment to the *philosophia perennis*.

14. However, Deussen's *Allgemeine Geschichte der Philosophie* adds to the quote from his earlier work the following statement: "A person would

perhaps be considered naive if he were to suggest that our present age, which has progressed 'so magnificently far' in every way, could learn something from the ancient Indians; yet a more general promulgation of the Indian world-view will certainly have *one* use: namely, to make us realize that we, with our entire religious and philosophical thought, are stuck in a colossal one-sideness, and that there may be quite another way of treating things than that which Hegel construed to be the only possible and reasonable way."[62]

Instead of the one *philosophia perennis* and the one common "nature of things," this statement emphasizes what is different and complementary in Indian thought. Deussen's reference to Hegel, however, demonstrates that the "colossal one-sidedness" which he hoped to alleviate through the study of Indian thought is not related to the Western tradition per se, but to a certain dominant trend of Western thought. Deussen himself took a position within this tradition, for which the Indian perspective seemed to provide confirmation and support – the standpoint of Schopenhauer's philosophy, which he considered to be the pinnacle of philosophical knowledge and the standard to be applied in the historiography of philosophy: "No wings can carry us higher – the path ends here, losing itself in the fog, yet not without hope, and it may thus be enough for us that we here, looking out and up from the highest peak within the finite, can discern the eternal stars through the ever thinner veil of clouds, clear enough to light our way through the night of existence."[63] But is Deussen really speaking from the position of Schopenhauer? Is he merely the latter's mouthpiece, distinguishable from him only by virtue of his more comprehensive and explicit historical work? The phrasing of the passage just cited, and specifically Deussen's reference to "the eternal stars," should be enough in itself to raise doubts. For as little as Deussen claimed to have reached a higher level of insight than Schopenhauer, in a certain sense he still could not avoid "looking down" upon him, and he placed Schopenhauer's thought into a context of historical understanding, of comparison, and of concordance that was not Schopenhauer's own.

15. For Deussen, Schopenhauer is the "Christian philosopher par excellence," "philosophus christianissimus";[64] and his "turning of the will towards negation" is nothing other than the καινη κτισις preached by the Apostle Paul in the New Testament. Indeed, Schopenhauer had held fast, "as if with iron bands," to the concept of God itself in his conception of the negation of the "will to live."[65] It is not our task here to investigate the extent to which Deussen reinterpreted Christian ideas in these assimilations; in any case, it is certain that Schopenhauer himself was reinterpreted, that the blade of his pessimism was blunted, and that his philosophy was furnished with a new sense of positive and inner-worldly fulfillment.

Deussen achieved a certain popularity in India. Several of his works have been translated into English, one even into Sanskrit.[66] In what has become known as the Neo-Vedānta, his thinking and his interpretive style have found a number of direct and indirect analogies. He also provided an effective example for the development of "comparative philosophy," which is presently in favor in India and North America. However, the search for what is essentially the same in both East and West is frequently carried out without the scientific rigor of Deussen or his attention to detail, and thus corresponds only too clearly to those abstract comparisons of the most universal categories so detested by Hegel.[67] Deussen's indefatigable commitment to the *philosophia perennis* may appear naive, his methodological approach obsolete, and the whole of his philosophizing epigonic. Nevertheless, his work shows a sense of direction and consistency which is exemplary from a philosophical point of view as well. We may illustrate this by comparing Deussen's work to that of his older contemporary F. Max Müller—a scholar who, unlike Deussen, had made Schopenhauer's personal acquaintance.[68]

16. We have already encountered Müller (1823–1900) as a descendent of the Romantic movement and its longing for the origins. Besides his Indological work, Müller also made a number of contributions to linguistics and religious studies, some of which have been quite influential.[69] At the same time, and fully in line with the British domination of India, he also had a well-developed sense of European progress and superiority. His admiration of India, and in particular of the Vedānta, was combined with fundamentally Christian convictions that occasionally took on an almost missionary form of expression, although this seems to have been much less significant in his later years.[70]

In 1882, eight years after he had completed his edition of the *Ṛgveda* together with Sāyaṇa's commentary (1849–874), his English translation of Kant's *Kritik der reinen Vernunft* appeared. His work on the latter project received philosophical assistance from the monist L. Noiré, who was himself indebted to Schopenhauer. In Müller's opinion *one* great line runs from the *Ṛgveda* to Kant. "While in the Veda we may study the childhood, we may study in Kant's *Critique* the perfect manhood of the Aryan mind."[71]

Time and again, Müller emphasized the inseparability of religion and philosophy. "We should damnify religion if we separated it from philosophy: we should ruin philosophy if we divorced it from religion."[72] For the idea of God is the ultimate goal of philosophical thought as well. The comparative study of religion which Müller championed was more than a matter of neutral historical research; it was committed to religion itself. Its primary aim was to uncover a common stock of truth: "If Comparative Theology has taught us anything, it has taught us that there is a common fund of truth in all religions . . ." The agreements among the various religions illustrate their common origin in "the human heart."[73] Müller rejected the notion of an "original revelation," and did not consider the unfolding of history to be a process of degeneration. It is in history itself that the "revelation" occurs and the idea of God is manifested and realized.[74] The historical and comparative study of religion is in itself a contribution to this manifestation. While engaging in the historical and objective study of religions, Müller remained convinced that he could intercept and to a certain extent neutralize historicism and the relativism that went with it. "There is one truth in all of them, the whole truth in none. Let each one cherish his own, purify his own, and throw away what is dead and decaying. But to give up one's religion is like giving up one's life."[75]

17. More specifically, Müller was interested in the compatibility between other religions and his own liberal view of Christianity, i.e., in the potential for Christianizing inherent in the non-Christian religions, the link that joined them to the truth of the Bible.[76] While Müller had praise for Schopenhauer's enthusiasm for Indian thought, and in particular for the Upaniṣads, he also welcomed Rammohan Roy's translations of the Upaniṣads which Schopenhauer had rejected, as the basis for a future Christianization of India.[77] In general, he viewed the nineteenth-century Indian reform movements (which he followed with a keen interest) as a sign of a growing approximation of Hinduism to Christianity. In his later development, Müller's thought increasingly tended towards eclecticism, while his ties to Christianity became looser, and his recognition of the Vedānta, which he described as the "acme" of human thought, more pronounced.[78]

Müller's main contribution to the historiography of Indian philosophy, his late work *The Six Systems of Indian Philosophy* (1899), does not have the clear philosophical and methodological contours which we find in Deussen's *Allgemeine Geschichte der Philosophie*. In general, Müller's doctrinal allegiance is much less pronounced and consistent that that of Deussen. He is more flexible and conciliatory and fluctuates between different historical and systematic perspectives and motivations, between an emphasis on historical processes and a commitment to the *philosophia perennis*.[79] There is, moreover, a significant rhetorical component in his vast and wide-ranging work.

To modern Hinduism, Müller has become the Western Indologist par excellence. His overall contribution to modern Indian self-understanding and self-appreciation has certainly been greater than that of Deussen.[80]

18. Few European Indologists of the latter part of the nineteenth and first half of the twentieth century subscribe to a philosophical position as pronounced as that of Deussen, and most of them appear more reserved and cautious even in comparison with Müller. The commitment to philological

exploration and historical understanding prevails even among those Indologists who take a special interest in Indian philosophical literature. Scholars such as Th. Stcherbatsky (1866–1942), whose allegiance to Kantian and Neo-Kantian ideas shaped his interpretation of "Buddhist Logic," and St. Schayer (1899–1941), who tried to analyze Indian modes of reasoning by applying modern formal and symbolic logic, are exceptions rather than the rule.[81] In different ways, their work illustrates N. Hartmann's idea of a "recognition of what has been cognized" ("Wiedererkennen von Erkanntem") and a "historical research which deals with the philosophical insights and achievements" ("Geschichtsforschung, die es mit den philosophischen Einsichten und Errungenschaften zu tun hat").[82] The philologists of Indian thought have criticized such commitment to specific Western doctrines and methods, and they have tried to abstain from it. But this does not mean that they were not themselves guided by and committed to more fundamental European standards and procedures. This is obvious, for instance, in R. Garbe's description of the Sāṃkhya system as "Indian rationalism," of H. Oldenberg's presentation of the transition from the *Brāhmaṇas* to the *Upaniṣads* in the light of, or in analogy to, the Greek shift "from myth to logos," or even E. Frauwallner's "strictly philological" exploration of early Vaiśeṣika.

19. Unlike Schopenhauer, Hegel has neither initiated a movement of enthusiasm for India, nor a tradition of Indological research. Instead, Hegel seems to have been succeeded by a tradition of neglecting India, especially within the historiography of philosophy. Those who followed him in this area usually accepted his claim—which he himself later modified—that there was no "real philosophy" in India, that the "freedom of the individual" which is the prerequisite of the "reality" of philosophy was never attained there, and that philosophy never freed itself from religion and mythology.[83] However, not all the traces which Hegel left in the historiography of Indian philosophy are negative. And this does not just refer to the fact that certain positive attitudes towards Indian thought developed in reaction against Hegel's philosophy and subordination of Oriental and especially Indian thought. Regardless of what Hegel said about or against Indian thought, his work set an example through its serious and thorough consideration of India within the framework of a philosophically conceived universal history of philosophy. With few exceptions, such as that of K. Rosenkranz (1805–1879), who included Indian literature in his works on aesthetics and the history of literature,[84] the Hegelians have not followed this example. Still, it did have an impact upon other philosophers and historians of philosophy whose ties to Hegel were less pronounced. Some authors whose interest in India was first awakened by Schopenhauer's and Schelling's thought subsequently came under

Hegel's influence or even attempted a synthesis of these approaches.

20. C.J.H. Windischmann (1775–1839), who undertook the project of a universal history of philosophy long before Deussen (although he never got beyond the "Orient" in his *Die Philosophie im Fortgang der Weltgeschichte. I: Die Grundlage der Philosophie im Morgenland*, Bonn 1827–1934),[85] was a Catholic disciple of Schelling. Yet he too came under Hegel's influence, especially during his later career. In fact, Schopenhauer, simplifying polemically, classified him as a "Hegelian."[86]

It was Windischmann's self-proclaimed aim to link the idea of the *philosophia perennis* with the concept of evolution and Schelling's doctrine of the odyssey of the spirit. "Truth is eternal; its perception and recognition by man indicates progress through time; man has a history of becoming aware of this truth . . . We must concern ourselves with the epochs of the spiritual awareness of truth and the ways in which the spirit gradually returns back home from its alienation abroad." To this extent, the history of philosophy is essentially a history of the aberrations of the spirit as well; it deals, as it were, with a "process of disease."[87]

In his presentation, Windischmann ranges widely through Indian mythology and religion. It is only the last part of his work which is dedicated to Indian philosophy in a more narrow sense, i.e., the classical systems. His work includes a number of German translations, some of them the very first ever made, of portions of the Upaniṣads as well as texts from the Nyāya, Sāṃkhya, and Vedānta. In preparing these, Windischmann was not only assisted by Chr. Lassen (who succeeded A.W. Schlegel to the Chair for Indology at Bonn), but also received the active support of his son, F.H.H. Windischmann (1811–1861), a scholar of Sanskrit and Iranian studies.[88]

Some of the leading historians of philosophy of the nineteenth century who did not completely or a priori exclude India from their picture of the history of philosophy were also more or less clearly indebted to Hegel. One example is H. Ritter (1791–1869), a student of Schleiermacher who became one of the leading historians of philosophy in the nineteenth century. Ritter included a careful and thoughtful survey of the state of research on Indian philosophy in the first volume of his twelve-volume *Geschichte der Philosophie* (Hamburg 1829–1853).[89]

21. V. Cousin (1792–1867) allied himself more clearly and explicitly with Hegel in his highly successful lectures on the history of philosophy, in which he also made extensive references to Indian thought.[90] To be sure, his "eclecticism" which links together the "surviving truths" of earlier philosophical teachings and movements would hardly have appealed to Hegel: ". . . that enlightened eclecticism which judges all doctrines with equity and benevolence, borrows from them what is common and true in

them, and neglects what is incompatible and false" ("cet éclectisme éclairé qui, jugeant avec équité et même avec bienveillance toutes les doctrines, leur emprunte ce qui elles ont de commun et de vrai, néglige ce qu'elles ont d'opposé et de faux").[91] For that matter, Cousin's description of the Orient as the "point of departure of civilization and philosophy" ("le point de départ de la civilisation et de la philosophie") and his remark that we should bow before its wisdom,[92] also deviate from Hegel's view.

A more complete survey than is presently intended would also deal with the position of the "Hegelian left"[93] and in particular Marxism vis-à-vis Indian thought. It would also have to pursue the question how the Marxist view of the non-European and especially Indian world relates to Hegel's own views. Marx himself was particularly attentive to the events which occurred in India during his lifetime. This interest in contemporary India is remarkable at a time when both philosophers and Indologists focused their attention on ancient and classical India. F. Engels noted that dialectical thought was already present among the Buddhists.[94] According to W. Ruben, one of the principal exponents of the contemporary Marxist interpretation of Indian philosophy, it was Marx who "turned Indology into a true science." Ruben has also made repeated and obviously sympathetic reference to Hegel's portrayal of India.[95] In his work *Die gesellschaftliche Entwicklung im alten Indien*, he tries to give an account of Indian philosophy within the framework of a comprehensive social history of ancient India and to thereby demonstrate the explanatory potential of dialectical materialism, and specifically of the Marxist doctrine of the superstructure.[96] As a whole, however, the Marxist "critique of ideologies" ("Ideologiekritik") has been applied to Indian philosophy on a relatively modest scale up till now.[97] Among Indian authors who have applied Marxist methods to the interpretation of the Indian tradition, we may mention Bhupendranath Datta, the younger brother of Svami Vivekananda, and, more recently, D.P. Chattopadhyaya.

22. Most of what Marx had to say about India is found in the newspaper articles which he wrote as the London correspondent of the *New York Daily Tribune*. In a letter to Engels, Marx claimed that he had written these casual pieces primarily for financial reasons and that India was "not his department."[98] Yet, there are some highly memorable passages in these articles. They illustrate his Hegelian background as well as his sharp focus on current developments and prospects for the future, and they have become famous not only within Marxism. In 1853, he concluded a series of articles on India with the following, more general observations:

> India, then, could not escape the fate of being conquered, and the whole of her past history, if it be anything, is the history of the successive conquests she has

undergone. Indian society has no history at all, at least no known history. What we call its history, is but the history of the successive intruders who founded their empires on the passive basis of that unresisting and unchanging society. . . . From the Indian natives, reluctantly and sparingly educated at Calcutta, under English superintendence, a fresh class is springing up, endowed with the requirements for government and imbued with European science. Steam has brought India into regular and rapid communication with Europe, has connected its chief ports with those of the whole south-eastern ocean, and has revindicated it from the isolated position which was the prime law of its stagnation. The day is not far distant when, by a combination of railways and steam vessels, the distance between England and India, measured by time, will be shortened to eight days, and when that once fabulous country will thus be actually annexed to the Western World. . . . Modern industry, resulting from the railway system, will dissolve the hereditary divisions of labour, upon which rest the Indian castes, those decisive impediments to Indian progress and Indian power. . . . The Indians will not reap the fruits of the new elements of society, scattered among them by the British bourgeoisie, till in Great Britain itself the now ruling classes shall have been supplanted by the industrial proletariat, or till the Hindoos themselves shall have grown strong enough to throw off the British yoke altogether. At all events, we may safely expect to see, at a more or less remote period, the regeneration of that great and interesting country, whose gentle natives are, to use the expression of Prince Saltykov, even in the most inferior classes, 'plus fins et plus adroits que les Italiens,' whose submission even is counterbalanced by a certain calm nobility, who, notwithstanding their natural languor, have astonished the British officers by their bravery, whose country has been the source of our languages, our religions, and who represent the type of the ancient German in the Jat and the type of the ancient Greek in the Brahmin.[99]

23. In 1853, the same year in which Karl Marx (1818–1883) wrote those words, his contemporary, J.A. de Gobineau, French diplomat, philosopher, historian and novelist (1816–1882), published the first two volumes of his "Essay on the Inequality of Human Races" (*Essai sur l'inégalité des races humaines*). Volumes 3 and 4 followed in 1855. This work, in particular its second volume, contains numerous conspicuous and ominous references to India.[100] As a matter of fact, India, the caste system and the Aryan invasion play a paradigmatic role in Gobineau's conservative and pessimistic ideology of history and race. While the first volume has appeared in several English translations,[101] the subsequent volumes have never been translated, and they have not had much resonance in the English speaking world. On the other hand, a complete German edition (1898–1901) has had considerable impact.

According to Gobineau, the "white race" is preeminent among the three major races of mankind (white, yellow, black) due to its ability to create and spread culture. However, in the process of imposing its values upon others, it cannot avoid intermixture and tends to lose its identity and strength. "Its inherent excellence drives it forth to world conquest, but that very conquest leads to its decline."[102] Gobineau sees the case of India as an exemplification of his theory: The Aryans, representing the highest potential of the "white race," invaded the Indian subcontinent and began to merge with the native population. Realizing the danger, the Aryan lawgivers implemented the caste-system as a means of self-preservation. Accordingly, the processes of bastardization and degeneration have been much slower in India than in other civilizations. The Brahmins, though far from the primeval glory of the ancient Aryans, succeeded in stabilizing their identity and superiority at a relatively early stage of decay.

Gobineau was convinced that India would ultimately survive the British challenge and reassert its identity against those European representatives of the "white race" whose superiority was in his own view only a temporary one: "A moment will come, in one way or another, when India will again live publicly, as she already does privately, under her own laws."[103] Britain, as well as other liberal, democratic and permissive nations, was destined for bastardization and decay. India was invoked against the ideals of the French Revolution and against that kind of progress which Marx and others tried to promote.

24. During Gobineau's life-time, the old theory of the Asian origin of the European languages and traditions, and of cultural movements from the East to the West, increasingly gave way to speculations on primeval movements from the West to the East, and on Aryan migrations from Europe, specifically Northern Europe, or even the North Pole, to India. According to these speculations, the European or Northern invaders gave their superior culture to the Indians and then lost their superiority through mixture with the original inhabitants and perished in a climate for which they were not suited. In 1903, E.de Michelis summarized this view by stating that Asia, and India in particular, was not the "cradle," but the "grave of the Aryans."[104]

The Aryan myth and speculative ideas about India continued to play a role in the race theories and doctrines of historical decadence which were developed in the late nineteenth and early twentieth centuries. They were particularly significant for the lunatic fringe of political and ideological movements around 1900, which contributed to the world view of National Socialism. Among these, the "Ariosophic" movement of G. Lanz-Liebenfels (1874–1954) deserves to be mentioned. During his years in Vienna, Hitler was a regular reader of the journal *Ostara*, in which Lanz developed his ideas about dark "Tschandalas" (*caṇḍāla*) and blond Aryans. In 1908, two issues of the journal dealt exclusively with "the law book of Manu and race cultivation among the ancient Indo-Aryans" ("Das Gesetzbuch des Manu und die Rassenpflege bei den alten Indo-Ariern"). Together with his older contemporaries A. Schuler and G. von List, Lanz was also an early propagator of the *svastika*.[105]

Not much later, references to "Jisnu Krischna," the Buddha, etc. which were partly derived from the mystifications of L. Jacolliot, appeared in the works of Mathilde Ludendorff and the ideology of the "Ludendorff Movement." A. Rosenberg's *Der Mythus des 20. Jahrhunderts* ("The Myth of the Twentieth Century"), which was first published in 1930 and became a leading ideological text-book of the Third Reich, frequently mentions the case of the Aryans in India as an illustration and as a warning. It also associates developments in Indian thought, such as the equation of *ātman* and *brahman* and the metaphysics of ultimate unity, with racial developments, and specifically with what it considers to be the loss of Aryan identity and assertiveness.[106] India is invoked in order to articulate and justify ideas and programs of unparalleled arrogance and destructiveness. This, too, is part of the history of European approaches to India.

It cannot be our task to pursue further ways in which ideas about ancient India found their way into modern ideological, spiritual and esoteric movements. Of these, the Theosophical Society, founded in 1875 by Mme. H. Blavatsky and Col. H.S. Olcott, played the most important role. It revived and rephrased the old idea of a primeval wisdom and revelation in which science and religion were undivided. It helped to popularize Indian psychological and cosmological ideas, the doctrine of karma and rebirth, and other Asian teachings in the West. Its impact both in India and in the West has been remarkable and complex.[107]

25. Hegel and Schopenhauer offer us diametrically opposed models of interpreting history, and equally divergent approaches to Indian thought. Yet, both of them still represent the tradition of metaphysics, and this tradition drew increasingly sharp criticism during the nineteenth and twentieth centuries. Numerous writers and intellectual movements proclaimed the transformation of philosophy into science, or into historical, sociological and "anthropological" modes of thinking and research.

In this context, the attempts of Auguste Comte (1798–1857) to establish a "positive philosophy" by systematically carrying out the suggestions of his teacher Saint-Simon have been particularly effective and exemplary. Comte's approach does not just provide us with a contrastive model to Hegel's system of development, it also exhibits certain structural similarities to Hegel's thought. According to Comte's doctrine of the three stages of human thought ("loi des trois états"), the "metaphysical stage" was preceded by a "theological stage" and will be superseded by a "positive stage" ("état positif"), which concerns itself strictly with what is actually given. In the *état positif*, there is no place for questions about the true nature of things, first causes, or absolute origins. The only concern is with the analysis of phenomena, with the discovery of similarities or causal relationships, and with the determination of regularities to serve for the future and provide technical and practical control over both the human and natural worlds.[108] Comte considered "sociologie," the study of man in his social existence, to be the supreme science, and for this reason it particularly needed to rise to a "positive" method of observation. Man himself became the object of a quasi-religious adoration, of a "Cult of Humanity," which Comte presented as the "Universal Religion" and described in great detail in his later works.[109]

26. Comte himself is not distinguished for any singular interest in India or the Orient in general. Moreover, G.H. Lewes (1817–1878), who of all the more successful nineteenth-century historians of philosophy most clearly embraced Comte's "positivism," did not include India in his presentation, arguing that only the Greeks had attained a truly scientific position.[110] Still, Comte did emphasize that his philosophy had created a fundamentally new and universal historical openness for "the whole of human evolution" ("l'ensemble de l'évolution humaine") which was also able to appreciate the oldest forms of human fellowship.[111] Comte's student E. Littré (1801–1881), who gained prominence primarily as a lexicographer and also studied under the Orientalist Chézy, stressed the merely "positive," i.e., humane, anthropological, and fundamentally anti-religious and anti-metaphysical interest which his philosophy had in the religious and philosophical systems of the East. Religion and theology, which had been overcome in their Christian guise, could not attain meaning again in a different garb and be imported to Europe. "Islam, Brahmanism, Buddhism are affected—however strange that may appear—, by all the blows which Christian theology receives in the Christian countries" ("l' islam, le brahmaisme, le bouddhisme sont touchés, quelque singulier que cela paraisse, par tous les coups que reçoit dans les pays chrétiens la theologie chrétienne.").[112] P. Leroux (1797–1871), a follower of Saint-Simon who edited the *Encyclopédie nouvelle* and the *Revue encyclopédique* together with J. Reynaud, wrote an article entitled "De l'influence philosophique des études orientales" in which he declared that Oriental Studies are just as important for the concerns of "humanity" as the discoveries of the natural sciences. By placing other works with equal rank and pretension alongside the Bible, such research illustrates the historical limits of Christianity and opens up a way for a religion at once more comprehensive and more humane.[113]

27. Of more importance and consequence, however, is the way in which the idea of the "positive," the commitment to "facts" and the project of exploring the variety and structure of the "human phenomenon" were adopted, transformed, and integrated into ethnological and sociological

research by such scholars as L. Lévy-Bruhl, E. Durkheim and M. Mauss.[114] Lévy-Bruhl published a study of Comte's philosophy, entitled *La philosophie d'Auguste Comte*, in 1900. These scholars, in particular Durkheim, represent a typically French combination of philosophy with sociology and ethnology; and they exemplify an intellectual style and a structural and comparative orientation which has had a major impact upon Indian studies in France. More recently, we find it in the influential work of L. Dumont.

Among French Indologists and historians of Indian philosophy, P. Masson-Oursel (1882–1956), a student of both Lévy-Bruhl and S. Lévi, was a vigorous advocate of the "positive" spirit, and he propagated the "comparative method" as the fulfilment of the "positive method." Although Masson-Oursel did not invent the expression "comparative philosophy," his *La philosophie comparée* (1923; translated as *Comparative Philosophy*, 1926) contributed greatly to its general acceptance and familiarity.[115] In his dual role as Indologist and "positivistic" philosopher, Masson-Oursel was for decades a kind of official spokesman for India and the Orient within the French historiography of philosophy.[116]

Masson-Oursel tried to explore the "totality of the human phenomenon" by analyzing and comparing its different manifestations in the great cultural traditions.[117] In doing so, he was primarily looking for recurrent isomorphic features, common structures, which he called "proportions," in mutually independent traditions.[118] His claim was to be a totally open-minded cartographer of the human mind, with a true universality, no longer bound by the restrictions of being part of one particular tradition. His thought seems to represent an objectifying, detached metaphilosophy, which no longer engages in any of the actual problems and subject-matters of the various philosophical traditions, but treats them all equally as objects of comparative anthropological inquiry.[119] However, in doing this he obviously followed one particular line of development in Western thought and took one particular, namely, anthropocentric, approach. In a sense, it was his abstract idea of a totally "objective" comprehension of facts, his projection of openness itself, which may have committed him to a peculiar kind of parochialism.

28. The most momentous sociological contribution to the study of India and its religious tradition has not come from the school of Comte, but from Max Weber (1864–1920). Weber has been celebrated as one of the founders of modern sociology, or even as the modern sociologist par excellence. His analysis of the role of religion in Indian social and economic life, and of the interaction of ideas and "social realities" in the history of Hinduism and Buddhism, is an important and exemplary part of his overall achievement.

"Interests (material and ideal), not ideas, directly determine man's action. But the world views, which were created by ideas, have very often acted as the switches that channeled the dynamics of the interests." This statement which Weber added in 1920 to the revised introduction of his *Die Wirtschaftsethik der Weltreligionen* ("Economic Ethics of the World Religions") and which was included in his *Gesammelte Aufsätze zur Religionssoziologie* ("Collected Essays on the Sociology of Religion"), provides a key to his approach in general.[120] It also applies to his study of Hinduism and Buddhism,[121] to his characterization of the social roles of the Brahmins and other "intellectuals," the directions of rationalization in the Indian tradition, the relation between the caste system and the doctrine of karma and rebirth. Even the various forms of criticism directed against this approach—which occasionally denounce it as a reflection of colonial attitudes and superimpositions—testify to its vitality and to its pervasive impact.[122]

However, in the present context we do not have to assess Weber's rank and influence in modern sociology. His work is also an event in the history of European self-understanding and self-questioning, as well as in the history of European encounters with India. It is, moreover, inseparable from the tradition of European philosophy precisely in the manner in which it attempts to transform and translate philosophical questions and perspectives into the language of empirical research. According to K. Jaspers, Weber was a philosopher "for the time in which he lived."[123]

It does not seem appropriate to call Weber a "Crypto-Hegelian."[124] But he certainly reflects and transforms the heritage of Hegel as well as that of Comte and Marx.

29. In his own way, Weber was trying to clarify and understand the uniqueness of Europe, the special direction Western history had taken, and the peculiar conditions of the modern world, "for in the last analysis Weber's program in the sociology of religion is intended to make us understand the uniqueness of modern occidental culture and to answer the question of why only in the Occident did there appear cultural phenomena 'which took a developmental path of universal importance and world-historical significance, at least as we like to think.'"[125]

Why did modern Europe develop its peculiar combination of theoretical and practical rationalism? Why and how did it develop its methods of rational, experimental and "value-free" science and research? Why, above all, did it develop the economic system of modern capitalism with its pervasive structures of planning and reckoning? There have been forms of "rationalism" and rational planning everywhere in the world, but in Europe, they have become universal and unrestricted. The fundamental problem of Western self-understanding concerns the origin and the consequences of this comprehensive "rationalization of the human spirit."[126]

In order to answer or even approach these questions, Weber found it necessary to refer to other, non-European traditions, those of East Asia, the Near East, and specifically India. He developed a vast comprehensive plan to compare the various cultures, and he executed some monumental fragments. He did this no longer from a standpoint of Hegelian self-assurance. While he was convinced of the uniqueness of the Western tradition, he was no longer sure of its goal and direction. The expectations which he associated with modern Western civilization and technology were ambiguous. He accepted the inherent logic of "value-free" research and scientific "progress," and its extension into rational planning and technological mastery. "Value-freedom," "value-neutrality" ("Wertfreiheit") was the responsibility and vocation of the modern Western or Westernized scholar, but it was also his predicament.

India was highly significant for Weber's comparative enterprise of European self-understanding. But it was not a potential supplier of meaning and values. India itself, like other traditions, was an object of "value-free" research and rational understanding.[127]

9. On the Exclusion of India from the History of Philosophy

1. As we have seen, P. Deussen is exceptional among the historians of philosophy of the nineteenth and early twentieth centuries. His *Allgemeine Geschichte der Philosophie* ("Universal History of Philosophy") is unique amid the literature of this field. His "ideal concept" of philosophy, which does not segregate religion from philosophy and thus allows him to include the metaphysical efforts of all peoples and times, was not shared by the academic historians of philosophy. Yet as we have also seen, there were a number of authors (not a few of whom were influenced by Schelling) who tried to trace philosophy back to its religious and mythical sources - and thus back to its pristine, Oriental state.[1] In this context, mention has been made of the names of C.J.H. Windischmann and Th.A. Rixner. K.Chr.F. Krause (1781-1832) also belongs in Schelling's camp (notwithstanding his later enmity), and was characterized as a Schellingian in E. Zeller's classification of nineteenth-century historians of philosophy.[2] Krause, an enthusiastic reader of Anquetil Duperron's *Oupnek'hat*, complained about the manner in which "the Indian science had . . . earlier . . . been given short shrift under the ignominious title of barbaric, i.e., non-Hellenic, philosophy."[3] E. Röth (1807-1858), a distant follower of the spirit of Schelling who possessed a very thorough philological background, also looked at the Orient in his *Geschichte unserer abendländischen Philosophie* ("History of Our Occidental Philosophy").[4] Yet whereas Schelling's thought may have indeed directed Röth and others to the Orient, their treatment was often merely a "pre-historical," childhood-oriented re-collection of early origins and basically in line with the Romantic view. The very title of Röth's work is symptomatic in this regard: a contemplation of the Orient is necessary in order to understand the developments that later took place in Europe as well as the European present. His search for his own philosophical roots, however, led him primarily to Egypt, and not to India.

What is more, Schelling's own position vis-à-vis India tended to remain reserved. The thoroughness and the extent of his explicit discussions of Indian thought are in no way comparable to that which may be found with Hegel and Schopenhauer. And, as the example of Th.A. Rixner illustrates, some of the authors who utilized Schelling as the starting point of their own approaches to the history of philosophy increasingly came under the influence of Hegel's thought.

2. Mention has already been made of the ambivalence in Hegel's treatment of India and the Orient and the repercussions it had during the nineteenth century. To be sure, Hegel does provide us with an example of a very serious and comprehensive discussion of Indian thought. Yet his historical segregation of philosophy from religion, his devaluation of any form of yearning for a lost unity, and his conviction that Europe, by unfolding the "actual," "real" philosophy committed to the spirit of free science, had essentially surpassed the Orient, instead contributed to a restrictive use of the concept of philosophy and to a self-limitation in the historiography of philosophy. As a part of this process, the academic historians of philosophy, in their role as caretakers of a specialized scholarly discipline, gave up the more comprehensive horizon of a phenomenology of the spirit and the world-historical perspective espoused in Hegel's history of philosophy in order to pursue a history of philosophy in its "true," "actual" sense. The willingness to concede India an "actual" philosophy as well, an attitude which Hegel occasionally gave utterance to during his later years,[5] generally received little notice, and an essentially restrictive view of the history of philosophy emerged which was to eventually dominate nineteenth and early twentieth century thinking and which explicitly excluded the Orient, and thus India, from the historical record of philosophy. Before we present a few examples from within this tradition, we should turn once more to those developments in the historiography of philosophy which took place prior to Hegel. In keeping with our subject, we shall primarily concern ourselves with the question as to how the compass of philosophy was delimited, in other words, with the problems of the "actuality" as well as of the origins of that which constitutes the subject matter of any history of philosophy. This obviously refers us back to the start of our presentation. i.e., to Greek doxography as represented in particular by Diogenes Laërtius As we have seen, Diogenes discussed the Orient and India in connection with questions about the origins and prehistory of Greek philosophy. In the final analysis, his quest for the origins of "actual" philosophy brought him back to the Greeks, and he concluded that the "barbarians" had no corresponding word or concept.[6]

3. At the close of our discussion of the approaches to Indian thought found in antiquity, we made a few brief remarks about the later effects of

Diogenes Laërtius' doxography. Walter de Burleigh's presentation of "The Lives and Characters of Philosophers" (*De vitis et moribus philosophorum*, first half of the fourteenth century) straddles the transitional period between the Middle Ages and the Renaissance and is little more than an excerpt of Diogenes' work, upon which it depends entirely. The first Latin translation was completed in 1431 by Ambrosius Traversarius Camaldulensis, and it was printed and reprinted several times before the year 1500. Many printed editions of the Greek text followed. Even long after 1498 and the increasing general knowledge of India which began around this time, Diogenes' work continued to exert an influence upon the doxographic literature and the historiography of philosophy because of both the information contained therein and the method in which this was presented. In fact, it often became superimposed in a variety of ways upon the newer material.[7] Thus, whereas Th. Stanley criticized Diogenes' work, setting Oriental philosophy at the conclusion of his work instead of at the beginning,[8] J. Brucker's (1696–1770) *Historia critica philosophiae* (1742–1744) was a much more typical work which had great influence in its time. It treated the non-European material, i.e., the non-Hellenic antecedents and the pre-history of philosophy, in a manner fully consonant with that of Diogenes.

In 1695, J. Jonsius presented the first survey of the "historiography" of philosophy;[9] another, more definitive, overview describing the state of the art during the period directly preceding Hegel is that of F.A. Carus (1770–1807). Considering the developments that were to follow, one of the most interesting things about the latter work[10] is the relatively large number of writings it mentions which treat, at least in intention, Oriental and Indian thought in some detail. Some of these even took on monographic proportions. The following examples are worth mentioning: O. Heurnius, *Barbaricae philosophiae antiquitates* (Leiden, 1600). This work discussed the Chaldeans and Indians and contains, in Carus' phrase, "trivialities;" G. Korthold, *Tractatus de origine et progressu et antiquitate philosophiae barbaricae* (Jena, 1651), which Carus describes as "little more than Heurnius;" E.D. Colberg, *Sapientia veterum Hebraeorum* (Greifswald, 1694), with the *Dissertatio de origine philosophiae*; the closing section of Stanley's history of philosophy, which deals with "barbarian" philosophy and appeared in a separate edition in Latin translation by Le Clerc entitled *Historia philosophiae orientalis* (Amsterdam, 1690); and G.J. Vossius, *De philosophia et philosophorum sectis* (Haag, 1657) in which philosophy is seen as having derived from the Orient.

4. The claims to present a universal human history become increasingly conspicuous in the seventeenth and eighteenth century literature on doxography and the history of philosophy. This trend is fully in line with the

more general tendencies of Rationalism and the Enlightenment,[11] yet such discussions often took place within a horizon of humanity defined by the Biblical account of creation. For example, whereas Stanley was content to begin his history of philosophy with Thales, the exposition by G. Hornius which appeared the same year (*Historiae philosophicae libri VII, quibus de origine, successione, sectis et vita philosophorum ab orbe condito ad nostram aetatem agitur* (Leiden, 1655) portrayed Adam as the first philosopher.[12] Chr. A. Hermann also intended to discuss the course of philosophy "from the beginning of the world" in his *Acta philosophica* (three journal volumes, Halle, 1715). Such claims find what is probably their most famous expression in J. Brucker's *Historia critica philosophiae a mundi incunabulis ad nostram aetatem deducta* (Leipzig, 1742–1744), in which Brucker even tried to include an account of "antediluvian philosophy." J.B. Capasso discussed the concept of a "universal history of philosophy" ("universalis historia philosophiae") in his *Historia philosophiae synopsis* (Naples, 1728). J. Chr. Gottsched also used an essentially open concept of a universal history of philosophy in his *Erste Gründe der gesamten Weltweisheit* (Leipzig, 1733; seventh ed., 1772; it includes a section on the "worldly wisdom of the Indians"), one of the most popular eighteenth-century works on the history of philosophy.[13] Some writings even asserted their claims to present a universal history of human thought in their titles, for instance, E.F. Schmersahl's *Historie der Weltweisheit überhaupt* (Celle, 1744). J.Aug. Eberhard's *Allgemeine Geschichte der Philosophie* (Halle, 1788; second ed., 1796) aspired to present a "universal history of worldly wisdom" ("Weltweisheit;" i.e., philosophy as distinguished from theology). F.A. Carus presented his "Ideas about a General History of Philosophy" and stated: "The general history of philosophy constitutes the natural history of thinking human reason, just as world history constitutes that of acting human reason." Its concern is with the "endeavors of human reason to realize the ideal of philosophy."[14] Such remarks illustrate a view of the history of philosophy and of the relationship of philosophy to its own history that was directly linked to Kant's philosophy and simultaneously paved the way for Hegel's conjoining of philosophy and the history of philosophy.

5. Kant, who gave the fourth article of the transcendental methodology of his *Kritik der reinen Vernunft* the title "The History of Pure Reason," more than once addressed the idea of a "rational" and not merely historical history of philosophy.[15] His most emphatic remarks on the subject are contained in the "Lose Blätter" ("Loose Leaves") published after his death. There, he speaks of an "a priori history of philosophy"[16] derivable from the nature of human reason whose successful attainment would, admittedly, necessitate a perfected self-knowledge of human reason, i.e., the perfection

of philosophy itself. Kant's suggestion was taken up in a particularly precise and acute form by J.C.A. Grohmann in *Über den Begriff der Geschichte der Philosophie* (Wittenberg, 1797): The history of philosophy, insofar as it has become possible in the sense of a rational construction, points to "the end of all philosophizing" and an "eternal treaty of peace" within the domain of philosophy.[17]

In spite of their claims to present universal human histories,[18] the doxographies and histories of philosophy which appeared in the seventeenth and eighteenth centuries often only hesitatingly applied the concept of philosophy to the Orient. Brucker, whose presentation encompasses such a far-ranging program, ultimately finds philosophy in its complete sense and with the "correct manner of philosophizing" only among the Greeks and the traditions which followed thereafter.[19] During the second half of the eighteenth century, the debate about the conceptual limits of philosophy and the scope of its history as well as about the legitimacy of including the Orient intensified, so that F.A. Carus was already in a position to recapitulate a tradition of discussion about the "admission of the pre- and non-Greek peoples" in his *Ideen zur Geschichte der Philosophie*, which appeared posthumously in 1809.[20]

6. In a comment of his own, Carus assumes that the "activity of reason" which is the concern of the history of philosophy is "nowhere completely" dormant, explaining: "Thus, after mutually comparing the reasons, it may be seen that the law of continuity which such a history must, like any other history, recognize, requires that some mention be made of the pre-Greek peoples. There as well, nature is not disjointed; there as well, the borders flow together."[21] Somewhat later, W.G. Tennemann (1761–1819), the leading German historian of philosophy in the period directly preceding Hegel, named Carus as a person who had provided a positive answer to the question of the inclusion of Oriental philosophy;[22] in 1814, Tennemann himself had been accused by C.F.Bachmann of not having adequately taken the Orient into consideration.[23] Tennemann referred to D. Tiedemann as a spokesman for the opposite, negative stance. Indeed, Tiedemann (1748–1803) was an advocate of a concept of "actual, real philosophy" ("eigentliche Philosophie")[24] which, by his own standards, could not be applied to the Orient, i.e., to those traditions which had not been shaped by the Greeks. Tennemann himself stated that among the peoples of the Orient, all wisdom "still conveyed the character of divine revelation"[25] and that "the philosophizing which we cannot deny them" had not led them "to any philosophy." "The beginning of the history of philosophy may thus be found among the Greeks, or more precisely, at that moment when a greater degree of reason developed from the culture of phantasy and intellect as clarity in concepts and the cohesion of knowledge was being striven after

and research into basic principles began. This took place during the time of Thales. This spirit of philosophical research, which has been transmitted from the Greeks to the more recent peoples via a variety of channels, is that which, in its different schools, forms, and effects, comprises the compass of the history of philosophy."[26] Another of the leading historians of philosophy during the period around 1800, J.G. Buhle, spoke somewhat more circumspectly and more along Carus' line. Buhle was in essence prepared to search for "the oldest philosophy of the peoples" in their religions; yet he also felt that Indian philosophy, at least as far as it was then known, contained "no original system of opinions" but instead referred back to borrowed ideas brought along by invaders, and that in any case more careful research and analysis was needed in this domain.[27]

7. There is no contradiction inherent in the fact that the ideas about "universal history" and the universality of reason in the seventeenth and eighteenth centuries eventually led to a decidedly restrictive definition of the compass of the history of philosophy. For reason, in whose name the history of philosophy is written, may indeed have been initially viewed as a universal human principle present in all times and places. Yet the "correct" manner of its development and use are something else entirely, and it was this which became the criterion for a concept of a "proper" and "actual" philosophy that was anything but universal. The confrontation between a universal human reason and the exclusiveness of its methodologically correct management and application is especially pronounced in Cartesianism,[28] and it is a symptomatic fact that two early and telling opinions opposing the inclusion of Oriental and pre-Hellenic thought – those of A. Gravius[29] and P.S. Regis[30] – came from the Cartesian camp: the methodologically ordered and progressive activity of reason first occurred among the Greeks, and did not reappear again until post-scholastic European philosophy.

Hegel, to whom we must now turn once again, integrated this traditional view of doxography and the history of philosophy, together with the associated problems as to the origin and domain of philosophy, into his own thought, which was as much systematic in nature as it was historical, thus raising it to a new level of reflection.[31] In his own system of thought, Hegel attempted to "preserve" not just the thought of India and the Orient, but also the ways in which Europe had approached it up until that point. Here, the "problem of applicability" is placed in a more thought-out and more differentiated context, insofar as Hegel, unlike most eighteenth-century historians of philosophy, did not start with any pre-defined concept of philosophy and then begin his search for Oriental "correspondences," but instead argued that the concept of philosophy itself has to be derived out of its historical development – in such a way that a re-collection of the

Orient is essential for its understanding, even though the concept of philosophy as such did not have to be present there. Of course, an understanding of philosophy as "unfolding of the idea" ("Entwicklung der Idee") is required before one may undertake a "definition of the history of philosophy" and determine "which of the infinite material and the manifold facets of the intellectual culture of the peoples is to be excluded from the history of philosophy." Such a concept, however, may only be presupposed to the extent that it is received and conceived of as the result of historical developments.[32]

8. Hegel gave intense thought to the question why it seems more appropriate to speak of philosophy when discussing Oriental and, in particular, Indian religious conceptions than when dealing with the corresponding conceptions from Christianity and Europe. He concluded that this was due to the fact that the individual, subjectivity, and the person were much less conspicuous in Indian religious thought than in its European counterpart, since the former was much more concerned with general essences and powers that appeared to be more closely connected with philosophy, which concerns itself with the universal and general. "This is the main reason why the conceptions of the Indians at once appear to be philosophical thoughts, to be general."[33] Admittedly, this generality is simultaneously undeveloped, pre-historical abstractness, and it thus reverts to the form of myth. For the historians of *philosophy*, the following criterion remains valid: "It is not our business to reduce the truths which are contained or expressed in such configurations to the form of thought, we are only concerned with recording those cases where thought is already present in the form of thought."[34]

The heights of reflection and the thoroughness which define Hegel's subordinating and, in a certain sense, dismissive exposition of Indian thought were rarely attained again by any of the nineteenth-century historians of philosophy who succeeded him. Typically, these were content with providing more or less explicit definitions of the domain of the history of "actual" philosophy, while their exclusion of the Orient was usually justified by a short statement of intent. What in Tennemann's eyes had still appeared to be rather the exception - a truly decisive and not just half-hearted demarcations vis-à-vis the Orient[35] - increasingly became the rule during the nineteenth and early twentieth centuries, and this trend accompanied the quick growth of factual knowledge about Indian thought in a peculiar and symptomatic manner. Even Th.A. Rixner, an early *Oupnek'hat* enthusiast who had initially extolled the Upaniṣads as the "original source of true knowledge"[36] was content in his later *Handbuch der Geschichte der Philosophie*[37] (recommended by Hegel himself), and thus in his new role as a professional and academic historian of philosophy, to make only brief references to these works. He described the teachings contained in the *Oupnek'hat* in a somewhat derogatory manner, speaking of them as "ancient mythical and phantastical monistic speculations by a kind of reasoning that has not yet come of age or ripened to understanding, not to mention attained the status of science."[38] In spite of the fact that new material had appeared in the interim, he took no notice of the later developments in Indian thought.

9. What follows is a compilation of exemplary opinions from some generally representative and well-known works on the history of philosophy, most of them from the nineteenth century. These testimonials speak largely for themselves. (Many works, by the way, simply begin their discussion with Thales without providing a word of explanation).

When and where does philosophy begin? . . . Obviously at that point when the first search for the final philosophical principle, for the ultimate reason for Being, was made in a philosophical manner. In other words, with Greek philosophy. The so-called philosophy (actually theology or mythology) of the Orient (China and India) and the mythical cosmologies of the most ancient Greeks are thus omitted from our (more limited) task. (A Schwegler)[39]

Our history of philosophy can only be the Greco-Roman-Christian one. We know neither the time of formation nor any kind of history about other, Asian philosophemes. Moreover, the simple beginnings of Greek philosophy, which developed from mythology, makes it unimportant for our purpose to ask whether this mythology did or did not have a foreign origin or how this development may have occurred. It is true that the greater cultivation of the Asian peoples was still making a strong impression upon the Greeks at the time of the great Attic thinkers, yet the Greeks thought for themselves and freely among themselves, and the Greeks alone found their way to clear scientific thought ... For this reason, I adduce to the laws of autonomous thinking alone, following which I see a youthful, healthy, and strong spirit assist and constitute itself in Greece. (J.F. Fries)[40]

All the same, we do not need to search for any foreign sources: the philosophical science of the Greeks may be completely explained by recalling the spirit, the devices, and the educational status of the Hellenic tribes. If there has ever been a people which was suited to generate its sciences on its own, it was the Greek. (E. Zeller)[41]

No Asian people . . . has lifted itself to the heights of free human contemplation from which philosophy issues; philosophy is the fruit of the Hellenic spirit. (F. Michelis)[42]

The human spirit may only be enticed and able to grasp its own nature in thought where it is conscious of its own specific dignity. Since, with the exception of the Jews, it did not come to this in the Orient, then neither the rules of decorum and the outward cultivation laid down by the Chinese sages, nor the pantheistic and atheistic doctrines which the Indian spirit attained in the Mīmāṃsa and, through Kapila, in the Sāṃkhya, nor the intellectual training to which it raises itself in the Nyāya, nor, finally, the confused, half-religious and half-physical teachings of the ancient Persians and Egyptians, can lead us to speak of a pre-Hellenic philosophy or even pre-

Grecian systems. Since it was the Greeks who first perceived the *γνωϑι σεαυτον*, philosophizing, or the wish to grasp the nature of the human spirit, means to think occidentally, or at least in a Greek way, and the history of philosophy thus begins with the philosophy of the Greeks. (J.E. Erdmann)[43]

10. Ancient philosophy is essentially Greek philosophy . . . That which the mind of other peoples and especially the Orient has aspired to in a related direction has remained more or less at the stage of the primeval phantasies of the peoples. Everywhere, they lack the freedom and the concomitant nobility of thought which tolerates the thralldom of myth for only a certain length of time and only in the infant stage of experience and thought. (E. Dühring)[44]

Philosophy, as a science, could not originate among the Nordic peoples, who are distinguished through their strength and courage, but do not have culture, nor among the Orientals, who are indeed capable of producing the elements of a higher culture but who tend more to passively preserve such elements rather than improve them through mental activity, but solely among the Hellenes, who harmoniously unite mental power and receptivity within themselves. (F. Überweg/M. Heinze)[45]

(In the most recent edition, which appeared in 1926 and was reprinted in 1967, the passage just cited was replaced by the following:[46]

Among the Orientals, speculation generally remains so much in the service of religion and the individual sciences that we cannot speak of them as having a philosophy in the actual sense. The Indians form an exception. While their thinking is also closely associated with religion, it is not bound to it to the same degree, exhibiting a very respectable cultivation, especially in the direction of metaphysics and logic.

To be sure, nothing of the substance of Indian philosophy is presented even in this, the latest complete edition of Überweg's *Grundriss*; an overview of the more recent secondary literature on Indian philosophy, compiled with the assistance of the Indologist E. Hultzsch and included in the bibliographic section appended to the work, is held to suffice.)

The first scientific treatment of metaphysics may be found among the Greeks. Here, for the first time, an endeavor was made to free metaphysics from its amalgamation with religious notions formed by the imagination, to place it on its own feet, and to bring it into scientific form by reflecting upon concepts in a reasonable manner. (E. von Hartmann)[47]

Even if one admits that the beginnings of moral philosophy raised themselves above moralizing among the Chinese and, moreover, the beginnings of logic rose above mere occasional reflection to scientific concept formation among the Indians – which is not what we intend to speak of here – these nevertheless remain so far removed from the self-consistent and self-contained course of European philosophy that there is no reason for a textbook to concern itself with these developments. (W. Windelband)[48]

"Just as its name, so philosophy itself is originally Greek." (J. Bergmann)[49]

11. Such opinions were by no means limited to the nineteenth century or to the study of the history of philosophy as practiced in the German-speaking countries. They were also expressed elsewhere, and well into the twentieth century. The histories of philosophy which were written in England and America are, in fact, often even more laconic and exhibit an even greater tendency to take the exclusion of India and the Orient from the history of philosophy for granted.

"It is the distinguishing peculiarity of the Greeks, that they were the only people of the ancient world, who were prompted to assume a scientific attitude in explaining the mysteries which surrounded them." (G.H. Lewes)[50]

"Philosophy originated in the ancient world among the Greek people." (S.G. Martin)[51]

"No one now will suggest that Greek philosophy came from India, and indeed everything points to the conclusion that Indian philosophy came from Greece ... Of course, the mysticism of the Upanishads and of Buddhism were of native growth and profoundly influenced philosophy, but were not themselves philosophy in any true sense of the word." (J. Burnet)[52]

"Even the theories of Oriental peoples . . . consist, in the main, of mythological and ethical doctrines, and are not thorough-going systems of thought."[53] (In the third edition of this work by F. Thilly, as revised by L. Wood,[54] the following change appears: ". . . are rarely complete systems of thought.")

"Philosophy begins with Thales." (B. Russell)[55]

Likewise, "Indian philosophy," together with some of its associated concepts, leads a rather unassuming existence within the philosophical lexica of the nineteenth and early twentieth centuries.[56] Thus, for example, W.T. Krug's *Allgemeines Handwörterbuch der philosophischen Wissenschaften*[57] includes a relatively detailed article on "Indian Philosophy or Wisdom" which can hardly be described as an adequate summary of the contemporary state of knowledge. One remarkable exception to all this is the article which B. Saint-Hilaire wrote for the *Dictionnaire des sciences philosophiques* (edited by A. Franck, 1844 ff.).[58] Entitled "Indiens (Philosophie des)," it closes with the words: "... in the history of philosophy, nothing is more novel and more important today than the study of the Indian systems" ("...rien dans l'histoire de la philosophie n'est aujourd'hui plus neuf ni plus important que l'étude des systèmes indiens.")

12. If we look once more at the passages cited above and the reasons which they present or presuppose to justify the exclusion of India and the Orient

from the history of philosophy, we will see that two factors may be noted which the authors themselves did not always clearly differentiate:

1. the exclusion of the Oriental world from the genetic context of the European history of philosophy;

2. the exclusion of the Orient from the domain to which the concept of philosophy is applicable.

The first of these two perspectives is clearly dominant, for example, in the statement of E. Zeller. Moreover, it is obvious that in his case such a demarcation was also made in the interest of responsible historical and philological research, and in opposition to theories of origins which were speculative in nature and too often dilettantish. Zeller's criticism was directed against the work of E. Röth,[59] but even more so against the numerous treatises of A. Gladisch, who posited relationships between key figures and movements of early Greek thought and various Oriental traditions, e.g., between Empedocles and the Egyptians,[60] Heraclitus and Zoroaster,[61] and the Eleatics and the Indians.[62]

At the same time, the motivation to maintain a closed and comprehensible framework and context for the history of philosophy as a discipline also became increasingly apparent, as in the justification for excluding India given by W. Windelband. The historiography of philosophy had increasingly turned into a specialized research discipline committed to stringent methodological criteria. There was no room for sweeping world-historical assessments and speculative comparisons. Instead, it was the task of the historian of philosophy to investigate the developmental histories of specific concepts and problems, and to clarify the genetic relationships between various teachings in a philologically responsible fashion. The internal history of Western, i.e., Greek and Judaeo-Christian thought, provided a suitable domain for this hermeneutical and methodological orientation, and its commitment to historical and philological mastery.

13. The increasingly pronounced philological research ethic resulted in the leading nineteenth-century historians of philosophy distancing themselves not just from Schopenhauer and Schelling but also more and more from Hegel.[63] Professional philosophers as well as historians of philosophy tended to avoid the speculative universalism of these thinkers, as well as the various ways in which they had opened themselves to the Orient and India.

The occasional excursions which the academic representatives of philosophy (with, of course, the exception of Deussen) made into the realm of Indian studies generally remained so dilettantish and so unacceptable for Indological research that they provided little incentive to continue such work, and actually served more as deterrents. This was the case, for example, with the "Indo-Greek study" by C.B. Schlüter entitled *Aristoteles' Metaphysik, eine Tochter der Samkhya-Lehre des Kapila* (Münster, 1874).

Discussing this work, A. Weber, one of the leading Indologists of the nineteenth century, remarked: "When a 'professor of philosophy' writes about a topic such as the one discussed in the present work, then one may especially request that he acquire the right material, that he not merely draw from second and third-hand sources, but go to the original sources themselves, which are available for the case. The present author, hoever, did not in any way do this."[64] Until well into the twentieth century, such work as that of the philosopher A. Dyroff, who linked his systematic philosophical deliberations (in this case concerning aesthetics) to specialized Indological research, viz. H. Jacobis' German translation of Ānandavardhana's *Dhvanyāloka*,[65] was a rare exception to the rule.

In a number of cases, the authors or editors of general works dealing with the history of philosophy found it expedient to leave Oriental thought to specialists who were better suited to the task. Since the turn of the twentieth century in particular, this division of scientific responsibility which no longer aims at a unified design has become prevalent in anthologies and other cooperative efforts. Here, we may recall such works at the *Allgemeine Geschichte der Philosophie*, edited by P. Hinneberg as a volume of his series *Kultur der Gegenwart*.[66] Therein, Hinneberg abdicated all claims to unity or integration, and assigned the task of writing the chapters on India, China, etc. to specialists in the respective areas. The *Geschichte der Philosophie in Einzeldarstellungen*, edited by G. Kafka, took a similar approach. For his *Histoire de la philosophie*, E. Bréhier asked P. Masson-Oursel to prepare a supplementary volume entitled *La philosophie en Orient*.[67] The specialists themselves, i.e., those Indologists who dealt with Indian philosophy, seldom took a stance vis-à-vis the opinions expressed by the historians of philosophy. To be sure, several Indologists did play an active role in the nineteenth-century discussion concerning the genetic relationships between Indian and Greek thought and the possibility of the two having influenced one another. Among the German-speaking Indologists who participated, we may mention the names of Chr. Lassen, A. Weber, L. von Schröder, and R. Garbe.[68] Yet it may not be claimed that the ideas advanced from the Indological camp met with great approval among the historians of philosophy or were even given serious consideration. Moreover, the Indological interest in these questions has also waned since the first decades of the twentieth century.

14. Apart from the question of genetic relationships, most of the remarks cited above seem to imply that the very *concept* of philosophy itself was fundamentally unsuited for dealing with the Indian and Oriental traditions. This is not just an expression of doubt concerning the factual occurrence of the "phenomenon" of philosophy in the Orient, but also a self-demarcation, self-representation, and self-assertion of Europe in the name of a particular concept of philosophy. At the same time, it reflects the European sense of

superiority characteristic of the nineteenth century. And not only in spite of the ever more extensively available non-European material, but also in response to it, some historians of philosophy concentrated their efforts even more exclusively upon their own tradition and origins while emphasizing the singularity and uniqueness of "philosophy."

The concept of philosophy was associated with a twofold concept of freedom:

1. a freedom from practical interests - from soteriological motives and from ordinary utilitarian interests; i.e., a "purely theoretical" attitude in which knowledge is sought for its own sake;[69]

2. a freedom from the grip of dogma, from myth, and from religious and other traditions; i.e., the freedom to criticize, to think rationally, and to think for oneself.

To a certain extent, this use of the concept of philosophy, which invokes the spirit of "pure theory" and of "autonomous thinking" and which has occasionally led to excursions into a "characterology" of nations and cultures,[70] can be traced back to the Greeks themselves and their self-understanding and self-assertion in the face of the Orient.[71] Furthermore, the notions of "pure science" and "true" philosophy reflect the Cartesian ideal of total freedom from prejudice. As we have already seen, Cartesianism led to some of the first of the modern demarcations against Oriental thought. As a result of this orientation, every type of traditionalism came to be viewed as unphilosophical or even anti-philosophical, a fact which also serves to explain why the Middle Ages were given such a short shrift by the leading nineteenth-century historians of philosophy.[72] It is a telling fact that the two most famous and monumental nineteenth-century works on the history of philosophy dealt with the history of Greek philosophy (E. Zeller) and the history of modern, i.e., post-Cartesian philosophy (K. Fischer).

15. Towards the end of his life, E. Husserl appealed to the spirit of Greek "theory" and Cartesian "freedom from prejudice" (the perfection of which he saw in his own phenomenology) in order to distinguish "European mankind" from the Indian and all the other Oriental traditions.[73] He proclaimed such philosophy, rooted as it was in an "attitude of pure theory" and founded upon the Greek sense of "wonder" as a genuinely European phenomenon, an "original phenomenon of intellectual Europe" ("Urphänomen des geistigen Europa"), and as something through which the Occident would have to rediscover its own teleology and its "universal human mission" ("menschheitliche Sendung").[74] Not long before this, F. Boll, a historian of science, presented a kind of programmatic retrospect and proclaimed the notions of pure theory and free research as constitutive for the identity and self-preservation of Europe.[75]

The ideas of pure theory and free science have also affected the leading Indologists of the nineteenth and twentieth centuries. Moreover, they set standards for those authors who are otherwise considered to be exemplary representatives of the historical and philological study of Indian philosophy and who do not explicitly involve themselves in the philosophical discussions about the concept of philosophy and the question of its applicability to the non-European traditions. This is as true for R. Garbe's treatment of the Sāṃkhya as "Indian Rationalism" as it is for H. Oldenberg's view of the transition from the Brāhmaṇas to the Upaniṣads or for H. Jacobi's attempts to find a program for an independent, theoretically-oriented science in the concept of *ānvīkṣikī*.[76] It is especially significant in the work of E. Frauwallner, who, like few others, has helped to historically and philologically open up the Indian philosophical literature while deliberately precluding all philosophical interpretation and evaluation from his research program: The orientation towards the concept of "pure theory" has not only shaped his view that the Vaiśeṣika is an originally and fundamentally unsoteriological system, it has also influenced his periodization of Indian philosophy. He tried to demonstrate that there had been a period of Indian thought characterized by purely theoretical, scientific interests upon which, however, soteriological motives later came to be superimposed. He thus found the spirit of "real philosophy" which the nineteenth-century historians of philosophy had thought to be lacking in the form of a kind of hidden layer lying within the history of Indian philosophy.[77] In an entirely different direction, such recent authors as B.K. Matilal have attempted to measure Indian thought by the standards of "scientific", analytical and purely theoretical philosophy and to vindicate its "truly philosophical" dimensions against the views of earlier historians of philosophy.[78]

16. There is no need for us to concern ourselves in any greater detail with the problems that have become increasingly obvious in the interim with respect to the concepts of pure theory or "value-free" science, nor shall we go into the ambivalence and dialectic inherent in the relationship between theory and practice that had already become manifest during the time of the Greeks. We shall also ignore at this point the historical changes these themes have undergone within the Western tradition,[79] and leave unanswered the question whether or to what extent the above-cited opinions about the applicability of the concepts of philosophy and theory actually correspond to the Indian material.[80] In the present context, our primary concern has been with ways in which Europe viewed and represented itself while responding to the question whether "there is" philosophy in India.[81]

The question as to whether and in what ways "there is" philosophy in traditional India has, however, not been decisive for the development of the European philosophical interest in Indian thought. From very different angles, and in the name of very divergent philosophies and ideologies, ideas and preconceptions about Indian thought have been enlisted as means of self-understanding, self-affirmation, and self-critique. The interest in, or dismissal of, Indian thought has been associated with the proclamation of one's own identity as well as the search for alternatives. Such crucial motifs as pantheism, quietism, and Stoicism, and questions concerning the "original revelation" and the relationship between philosophy and religion have also been tied to the study of India in a variety of ways. Regardless of the question whether there has been an equivalent to Greek-European "philosophy" and "theory" in India - the idea of India has had a significant impact upon the manner in which Europe has articulated, defined, and questioned itself and its fundamental and symptomatic concepts of theory, science, and philosophy.

10. Preliminary Postscript: The Hermeneutic Situation in the Twentieth Century

1. It is obvious that the conditions of the encounter and "dialogue" between India and the West have changed drastically during the twentieth century. An analysis of these developments, and of the complexities of the current situation, will not be attempted in this book.[1]

The two world wars, the end of colonialism, India's indepencence have affected the identity of the participants in the dialogue. European self-questioning and self-destruction have progressed rapidly. The emergence of America, Russia and Japan as protagonists of the modern world has changed the meaning of "East" and "West." There has been an unprecedented multiplication of channels of international communication and interaction, and an explosion of easily accessible information. In the world of modern technology, "encounters" and "dialogues" have become much easier, but also much more ambiguous and questionable.

During this period, Indological research has been carried on from different angles and at different levels, and it has made available to the West a vast amount of data and interpretations concerning India. There is still the historical and philological approach, which continues to derive its data and its direction from the Indian texts themselves and is primarily interested in historical reconstruction. In addition, anthropological and sociological approaches have become increasingly important; they focus on the Indian cultural and religious tradition in its actual manifestations, and they try to understand it in a functional manner, with reference to or even in terms of social, economic, ethnographic, and behavioral phenomena. And there are, of course, the existentially or ideologically involved approaches, which find in the Indian tradition a genuine religious, philosophical or theological challenge and respond to it from the angle of specific world-views or religious convictions.

Academic research is only one mode of presence of the Indian tradition in the Western world. In addition, we have its presence in the arts, literature, popular cults, methods of meditation, sectarian movements, "transpersonal psychology," the syndrome of "ancient wisdom and modern science," and so forth. There are, moreover, the many ways in which Indians themselves present and interpret their tradition to the West. Are the boundaries finally dissolving? Has there been a genuine "fusion of horizons"? Have the errors and preconceptions of the past been replaced with openness and understanding? Or is the sheer quantity and diversity of the available information in itself a threat to the "living spirit" of the encounter and dialogue?

2. How do Western philosophers respond to the new situation? Have they learned to include Indian thought in their horizon, to appreciate it *as* philosophy, or to accept it as a challenge and alternative to what they call philosophy? Is the attitude of Eurocentric exclusivism among the historians of philosophy, which we have described in the preceding chapter, a matter of the past? Has it been superseded once and for all?

As stated earlier, we are not dealing in this book with the most recent developments and the current status of the encounter between India and the West. Our presentation is an historical introduction which leads us only to the threshold of the twentieth century. Accordingly, we will not try to answer these questions in a comprehensive fashion. We will only try to indicate briefly certain basic trends and prospects and, above all, to articulate some open questions.

It is undeniable that there is currently a greater willingness to credit India with a philosophical tradition of its own, and to include some information about it in general reference works on philosophy and its history. Exclusivistic statements such as those which we quoted in the preceding chapter have, indeed, become rare in our days. While P. Edwards' *Encyclopedia of Philosophy* (New York, 1967) offers at least a survey article on "Indian Philosophy," the monumental *Historisches Wörterbuch der Philosophie* ("Historical Dictionary of Philosophy") which was founded by J. Ritter, has, in addition, a number of more specific articles on Indian concepts.[2] The currently most comprehensive bibliographical work on the general history of philosophy, W. Totok's *Handbuch der Geschichte der Philosophie,* contains a lengthy section on the "philosophy of the Indians." The compiler introduces this section with the following programmatic statement:

> The philosophical historiography of the Orient has included Indian thought in its domain of scholarly investigation only late and with hesitation. The reason for such hesitation was partly the insufficient philological exploration of the sources, and partly the special method of Indian philosophizing, which is in various respects different from the European one. The research work of several generations of European and Indian scholars was necessary to secure for Indian philosophy the recognition which it deserves as one of the most outstanding documents of the human speculative spirit.[3]

F. Überweg's *Grundriss der Geschichte der Philosophie*, for more than a century one of the most authoritative academic handbooks on the history of philosophy, provides an interesting illustration. While its earlier editions followed the common practice of excluding India, its new edition, which is currently under preparation, will deal extensively with Indian thought.[4] It has also become more familiar to find Indian contributions included in historical surveys of specific philosophical disciplines, for instance in I.M. Bochenski's history of logic (*Formale Logik*, Freiburg, 1956; second edition: 1962). In the last (and unfinished) major work by K. Jaspers, *Die grossen Philosophen* ("The Great Philosophers," Munich, 1957), we find chapters on the Buddha and Nāgārjuna.[5]

3. The basic trend exemplified by these works has, however, not affected the teaching of philosophy and its history in the European, and specifically German, universities. There is currently no professor of philosophy in Germany whose dedication to Indian philosophy could in any way be compared to that of P. Deussen in the early decades of this century. To a certain extent, and in accordance with the role of A. Schopenhauer, interest in Indian thought is still associated with non-academic philosophy; as an example we may mention the work of J. Gebser.[6]

The situation is somewhat different in North America, although the prevailing climate of analytic and science-oriented philosophy is not generally favorable to the study of Indian philosophy. Since the end of the nineteenth century, Harvard University has developed a certain tradition of including India in the teaching of philosophy. W. James (1842–1910) often referred to Indian thought in his lectures and publications, although his attitude was not particularly sympathetic.[7] J. Royce (1855–1916), G. Santayana (1863–1952) and W.E. Hocking (1873–1966), who were also associated with Harvard, showed a remarkable interest in and appreciation of the Indian tradition.[8] J.H. Woods (1864–1935), who taught in the Department of Philosophy at Harvard and served as its chairman, devoted his scholarly energies primarily to Indian thought. His most significant contribution was published in 1914 under the title *The Yoga System of Patañjali*; it is a translation of the *Yogasūtras* together with the commentaries of Vyāsa and Vācaspatimiśra. In his own way, Woods tried to continue the work of P. Deussen, who was one of his teachers.[9]

Numerous other representatives of academic philosophy in America have dealt with Indian ideas more or less explicitly, for instance W.B. Savery, E.A. Burtt, F.S.C. Northrop, Ch. Hartshorne, A. Danto, and—again at Harvard—R. Nozick.[10] The *Encyclopedia of Indian Philosophies*, edited by K.H. Potter, is primarily meant for Western philosophers taking an interest in Indian thought.[11] Moreover, American universities, unlike European universities, employ a considerable number of Indian and other Asian scholars teaching Indian, Western and "comparative" philosophy.[12]

4. An increasing number of Western scholars try to do justice to Indian philosophy by treating it simply "as philosophy," regardless of its cultural and historical origin and context, and dealing with it in terms of truth and validity. In most cases, this amounts to an application of methods and criteria of modern logic and epistemology or, more specifically, of current Anglo-Saxon analytic philosophy. This perspective focuses on the technical, systematic achievements of Indian philosophy, and it tries to measure and clarify them by using the "most advanced" standards of modern Western thought. Almost inevitably, Indian thought appears as a more or less successful approximation to these standards.[13]

Others expect from India alternatives to the Western attitudes and preoccupations. They hope to find human possibilities and dimensions of meaning which are less developed or even absent in the West. They look for synthesis, dialogue, mutual supplementation, even therapy. In this sense, F.S.C. Northrop invokes "the meeting of East and West."[14] W.E. Hocking says that "we need not only two but many eyes," and he refers to a hierarchy of three historic attitudes towards foreign cultures, specifically the East: 1. "This is strange and alien—avoid it." 2. "This is strange and alien—investigate it." 3. "This appears strange and alien—but it is human; it is therefore kindred to me and potentially my own—learn from it."[15]

Hocking's statements appeared in a volume edited by Ch. A. Moore (1901-1967), who was one of the most dedicated advocates of a "meeting" of Asia, specifically India, and the West. Since 1939, he organized "East West Philosophers' Conferences" at the University of Hawaii. He also founded the journal *Philosophy East and West* and edited *A Source Book in Indian Philosophy* (with S. Radhakrishnan; first published in 1957). Throughout his career, he tried to further the cause of "synthesis" and "comparison" and to naturalize Indian thought in American academic and scholarly life.[16] Moore's unbroken optimism, his faith in the philosophical and "synthetic" potential of organized meetings, his unquestioning reliance on "personal representatives" of Eastern religious and philosophical traditions, his immunity from hermeneutical scruples—this in itself is a remarkable and symptomatic phenomenon. In a sense, Moore's efforts continued the tradition of the first "World Parliament of Religions" which was held in Chicago in 1893.[17]

Are we ready for meetings and synthetic efforts of this kind? Are we ready for philosophical evaluations and comparisons? Are the "personal representatives" of the Indian and other Asian traditions ready to transmit the authentic meaning of these traditions to the West? Or should we follow the example and explicit advice of E. Frauwallner (1898-1974) and other leading philologists of Indian thought who demonstrate through their work the significance of patient textual work, and its priority over all generalizations and comparative evaluations?[18]

5. Is it still too early for serious and significant philosophical responses to Indian thought? Is this field not yet ready for Western philosophers? Should we await further advances in the philological exploration of the Indian sources? Or is it the progress of Indological research itself which teaches us to be more modest and cautious, and to abstain from applying our own philosophical notions and perspectives?

In a statement published in 1949 and referring to the work of W. Dilthey, H.-G. Gadamer says:

> Although in the meantime the research in Eastern philosophy has made further advances, we believe today that we are further removed from its philosophical understanding. The sharpening of our historical awareness has rendered the translations or adaptations of the texts . . . fundamentally problematic. . . . We cannot speak of an appropriation of these things by the Occidental philosophy. What can be considered established is only the negative insight that our own basic concepts, which were coined by the Greeks, alter the essence of what is foreign.[19]

It would hardly serve the cause of Indian thought in the West, and of a philosophical "dialogue" with the Indian tradition, if we would simply dismiss such considerations or leave their dissipation to the progress of Indological reaearch. The recognition of the other, the foreign as such is a decisive step on the way to its understanding. It is the lack of such recognition which accounts for the naive and superficial character of so many statements on Indian and "comparative" philosophy. In the context of hermeneutics, Gadamer's apparently negative and destructive critique has, nevertheless, a positive potential: It can encourage us to see the fact that, in approaching Indian thought, we carry with us our Western perspectives and presuppositions not merely as an impediment and aggravation, but as a necessary and positive ingredient of understanding itself.[20]

Gadamer's hermeneutics teaches us to accept "prejudice" ("Vorurteil") as something indispensable, and to discard the abstract and vacuous ideal of an entirely open and "unprejudiced" understanding. It shows that understanding cannot amount to slipping into somebody else's skin, as it were, and to comprehend or experience the foreign, the other simply in its own identity, or by coinciding with it. Understanding ancient Indian thought cannot mean "becoming like the ancient Indians," thinking and seeing the world exactly like them. We are not capable of such "objectivity," and if we were, we would obviously *not* be "like the Indians." The goal of a radical "philosophical εποχη,"[21] an unqualified abstention from one's own background and presuppositions, is unrealistic and undesirable. We cannot and need not "disregard" ourselves in the process of understanding.[22] Postulates like that of Betty Heimann, that India ought to be explained "exclusively out of its own peculiarity" ("ausschliesslich aus seiner Eigenart"),[23] are questionable not only because of the many practical obstacles which stand in their way.

6. What we need is not sheer "neutrality" and "extinction of one's self," but "the conscious assimilation of one's own fore-meanings and prejudices": "The important thing is to be aware of one's own bias, so that the text"—and why not an Indian text?—"may present itself in all its newness and thus be able to assert its own truth against one's own fore-meanings."[24] Should Gadamer's concepts of "hermeneutical conversation" or "dialogue" ("hermeneutisches Gespräch") and "fusion of horizons" ("Horizontverschmelzung"), which he develops in his controversial classic *Wahrheit und Methode* ("Truth and Method"), not also be pertinent to the interpretation of Indian thought and its literary documents?

In utilizing these concepts, and in executing his project of a "philosophical hermeneutics," Gadamer confines himself to the Western tradition which originated with the Greeks. He responds to "the tradition from which we come" ("Überlieferung, aus der wir kommen"). He explores and practices the "fusion of horizons" as it occurs between different periods or layers of the Western tradition, i.e. with reference to a past which has to be assimilated by the present: " . . . the horizon of the present cannot be formed without the past. There is no more an isolated horizon of the present than there are historical horizons. Understanding, rather, is always the fusion of these horizons which we imagine to exist by themselves."[25]

The exclusion of non-European materials from Gadamer's work has obviously contributed to its impressive density and cohesiveness. There is, however, no compelling reason why its hermeneutical concepts and perspectives should not be applicable in a wider, trans-cultural context. Indeed, we belong to the European tradition which has its origins in Greece. But this tradition has its own modes of openness and self-transcendence. Within the European tradition itself, there has been a "fusion" of different cultural horizons—Greek, Roman, Hebrew, etc. That we relate to other traditions, does not imply that we are estranged from "our own" tradition. The phenomena of understanding and misunderstanding, which occur "within" a particular tradition, need not be fundamentally different from those which we encounter when we try to approach other traditions. We have no reason to assume more than a difference in degree, which may, however, be very significant. Just as the access to texts in foreign languages, the access to foreign traditions represents "simply an extreme case of hermeneutical difficulty, i.e. of alienness and its conquest."[26]

7. Gadamer himself says: "Just as the individual is never simply an individual, because he is always involved with others, so too the closed horizon that is supposed to enclose a culture is an abstraction. The historical movement of human life consists in the fact that it is never utterly

bound to any one standpoint, and hence can never have a truly closed horizon. The horizon is, rather, something into which we move and that moves with us."[27] Regardless of all specific problems of communication and interpretation, this statement obviously applies to the general encounter between India and Europe, and to the "horizon" of Western self-understanding in its relationship with the Indian tradition.

Understanding, as well as misunderstanding, takes place in the European encounter with Indian and Oriental thought, just as it takes place in Europe's relationship with its own Greek sources, and just as it has taken place in the encounter between other traditions. In a general sense this is obviously correct. But it is not necessarily adequate, and it leads us to further questions. Is the relationship between India and the West indeed an encounter between two traditions? Is the modern West still a tradition? Are its ways of dealing with other traditions, it methods of objectifying historical and anthropological research, still ways of intercultural communication, interaction or even domination? Is it not their inherent claim to provide something more universal—a global medium and framework of communication, the freedom to approach and "understand" *any* tradition in an "objective," scientific manner? Or does this achievement of universality conceal another, perhaps more fundamental and elusive problem of communication—that between objectifying and detached "research" on the one side and commitment to a living tradition on the other? In other words, is the distance between "tradition" and "modernity" greater than that between any particular traditions?

According to Gadamer, historical research and the "scientific attitude to the past" have more in common with the living continuity of traditions than is obvious at first sight.

> At the beginning of all historical hermeneutics, then, the abstract antithesis between tradition and historical research, between history and knowledge (about it), must be discarded. The effect of a living tradition and the effect of historical study must constitute a unity, the analysis of which would reveal only a texture of reciprocal relationships. Hence we would do well not to regard historical consciousness as something radically new—as it seems at first—but as a new element within that which has always made up the human relationship with the past.[28]

Modern historical research itself continues to be "transmission of tradition" ("Vermittlung von Überlieferung").[29]

8. The attitude of historical research and "understanding" is a particular way of being *in* the European tradition. It arose at a particular point in its history and is certainly not a total break with it.[30] Is it also a universal human potential which happened to become fully manifest in Europe, but is the implicit *telos* of other traditions as well? Does it fulfil their own aspirations to be "understood" in this sense? Or is this enterprise of historical

"understanding" inseparable from its origin and fundamentally Eurocentric? Does this refer us back to Hegel?

In statements quoted by J.L. Mehta, M. Merleau-Ponty refers to Europe's "onerous task of understanding others" and its "idea of truth which requires and authorizes it to understand other cultures"; and he presents what Mehta calls a "classic formulation of the Western concern with understanding" the traditions of Asia:

> China and India are not entirely aware of what they are saying. What they need to do to have philosophies is to try to *understand* themselves and everything else. Although these remarks are commonplace today, they do not settle the question. They come to us from Hegel. He was the one who invented the idea of 'going beyond' the Orient by 'understanding' it. It was Hegel who contrasted the Western idea of truth as the total conceptual recovery of the world in all its variety to the Orient, and defined the Orient as a failure in the same understanding.[31]

Unlike Merleau-Ponty, E. Husserl does not invoke Hegel when he refers to the "innate entelechy" of Europe, which directs it towards an "absolute idea," a universality above and beyond all "merely empirical anthropological" types such as "China" and "India."[32] The European tradition is not simply a cultural tradition among others. It owes its identity to the ideas of "philosophy" and "pure theory," and it has a unique global mission. Europe alone can provide other traditions with a universal framework of meaning and understanding. They will have to "Europeanize themselves, whereas we, if we understand ourselves properly, will never, for example, Indianize ourselves."[33] The "Europeanization of all foreign parts of mankind" ("Europäisierung aller fremden Menschheiten") is the destiny of the earth.[34]

M. Heidegger, too, refers to the "complete Europeanization of the earth and of mankind" ("vollständige Europäisierung der Erde und des Menschen");[35] and he agrees with Husserl in crediting only the Greek-European tradition with a genuine concept of philosophy. But his assessment of this situation has little in common with Husserl's proclamation of the global mission of Europe. Moreover, his understanding of the relationship between "natural" and "historical" sciences, and of the role of "science" and "research" in the modern world, is significantly different from that of Gadamer, who is otherwise deeply indebted to him.

In spite of its notoriously enigmatic and elusive character, Heidegger's thought opens more radical perspectives on the situation of the modern world and the possibility of "dialogues" with the East than that of Gadamer or Husserl.[36]

9. In accordance with W. Dilthey, Gadamer proclaims the peculiar character and the special dignity of historical understanding, as we find it in the "human sciences" ("Geisteswissenschaften"). He emphasizes the "ele-

ment of tradition" in the "Geisteswissenschaften" and the fact that unlike the natural sciences they are not dominated by the ideas of "research and progress."[37] He even criticizes Dilthey for the concessions which he made to the goals and methods of the natural sciences, and for his attempts to turn history itself into "an object."[38]

Heidegger, on the other hand, is far less concerned with distinguishing "natural" and "human sciences." Instead, he emphasizes the pervasive character of calculating, objectifying, "representational" methods of "research" in all sciences: "Knowledge as research calls reality to account how and to what extent it can be made available to representational thinking." ("Das Erkennen als Forschung zieht das Seiende zur Rechenschaft darüber, wie es und wie weit es dem Vorstellen verfügbar zu machen ist.")[39] It is part of the globalized situation of the modern technological world, which is dominated by what Heidegger calls the "Gestell," or more fully: "vor-, her- und bestellbares Gestell" ("representable, produceable and operable constellation"). This universal technological "constellation" does not distinguish between "natural" and "human sciences." There is no simple retreat from it – neither into "historical understanding" nor into an inner world of contemplation or meditation. And no calculated methods of self-transformation, or of importation and application of Eastern ways of thinking, can help us gain freedom from the constellation of the modern world.

Science and technology are the marks of Westernization. They have brought about the "Europeanization of the earth." Unlike Husserl, Heidegger does not present such "Europeanization" as a proud and unambiguous achievement. Science and technology are the ultimate expression and consequence of those ways of representational, objectifying, "metaphysical" thinking which began in ancient Greece and which constitute the essence of philosophy in its genuine, i.e. Greek-European sense. Philosophy in this sense, which implies a deep "forgetfulness of being" ("Seinsvergessenheit"), is the mother of science and technology, and of the "Atomic Age." There is no non-European philosophy of this kind, "neither Chinese nor Indian."[40]

> The phrase 'Occidental-European philosphy' which one so often hears is in truth a tautology. Why? Because 'philosophy' is in essence Greek . . . To say that philosophy is in essence Greek is the same as to say that the Occident and Europe, and they alone, are in their inmost historical course originally philosophical. This is proved by the rise and domination of the sciences. Because they originate from the inmost Occidental-European course of history, namely the philosophical, therefore they are today in a position to give their specific stamp upon the history of man on the whole earth . . . The word φιλοσοφια appears as it were as the birth-certificate of our own history; we might even say, as the birth-certificate of the contemporary epoch in world-history which calls itself the Atomic Age.[41]

10. Heidegger's thesis concerning the Greek-European origin and essence of "philosophy" and "science" is no longer a self-confident proclamation of the uniqueness of Europe as it was for the historians of the nineteenth century and still Husserl. It is, rather, a statement concerning a global predicament. Europeanization "eats away all substance from things."[42] Metaphysics is "one single, but perhaps also the necessary predicament of the Occident, and the condition of its planetary domination."[43]

We have to go back to the Greek sources of the modern world. We have to understand its origination out of certain fundamental constellations and decisions of early European thought. This Western self-exploration, this "dialogue with the Greek thinkers," has "hardly been prepared"; and yet it is only the prelude to "the inescapable dialogue with the East Asian World."[44] In the words of J.L. Mehta, Heidegger sees early Greek metaphysics "as pregnant with the entire development which, through its culmination in the scientific and technological mode of thinking dominating the man of today, has assumed a planetary importance, far exceeding the limits of a geographically or historically localized 'culture' or 'civilization.'"[45] How can there be a "dialogue" with Asia if the European "mode of thinking" has already attained planetary domination?

In the modern planetary situation, Eastern and Western "cultures" can no longer meet one another as equal partners. They meet *in* a Westernized world, under conditions shaped by Western ways of thinking. But is this "universality" the true *telos* of mankind? Could it be that the global openness of modernity is still a parochially Western horizon? Or was Europe itself somehow left behind by the universality which it had inaugurated? Did it help others to gain freedom and distance from their traditional foundations, while it remained committed to its own roots and—paradoxically—within its "traditional" horizon?[46]

Heidegger refers again and again to the global, universal domination of the Greek-Western "scientific" way of thinking. But he also makes it very clear that this in itself cannot constitute the framework and medium for the future dialogue with the East. The "thinking of the future," which will be ready for this dialogue, can no longer be "philosophy because it thinks on a more fundamental level than metaphysics—a term which means the same."[47] Neither the language of "science," nor that of "metaphysics," nor that of "historical understanding" can provide the proper medium for a dialogue in which all these ideas themselves will have to be questioned. We have to transcend "what is European" ("das Europäische"); we have to reach "beyond Occident and Orient."[48] Yet, neither Orient nor Occident seems capable of opening and establishing a medium and "sphere of their possible dialogue" ("Bereich ihrer möglichen Zwiesprache").[49]

In his own way, Heidegger accepts the Hegelian diagnosis that there is no escape from history and the global presence of European thought; but to him, this does not mean that ancient or non-Western traditions are superseded by, "aufgehoben" in modern Western thought. They may, in fact, reach far beyond our current capacity of comprehension. They may not be accessible to the very ideas of "research" and "theoretical mastery." We have to detach ourselves from the spell of methodic research and progress. The enigmatic future "dialogue" with the East, to which Heidegger refers, cannot be planned and organized. What we may have to learn above all is "Gelassenheit," a serene willingness to wait, and *not* to plan for this future.[50]

II

The Indian Tradition and the Presence of Europe

11. Traditional Indian Xenology

1. The changing attitudes towards India and the various manifestations of interest in, or "search" for, the Indian tradition which we have explored in the preceding chapters are also expressions of European self-understanding, self-affirmation and self-criticism. They accompany European history from its Greek beginnings, and they reflect basic changes in European thought and life. There is no parallel or analogous development of Indian interest in or speculation about Europe. Thus there can be no symmetry in the historical presentation of the encounter between Europe and India and their mutual approaches and responses in the areas of religion and philosophy.

Traditional Hinduism has not reached out for the West. It has not been driven by the zeal of proselytization and discovery, and by the urge to understand and master foreign cultures. It has neither recognized the foreign, the other as a possible alternative, nor as a potential source of its own identity. "It has at no time *defined itself* in relation to the other, nor acknowledged the other in its unassimilable otherness."[1] India has discovered the West and begun to respond to it in being sought out, explored, overrun and objectified by it. Its initial position in the encounter was that of a target of European interests and expectations. It was not the course of Indian history, nor the inner dynamism of the Hindu tradition, that led to the encounter. Europeans took the initiative. They went to India. This is a simple and familiar fact. Yet its fundamental significance for the hermeneutics of the encounter between India and the West is often forgotten.

2. The period around 1800, which saw the full establishment of European power and presence in India, also saw the beginnings of modern Indology, i.e. the scientific exploration and objectification of India's past. The combination of these two events, which is more than a temporal coincidence, had a fundamental impact upon Indian attitudes towards themselves and the "other." Indians took a more and more active part in the European

enterprise of exploring India's past, and they began presenting themselves to the world in a new fashion. They tried to disengage themselves from the status of mere objects or instruments of Western curiosity, and they took more distinctive initiatives to interpret their identity for the Europeans, and to defend and affirm it against them. They began to demarcate themselves against the foreign and to recognize the other, but in a new sense they also tried to comprehend and assimilate the Western ideas within the framework of their own tradition. They responded to the universalistic claims of Western thought with a universalism of their own. They opened, even exposed themselves to the West. But this very openness appeared as a confirmation and consummation of their own tradition, its potential of universality and inclusiveness. Today, the presence of European ideas in Indian thought is far more pervasive than the presence of Indian ideas in the West. What is the meaning of this "Westernization," this apparent intellectual subjugation of India by the West? Is it sheer alienation, or does it conceal an underlying strength and flexibility of the Indian tradition?

The Indians reinterpreted key concepts of their traditional self-understanding, adjusting them to Western modes of understanding. By appealing to the West, by using its conceptual tools, they tried to secure and defend the identity and continuity of their tradition. Were they successful? Did they preserve and perhaps enrich their tradition by presenting it to the West? Did they rediscover their identity in this new and unprecedented exposure to the other? What was new in the encounter with the West, as it occurred around 1800? How does the new response to the Europeans, specifically the British, differ from earlier encounters with foreigners? Was it a radical transformation, perhaps even denial of traditional Indian "xenology"? What precisely was the nature and development of traditional Indian "xenology,"[2] of responding, or failing to respond to the foreign, the other?

3. As we have stated earlier, there is no history of an Indian search for, and exploration of, Europe which could be placed side by side with the European "search" for India. The Indian perspectives on Europe call for another method of presentation than the European attitudes towards India. The situation of the encounter and "dialogue" between India and Europe is an uneven, asymmetrical one. The two parts of this book require different approaches. The second part cannot run parallel to the first.

We will begin by giving a survey of traditional Indian xenology, and more specifically, the traditional Hindu ways of dealing with, or avoiding recognition of, foreigners. The new historical and hermeneutical conditions of the period after 1800 will then be explored and illustrated by presenting the case of the so-called "father of modern India," Rammohan Roy. The subsequent development of "modern" Indian thought and is xenological implications will only be discussed in a cursory fashion. Instead, we will focus on exemplary conceptual developments, specifically the modern Hindu reinterpretations of the concepts of *dharma* and *darśana* and their ambiguous association with the Western concepts of "religion" and "philosophy." For external and practical reasons, too, the second part of this book will have to differ from the first. We have to make adjustments to the different state of research in both areas, to differences in the accessibility and familiarity of the sources, etc. On the one hand, the discussion of the Indian attitudes and responses has to be more selective, on the other hand, we will have to pay more attention to controversial and unfamiliar details.

Our presentation will try to balance its commitment to, and distance from, the Indian and European sources. We will, however, not pursue the evasive and vacuous goal of absolute neutrality and impartiality. Our survey is itself part of the unfolding and continuing historical and hermeneutical processes with which it deals. Absolute neutrality and "objectivity," if it were possible, would be utterly abstract; or it would again be one-sided and an expression and continuation of that very Eurocentrism which it tries to avoid.

4. Again and again, Indians have been exposed to the experience of foreigners and "outsiders"; again and again, non-Indians have interfered with the course of Indian history. Long before the "Aryan" invasion and the encounter of the Vedic people with the foreign world of the Indian subcontinent, the Harappan civilization was part of a wide network of trade relations and other "international" connections. After the Aryan invasion in the second milennium B.C., foreigners have come to India in steady succession—Greeks, Persians, Central Asians, different waves of Muslims, Portuguese, Dutch, French, British. They came as conquerors, raiders and merchants, but also as refugees and pilgrims.

The Indian role was not always a passive one: In ancient and classical times, we find not only Roman merchants in India, but also Indians in the Mediterranean world. There was, moreover, the "missionary" religion of Buddhism which spread Indian ideas over vast areas of Asia and established its own network of intercultural contacts. And there was the remarkable and still enigmatic phenomenon of "Greater India"—the spread of Indian institutional and cultural phenomena and the establishment of Indianized empires in other parts of Asia, specifically in Southeast Asia. This involved the participation of Indians, including Brahmins, as advisors, craftsmen, teachers, astrologers. Finally, we have the less conspicuous, but highly significant process of assimilation of "foreign" groups in India itself—the gradual "Hinduization" of autochthonous outsiders.

How was this steady succession of contacts with foreigners and foreign challenges reflected in traditional Indian thought? How did it affect traditional Hindu self-understanding? How did the Indians refer and respond to the foreigners? Within the limits of this study, we cannot attempt a comprehensive account of the traditional Indian ways of interacting with foreigners. We can only refer to basic trends and representative ideas, and we will focus on Hindu xenology in its theoretical and normative aspects, as we find it documented in Sanskrit literature.

5. In the documents of the Vedic period, we do not find any conspicuous interest in foreign countries and cultures. But there is a clearly recognizable, though somewhat mythical awareness of the surrounding world and of foreign or hostile powers or groups or people. Vedic men referred to themselves as *ārya* (i.e., *ariya* in old Iranian), "pure," "noble," or *mānuṣa*, descendents of Manu or Manuṣ, the progenitor of the "Aryans."[3] They were a closely knit group of conquerors and immigrants who gradually took possession of the Indian sub-continent.[4] They defined their identity against its original inhabitants, the *dasyu* or *dāsa*. In the perspective of the "Aryans," these represent the foreign, the other as such and in its negative connotations. They appear as the enemies of the gods, and they are vanquished and subdued by Indra and Agni. They are excluded from the Aryan community (*amānuṣa*) and its ritual performances, vows and sacrificial offerings (*aśraddha; ayajña; avrata; anyavrata; akarman*).

Already in the Vedic period, the term *dāsa* assumes the meaning "servant" and "slave." According to later authors and lexicographers, *dasyu* and *dāsa* also refer to low castes and occupations in general.[5] Another important and ambiguous term in Vedic xenology is the word *ari*, which underwent remarkable and symptomatic semantic changes: "While in Greece the word for foreigner (ξεvFoς) becomes the word for 'guest' or 'host' (Gastfreund), the corresponding word in India becomes a term for the enemy or—in popular locution—an impolite reference to somebody whom one does not deem worthy of respect."[6] A peculiar Vedic scheme, which was already controversial in ancient time and became obsolete in the post-Vedic period refers to "five tribes" or "nations" (*kṣiti; kṛṣṭi; jana; jāta*).[7] According to the commentators, this classification may either comprise certain groups within mankind, such as the four theoretical castes (*varṇa*) and, in addition, the *niṣāda* or *niṣadha*, or it may include the totality of terrestrial and celestial beings in general. Already Yāska's *Nirukta* (fifth century B.C.) recognizes this alternative.[8]

6. Since the period of the *Brāhmaṇas* around 800 B.C., the xenological concept of *mleccha* gains increasing prominence. It refers to the foreigner, the outsider who is not part of the ritual, religious, social and linguistic community of the Aryans, who does not speak Sanskrit and does not follow the Vedic norms of the "order of castes and stages of life" (*varṇāśrama-dharma*). Occasionally, for instance in Manu, *mleccha* refers to a specific

group within the *dasyu* who are excluded and deficient for linguistic reasons.[9] The etymology of this word, which appears also in several Middle Indian variants (*milakkha, milakkhu, milāca, meccha*), remains dubious.[10] The term *barbara* (Pali *babbhara*), which has conspicuous non-Indian parallels, also refers to foreignness or exclusion from a linguistic angle.[11]

Among the later xenological terms, *yavana* (Pali *yona*) is by far the most important one. It became familiar since the early epic period and began to rival and supplement the word *mleccha*. Its foreign origin is beyond question: It is derived from Greek 'Ιαων/'Ιαονες—although probably not directly from the Greek, but through Old Persian *yauna*. The Indians probably borrowed the term when they came into contact with Greeks during the reign of the Persian king Darius I. The first Indian equivalent of *yauna* was Prakrit *yona; yavana* was then introduced as a Sanskritization of the Middle Indian form *yona*.[12] The connotation "Ionians," i.e., Greeks, or at least "invaders from the North-West," is obvious in the older usages of *yavana* or *yona*. They appear often among other border people and invaders, e.g. in Manu X, 44. Here they are mentioned together with the Central Asian *śaka*, South Indian *draviḍa*, the *darada* of the Afghan region, the *pahlava* (Persians) and *cīna* (Chinese?). All these groups are explained and classified as fallen members of the warrior caste (*kṣatriya*). Similar lists appear, for instance, in the *Mahābhārata*.[13] In these texts, the *yavana*, just like the *śaka* etc., seem to be different from the *mleccha*, who are foreigners, outsiders in a more radical sense. However, in later texts, *yavana* may also be used as a synonym of *mleccha*, and without the earlier differentiations, it refers to the "barbarian" as such who is in no way committed to the *dharma* and not genetically related to the caste system. Quite frequently, *yavana* also refers to the Muslims whose invasions began in the eighth century.[14]

7. Surveying the various older usages of *mleccha* and *yavana*, it is clear that they not only come from different sources, but also represent significantly different attitudes to foreigners. *Yavana* is a more descriptive concept which refers to specific groups of foreigners, recognizes their factual peculiarity among other such groups, and indicates a certain degree of curiosity and readiness to differentiate. *Mleccha*, on the other hand, implies a much stronger value judgement, a religious-tabooistic exclusion. It identifies the foreign, the other as violation of fundamental norms, as deficiency, deviation and lack of value. In the older literature, the *yavana* appear usually as one group among others; the *mleccha* represent the foreign as such, in its undifferentiated otherness and exclusion.

The *yavana*, though foreigners, have nevertheless become naturalized in India, at least in its border areas, and they have become part of the Hindu sense of tradition. Therefore, from an early time on, they have been genetically derived from the caste system and claimed and explained as mixed castes or fallen *kṣatriyas*.

Already Gautama's *Dharmasūtra*, a text which seems to predate Alexander's Indian campaign (327–325B.C.), mentions the theory that the *yavana* are descendents of *kṣatriya* fathers and *śūdra* mothers.[15] Even if this passage should be an interpolation, we have no reason to question its relatively ancient and, at any rate, pre-Christian date of origin.[16] Other *Dharmasūtra* texts, for instance that by Āpastamba, do not recognize the interpretation of the *yavana* as a mixed caste.[17] In a curious and conspicuous statement, Patañjali's *Mahābhāṣya* (second century B.C.) on Pāṇini 11,4,10 (*śūdrāṇām aniravasitānām*) presents the *yavana*, together with the *śaka*, as "śūdras who are not excluded" (*aniravasita*). The chronological implications of this reference have been the subject of much debate.[18]

There is, however, no definitive terminological distinction between *yavana* and *mleccha*. The *mleccha*, too, do not always appear as foreigners *per se* in their undifferentiated otherness. Occasionally, the term also refers to a specific group of outsiders among other groups in India.[19] Emphasizing the scientific achievements of the Greeks, Varāhamihira's *Bṛhatsaṃhitā* (sixth century A.D.) declares that the *yavana* are indeed *mleccha*,[20] i.e., a specific group among the foreigners in general. This statement of inclusion leaves the conceptual distinction between *mleccha* and *yavana* intact. The fact that this distinction is increasingly blurred is itself a symptom of later Hindu xenology.

8. In "orthodox" (*smārta*) Hinduism, the exclusion of the *mleccha* also follows geographical criteria. *Bhārata*, India, is the area in which the *ārya* has his true and proper home, which supports and upholds his status as an "Aryan." Within Bhārata, *āryāvarta*, the area north of the Vindhya mountains, plays a special and, in older literature, clearly privileged role.[21] The Aryan or "twice-born" (*dvija*) who hails from this country preserves his identity and status only as long as he lives in it. According to the sacred cosmography of Hinduism, only Bhārata is fit for ritual performances and soteriological activities. It is privileged as *karmabhūmi*, the land of ritual and religious works and decisions, in which people can influence, master or even cancel their karma, the power of their past deeds, and in which they can embark on the path to final liberation from the cycle of births and deaths (*saṃsāra*). Bhārata is the land of *dharma*, and as such, it has a unique ritual, religious and soteriological status.[22]

The *śūdras*, whose share in the structure of *dharma* is only a limited and restricted one, are, on the other hand, less restricted geographically than the Aryan, "twice-born" members of the three higher castes.[23] The *mlecchas*, who have no share at all in the "dharma of castes and stages of life," also have no proper place in Bhārata. If they reside in India, this implies that the dharmic norm is not fully upheld and weakened or jeopardized.[24] On the other hand, the *yavanas*, just like the non-Hindu aborigines, are sometimes credited with a certain legitimate presence in India. According to the Purāṇas, they have a legitimate place in the West of Bhārata, just as the Kirātas have their place in the East.[25]

The possibility that a Hindu king might conquer or administer regions inhabited by "barbarians" poses further problems. How can he apply the rules of *dharma* to the *mlecchas*, who are essentially without *dharma* and have no part in its hereditary order? As we might expect, this possibility plays no significant role in the normative legal and religious literature of Hinduism. Moreover, conquering campaigns of Hindu rulers outside of India have indeed been rare. Yet, the possibility of extending the caste order beyond its original domain has occasionally been discussed in *Dharmaśāstra* literature.

A characteristic, though in some respects extreme and unusual statement is found in Medhātithi's commentary on Manu's law-book (II,22–23). Medhātithi (ninth century) first defines Āryāvarta as that region which naturally produces Aryans, and in which foreign, non-Aryan invaders will not stay permanently, not even very long.[26] Then he says: If a king whose conduct has been blameless defeats the *mlecchas*, establishes the order of the four castes in their country and assigns to the *mlecchas* a status which corresponds to that of the *caṇḍālas* in Aryāvarta, then the occupied country can become suitable for Vedic rituals. According to Medhātithi, the foreign soil as such, apart from the contact with those who occupy and pollute it, is not impure.[27] The text does not enlarge on the implications of this passage which has few parallels in *Dharmaśāstra* literature. In general, such considerations are essentially retrospective. They try to rationalize what has actually taken place—the extension of the caste order beyond its original limits, and the inclusion of "barbarian" regions under its rule. It is obviously not the concern of the *Dharmaśāstras* to present perspectives or incentives for the future conquest of foreign lands or for missionary and colonial initiatives.[28]

9. As we have seen, language is a central criterion for the definition of the Aryan. It is essential for preserving his ritual power and identity against the *mlecchas*. The continuity of the tradition, the identity and stability of the Aryan *dharma*, depends on its linguistic vehicle, the Sanskrit language. The purity and propriety of the Aryan way of life cannot be separated from the purity of its sacred language. This association has been essential for the extraordinary development of grammar and philosophy of language in India.

Patañjali, the exponent of the "Sanskrit renaissance" in the second century B.C., states that one ought to study grammar (i.e., the grammar of Sanskrit) in order not to become a *mleccha: mlecchā mā bhūma-ity adhyeyaṃ vyākaraṇam*.[29] Already the *Śatapatha Brāhmaṇa* relates that the "demons" (*asura*) were defeated by the gods because their ritual language was incorrect and corrupt. A Brahmin should not use such language (which itself may be called *mleccha*), in order not to become a *mleccha* or *asura*.[30] Much later, the *Kathāsaritsāgara* by Somadeva (eleventh century) presents the *mlecchas* of its time, i.e., primarily the Muslims, as resuscitated *asuras*.[31] In general, one should avoid contact with the *mlecchas*. According to a warning first found in the *Bṛhadāraṇyaka Upaniṣad*, one should not travel to "the ends of the world," the foreign lands beyond the horizon of the Aryans, in order not to incur evil, sin and death.[32] The teachers of *Dharmaśāstra* and *Mīmāṃsā* often repeat such warnings and prohibitions. One should not learn the language of the *mlecchas: na mlecchabhāṣāṃ śikṣeta*.[33] One should not converse with them, nor visit their countries.[34] Furthermore, it is not desirable to make the Sanskrit language accessible to the foreign barbarians.

In the "orthodox" understanding, Sanskrit is not just one language among others. There is no independent and parallel potential of meaning and correctness in these other languages. According to one familiar, but controversial theory, the languages of the *mlecchas* represent extreme cases of deformation or corruption (*apabhraṃśa*) of Sanskrit, *the* language par excellence. In order to clarify these derivative and defective languages, one should extrapolate and apply the model used by the grammarians of the Middle Indian Prakrit languages, and treat them as distant offshoots of Sanskrit.[35] However, the attempt to derive all *mleccha* words from Sanskrit roots and to construe their meanings "etymologically" and regardless of their actual usage by the *mlecchas* is usually rejected by the leading exponents of the Mīmāṃsā school.[36]

10. Post-Vedic Hindu xenology is inseparable from the concept of *dharma* and the system of the four major castes (*varṇa*). On the other hand, the classical *varṇa* system itself reflects ancient encounters with foreigners and ambiguous attempts to respond to their foreignness. This applies most of all to the *śūdras* and the role which they play in relation to the three higher castes of the "twice-born." The oldest texts emphasize the unity and identity of the Aryan community against the hostile foreigners, the *dasyu* or *dāsa*. The *Ṛgveda* even refers to one single "Aryan *varṇa*," whose purity Indra protects against the *dasyu*.[37] Those "others" who are thus excluded from the Aryan community and social identity are subsequently affiliated with it and, to some extent, included in it. Assimilated as *śūdras*, they become part of the complex, internally differentiated *varṇa* system. Their initial foreignness and exclusion is projected into the system and reflected in the tension between the *śūdras* and the "twice-born" members of the three higher castes. In passages first pointed out by Th. Benfey, the *Atharvaveda* contrasts *ārya* and *śūdra* in the same manner as other, more frequent statements contrast *ārya* and *dasyu/dāsa*.[38]

We have already noticed that later commentators often identify the *dasyu* as *śūdras* and project them into the context of the caste system. The existence of this system in its developed form can certainly not be presupposed for the older Vedic period, to which the earlier references to *dasyu* and *dāsa* seem to date back. Yet it seems likely and would agree with the views of authorities such as P.V. Kane that many "non-Aryan" foreigners or aborigines to whom the term *śūdra* may have originally referred did indeed become members of the *śūdra* caste.[39] As such, they remained excluded from significant aspects and functions of the ritual community. Part of the tension and opposition between "one's own" sphere and the "other" has thus been preserved as well as superseded within the "own" system.[40]

Corresponding to this "internalization" of foreigners and outsiders, and as an open-ended extension of the concept of *śūdra*, some texts classify all human beings who are not "twice-born" Aryans as *śūdras*. The idea that all lower strata of mankind, including all non-Indians, should be viewed as fallen *āryas* and assigned to the *śūdra* "caste" occurs, for instance, in the work of Bhāruci, the oldest extant commentary on Manu.[41] Numerous other texts seem to take this idea for granted, though in a vague and evasive sense. As we have noted earlier, it is a familiar idea that the *mleccha* status of the *yavanas* is due to a process of "śūdraization" (*śūdrībhāva*) of *kṣatriyas*, i.e., a violation and loss of their appropriate *dharma*.

11. But even if the *mlecchas* are not included in, or genetically derived from, the *varṇa* system, they are seen in accordance with, and as an extrapolation of, this system. They appear as marginal phenomena below or beyond the lowest strata of the caste hierarchy, lower even and more removed from the ritual norm than the *caṇḍālas*. Instead of referring to a vertical, hierarchical order, we may also try to visualize this scheme of social and xenological thinking as a sequence of concentric circles, which surround the center of ritual purity and perfection. Seen from this center, the most distant members of the social structure, the *caṇḍālas*, constitute the transition to the *mlecchas*. These in turn form the transition to the realm of the animals.[42] The perspective is, of course, that of the Brahmins who were the authors of the majority of texts on which our presentation is based. They see themselves at the center of this system of concentric circles, in which foreigners appear as an extension or continuation of the internal structure of Hindu society.

There is, however, one very significant difference between the *mlecchas* and the indigenous outcastes (*caṇḍāla* etc.) Even in their exclusion from the rituals and the sources of the sacred tradition, the *caṇḍālas* are part of the dharmic system, though in a negative fashion. They participate in it insofar as they accept their exclusion; they subject (or ought to subject) themselves to the ritual norms of exclusion and prohibition, and they are recognized as negative constituents of the system. The *mlecchas*, on the other hand, do not accept and recognize their exclusion and are not supposed and expected to do so. They participate in the order of *dharma* not even in a negative manner, i.e., by accepting and obeying prohibitions.

The "orthodox" Hindu view of the four main castes (*varṇa*) as quasi-biological species applies in an analogous fashion also to the *mlecchas*: They are different from the Aryans not only by virtue of ethical and cultural criteria, but also of hereditary and "biological" attributes.[43]

12. The basic rules of "purity" which have to be observed with regard to *śūdras* and outcastes also apply to contacts with *mlecchas*. They, too, are "impure" and "polluting,"[44] and there is a tendency to depict them as utterly beastly (*paśudharmin*) and indecent creatures.[45] However, since they are not part of the system and not even attached to it in a negative manner, references to them are infrequent and vague. The restrictions and prohibitions concerning the interaction with the foreigners are far less explicit and detailed than those regarding the *śūdras* and *caṇḍālas*. As a matter of fact, this relative vagueness leaves room for a certain indifference, and for exceptions and adjustments. We have already referred to Manu's notion of "fallen *kṣatriyas*" and Patañjali's presentation of the *yavanas* and the *śakas* as "śūdras who are not excluded."[46] – P. Hacker characterizes the "orthodox" norm of behavior towards the foreigners as "passive intolerance:" "It is not required that he who adheres to foreign customs and foreign faith should be actively encroached upon, but human interaction with him is prohibited."[47]

The *Arthaśāstra*, a more pragmatically oriented work on political and administrative methodology, leaves it to the discretion of the ruler to collaborate with *mlecchas*. But such collaboration is also allowed in the case of jungle tribes or gangs of thieves, and it corresponds to the general maxim that the political goal justifies many different means.[48]

In accordance with their different assessment of the caste system, the approach of the Jainas and Buddhists to foreigners is, of course, significantly different from that of the Hindus and specifically the Brahmins. In the Buddhist view, ethical and characterological criteria superseded the hereditary element. This applies as much to the concept of the *ārya* (and *mleccha*), as it applies to the Buddhist idea of the "true Brahmin."[49] Ethical, geographical, ethnic and other criteria are combined in a peculiar fashion in the Jaina interpretation of the difference and relation between *ārya* and *mleccha*..[50]

13. Our preceding presentation has been largely based upon works of a normative and idealizing character. From these texts we cannot expect reliable historical accounts of factual encounters between Indians and foreigners, and of the practical aspects of their interaction.[51] Yet it would be quite wrong to deny that these texts have "real" historical value, or that

they can provide insight into the realities of Indian thought and life. They may be "theoretical"; nevertheless they are significant historical documents of Indian self-understanding. They reflect an orientation which has had great importance for the "realities" of Indian history, and which is confirmed not only by other branches of Sanskrit literature, but also by other documents of Indian history.

The themes on which it is silent are among the more conspicuous features of classical Indian, specifically Sanskrit literature. The legendary biography of Alexander the Great, which gained great popularity in large areas of Asia (including Indian Islam), has remained virtually unnoticed in Hindu India, one of the targets of Alexander's campaigns.[52] There are no Hindu accounts of foreign nations and distant lands. The Indian cultural "colonization" of East and Southeast Asia and the spread of Buddhism are not at all reflected in Sanskrit literature. Even the Muslims, who were not only present in India for many centuries, but were its actual rulers, appear only in vague and marginal references. In spite of various forms of factual symbiosis and occasional scholarly collaboration, we find no serious philosophical or religious debate with Islam in traditional Hindu literature.[53] By and large, this applies also to the activities of the Europeans and the Christian missionaries up to the beginning of the nineteenth century. What Indian literature offers in this respect, is a tradition of silence and evasion.[54]

The rare and unusual passages which seem to contain specific historical or geographical references to the Western world are generally questionable as to their precise implications or their authenticity. For instance, this may be said about the alleged reference to Apollonius of Tyana in a Vedānta text which was first noticed by M. Hiriyanna.[55]

The lists of mythical regions and peoples which we find in the cosmography of the Purāṇas and other texts do not indicate any specific xenological interest, or any concrete curiosity concerning the foreign world. On the contrary, they present us with more or less speculative variations of Hindu society—transempirical, mythical projections with which there can be no concrete interaction. To be sure, certain historical reminiscences may have found their way into some of these traditions, for instance those concerning the mythical regions *Śākadvīpa* and *Śvetadvīpa*, but this does not change the general picture.[56] This open diversity of possible worlds does not imply a relativistic distance from one's own tradition, and it does not indicate any readiness for alternatives and historical changes as we find it in European Utopian literature.

14. Why should a Hindu who sees himself as part of an all-inclusive tradition and is committed to a truth which is timeless and complete be interested in foreign customs and traditions? Why should he explore the amorphous multitude of the countries of the *mlecchas*?[57] What could he possibly learn

from them? Certainly nothing that could affect his understanding of *dharma*—the sacred norm, the hereafter, those goals and means of human existence which are not accessible to empirical knowledge. The Veda is the only legitimate source of transempirical cognition. This is, above all, the view of the Mīmāṃsā. Yet this most "orthodox" philosophical school of Hinduism, which specializes in the exegesis of the Veda and the exposition of the *dharma*, pays more attention to the *mlecchas* than any other traditional philosophical system (*darśana*) of Hinduism. In spite of its emphasis on the uniqueness of the Veda and the exclusivity of the *dharma* which it teaches, this system is ready to concede that the *mlecchas* have a certain status of their own, and a potentially superior competence, as far as worldly, empirical matters are concerned.

The greatest of all Mīmāṃsā philosophers, Kumārila (seventh century) discusses the status of the *mlecchas* in a section of his *Tantravārttika*.[58] This is not only the most significant xenological text in the history of Mīmāṃsā, but also one of the most remarkable expositions of its kind in Indian philosophical literature in general. Although it has not had a major impact upon later developments, not even in Mīmāṃsā itself, it clearly deserves a more detailed presentation and discussion.

15. As it happens often in the works of Kumārila, an issue of general importance is introduced in connection with a specific problem of Vedic exegesis. *Mīmāṃsāsūtra* I,3,10 and the oldest extant commentary on it, Śabara's *Bhāṣya* (ca.500A.D.), pose and discuss the problem whether the meaning of certain Vedic words, which are not common among the *āryas*, but well known among the *mlecchas*, should be derived from Sanskrit roots or from their actual usage among the *mlecchas*. Should the meaning of such words as *pika* and *nema*, which are not generally at home in Sanskrit, be learned from the *mlecchas*, or should it be construed on the basis of Sanskrit etymologies, i.e., from elements of *the* language par excellence?

Śabara argues that it is perfectly legitimate to follow the linguistic usage of the *mlecchas* in such secular matters, where there can be no real conflict with the sacred tradition of the *āryas*. In his view, the *mlecchas* may indeed be credited with equal or even superior competency in certain worldly activities, such as the catching and rearing of birds. Kumārila agrees with Śabara's interpretation, but puts it into a much wider and more complex philosophical context. First, he elaborates the opposite view (*pūrvapakṣa*) introduced by Śabara. The *pūrvapakṣin* argues that it would be illegitimate, if not impossible, to learn about the *mleccha* usage of words. Does not the Veda itself prohibit conversing and interacting with them? And who would be able to find his way in the endless variety of their regions and languages? Are the *mlecchas*, who are not committed to the norms of dharma not equally unreliable in matters of linguistic usage? Sanskrit etymologies have been proposed for South Indian, Dravidian words. Is the same procedure not equally appropriate and ultimately unavoidable for more distant languages, such as those of the Persians (*pārasīka*), Greeks (*yavana*) and Romans (*raumaka*)? Should it not be a matter of principle to disregard the linguistic usage of the *mlecchas*?

16. In his response to the *pūrvapakṣa*, Kumārila first reiterates what he had already emphasized in his commentary on the preceding *sūtra* – that nothing can be learned from the *mlecchas* about the *dharma*, and that their traditions cannot claim any transempirical validity. However, this is not true as far as worldly, empirical transactions (*dṛṣṭārthavyavahāra*), such as agriculture, are concerned. The *mlecchas* may even be more qualified when it comes to providing certain services, building houses, etc. And insofar as certain products, such as silk products (*patrorṇa*), or harnesses (*vārabāṇa*), have their origin among the *mlecchas*, they should also be credited with the ability to provide the appropriate words for these products.[59]

Kumārila's Mīmāṃsā thus shows a certain degree of xenological flexibility in the "secular" (*laukika*) realm; but it does not accept any compromise with regard to the *dharma*. The sacred ritual norm can only be learned from the Veda, which is accessible only to those who have a hereditary qualification for it. The Veda teaches what the "twice-born" Aryans have to do in order to be Aryans, and in order to reach certain goals which are not susceptible to worldly, empirical means of cognition. It does not provide information on ordinary matters of fact, i.e., the domain of the worldly means of knowledge (*pramāṇa*). It leaves this domain to its own rules and standards. This is a realm which the "twice-born" Aryans share with the foreigners and outsiders. The *mlecchas*, too, are guided by, and can be competent users of, the worldly means of knowledge (*pramāṇa*). This is also recognized by Vātsyāyana Pakṣilasvāmin (ca.400A.D.) and other Nyāya commentators: In the field of ordinary sense perception, the testimony of *mlecchas* can, indeed, be acceptable; just like the *ṛṣi* ("seers") and *ārya*, they can be reliable witnesses of what they have actually seen.[60]

In the context and under the peculiar conditions of the Hindu tradition, the impact of this approach was inevitably limited. The practice of traditional Hindu life leaves hardly any room for a purely "secular" field of human transactions which would not be affected by the rules and restrictions of dharma. Kumārila's separation of the "worldly" (*laukika*) and "Vedic" (*vaidika*) realms is by no means typical of Hinduism; even in Mīmāṃsā its significance has been limited and ambiguous.

17. For an adequate assessment of Kumārila's presentation, it is essential to be aware of one of its fundamental premises – the absolutistic conception of language to which the Mīmāṃsā tradition generally adheres. Śabara and Kumārila do not want to suggest that other languages are vehicles of mean-

ing in the same full sense as the Sanskrit language, or that Sanskrit is just one among other languages. What is at stake is the question whether the *mlecchas* can provide certain linguistic supplements, or whether they have been able to preserve elements of the language par excellence, i.e., Sanskrit, which its proper guardians, the *āryas*, have failed to preserve and remember.

The theory that the semantic status of the *mleccha* languages is fundamentally the same as that of the Sanskrit language is rejected in Kumārila's commentary on the preceding *sūtra* (I,3,9).[61] The *ārya*, especially the well-educated *śiṣṭa*, can certainly claim an essentially higher authority for his own language. There can be no real conflict (*vipratipatti*) or rivalry between the usages of the *āryas* and the *mlecchas*. If there are discrepancies, the authority of the *ārya* is always the higher one. Kumārila thus advocates an intermediate position between the recognition of an equal or comparable status of other languages (*pūrvapakṣa* on I,3,9) and the uncompromising and exclusive reliance on Sanskrit etymologies (*pūrvapakṣa* on I,3,10).

Kumārila does not have much to say on the question asked by the *pūrvapakṣin* on I,3,10—how an Aryan who is supposed to honor the injunctions against conversing with foreigners can legitimately acquire a knowledge of their languages. He refers only casually to such Aryans who happen to be "bilingual" (*dvaibhāṣika*) and do not require any illicit contacts with foreigners in order to make competent statements on languages other than Sanskrit.[62] Kumārila refers here to a phenomenon which is of extraordinary significance in the Indian tradition, but treated with caution and reserve, or passed over in silence, by the representatives of "orthodoxy." It is the fact that the guardians of the sacred tradition and its linguistic vehicle, the Sanskrit language, were usually "diglossic"; in addition to Sanskrit, they also knew other, and often very different, languages, such as the Dravidian ones.

Apart from this, Kumārila's statements reflect a historical situation in which some factual information about the non-Indian world was available. As we have noticed, even the Romans (*raumaka*) are mentioned, probably based upon their extensive trade relations with South Indian, for which we have much numismatic and other evidence. However, in Kumārila's days the actual contacts with the Romans and other Westerners were already a matter of the past.

18. Although Śabara's and Kumārila's xenological statements are somewhat unusual in philosophical Sanskrit literature, they are not entirely isolated. There is considerable evidence that for a number of centuries Indians were indeed aware of, and interested in, the scientific, technical and other worldly achievements of foreign nations, for instance the astronomy of the *yavana*, i.e., the Greeks and other Westerners. In this connection, the

assessment of al-Bīrūnī (eleventh century) is significant. He first emphasizes the extraordinary ethnocentrism of the Hindus, their tendency to overestimate and isolate themselves, and not to recognize the achievements of other traditions. But then he adds that this was not always the case. There were times when the Hindus were ready to learn from the scientific achievements of the Greeks. He quotes a verse from Varāhamihira's *Bṛhatsaṃhitā* (sixth century) which Varāhamihira himself attributes to his predecessor Garga.[63] It says that the Greeks, though impure barbarians, deserve respect because of their scientific capabilities. How much more would such respect be due to a learned Brahmin, who combines scientific and scholarly competence with ritual purity! According to Bīrūnī, this verse demonstrates how a certain openness for the foreign world relapses into isolationism and conceit.

At any rate, there can be no doubt that in astronomy, astrology and some branches of mathematics the Indians have learned from the West, specifically from Babylonia and later on from the Mediterranean world. In these sciences, we even have the rare phenomenon of Sanskrit translations or adaptations of foreign, primarily Greek originals. From Varāhamihira's *Pañcasiddhāntikā*, we know about the *Romakasiddhānta* and the *Pauliśasiddhānta*, two works which preserve elements of Greco-Babylonian astronomy and seem to have been based upon Western originals.[64] The *Yavanajātcka* by Sphujidhvaja, "a text based in large part on the translation of a Greek text from Alexandria made by Yavaneśvara in 149/150," was recently edited and translated by D. Pingree.[65] In spite of Bīrūnī's statements on Hindu isolationism, examples of openness and receptivity can also be found during the period of Islamic rule. For instance, around 1700 Jagannātha, who was commissioned by the Mahārāja of Jaipur, translated an Arabic version of Euclid's *Elements* into Sanskrit (under the title *Rekhāgaṇita*). Many centuries earlier, the *Mahābhārata* and other texts had already recognized the *yavanas* as able soldiers, craftsmen, artisans, etc.[66]

19. In general, however, the commitment to the rules of *dharma* and to transempirical, soteriological goals limits or supersedes the interest in science and technology, and with it the openness for the scientific achievements of foreigners. Furthermore, the traditionalistic tendency to regard all "sciences" (*vidyā*) as timeless, all-inclusive configurations of knowledge is incompatible with the ideas of progress and an open-ended empirical accumulation of knowledge.

As for the *dharma* and the path to final liberation, there can be no compromise with the *mlecchas*. Their traditions have no validity; their practices and beliefs do not constitute alternate routes to one ultimate goal.[67] Around 1600, Madhusūdhana Sarasvatī, who may have had contacts with the court of the Mogul emperor Akbar, explicitly excludes the Buddhists and others from the harmonizing scheme of his *Prasthānabheda*. As to the paths or methods (*prasthāna*) of the *mlecchas*, Madhusūdana simply takes it for granted that they are invalid, and he does not consider it necessary to argue for their exclusion from his concordance.[68]

According to Appaya Dīkṣita, who lived one generation earlier, it goes without saying that the languages of the *mlecchas*, even more so than corrupt Indian vernaculars, are unfit to provide valid and effective soteriological instruction.[69]

20. A comparison with the classical Hellenic notion of the "barbarian" (βαρβαρος) can help to illustrate the xenological peculiarity of the Hindu concept of *mleccha*. Even as objects of hate and contempt, the barbarians are, so to speak, mirrors in which the Greeks reflect their own identity.[70] They have, as foreigners and manifestations of "the other," an undeniable stature and concreteness, against which the Greeks assert and define themselves. In post-classical times, they often appear in a more positive light and may be associated with a search for social and ethical alternatives, or for the roots of one's own identity. The concept of *mleccha* represents a much more radical type of exclusion and utter disregard.

The Indocentrism developed in "orthodox" Hindu thought transcends by far what is ordinarily called "ethnocentrism."[71] It is not simply an unquestioned perspective or bias, but a sophisticated theoretical structure of self-universalization and self-isolation. Seen from within this complex, highly differentiated structure, the *mlecchas* are nothing but a faint and distant phenomenon at the horizon of the indigenous tradition. They do not possess an "otherness" against which one's own identity could be asserted, or in which it could be reflected. They are neither targets of possible conversion, nor sources of potential inspiration. The "otherness" is a negative and abstract one; it does not contain any concrete cultural or religious challenges. Classical Hindu thought has developed an extraordinary wealth of schemes and methods of religious and philosophical subordination and coordination, of inclusion, hierarchization and concordance of world-views. But in this process, it has developed a complex, internally differentiated framework of orientation, a kind of immanent universe of thought, in which the contrast of the "indigenous" and the "foreign," of identity and otherness, seems a priori superseded, and which is so comprehensive in itself that it is not conducive to any serious involvement with what is different and apart from it—i.e., the "other" in its otherness.

21. The case of Buddhism is, of course, substantially different from that of Hinduism or Brahmanism. A Buddhist should not only have a different understanding of the caste order *in* India, but also of the concepts of the "foreigner," and of the contrast between *ārya* and *mleccha*. He is no longer

committed to the ethnic and hereditary connotation of these concepts, and he is also more open in terms of language and sacred geography.

In the third century B.C., the Buddist emperor Aśoka showed a remarkable awareness of non-Indian groups, specifically those in the North-West of his empire. He even took their languages into consideration. In one of his numerous edicts, the bilingual edict of Kandahar in Afghanistan, which was discovered in 1953 and first published in 1956, he used the Greek and Aramaic languages.[72] Moreover, he was willing to tolerate and protect many different forms of religious belief and practice. But vis-á-vis this legitimate variety of "sectarian" groups (*paṣaḍa*), he propagated the suprasectarian unity of the Buddhist *dharma*, which in his view was primarily a universalistic ethics.[73] He paid little attention to the more specific metaphysical teachings of Buddhism.

There is a universalistic and missionary attitude already in early *Hīnayāna* Buddhism, and it becomes much more conspicuous in *Mahāyāna* Buddhism. The ideal Buddhist teacher should be able to adjust his teachings to the modes of understanding of his disciples. He should be willing and able to learn their languages and to instruct them in accordance with their own ways of thinking. The Buddha himself did not teach in Sanskrit, but in a vernacular language spoken by the people of Eastern India. The Buddha's pedagogic flexibility assumes mythical proportions in the *Mahāyāna* Buddhist ideal of "skill in means" (*upāyakauśalya*): It postulates that the Buddha or Bodhisattva is capable of speaking all languages, including those of the non-Indian "barbarians," or that he speaks a "transcendental" language which the listeners understand in accordance with their own linguistic capabilities.[74] According to a verse from Āryadeva's *Catuḥśataka*, which is quoted by Candrakīrti and others, the *mleccha* has to be addressed in his own language in order to guide him to understanding. Similarly, "worldly" means of instruction are necessary to teach those with worldly attitudes and attachments.[75]

22. Already the Theravāda canon contains occasional comparisons between Indian and non-Indian practices and beliefs. It employs these specifically in its criticism of the Hindu theory of a hereditary caste hierarchy. In the *Majjhimanikāya*, we are told that the Greeks and the Kambojas of Eastern Iran do not accept four castes (*varṇa*), but recognize only two basically non-hereditary segments of the population—masters and slaves.[76] Later Buddhist writers also use references to the *mlecchas* in their polemics against the brahminical reliance on the Veda, which already the *Tevijjasutta* characterizes as utterly blind. Dharmakīrti states that there is nothing in the Vedic tradition which would distinguish it from the ancient customs and beliefs of the *mlecchas*, and support its claim to a status of timeless, superhuman, "authorless" validity (*apauruṣeyatva*).[77] Similar references are

occasionally found in the argumentation of Nyāya authors against the Mīmāṃsā theory of language and tradition.[78]

Yet even Dharmakīrti associates the *mlecchas* with immoral forms of life. He and other—later as well as earlier—Buddhist writers refer specifically to the "Persians" (*pārasīka*), and they compare or even equate their alleged practices of ritual killing, "marrying one's own mother" (*mātṛvivāha*), etc., with Vedic customs and injunctions. In their view, both represent a perverted traditionalism.[79] However, the argumentation is for the most part *ad hominem*, and it does not indicate any genuine interest in the peculiarities of foreign cultures as such. Other texts, specifically in Jainism, refer in a similar fashion to practices of the "Turks" (*turuṣka*).[80]

23. In general, we may say that the more universalistic Buddhist approach to foreign nations, languages and cultures has not brought about a radical change in Indian xenology. Apart from the fact that Buddhism virtually disappeared from its Indian homeland, it is also true that it adjusted in various ways to the Hindu milieu, its inherent traditionalism and its commitment to one sacred language. In orthodox Theravāda Buddhism, the prevailing view is that the sacred teachings should be transmitted in that language only which was allegedly spoken by the Buddha himself, i.e., the Pali language. The great commentator Buddhaghosa justifies this view in a controversial and questionable interpretation of a canonical passage attributed to the Buddha himself.[81]

There is little resonance of the Buddhist activities outside of India in Indian Buddhist literature. The advances of the missionaries, the great translation projects, the enthusiasm with which the Buddhist *dharma* was welcomed by so many Asian traditions--all this is hardly ever mentioned in India itself, and it has had few repercussions upon the debates between Hinduism and Buddhism, which were carried on in the Indian motherland.

As one would expect, the philosophical literature of Hinduism pays even less attention to the spread of Buddhism. In the orthodox view, the adoption of Buddhism by innumerable *mlecchas* does not at all speak in its favor, but should be regarded as an embarrassment to the Buddhists. A casual and laconic remark which is found, with minor variants, in several works of the great commentator Vācaspatimiśra (ninth/tenth century), illustrates this point. Vācaspati says that the teachings of the Buddha and others cannot be recognized as utterances of authoritative teachers simply because they have been adopted by such creatures as the *mlecchas*, who are the scum of mankind and akin to the animals (*kaiścid eva mlecchādibhir manuṣyāpasadaiḥ paśuprāyaiḥ parigrahān na-eteṣām āptoktatvasambavaḥ*).[82]

24. Once more, we may refer here to the intriguing phenomenon of "Greater India," that enigmatic expansion of Indian culture over vast areas of Asia which went more or less unnoticed in India itself. According to G.

Coedès, one of the major authorities on Southeast Asian history, the following features characterize the cultural phenomenon of "Greater India" or, as he prefers to call it, "Farther India": "the importance of the Sanskrit element in the vocabulary of the languages spoken there; the Indian origin of the alphabets with which those languages have been or still are written; the influence of Indian law and administrative organization; the persistence of certain Brahmanic traditions. . . ; and the presence of ancient monuments which, in architecture and sculpture, are associated with the arts of India and bear inscriptions in Sanskrit." Coedès goes on to call "the expansion of Indian civilization . . . one of the outstanding events in the history of the world" and he quotes the exuberant words of Sylvain Lévi, one of the rediscoverers of "Farther India": "Mother of wisdom . . . India gave her mythology to her neighbors who went to teach it to the whole world. Mother of law and philosophy, she gave to three-quarters of Asia a god, a religion, a doctrine, an art." However, on the following pages, Coedès refers to the other side of his phenomenon, which is no less remarkable than the expansion itself: "Curiously, India quickly forgot that her culture had spread over such vast domains to the east and southeast. Indian scholars have not been aware of this fact until very recently."[83] In India itself, Vivekananda and others contributed to the revival of these lost memories, and to the idea of "Farther India."

25. Concerning the question *how* this "Indianization" took place, and to what extent the Indians themselves were involved in it, Coedès is rather cautious. But again and again, he suggests that there were not many Indians involved, that we are not dealing with "colonies Indian in population," but "Indianized native societies," and that the "penetration of Indian culture" was to a large extent "the work of natives impressed by a superior civilization."[84]

Other Western scholars, for instance J.C. van Leur, have emphasized the non-Indian initiatives in this process even more strongly.[85] Indian scholars, on the other hand, have shown a natural and understandable tendency to emphasize and perhaps overestimate the direct Indian share in the cultural expansion. Apart from the extensive work done by Indian historians in this field, such as R.C. Majumdar and, more recently, H.B. Sarkar, the rediscovery and ideology of "Greater India" has been a significant element in Neo-Hindu self-understanding and self-assertion.[86] Vivekananda was one of the first to invoke the forgotten glory of this cultural empire. In 1926, the "Greater India Society" was founded, and Rabindranath Tagore wrote the nostalgic foreword to the first issue of its *Journal*: "To know my country in truth one has to travel to that age when she realized her soul, and thus transcended her physical boundaries; when she revealed her being in a radiant magnanimity which illumined the eastern horizon making her recognized as their own by those in alien shores who were awakened to a great surprise of life; and not now when she has withdrawn herself within a narrow barrier of obscurity, into a miserly pride of exclusiveness, into a poverty of mind that humbly revolves round itself in an unmeaning repetition of the past that has lost its light and has no message to the pilgrims of the future."[87]

Modern Hindu authors often trace such loss of cultural dynamism to the presence of Islam.[88] As a matter of fact, the withdrawal and self-isolation deplored by Tagore had begun long before the appearance of the prophet Mohammed.

26. In a sense, the effect of Buddhist universalism upon Hindu xenology has itself been a negative one. In response to this universalism, Hindu "orthodoxy" has become more rigid and exclusivistic; and there has been a theoretical consolidation of that introverted traditionalism which for centuries has secluded Hindu thought in itself and reduced the foreign world to an insignificant and marginal phenomenon.

Buddhism itself has been included, assimilated, superseded and at the same time excluded and disregarded by Hindu thought. This process illustrates the potential and the limits of the traditional Hindu way of dealing with "heterodox" teachings. It leaves room for many different views and standpoints, but always tends to include them in hierarchic or perspectivistic schemes, and to subordinate them to one ultimate truth, frequently that of Advaita Vedānta. The "other" teaching is usually not recognized in its otherness, but claimed as an aspect of, approach to, or abberration from the truth contained in the "own" doctrine. Moreover, these traditional schemes of inclusivistic doxography never go beyond the field of indigenous Indian "heterodoxies."[89]

In the so-called orthodox philosophical systems (*darśana*) of Hinduism, there has been no development of new xenological perspectives, of new ways of recognizing the foreign and the other. If there are innovations and significant variations, they occur usually outside of the mainstream of "orthodox" Hindu-Brahmanic thought, in the sectarian systems and in Tantrism.[90] To be sure, the inclusivistic model is found even here, and adjusted and modified in accordance with the various theistic positions of Śaivism, Vaiṣṇavism, etc. But there are also perspectives of religious and doctrinal antagonism, and of facing the "other" in his otherness, for which there is no precedent in the "orthodox" scholastic tradition. Above all, this holds true with regard to the rivalries and mutual attitudes of Hindu sectarian groups. But in some cases, non-Hindu groups, specifically the Muslims, have also been included in this process.

27. The term *pāṣaṇḍa* (also *pākhaṇḍa*) which Aśoka had used (in Middle Indian variants, such as *paṣaḍa*) to refer to the various religious groups in

his empire, now assumes an increasingly negative, pejorative connotation.[91] In the sectarian perspective, it refers to "heretics," "godless" people, to religious rivals and enemies, and most specifically to the Muslims. It indicates an atmosphere of religious competition and exclusivism which may be conducive to missionary, or quasi-missionary, activities. As a matter of fact, such sectarian groups as the *Vallabhīyas* and *Gauḍīya Vaiṣṇavas* (both originating around 1500) have made efforts to proselytize or at least *re*convert--not only among other Hindu groups, but occasionally also among the Muslims. The attitude of the Bengali Vaiṣṇavas has been criticized as "militant sectarianism and bitter intolerance."[92] Yet this spirit of confrontation and rivalry also opens new possibilities of self-demarcation, self-definition and recognition of the other as other.

In this climate of "sectarian" strife and search for identity, the word "Hindu" which so far had been used by foreigners, specifically Muslims, was first employed by the Hindus themselves.[93] This word goes, of course, back to the river name *sindhu*, i.e., Indus, and it is the Persian-Arabic equivalent of Greek 'Ινδος and Latin *Indus*. The Hindus now start using this foreign term as a device of asserting and defining their identity against the foreigners; the fact that they are named, excluded and defined as "others" by these foreigners provides them with a new sense of their own identity, as well as a new perspective on the otherness of others. This sense of identity against others, and among competing groups, is different from the old self-understanding of the *ārya*, or the "orthodox" self-identification in the framework of the one absolute, i.e., Vedic *dharma*.

28. *Dharma* is no longer the one and only, all-comprehensive *dharma*, but one *dharma* among others. The word *dharma* now starts appearing in the compound *hindudharma*. Again, this indicates a potentially new recognition of one's own being-for-others, as well as the otherness of others.

J.T. O'Connell says about the occurrences of the word "Hindu" in Bengali *Vaiṣṇava* literature: "Most occurrences are in episodes of strained relationships between Hindus and Yavanas or Mlecchas, as the Muslims are called. The strains are usually resolved satisfactorily. The word 'Hindu' never appears in a purely intra-communal Hindu context and has no significance in the central religious concerns of the texts, the expositions of bhakti."[94] The word appears also in seventeenth-century Maharashtra, where Śivājī (1627–1680) and his followers led successful campaigns against the Mogul rulers. Śivājī was associated with the religious teacher Rāmadāsa (originally Nārāyaṇa).[95]

However, the term "Hindu" remained generally excluded from mainstream Sanskrit literature. The two great Pandit encyclopedias of the nineteenth century, *Śabdakalpadruma* and *Vācaspatya*, cannot city any other text than the obscure *Merutantra*.[96] Even in the tradition of

Gauḍīya Vaiṣṇavism, Sanskritic Vedicizing tendencies became increasingly significant, and this affected the xenological attitudes of later Bengali Vaiṣṇavas. In the second half of the eighteenth century, i.e., in the decades preceding the beginning of the modern era of Indian thought, Baladeva Vidyābhūṣaṇa tried to affiliate the tradition of Kṛṣṇa Caitanya with "official" Advaita Vedānta. He refers neither to the Muslims nor to the Europeans, and he does not use the word "Hindu."

Some modern Indian nationalists, most notably M.S. Golwalkar and V.D. Savarkar, have argued vehemently that the word "Hindu" was *not at all* adopted from the Muslims and was *not* originally used by non-Hindus. Instead they claim that it is a genuinely Indian term, reflecting "the unity, the sublimity, and the specialty" of the Indian people.[97] This thesis, together with the arguments meant to support it, is a symptomatic expression of one significant trend in Neo-Hindu apologetics.

29. The commitment to the hereditary caste system may be less rigid in the sects than in mainstream "orthodoxy." This affects their xenological attitudes. The chosen membership in the religious or soteriological community can be more significant than the hereditary caste membership. Such openness and flexibility is occasionally extended beyond the confines of the Indian world, and even the *mlecchas* are at times recognized as potential members of the soteriological community.[98]

According to the *Kulārṇavatantra* and the *Mahānirvāṇatantra*, Śaivite texts of questionable date of origin, all men are fit to join the community of *kaulas*. It is a transgression for a *kaula* to exclude a *caṇḍāla* or *yavana*.[99] However, the unquestioned association of the foreigners with the *caṇḍālas* shows the continued relevance of the traditional xenological perspectives. In Tantrism, the boundaries between Hinduism and Buddhism are often less clear and rigid, and the soteriological universalism of *Mahāyāna* has left its traces. As a matter of fact, there are Tantric texts which have become popular both in Buddhism and Hinduism, e.g., the *Tārātantra*.

In this literature, we find occasional traces of a more concrete interaction with the non-Indian world. The *Kubjikāmatatantra* hints at the introduction of non-Indian practices into Indian Tantrism. The *Jayadrathayāmala* (twelfth century and later) gives a relatively detailed description of Tibetan practices, and it contains numerous words which seem to be of non-Indian origin.[100] The *Māyātantra* has a special mantra for foreigners (*yavana*; probably Muslims) "who delight in impure food and evil conduct."[101]

In various ways, Tantrism has softened or circumvented the rigid xenological restrictions of "orthodox" (*smārta*) Hinduism. It may even have influenced the new universalism of figures like Rammohan Roy, who often referred to the *Mahānirvāṇatantra*.[102] Yet, it has not brought about fundamental changes and it does not exemplify Indian thought in general. On the eve of the modern period, while actual contacts were rapidly intensifying, Hindu xenology still followed largely traditional patterns. Two relatively late texts, which show familiarity with the British, i.e., the *Bhaviṣyapurāṇa* and the *Sarvadevavilāsa*, can illustrate this.

30. The *Sarvadevavilāsa*, which was written in Madras around 1800 and edited by V. Raghavan,[103] contains some exemplary responses of Brahmin "orthodoxy" to the more and more frequent appearances of Europeans in that region of India. The seizure of power by the "low," "vile" (*nīca*) foreigners, i.e., primarily the British, is presented as a danger to the "order of castes and stages of life" (*varṇāśramadharma*) and associated with the reign of the demon Rāvaṇa, as depicted in the great epic *Rāmāyaṇa*.[104] The Europeans are referred to as "pale-faced" (*śvetamukha, sitāsya*) or "huns" (*hūṇa*).[105]

The treatment of the Europeans and of Christianity is more complex and problematic in the *Bhaviṣyapurāṇa*. Several manuscripts and printed editions of this text contain sections which seem to have been added in the nineteenth century to a much older basis. These interpolations continue a tradition of revisions and actualizations of the *Bhaviṣyapurāṇa*, a text which claims to deal with the "future" (*bhaviṣya*) and to contain ancient predictions concerning future events.[106]

The work, which also deplores the growing power of the foreigners over the Aryans, contains a number of Biblical names and stories, uses the expression "son of the Lord" (*īśaputra*), and presents Adam and Eve as the progenitors of a pedigree of *mlecchas*. More specifically, it refers to the *mahāmada* ("Mohammedans")[107] and the *guruṇḍa* ("European barbarians" according to the interpretation of H. Hoffmann).[108] The text itself gives an "etymology" of the word *guruṇḍa* and suggests that it points to the "mutilation" (*ruṇḍa*) of "cows" (*go*), the despicable practice which accounts for the barbarian status of these foreigners.[109] Furthermore, we are told that the *guruṇḍa* have come to India "for the sake of trade" (*vāṇijyārtham*) and that they are adherents of Buddhism.[110] We even get samples of their language, for instance the words *saṇḍe* and *siksaṭī* which corresponds to the English words "Sunday" and "sixty."[111]

31. Regardless of the age and authenticity of those passages in the *Bhaviṣyapurāṇa* which refer to Christianity and the Europeans, its association of the foreigners with eschatology and disintegration is also found in many other texts, and it corresponds to the general ideology of decadence and degeneration which we find in the doctrine of the four ages of the world (*yuga*). The *Kaliyuga* which started approximately 5000 years ago is the last and worst of these periods. The growing power and presence of foreigners in India epitomizes the nature of the *Kaliyuga* and the concurrent decline of *dharma*.[112] At the same time, however, there is hope that Viṣṇu, in his "in-

carnation" (*avatāra*) as Kalkin, will appear once again at the end of the current world period, eradicate the *mlecchas* and bring back the pristine purity of *Bhāratavarṣa*.[113]

These mythological schemes do not provide any positive prospects for future encounters with foreign cultures and religions; they do not leave room for any kind of synthesis, reconciliation, or dialogue. The languages, practices and beliefs of the foreigners are nothing but threats to the identity of the tradition, and symptoms of the decline of *dharma*.

In spite of this gloomy mythological vision and the deep-rooted xenophobia among the theoretical guardians of the tradition, there has been a certain degree of collaboration with Muslims and subsequently also with Christian missionaries. Much of this is anonymous and scarcely documented. But we have the names of numerous Brahmin pandits who worked for the Mogul rulers.[114] There is also some information on Padmanābha, Abraham Roger's friend and informant in the seventeenth century, and the dialogue partners of R. de Nobili, F. Bernier and B. Ziegenbalg.[115] We know even more about collaborators of the French in the eighteenth century. One of them, Ānandaraṅga Piḷḷai (1709–1761), left a detailed private diary, in which he recorded his impressions of the Europeans—with a remarkable openness, but also with a clear sense of Hindu identity and distance from the Europeans.[116]

However, we know of no Hindu, and certainly no Brahmin, prior to the period of Rammohan Roy (1772–1833), who actually travelled to Europe and recorded his experiences in writing; occasional references to predecessors of Rammohan remain entirely vague and anonymous. Even the Christian converts who came to Europe in the eighteenth century—for example as students of theology at the University of Leiden—did not leave written accounts. The first known Indian who left a report of his experiences in the West was the Bengali Muslim Itisām al-Dīn, who traveled to England in 1765. A much more detailed account was given by another Indian Muslim, Mirza Abū Tālib Khān (born 1752 in Lucknow, but of Persian and Turkish descent). He spent three years in Europe, mainly in England, and expressed his bewilderment at the European belief in historical progress and various manifestations of Western materialism; nonetheless, he was impressed with the industrial and technological achievements of the British.[117]

32. The overall picture remains the same: In traditional Hindu thought and literature, there has been virtually no interest in foreign countries, societies, cultures or religions. There has been no accumulation of information about the non-Indian world, no differentiation of xenological understanding. As we said in the introduction of this chapter, India has not reached out for the West; it has not actively prepared the encounter and "dialogue" with the Christian-European, or any other foreign tradition.

The lack of xenological interest and initiative in traditional Hinduism is obviously connected with its lack of historical interest and motivation. The historical literature of other countries is often linked with an affirmation and documentation of the own identity vis-à-vis foreign powers and cultures.[118] As we have seen, this plays hardly any role in traditional Hindu self-understanding. Hegel has claimed that the Indian tradition is fundamentally "static" and ahistorical, and that it represents, as it were, a petrified state of origin and "childhood." We know today that this thesis is untenable and that India has seen periods of great dynamism and extraordinary changes. Yet we may say that in its history and through periods of great upheaval Indian thought has become increasingly traditionalist, introverted, "static." In its own way, this apparent withdrawal from the challenges of history and the foreign world, this xenological passivity and growing introversion, may be as significant for the hermeneutical situation of the encounter and "dialogue" with Europe as the Western restlessness and aggressiveness.

12. Rammohan Roy and His Hermeneutic Situation

1. As we have seen, the contrast between an originally pristine and rich past and a subsequent history of obscuration and decay is a recurrent theme within the European interpretation of India. It may be found in the missionary literature, during the Enlightenment, and among the early Orientalists swayed by Deism. It was especially pronounced during the Romantic period. For the thinkers of the Enlightenment, the development of Indian thought constituted no less than the very paradigm of the theme of decay as well as an exotic illustration of the situation in Europe. During the Romantic era, the interest in India was an interest in Europe's own origins - and in the past per se. In essence, India spoke from a position in the remote past, via its distorted present, to the European present.

In Hegel's philosophy, India's relegation to the past assumes new dimensions, and it appears in a peculiar transformation. According to Hegel, there is not even progress in decay in India, and all tension between the present and the past is lacking. Indian thought as such represents a principle of a "past" which is historical as much as it is systematic. It is a principle which is left behind on the path of the spirit and superseded by its further development. Hegel was convinced that there could be no "return" to Indian thought; nor was there any way to resuscitate or reactivate it, or to endow it with a new presence and modernity of its own. Of course, Hegel considered the expansion and universalization of "modern," "contemporary" European thought (also in the form of a colonization of non-European peoples) to be not only legitimate, but also inevitable. This seems to imply that Europe would eventually have to bring India and the other remaining cultures of the "past" into its own present. However, Hegel does not go into detail about the problems associated with such a "modernization" (i.e., Westernization) of cultures which did not find their own way into modernity and the present.[1]

In contrast, Hegel's antipode Schopenhauer linked his expectations of a new Renaissance to a better understanding of "pristine" Indian thought. Yet this was a Renaissance that was to occur primarily in Europe; Europe had to rediscover Indian thought, and extricate it from its past. In spite of his criticism and distaste for his own European present, it was there and there alone that Schopenhauer saw the power for the appropriation, actualization, and "rebirth" of Indian thought.

2. Hegel's lifetime (1770–1831) coincides almost exactly with that of a man who, like no other, has been celebrated as the pioneer of the Hindu "Renaissance" and as the herald of modernization in India: Rammohan Roy (1772–1833). Hegel himself never spoke of Rammohan, who was also an associate and contemporary of the British Orientalists and took active part in the pioneering achievements of Indology. The only references to him made by Schopenhauer were derogatory in nature; those of Schelling were not much more complimentary.[2]

This Bengali "reformer" and "father of modern India" appears upon the scene of philosophical and religious debate as a representative of the living India of the present who places the tension between the origins and decay, between the past and the present, at the focal point of his thought and activity, who faces the Europeans as an interpreter of the Indian past and, simultaneously, as a representative of the Indian present. By contrasting the present conditions with the "original" sources of his tradition, he also attempts to open up new perspectives for the future for his Indian (and in particular Bengali) countrymen. He publishes extensively, enters into polemic debates with representatives of Hindu traditionalism as well as with missionaries and other Europeans, makes use of the English language, and travels to Europe (remarkable enough in the eyes of the Europeans, scandalous to his fellow Indians), dying in Bristol, England in 1833.

The stir which his personal appearances as well as his publications caused in Europe and even in America was considerable, and not surprisingly, it was particularly pronounced in the context of missionary and theological interests and controversies. The Unitarians greeted him as an ally; but for those more orthodox missionaries who initially saw in him a sign of hope for the Christianization of India, he later became a symbol of frustration and of Hindu self-assertion in the face of Christianity.[3]

3. Rammohan Roy also left his traces in the philosophical literature of the nineteenth century. During his own lifetime, he was the subject of an article in W.T. Krug's philosophical encyclopedia, *Allgemeines Handwörterbuch der philosophischen Wissenschaften*, while an additional article was added later.[4] He was described as a "Hindustani philosopher reputed to be the most excellent of those currently alive": "It may be that this extraordinary man is fated to carry out or at least to begin the Reformation his people so

dearly need." In addition, the later article emphasized that Rammohan wanted to return to the "original rationalism" of the Indian tradition.[5] Several years after this, Count Björnstjerna declared that Rammohan's attempt to reform "Brahma's teachings" and "like Luther, return these to their original purity," had failed.[6]

Rammohan corresponded personally with J. Bentham, who saw in him a comrade-in-arms for the cause of humanity and for his utilitarian principle of the "greatest possible happiness for the greatest possible number."[7] For Schelling, he was an advocate of "pure theism" and an abstract "religion of reason."[8]

C.J.H. Windischmann remarked that Rammohan had wanted to find "pure deism" in the Vedas, and he disapproved of the fact that Rammohan, as a Unitarian, was not ready for the Christian trinity. He concluded that with the appearance of Rammohan, India had indeed gone beyond the ancient "magical principle," although it still had quite a long way to go on the path to Christianity.[9] According to these and a number of other similar comments by Europeans, India had, so to speak, shaken off its ancestral inertia and was proceeding to a new stage of religious and philosophical consciousness (one which Europe, of course, had already attained). For many of the European observers, this was the key to their interest in Rammohan Roy and his successors: the assumption that India had finally attained a transitional stage on the way to Christianity and to other plateaus of thought that the West had long since achieved.

The judgement of Max Müller is, in comparison, more accommodating, for he saw in Rammohan "the first who came from East to West, the first to join hands and to complete that world-wide circle through which henceforth, like an electric current, Oriental thought could run to the West and Western thought return to the East."[10] M. Monier-Williams declared that Rammohan was "the first earnest-minded investigator of the science of comparative religion that the world has produced."[11] Yet even these opinions did not reflect complete religious neutrality, but rather a universality in the spirit of Christianity. Thus, we may once again see that the interest in Hindu reform was linked to the possibility of Christianizing India.[12]

And yet accusations that Rammohan was willing to compromise with Christianity did not just arise from the side of the orthodox Hindus, but also from voices in the West. Schopenhauer, for one, was highly critical of Rammohan's concessions to Christianity, describing him as a "Brahmin turned Jew" and accusing him of falsifying the Upaniṣads in a theistic and biblical fashion.[13]

4. In the context of modern Hindu self-awareness, the role played by Rammohan often assumes mythical proportions. He is usually placed at the beginning of the histories of "modern" or "contemporary" Indian thought

that are written by Indian authors; he appears as the very apotheosis of innovation and modernization, as the "father of modern India," and as the person who woke Hinduism from its long torpor.[14] He has become a kind of focal point for a retrospective glorification and the personification of many of the most important aspirations of modern Hinduism, in particular its claim to a comprehensive and harmonizing openness and universality: in him, the potential for such superior openness seems to have been fully actualized, and demonstrated to the modern world. He appears, to use the formulation of B.N. Seal, as "the universal man."[15]

In contrast, recent research exhibits a clear tendency towards a more sober assessment which emphasizes the "influences" upon Rammohan, or even reduces his approach to pre-existing, especially Western models. D. Kopf, in particular, has stressed his dependence upon the British Orientalists.[16] S. Hay has even gone so far as to say that the beginning of the "Bengali Renaissance," traditionally associated with the name of Rammohan Roy, may be more precisely dated to the publication in 1805 of H.Th. Colebrooke's treatise on the Vedas.[17] In J.T.F. Jordens' eyes, Rammohan's program contains practically nothing that is specifically Hindu, being essentially reducible to deistic and Unitarian ideas from Europe.[18] Islamic thought, too, and even Freemasonry have been suggested as sources of Rammohan's inspiration.[19] Other authors have emphasized that the reform movement initiated by Rammohan, the Brāhma Samāj, has remained largely – among "99.9%" of the Hindus – without success,[20] i.e., that it has neither attracted a large number of members, nor resulted in any fundamental changes within Hinduism.

5. It is not our intention to render a judgement on Rammohan Roy's originality or lack of it, to compare the Indian and non-Indian elements in his thought, or to provide a general analysis of the historical and biographical factors and circumstances relating to his life and work. Instead, our primary concern lies with the complexity and peculiarity of his hermeneutic situation and the structure and position of his thought between India and Europe as mirrored in his writings. As indispensable as the historical surveys and the psychological and biographical analyses of "influences" may be in this regard, they alone do not suffice for an understanding of the central hermeneutic question: this is not just a matter for factual "research"; more than that, it calls for philosophical reflection and clarification.

No matter what the originality or dependency of Rammohan's thought may be, and no matter what the ways were in which it was received or reinterpreted in the period which followed him, his thinking and self-presentation are so exemplary in terms of their cross-cultural hermeneutic structure and provide so many clues for the subsequent developments that they form the natural starting-point for our presentation. Even the ways in which Rammohan's work was misunderstood and rejected are of importance for an understanding of nineteenth-century India. For the purposes of this study, it is not necessary to discuss in detail the extent and significance of the various "influences" upon Rammohan's thought. Even so, the following presentation should be capable of demonstrating that any reduction to Western models is a simplification as inappropriate as the neo-Hindu mythicizing is unacceptable. For in fact, this type of reductive inquiry into "influences" itself can prove to be one-sided and misleading.

In order to provide a background and framework for the following discussion, some information concerning the external circumstances of Rammohan's life is indispensable. We shall, however, not attempt a biographical or developmental *explanation* of his work. Moreover, we must bear in mind that our knowledge of some important periods of his life, and particularly of his early development, is fragmentary and inadequately documented.[21]

6. Rammohan was most probably born in 1772.[22] At this time, the reign of the Moguls was approaching its end and was already de facto over. The English had been without serious rivals in India since the Battle of Plassey (1757) and were stabilizing and institutionalizing their rule over Bengal. Rammohan himself came from a Brahmin family – a fact which is of great importance for the ways in which he later presented himself – although his family had long since overstepped the bounds of strict orthodoxy as a consequence of their business (as well as linguistic and cultural) exchange with the Muslims. Rammohan was also a successful businessman, real estate agent, lender, and broker, especially after he received his share of his father's inheritance (1796), and he thus came into contact with the British East India Company, specifically, with its civilian officers Th. Woodforde and J. Digby. To his earlier mastery of Persian and Arabic, he now added a thorough knowledge of the English language. After 1815, he lived financially secure in Calcutta, devoting his time primarily to his scholarly and journalistic activities, which resulted in several controversies with orthodox Hindus and Europeans. His campaign against the practice of "suttee" (*satī*) earned him a wide reputation. In 1828, he founded his reform movement, the Brāhma Samāj (which succeeded the earlier Ātmīya Sabhā). Soon thereafter, he traveled to England; as we have noted earlier, he died in Bristol in 1833.

At the time of his death, Rammohan Roy was one of the most famous and controversial figures in India. He left behind a relatively small group of dedicated followers, and a larger group of vehement opponents. Yet even those who did not accept his ideas were drawn into the historical and hermeneutical movement which he reflected more intensely, and articulated more acutely, than any of his contemporaries. Quite naturally, his impact was most visible in Bengal. But responses from other areas of India were by no means lacking. They came, for instance, from the new urban centers in the South and West, Madras and Bombay. Bal Gangadhar Jambhekar (1812–1846), who has been called the "father of modern Maharashtra," responded to Rammohan in an article published in the *Bombay Durpun* in 1832: "With the love of general literature, he indulged also in reflection on religious subjects, which induced him at last totally to forsake the faith in which he was born and to embrace Deism." The subsequent Marathi version of this article rendered the term "Deism" as *vedāntamata.*[23]

7. Rammohan's first publication was a short treatise in Persian, *Tuhfatu'l muwāhhidīn* ("Gift to the Deists," 1803/04); in it, he refers to an even earlier, apparently unpublished work in Persian entitled *Manazarātu'l adiyān* ("Discussion on Various Religions"). The orientation of the *Tuhfat* is deistic, and it may reflect an acquaintance with the *Dabistān* (1645), specifically with its treatment of Akbar's ideas on religious concordance and universal monotheism.[24] The *Tuhfat*, too, tries to find the idea of the one true God in all religions, although with various degrees of clarity and obscuration. In Rammohan's later publications, Islam and the Persian language do not play any noticeable role. However, some remarkable quotes in Arabic in the *Second Appeal to the Christian Public* still indicate his familiarity with the Koran.

In 1815, two presentations of the Vedānta appeared in Bengali that were based upon the *Vedāntasūtras* and Śaṇkara's commentary: the more extensive *Vedāntagrantha* and the shorter and more succinct *Vedāntasāra*. An English version of the *Vedāntasāra*, together with a new preface, followed in 1816 under the title *Translation of an Abridgement of the Vedant.*[25] Bengali translations of five Upaniṣads (*Kena, Īśā, Kaṭha, Māṇḍūkya*, and *Muṇḍaka Upaniṣads*), together with short paraphrases based upon the commentaries by Śaṅkara, were published between 1816 and 1819. With the exception of the *Māṇḍūkya Upaniṣad*, these works also appeared in English. A number of other tracts and pamphlets followed in both English and Bengali. The most important and exemplary of these include *The Precepts of Jesus, the Guide to Peace and Happiness* (1820), an interpretation of the New Testament concentrating entirely upon ethical and practical matters which was greeted with enmity by the missionaries in Serampore.[26] The *Gosvāmīr sahita vicāra*, a short but significant debate with a Vaiṣṇava of the Caitanya school, which refutes the claim that the *Bhāgavatapurāṇa* should be viewed as a genuine commentary on the *Brahmasūtras*, appeared in 1818. Other titles worthy of mention are the Bengali work *Cāri praśner uttara* (1822), which offers several important clarifications on ethical and social themes as an answer to the "four questions" posed by a critic, and a very short work with the characteristic title *The Universal Religion: Religious Instructions Founded on Sacred Authorities* (1829). This latter work draws its deistic and universalistic claims entirely from Hindu sources.[27]

Rammohan's reform movement, the Brāhma Samāj, continued to survive schisms and changes until after 1900, although admittedly not as a popular movement. Instead, it served as a catalyst for the Bengali intelligentsia and as a springboard for a number of later movements, both along its lines and in opposition to it.[28]

8. As we have stated earlier, our chief concern here is not with Rammohan's "originality" or the extent of his "influence," but rather with his work as an exemplary mirror of a hermeneutic situation which had no real precedent on either the Indian or the European side, a situation in which India and Europe, the traditional and the contemporary, self-understanding and awareness of the other were linked to one another in new and peculiar ways. What is of importance here is not only the reception and transmission of individual doctrines and concepts, but also the encounter and in part interweaving of contexts and horizons of understanding. We are not simply dealing with Western "influences" upon Rammohan's thought, or with his understanding and evaluation of foreign, Western ideas, but also, and perhaps more significantly, with ways in which the foreign came to be adopted as a means of *self*-understanding and *self*-presentation and how Rammohan's thought thus achieved its peculiar cross-cultural ambiguity.

Even a cursory glance at Rammohan's works and the variety and interplay of languages which he used shows that we are faced here with a hermeneutic situation which is fundamentally different from that of Western scholars and thinkers attempting to understand the Hindu tradition; nor is it simply a Hindu parallel or counterpart to their situation. It is not so much Rammohan's multilingualism as such which is remarkable, but rather the peculiar function which it serves: for Rammohan, English, the "foreign" language, is not just a means of communicating with a foreign culture, it also serves as a medium in which he articulates his self-understanding and reinterprets his own tradition. What is more, he uses English and Bengali not simply as vehicles for translation, but also as devices for applying and actualizing the classical Indian tradition and of opening it up and reclaiming it for the present.

> The greater part of Brahmins, as well as of other sects of Hindoos, are quite incapable of justifying that idolatry which they continue to practise. When questioned on the subject, in place of adducing reasonable arguments in support of their conduct, they conceive it fully sufficient to quote their ancestors as positive authorities! And some of them are become very ill-disposed towards me, because I have forsaken idolatry for the worship of the true and eternal God! In order, therefore, to vindicate

my own faith and that of our early forefathers, I have been endeavouring, for some time past, to convince my countrymen of the true meaning of our sacred books...

These words open the first of Rammohan Roy's English works, the *Translation of an Abridgement of the Vedant* (Calcutta 1816). As he explains it, the "sacred books" were systematized and summarized in an authoritative manner by "Byas" (i.e., Vyāsa). "But from its being concealed within the dark curtain of the Sungscrit language, and the Brahmins permitting themselves alone to interpret or even to touch any book of the kind, the Vedant, although perpetually quoted, is little known to the public: and the practice of few Hindoos indeed bears the least accordance with its precepts!"[29]

Here we find a programmatic characterization of important aspects of Rammohan's activities as a writer and translator: The "dark curtain of the Sungscrit language" should be lifted so that the meaning of the most important texts may (through translations into the various Indian languages) be made available to the masses of Hindus[30] and (through translations into English) to the Europeans. By being confronted with the true sources of their own tradition, the Hindus would be awakened from "their dream of error"[31] and led to a regeneration of their religious and social life. At the same time, the Europeans should be shown that the "pure spirit" of Hinduism is not to be confused with certain contemporary practices of its followers.[32]

10. The authoritative texts, as Rammohan repeatedly assures his readers, do not offer any justification for the proliferation of ritualism, the polytheistic "idolatry," or the unrestrained "superstition" of modern Hinduism. For Rammohan, the "authoritative texts" are, above all, the "Veds" and the "Vedant," i.e., those portions of the Vedic literature knows as the Upaniṣads, and the *Vedāntasūtras* of Bādarāyaṇa with the commentary of Śaṅkara. It is for these texts that he provides his Bengali and English translations, paraphrases, and summaries. In addition, however, he also draws extensively upon the *Bhagavadgītā*, the Law Book of Manu, and other *smṛti* texts, and makes reference to the Purāṇas and Tantras as well: "The Purana and Tantra etc. are of course to be considered as Shastra, for they repeatedly declare God to be one and above the apprehension of external and internal senses."[33] Special importance is attached to two Śaivite Tantric texts, the *Kulārṇavatantra* and especially the more recent *Mahānirvāṇatantra*. Hariharānanda Bhāratī, the commentator of the latter text, was personally associated with Rammohan.[34]

In spite of his repeated references to what is most ancient and original, Rammohan did not concern himself with historical and philological differentiation; nor did he play the older and newer layers of the Indian religious literature (for example, the Vedas and the Purāṇas) against one another. Tantras and Purāṇas were included in the corpus of authoritative texts. Although Rammohan took an active interest in the work of the early European Indologists, he did not share the generally pejorative assessment of the Tantras which we find with such European authors as Colebrooke. Occasional derogatory remarks about the Purāṇas which appear in his English writings seem to be addressed primarily to European readers.[35] Later commentators, however, were rebuked as innovators and adulterators of the tradition. In particular, Rammohan criticized the works of Raghunandana (who lived in the sixteenth century, but was assigned to a more recent date by Rammohan), which were popular in Bengal and widely used by his "orthodox" and traditionalist opponents. In doing so, he tried to reciprocate and reverse one of the major accusations which his opponents had raised against him – that of being an "innovator."[36] In reality, Raghunandana and his followers were innovators – not he, who went back to the genuine sources, the truly authoritative texts.

The confrontation here is primarily between precept and practice, between the authoritative texts and mere custom and convention, between true meaning and false interpretation. "What can justify a man, who believes in the inspiration of his religious books, in neglecting the direct authorities of the same works, and subjecting himself entirely to custom and fashion, which are liable to perpetual changes, and depend upon popular whim?"[37]

For Rammohan, pure, monistically oriented monotheism – which is what he conceives as the true meaning of the "religious books" – is manifested particularly clearly in the "Veds" and in Śaṅkara's Vedānta. Yet it may also be found in the Purāṇas and other texts as well, if they are but correctly understood, i.e., if one keeps in mind the extent to which their means of expression and representation are merely figurative and allegorical and are an appeal to all those who are not yet in a position to attain "pure" understanding; for all of the decisive texts ultimately teach the unity of God and "the rational worship of the God of nature."[38]

11. Rammohan repeatedly states his conviction that reason and common sense go hand in hand with the true meaning of the sacred texts. Apart from a certain "natural" inclination of the ignorant," it has been above all the egotism of the brahmins and pandits which has obscured this true meaning.[39] The Brahmins have usurped the study and the transmission of the Vedic texts as one of their prerogatives. They have tried to conceal the sacred tradition behind the "dark curtain of the Sungscrit language," although they themselves have long since lost access to its real meaning.

It was one of Rammohan's most important goals to circumvent and ultimately abolish the restrictions of *adhikāra*, i.e., the rules of caste-based, hereditary "qualification" for studying the Veda which were perpetuated by brahmins and "selfish scholars" (*svārthapara paṇḍita*).[40] Already in his *Tuhfatu'l muwāhhidīn* (1803/04), Rammohan had tried to promote religious and soteriological egalitarianism. Now he sought sanction for it in the authoritative texts of Hinduism, for instance, in the *Kulārṇavatantra* and the *Mahānirvāṇatantra*, but especially in Śaṅkara's writings.[41] In doing so, he was forced to deal very selectively with these texts; the very explicit and emphatic passages in Śaṅkara's commentary on the *Brahmasūtras* which support the restrictions of the *adhikāra*[42] were passed over in silence.

To justify his program, Rammohan also made mention of the religious behavior of other peoples and communities. For example, to support the possibility of the "non-idolatrous" worship of God he considered to be so crucial, he referred to the practices of the Muslims, Protestants, Sikhs, etc.: "If so, how can we suppose that the human race is not capable of adoring the Supreme Being without the puerile practice of having recourse to visible objects?"[43] In a complete reversal of the Indocentric and xenophobic attitude of such classical Hindu thinkers as Vācaspati, he reminded his fellow Bengalis that India was less than "one twentieth of the world," and that "outside Hindustan, the people of more than half the world worship one pure supreme God."[44]

One especially well-known and exemplary domain to which he applied his critique was the controversy concerning the legitimacy of "suttee," the practice of cremating a widow together with her husband. Here, the way in which he cites authoritative passages and plays them off against one another is reminiscent of the exegetic patterns of the traditional Pūrvamīmāṃsā. However, the close of his arguments then consists in an appeal to "compassion" and a reference to the "civilized nations on the surface of the globe."[45]

12. As we have already noticed, the call to return to the sources of tradition is at the same time an appeal to reason and to common sense. It is a call to liberation from the blind attachment to custom and prejudice; merely continuing the behavior of one's ancestors would be, as the earliest publication on the Vedānta, the Bengali *Vedāntagrantha* (1815), explains, appropriate for animals.[46] In fact, Rammohan's choice of texts and his interpretation of the "true meaning" of the sacred tradition are committed to an idea of reason and rationality which bears the stamp of eighteenth-century European thought. The concepts of reason and common sense, together with a utilitarian and pragmatic sense of social good and public welfare, also allow Rammohan to transcend the domain of the Hindu sources and place these in an open horizon of religious and social teachings of mankind in general. In the *Precepts of Jesus*, they guide him in his attempt to draw additional inspiration from the New Testament and to complement the teachings of Hinduism in terms of ethical and social practice. To be sure, Rammohan also points out the limits of reason and common sense, making it

clear that they are by no means in any position to supersede religious tradition and the authoritative texts and to provide the guidance and orientation which we need: "When we look to the traditions of ancient nations, we often find them at variance with each other; and when, discouraged by this circumstance, we appeal to reason as a surer guide, we soon find how incompetent it is, alone, to conduct us to the object of our pursuit."[47] "Reason" and "common sense" are concepts linked to eighteenth-century European thought. They appeal to European readers, and they have their natural context in Rammohan's English works. In his Bengali works, on the other hand, the Sanskrit terms *yukti* and *śāstra* are used to indicate the tension between "reason" and "authoritative tradition."

As we have seen, Rammohan has no desire to be an "innovator." And yet at the same time, he is fully willing to assume the role of reformer, and he finds orientation in the example of the European Reformation, which, as he sees it, did away with distortions of Christianity and restored it to its original purity: "I begin to think that something similar might have taken place in India; and similar results might follow from a reformation of popular idolatry."[48]

13. Western religious and philosophical concepts and models are a constant part of Rammohan's presentation, penetrating deep into his self-understanding. The mark of European thought may be seen in his program of a return to the purity of the original sources, his universalism, his concept of God, his style of interpretation, etc. In particular, the approach of the British Orientalists provided a model for him. Nevertheless, it is one-sided and inadequate to emphasize the merely receptive and imitative side of his work.

No matter what Rammohan may have adopted, he brought it into his own particular hermeneutic situation of appealing to and reflecting upon different traditions, of appropriating the alien, and of asserting himself against that alien. This occurred within the context of a fundamental "multilingualism" constitutive for his thought. In the various languages he makes use of, and especially in Bengali and English, his statements assume specific strategic and pedagogic functions and meanings; these various languages are not neutral vehicles carrying an identical message; the choice of Bengali or English has doctrinal implications. It entails conceptual and interpretive variations corresponding to the different associational and conceptual horizons of English and Bengali. Thus, when interpreting Rammohan's thought, and in particular such concepts as that of God, it is not enough to consider his English texts alone. It is also inappropriate to look for strictly systematic and theoretically neutral expressions of his "doctrine." Rammohan's hermeneutical situation leaves little room for detached systematic and theoretical thinking or strictly text-oriented interpretation. He conceives and articulates his ideas "for others" and with an eye on different horizons of reception and expectation. He presents the Indian past for the Indian present, and he interprets and affirms his own tradition for as well as against the Europeans and within their religious and philosophical horizon of expectations. And in the act of presenting himself and his tradition to the foreigners, he learns, as it were, to see himself with foreign eyes.

Rammohan's contribution to the encounter between India and Europe is not to be found in any teachings *about* the relationship between the two, nor in any theoretical model of cross-cultural or interreligious understanding. The essence of his contribution lies instead in the variety and interplay of his means of expression, in the rupture and tension in his hermeneutic orientation, in his practice of responding and appealing to different traditions and horizons of expectation, and in the exemplary openness and determination with which he avails himself of the historical situation and its hermeneutical opportunities.

14. We have already pointed out the role which such concepts as "reason" and "common sense" play in Rammohan's English works. Other concepts, such as that of the "dignity of human beings,"[49] similarly reflect the European Age of Englightenment. The concept of God, with its deistic and rationalistic associations, also fits this context. And yet when speaking of God or the Absolute in his English works and translations, Rammohan clearly takes the Christian commitment to the idea of the person into consideration: In spite of all his references to the principles of the Vedānta on the one hand and the "natural light" on the other, the God he portrays is a personal God. Even in those places where the Sanskrit text of the works translated and paraphrased by Rammohan uses the term *brahman* in the neuter case, he consistently uses the masculine form ("he") in his English works, in effect replacing the monistic principle of reality with the God of monotheism.[50] We have already mentioned Schopenhauer's vehement reaction against this personalization, which he regarded as inadmissible;[51] in the *Oupnek'hat*, the neutral "id" appears at each of the corresponding places. Schopenhauer would have found less reason for his indignation in the Bengali language, which in this case does not distinguish between the masculine and the neuter. The original Upaniṣads themselves are much less concerned about the distinction between the genders, or the "impersonal" and the "personal" *brahman*, than Schopenhauer.

Doctrines peculiar to India, such as those concerning the *om*, the distinction of levels of soteriological qualification (*adhikāriviśeṣa*), and metempsychosis and reincarnation, are not fully omitted from the English translations and presentations,[52] yet they are less conspicuous here than in the corresponding portions of the original texts or the Bengali versions.[53] In general, ritual themes are disregarded entirely. When discussing the concept of absolute liberation (*mokṣa, mukti*), the English texts are considerate of Christian and European conceptions (as when they speak of "everlasting beatitude") in a way not present in the Bengali texts.[54]

When we look at the four Upaniṣads which Rammohan translated into English as well as Bengali, we may find a progressive accommodation to the European reader. In the last of these translations, that of the *Muṇḍaka Upaniṣad* (1819), this accommodation appears to have attained a kind of high-water mark. Moreover, it is symptomatic that the *Māṇḍūkya Upaniṣad*, which deals with the sacred syllable *om* as well as the four states of consciousness (including the meditative state of *turīya*), and which is especially Indian in its contents and its structure, appears in Bengali but not in English.

What is common to both the English and the Bengali works is the fact that they (in contrast to Śaṇkara) relate the contents and the study of the Upaniṣads to practical and earthly matters, in particular to social goals, and not just to the goal of liberation. Here, soteriology and utilitarianism are linked together; for *all* "human goals" (*puruṣārtha*), and not just *mokṣa*, may be advanced through the study of the Upaniṣads and the Vedānta. Again and again, Rammmohan emphasizes that being a householder, living a practical life, having worldly, temporal goals is *not* incompatible with knowing the supreme *brahman*.[55] In general, we should not forget that the English translations were not intended for Europeans alone. They also contain key elements of Rammohan's appeal to the Hindus, for whom the medium of English was quickly gaining in power and importance.

15. We have repeatedly noticed that the idea of a "natural light," thought to have been originally present in the Indian tradition, but lost or obscured in later times, was one of the most important points to which the missionaries in India attached their hopes.[56] An Indian return to the sources of their own tradition was supposed to contribute to their liberation from superstition and "idolatry" and thus pave the way for the "divine light" of the Christian revelation.

Because he initially appeared to promote this process from the Indian side, some missionaries viewed Rammohan Roy as nothing less than an instrument of Divine Providence.[57] And thus, their disappointment was even greater when he stopped, so to speak, half-way, for he never recognized such specifically Christian beliefs as the doctrine of the Holy Trinity, adhering instead to a Unitarian, deistic concept of God and lines of reasoning which had been used to challenge Christianity within Europe.[58] His pamphlets against Christian missionaries and dogmatists, which were simultaneously documents promoting a "pure" Hinduism, show Rammohan at the peak of his polemic and literary abilities;[59] and within the movement which he led, and in particular in its major publication, the Bengali journal *Tattvabodhinī Patrikā*, the discussion with Christian (and especially Anglican and Baptist) orthodoxy became an important medium for Hindu self-presentation and self-assertion.[60] *The Precepts of Jesus* (1820) and their appendix, the *Final Appeal to the Christian Public*, show the extent and seriousness of Rammohan's Biblical studies, but they also demonstrate his exclusive focus on ethics, and his disregard for matters of Christian faith and dogma: "I feel persuaded that by separating from the other matters contained in the New Testament, the moral precepts found in that book, these will be more likely to produce the desirable effect of improving the hearts and minds of men of different persuasion and degrees of understanding."[61] Referring to Rammohan and his followers, Bishop Heber said that the "deistical Brahmins" were the "chief hindrances" of the missionaries.[62]

More important for an understanding of Rammohan's Indian context are his discussions with spokesmen of traditional Hinduism, and the arguments which these traditionalists raised against him. The most significant example of this is provided by the *Vedāntacandrikā*, a Bengali work with an attached English translation (*An Apology for the Present System of Hindoo Worship*) that appeared in Calcutta in 1817. Although written anonymously, this work was quickly, albeit not with absolute certainty, ascribed to Mṛtyuṃjaya Vidyālaṃkāra, the "head pandit" of the College of Fort William.[63] Rādhākānta Deva (Radhakant Deb) may have contributed to this work. The translation was by W. H. Macnaghten.

16. In taking his stand with respect to the Indian present, Rammohan invokes the authority of the oldest and purest traditions of Hinduism; he argues polemically against such "modern" commentators and compilers as Raghunandana, whose innovations, in Rammohan's eyes, had only contributed to an obfuscation of the meaning of the tradition. Yet at the same time, it is no surprise that the criticism brought against him from the ranks of the traditionalists refers to him as an innovator, and it is with regard to these aspects of "innovation" and "modernness" that this attack is the most intense. *Ādhunika* and *idānīntana* (usually rendered as "moderns" in the English edition) are words which are programmatic within the polemic of the *Vedāntacandrikā*.[64]

To the extent that he is an "innovator", Rammohan appears in the *Vedāntacandrikā* – where he is not mentioned by name – as a symptom of the approaching *Kaliyuga*, the fourth and most evil of the ages of the world. During the *Kaliyuga*, the rules of the *adhikāra*, the right to study the sacred scriptures granted on the basis of caste membership, break down; and thus Rammohan's attempt to democratize such holy knowledge and his introduction of a "market-place theology"[65] both reflect and promote this process of decay of the *dharma* and the social and soteriological order which is its manifestation.

In the opening comments of the tract, the "innovator" is confronted by the *śiṣṭa*, the person educated in the tradition and committed to it.[66] The innovator or "founder of new doctrines" (*nūtanasampradāyakārī*) propagates his own delusions (*svakapolakalpita*) and aims at the fulfillment of his own goals (*svaprayojanasiddhi*).[67] In this way, Rammohan's own censure of the "egotistic" pandits is turned around and against him.

The *Vedāntacandrikā* emphasizes and denounces the fact that Rammohan himself stresses the absoluteness and omnipotence of God yet is not willing to accept these in the sense of an omnipresent immancence within the things of this world, that he recognizes the unity (*advaita*) of the Absolute, but rejects its concrete universality: "The argument therefore of him is not easily comprehended, who denies that the worship of the Supreme Being is involved in the worship of beings endued with forms and properties; who professes to believe in the Vedanta; who professes Unity, and who denies the doctrine of universality. Possibly some new Vedanta may have sprung up, which inculcates an unheard of Unity." The corresponding Bengali passage uses the expression *abhinava svabuddhikalpita vedānta*.[68]

17. According to the *Vedāntacandrikā*, Rammohan juxtaposes the unity of the Absolute and the universal multitude of its forms and presences; the pure and abstract unity of the Supreme Being is, as it were, isolated from its manifestations and invoked against them. Ultimately, as the *Vedāntacandrikā* emphasizes, the "polytheistic" idolatry of the Hindus is also concerned with the one God.[69] Whoever worships his "idol" or his particular God with a pure and full heart thus also worships the *one* God; there is no need for any artificial changes or reforms. It is obvious that such a position contains elements which will later reappear with more force and universality in Ramakrishna's criticism of the teachings of the Brāhma Samāj.

Rammohan's answer to the *Vedāntacandrikā* is contained in his *Second Defence of the Monotheistical System of the Veds* and the corresponding Bengali text, *Bhaṭṭācāryer sahita vicāra*. It restates and defends once again his fundamental views as discussed in the preceding sections, so that there is no need to discuss them here in any more detail.

What is important in Rammohan's debate with his traditionalist critics is the fact that they themselves no longer adhered to the rules which they in turn accused him of violating. For example, such pandits as Mṛtyuṃjaya Vidyālaṃkāra were already working with the Europeans and the missionaries, permitting the Europeans to pay them for their services as teachers and scholars, and in this way violating the restrictions of the *adhikāra*: ". . . it cannot be passed unnoticed, that those who practise idolatry and defend it under the shield of custom, have been violating their customs almost every twenty years, for the sake of a little convenience, or to promote their worldly advangage."[70]

Rammohan's response to the *Vedāntacandrikā* is supplemented by his debate with a *Gauḍīya Vaiṣṇava* "traditionalist" in *Gosvāmīr sahita vicāra*. Here, as well as in his Bengali introductions to the *Māṇḍūkya Upaniṣad* and the *Vedāntagrantha*, he accepts the principle of *adhikāribheda*, the relative value of image worship for those of lesser qualification, and the fact that the Purāṇas and other texts present God anthropomorphically and encourage image worship. Yet he insists that these texts themselves transcend such statements and relegate them to lower levels of understanding. While the merely pedagogical and symbolical use of images was understood "in the past," recent tradition in Bengal has blurred the distinction between symbolic representation and actual presence, and raised the images to the status of deities.[71]

Rammohan's propagation of pure, uncompromising monotheism, and his rejection of image worship, imply the claim that the *adhikāribheda*, and the distinction between "levels of truth," can and should be overcome. The need for images and similar pedagogical concessions to lower levels of qualification should be eliminated by educating those who are less qualified, and by enabling them to recognize the reality and unity of God without such "puerile" devices. The idea that the "absolute" truth can thus be made available to everybody, and that "mass education" and social progress can bridge the gap between the different levels of understanding and qualification, is one of Rammohan's most radical deviations from traditional Hindu thought, and more specifically, from Śaṅkara's Advaita Vedānta.

18. In a remarkable dialectical maneuver, Rammohan tries to show that one of the key strategies of his ostensibly traditional opponents — namely, the argument that the polytheistic multitude of Hindu idolatry is "ultimately" monotheistic – can itself be traced back to European influences. Referring to certain liberal Europeans, Rammohan states:

> They are willing to imagine, that the idols which the Hindus worship, are not viewed by them in the light of gods or as real personifications of the divine attributes, but merely as instruments for raising their minds to the contemplation of those attributes, which are respectively represented by different figures. I have frequently had occasion to remark that many Hindoos also who are conversant with the English language, finding this interpretation a more plausible apology for idolatry than any with which they are furnished by their own guides, do not fail to avail themselves of it, though in repugnance both to their faith and to their practice.[72]

The type of liberal and, in his opinion, overly benevolent European which Rammohan refers to here is represented by W. Jones and the anonymous author of the *Vindication of the Hindoos from the Aspersions of the*

Reverend Claudius Buchanan (London 1808; "by a Bengal Officer"). Jones had remarked that the Hindus were willing to allow the validity of the Christian message, adding:

> . . . the deity, they say, has appeared innumerable times, in many parts of this world and of all worlds, for the salvation of his creatures; and though we adore him in one appearance, and they in others, yet we adore, they say, the same God, to whom our several worships, though different in form, are equally acceptable, if they be sincere in substance.[73]

Even earlier than this statement, Ch. Wilkins noted in the introduction to his pioneering translation of the *Bhagavadgītā* (1785), that "the most learned Brahmins of the present times were Unitarians according to the doctrines of Kreeshna", but he added that, by "outwardly" performing Vedic ceremonies, they were exploiting the ignorance and superstition of ordinary people.[74]

An important example of the opposing view is provided by the Abbé Dubois. Rammohan appreciated Dubois' acutely negative opinion of Hindu religious life, and is said to have spoken of him as "the European who best knew the Hindus."[75] Dubois, on the other hand, despised Rammohan and was generally pessimistic about the Hindu potential for "reform."[76]

19. The Hindu cooperation with the "Orientalists" and other Europeans, the willingness to work on Indian material on behalf of the Europeans, and the self-presentation for the Europeans had, following a period of hesitation and restraint, already become very visible in Rammohan's day. Even before 1800, such works as the *Purāṇaprakāśa* and the *Code of Gentoo Laws* bear witness to the cooperation with W. Hastings and the early Orientalists.[77] There is hardly any explicit response to, or intellectual interaction with, the foreigners in these works; and yet this type of self-representation vis-à-vis the Europeans was an important starting-point for the intellectual encounter with them. The cooperation with Europeans became increasingly institutionalized through such facilities as the College of Fort William. This simultaneously opened up channels for the entrance of Western ideas, something which was especially true of the Hindu College in Calcutta (founded in 1816). It was there that H. Derozio displayed his controversial activity that was often considered anti-religious and which Rammohan himself disavowed.[78]

In 1823, the Committee of Public Instruction presented its plan to establish institutions in India which were dedicated to the dissemination of the English language and European science and philosophy.[79] In a famous letter to Lord Amherst, Rammohan himself argued emphatically in favor of the introduction of the English system of education and against the expansion of the traditional system of Sanskrit education and the instruction in the orthodox schools of Hindu philosophy. However, he was primarily referring to questions of elementary and mass education, and we should not see this letter as Rammohan's only or definitive statement on the value of the Sanskrit tradition, especially the Vedānta.[80]

In contrast to the pandits who were employed by the British as teachers, translators, or "resource persons", and thus served as mere instruments, Rammohan took a determined *initiative* to present and interpret the Indian tradition for the West.[81] What is more, this initiative was linked with an unprecedented willingness to assimilate and adopt Western means of self-representation.

20. As we have already seen, Rammohan's translations into English and Bengali are an expression of the multilingualism that characterizes his hermeneutic situation, and it corresponds to a dual motivation behind his thought and activity: the "Veds", which were thus presented to two different audiences, serve as vehicles of receptivity and reform as well as of self-assertion in the face of the West. Both of these motivations are closely linked in Rammohan's work; yet in the course of his development it appears as if the motif of Hindu self-assertion gradually became more important than that of receiving or assimilating.

The return to the sources of tradition at first appears to have the primary purpose of waking up Rammohan's Indian and in particular Bengali contemporaries from their social and religious degeneration and to aid them in becoming more willing to learn from the West and prepare them for a social and religious revival and reform. This appears to have been a concern which preceded that of Hindu self-assertion, and it is also symptomatic that the Bengali translations and paraphrases all appeared earlier than the corresponding English works. The Upaniṣads and other "holy texts" are "of unquestionable authority amongst all Hindoos" and are sacred and inspired "in the opinion of the Hindoos";[82] the message which may be proclaimed through them or with their aid thus has special import. Rammohan's choice of the "Veds" was a natural one because they were authoritative for the Indians and appeared to contain precisely those ideas and values which he tried to propagate and which he had embraced prior to his adoption and systematic study of the Upaniṣads and Śaṅkara.

Of course, we would be going too far if we were to suggest that Rammohan's concern with these texts was based solely upon pragmatic and tactical considerations. His self-understanding as a "Vedāntin" seems to have been genuine. It should also be remembered that the role of the Vedānta as a source of authority was ambivalent in Bengal in the period around 1800. The *Navyanyāya* was predominant in scholastic teaching, and the systematic study of the Vedānta did not play a conspicuous role. The more general orientation was largely shaped by Tantric works. In contrast to the situation in Benares and in particular in South India, there were few pandits in Bengal at this time who were fully competent in the field of the Vedānta.[83] And yet no matter how slight the actual knowledge of his countrymen may have been, Rammohan was able to appeal to fundamental and widely familiar associations of authority and sanctity which were linked to the Veda, the Vedānta, and the name of Śaṅkara.[84]

21. Regardless of the precise character and development of his allegiance to the Upaniṣads and Śaṅkara's commentaries,[85] in his presentation of these texts to his fellow Indians as well as to the missionaries and other Westerners, Rammohan became increasingly open to the idea of a superior universality and originality which gave Hinduism the ability to respond to the Western and Christian claims to universality and superiority. In an open letter published in 1823 which was one of the most pronounced expressions of his Hindu self-assurance, he declared that the Indians were certainly indebted to the English for the introduction of "useful mechanical arts" but by no means for achievements within the fields of "science, literature, or religion." Rather, the "first dawn of knowledge" had been seen in India, and in these areas, the rest of the world owed a debt to the Indians.[86] In this connection, it is characteristic that one of Rammohan's latest publications, *The Universal Religion: Religious Instructions Founded on Sacred Authorities* (1829), was based exclusively on Hindu sources.

Quite obviously, these sources did not simply serve as vehicles for propagating reformatory impulses and Western ideas. By using the "sacred texts" of Hinduism in this way and defending them against missionaries and other Western critics, Rammohan credits them (albeit never really explicitly) with a function and meaning that became ever more pronounced among later authors: that of a framework, a context for the encounter, and a universalism superior to the possibilities of Western and Christian understanding. The framework and potential for the encounter and reconciliation of the traditions is now sought *within* the Hindu tradition; receptivity and openness themselves appear as constituents of the Hindu identity and as principles of self-assertion. The encounter with the foreign, the alien, which had previously been and was seen still by many of Rammohan's contemporaries in an apocalyptic light,[87] now came to be seen as a positive challenge and as an opportunity for preserving and actualizing Hinduism's own potential.

Rammohan's most important and, in a sense, revolutionary step within the field of Hindu xenology was that he tried to guide India and Hinduism into the open arena of the "great wide world," that he exposed his own tradition to comparisons and contrasts with other religious and cultural traditions, and that he called for an openness towards and a willingness to learn from Western science and the Christian ethic. He was convinced that the sources of his own tradition were suitable for promoting and legitimizing such an openness; in his eyes, this was a confirmation of their own power and validity in the face of the challenge from abroad. In this sense, they were not just vehicles of receptivity, but also became sources of inspiration and instruction for the non-Indian world, able "to impart divine knowledge to mankind at large."[88]

13. Neo-Hinduism, Modern Indian Traditionalism, and the Presence of Europe

1. The hermeneutic situation which is expressed in Rammohan Roy's "multilingualism," his cross-cultural horizon of self-understanding and appeal, his position between receptivity and self-assertion, "Westernization" and "Hindu revivalism," forms the background and basic condition of modern Hindu thinking and self-understanding. Rammohan's own role as "father of modern India" has often been exaggerated, and it has assumed almost mythical proportions. Yet his life and work represent more than just a chronological starting-point for the development of modern Hindu thought.

Since Rammohan's time, it has become increasingly obvious that the European, i.e., primarily British, presence in India was not just another case of foreign invasion and domination, or of cross-cultural, interreligious "encounter." Instead, it was an encounter between tradition and modernity, i.e., an exposure to new forms of organization and administration, to unprecedented claims of universality and globalization, to rationalization, technology, and a comprehensive objectification of the world. It also meant the advent of a new type of objectification of the Indian tradition itself, an unprecedented exposure to theoretical curiosity and historical "understanding," and to the interests of research and intellectual mastery.

The European presence in India since Rammohan Roy has been vastly different from the Indian presence in Europe. And this is not just due to Europe's superior political and administrative power, nor is it a matter of factual information *about* Europe. It is a presence which is spread through a variety of institutions, technical innovations, missionary activities, educational policies, and other direct and indirect channels. Accordingly, the Indian response has many levels and facets, and it is as complex and differentiated as India itself. It reflects the linguistic and religious, the social and cultural variety of the Indian tradition. It is expressed in English, Sanskrit, and numerous vernaculars, in art, literature, and philosophy, in social, political, and religious movements, through cooperation with, and withdrawal from, the Europeans, through innovations in traditional garb, and the rearticulation of traditional ideas in Europen terms and concepts. It occurs in statements about, and adaptations of, Western ideas, but also in reaffirmations and reinterpretations of the Hindu tradition and identity, in active participation in Western "civilization" and the globalization of science and technology, or in its critique and rejection. It is represented by poets, pandits, and politicians, by theorists and practitioners, by popular and elitist movements. For modern Indians, dealing with the West is not a matter of choice or predilection: it is a historical necessity and predicament.

2. The wide variety of attempts to respond to the West and to articulate or reinterpret the meaning and identity of the Hindu tradition in the modern world can be exemplified by the following brief and selective list of names: Radhakant Deb (Rādhākānta Deva), I.C. Vidyasagar (Īśvaracandra Vidyāsāgara), and Debendranath Tagore (Devendranātha Ṭhākura), who criticized, modified, and continued Rammohan Roy's work; proponents of Tantric and Vedantic "experience" like Ramakrishna (Rāmakṛṣṇa; i.e., Gadādhara Caṭṭopādhyāya) and Ramaṇa Maharṣi; Vedicizing reformers, most notably Dayānanda Sarasvatī; Bhaktivinoda Ṭhākura and numerous other Vaiṣṇava reformers and universalists; B.G. Tilak, M.K. Gandhi and other nationalists and political leaders; poets and thinkers like Bankim Chandra Chatterji (Bankimcandra Caṭṭopādhyāya) and Rabindranath Tagore (Ravindranātha Ṭhākura); the great international spokesmen of Neo-Hinduism, such as Vivekananda, Aurobindo, and Radhakrishnan, who expressed themselves primarily in English; encyclopedic scholars and reformers like S.V. Ketkar (Śrīdhara Vyaṅkateśa Ketakara) and Laxman Shastri Joshi (Lakṣmaṇa Śāstrī Jośī); leading Sanskrit pandits, such as Vāsudevaśāstrin Abhyaṅkara, Anantakṛṣṇa Śāstrin, and Gopīnātha Kavirāja; academic teachers of philosophy, such as K.C. Bhattacharya.

It would be preposterous to attempt a complete or even representative account of the xenological, philosophical, or ideological positions and perspectives indicated by these names; nor is it necessary in the context of this study. We can and must be more selective. We will focus our attention on a few important movements and leading individuals who have articulated their xenological positions in an exemplary fashion and who have responded explicitly and specifically to the European ideas of philosophy, science, and religion. In particular, we will deal with the xenological implications of the phenomenon commonly referred to as "modern Indian philosophy," and with some representative and factually influential models of the accommodation, universalization, self-assertion, and reinterpretation of the Hindu tradition. In addition, we will also refer, though much more briefly, to some scholars and thinkers who have not appealed, at least not explicitly, to Western ideas and audiences, and who have not made any significant use of the English language. This will include references to modern pandits who have tried to cope with the modern world from within the framework of traditional "orthodoxy" and through the medium of Sanskrit.

We will not deal in any detail with the actual spread of Western ideas, the educational policies of the British, the activities of the missionaries, the various channels through which European ideas were disseminated, or the various modes of reception by the different strata of Indian society and in the different areas of India. Islamic revivalism and modernism in India will remain excluded from our presentation.[1] Following our selective survey of important personalities in chapters 13 and 14, we will focus on the role of two fundamental concepts in modern Hindu thought - the concepts of *dharma* and *darśana*, which serve as translations for, but also as devices of self-assertion against, the Western concepts of religion and philosophy.

We will also observe chronological limitations. We will focus on developments in the nineteenth and early twentieth centuries. In general, this study does not deal with the current situation as such, but with its historical antecedents and conditions, and with its hermeneutic background.

3. In a broad classification, Paul Hacker has divided modern Indian thought, and the Indian attitudes towards the West, into "Neo-Hinduism" and "surviving traditional Hinduism." Occasionally, Hacker also speaks of Hindu Modernism (by which he likewise means "Neo-Hinduism"); he avoids the terms "Renaissance" and "Reformation", so preferred by other authors in this context.[2] Neo-Hinduism and Traditionalism are the two main trends in modern Hindu thought, two ways of relating to the Hindu tradition while encountering the West. Whereas Neo-Hinduism has had more "publicity abroad," "surviving traditional Hinduism" has retained a much greater vitality within India itself. Today, both of these approaches find themselves confronted by Marxism.[3]

Hacker stresses that the distincton between Neo-Hinduism and Traditionalism is not based upon any particular teachings: ". . . we should lose sight of the essentials if we were to try to find the decisive difference in the area of doctrine."[4] Thus, for example, the tenets of the essential unity and equality of religions and of a tolerance essentially intrinsic to Hinduism, both of which play such a major and obvious role in Neo-Hinduism, are by no means foreign to Traditionalism.

Traditionalism, it should be noted, has also taken in and assimilated new elements, and is by no means a mere continuation of that which existed before the encounter with the West. Similarly, it is *not* possible to describe

Neo-Hinduism as a rigorous break with the past and its transmission. What distinguishes Neo-Hinduism and Traditionalism are the differrent ways in which they appeal to the tradition, the structures which they employ to interrelate the indigenous and the foreign, and the degree of their receptivity vis-à-vis the West. Modern traditional Hinduism has preserved an essentially unbroken continuity with the tradition,[5] and it builds upon this foundation, carries on what is already present in the tradition, even though additions are made and extrapolations occur.

4. To be sure, Neo-Hinduism also invokes the tradition, tries to return to it, and hopes to find in it the power and context for its response to the West. Yet as Hacker emphasizes, this return is the result of a rupture and discontinuity. More important than the fact that foreign elements have been added to the tradition is that basic concepts and principles of this tradition have been reinterpreted and provided with new meanings as a result of the encounter with the West: "Neo-Hinduism . . . always implies reinterpretation."[6] The link which the "Neo-Hindus" find to their tradition is, one may say, an afterthought; for they first adopt Western values and means of orientation and then attempt to find the foreign in the indigenous: ". . . afterwards they connect these values with and claim them as part of the Hindu tradition."[7] The ways in which they make use of the key Hindu concept of *dharma* (which shall be discussed in detail below) is especially symptomatic of this. To be sure, the traditionalists have also added new meaning to this concept, and relate it to the non-Indian world in a new manner, for instance in the *sanātanadharma* movements;[8] in contrast to the "Neo-Hindus," however, they do not assign it any essentially new interpretation oriented primarily around Western models.

Hacker's two categories are not mutually exclusive and not always clearly distinguishable. There are possibilities of transition, overlap, or combination. There may indeed be instances of a relatively "pure form of Neo-Hinduism," perhaps Radhakrishnan or Aurobindo,[9] and there are also certain very pronounced forms of confrontation and polemic between Modernism and Traditionalism. Yet it is also possible "that one and the same person combines elements of both ways of thinking."[10] And it is precisely this which so marks the peculiar ambivalence and range of variation which may be seen in modern Indian thought: orthodoxy and receptivity, openness and self-assertion, the new interpretation of indigenous concepts and a Hinduization of Western concepts, all these intermix in a variety of ways.

We should also bear in mind that Neo-Hindu "modernism" by no means advocates an extreme of Westernization: on the one hand, while it may indeed be contrasted with traditionalism,[11] it may also be distinguished from more radical forms of "modernization," secularization, and the adoption of

Western model – Hacker himself mentions Marxism. In general, it is obvious that Hacker's scheme is a simplification, although a useful and convenient one.

5. Referring to his choice of the word "Neo-Hinduism," Hacker says: "I do not know who invented the term Neo-Hinduism. I found it in an informative article by Robert Antoine who presented the Bengali writer Bankim Candra Caṭṭopādhyāya (Chatterjee) as a 'pioneer of Neo-Hinduism.'"[12] Bankim Chandra lived from 1838–1894. Older authors, e.g., Rammohan Roy and his successors, were merely "forerunners" in Hacker's eyes. They could not have been Neo-Hindus in the complete sense of the term because the nationalism which Europe was bringing to India had not yet attained its full bloom in their day; Neo-Hindu nationalism in turn is inseparable from modernization and Westernization.[13]

The appropriateness of this historical differentiation is beyond question. Rammohan Roy, the "father of modern India," was certainly not a nationalist, notwithstanding any subsequent claims that he was indeed the founding figure of Indian nationalism. For Rammohan greeted the British as instruments of Divine Providence and considered their rule over India and the introduction of a European educational system into India to be both necessary and good. Yet there are also a number of reasons to consider him a "forerunner" of Neo-Hinduism, not the least because he helped pave the way for Neo-Hindu nationalism: In Rammohan's work, and in particular in his later development, that cultural and religious self-assertiveness which would later be transformed into modern Indian nationalism became increasingly pronounced; and along with his conviction that the British rule was historically necessary was linked the hope that precisely through this – "from constant intercourse with Europeans"[14] – the will to national self-assertion would ultimately be strengthened. In any case, it is not correct to ascribe to Rammohan a completely indifferent attitude – "this indifference to the 'native' or 'foreign' character of traditions"[15] – in this regard. The practice of reinterpretation which is such an essential element of Neo-Hinduism may also be found in Rammohan's work; and in his view, the introduction of European means of orientation in the fields of politics and ethics, science and technology has to be mediated by a new appropriation and "actualization" of the original teachings of Hinduism. While there is nothing in Rammohan's work as pronounced as Vivekananda's idea of the "practical Vedānta," the foundations of a program for deriving practical consequences from the metaphysics of the Vedānta are already apparent. And it is thus not surprising that the first explicit signs of a confrontation between modernism and traditionalism appear in the controversies initiated by Rammohan, viz., in the *Vedāntacandrikā* and its criticism of the *ādhunika* and *idānīntana* ("innovator", "modernizer").[16]

6. As for the term "Neo-Hinduism," which was employed by R. Antoine and P. Hacker, it appears that the term itself cannot be traced back to Rammohan's time, although the closely related expression "Neo-Vedānta" (as well as "new Vedānta," "Neo-Vedantism") can. Both Christians and Hindus make use of it in their critical and polemical descriptions of a "modernistically" reinterpreted Vedānta.

Already the *Vedāntacandrikā* (1817) itself characterizes Rammohan's pure and imageless monotheism as a "new Vedānta" (*abhinava vedānta* in the Bengali version).[17] Following Rammohan's death, the term "Neo-Vedantism" is used in the debates between the missionaries and the Brāhma Samāj. Thus, for example, a "notice" in the *Calcutta Review* makes a comparative reference to "Neo-Platonism" and continues: "So, in like manner, ought much of what, nowadays, is made to pass for Vedantism, – consisting as it does of a new compound arising from an incorporation of many Western ideas with fragments of oriental thought – to be designated Neo-Vedantism to distinguish it from the old."[18] In the following decades, the more fully developed Neo-Vedānta takes up the challenge from both sides and attempts to prove that its "innovations" in no way represent an external addition of Western elements, but rather draw from the potential originally contained in Hinduism and the Vedānta.

Our discussions below will primarily consider Neo-Hinduism and, specifically, the Neo-Vedānta. This is not due so much to the fact that it, as Hacker has correctly stressed, has attracted more publicity in the West, but rather because it provides an explicit and exemplary demonstration of the relationship with the Western world and the hermeneutic problems involved in the confrontation with it. Standing between traditionalism and orthodoxy on the one hand and a mere mimicry of Western models on the other, it represents, so to speak, the xenological core of modern Indian thought.

Before we begin with our discussion of the concepts of *dharma* and *darśana*, concepts that provide such prime illustrations of the hermeneutic and xenological orientation of modern Hinduism, we shall first present a short survey of some major religious and intellectual movements in the period following Rammohan Roy. Our main focus will be upon the following thinkers and developments: Debendranath Tagore, Keshab Chandra Sen, and the development of the Brāhma Samāj; Bankim Chandra Chatterji and "Humanism" and "Positivism"; Ramakrishna, Vivekananda, and their successors; and Dayananda Sarasvati and the Ārya Samāj; we shall also look briefly at some twentieth-century figures, i.e., Aurobindo, Radhakrishnan, Coomaraswamy, and K.C. Bhattacharya. In addition, we shall also refer to testimony from the orthodox and pandit literature, and to other instances of a more traditionalist xenology.[19]

7. One question that was of central importance for later developments emerged in Rammohan's work, although he did not discuss it in a fully explicit and thematic fashion. This question concerns the basis and the extent of the binding "revelation" in Hinduism and its relationship to the "revelations" of other religions traditions, as well as the true sources of religions conviction in general.

This theme acquired a central significance with Debendranath Tagore (Devendranātha Ṭhākura, 1817–1905),[20] probably the most important leader of the Brāhma Samāj after Rammohan's death. In 1839, Debendranath founded the Tattvabodhinī Sabhā, an organization that was closely linked to the Brāhma Samāj and whose magazine, the *Tattvabodhinī Patrikā*, represented the views of the Samāj. In contrast to Rammohan, Debendranath posed the question as to the authority of the Hindu holy scriptures in a very direct and explicit manner. Together with his friends, he tried to determine how much of the traditional material was indeed binding and reliable and could be accepted once and for all as the valid vasis of the "religion of the believers in Brahma." In further contrast to Rammohan, Debendranath quickly broke with the Vedānta philosophy of Śaṅkara, whose non-dualism appeared completely unsuited to the establishment of a new religious and social life. He concluded that he should replace Śaṅkara's commentaries to the Upaniṣads with interpretations of his own.[21] Other texts and groups of texts also were inadequate in his eyes; no text speaks for itself, none proves its own authority: the principle of selection, the criterion of authority, i.e., the foundation of religious conviction, is not to be found *in* the texts:

> I came to see that the pure heart, filled with the light of intuitive knowledge (*ātmapratyayasiddhajñānojjvalita viśuddha hṛdaya*), — this was its basis. Brahma reigned in the pure heart alone. The pure, unsophisticated heart was the seat of Brahmaism (*brāhmadharmer pattanabhūmi*). We could accept those texts only of the Upanishads which accorded with that heart. Those sayings which disagreed with the heart we could not accept.[22]

The Upaniṣads themselves contain as it were reports about that which the ancient seers (*ṛṣi*) have experienced and tested (*parīkṣita*), and they encourage each of us to follow the "test" or the "experiment" of his own heart (*hṛdayer parīkṣā*).[23]

8. Debendranath places himself in the position of a "seer" and attempts to personally realize and reactualize what is documented in the Upaniṣads - at least as far as they are true and acceptable: "Thinking thus, I laid my heart open to God, and said: 'Illumine Thou the darkness of my soul.' By His Mercy my heart was instantly enlightened... Thus by the grace of God, and through the language of the Upanishads, I evolved the foundation of the

Brāhma Dharma from my heart."[24] The source of truth, that site of divine inspiration, may be found in one's "own heart," and in the final analysis, what the Upaniṣads actually provide is merely a linguistic medium, a means of expression. Of course, it is obvious that the immediacy and authority of religious experience which Debendranath claims to have located in his "own heart" contains European ingredients. It is inspired by the modern European search for certitude, as well as by various Western conceptions of inspiration and intuition, and, more specifically, by the ideas of the Scottish school of common sense. In his critical approach to the authority of "sacred texts," he was, moreover, influenced by the views of his companion Aksay Kumar Datt, who was a much more radical "Westernizer" and "modernizer."[25]

On the other hand, European conceptions are recast as vehicles for Hindu self-assertion; for example, the term *ātmapratyaya*, which appears in the *Māṇḍūkya Upaniṣad* as part of the compound *ekātmapratyayasāra*, is utilized to translate and Hinduize the concept of intuition. Debendranath reinterprets this term, which was originally understood as the non-dualistic self-presence of absolute consciousness.[26]

Debendranath's self-assertion as a Hindu is much more pronounced than Rammohan's. In the *Brāhmadharmagrantha*, which appeared in two parts between 1850–1852 and was intended to serve as the basic text-book for the Brāhma Samāj, he made almost exclusive use of Hindu sources, although he occasionally modified and rephrased the original texts.[27] At the same time, his doctrine of intuition and his interpretation of religious texts as documents of inner experience opened up new dimensions of universality and of interaction with other religions, and it paved the way for such exemplary Neo-Hindu views as that of Radhakrishnan, who saw all valid religious documents, both within and without Hinduism, as records of "experiences," and thus understood "intuition" and "experience" as the basis and the common denominator of all religions.[28]

9. Debendranath represents what might be termed a conservative universalism; he was not inclined to change the forms of Hindu social and religious life in a radical manner or to reduce them to syncretisms or "common denominators" with other religions. Rajnarain Bose, who was closely associated with Debendranath and advocated Unitarian universalism as well as Indian nationalism, stated: "Although Brahmoism is a universal religion, it is impossible to communicate a universal form to it. It must wear a particular form in a particular country."[29]

The universal as well as syncretistic potential inherent in Debendranath's approach became much more manifest in the work of a man who was Debendranath's partner and complement in the development of the Brāhma Samāj and yet also his antipode: Keshab Chandra Sen (1838–1884).

The development which became clear with Roy and Devendranath – although in some ways only implicitly – gained greater significance with Keshab: While Roy had not yet thematically conceived the contrast between scripture and intuition, Devendranath entertained open doubts about the infallibility of the Veda. Keshab expanded this view even more by granting inspired intuition a general precedence over all written 'revelation.'[30]

Keshab was much more inclined than Debendranath to search for "inspired" sources outside of Hinduism as well and to demonstrate the universal harmony among the traditions by compiling exemplary records of religious experience. In 1866, he founded his own branch of the Brāhma Samāj, within which a new schism occurred in 1878.[31] In 1880, he proclaimed the "New Dispensation (*nava vidhāna*) which, as the third "dispensation" following the "dispensations" of the Old and the New Testaments, was intended to establish the universal church and the harmony of all religions. Keshab's *Ślokasaṃgraha*, a counterpart of Debendranath's *Brāhmadharmagrantha*, offers a collection of quotes from Hindu, Buddhist, Jewish, Christian, Islamic, and Chinese religious sources.[32]

I believe in the Church Universal which is the deposit of all ancient wisdom and the receptacle of all modern science, which recognizes in all prophets and saints a harmony, in all scriptures a unity and through all dispensations a continuity, which abjures all that separates and divides, always magnifies unity and peace, which harmonizes reason and faith, yoga and bhakti, asceticism and social duty in their highest forms and which shall make of all nations and sects one kingdom and one family in the fullness of time.[33]

10. With this, it is obvious that Keshab has arrived at an understanding of history and soteriology that is no longer Indian. He comes closer to Christianity – which he considers to be the "religion of Humanity," the "worship of Humanity"[34] – than any other leader of the Brāhma Samāj, and yet through his universalism he simultaneously distances himself from the Christian tradition. Jesus is a great seer, a *ṛṣi* – along with others, along with Buddha, Caitanya, Moses, Kabīr, etc., all of whom have been drawn together into an "indissoluble organic unity" through the "power of the heart."[35]

In his attempts to find a criterion for the truth and validity of "intuition" and the "voice of the heart" which he perceives in himself and in the testimony of the "seers," Keshab, like Debendranath before him, adheres to such eighteenth and nineteenth century Western philosophical conceptions as "instinctive belief," "common sense," "a priori truths," "moral sense," "primitive cognitions," and a complete arsenal of corresponding concepts.[36]

The East and the West, and especially India and Europe, should complement and correct one another. Europeans should teach the Indians science and exact thought, while learning in turn "ancient wisdom from India."[37]

> Europe, the Lord has blessed thee with scholarship and science and philosophy, and with these thou art great among the nations of the earth. Add to these the faith and intuition and spirituality of Asia, and thou shalt be far greater still. Asia honours thy philosophy; do thou honour, o Europe, Asia's spirituality and communion. Thus shall we rectify each other's errors and supplement mutual deficiencies.[38]

This model of a mutual supplementation of scientific and analytical thought and religious spirituality, in particular as presented by Vivekananda, has become typical of Neo-Hindu self-awareness and the Neo-Hindu interpretation of the relationship between India and Europe. P.C. Mozoomdar/Majumdar (Pratāpacandra Majumdāra; 1840–1905) continued Keshab's work in his publications, specifically *The Oriental Christ*, and on several journeys to Europe and America. In 1893, he represented the Brāhma Samāj at the World Parliament of Religions in Chicago.[39]

11. In spite of his great willingness to accommodate Christianity, in spite of the affiliation of his "New Dispensation" with the "dispensations" of the Old and the New Testaments, Keshab considered himself to be essentially the fulfiller and executor of Hinduism: Hinduism alone has been called to lead Christianity to its true universality and to simultaneously perfect itself therein. Speaking of Christ, Keshab states: "The Acts of his Hindu Apostles will form a fresh chapter in his universal gospel. Can he deny us, his logical succession?"[40] The Hindu tradition of inclusivism is placed under the name of Christ: the "Christianization" of India is simultaneously the Hinduization of Christianity. Keshab's program was illustrated and radicalized in an idiosyncratic fashion by Brahmabandhab Upadhyay (1861–1907), a nationalist and journalist who converted to Christianity – first to Protestantism, then to Catholicism – and yet remained convinced that he had not compromised his being Hindu: he had merely actualized and fulfilled the spiritual universalism immanent in his "Hinduism." On the other hand, Brahmabandhab produced some of the sharpest anti-British polemics of his day.[41]

In the later part of his life, Keshab had numerous encounters with Ramakrishna (i.e., Gadādhara Caṭṭopādhyāya, 1836–1886), who was probably the most famous representative of "living Hinduism" and has become the very symbol of the potential of undogmatic religious experience and ecstasy contained within the Hindu tradition.[42] In Keshab's eyes, Ramakrishna seems to demonstrate that his idea of the harmony of religions, his *nava vidhāna*, could be fulfilled and lived within Hinduism; conversely, Keshab is one of the most frequently mentioned personalities in the so-called *Gospel of Sri Ramakrishna.*[43] P.K. Sen has correctly contested the assumption that Ramakrishna had a profound influence on Keshab: long before the two ever met, Keshab had already found his own way to the "Religion of Harmony."[44] And in spite of their well-attested mutual affection, it is the differences in their behavior and their orientations that strike one most. Nevertheless, both of these figures demonstrate the themes of self-assertion and universalism, of receptivity and preservation and fulfillment of the tradition, that were imposed by history upon nineteenth-century Hinduism.

12. In contrast to Keshab, Ramakrishna did not affiliate himself with the Brāhma Samāj: instead, he was among its most effective critics. In a certain sense, the restorative features of his criticism were a continuation of the tradition exemplified by the *Vedāntacandrikā.*[45]

The world, as the living play and manifestation of God, neither requires "reform," nor is it receptive to it. Ramakrishna had little more than mild irony when speaking of the will to social and religious reform exhibited by so many of his contemporaries: he viewed this as just one form of attachment to the world, and a lack of freedom for the divine. In his eyes, the Brāhma Samāj's program of reform was an abstraction which isolates *one* aspect of the divine and the religious from the concrete multiplicity of its manifestations: from the rich melody of Hinduism, it offers but a single note.[46] The value and richness of Hinduism cannot be reduced to the abstract purity of its pristine sources; instead, in consists in its organic totality, which Ramakrishna conceives in the sense of a non-historical inner perfection, the timeless of presence of the *sanātana dharma* ("eternal religion").[47] Even without "reform," Hinduism is prepared for the encounter with Christianity and the other religions of the world; its potential of "experience" and its inner diversity offer room enough for the inclusion and recognition of other names and forms of worship. Ramakrishna saw no problem in adding the worship of Jesus to the various cult forms of Hinduism, and he was convinced that his own meditative experiments could demonstrate that the various religions were all paths to the same goal. The metaphor of the different expressions for the *one* water which all drink,[48] together with other parables and metaphors, illustrates the Unity of God in the diversity of forms of worship.

This should not be mistaken for an example of deistic "tolerance"; instead, this is one of the most impressive examples of "inclusivism" in the nineteenth century. Its very "openness" is a form of self-assertion; and it proved to be one of the major obstacles to the efforts of the Christian missionaries. Nor is this a syncretism in the sense of Keshab, but an extrapolation of Hinduism itself, an answer to the Europeans coming out of the tradition of Tantric Vedānta. The Hinduism which Ramakrishna exemplifies, in particular in the stylized and mythicizing presentation by his successors, appears as an open, yet in itself complete, framework of encounter and reconciliation with other traditions, as the timeless presence of the religious per se, to which nothing new can accrue.[49]

13. Vivekananda (actually, Narendranātha Datta, 1863–1902), Ramakrishna's most famous and effective apostle both in India and in the West, was an untiring herald of this message. Next to Rammohan Roy, Vivekananda became one of the leading figures of modern Hindu thought and self-awareness and an exemplary exponent of Hindu self-representation vis-à-vis the West. His appearances in the West, his self-understanding, and his activities within India are all interwoven in a peculiar way: "During his first visit to the West, Vivekananda became the man who made history: the most influential shaper and propagandist of the Neo-Hindu spirit."[50]

The literature concerning Vivekananda is voluminous, although the great majority of it is the work of disciples and admirers. In the Indian portrayals, he is often presented in a stereotyped and glorifying manner as the herald of a Vedānta rejuvenated with new vigor and vision and capable of leading to a world-wide synthesis,[51] and as the founder of a renewed and well-grounded Hindu self-assurance. Even in the West, he is not infrequently celebrated as the teacher of a "universal gospel" and the proclaimer of the "harmony of religions."[52]

In contrast, critical assessments and attempts to "demythologize" Vivekananda are much more rare,[53] and rarer still are examples of a thorough historical analysis and hermeneutic clarification of Vivekananda's work. It might seem as if Vivekananda's work does not offer any really worth-while tasks for historical research or philosophical reflection; in many parts, it is rhetorical and popularizing, reducing the complexity of classical Vedānta to simple and occasionally superficial formulas. Whoever searches here for theoretical consistency or philosophical originality may find himself as disappointed as with Rammohan Roy; similarly, the tangible historical and practical success with which Vivekananda met may be as questionable as that attained by Rammohan.

14. This notwithstanding, the critical studies of P. Hacker have shown that historical research and hermeneutic analysis are faced here with important tasks.[54] And it may be seen that Vivekananda's work, like that of Rammohan Roy, is an exemplary reflection and expression of an historical and hermeneutic situation. In this sense it has important implications for the modern world, no matter what its practical relevance or theoretical conclusiveness may be.

In comparison to Rammohan, Vivekananda tends much more to explicitly assert himself as a Hindu and to derive his teachings and practical programs from the sources of Hinduism. Vedāntic "inclusivism" is the very framework and basis for Vivekananda's encounter with the West. At the same time, his "missionary" impulse is much stronger than Rammohan's; he is committed to propagating Hindu principles beyond the borders of India and to utilizing their international recognition in his efforts to regenerate Hindu self-awareness and self-confidence.[55] In general, Vivekananda's references to the mutual relations, and the similarities and dissimilarities, between India and the West, both in terms of India's self-representation *for* the West and its self-assertion *against* it, are much more explicit than was the case with his predecessors.

His travels to the West play an exemplary and programmatic role in Vivekananda's life. Again and again, he speaks to Western audiences about India and Hinduism,[56] to his own countrymen about the West, and to both sides about their mutual relationship. He simplifies and schematizes. He lives and practices the problematic and ambivalent position which Neo-Hinduism occupies between India and the West. He adopts Western motifs of self-criticism and the search for India and transforms them into aspects of Hindu self-assertion. He appeals in a rhetorically effective manner to ideas and values which many Europeans find lacking in their own tradition and present, and he demonstrates the extent to which the Neo-Hindu "dialogue" with the West employs or presupposes Western means of self-reflection and self-critique.

Vivekananda's treatment of the interrelations of understanding and the mutual reflections of Indian and European self-awareness remains without explicit hermeneutic reflection, and he pays little theoretical attention to the intercultural and interreligious situation which he represents, so to speak, in practice.

15. Whereas Rammohan Roy often referred to his descent from the Brahmin caste, Vivekananda liked to present himself as a *kṣatriya*, a member of the caste of warriors and kings. Actually, he was born into the caste of the *kāyastha*, whose membership in the *kṣatriya* caste is highly questionable.[57] It was important for his education that he became acquainted with the works of such representatives of European critical and positivistic (i.e., secular and progress-oriented) thought as J. St. Mill and H. Spencer at Presidency College in Calcutta. During this period, he also became familiar with the teachings of A. Comte, who was well known in Bengal at this time.[58] Parallel to this, he acquired a good, but not very comprehensive knowledge of traditional Sanskrit scholarship. As a member of the Ramakrishna circle, he became acquainted with the *Yogavāsiṣṭha* and the *Aṣṭāvakragītā*, Vedānta texts outside of Śaṅkara's "orthodox" tradition.

Vivekananda's knowledge of European philosophy remained important for him even after he had the encounter with Ramakrishna that was to be so crucial for his religious and philosophical orientation and his self-awareness as a Hindu. He became Ramakrishna's favorite student and presented himself as his instrument. In India and on his journeys to Europe and America, most conspicuously at the World Parliament of Religions in Chicago (1893), he appeared as the herald of the Hinduism which Ramakrishna embodied. And in Ramakrishna, he found a secure tenure where there had previously been only searching and doubt, and a kind of Indian answer to Europe which did not even require verbalization and conceptualization.

Vivekananda taught that Ramakrishna was the living commentary to all of the sacred texts of the Hindus; he encompassed within himself all that which had been lived in the millenia of Hindu religious life; with his birth, the Golden Age, the 'Age of Truth,' had dawned once again.[59]

In Vivekananda's eyes, Ramakrishna was the inner fulfillment of the Hindu tradition, and the living demonstration that India was ready for Europe without ever having searched for it and was thus equal to the challenge which the encounter between the two represented: Through its embodiment in Ramakrishna, Hinduism did not just demonstrate its potential of receptive openness, but also the power to go beyond itself and to affect or even transform the West:

The time was ripe, it was necessary that such a man should be born, and he came; and the most wonderful part of it was that his life's work was just near a city which was full of Western thought, a city which had run mad after these occidental ideas, a city which had become more Europeanized than any other city in India. . . . Let me now only mention the great Shri Ramakrishna, the fulfilment of the Indian sages, the sage for the time, one whose teaching is just now, in the present time, most beneficial. And mark the divine power working behind the man. The son of a poor priest, born in an out-of-the-way village, unknown and unthought of, today is worshipped literally by thousands in Europe and America, and tomorrow will be worshipped by thousands more.[60]

16. There is no reason to doubt that Vivekananda's veneration of Ramakrishna was genuine and in keeping with the Indian tradition of revering one's guru. But it is equally true that he stylized and used his guru in his own peculiar way and that his own personal work, the 1897 "founding of the Ramakrishna order for the purpose of preaching Hinduism in India and abroad, for the purpose of general mass-education and philanthropic activity..., was in no way directly inspired by Ramakrishna's ideas."[61] Ramakrishna himself can hardly be counted among the spokesmen of Neo-Hinduism; yet through Vivekananda he became the instrument and leading figure of Neo-Hinduism in its encounter with Europe.

Ramakrishna is the representative and quintessence of that "spirituality" which Vivekananda time and again – using often stereotypical phrases – presents to the Europeans as the true message of India: teachings about the spirit, the soul, God; that is what India has to offer to the world and especially to the West and what, moreover, the modern West particularly needs.

Let others talk of politics, of the glory of acquisition of immense wealth poured in by trade, of the power and spread of commercialism, of the glorious fountain of physical liberty; but these the Hindu mind does not understand and does not want to understand. Touch him on spirituality, on religion, on God, on the soul, on the infinite, on spiritual freedom, and I assure you, the lowest peasant in India is better informed on these subjects than many a so-called philosopher in other lands. I have said. . . ., that we have yet something to teach to the world.[62]

Closely related to this, and linked as well to Ramakrishna's thought, is Vivekananda's claim that the idea and practice of tolerance and universal brotherhood is India's gift to the world:

India alone was to be, of all lands, the land of toleration and of spirituality . . . in that distant time the sage arose and declared, *ekaṃ sad viprā bahudhā vadanti* - 'He who exists is one; the sages call him variously.' This is one of the most memorable sentences that was ever uttered, one of the grandest truths that was ever discovered. And for us Hindus this truth has been the very backbone of our national existence... our country has become the glorious land of religious toleration.[63]

17. As Vivekananda sees it, "the world is waiting for this grand idea of universal toleration"[64] and spirituality to be passed on by India.

The other great idea that the world wants from us today . . . is that eternal grand idea of the spiritual oneness of the whole universe . . . This is the dictate of Indian philosophy. This oneness is the rationale of all ethics and all spirituality. Europe wants it today just as much as our downtrodden masses do, and this great principle is even now unconsciously forming the basis of all the latest political and social aspirations that are coming up in England, in Germany, in France, and in America.[65]

The time is ripe for Ramakrishna and the Vedānta. And while the West may have conquered India, it still needs India as well; it is waiting for India without realizing its need. For Vivekananda, this means that it is waiting for the Vedānta and its "idea of the spiritual oneness of the whole universe." The truth of the Vedānta may already be seen in the efforts at social reform and in the beginnings of self-correction displayed by modern Western thought, without, to be sure, being discovered and formulated as such. The Indian tradition – perfected through Ramakrishna – is called upon to steer these beginnings, to develop them and trace them back to their metaphysical basis and in this way show Europe a way out of its historical aberration.

Vivekananda often speaks of what he sees as the one-sided materialism, hedonism, secularism, and rationalism of the West. The Western nations are ruled by the pursuit of profit and the desire to control, by a concentration upon external things, by the "ideal of eating and drinking"; they are presently "...almost borne down, half-killed and degraded by political ambitions and social scheming... Ay, in spite of the sparkle and glitter of Western civilisation, in spite of all its polish and its marvellous manifestation of power, standing upon this platform, I tell them to their face that it is all vain."[66]

18. However, materialism and secularism are only *one* side of the Western world, for it also boasts of that energy and dynamism which Vivekananda would so like to awaken in his own countrymen. And while he may indeed feel that nationalism, accompanied as it is by intolerance and the desire for power, is one of the evils of the Western world, he also admires the vigor and the dynamism associated with the Western sense of national identity. The Indians have lost their "individuality as a nation"; this is the reason behind their degeneration and humiliation, the "cause of all evil in India." The Indians must learn from the other nations, and in particular the nations of the West, to be a genuine and full-fledged nation.[67] In order to help his people in this regard, Vivekananda is ready to adopt all suitable means and ways of motivation from the West. In this context, he sees no alternative to learning from the West; his orientation here is shaped entirely by Western models.

The Hindus should make the organizational abilities, the pragmatic orientation, the work ethic, the social virtues, and the scientific and technical knowledge of Europe and America their own. They should overcome their own indifference and lethargy and advance to new vigor and self-confidence. They should follow the example of Japan, which had successfully assimilated Western science *and* rediscovered its own strength and identity.[68]

Vivekananda's call to initiative, will-power, and faith in India's own abilities appears frequently throughout his work and in memorable formulations: "Have faith in yourselves, and stand up on that faith and be strong; that is what we need. Why is it that we three hundred and thirty millions of people have been ruled for the last one thousand years by any and every handful of foreigners who chose to walk over our prostrate bodies? Because they had faith in themselves and we did not."[69] Americans and Europeans exhibit this self-confidence to a particularly high degree. This is what lies behind their prosperity and their national power and identity.

As Vivekananda often stresses in his letters and travel reports, Americans are especially exemplary in their readiness to practical philanthropy, their organizations for educating the public, etc. In fact, the establishment of the Ramakrishna mission in 1897 was directly influenced by his experiences in America. And yet he also has recourse to socialist conceptions, especially during his later years, when he was influenced by his personal acquaintance with the Russian anarchist and utopist Kropotkin. He spoke of himself as a "socialist" and concurred with the Marxist prognosis concerning the coming rule of the proletariat, which he tried to link to traditional Hindu concepts by describing it as the "rule of the Śūdras."[70] He never mentioned, however, Marx or Engels.

19. The materialistic West, successful in the mastering of external situations, stands opposed to the spiritual and religious East, which has degenerated in social and practical respects. This contrast forms the basis for Vivekananda's conceptual model of a mutual complementing and synthesis, a model which occasionally, especially before Western audiences, takes on the form of a trade exchange.

> Therefore it is fitting that, whenever there is a spiritual adjustment, it should come from the Orient. It is also fitting that when the Oriental wants to learn about machine-making, he should sit at the feet of the Occidental and learn from him. When the Occident wants to learn about the spirit, about God, about the soul, about the meaning and the mystery of this universe, he must sit at the feet of the Orient to learn.[71]

As we have seen, similar models of contrast and complementing were already a distinctive part of Keshab Chandra Sen's work, although they were there included in a context of thought that aimed more at syncretism than at religious and national self-assertion. The missionary Christianity which Keshab was so willing to accommodate is, in Vivekananda's view, too closely tied to the materialism and intolerance of the West to represent true religiosity. And to the extent that it really is religion — is it not an absurd suggestion to introduce it into a country which is in its very essence and, as it were, by definition religious, whose national identity Vivekananda seeks to establish through its religiosity?[72]

But even when referring to the introduction of scientific and technical knowledge or the adoption of Western self-confidence and Western vigor, Vivekananda is not satisfied with a mere syncretistic annexation. What appears as an introduction of foreign achievements is also a rediscovery of the forgotten potential of the Indian tradition. In order to be truly appropriated, apparently foreign elements must be founded upon and communicated through the richness of one's own tradition. To a certain degree, this also pertains to the field of the exact sciences; although Vivekananda does not go so far in this regard as Dayananda Sarasvati. Yet he, too, assures his fellow Indians that such sciences as arithmetic and astronomy were already laid out in the Veda and that, in any case, the Indians were not dependent upon the Greeks in this regard.[73]

20. However, science is not the central issue in Vivekananda's rediscovery and reinterpretation of the Indian tradition. It is ethics, social commitment, and national identity itself, which he tries to draw from the sources of Hindu religious and metaphysical thought. The sense of identity and social initiative which he tries to awaken in his fellow Indians must not be a borrowed or derivative one. It must coincide with a sense of rediscovery and reacquisition of their own heritage – and this means, above all, the heritage of Advaita Vedānta, the tradition of Śaṇkara.

Ethics, self-confidence, and brotherly love find their true and binding foundation in Advaitic non-dualism; the Indians have discovered the true and metaphysical principle for that which appears at the surface in the ethical and social efforts of the West. They only have to readopt and transform into social action that which was always in their possession. Their Vedānta must become a "practical Vedānta."[74]

In the same above-cited context in which Vivekananda makes reference to the exemplariness of Western self-confidence and Western will-power, he also states:

> That is what we want, and that can only be created, established and strengthened by understanding and realizing the ideal of the Advaita, that ideal of the oneness of all. Faith, faith, faith in ourselves, faith in God – this is the secret of greatness . . . We have lost faith in ourselves. Therefore to preach the Advaita aspect of the Vedānta is necessary to rouse up the hearts of men, to show them the glory of their souls. It is therefore, that I preach this Advaita. . .[75]

Self-confidence is ultimately confidence in one's own identity with the divine One. Because the Advaita Vedānta teaches this identity with complete clarity, it offers the principle behind that which appears in practice in the West; and what appears to have been borrowed from the West was thus in actuality always encompassed and preserved within the Indian tradition: in other words, it is merely the fulfillment of that which the Vedānta "in itself" had always called for and upheld.

21. With this idea of a "practical Vedānta," Vivekananda takes a step which clearly goes beyond not just the teachings of the classical Vedānta, but also those of his master Ramakrishna: As we have seen, Ramakrishna considered such an engagement in the world and for the world as merely one form of attachment to the world.

Yet it is not only this program of practical and applied Vedānta which distinguishes Vivekananda from Ramakrishna. Together with his will to social reform, Vivekananda develops a tendency to contrast pure origins with later forms of degeneration for which his master most certainly did not provide an example or a justification: Whereas Ramakrishna generally adhered to the evolved whole of Hinduism, Vivekananda comes close to the search for origins and the awareness of degeneration expressed by Rammohan Roy. Śaṅkara is his great example, as he desired to return the Indian world to its "pristine purity."[76] Vivekananda deplores that the truly authoritative Veda is eclipsed in its validity by the Purāṇas and Tantras, documents of an increasing historical degeneration.[77]

In this context, Vivekananda severely reproaches Buddhism, to which he assigns considerable responsibility for the degeneration of Hinduism, and especially for the corruption of Tantrism and the "Brahmanic idolatry." In his opinion, as Buddhism itself degenerated, it infected, as it were, Hinduism.[78]

On the other hand, Vivekananda also refers to Buddhism as nothing less than the "fulfillment of Hinduism" and as a source of energy and inspiration: "Hinduism cannot live without Buddhism, nor Buddhism without Hinduism."[79] In order to resolve and explain this contradiction, we should first recall that Vivekananda repeatedly makes an emphatic distinction between the Buddha himself, the great teacher and practitioner of compassion, and the errors and shortcomings of his followers.[80] Besides, it is a striking and symptomatic fact that his friendly and approving comments are usually presented to Western, primarily American, audiences, while his criticism and warnings find their expression mostly in India. There are equally symptomatic changes and ambiguities in his attitude towards Tantrism, which he often condemned in public and yet accepted and valued as an essential ingredient of his Indian, specifically Bengali identity.

22. This agrees with the above-mentioned fact that Vivekananda's comments contain elements that are essentially rhetorical, were composed with strategic and tactical considerations in mind, and paid heed to the occasion and the expectations of his listeners. It also provides an indication of the ambivalent hermeneutic situation in which Vivekananda finds himself: his references to Buddhism, both in India and in the West, bear the mark of his discussion with the West and his broken and apologetic relationship to his own tradition. Speaking to his fellow Indians, it is not so much Buddhism per se which he rejects as it is Western attempts to play off Buddhism against Hinduism.[81] On the other hand, in his appearances before Western audiences, Buddhism serves to demonstrate the universal reach and inclusivist power of Hinduism. The Hindu relationship to Buddhism is utilized as an example of a successfully completed absorption and neutralization of a great missionary religion: "But in India this gigantic child was absorbed, in the long run, by the mother that gave it birth, and today the very name of Buddha is almost unknown all over India."[82] Vivekananda repeatedly stresses that Buddhism is the oldest and most successful of all

missionary religions, having spread at an early date over the "civilized world" of its time – "from Lapland to the Philippines."[83] Within India itself, however, this world-wide religion was nothing more than a "sect."[84]

Implied in these statements are references to Christianity and its missionary claims; and such references do not at all remain merely implicit. Invoking Western authors, Vivekananda also makes the attempt to historically and genetically derive the basic doctrines of Christianity and its missionary impetus from Buddhism.[85] In this way, Buddhism becomes a vehicle for historical reductionism and an inclusivistic neutralization of Christianity.

In general, the way in which Buddhism is treated has a symptomatic role to play in the development of modern Hindu thought. Whereas Ramakrishna's comments remained within the traditional framework, Bankim Chandra Chatterji already exhibited the same petulant reaction to Western interpretations of Buddhism that may be found with Vivekananda.[86] The attitude of Rabindranath Tagore was more positive, while S. Radhakrishnan concerned himself with Buddhism in an especially detailed and yet quite ambivalent manner.[87]

23. Vivekananda's Neo-Hindu self-awareness is also characterized by the manner in which he takes up the traditional concept of the *mleccha*. The inconsistency of those modern traditionalists who theoretically adhere to their ancient exclusivism but in practice have long since acceded to cooperate with their foreign rulers provides him with an obvious occasion for critique: "And to the Brahmins I say, 'Vain is your pride of birth and ancestry. Shake it off. Brahminhood, according to your Shastras, you have no more now, because you have for so long lived under Mleccha kings.' "[88] If they were to take their own prescriptions seriously, then they would have to follow the reputed example of Kumārila and burn themselves slowly in the *tuṣa* fire in order to atone for this defilement. "Do you know what the Shastras say about people who have been eating Mleccha food and living under a government of the Mlecchas, as you have for the past thousand years? Do you know the penance for that?"[89]

Here, Vivekananda is contrasting the theoretical pride of the Brahmins with their factual and practical humiliation. He has only scorn and contempt for this type of thinking, emphasizing purity and exclusivity as it does: It is an essential element of his message and of the life he lives that India must fully accede to the contact and intercourse with other nations and religions in order to fulfill its own religious and national potential, in order to become a nation and to demonstrate the power and fullness of Hinduism. From time to time, he also refers to passages in the traditional literature which he finds incompatible with the ethnic exclusivism and the pejorative treatment of the *mleccha*; for example, he asserts in a curious misinterpretation of a passage in the *Nyāyabhāṣya* that Vātsyāyana, its author, stated that the *mleccha* have "seers" (*ṛṣi*) of a Vedic caliber.[90]

Vivekananda repeatedly advances an ethical and spiritual reinterpretation of the contrast between "Aryan" and "non-Aryan" that is reminiscent of Buddhist procedures: "He is of the 'arian' race, who is born through prayer, and he is a nonarian, who is born through sensuality."[91]

24. Yet it becomes clear time and again that for Vivekananda, such ethical and spiritual demarcations coincide with ethnic and national delimitations. A definition of the *mleccha* based merely upon factors of ethnicity or birth should be replaced by a concept of *ārya/mleccha* of a higher order. This higher concept should then in turn be utilized to call the Indians to a new ethnic and national self-awareness. By the way, this double step from ethnic to ethical and spiritual and then again to ethnic/national is not uncommon in Neo-Hinduism.

The *true* Aryans are those who have attained a knowledge of the nature of the divine Self: In Vivekananda's view, however, these are de facto the Indians, who have preserved their sacred knowledge within the Sanskrit tradition.

There was, from the earliest times, a broad distinction between the Aryas and the non-Sanskrit speaking Mlecchas in the conception of the soul. Externally, it was typified by their disposal of the dead — the Mlecchas mostly trying their best to *preserve* the dead bodies either by careful burial or by the more elaborate processes of mummifying, and the Aryas generally burning their dead. Herein lies the key to a great secret — the fact that no Mleccha race, whether Egyptian, Assyrian, or Babylonian, ever attained to the idea of the soul as a separate entity which can live *independent* of the body, without the help of the Aryas, especially of the Hindus.[92]

Admittedly, both here and in similar contexts, the concept of the Arya is not simply identified with that of the Hindu, and it appears as if Vivekananda is here making an at least implicit concession to the recent European use of the term "Aryan." On other occasions, however, he rejects such a Western usage and emphasizes that the word "Arya" may only be applied to the Hindus.[93] In general, there can be no doubt that Vivekananda frequently used the word "Arya" to appeal to the self-esteem of the Indians *as* Indians — in a sense in which even the Europeans, who in his view had never by themselves realized the true nature of the "soul," i.e., the *ātman*, were *not* Aryans: "What we call Manas, the mind, the Western people call soul. The West never had the idea of soul until they got it through Sanskrit philosophy, some twenty years ago."[94]

East and West, India and Europe - these are geographical and ethnic notions. For Vivekananda, however, they also represent ethical, spiritual, and metaphysical categories.

25. Vivekananda preaches universal tolerance and openness, the harmony of the religions, and the synthesis of East and West. Yet at the same time, he finds in this program the essential confirmation and fulfillment of his own tradition – of the Hinduism identified with the Vedānta – which he considers to be not just a particular religion, but rather religion per se. He aspires to a harmony in the sense of this tradition and within the framework it provides. And in doing so, he sees himself as the spokesman for a people which owes its ethnic distinction to the possession of this tradition and which should assert its national self-esteem by reflecting upon this tradition and by proclaiming and propagating it outside of India.

The spread of the supposedly Vedāntic ideas of spirituality, tolerance, and harmony amounts to a conquest of the world by Hinduism. The Indians are repeatedly called upon to "conquer" the world, and in particular the West, with their spirituality.[95] Western colonialism and imperialism is thus up against a kind of spiritual expansionism and "imperialism." Here, Vivekananda's primary concern is not with winning converts to Hinduism – notwithstanding the fact that he occasionally alludes to the idea of a "conversion" to Hinduism.[96] More important is his conviction that Hinduism does not require any conversions at all, that the remaining religions are all in truth encompassed by Hinduism from their very inception and, moreover, that Hinduism in principle already anticipates all future developments within itself. Thus, it may face the challenges posed by history and the world with calm self-assurance. Here we find the successor to Ramakrishna speaking, who provides the inclusivism embodied by his master with its most exemplary expressions:

> Ours is the universal religion. It is inclusive enough, it is broad enough to include all the ideals. All the ideals of religion that already exist in the world can be immediately included, and we can patiently wait for all the ideals that are to come in the future to be taken in the same fashion, embraced in the infinite arms of the religion of the Vedānta.[97]

In a sense, the world has already been conquered by Hinduism without even knowing it.

26. Vivekananda agrees with Ramakrishna's criticism of the Brāhma Samāj. He is particularly offended by the imitative and syncretistic elements in this and similar movements – by the degree in which they take the premises and expectations of their English colonial lords into consideration. Imitation and conformity cannot lead to new strength, but are instead symptoms of humiliation and decay. "O India, this is your terrible danger. The spell of imitating the West is getting such a strong hold upon you, that what is good or what is bad is no longer decided by reason, judgement, discrimination or reference to the Shastras. Whatever ideas, whatever manners the white men

praise or like, are good; whatever things they dislike or censure, are bad!"[98] To be sure, the search for confirmation and recognition in the West is, as we have seen, a central motif in Vivekananda's own activities. Although he is concerned with a self-assertion of Hinduism based upon Hinduism's own sources, the way in which he returns to these sources is mediated by his encounter with the West and shaped by Western models and expectational horizons. This is particularly true of Vivekananda's program for a "practical" and ethically and socially "applied" Advaita Vedānta.

P. Hacker's views concerning the systematic and historical implications of this specifically Neo-Hindu program are both penetrating and provocative.[99] His thesis is that the doctrine of an ethical and social applicability of the Vedānta philosophy of identity was not only inspired in a more general sense by the encounter with the West, but that the Western starting point can be precisely identified and a date provided for the beginning of its influence upon modern Indian thought: The first person who attached the idea of ethical applicability to the Indian doctrine of identity and its formulation as *tat tvam asi* was A. Schopenhauer, who was working within the context of his own system of ethics. In turn, Schopenhauer's follower P. Deussen adopted this idea and introduced it into modern Indian thought on February 25, 1893 through a speech in Bombay and on September 9, 1896 during a personal conversation with Vivekananda.[100]

To support and illustrate his thesis, Hacker provides a survey and interpretation of passages from Sanskrit literature which link ethical maxims, in particular those concerning compassion and selflessness, with metaphysical and theological teachings. His conclusion is that in none of these passages is the identity principle expressed in *tat tvam asi* used as a metaphysical justification to support ethical demands: When a "reason" is provided in these cases, then it is based upon an assimilation or approximation to the other based upon the common presence of God in all persons, but not through any identification with God. Hacker concedes that the *Bhagavadgītā* contains the rudiments of a panentheistic justification for ethics - but not one based upon the philosophy of identity. In another work, sc. his important study of the myth of Prahlāda, he traces the role and development of this panentheistic argument within the Vaiṣṇava tradition.[101]

27. The challenge expressed here has not yet been taken up by the representatives of the Neo-Vedānta, and a historical and philological discussion is hardly to be expected from this camp. The basic significance and pertinence of Hacker's observations is undeniable. Yet his thesis, which involves questions concerning the interpretation of Schopenhauer as well as the Indian tradition and Neo-Hinduism, calls for further reflection and has to be modified in certain details. Hacker himself amended his view on a later occasion: "I would just like to note that I, when I wrote that arti-

cle, had not yet recognized the *apposition* of Schopenhauer's moral justification with Vivekananda's positivistic ethic and the imperative of believing in one's own self."[102]

Such an apposition is significant indeed: there is no single or fully unified foundation of ethics in Vivekananda's thought. Instead, several motives appear in juxtaposition. Often, one or the other is taken up for tactical or rhetorical purposes, in accordance with a particular audience; and the fact that *one* viewpoint is occasionally given more emphasis than another by no means implies that it alone is of central importance. *One* single event was not enough to bring Vivekananda onto the path of his "practical Vedānta." Apart from Western sources, such Indian texts as the *Yogavāsiṣṭha* and the *Aṣṭāvakragītā* had prepared him for the possibility of combining ethics and metaphysics. Deussen's ideas, and specifically the conversation of 1896, provided additional support and further encouragement not only for his practical program, but also for his Hindu self-assertion against the West.

It is, however, obvious that a certain change in style and emphasis took place under the influence of Deussen's arguments. In the *Karmayoga*, based upon a series of lectures, Vivekananda was still expounding a theory of action which, with its postulate of disinterested action and its repeated assurance that, ultimately, the world was not to be helped, was largely indebted to the *Bhagavadgītā* and, moreover, to the teachings of Ramakrishna.[103]

The impressions made by his stay in the West apparently contributed to a certain "secularization" of his position: Acting within the world no longer served primarily as a means to a soteriological end; instead, religious and spiritual means were sought to fulfill worldly and social ends.

28. Hacker states that traditional Advaita Vedānta and Hinduism in general "had certainly not ethically applied the tat tvam asi before the beginning of European influence..., at least not in the sense of Schopenhauer's understanding."[104] And in fact, several of Vivekananda's direct predecessors, including Debendranath Tagore and Dayananda Sarasvati, had taken exception to Śaṅkara's Advaita Vedānta precisely because they considered it to be unsuited for ethical and social practice. But as we have noticed, Vivekananda's understanding of the Vedānta was not only shaped by Śaṅkara, but also by the *Yogavāsiṣṭha* and the *Aṣṭāvakragītā*. Moreover, we have not yet determined the exact sense in which one may speak of Schopenhauer's "applying" the *tat tvam asi*. His view is that philosophical ethics is essentially descriptive, even contemplative. It does not prescribe what ought to be done, and, moreover, is not concerned with putting metaphysical principles into practice. Schopenhauer's essentially negative view of the empirical world rules out a practical interest in it; he rejects the attempts of traditional philosophical ethics to advance a "universal

recipe to generate all the virtues."[105] Accordingly, he is not concerned with deriving practical *demands* from the *tat tvam asi*. He refers instead to the metaphysical truth expressed in this sentence in order to *explain* what he considers to be the central ethical phenomenon of compassion and selfless action – namely as a manifestation of the fundamental unity of reality which has not yet achieved the full clarity of knowledge.

It is Deussen and not Schopenhauer who is concerned with "conclusions" of an ethical nature that could lead to an improvement of the empirical world. It is Deussen who cites the Biblical phrase "and you shall know them by their fruits" and tries to combine Schopenhauer's metaphysics of the absolute will with the Christian ethic of charity in a "harmonious whole,"[106] and who calls upon the Indians to draw the appropriate ethical conclusions from their metaphysics of unity. The "metaphysical foundation" thus reveals itself to be a utilitarian appeal to common sense as well, insofar as according to the identity principle one ultimately does something good for oneself by helping others.

The special importance which Deussen's view that the Vedānta contains the "purest form" of morals gained for Vivekananda can only be assessed when one recalls the extent to which the Christian missionaries of the nineteenth century had stressed the ethical and social deficiency of the Vedānta and turned the criterion of utility *against* it: "Let Utility then answer if she prefers Vedantism to Christianity."[107] Time and again, allusions were made to various ethical, social, and civilizing "consequences" in order to propagate the superiority of Christianity over the Vedānta.[108]

Ultimately, the practical thrust in Vivekananda's thought and its articulation in the form of a "practical Vedānta" also provided an answer to this challenge. In essence, Vivekananda was not concerned with merely appending an ethical and social dimension onto Hindu thought, but rather with deriving this from the most basic principles of Hinduism itself. To this extent, his relationship to practice is pivotal to his relationship with the Western world.

In general, the role of ethics is central for the self-understanding and self-articulation of modern Hindu thought. We may recall here the efforts of Rammohan Roy, but also those of more traditional "reformers," for instance Svāminārāyaṇa (1781–1830) in Gujarat or, among Vivekananda's contemporaries, Nārāyaṇa Guru (1854–1913) in Kerala. In Maharashtra, Viṣṇubāvā Brahmacārī (i.e., V.B. Gokhale, 1825–1892), "proposed an utopian socialism based on Vedāntic monism." B.G. Tilak (1856–1920), who was familiar with Deussen's lecture in Bombay and whom Hacker includes in his argumentation concerning the origins of "practical Vedānta," found inspiration for an ethically applied monism in the *Jñāneśvarī*, the great Marathi commentary on the *Bhagavadgītā* completed in 1290.[109]

29. Vivekananda stands at the end of the same century whose beginning was witnessed by Rammohan. During this time, Rammohan's receptivity, which exhibited only the cautious beginnings of universalist self-assertion, had been replaced by a much greater initiative towards the outside world, and the West in particular, an expansive sense of mission and destiny. Vivekananda was aware of the fact that in his undertaking to carry Indian spirituality into the West, he had seized an historical opportunity created by Europe itself, he had to utilize channels of communication which were provided by the West. "Owing to English genius, the world today has been linked in such a fashion, as has never before been done. Today trade centres have been formed such as have never been before in the history of mankind, and immediately, consciously or unconsciously, India rises up and pours forth her gifts of spirituality, and they will rush through these roads till they have reached the very ends of the world."[110]

However, Vivekananda does not present us with any hermeneutic reflections as to how far the *contents* of his "spiritualistic" message have been affected by Western categories and expectations: He is not willing or able to see how far he has removed himself from the position of Śaṅkara and how much he has yielded to those Western means of orientation against which he desires to assert Hinduism. Critics have characterized his doctrine as a "so-called Vedānta," and they have referred to the "hasty improvisation" with which he and other representatives of Neo-Hinduism have tried to combine Western impulses with "inherited spiritual goods."[111] Indeed, Vivekananda wants to avoid compromising with Western secularism, but cannot avoid the following unresolved dilemma: India should prove its secular value as a nation using the standards of the West; but it should also preserve its spirituality and avoid the Western entanglement in *saṃsāra.*[112] The secularization of the Vedāntic tradition is yearned for and yet again shunned. The ambivalence and "improvisation," which is so characteristic of Vivekananda's thought, appears as if caricatured among several of his numerous successors and imitators, e.g., Svami Ramatirtha (1873–1906), who visited America soon after Vivekananda and taught: "Domestic, social, political or religious salvation of every country lies in Vedānta carried into effect."[113]

Yet it would not be appropriate to judge Vivekananda's achievements primarily against the standards set by the teachings and the intellectual level of Śaṅkara. In spite of all "hastiness" and imbalance, his work represents a genuine and exemplary manifestation of the encounter between India and the West.

30. Before we turn to a short survey of developments in the twentieth century, and to a few recent instances of pandit traditionalism, we should first mention two figures who provided a contrast to Vivekananda during the

nineteenth century: Dayananda Sarasvati and Bankim Chandra Chatterji (Bankimcandra Caṭṭopādhyāya).

The Bengali author and thinker Bankim Chandra Chatterji (1838–1894) may not be as well-known outside India as Vivekananda, yet he was just as important for the development of Neo-Hindu thinking. In contrast to Vivekananda, Bankim primarily employed the Bengali language; yet his readiness to adopt and appropriate the Western natural scientific point of view surpassed that of Vivekananda; and the Hindu self-assertion and willingness to reform which he advocated were more unreservedly secular. Ramakrishna held a correspondingly negative opinion of Bankim.[114]

The *dharma* concept, which is one of the fundamental notions of traditional Hinduism, appears in Bankim's thought as a vehicle of appropriating European "Humanism" and "Positivism," in particular that represented by A. Comte, who for a while enjoyed great popularity in Bengal. The role which *dharma* plays in Bankim's thought shall be discussed in more detail below in connection with our systematic discussion of the Neo-Hindu reinterpretation of this concept.[115]

At the focal point of Bankim's new approach lies the concept of *anuśīlana*, which appears in the subtitle of his main philosophical work *Dharmatattva* and which he utilizes in his attempts to reconcile the Western ideas of "culture" and secular progress with the traditional Indian context. For Bankim, the "cultivation" of one's self and one's own potential and thus the realization and actualization of one's humanity or "humanness" (*manuṣyatva*) is part and parcel of the concept of man.[116] This in turn he tries to legitimize from within the Hindu tradition by invoking the humanistically and positivistically re-interpreted concept of *dharma*. In it, he finds the ideas of "duty" and "essence" (i.e., "essential attribute") to be interwoven. Bankim emphasizes the importance of the physical and worldly for the attainment of full "humanness" and as a precondition for the possibility of religious development. He is convinced that India must look to its foreign lords, the British, in order to obtain knowledge about and proficiency in this domain, which is also indispensable for the "cultivation" (*anuśīlana*) and securing of India's own national strength and autonomy.[117]

31. In his literary work and his activity as editor of the journal *Baṅgadarśana*, Bankim Chandra adheres firmly and intentionally to the Bengali language. This is a fundamental component of his program of "patriotism" (*svadeśaprīti*) and self-assertion vis-à-vis the Europeans. On the other hand, he also considers it imperative that this vehicle of self-assertion be opened up for the acceptance and transmission of Western concepts and terms. He often includes long English quotes in his Bengali philosophical works and makes use of corresponding English expressions

when explaining problematic Bengali terms or neologisms. Unlike Vivekananda, he develops a clear hermeneutic awareness of problems concerning the intercultural correspondence of terms and concepts.[118] He often discusses in detail the contemporary scientific and philosophical literature of Europe, without exhibiting Vivekananda's rhetorical and popularizing tendencies. He also speaks of European Indology, of India's role as an object for European research, using a largely critical tone.[119]

The humanitarian and nationalistic aspects of his philosophical and literary program are interwoven with one another in an idiosyncratic fashion, although nationalism seems to occupy the primary position: Patriotism (*svadeśaprīti*) and the love of mankind (*manuṣyatva*) are to be cultivated equally and integrated in one another; if this were to succeed, India would accede to the highest rank in the world.[120] The Indians should adopt the concepts of national independence and freedom from the British; yet they should also try to recreate and legitimize them out of their own tradition in such a way that they may utilize them against the British with complete self-assurance.[121]

Bankim derives his claims to national self-assertion and superiority largely from the universal and "inclusivistic" wealth of the *religious* tradition of Hinduism (to which he tries to give a new secular meaning). He stresses the Hinduism of the Purāṇas and its evolved totality against what he sees as the abstract and other-worldly teachings of the Vedānta. The emphasis on the *Bhagavadgītā* is much stronger and more pronounced than among his predecessors. Kṛṣṇa becomes the very epitome of Hindu self-awareness;[122] he represents the superior richness of Hinduism, its comprehensive power of integration, against the religious and philosophical claims of the Europeans.

Yet the model for Bankim's presentation is that of a "humanistically" influenced European picture of Christ which arose in the nineteenth century.[123] While Bankim may claim the evolved whole of Hinduism as the basis of national self-awareness, Hinduism is and remains filtered by Western concepts and goals. Ramakrishna's criticism of Bankim's presentation of Kṛṣṇa and Hinduism is exemplary: Who can really be a Hindu who accepts Kṛṣṇa but not the Gopīs?[124]

Naturalism and secularism and the corresponding reinterpretation of the concept of *dharma* acquire much more pronounced forms among such thinkers and writers as Aksay Kumar Datta.[125]

32. Admittedly, Dayānanda Sarasvatī (1824–1883), the founder of the reform movement Ārya Samāj whose work we shall discuss at the close of this chapter, can hardly be numbered among the representatives of modern Indian *philosophy*. This notwithstanding, he provides a lucid, exemplary, and somewhat naively exaggerated illustration of some of the main motifs and tensions in modern Indian thought: traditionalism and modernism,

self-assertion and receptivity, nationalism and universalism — all are interwoven in his thought in a very characteristic fahsion; efforts towards reform, assimilation, and progress are linked with an uncompromising, yet radically reinterpreted adherence to the oldest sources of his own tradition.

Dayananda, an unusually prolific author and polemicist from Gujarat, adhered primarily to the Vedic *Saṃhitās*, those superior teachings of the Indian "Aryans" which were never created and predate all historical developments, having been originally communicated by God.[126] It is from these Dayananda considered human knowledge and human civilization to have been ultimately derived. However, the Indians themselves, the original recipients and guardians of the Vedic revelation, have failed to preserve its proper understanding. The "polytheism" of the Purāṇas and the escapism of the Advaita Vedānta have obscured and concealed what is actually a message of pure monotheism and the mastering of the secular world. As a consequence, this message has been forgotten, and the Neo-Vedāntic "reformers" have kept it in oblivion.

Even the Europeans ultimately owe their technological and scientific achievements and thus their present superiority over the Indians to their having originally been instructed by the Indians. Of course, they have become entangled within a historically derivative and degenerate religion — Christianity — which Dayananda sharply criticizes and compares to the Hinduism of the Purāṇas.[127] The motif that the Western sciences and all civilizations in general are ultimately dependent upon India and the Veda is taken up with an even greater resolve by Dayananda's follower Gurudatta and linked to a sharp criticism of Western Indological research.[128]

Dayananda emphasizes the universal, global significance of the Vedic teachings; he is critical of the historically developed forms of the caste system. And yet his orientation remains essentially ethnic. He reverts emphatically back to the old concept of *ārya* — which he views as a concept largely determined by ethnicity and geography — as well as the equally ancient contrasting concept of *dasyu*.[129] The message of the Vedas is that of the universal and rational religion which embraces all peoples and groups; because of their original possession of this message, however, the Indian "Aryans" were and still are prominent among all peoples. Still, for the historical situation in which India finds itself and for the purpose of its national regeneration, Dayananda recommends that the Indians learn from the virtues and achievements of the Europeans;[130] ultimately, however, all of humanity must learn from those ancient and sacred sources which anticipate in principle all future developments and whose original guardians were the Indians.

33. In addition to his Hindi works, Dayananda is also the author of numerous Sanskrit works, specifically of commentaries to the Vedas. His approach is much more archaizing than that of Vivekananda or Bankim

Chandra; he frequently follows the teachings and exegetic principles of the traditionalist Pūrvamīmāṃsā, and he criticizes the Westernization and the syncreticism of the Brāhma Samāj. Nevertheless, he may also be counted among the representatives of Neo-Hinduism in a number of important points; indeed, there were various controversies between his movement and the exponents of "orthodoxy" and traditionalism.[131]

In the introduction of his Sanskrit commentary to the *Ṛgveda*, Dayananda attempts to demonstrate in detail that substantial elements of modern science and technology may be found in the Veda; among other things, he speaks of the Vedic teachings about telecommunications (*tāravidyā;* "transmission knowledge"), about the construction of ships and aircaft (*nauvimānavidyā*), and about gravity and gravitational attraction (*ākarṣaṇa, anukarṣaṇa*). He also provides examples of Vedic achievements in the fields of administration and politics.[132] In each of these cases, Dayananda maintains that such later Hindu commentators as Sāyaṇa completely misunderstood the original meaning of the Vedic revelation. Moreover, he also assumes that an analogous process of adulteration and false interpretation has affected the Vedic auxiliary sciences and supplements (*vedāṅga, upaveda*) as well as the philosophical systems (*darśana*, assigned to the Vedas as "additional limbs," *upāṅga*); and within these disciplines, he makes a rigorous distinction between the basic texts and what he considers to be counterfeit commentaries.[133] Outside of the Ārya Samāj, Dayananda's theses are usually considered a curiosity among the exegeses of the Veda and have been subjected to ridicule; disregarding their "curiousness," however, they also possess a symptomatic importance, for they illustrate the central role which modern science and technology play within the challenge to India that is posed by the West and for the self-understanding and self-representation of Hinduism vis-à-vis the West. The fascination with science and technology was already great with Rammohan Roy; Keshab Chandra Sen and Vivekananda attempted to meet it with models stressing the mutual complementing of East and West. On the other hand, some Europeans were convinced that introducing European scientific thought into India would help pave the way for the reception of Christianity,[134] and they presented scientific and social progress as the concomitant and consequence of Christianity. However, this strategy was not very effective. The Hindu reaction consisted in viewing Western progress as being independent of Christianity as well as in attempts to show that the Indian tradition does not merely provide a potentially equal or superior substratum for such achievements, but was actually their historical basis. Dayananda's exegesis of the Veda illustrates this in an extreme, yet exemplary fashion.

14. Supplementary Observations on Modern Indian Thought

1. Our presentation has brought us to the threshold of the twentieth century. We have focused on thinkers and religious "reformers" who have come to symbolize the achievements of modern Hindu self-affirmation, but also the problems and ambiguities of assimilation and adjustment. In both respects, Vivekananda, who died in 1901, exemplifies and summarizes the developments since Rammohan Roy.

We have not dealt with other writers, thinkers, educators, political leaders who, though perhaps not as well known as Vivekananda, are by no means less significant. One of the greatest educators and most efficient "reformers" stands chronologically between Rammohan and Vivekananda—Ishvar Chandra Vidyasagar (Īśvaracandra Vidyāsāgara, 1820-1891). In 1849, Vidyasagar published a Bengali biography of "great Europeans." He was one of the first Indians to apply Western historical and critical methods. His "Introduction to Sanskrit Grammar" (*Saṃskṛta vyākaraṇer upakramaṇikā*) and his "History of Bengal" (*Baṅglār itihāsa*), also in Bengali, are works without precedent in the Indian tradition.[1] Vidyasagar never visited Europe and never abandoned his confidence in what he considered to be superior European learning and rationality. His contemporary, the poet Michael Madhusudan Datta (1824-1873), did go to England and subsequently expressed his disenchantment with the West, his deep personal tension between India and Europe, and his search for new modes of self-assertion. As a writer, he abandoned the English language and returned to his native Bengali.[2] A few decades later, the young Rabindranath Tagore (Ṭhākura, 1861-1941), who was to become the most celebrated poet of modern India, visited England and recorded his impressions as follows: "I had thought that the island of England was so small and the inhabitants so dedicated to learning that, before I arrived there, I expected the country from one end to the other would echo and re-echo with the lyrical essays of Tennyson; and I also thought that wherever I might be in this narrow island, I would hear constantly Gladstone's oratory, the explanation of the Vedas by Max Mueller, the scientific truth of Tindall, the profound thoughts of Carlyle and the philosophy of Bain. I was under the impression that wherever I would go I would find the old and the young drunk with the pleasure of 'intellectual' enjoyment. But I have been very disappointed in this."[3]

In addition to Bankim Chandra Chatterji (1838–1894), Dayananda Sarasvati (1824–1883) and Bal Gangadhar Tilak (1856–1920), numerous other authors have combined the reinterpretation of the religious and philosophical tradition with nationalism and political activities; for instance, Madan Mohan Malaviya (1861–1946), patriot, educator and founder of Banaras Hindu University, or Bipin Chandra Pal (1858–1932), political ideologist and activist in Bengal.[4] We cannot discuss the activities of these personalities and their contributions to the independence movement which culminated in the work of Gandhi (1869–1948). Nor can we discuss the complex state of Hindu thought and xenology in the twentieth century. As we have stated before—this study does *not* deal with contemporary Indian thought, or the current state of the "East-West dialogue," but only with the historical antecedents and the hermeneutical presuppositions of the current situation.[5]

In the following brief supplement to our discussion of nineteenth-century Indian thought and xenology, we will present some preliminary observations concerning the work of two leading Neo-Hindus, Aurobindo and Radhakrishnan, and then turn briefly to some more conservative and traditionalistic expressions of modern Indian thought.

2. Aurobindo Ghose (Sri Aurobindo, 1872–1950) and Sarvepalli Radhakrishnan (1888–1975) are the two most representative Neo-Hindu thinkers of the twentieth century. In different ways, they exemplify the potential and the problems of Neo-Hinduism. Let us first turn to Aurobindo. The very dates of his life are telling, if not ominous: Born in Calcutta in 1872, he spent the period between 1879 and 1893 in England, after which he returned to India, where he became a passionate spokesman of nationalism and a political revolutionary. In 1908, he was arrested by the colonial authorities and jailed in Alipur for approximately one year. In 1910, he escaped British jurisdiction by resettling in the French possession of Pondicherry. There, he led a non-political life dedicated to meditation and inner search until his death in 1950. He became the center of an institutionalized circle of students, the Sri Aurobindo Ashram, the practical organization of which was left to Mira Richard, better known as the "Mother."[6]

In contrast to Vivekananda—whom he clearly exceeds in intellectual and visionary power—Aurobindo does not go "missionizing" into the West; instead, he returns to India from Europe and discovers his own tradition as a kind of foreigner. English is the language through which he is introduced to the great works of the Sanskrit tradition. From the West, he also brings key elements of his radical *political* will to self-assertion.

Aurobindo transforms the spiritual nationalism of Vivekananda, one of his major inspirations,[7] into revolutionary praxis, which he interprets as the historical actualization of religion and the Vedānta. Nationalism itself becomes a kind of religion, the engagement for a political and national liberation of India a religious and soteriological act, a "political Vedantism" which gives new meaning to the concept of "salvation" (*mokṣa*).[8] Just as with Vivekananda, the motif of inclusivism serves as a device of religious and national self-assertion. Hinduism, the "eternal religion," the "universal religion," the *sanātana dharma*, encompasses and anticipates all other religions, just as it encompasses and anticipates the "discoveries of science and the speculations of philosophy." In this sense, it must manifest itself as nationalism.[9] And the national awakening of Hindu India is fundamentally superior to the nationalistic endeavors of other countries insofar as it concerns the regaining and actualizing of a spirituality and universality which is destined to be "poured out" over the entire world.[10]

3. As we have seen, Aurobindo's political activism ceased during the second half of his life, the period he spent in Pondicherry. Yet the meditative experimentation which he carried out in those years and through which he hoped to actualize and demonstrate the spiritualistic potential of Hinduism was in itself a kind of Hindu self-assertion. Hindu nationalism and spiritualistic universalism dominate the two major phases in Aurobindo's exemplary Neo-Hindu life. They are distinct from one another and yet are interrelated and complementary means of self-assertion.

Impressive testimony of his experience of alienation, his search for a truly intrinsic, genuine sense of identity, invocations of the lost glory and autonomy of India, and sharp criticism of the Neo-Hindu tendency to half-heartedly imitate and "hastily improvise" are common in Aurobindo's early writings:

> We have tried to assimilate, we have tried to reject, we have tried to select, but we have not been able to do any of these things successfully. Successful assimilation depends on mastery; but we have not mastered European conditions and knowledge, rather we have been seized, subjected and enslaved by them . . . Let us not . . . select at random, make a nameless hotchpotch and then triumphantly call it the assimilation of East and West . . . India can never cease to be India or Hinduism to be Hinduism, if we really think for ourselves. It is only if we allow Europe to think for us that India is in danger of becoming an ill-executed and foolish copy of Europe.[11]

In his attempt to establish the identity of Hinduism and its importance for the modern world, Aurobindo does not advocate a return to earlier phases of its history, nor does he merely assert its timeless validity: Instead, he tries to provide it with a new sense of vitality and change, with a new, or at least revived, openness for questions and experiments. If this is a restoration or return, then it is, according to Aurobindo, a return to the sources of experience themselves, from which Hinduism won its former creative power and autonomy and which alone can open it new perspectives for the future. Not only should this potential of experience be asserted, it should be manifested and activated in the practice of inner experimentation, i.e. the exploration of the dynamics of awareness, and thus become a part of the actuality of the modern world. Such an experimenting with consciousness, understood as a renewal and actualization of the Hindu tradition, would also take up and neutralize the challenges posed by the experimental natural sciences and technological achievements of the West. In a sense, Aurobindo tried to revive and concretize the ancient ideal of the *ṛṣi* for the modern world.[12]

4. In spite of the inclusivistic statements made during his youth, Aurobindo does not accept the presumption that "true Hinduism" has already anticipated all future developments. He develops a new sense for the temporal and historical, for the human and social shaping of the Divine. In this regard, he does not agree with other Neo-Hindu thinkers. In contrast to Vivekananda, he is greatly influenced by the nineteenth-century Western evolutionists, and the historical perspective of Hegel and some of his followers is an important element in his thought.[13] He does not accept the timeless presence of the Absolute in the sense of Śaṅkara; in his eyes, the Absolute manifests itself in the historical development of man and the world. Here, the Western ideas of evolution and "progress" attain a new and peculiar significance. On the other hand, the increasing secularization, objectification and externalization of the natural and the social world which has accompanied the sciences in the West should be supplemented, fulfilled, and ultimately superseded by developments and discoveries in the spiritual realm, in the inner reality of the self.

We do not need to go into details concerning the special and sometimes highly speculative theories and methods which Aurobindo developed in this context.[14] What is particularly noteworthy is that the ascent to new stages and dimensions of consciousness, the thrust into the "supramental" etc., is presented as a concrete historical task not limited to the inner world of the individual but involving the cosmos and mankind as well. Aurobindo is convinced that the spiritual realities can be made manifest in the actual, current world, and that in this process Hinduism can prove its concrete historical potential. Like few other modern Hindu thinkers, Aurobindo exerts himself to develop a new and authentic approach to his own tradition; and it is in precisely this way that he responds to and acknowledges the European challenge.[15]

5. "There can be no doubt that the most original Neo-Hindu thinker is Aurobindo; but Radhakrishnan seems to be the most typical."[16] Regardless of the question of originality, it is evident that Radhakrishnan has been a most successful spokesman of Neo-Hinduism in the West, and that he has produced some of the most memorable and persuasive formulations of Neo-Vedāntic thought. On the other hand, his work exemplifies some of the fundamental dilemmas and ambiguities of Neo-Hinduism.[17] Unlike most of the exponents of Hinduism we have discussed so far, Sarvepalli Radhakrishnan (1888–1975) was not from Bengal, but from South India. Born into a family of devout Vaiṣṇavas, he was educated at various schools and colleges. He was enrolled at Madras Christian College in 1904 and received his master's degree in 1909. His most important teacher was the liberal theologian and philosopher A.G. Hogg (1875–1954), a prolific author who was generally sympathetic towards Hinduism, but critical of what he considered to be its ethical deficiencies. Just as Aurobindo, Radhakrishnan first studied classical Indian texts in translations. All his publications were in English. Raised with Tamil and Telugu, he never learned Hindi, the national language of independent India.[18]

We need not discuss in detail Radhakrishnan's extraordinary career as a scholar, teacher, diplomat and statesman. He occupied prestigious positions at Indian and Western universities, for instance in Calcutta and Oxford, and served as the president of UNESCO, the Indian ambassador to Moscow, and finally as the Vice-President and President of the Indian Republic. He received numerous honors and was celebrated as the embodiment of a new cross-cultural and interreligious openness and universality, as the "ambassador between East and West," "the Thomas Aquinas of the modern age."[19] etc. Even the relatively rare cases of criticism of his work still reflect his wide recognition and his exemplary position in the encounter between India and the West.[20]

Radhakrishnan's very first articles—sections from his M.A. thesis which he published in 1908, while he was still a student—already articulate two fundamental themes of his Neo-Hindu apologetics: the importance of philosophy for the identity and self-affirmation of modern India, and the significance and potential application of Advaita Vedānta in the area of ethics and social practice.[21] Like Rammohan and Vivekananda before him, Radhakrishnan was also deeply hurt by the European verdict that Hinduism was ethically deficient and incompatible with social and scientific progress.

Like Vivekananda, Radhakrishnan was not satisfied with rejecting this criticism. Instead, he derived his demand for social reform from it, but also tried to neutralize it by showing that Hinduism, specifically Advaita Vedānta, was not only compatible with ethics, social improvement and international understanding, but capable of providing them with a firm metaphysical basis and framework.

6. In his interpretation of authoritative Indian texts, Radhakrishnan often refers to the realities of the twentieth century. Speaking of his presentation and exegesis of the *Brahmasūtras*, he says: "It has grown out of vital urges and under the pressure of a concrete historical situation."[22] The motif of "actualization," which implies "legitimization" and compensation for the historical humiliation of Hinduism, is quite central. Such "actualization" of the sources of the Vedānta is not meant to serve the regeneration of India alone, but also the regeneration and reconciliation of the entire modern world.

The fact that Radhakrishnan used the English language and often addressed Western audiences had a deep impact upon his thought. He adapted himself to Western premises and expectations, and used Western concepts and terminology for his cross-cultural interpretation and reinterpretation, as well as for his own understanding, of traditional Indian concepts. In his presentations of Indian thought, he usually cites from a wide spectrum of Western literature, most frequently from the Bible. His notes on the *Bhagavadgītā* contain more than thirty quotes from the Bible along with numerous other citations from more than fifty Western authors ranging from Plato to Rilke. In these quotes and references, Radhakrishnan does not pay much attention to philological or historical criteria, and he is not concerned with historically "objective" parallels between the religious and cultural traditions. Instead, he wants to show the concordance of the authoritative texts of Hinduism with exemplary expressions of Western religion and philosophy, as well as with the achievements of modern science.[23] His parallels and identifications are meant to demonstrate and actualize the universal openness, as well as the inclusivistic fullness, of his own tradition.

7. In his attempt to "actualize" Hinduism and its potential for reconciliation and synthesis, Radhakrishnan often extrapolates and universalizes exegetic methods and schemes of concordance which were traditionally used within the limits of specific Indian traditions, and certainly not applied to non-Indian doctrines. In particular, Radhakrishnan focuses on the concept of *samanvaya*, which appears often in the Vedānta and which was chiefly used to harmonize passages in the Upaniṣads:

> Today the samanvaya or harmonisation has to be extended to the living faiths of mankind . . . As the author of the Brahma Sūtra tried to reconcile the different doc-

trines prevalent in his time, we have to take into account the present state of our knowledge and evolve a coherent picture.[24]

Radhakrishnan takes it for granted that such an extension or extrapolation of the traditional *samanvaya* is nothing more than an adjustment to the current state of knowledge and thus a simple and obvious step which is fully warranted by the Hindu tradition itself. In this regard, he presents himself as the successor to such classical Vedānta commentators as Śaṅkara and Rāmānuja.[25] He never acknowledges the exclusivism which is just as characteristic of traditional Hinduism, its exclusion or disregard of the *mleccha*, etc.; in those rare cases where he does make note of traditional statements about the non-Indian world, he either reinterprets them in an idealizing fashion, or simply misinterprets them.[26]

In his notes on the *Bhagavadgītā*, Radhakrishnan cites a well-known Vaiṣṇava verse which he incorrectly attributes to Udayana, according to which the various religious and philosophical groups in India are all ultimately concerned with one and the same God; he adds that had Udayana lived in our time, he would have amended his discussion of Indian sects to include the Christian and Islamic faiths.[27] Obviously, Udayana could have referred to Islam in his time. Yet he did not, just as no other representative of traditional Hindu thought ever seriously considered the non-Indian religions. Radhakrishnan disregards the fact that traditional Hinduism was not used to making explicit adjustments to "current historical situations" or "current states of knowledge." That "actualization" which he presents as such an obvious and unproblematic step has hardly any precedent within traditional Hindu thought; it is itself a step towards "Westernization."[28]

8. At the heart of Radhakrishnan's program of harmonizing lies the concept of "experience." In his eyes, all genuine religious texts are documents of authoritative experiences by "seers"; experience is the "soul of religion."[29] Again, Radhakrishnan utilizes and universalizes traditional concepts in a manner which can hardly be called traditional. He claims the concept of experience as an important means of Neo-Hindu self-assertion: while all religions have their roots in "experience," Hinduism is the religion of experience par excellence, the one religion which remains faithful to its "experimental basis" and preserves an "empirical," undogmatic openness.[30] "Experience" in this sense may also be associated with "science," and even with the modern Western ideas and ideologies of liberalism and "democracy."[31]

The manner in which Radhakrishnan contrasts Hinduism with Christianity and other religions is more conciliatory than that of Vivekananda. Nevertheless, the inclusivistic claim to superiority which we found in Vivekananda's work also appears in Radhakrishnan's writings. In a passage whose formulation is reminiscent of Vivekananda, Radhakrishnan declares that the

Bhagavadgītā is a document of the universal and eternal religion, whose synthetic fullness encompasses the "whole gamut of the human spirit."[32] In a related remark about the Vedānta, we are told that it is "not a religion, but religion itself in its most universal and deepest significance."[33] Radhakrishnan seems convinced that the exemplary universalism of the Vedānta has the power to reveal the hidden universalistic potential and the *philosophia perennis* in the other religions and philosophies as well.[34]

9. Fact and norm, description and idealization, statement and appeal are inseparable in Radhakrishnan's style of thought and presentation;[35] and the rhetorical elements that have been part of Neo-Hinduism since its beginnings in the nineteenth century are very conspicuous and significant in his work. Just like Vivekananda, Radhakrishnan ignores the distinction between the metaphysical and absolute (*paramārtha*) and the empirical (*vyavahāra*) that is observed in traditional Advaita Vedānta; the very presupposition of Radhakrishnan's Neo-Hinduism is that the metaphysics of unity is also capable of offering guidelines for social and political practice.

Radhakrishnan's program of a social and political application and a general "actualization" of the Vedānta has often been glorified and imitated.[36] One of the much less frequent cases of *criticism* of Radhakrishnan is the defense of the Hindu tradition presented by A.K. Coomaraswamy (1877–1947).

As Coomaraswamy, who came from Ceylon, had an English mother, and spent a large part of his life in America, sees it, the "Orient," and especially "India," are the very equivalent of traditionality. In his view, the antithesis of the Orient and Occident is tantamount to the antithesis between traditionality and modernity. The Occident has lost the sense of tradition which it once possessed. It is now the special responsibility of the Orient to preserve and defend its traditionality. Yet this is precisely what such authors as Radhakrishnan, who were trying to "actualize" and "modernize" the Hindu tradition, had failed to do.[37] Closely tied to his concept of tradition are Coomaraswamy's concepts of metaphysics and the *philosophia perennis*. Metaphysics must be distinguished from "mere" philosophy precisely because it is timeless and universal; it represents the *philosophia perennis* and is capable of nourishing the continuity and traditionality of traditional cultures.

10. We do not need to discuss Coomaraswamy's view of tradition, and defense of traditionality, as they are implied or articulated in his wide-ranging work as an art historian and comparative interpreter of Asia and Europe. It is obvious that his professed traditionalism and his invocation of the *philosophia perennis* is by no means a mere continuation of the Hindu tradition. In its own way, it reflects the comparative awareness of a multitude of traditions and the threat of "traditionlessness" and relativism.

It also responds to the modern Western sense of loss of orientation and objective guidance. Coomaraswamy's defense of tradition converges with the European self-critique found in the writings of R. Guénon and F. Schuon; Guénon's "traditionalism" received its first full exposition in his *Introduction générale à l'étude des doctrines hindoues*, which appeared in 1921.[38] In Europe itself, deliberate and explicit "traditionalism" has been a recurrent phenomenon. We may recall here the idea of tradition and traditionality, which such authors as de Bonald, de Lamennais and Ventura di Raulico invoked against the Age of Enlightenment and the French Revolution, and in general against secularism and rationalism.

M.K. Gandhi (1869–1948), the celebrated leader of the independence movement, also tended to substitute the dichotomy between tradition and modernity for that between East and West. However, his manner of advocating tradition was different from that of Coomaraswamy. He did not claim that India was the sole legitimate guardian of traditionality. After many years of living abroad, he declared that there was no such thing as Western or European civilization, but just modern civilization as such—a universal, global phenomenon which he despised. He expressed his rejection of modern civilization and technology already in his first book, *Hind Swaraj or Indian Home Rule*, which appeared in 1909, while he was in South Africa. Gandhi was convinced that the meeting and assimilation between India and Europe which was to occur within the framework of modern civilization would be a shallow and deceptive one. There was the potential for a more profound meeting and mutual understanding if both East and West were free from the spell of modernity, i.e. technology, industrialization, historical "progress," etc. However, the deep problems and the complexity associated with Gandhi's thought and personality are not among the topics of this study.[39]

11. Both Radhakrishnan and Coomaraswamy exemplify an important aspect of modern Hindu thought through their persistent interest in transhistorical comparison and concordance, although their understanding of the *philosophia perennis*, to which they seem equally committed, is rather different. Radhakrishnan himself served as co-editor of a two-volume *History of Philosophy, Eastern and Western* (1952–1953) and of *The Concept of Man: A Study in Comparative Philosophy* (1966, with P.T. Raju). A number of comparative presentations were dedicated to him. His follower and collaborator P.T. Raju wrote an *Introduction to Comparative Philosophy*.[40] In general, "comparative philosophy"—an expression probably introduced by an Indian author—plays a paradigmatic role in modern Hindu thought and self-understanding, and it is an important vehicle of apologetics and cultural self-affirmation.[41]

The concept of philosophy itself has often been associated with cultural and national self-assertion. Important figures of the independence movement and national leaders, such Gandhi or Nehru, have been referred to as "philosophers" and included in presentations of "modern Indian philosophy," even if they personally rejected the classification as "philosophers" and did not show an interest in theoretical thought. On the other hand, academic philosophers often associate their work with the motif of independence; even a deeply theoretical thinker like K.C. Bhattacharya (1875–1949), who was not involved with apologetics, was nevertheless committed to the ideal of *svātantrya*, "sovereignty," "autonomy" in ideas.[42] Of course, many modern Indian thinkers simply participate in the Western enterprise of philosophy; or they cultivate what they consider the neutral, universal, "objective" ground of logic, epistemology and linguistic analysis. Others apply the seemingly objective, transcultural standards of modern philosophical analysis to the study of classical Indian thought. However, in focusing on the analytical achievements of Indian philosophy, they are not always without apologetic motivation.[43]

12. It is not our aim here to discuss the development of the educational system in modern India, the introduction of Western philosophy and science into Indian schools and universities, or the current situation of philosophy in Indian academic life. A few reminders may suffice.

Various factors and shifting constellations have determined which European thinkers have become known and gained influence in India.[44] At first, the initiative in the transmission of European—and Western—knowledge and thought lay in the hands of the missionaries. Subsequently, "secular" institutions, such as the Hindu College in Calcutta (where H. Derozio exhibited his short but consequential activity) came to play an increasingly important role. In 1835, English was "officially" introduced as the language of higher education—an event that is associated with the name of Macaulay. As a result—and in accordance with the recommendations of Ch. Wood (1854)—universities were set up along English lines. Since the times of Rammohan Roy, such Western initiatives have also been supplemented by a variety of forms of cooperation and autonomous efforts from the Indian side.

The reception of European thinkers first took place primarily in Bengal. This, for example, was the case with Th. Paine, whose *The Age of Reason* (1794) was translated into Bengali in various installments.[45] At Hindu College, Derozio presented the ideas of D. Hume. For several decades, A. Comte and his "Positivism" had a dedicated and intellectually influential following in Bengal.[46] H. Spencer, J. St. Mill and A. Bain also became famous; and Rammohan himself corresponded with J. Bentham. Since the close of the nineteenth century (reflecting developments in the English universities) the English Hegelians, and especially F.H. Bradley, have played a significant and influential role. Like Kant afterwards, they have been used in comparisons with the Advaita Vedānta. The name of that great Indophile, A. Schopenhauer, has received frequent mention, although few Indians were actually acquainted with his philosophy. The works of such currently less known writers as J.R. Seeley and J. Ruskin gained considerable influence. Marx has been a topic of discussion since the beginning of the twentieth century.[47] Most recently, Wittgenstein, Austin, "linguistic analysis," etc. have also gained considerable prominence in Indian academic life, as well as in philosophical periodicals.[48]

13. In contrast to Neo-Hinduism and other, less reserved forms of adopting Western ideas which may amount to a complete neglect of traditional Hindu thought, there are ways of survival or deliberate continuation of the Indian tradition in which European concepts and orientations play apparently no role at all and in which the European foreigners are referred to only in accordance with traditional xenology and its basic concept of the *mleccha*. Yet, the absence of explicit forms of assimilation and ostensible influences does not mean that such "traditionalism" has remained entirely unaffected by the Western presence.

What P. Hacker calls "surviving traditional Hinduism," is itself a multifaceted phenomenon, which reflects the Western presence in a variety of ways. It also contains various forms of disagreement with, or even explicit responses to, Neo-Hinduism and its assimilation of Western thought. "Surviving traditional Hinduism" has found its literary articulation in popular tracts in Indian vernaculars, in explications and reinterpretations of myths and rites, in devotional poetry, as well as in commentaries and treatises in Sanskrit—i.e., in what may be called modern pandit literature. For a contrast with the Neo-Hinduism of Aurobindo and Radhakrishnan, this pandit literature in Sanskrit seems particularly appropriate. It has not been considered and cited at all by Hacker; and it has in general found very little attention in the surveys of modern Indian thought and literature. Neither its factual variety nor its basic hermeneutic potential have hitherto been explored.[49]

Since the days of Rammohan Roy, there have been attempts by "traditionalists" to accommodate the Western presence in their own way. Rammohan himself criticized those representatives of the "orthodox" tradition and the community of brahmin scholars, for instance Mṛtyuṃjaya Vidyālaṅkāra, who worked for the European *mlecchas* and made a variety of tacit concessions without being willing and able to enter into an explicit dialogue. There were, however, other Sanskrit traditionalists who did respond explicitly, specifically in oral or written debates with Christian missionaries who for some time were trying to challenge them on their own territory, in their own horizon of thinking, and in Sanskrit. In particular, we may mention those representatives of "resistant Hinduism" whose work was explored by R.F. Young—pandits of the period around 1840 who responded to J. Muir's missionary Sanskrit treatise *Mataparīkṣā*.[50] Regardless of their rejection of the Christian teachings, and in spite of their attempt to respond within the traditional Indian framework of debate—the very fact that they did respond to the *mlecchas* in writing and even in printing constitutes a change and a concession to the Europeans.[51]

14. The history of modern Sanskrit literature, and of the continuation of traditional commentarial and exegetical forms in modern times, has not yet been written. The developments which have taken place within these traditional forms, and in the framework of the traditional schemes of "sciences" (*vidyā*), have not yet been explored. Although much of this seems to be a mere continuation of traditional exegesis and explication, unaffected by the encounter with the West and the modern world in general, there have also been signs of cautious change and reorientation. Some of the guardians of traditional philosophical learning, such as Phaṇibhūṣaṇa Tarkavāgīśa and Anantakumāra Bhaṭṭācārya,[52] were not only aware of, but also keenly interested in modern Western philosophy. Other Sanskrit pandits, for instance Vivekananda's contemporary Upendradatta Pāṇḍeya (1860–1901), went so far as to call for a new, non-scholastic creativity and rationality among traditional Sanskrit scholars.[53]

We should also remember that numerous pandits who continued the commentarial tradition in Sanskrit were employed by the British or other Westerners as editors, "resource persons," etc. In some cases, they worked as translators into English, or they even translated European philosophical literature, for instance Francis Bacon, into Sanskrit. Such towering figures as Gaṅgānātha Jhā and Gopīnātha Kavirāja transcended the role of textual specialists and became living symbols of the breadth and comprehensiveness of the Sanskrit tradition.[54]

For such scholars, continuing the tradition in the face of the growing Western presence and the increasing Indian accommodation and assimilation was itself a deliberate act and an implicit response. H.G. Gadamer's general observations on tradition and its preservation certainly apply to the situation of the modern Indian "traditionalists." "Even the most genuine and solid tradition does not persist by nature because of the inertia of what once existed. It needs to be affirmed, embraced, cultivated. It is, essentially, preservation, such as is active in all historical change. But preservation is an act of reason, though an inconspicuous one."[55] For Indians, we may add, such preservation is also an act of responding to the West. In modern times, responding to the Western presence and the global phenomenon of Westernization is no longer a matter of personal choice or predilection. Even withdrawal and silence, and affirmation and continuation of traditional forms, are ways of responding.

15. That conscious conservatism and traditionalism do not necessarily go hand in hand with xenological self-isolation or an opposition to reform is clearly demonstrated by the example of Rammohan's younger contemporary and antagonist Radhakant Deb (Rādhākānta Deva). This conservative Bengali, who compiled the monumental Sanskrit encyclopedia *Śabdakalpadruma* (1822–1852), rejected Rammohan's ideas yet exerted himself to renew the Indian system of education. Radhakant, who had a command of the English language and was obviously impressed by the Western sciences, represents what might be called liberal orthodoxy. He corresponded with such Western Indologists as H.H. Wilson, E. Burnouf, and M. Müller, and while he did indeed consider them *mleccha* in the traditionalist sense of the word, he nevertheless tried to approach them in a way justified by the xenological tradition of Hinduism itself: In a letter to Müller in which he thanks him for his edition of the *Ṛgveda*, he explains that it is indeed strange to study the holy scriptures in an edition published by a far-distant *mleccha* on the banks of the Thames, but adds that this *mleccha* was the descendent of fallen *kṣatriyas*, and that his original kinship with the Hindu race had been confirmed by modern linguistic and philological research. And, in the same manner that "Yavanācārya" (i.e. Yavaneśvara) had once communicated to the Hindus his system of astronomy, now the "German Bhaṭṭa" was presenting the Indians with his edition of the *Ṛgveda*.[56] In his own cautious way, Radhakant tried to recover a lost sense of openness and receptivity, and the potential for reform, from the tradition itself.

16. The work of Max Müller and other Western Indologists and historians of ancient India generally became a point of contact for conservative Hindus, and the European interest in the most ancient Indian past became for them a factor of self-affirmation and apologetics, which could also be utilized as an argument against modernization and Westernization. Müller in particular has become one of the heroes of the Indian rediscovery of the past, and of Hindu "revivalism." Specifically in Bengal, J. Tod's *Annals and Antiquities of Rajasthan* (2 volumes, 1829–1832), a work which celebrates the Rajputs and their traditional chivalry, has contributed greatly to a new sense of cultural pride and national identity. Its impact upon Bengali literature has been deep and pervasive.[57]

On the other hand, the critical, historical, and often reductive work of Western Indologists has met with passionate rejection by conservative Hinduism and been seen as part of a strategy of Western domination and suppression.[58] Against this, other Western writers who have tended to glorify India and mythify its ancient origins have again been invoked as witnesses and allies.[59] In general, a history of the reception of Western Indology in India would provide ample opportunity to demonstrate further and exemplify important developments and attitudes within modern Indian thought.

Problems associated with the presence of the European *mleccha* and the self-assertion and purification of the Hindus against them have also been discussed in the twentieth century by some of the greatest traditional pandits using the standards of the *Dharmaśāstra*, e.g., by Vāsudeva Śāstrin Abhyaṅkara in his *Dharmatattvanirṇaya*.[60] Essentially, this work stresses the birthright and the hereditary aspects of Hinduism, with the author determining that Hinduism cannot be approached through mere "initiation" (*dīkṣā*).[61] Special consideration is given to the question as to how far one may go in dealing with the *mleccha* without endangering the metaphysical essence of Hinduism, i.e., the hereditary caste membership, and without reaching a point of irreversible degeneration into the *mleccha* state (*mlecchabhāva*), at which purification through ceremonies of atonement (*prāyaścitta*) would become impossible.[62] At the same time, it is argued (in a manner which seems appropriate for pandits who not infrequently serve the Europeans) that the norms of "purity" which regulate the interaction with the "lowest" (*antyaja*), i.e., the outcastes, within the Hindu system do not necessarily apply to contacts with foreigners.[63] In addition to his *Dharmatattvanirṇaya*, V.S. Abhyaṅkara made numerous other significant contributions to various branches of traditional Sanskrit learning, e.g. his *Advaitāmoda* and his commentary on the *Sarvadarśanasaṃgraha*.[64]

The *Dharmapradīpa*, written by Anantakṛṣṇa Śāstrin, Sītārāma Śāstrin, and Śrījīva Bhaṭṭācārya, three of the leading pandits of their time, also bears mention.[65] In this work, questions of "purification" (*śuddhi*) and rehabilitation of Hindus who have joined a "mleccha religion" (*mlecchadharma*) or been coerced into giving up their ways of life and belief are discussed in great detail.[66] The conversion of persons who were *born* into a foreign religion is not taken into consideration at all.

17. Generally, the authors of these and similar works of modern Sanskrit literature warn against the practice of reinterpretation (for instance, of the four main "castes," *varṇa*), that is so common in Neo-Hinduism, and against the introduction of "new sectarian traditions" (*nūtanasampradāya*):[67] Against these practices of the Westernizers and modernizers, they refer to themselves as "followers of the eternal religion" (*sanātanadharmīya, sanātanadharmāvalambin*) and true "Hindus" (*hindu, hindū*)[68] But this in itself indicates a self-understanding which is not as "traditional" and unaffected by the Western presence as it might appear at first sight.

The modern pandit tradition is *not* just a tradition of memorization and textual learning, of passive possession and thoughtless perpetuation of inherited knowledge. But regardless of all individual differences, the more fundamental question remains: Can those who preserve the traditional schemes of knowledge not just as contents of historical awareness, but as ways of seeing the world—can those guardians and representatives of the tradition and its authoritative language provide it with a living presence? Can they, who speak the language of the tradition, also speak for it in the modern world? Can they present it to the West and the Westernized world without simply being used as sources of information or objects of historical curiosity? Can they in turn comprehend this world within the horizon of their own inherited knowledge? Do they possess traditional means of understanding which are sufficient to respond to and interpret the modern world? Does the tradition itself provide such a framework of understanding? Is the tradition of the Sanskrit pandits the most authentic form of survival of traditional Hinduism? Are they more qualified to speak for the tradition than the Neo-Hindus? Do they represent the continued life and strength of the tradition – or its final petrification?

18. To close this chapter, we shall cite two modern Indian authors who, from the experience of their own thought and life, have articulated the peculiar hermeneutic brokenness of modern Indian self-understanding with impressive clarity and intensity. Our first author, Nirmala Varmā, was born in 1929 and has published novels, short stories and essays in Hindi. In an essay entitled *Atīta: eka ātma-manthana* ("The Past – A Self-Examination"), he discusses the dichotomy between the traditional Indian understanding of the past and the modern Western orientation towards the future (*bhaviṣya*) and towards progress, the Western attempts to transform the Indians into "historical men" (*aitihāsika manuṣya*), and the alienation of modern Indians from their living past. He charactarizes the development beginning with Rammohan Roy as follows:

> Rammohan Roy and the liberal intellectuals of his generation were aware of this dichotomy, but the way which they chose to resolve it was a deceptive one – it has led us in a direction from whose consequences we have to suffer today. Facing the 'progress-oriented' (*vikāsonmukha*) standards (*ādarśa*) of Western civilization, these intellectuals felt very inferior. In order to free themselves from this sense of inferiority (*hīnabhāva*), they tried to revive the greatness of the entire Indian past. They wanted to demonstrate to their foreign rulers that the glory of their by-gone culture could bear comparison with modern European values. But they were also attracted by these 'modern European values,' regarded them as a symbol of a superior civilization, and wanted to be accepted and 'respectable' in front of them. On the one hand, the intellectuals of the Bengali Renaissance pleaded for the Vedas and Upaniṣads, on the other hand, they adopted the doctrines of John Stuart Mill and were keen to apply them to their own social order. On the one hand, they were proud of their own past; on the other hand they wanted to exchange this pride for European values and thus shape the future of their country. This movement of Indian intellectuals of the nineteenth century is usually called a 'movement of harmonization' (*samanvaya kā abhiyāna*). It was an external and superficial harmonization, but also a very deceptive and destructive one . . .[69]

At the conclusion of his pessimistic retrospective, Varmā says that the time has come for a "churning" or "stirring" of one's ideas (*ātmamanthana*), and that a period of silence (*khāmośī*) may be necessary to prepare future articulations of authenticity and truth.[70]

19. Our second author, J.L. Mehta (born in 1912) was a professor of philosophy at Banaras Hindu University, but has also taught in the United States. Most of his publications, including a major study of Heidegger, are in English. Again and again, they address the central questions of modern Indian self-understanding. Can modern Hindu thought rediscover and redefine itself in the Westernized world? Should it even try to assert itself, to find or preserve an identity of its own? Is this a matter of choice or of historical necessity?

> Can we simply turn our backs on our past, just discard it, and appropriate the final fruits of Western self-understanding as *the* inner telos of man universally and as such, or shall we reject the spiritual-philosophical endeavor of the West altogether as of no consequence and seek to entrench ourselves into a specifically Indian philosophizing in the language of the past and supposedly undisturbed by the alien world of meanings embodied in the English language we employ for the purpose? Or shall we begin to *understand* both in their mutual otherness, to learn the language of each and so to evolve ways of thinking and talking which will be truly appropriate to our membership of both worlds, striving in such fashion to transform it into one?[71]

Elsewhere, Mehta describes the hermeneutic situation of modern India as follows:

> The coming of modernity to India signified not merely the impingement of an alien world of knowledge, ideas, and ideals upon the Indian consciousness, but of a world which was itself rapidly reaching out toward a newly conceived future, as well as spreading out its tentacles to encompass the whole world. Under the colonial origins of his modernization, the Indian encountered 'philosophy' and 'religion' and began forthwith the long journey of reinterpreting his tradition in terms of these Western categories. Most importantly, he began thinking about it in the English language, not just to expound it to English scholars, but as the principal medium of his own self-understanding. Such self-understanding was reflected back in new meanings given to ancient words in the Indian languages and it also expressed itself in the way traditional meanings were themselves reflected in his use of concepts embedded in English words. In this interplay between the one and the other, between the traditional and the modern, between one's own and the alien, between the present and the past, what was happening to the truth of that tradition and to its manner of speaking to us? Was it being gradually covered up and hidden from our view, or was it being brought now to shine forth, at least in promise, in its real purity?[72]

15. *Darśana, Ānvīkṣikī,* Philosophy

1. While the European historians of philosophy in the nineteenth and early twentieth centuries still question whether the concept of philosophy can be applied beyond the tradition of European, fundamentally Greek thought, a process of globalization takes place in which non-European traditions not only adopt European philosophical concepts and teachings, but also reinterpret and reconceive their own ways of thinking *as* philosophy. India has played a conspicuous and significant part in this process. Indians have responded not only to specific philosophical ideas, but above all to the term and concept "philosophy" itself. For modern Hinduism, the concept of philosophy has become a vehicle of self-understanding, of assimilation and "Westernization," but also of self-affirmation against the West.

In modern Indian vernaculars as well as in modern Sanskrit, the word *darśana* is widely used as translation of "philosophy." *Darśana* is considered to be the traditional Indian word for "philosophy"—not merely in the sense of a lexicographic equivalent, but also as an answer which the Indian tradition has held in stock for its encounter with what is called "philosophy" in the European tradition. On the one hand, the word serves as a terminological device for the reception and assimilation of the European concept of philosophy, as an indigenous linguistic receptacle for foreign conceptual contents. On the other hand, specifically Indian apologetic claims are associated with the usage of this word. We often hear that *darśana* has to be understood in its etymological affiliation with *dṛś*, "to see," i.e. as "vision," "intuition," "realization," and that this meaning indicates something genuinely Indian, and characteristically different from the analytical, discursive, theoretically objectifying spirit of European philosophy.[1]

2. Among Western historians of Indian philosophy, the terminological and conceptual correlation between "philosophy" and *darśana* is not normally accepted. Even those historians who are willing to concede that there

is, or has been, philosophy in India, often maintain that there is no indigenous Indian word or concept corresponding to what we call "philosophy."[2] It was only for a short period that, following H. Jacobi's suggestion, the word *ānvīkṣikī*, as used in Kauṭilya's *Arthaśāstra*, was taken seriously as a possible terminological equivalent. It is obvious that Jacobi was focusing on the critical and methodological implications of *ānvīkṣikī*, and he wanted to associate them with the ideas of critical, autonomous reasoning and "pure" theory which the European historians of philosophy tended to regard as criteria of "real" philosophy.

Jacobi's interpretation has been discussed in detail and rejected by P. Hacker.[3] Nevertheless, the issue is certainly not closed. The different approaches to the concepts of *ānvīkṣikī* and *darśana* reflect not only differences in the interpretation of classical Indian philosophy, but also in European self-understanding, and in the assessment of the encounter between India and Europe. Considering the great and symptomatic significance which *darśana* has gained for the Neo-Hindu self-understanding and self-definition, it seems surprising how little has been done to examine and clarify the traditional role and background of *darśana* and to trace and explain the hermeneutical processes of interpretation and reinterpretation which have led to the modern Indian adoption of *darśana* as a terminological equivalent or analogue of "philosophy."

3. An obvious basis for the semantic association between "philosophy" and *darśana* is given by the fact that *darśana* is a familiar and characteristic term in Indian doxographic literature, i.e. in that literature which summarizes and classifies the main schools or systems of what is commonly called "Indian philosophy." Most of the traditional Indian doxographies use the word *darśana* in their title, in particular those two which are the best known as well as the most interesting and significant ones: Haribhadra's *Ṣaḍdarśanasamuccaya* (eighth century) and Mādhava-Vidyāraṇya's *Sarvadarśanasaṃgraha* (fourteenth century). The short compendium by the Jaina Haribhadra is not only the older one of these two, but the oldest of all the Sanskrit doxographies which we have or about which we know.[4]

The fact that Haribhadra chose the word *darśana* for the title of his doxographic treatise shows that by the time of the eighth century it had become a well-known designation for "philosophical" systems or doctrines. If we look, however, at earlier and contemporary and even at some later works, it is equally clear that it had by no means become *the* generally accepted standard term for the traditional systems of Indian philosophy. In fact, it plays no noticeable role in the self-characterization of the leading exponents of these systems. The philosophers themselves hardly ever use it when they refer to what they and their partners and opponents in debate, i.e. the representatives of other systems, are doing. It is generally absent in the older literature of the systems, i.e. in the *sūtras* and their immediate commentaries. Instead, we find—often within compounds—terms like *tantra, mata, vāda, siddhānta* or *śāstra*; these terms have obviously no specific reference to the method or subject-matter of philosophy.[5]

Haribhadra's commentators, Maṇibhadra and Guṇaratna, often use *mata* to paraphrase *darśana*. Haribhadra himself uses both terms interchangeably. On the other hand, Haribhadra distinguishes or even contrasts two meanings of *darśana* in the introductory verses of his work, when he first salutes the Jina Mahāvīra as one who is *saddarśana*, i.e. has true and complete insight, and then proceeds to announce his program of describing the various philosophical "views" (*darśana*).[6]

4. The terminology of Śaṅkara, who may have been a contemporary of Haribhadra, provides additional information.[7] In his references to the philosophical teachings of others, as well as to the system which he himself advocates, Śaṇkara normally uses the terms *tantra, siddhānta, śāstra, pakṣa, mata,* or *samaya*—mostly in compounds, such as *vedāntavāda, sāṃkhyatantra*, and *sugatasamaya*.[8] In one significant passage, however, he uses repeatedly the word *darśana*, even referring to the philosophical tradition advocated by himself as "our *darśana*" (*asmadīyaṃ darśanam*) or "the Upaniṣadic *darśana*" (*aupaniṣadaṃ darśanam*). However, this passage is a response to the statement of an opponent who had criticized the Vedāntic viewpoint as incoherent (*asamañjasam idam aupaniṣadaṃ darśanam*), and seems to adopt the opponent's own terminology.[9] In another passage,[10] Śaṅkara refers to the "systems (or 'views') like Sāṃkhya, etc., which are opposed to right insight" (*saṃyagdarśanapratipakṣabhūtāni sāṃkhyādidarśanāni*). It is evident that he is playing here on different connotations of *darśana*: As *samyagdarśana*, as the one true insight and realization, *darśana* appears appropriately in the singular, and it is to be distinguished from, and even contrasted with, that plurality of mere views which constitute the subject-matter of doxographic enumeration.

In the seventh century, and approximately one century earlier than Śaṅkara, the great Buddhist Madhyamaka commentator Candrakīrti referred to his own system, or rather method, as *madhyamakadarśana*—a method which avoids the "false theories of the dichotomy of existence and non-existence" (*astitvanāstitvadvayadarśana*) and is thus different from the "mere views," i.e. "false theories" of the Vijñānavādins etc. (*vijñānavādidarśanādi*).[11] Again a century earlier, the Vaiśeṣika teacher Praśastapāda referred to the false "views of the Buddhists, etc." (*śākyādidarśana*), which are "incompatible with the (true) Vedic insight" (*trayīdarśanaviparīta*).[12]

The passages which we have quoted indicate that at the time of the composition of the *Brahmasūtrabhāṣya* the word *darśana* had already assumed a certain doxographic connotation. But it had obviously not assumed such a role that it could have led Śaṅkara to use it more or less exclusively, and instead of such terms as *tantra* or *vāda*.

At any rate, *darśana* in the doxographic sense, i.e. as "(mere) view," without qualifying epithets, such as *samyag-*, is clearly distinct from *darśana* in the sense of *samyagdarśana* or *tattvadarśana*, i.e., of right vision or realization. The doxographic meaning is a basically neutral, occasionally even pejorative meaning. The combination and merger of these two meanings, or the interpretation of the doxographic usage in the normative sense of "right vision," "realization," is a symptomatic innovation of Neo-Hinduism.

5. Our observations on the traditional usage of *darśana* may be supplemented by referring to its close relative *dṛṣṭi* (Pali *diṭṭhi*), which is used most conspicuously, but by no means exclusively, in Buddhism. *Dṛṣṭi/diṭṭhi*, as used in chapter 27 of Nāgārjuna's *Madhyamakakārikā* or in the *Brahmajālasutta* of the *Dīghanikāya*, indicates something which is not only neutral or irrelevant, but soteriologically harmful—speculative views, mere theories which—by virtue of the fact that they are mere views and conceptualizations—constitute elements of bondage and obstacles on the way to liberation.[13] With these "mere views," the Buddhists contrast the "right," i.e. soteriologically meaningful and helpful "view" or "orientation" (*samyagdṛṣṭi*, Pali *sammādiṭṭhi*), which is the first part of the "eightfold path" to final liberation (*nirvāṇa*). Although *dṛṣṭi* is much less conspicuous in Hindu philosophical literature, it occurs here, too, in the meaning "view" or "mere view."[14] The same connotation of "speculation," "mere theory" may also occasionally be found in the usage of *darśana*.[15]

The Jainas and Vedāntins who produced most of the doxographic literature do not normally use the word *darśana* in a pejorative sense. They tend to use it in a neutral, non-committal sense, and certainly without any normative or idealizing implications. As a matter of fact, the Jaina doxographers sometimes claim a complete and uncompromising neutrality, an attitude *sine ira et studio*, for their way of dealing with the various philosophical views. A verse from Haribhadra's *Lokatattvanirṇaya*, which both Guṇaratna and Maṇibhadra quote in their commentaries on the *Ṣaḍdarśanasamuccaya* and which is possibly based upon an older Buddhist verse, states that there is no partiality in favor of the Jina Mahāvīra nor any dislike or bias against teachers like Kapila.[16] Such statements should certainly not be interpreted as programs for historical and critical research. Yet it is true that Jainism has developed a remarkable tradition of dealing with and relating to other schools and doctrines not just in order to criticize and refute them, but to put them into a systematic order and framework. And it is in this systematically coordinating, comprehensive and inclusive treatment of other doctrines that the Jainas find their own perspectivism, the *anekāntavāda*, fulfilled and confirmed.

6. Already the Jaina canon has long and detailed lists and classifications of various doctrines or viewpoints (*vāya*; Sanskrit *vāda*). Even the word *darisaṇa,* the Ardhamāgadhī equivalent of *darśana*, is used in these passages—appearing alone as well as in such compounds as *kiriyāvāidarisaṇa* (Sanskrit *kriyāvādidarśana*).[17] In addition to such usages, *darśana* has, of course, more specific and at times problematic, functions within the philosophical terminology of Jainism. In the threefold scheme of *darśana, jñāna* ("knowledge") and *cāritra* ("conduct") which describes the soteriological path of the Jainas, *darśana* has the meaning "attitude," "outlook," "orientation," and it is explained as *śraddhāna*, "faith."[18] As "right outlook" (*samyagdarśana*), it leads to "right knowledge" (*samyagjñana*), and it opens the way to salvation or liberation.

The enumerations of various "teachings" or "views" (*vāya; darisaṇa*) in the older texts are still primarily for the sake of criticism and refutation. We do not yet find the later claims to openness and inclusiveness with regard to the views of other, competing schools. Nevertheless, a tendency to recognize other teachings as expressions of partial truths is clearly present at a very early time, and it may be contrasted with the Buddhist tendency (as developed most clearly in Nāgārjuna's *Madhyamaka* school) to refute not only *other* views, but "mere views" per se.[19] Yet the Buddhist approach has also produced rich doxographic materials (though not "doxographies" in the strict sense), most conspicuously in the work of Nāgārjuna's follower Bhavya (or Bhāvaviveka) and in Śāntarakṣita's *Tattvasaṃgraha*, together with its commentary by Kamalaśīla.

The philosophical consummation of the Jaina approach is reached in the perspectivistic theory of world-views (*naya*) which we find most fully developed in the works of Siddhasena Divākara and Mallavādin. Here, the enumeration of historically factual viewpoints merges with the construction of systematically possible standpoints in philosophy. Jainism is credited with a special and unique manner of coordinating, systematizing and completing the other world-views, of showing their attachment to partial truths and mere aspects, and of salvaging them from their self-imposed isolation and one-sidedness.[20]

The conception of *naya*, and the procedures associated with it, are among the more distinctive contributions of Jainism to Indian philosophy, and their significance is not confined to the Jaina tradition. As for the word *naya* itself, it has also become quite familiar in non-Jaina doxographic and philosophical literature; it is frequently used as a virtual synonym of *darśana* and *mata.*[21]

7. Quite obviously, the Jaina tradition provided a natural setting for the development of doxographic literature, as we find it represented by Haribhadra's *Ṣaḍdarśanasamuccaya.* Yet Haribhadra avoids the term *naya* with its systematic and "constructive" connotations, and uses *darśana* and *mata* instead. Haribhadra was a Brahmin by birth and education, and in his later career as one of the most learned and prolific Jaina authors he obviously tried to place Jainism in the broader framework of the Indian tradition, deemphasizing a terminology and phraseology which might have appeared as too technically and parochially Jainist. And it is not only the term *naya*, but also the systematic and constructivist claims of the *naya* theory which his doxography avoids. In choosing *darśana* as his doxographic titleword, Haribhadra did not simply continue or resume the old usage of *darisaṇa*, but he also referred to a usage which had gained momentum outside of Jainism, and which had prepared the word *darśana* for its special doxographic role. The greatest representative of the Śabdādvaita tradition, Bhartṛhari (who lived most probably during the second half of the fifth century), provides early and informative testimony for this usage.

Bhartṛhari was not a doxographer, and he did not use the word *darśana* in an explicitly doxographic sense. But his work shows us this doxographic usage *in statu nascendi* and in preliminary stages of development, and in a peculiar affiliation with the philosophy of the absolute "word." In his *Vākyapadīya*, as well as in his commentary on Patañjali's *Mahābhāṣya*, Bhartṛhari uses *darśana* in the sense of "view" and "perspective," and then also of "way of thinking" and "doctrine." There are various "views," or "ways of seeing," with reference to one and the same "visible" object: *ekasmin api dṛśye 'rthe darśanaṃ bhidyate pṛthak.*[22] The "seeing" and understanding of time varies: *bhinnaṃ kālasya darśanam.*[23] We find different perspectives, different ways of seeing the same reality in many areas.[24] There is the "perspective of unity" (*ekatvadarśana*) as well as the "perspective of aggregation" (*saṃsargadarśana*); in such and similar compounds, *darśana* is used in a way which recalls the Jaina concept of *naya.*[25] In his commentary on the *Mahābhāṣya* Bhartṛhari also uses the more specifically doxographic expressions *vaiśeṣikadarśana* and *mīmāṃsakadarśana.*[26] Towards the end of the second *kāṇḍa* of the *Vākyapadīya*, he refers to his *guru* as having studied other traditions as well as his "own system" (*svaṃ ca darśanam*), i.e. the tradition of grammatical philosophy; and he adds the general observation that insight gains distinctness from (the study of) different traditional views: *prajñā vivekaṃ labhate bhinnair āgamadarśanaiḥ.*[27]

This statement sounds almost like a motto and a programmatic justification of the future doxographies, in particular if we consider the perspectivistic approach of the Jainas. It may be worth noticing in this connection that Bhartṛhari's commentator Helārāja uses *darśana* and *naya* as interchangeable terms.

8. Indian as well as Western authors have emphasized that the philosophical "views" or "systems" which are the subject-matter of the Sanskrit doxographies should not be interpreted as systems of "pure theory" in the Greek-European sense. Indeed, the soteriological and practical perspective is as obvious in the basic texts of the systems (*darśana*) as in their doxographic recapitulations. Yet, in contrasting "pure theory" and "soteriological orientation," we have to be more cautious and discriminating than is often the case on both the Indian and the Western sides.

We do not have to repeat here the statements of those historians of philosophy who saw the "purely theoretical" attitude, the interest in "knowledge for the sake of knowledge," as a uniquely and exclusively European phenomenon. On the other hand, modern Hindu authors have invoked the traditional Indian disregard for "pure theory" as an element of Hindu self-affirmation. From their perspective, "knowledge for the sake of knowledge" and "value-free science" appear as idle curiosity, as compared to the soteriological commitment of Indian thought.[28]

Indeed, declarations like those of Plato and Aristotle about "wonder" (θαυμαζειν) as the ground of philosophy, about the "desire to know" as a natural and inherently legitimate distinction of man, and about the ideal of the "theoretical life" (βιος θεωρητικος) are absent in Indian literature. Instead, Indian philosophers usually take it for granted, or even postulate explicitly, that the desire to know has to be motivated and guided by a goal or purpose (*prayojana*). For the majority of philosophical systems (*darśana*), the ultimate purpose is final liberation (*mokṣa, mukti, apavarga*) from the cycle of rebirth and its inherent deficiency and distress (*duḥkha*).

9. This soteriological motivation, which gained central importance in ancient Buddhism, is also generally present in the major works of classical Hindu philosophy, and it often appears as their starting-point and source of legitimacy. The *Sāṃkhyakārikā* by Īśvarakṛṣṇa provides one of the more conspicuous and memorable examples. It begins with the word *duḥkha* and presents suffering, and the desire to overcome it, as the basic incentive for the "pursuit of knowledge" (*jijñāsā*). A soteriological formula which seems to echo Buddhist ideas is among the opening statements of the *Nyāyasūtras*. Classical Vaiśeṣika tries to demonstrate its soteriological significance and to dispel doubts about its soteriological status which were raised in the *Nyāyabhāṣya* and other texts.[29]

In contrast to the natural human urge to know which Aristotle proclaims in the first sentence of his *Metaphysics*, Indian philosophers tend to emphasize that the cognitive motivation is inseparable from the desire to obtain what is pleasant and to avoid what is unpleasant; just as human activities in general, intellectual, cognitive endeavors are said to be directed towards "fruits" or "results" (*phala*).[30] On the other hand, the attainment of results and goals—and ultimately the goal of final liberation—depends upon right insight and cognition.[31]

Indeed, the fact that traditional Indian self-understanding associates the "philosophical systems" (*darśana*) with practical, soteriological motivations, and even with the idea of a "science of final liberation" (*mokṣaśāstra*), cannot be disputed. Yet, this does not invalidate our earlier observation that the confrontation of "pure theory" and "soteriological orientation" requires caution and discrimination. In order to avoid misleading simplifications, we have to be aware of the historical complexity and variability of both the Indian and the Western approaches, and of the deep problems and ambiguities associated with the concept of "theory," or "pure theory." The fact itself that the soteriological motivation has been postulated and proclaimed so explicitly in the Indian tradition, and that it has in turn become the object of *theoretical* inquiries, involves questions which are significant with regard to the historical development of Indian thought, as well as with regard to the conceptual relationship between "theory" and "practice."

10. The ideas of "pure theory" and "knowledge for its own sake" can hardly be considered as definitive and self-evident achievements of the European tradition; nor are they unquestionable standards for assessing or disqualifying non-European traditions. In the present context, we do not have to discuss the extent to which these ideas have been stylized by the historians of European and especially Greek thought.[32] Nor do we have to investigate whether or how these historians have combined and contaminated fundamentally different phenomena and ideas—the Greek "theory" (θεωρια), the Christian idea of contemplation, and finally the modern and secularized ideas of "science without presuppositions" and "value-free research." It will be sufficient to recall some exemplary questions which modern Western thinkers have raised with regard to the ideas of "pure theory" and "theoretical knowledge," and about the relationship between theory, practice, and human interests.

One of the most radical and challenging approaches to these questions is found in the work of M. Heidegger. Already in *Sein und Zeit* ("Being and Time"), he characterizes the theoretical contemplation of the object, the objectification which seems to be without any practical motivation, as a derivative mode of praxis. In Heidegger's later critique of the history of European metaphysics, the unfolding of theoretical objectification and of "re-presentational" thinking ("*Vor-Stellen*") appears as an increasing claim to power over the objects: Thus, "theory" cannot be separated from the technological drive towards mastery and domination. Descartes' attempt to establish man, through theory and metaphysics, as the "master and owner of nature" ("*maître et possesseur de la nature*") provides a conspicuous illustration. What is at the center in this case is not theory per se, but its methodological, technical and anthropocentric "application." But such application is by no means a secondary phenomenon.

J. Habermas has distinguished some basic modes of interest which have determined the cognitive enterprise in the European philosophical and scientific tradition: the Greek "theoretical" interest in cosmic mimesis, i.e. in cognitive assimilation to the structure of the universe; the technical interest which dominates the natural sciences, i.e. "the cognitive interest in technical control over objectified processes"; the practical hermeneutical interest in the cultural sciences; the "emancipatory" interest, which modern philosophy shares with the critically oriented social and psychological sciences, which manifests itself in self-reflection, recognizes the illusory nature of "pure theory," and accepts the inseparability of knowledge and human interests.[33] M. Scheler has distinguished soteriological knowledge ("*Erlösungswissen*"), as the highest type of knowledge, from knowledge which aims at technical mastery ("*Leistungswissen*," "*Machtwissen*"), and knowledge which is committed to cultural ideas ("*Bildungswissen*").[34] Numerous other attempts have been made to define the relationship between theory and practice, knowledge and human interests, truth and relevance, and to clarify the ambiguities and complexities of this relationship. Regardless of the details—we cannot simply contrast the Indian "soteriological" commitment with the "purely theoretical" orientation of the West. There are various, often implicit forms of interaction and confrontation between theory and practice on both sides. We certainly can compare and contrast these, and the different historical directions which the relationship between theory and practice, or knowledge and its goals and uses, has taken in India and in Europe.

11. E. Frauwallner has tried to demonstrate that, prior to its domination by religious and soteriological interests, Indian thought went through a period of theoretical and "scientific" orientation.[35] In particular, he has tried to interpret the old Vaiśeṣika system as a fundamentally unsoteriological doctrine. Frauwallner's approach is obviously influenced by the ideals of "pure theory" and "objective science" as they were advocated by traditional European historians of philosophy, and it can hardly be justified in its entirety. Nevertheless, it raises important and legitimate questions.

It seems evident that the basic text of the Vaiśeṣika system, the *Vaiśeṣikasūtra*, contains numerous later additions and interpolations, and that attempts were made to strengthen and emphasize the religious and soteriological dimension of the system. The development of the Vaiśeṣika concept of *adṛṣṭa*, its increasing association with ethical and soteriological functions, and its identification with the principle of *karman* illustrate this. In general, the theory of *karman* and rebirth becomes an unquestioned premise of Vaiśeṣika physics and cosmology. "Retributive" causality supersedes "natural" causality. The world becomes more and more a stage for karmic and soteriological processes.[36] In the course of this development, the Vaiśeṣika also responds to the explicit doubts concerning its soteriological relevance which were raised in Vātsyāyana Pakṣilasvāmin's *Nyāyabhāṣya*.[37] The Nyāya itself posits and emphasizes its soteriological commitment in a manner which appears somewhat forced. The Nyāya as well as other systems obviously tried to respond to and to neutralize the challenge of more genuinely and deeply soteriological movements, especially Buddhism.

More than other traditions, Buddhism has developed its critique of theory and speculation, and of merely factual knowledge. As Dharmakīrti states, "precise knowledge of the number of insects" (*kīṭasaṃkhyāparijñāna*) etc. is not part of the enlightenment which the Buddha teaches and exemplifies.[38] Earlier in this chapter, we have referred to the role of *dṛṣṭi/diṭṭhi* in Buddhism. *Dṛṣṭi*, "speculation," "theorizing," "conceptualization," implies soteriological negligence and irresponsibility, and in general a waste of time. Beyond that, it also stands for the representational, reifying and possessive positing of objects and the relations between objects, the projection and reflection of that primeval "thirst" which attaches us to the world of passion and pain, the formation of a network of ideas in which the owner himself, the thinking and theorizing subject, gets caught.

12. Against all forms of theorizing and calculating attachment to the world, and regardless of all assurances that knowledge has to have a goal and purpose, and be a means to an end, the Indian tradition has developed conceptions of knowledge and ideals of contemplation which radically eliminate and transcend all goal-oriented interests, and the means-ends-relationship itself. This is not knowledge as "soteriological technique," but knowledge which tries to supersede all technique and instrumentality. Liberation cannot be attained through causal techniques, or the mastery of means-ends-relationships; but it means freedom from such relationships themselves, and from a world which functions and exists through them. It means pure, free, disinterested contemplation in which all causal and instrumental relations, and with them the world itself, become transparent and irrelevant. Accordingly, the soteriology of Sāṃkhya and Yoga postulates that the "spirit" (*puruṣa*) should withdraw from "being an actor" (*kartṛtva*) as well as from "being an enjoyer" (*bhoktṛtva*) and in general from all participation in the causal world. The same ideas are developed more radically in some schools of Buddhism and, within Hinduism, in Śaṅkara's Advaita Vedānta. Śaṅkara teaches that "knowledge" (*jñāna*)

which coincides with liberation is something utterly incompatible with "works" (*karman*) which are accomplished in accordance with the means-ends-relationship (*sādhyasādhanabhāva*). Such "knowledge" can neither be a means for something else, nor can it be brought about by means or instruments. "Works" and "knowledge," *karman* and *jñāna* belong to fundamentally different contexts. Knowledge is not something to be done or performed; it is openness for absolute reality (*brahman*), i.e. a reality which is not a function and projection of "works" and desires.[39]

Such "pure" knowledge abandons all claims to causal and conceptual mastery and explanation, and it transcends the world which is the realm of such apparent mastery and explanation, i.e. the world of empirical transactions (*vyavahāra*) and of *māyā*. Śaṅkara's predecessor Gauḍapāda, who is greatly indebted to the Buddhist Madhyamaka school, explicitly identifies "worldly existence" (*saṃsāra*) with "intentness upon," or even absorption by "causes and effects" (*hetuphalāveśa*).[40] The soteriological orientation of Advaita Vedānta and Madhyamaka Buddhism is fundamentally different from a mere "technology of liberation." It implies an extraordinary level of "theoretical" awareness, and intense and uncompromising reflection upon the relationship between "knowledge" and "works," "theory and practice."[41]

13. The doctrines and systems which the Indian doxographies present under the title *darśana*, provide clear and specific parallels to what is commonly called "philosophy" in the West: They are theoretically oriented, systematized "world-views," and they exclude more or less matters of religious practice. However, we are dealing here with "philosophy" as something given by tradition, i.e. as a certain spectrum of firmly established, fully developed doctrinal structures; we are not dealing with "philosophy" as an open-ended process of asking questions and pursuing knowledge. *Darśana*, as used in the doxographies, is a fundamentally retrospective concept. It refers to what others have thought in the past, to views and systems which have been inherited from the past. There is no suggestion of progressive, future-oriented thought, and there are hardly any methodological implications in the doxographic usage of *darśana*.

On the other hand, there are obvious methodological implications in the concept of *ānvīkṣikī*—the concept which H. Jacobi tried to interpret as the proper Indian equivalent of "philosophy." Jacobi relied primarily on a passage in Kauṭilya's *Arthaśāstra*. Soon after the first publication (1909) of this work on government and politics, which had been considered lost for a long time, Jacobi referred to this passage,[42] translated *ānvīkṣikī* as "philosophy," and was obviously convinced that there was a precise conceptual correspondence. Several translations of the *Arthaśāstra* also render *ānvīkṣikī* as "philosophy."[43]

The discussion was continued by M. Winternitz,[44] who dealt primarily with the relationship between the methodological notion of *ānvīkṣikī* and the soteriological idea of a "science of the self" (*ātmavidyā*). Winternitz rejects Jacobi's translation of *ānvīkṣikī*, and he warns against a superimposition of the European dichotomy of theology and philosophy. Even prior to the rediscovery of the *Arthaśāstra*, J. Dahlmann discussed the relationship between *ānvīkṣikī* and *ātmavidyā* on the basis of passages in the *Mahābhārata*.[45]

The most penetrating study of *ānvīkṣikī* which we have to this date was published by P. Hacker in 1958. Hacker's discussion, which provides a thorough critique of Jacobi's approach, not only supersedes most of the earlier work on the topic, but also various more recent contributions, such as the superficial observations by A.K. Warder.[46] Like Winternitz (of whose contribution he was apparently not aware), Hacker rejects Jacobi's correlation or identification of *ānvīkṣikī* and "philosophy." He emphasizes that *ānvīkṣikī*, as used by Kauṭilya, does not represent a generic concept, covering different "philosophical" systems, but "something that can be applied more or less,"[47] a method which is not restricted to any particular domain, and which has no specific affinity to the topics of philosophy. Concerning the role of *ānvīkṣikī* in the Nyāya system, Hacker argues that the Nyāya borrowed the term from the "science of politics" and adopted it for its own "self-definition."[48]

14. Hacker summarizes his argumentation against Jacobi as follows: "The origin of all false conclusions and improbable constructions in Jacobi's 'Frühgeschichte der indischen Philosophie' is his inadequate rendering of *ānvīkṣikī* as 'philosophy'—with which he then contrasts a 'theology' which he finds in *trayī*. His ingenious reflections tell much more about their author (i.e., that he was obviously so impressed with the Occidental emancipation of philosophy from theology that he projected this conflict into his own area of research, India) than about actual events in the history of Indian thought, which is still quite obscure as far as those centuries are concerned."[49] Hacker's challenging argumentation provides an appropriate starting-point for a renewed discussion of this highly significant and intriguing topic.

Kauṭilya introduces the word *ānvīkṣikī* while giving a list of "sciences" which he recognizes, and which includes his own "science of government and politics" (*daṇḍanīti*): *ānvīkṣikī trayī vārttā daṇḍanītiś ca-iti vidyāḥ*.[50] While the explanation of *trayī* as "science of the three Vedas" and *vārttā* as "science of material welfare" (i.e., trade and agriculture) does not pose major problems, the definition of *ānvīkṣikī* turns out to be more difficult and elusive. Kauṭilya first presents an enumeration of three schools of thought, which are subsumed under, or at least associated with, the concept of *ānvīkṣikī; sāṃkhyaṃ yogo lokāyataṃ ca-ity ānvīkṣikī*. "Immediately thereafter, he describes, also in an etymologizing manner, what happens in *ānvīkṣikī*: 'The investigative science *investigates with reasons* what is right and wrong in the field of Vedic knowledge, what is advantageous and disadvantageous in the science of material acquisitions, and appropriate or inappropriate in the science of government, and moreover, the strengths and weaknesses of these (three sciences) . . ." (*dharmādharmau trayyām arthānarthau vārttāyāṃ nayānayau daṇḍanītyāṃ balābale ca-etāsāṃ hetubhir anvīkṣamāṇā*).[51] Concluding this section, Kauṭilya cites a verse which is obviously taken from an older source: "The investigative science has always been considered as a source of light for all sciences, an instrument for all activities, a foundation for all religious and social duties" (*pradīpaḥ sarvavidyānām, upāyaḥ sarvakarmaṇām/āśrayaḥ sarvadharmāṇāṃ śaśvad ānvīkṣikī matā*). This implies that *ānvīkṣikī* is not a special "science," side by side with other "sciences" and with an equally specific subject-matter, but a methodology which these other sciences themselves can and should utilize.

15. Already Jacobi has noticed that the verse quoted by Kauṭilya appears also, with a variant appropriate to the new context, in the *Nyāyabhāṣya* by Vātsyāyana Pakṣilasvāmin (ca. 400 A.D.); now it is the Nyāya itself which is presented as the fulfillment of that sense of *ānvīkṣikī* which the old verse describes.[52] But there are also other ways in which the *Nyāyabhāṣya* supplements and modifies the information found in the *Arthaśāstra*. Vātsyāyana and his commentator Uddyotakara also define *ānvīkṣikī* as an "investigative," "reflective" science which reconsiders, re-examines what has been grasped through sense-perception and sacred tradition, and which applies valid criteria (*pratyakṣāgamābhyām īkṣitasya-arthasya-anvīkṣaṇam*; *pramāṇair arthaparīkṣaṇam*), and they assert that without its peculiar discipline of reasoning and argumentation the Nyāya would not be different from the Vedic-Upaniṣadic "science of the (supreme) self" (*ātmavidyā, adhyātmavidyā*).[53]

Vātsyāyana emphasizes repeatedly that the Nyāya is indeed *ātmavidyā* and oriented toward the goal of final liberation (*apavarga*). The Nyāya, too, deals with the absolute self; as far as its goal and its subject-matter are concerned, it cannot and should not be distinguished from the Upaniṣads. Instead, its distinguishing feature is its methodology, to which it also owes its status as a general "auxiliary science," or even as a "meta-science." Hacker's statement that Vātsyāyana claimed a "special object" ("*besonderer Gegenstand*," i.e. subject-matter) for his system, on which he based its distinctive status,[54] has thus to be taken with some caution. To be sure, the sixteen "themes" (*padārtha*) of the Nyāya system are indeed characterized as actual objects (*vidyamānārtha*), and they are presented as the special domain of the system. However, Vātsyāyana adds that liberation will result only from the adequate knowledge (*tattvajñāna*) of those twelve soteriologically relevant entities which are called *prameya*, "objects of knowledge," i.e. the self (*ātman*), body (*śarīra*), etc. The *prameya* are those entities which the Nyāya recognizes as objects in the full metaphysical and soteriological sense. The other – essentially logical or dialectical – "themes" of Nyāya are "objects" in a different sense and on a different level of reflection: They are thematized factors of knowledge, methods and perspectives of argumentation; the Nyāya has a special status insofar as it *objectifies* or thematizes them, insofar as it deals with them in an explicit and technical fashion. Uddyotakara defines the peculiar character of this "objectification" more clearly than Vātsyāyana; what distinguishes Nyāya is not the occurrence of "means of knowledge" (*pramāṇa*), etc. per se (they are implicitly recognized by the other systems as well), but their explicit thematization and systematic refinement.[55]

Vātsyāyana adds to the list of sixteen "themes" (*padārtha*) an enumeration of four "relevant matters" (*arthapada*), using a term which inverts the parts of the compound *padārtha*. This enumeration, just like a similar scheme in Vyāsa's *Yogabhāṣya*, clearly reflects the "four noble truths" of Buddhism (i.e., the truths of suffering, its origin, its cessation, and the way leading to this cessation).[56] Several Nyāya authors have tried to coordinate all relevant "objects of knowledge" (*prameya*), or even all sixteen "themes" (*padārtha*), with the four *arthapada*, or to subsume them under these soteriologically "relevant matters," and thus to establish the pervasive soteriological significance of the Nyāya system in all its details. Bhāsarvajña (probably around 900 A.D.) discusses the issue in remarkable detail, and he refers explicitly to the "four noble truths" of the Buddhists.[57]

16. Hacker maintains against Jacobi that Vātsyāyana's association of *ānvīkṣikī* and *ātmavidyā* should not be seen as an artificial and retroactive harmonization, or as an attempt to revoke a process of philosophical emancipation. He reminds us that this association fully agrees with a tradition which is documented by Kauṭilya himself: *Arthaśāstra* I,2 mentions that the school of the Mānava recognized only three sciences, and that it regarded *ānvīkṣikī* as a special kind of "Vedic science" (*trayī*). Kāmandaki explains *ānvīkṣikī* repeatedly as *ātmavidyā* or *ātmavijñāna*. In this sense, we may also understand Manu's phrase *ānvīkṣikīṃ ca-ātmavidyām* . . .[58] There has also been a tradition which tried to coordinate the "investigative" *ānvīkṣikī* with the Vedic *trayī* in a manner analogous to the relationship between Pūrvamīmāṃsā and Uttaramīmāṃsā, or to associate it with *manana*, the "reflection" which, according to the Vedānta, should follow the "hearing" (*śravaṇa*) of the Vedic texts.[59] Numerous other passages could be added to Hacker's references, especially from the Mahābhārata. Here, the term *ānvīkṣikī* is applied to questions of an Upaniṣadic type, and

we hear about the "churning" of an Upaniṣad for the purpose of the "supreme ānvīkṣikī" (*ānvīkṣikī parā*).[60] *Ānvīkṣikī* in these obscure passages seems to have a special connection with the *jñānakāṇḍa*, the Upaniṣadic "knowledge portion" of the Veda.

The Mahābhārata also contains Kauṭilya's list of "four sciences" (*trayī, vārttā, daṇḍanīti, ānvīkṣikī*), as well as the threefold list, which Kauṭilya ascribes to the Mānava and which does not recognize *ānvīkṣikī* as a separate "science."[61] It is remarkable that the fourfold list emerges again in the *Vedāntacandrikā*, the anonymous pamphlet against Rammohan Roy which was published in 1817; in W.H. Macnaghten's attached English translation, *ānvīkṣikī* appears as "reasoning power", but also as "philosophy."

The concept of *ānvīkṣikī* which the classical Nyāya system adopts for its self-definition is certainly no emancipatory and anti-traditional concept: Any "investigation" or reasoning which is incompatible with sense perception and with authoritative tradition (*pratyakṣāgamaviruddha*) can only be "petty," "trivial" reasoning (*kṣudratarka*), and it would be a "spurious Nyāya" (*nyāyābhāsa*).[62] "Reasoning" and "investigation" have to accept and "follow" what is given by perception and tradition; this is an implication which the "orthodox" Naiyāyikas also find confirmed by the connotation of the prefix *anu-* within the word *ānvīkṣikī*.[63]

17. Does all this mean that the question of the autonomy of methodical thinking and critical reasoning, and of its emancipation from the authority of religious and soteriological tradition, is a Eurocentric question which should not be applied to the Indian situation? Indeed, Jacobi's way of posing, or presupposing, this question reflects his European background and, more specifically, the actual historical conditions of his work as an Indologist. It reflects an obvious "prejudice"—but one which may still be useful, or even indispensable, as a heuristic device.

We have introduced our discussion of *ānvīkṣikī* by referring to its methodological implications. Most of our subsequent quotes postulate that such "methodological" and "investigative" reasoning should be compatible with the sacred tradition, should try to justify it, or at least be neutral. However, Kauṭilya himself is clearly less concerned about such compatibility than the Naiyāyikas and other "orthodox" groups; his *ānvīkṣikī* has a more independent status.[64] Numerous references, accounts and allusions in ancient and classical Sanskrit literature, for instance in the great epics, document that this was by no means an isolated phenomenon. As a matter of fact, others had much more radical ideas about independent, critical reasoning than Kauṭilya, and in many instances, *ānvīkṣikī*, together with the closely related notions of *hetuvidyā* and *tarkaśāstra*, is clearly incompatible with, and opposed to, the Vedic tradition, or to the soteriologically relevant "science of the self" (*ātmavidyā*).

Kauṭilya's own presentation in the *Arthaśāstra* focuses on the "neutral" methodological aspect of the "investigative science," on the applicability and usefulness of *ānvīkṣikī* for other sciences which play a role in the education of the prince and in the successful conduct of government and administration. In this particular context, Kauṭilya is not interested in discussing the soteriological relevance of *ānvīkṣikī*, or its compatibility with the Vedic *ātmavidyā*. His primary concern with methodology is also illustrated by his list of schools of thought in which he finds *ānvīkṣikī* exemplified. The Sāṃkhya school, which he mentions first, has made important contributions to the formalization and systematization of the *pramāṇa* theory (i.e., the doctrine of the "valid means of knowledge"); it is, however, also a genuinely soteriological system. Such soteriological commitment is absent in the Lokāyata tradition, which Kauṭilya mentions last. The Lokāyata represents an openly secular attitude, which is critical towards the Veda and the traditions of *ātmavidyā*. What Kauṭilya means by *yoga*, the second item in his list, is not easy to determine. In a general sense, it is important to remember that the word *yoga* is by no means exclusively associated with the Yoga system of Patañjali, or with other doctrines and techniques of meditation and inner discipline. Its root *yuj-* also accounts for the word *yukti*, "reasoning"; and likewise, the word *yoga* itself is occasionally used to refer to disciplines of "reasoning" and "argumentation," such as Nyāya and Vaiśeṣika. This usage is documented in older as well as in more recent texts.

For instance, in his commentary on *Nyāyasūtra* 1,1,29, Vātsyāyana mentions "system-specific teachings" (*pratitantrasiddhānta*) of the "Yogas" which are obviously different from, and incompatible with, the teachings of Pātañjala Yoga.[65] In the doxographic literature of the Jainas, the *Naiyāyikas* and *Vaiśeṣikas* are often referred to as "Yogins" or, more specifically, as *Śaiva* and *Pāśupata* Yogins; and their teachings are presented as doctrines of "Yoga."[66]

18. For the "orthodox" groups, the methodological "neutrality" of Kauṭilya's *ānvīkṣikī*, i.e. its openness to different uses and interpretations, is in itself objectionable. On the one hand, reasoning can become an end in itself, and degenerate into sheer intellectual vanity; on the other hand, it can serve anti-traditional, anti-Vedic purposes. There is ample evidence that such developments have, indeed, taken place in ancient India.

We do not have to discuss in detail the various forms which the critique of tradition and traditionalism, and the emancipation of reasoning and argumentation have taken in India since the time of the Buddha and the Jina Mahāvīra, and how this relates to various movements of scepticism and materialism.[67] Together with expressions like *tarkavidyā* ("science of reasoning"), the word *ānvīkṣikī* is directly associated with these tendencies. The "sophists" (*haituka*) who are addicted to "investigative reasoning" (*ānvīkṣikī tarkavidyā*) appear as "scorners of the Veda" and as persons who reject its authority (*vedanindaka, nāstika*).[68] The "investigative intellect" (*buddhir ānvīkṣikī*) leads its "worldly," "secularizing" (*lokāyatika*) followers to a harmful anti-traditionalism.[69] The Buddhists, too (whom the "orthodox" Hindus classify as "heterodox" addicts of reasoning), criticize and reject unrestricted critical reasoning and argumentation. Already in the Pali canon, the *takkin* (Sanskrit *tarkin*; from *tarka*, "reasoning"), with his addiction to argumentation and his delusion of intellectual sovereignty, typifies a dangerous aberration.[70] Manu II, 11 censures those who invoke the "science of logical reasons" (*hetuśāstra*, "dialectics") against the sacred tradition, and who deny the authority of the Veda. Gautama's *Dharmaśāstra* juxtaposes the "Vedic science" (*trayī*) and *ānvīkṣikī* as distinct alternatives.[71] "Sophists," "reasoners," "logicians" (*haituka, tārkika*, etc.) are often brought together with "heretics" (*pāṣaṇḍa*).[72] The increase of reasoning and argumentation appears as a symptom of the *Kaliyuga*, the worst world period, and of the religious degeneration by which it is accompanied.[73] Out of "fear of the science of reasoning" (*tarkavidyābhaya*), people seek refuge with the sources of tradition, with the Upaniṣadic "revelation."[74]

In their usage by the critics of "autonomous," unrestricted reasoning, the terms *ānvīkṣikī, tarkavidyā, hetuśāstra*, etc., are closely related or even appear as synonyms. However, the pejorative connotation of *tarka* is more pronounced than that of *ānvīkṣikī* (or *yukti*). On the other hand, the Nyāya system, which adopts a positive and "orthodox" notion of *ānvīkṣikī* for its self-definition, also uses the term *tarka* with positive, "respectable" connotations, for instance in numerous titles of works.[75]

19. Some of the most memorable invectives against all attempts to establish the fundamental metaphysical and soteriological truths without the guidance of the sacred texts, and against the vanity of "dry," fruitless," "groundless" reasoning (*śuṣkatarka*, etc.)[76] come from the great Śaṅkara. The sophist or dialectician (*tārkika*) who disregards the sacred tradition gets entangled in the fictions and constructions of his own intellect, and he falls into vanity, heresy and self-deception.[77] Analytic reasoning alone, which is committed to the method of "positive and negative concomitance" (*anvayavyatireka*), cannot lead us to the truth about the absolute self. Only the Vedic-Upaniṣadic revelation provides access to this goal; and only that reasoning which understands itself as being grounded in this revelation, and applies the *anvayavyatireka* method as an auxiliary device, is legitimate and fruitful.[78]

"Reasoning" and "inference" are never final; they are never safe from future correction and refutation. It is in the very nature of human reasoning to constantly outdo and disprove itself, and to be unable to find a firm and permanent position.[79] Several centuries before Śaṅkara, Bhartṛhari observed that anything established by skilled "logicians" (*anumātṛ*) was bound to be explained differently by other, even more ingenious ones; Bhartṛhari also used the expression *śuṣkatarka*, "dry," "fruitless" reasoning.[80] Śaṅkara's statement in his commentary on *Brahmasūtra* II,11,11 that independent, unrestrained reasoning, i.e. human reasoning as such, is unstable and unfounded, is part of his response to an opponent who gave a positive interpretation to this phenomenon: In his view, the so-called instability of reason is in reality a distinction (*ayam eva tarkasya-alaṃkāro yad apratiṣṭhitatvaṃ nāma*), since it means openness for the correction of mistakes, i.e. for future progress. The fact that a predecessor was in error and confusion does not imply that we ourselves have to go astray (*na hi pūrvajo mūḍha āsīd ity ātmanā-api mūḍhena bhavitavyaṃ iti kiṃcid asti pramāṇam*).[81] This statement of a defender of reasoning and "progress" may appear as a somewhat isolated curiosity; but even as such, it is worthy of notice.

Śaṅkara himself, as well as other leading advocates of Advaita Vedānta, also use *tarka* in their argumentation. But such usage is primarily a negative one, meant to refute or neutralize opposing doctrines. The rules of critical reasoning and argumentation are invoked against those systems which claim to be built upon reason; their own standards are used to demonstrate their deficiencies. In such contexts, reasoning and argumentation (which may also serve important exegetic, i.e. positive, functions) are used as devices of a *reductio ad absurdum*. After Śaṅkara, the great Vedāntic dialectician Śrīharṣa perfected this reductive use of reasoning (*vitaṇḍā*), this uncovering of undesirable consequences (*prasaṅga*) in accordance with the methods developed by Nāgārjuna and his Madhyamaka school.[82] The Vedāntins seem convinced that by using *tarka* against their opponents they are only fulfilling and making explicit what those who rely on "groundless" reasoning are doing to themselves and to each other. Without any soteriological commitment, Jayarāśi, possibly Śaṅkara's contemporary, demonstrates a merely negative, reductive, dilemmatic use of reasoning in his *Tattvopaplavasiṃha*.

20. The autonomy of human reasoning, the freedom from the forces of tradition, and the separation of philosophy and religion which the historians of philosophy in the nineteenth century saw as criteria of true philosophy, have not been proclaimed in the classical systems of Indian philosophy. Of course, religion and sacred tradition in India did not possess such uniformity and dogmatic compactness that they could have challenged and polarized critical reasoning in the same way as in Europe. There was less scope for conflict, less inducement for emancipation. And moreover, Indian mythology seems to be more susceptible to gradual transitions and reinterpretations than to confrontation with rationality, or to replacement by it. Nevertheless, the question of the autonomy of philosophical thinking

and critical rationality which determined Jacobi's interpretation of *ānvīkṣikī* is not entirely inappropriate for the Indian situation. Although the tension between "free thinking" and the acceptance of tradition has never become as pronounced in India as in Europe, it has not been entirely absent. Of course, we have to view the relationship between "free thinking" and tradition, reason and revelation in a more cautious and balanced manner than many European historians of philosophy, whose treatment of the Pre-Socratic step "from myth to logos" and of the Cartesian freedom from prejudice has often been rather stereotyped and simplistic. In the meantime, the significance of "mythical" premises in the thought of the Pre-Socratics, or of "traditional" presuppositions in Cartesianism, has become increasingly evident. In general, there has been a new openness for the positive implications of "tradition," and a new readiness to acknowledge the constitutive role of "prejudice" in the pursuit of knowledge.[83] On the other hand, the fact that there were no Cartesian "declarations of independence" of rationality in India does not mean that there was no critical search for the foundations of knowledge, for valid criteria, and no ability to reflect upon and question traditional sources and presuppositions.

21. We must not limit our attention to explicit forms of anti-traditionalism and to programmatic declarations concerning the "independence" of critical thinking. Distance and alienation between reason and tradition can also be indicated by the deliberate effort to defend tradition and to restore its authority, and in general by its explicit thematization. A good deal of classical Hindu philosophy is, indeed apologetics and restoration in this sense.

The extent to which tradition and revelation become thematic, and the focus of conceptual efforts of clarification and justification, testifies to the presence of a reflection which has by no means blindly surrendered to tradition. The commitment to tradition is not a mere habitual continuation of past ways of thinking. It is something actively asserted and pursued, something questioned, justified and rationalized. In a variety of ways, philosophers have tried to reconcile the acceptance of the Veda, or of other traditions and "revelations," with the spirit of critical argumentation which prevails in the classical systems and which is also reflected in the idea of *ānvīkṣikī*.

The Nyāya school takes an active part in these attempts. It tries to defend the Veda by using the means and standards of "rational" argumentation, and it tries to demonstrate that its teachings are fully compatible with the data of sense perception and inference (*pratyakṣa; anumāna*). It also tries to anchor the truth and authority of the Veda in the idea of an omniscient and benevolent divine author (*īśvara*), who is by definition without error and deceit.[84]

Likewise, the founders of particular schools of thought are often raised to the status of omniscient "seers" (*ṛṣi*). Yet this does not imply that their teachings are supposed to be inaccessible to rational scrutiny and justification. For instance, the Sāṃkhya tradition invokes the authoritative insights of its mythical founder Kapila, whom it regards as the "primeval sage" (*ādividvān*); but it continues to maintain that the Sāṃkhya teachings are based upon and justifiable by sense perception and inference. On account of this claim, R. Garbe, the European pioneer of Sāṃkhya studies, has applied the somewhat misleading designation "Indian rationalism" to this system.[85]

22. Another, more radical attempt to justify and safeguard the Vedic tradition is represented by the Mīmāṃsā; this school of exegesis and apologetics tries to secure a domain for the Veda which is fundamentally inaccessible to the "worldly" means of knowledge (*pramāṇa*), and thus to reasoning and argumentation. However, reasoning and argumentation are indispensable in this process. They are needed to remove the contents of the Veda from the scope of sense-perception and inference, and of rational critique as well as rational justification. They are, in a sense, invoked against themselves. The authority of the Veda relates to the transempirical domain of the *dharma*, of what has to be done, i.e., primarily the ritual norms and duties. In this domain, there can be no conflict with the results and criteria of "worldly," i.e. empirical and rational cognition. The *dharma* is as inaccessible to "worldly" proof and justification, as it is to empirical and rational refutation. Moreover, the authority of the Veda does not imply that it is the work of an omniscient and absolutely reliable author. The Veda stands and speaks for itself as the timeless and uncreated testimony of *dharma*. It does not have an author; for this very reason, it has no room for error and deception. Outside of the domain of *dharma* and the exegesis of the Veda, the Mīmāṃsā has shown great openness for empirical criteria and for independent argumentation, and the school tradition has accomodated numerous innovations and variations.

In two different ways, the Nyāya and the Mīmāṃsā respond to the argumentation of the Buddhists and other "heterodox" groups, who criticized the Vedic tradition on the basis of sense perception, inference, common sense, etc. Of course, the Buddhists themselves developed a wide spectrum of ideas concerning tradition and revelation, as well as attempts to clarify and resolve the relationship between reason and revelation. In the epistemological school of Dignāga and Dharmakīrti, we find the remarkable notion that the true doctrine of the "means of knowledge" (*pramāṇa*), and the proper use of sense perception and inference, ultimately coincide with, and amount to, the revelation of the Buddha.[86]

The tradition of Advaita Vedānta, which eventually took the lead among the "orthodox" systems of Hinduism, adopts the Mīmāṃsā theory of the "authorlessness" (*apauruṣeyatva*) of the Vedic texts.

23. The emphasis on the inseparability of *ānvīkṣikī* and *(adhy) ātmavidyā* which we found in the classical Nyāya texts is obviously part and symptom of a wider historical phenomenon, a process of returning to authoritative sources and traditions, and of restoring and defending a unity and harmony between revelation and reason, tradition and argumentation which had been challenged and threatened.[87] In this process, the Vedic sources themselves whose authority is invoked and proclaimed undergo a far-reaching reinterpretation. They are associated with views and orientations for which they provide little recognizable evidence; and they are invoked to support a historical stability and continuity, and a deliberate traditionalism, which seems to have little in common with their own spirit.

As we have seen, the Nyāya establishes its identity and peculiarity against other types of "orthodox" thought by systematically developing the element of *ānvīkṣikī*, of "investigation" and argumentation. On the other hand, it constitutes itself as an "orthodox" system by postulating that its *ānvīkṣikī* is fully committed to the tradition, and nothing but a special kind of *ātmavidyā*. The suspicion to which *ānvīkṣikī* could easily be subject has to be eliminated. "Logic" and "reasoning" themselves, which so often appear to be allied with anti-Vedic movements, have to be "orthodox." They have to prove themselves against the "petty reasoning" (*kṣudratarka*) of the heterodox Cārvākas and against the "logical path" (*anumānamārga*) of the Buddhists.[88] Logic and dialectic, if used properly, support the validity of the sacred texts. Argumentative and "questioning" thought,[89] which seemed to be on the verge of a radical "emancipation," has once again committed itself to the tutelage of the tradition, and to religious goals and contents.

24. In his argumentation against Jacobi, Hacker emphasizes the central and symptomatic significance of the question how to relate the two terms *ānvīkṣikī* and *ātmavidyā* in Kāmandaki's statement *ānvīkṣiky ātmavidyā syād* . . . Against Jacobi's translation "Die Philosophie soll eine *ātmavidyā* sein" ("Philosophy should be an *ātmavidyā*"), Hacker insists that *ānvīkṣikī* is not the subject of this sentence, but its predicate nominative.[90] The implications of this alternative are clear: Does Kāmandaki demand that *ānvīkṣikī*, i.e. an independent, investigative, "philosophical" science, should commit itself to religious and soteriological goals? Or does he suggest that a fundamentally unbroken, soteriologically committed "science of the absolute self" should be "methodical" and "investigative"? Immediately following, Hacker refers to the phrase *ānvīkṣiky ātmavidyā* in Manu VII,43 and he claims that here, too, *ānvīkṣiki* is used "in its original function as the feminine form of an adjective."[91] It seems, however, evident that both Manu and Kāmandaki allude to Kauṭilya's fourfold list of sciences, that

ānvīkṣikī, not *ātmavidyā* is the primary theme of their statements, and that *ātmavidyā* qualifies *ānvīkṣiki*, not vice versa. Accordingly, Manu's commentator Medhātithi explains that the *ānvīkṣiky ātmavidyā* is that *ānvīkṣikī* which is "good for the self" (*ātmane yā hitā*) and thus different from the *tarkavidyā* of the Buddhists and Cārvākas.[92]

Ānvīkṣikī is legitimized as well as neutralized in this coordination with *ātmavidyā*. It is characteristic that later commentators no longer see the need for such neutralization. They often tend to explain *ānvīkṣikī* and *ātmavidyā* as two different sciences—an interpretation which already Medhātithi considered as a possibility.[93] And even if they preserve the combination and coordination of the two terms—they are no longer aware of the historical situation in which *ānvīkṣikī*, together with *hetuvidyā, tarkaśāstra*, etc., was a living challenge and a threat to the stability and continuity of the tradition. By the end of the first millenium A.D., *ānvīkṣikī* itself, together with other forms of critical, investigative and heterodox thinking, was more or less fossilized. It was itself part of the tradition, included in a timeless framework and inventory of legitimate "sciences" and possible views and orientations, superseded by the emerging "structure of Hindu traditionalism" which we will discuss in another chapter.[94]

25. In spite of its critical and methodological potential, the concept of *ānvīkṣikī* did not come to represent an open-ended, future-oriented attitude of thought. The retrospective tendencies of the Hindu tradition prevailed in this case, too. In Kauṭilya's *Arthaśāstra, ānvīkṣikī* was a method not confined to one particular domain of objects, and to be used by various branches of learning. But in its adoption by the "orthodox" Nyāya school, it became the name of *one* traditional system, *one darśana, one śāstra*; in this sense, Jayanta speaks of the *śāstram ānvīkṣikam*.[95] *Ānvīkṣikī* and *tarka* appear as titles of traditional "orthodox" branches of learning in the lists of fourteen or eighteen "sciences" (*vidyā*) which have become canonical in classical Hinduism, and they signify the Nyāya or the "expanded" Nyāya (*nyāyavistara*), which includes the Vaiśeṣika.[96] *Ānvīkṣikī, tarka* and *nyāya/nyāyavistara*, as used in these lists, are basically synonymous.

Jayanta explains that the list of fourteen sciences is a list of soteriologically relevant branches of learning, in which Kauṭilya's merely secular and empirical sciences of government (*daṇḍanīti*) and material welfare (*vārttā*) would be out of place. Kāmandaki's *Nītisāra* subsumes the entire fourteenfold list under the science of the three Vedas (*trayī*).[97] Unusual in its time, but much closer to Kauṭilya's own treatment of *ānvīkṣikī*, is the procedure of Rājaśekhara (tenth century?). He uses *ānvīkṣikī*, just like *tarka*, as a generic term for the "orthodox" systems of Sāṃkhya, Nyāya, and Vaiśeṣika, as well as the "heterodox" systems of Buddhism, Jainism and

Lokāyata; that means, he uses it for all the argumentative disciplines of the Indian philosophical tradition, insofar as they are different from the exegetic disciplines of Mīmāṃsā and Vedānta.[98]

Regardless of the role which the concept of *ānvīkṣikī* has played in certain periods of Indian history, and regardless of its undeniable association with tendencies of "autonomous" reasoning and critique of the tradition—its significance as an indicator of rational and methodological attitudes and programs has been ambiguous and temporary. As far as its overall historical role is concerned, it can hardly be considered as an equivalent to "philosophy."

26. Hacker concludes his article on *ānvīkṣikī* as follows: "It is a characteristic trait of the Hindu culture that it knew the concept of philosophy, but no word which expressed this concept fully and exclusively."[99] Earlier in his article, he notes in connection with a critical reference to Jacobi that philosophy in India was recognized as a "special science" ("besondere Wissenschaft"), but that the Indians did not have "a *word* which would have described this domain—*only* this domain, but in its entirety."[100]

Hacker's statements are intriguing as well as problematic, even if we disregard the philosophical implications and ramifications of the question whether or how there can be, in this particular context, a clearly identifiable concept without a corresponding word. What seems to be at stake in Hacker's statements is the claim that philosophy was present in India in the sense of a clearly identifiable and distinguishable cultural phenomenon, as a distinctive discipline which, though without the proper linguistic label, was actually pursued and cultivated. How essential is a linguistically or conceptually explicit self-awareness and self-definition for the "reality" of philosophy? What would the reality of philosophy be like without explicit reflexivity? Whatever we may define as philosophy—a certain level of reflexivity and of explicit self-positing seems to be indispensable. In this loose sense, a "concept" of philosophy (which would not require a precise terminological label) would, indeed be part of philosophy itself in a manner in which, for instance, a concept of painting is *not* part of the actual art of painting. Yet it would hardly be appropriate to say that philosophy cannot occur without a clearly corresponding, explicit term and concept. Even in the history of European philosophy, there has been much retrospective application and extrapolation of the term and concept of philosophy. Ways of thinking and intellectual orientations and pursuits which were not originally under the guidance of an "idea" of philosophy were interpreted, adapted and assimilated as philosophy. In an exemplary and highly significant sense, this has happened in the early period of Greek thought, when Plato and Aristotle adopted and appropriated Pre-Socratic thought *as* philosophy. The retrospective application and historical expansion of the concept of philosophy is also part of the reflexive self-positing of philosophy. Its self-definition is an ongoing historical process, and it is much more than a series of attempts to define an academic discipline or a specific conceptual domain. At important junctures in the history of European thought, the attempts to define and understand what philosophy is coincide with European self-proclamations and with attempts to comprehend the meaning and direction of the entire European tradition.[101] Regardless of the conceptual correspondences between *darśana* or *ānvīkṣikī* and "philosophy," neither of these concepts has played a role in India which would be historically comparable to the role of "philosophy" in Europe.

Today, it is no longer necessary to argue that there was philosophy in India in a sense which is fully compatible with what European philosophers have actually been doing, and with what is documented in European philosophical literature. There has been practical wisdom and conceptual sophistication in India, constructive metaphysics as well as critical epistemology, ontology as well as linguistic analysis: and in general, there has been a level of reflexivity and conceptual articulation which is fully commensurable with what we find in Europe. This commensurability of actual philosophical thinking, and the peculiar and distinctive role which philosophy, as well as its name and concept, have played in Europe are equally fundamental premises for the comparative study of Indian and European thought, for any future cooperation of Indology and philosophy, and for the philosophical "dialogue" between India and the West.

16. The Adoption of the Concept of Philosophy in Modern Hinduism

1. Since the first half of the nineteenth century, and in particular since the introduction of English as the language of higher education (1835) and the inauguration of English-language universities (after 1854), philosophy in the European sense and, moreover, the word and concept of "philosophy," has taken up an ever firmer place in Indian intellectual life.[1] A Department of Philosophy, primarily devoted to the study of Western philosophy, is a part of the regular faculty of every major university. Philosophical congresses are held; numerous journals and series have been published on philosophy and the history of philosophy. The literature which lays claim to the concept and name of philosophy is voluminous, and philosophy also has an important role to play in the vocabulary of many of the leading figures of public life. In this area, India is among the most productive nations today (at least in a quantitative sense). As a result of the colonial policies on education, European philosophy has been adopted and cultivated as a foreign way of thought. Yet at the same time, India's own, indigenous tradition has also been rediscovered and reinterpreted as philosophy, and it has thus been presented anew, and related to Western philosophy in a multitude of ways, involving comparison, identification, parallelization, or contrasting and neutralization.

Subsequently, and oriented around an originally European conceptual world and terminology, these developments have also been taken up and continued within the modern Indian languages. Here, following a number of other attempts which shall be discussed below, and with certain exceptions and regional variations, the term *darśana* (and *darśanaśāstra*) has established itself as the most important terminological analogue to "philosophy," specifically in Hindi and Bengali. A fast growing number of presentations of both Indian and European philosophy has appeared in Hindi and other Indian languages; and topics involving philosophy or the history or philosophy have increasingly come to be discussed in Indian terminology. In turn, this lexicographic Indianization has raised questions concerning the compatibility and correlation of philosophy in the European sense with the Indian tradition. Especially since India attained independence in 1947 Hindi has gained increasing importance as a medium of philosophical instruction and a language for philosophical publications, including translations from English as well as Sanskrit. More recently, Sanskrit itself has gained new visibility in publishing and teaching, and through various attempts to revive it as a language of higher learning.

2. The vast majority of the available literature on Indian philosophy, of the "histories" of Indian philosophy, etc., is the work of Indians. Here, it is sufficient to recall the well-known works by S.N. Dasgupta, M. Hiriyanna, S.C. Chatterjee and D.M. Datta, U. Mishra, J.N. Sinha, etc. Many of these works have also been translated into Hindi.[2] In addition, there are a number of presentations of Indian philosophy which originally appeared in Hindi or other modern Indian languages, along with philosophical journals, etc., in which *darśana* frequently appears in the title. Examples of this include the quarterly journal of the Indian Philosophical Association *Akhila Bhāratīya Darśana Pariṣad*, entitled *Dārśanika traimāsika*, and the Bengali quarterly *Darśana*.[3] Still, even those presentations which were not translated from English are oriented largely around English works, seldom go beyond these, and are in many cases adaptations of them. Many of these works are introductory texts or general surveys intended to serve the purpose of classroom instruction. And thus, the Hindi literature on philosophy and the history of philosophy continues to be overshadowed by the English. Even the numerous recent Hindi translations of Sanskrit works are often retranslations of works that were previously translated into English. At any rate, it is remarkable that translations into Hindi have now become more frequent and common than those into English.

In spite of the growing importance of Hindi, there is still a natural inclination to publish original research contributions which address an international context and are aimed at generating an international response in English. A number of authors work in several languages. Of course, many of the traditional teachers have little or no concern with English, expressing themselves instead in one of the Indian languages; and some of the studies, commentaries, or paraphrases of classical works of Indian philosophy that have appeared in Hindi, Bengali, or Gujarati bear witness to an extraordinary degree of traditional learning and command of texts.[4]

3. Most of the presentations of "Indian philosophy" (Hindi: *bhāratīya darśana*) written in one of the modern Indian languages offer doxographically arranged surveys which range from the Vedic literature (or at least the *Bhagavadgītā*) to the main schools of theistic Vedānta, with

special consideration being given to the classical systems (*darśana*). Modern Indian philosophy is relatively seldom included in such works or in their English prototypes and counterparts.

One Hindi presentation which dates prior to independence yet is still widely known and used is Baladeva Upādhyāya's *Bhāratīya darśana*. This work, which first appeared in 1942, has since appeared in a number of new editions and reprints (the last in 1977 in Benares); it covers the spectrum from the Vedic literature to the philosophical teachings of Vaiṣṇavism and also offers comparative references to European philosophy in an appendix. The same author published a shorter survey entitled *Bhāratīya darśanasāra* in New Delhi in 1962.[5]

The number of analogous works that have been published since independence was won, and in particular since 1960, is much larger. These include Vācaspati Gairolā, *Bhāratīya darśana* (Allahabad, 1962); Arjuna Miśra, *Bhāratīya darśana ke mūla siddhānta* (Lucknow, 1962; as the title itself indicates, this is a presentation of the "Fundamentals of Indian Philosophy" which ranges from the Veda to the Viśiṣṭādvaita); H.P. Sinha, *Bhāratīya darśana kī rūparekhā* (Calcutta, 1963); S.L. Pāṇḍeya, *Bhāratīya darśana kī kahānī* (Allahabad, 1964); Haridatta Śastrī, *Bhāratīya darśanaśāstra kā itihāsa* (Merut, 1966); Divānacanda, *Darśanasaṃgraha* (Lucknow, second ed., 1968).[6] Umeśa Miśra, the author of an ambitious, although unfinished English *History of Indian Philosophy*, has also written a shorter Hindi presentation entitled *Bhāratīya darśana*.[7] A number of representative contributions dealing with Indian philosophy are contained in *Bhāratīya darśana*, edited by N.K. Devaraja (Lucknow, 1975).

Similar works are available in other modern Indian languages, especially in Bengali, Gujarati, and Marathi, although their numbers are not so large. S.N. Dāsagupta (Dasgupta), the author of the famous five-volume *History of Indian Philosophy*, has also written an "Introduction to Indian Philosophy" in Bengali – *Bhāratīya darśaner bhūmikā* (Calcutta, no date). Another Bengali work published in the same city is N.V. Cakravartī, *Bhāratīya darśana*. Perhaps the most important history of Indian philosophy in Bengali is T.C. Rāya (Tarak Chandra Roy), *Bhāratīya darśaner itihāsa* (Calcutta, 1958; 2 vols.). A presentation of Indian philosophy in Gujarati is found in C.V. Rāvaḷa, *Bhāratīya darśana* (Ahmedabad, 1965); another work in Gujarati is *Hinda tattvajñānano itihāsa* by N.S. Mehta (Narmadāśaṅkara Mehatā, 1871–1939), probably the first history of Indian philosophy in an Indian vernacular. Works in Marathi rarely use the word *darśana*, preferring *tattvajñāna* (or *tattvavidyā*, "the knowledge of truth") instead. An example of this is N.C. Kelkara, *Bhāratīya tattvajñāna* (Bombay, 1934). The great "Marathi Encyclopaedia of Philosophy" of D.D. Vāḍekara, by far the most ambitious and comprehensive undertaking of its kind in modern India, also has *tattvajñāna* in its title: *Tattvajñāna mahākoṣa* (3 vols., Poona, 1974). The terms *tattvajñāna, tattvavidyā*, and other compounds using *tattva* continue to play a role in other languages as well; in Gujarati, the important Jaina scholar Sukhalāla Sanghavī (Sukhlal Sanghvi) wrote a presentation of Indian philosophy entitled *Bhāratīya tattvavidyā* that was later translated into English. Various specialized dictionary projects have been undertaken in Bengali, Hindi, and other languages.[8]

4. Most of these "histories" of, and introductions to, Indian philosophy are surveys of classical Indian philosophy which do not, as a rule, historically trace Indian thought into the present and its encounter with European thought. Recent and contemporary Indian philosophy has been dealt with separately in numerous anthologies, surveys, etc. One representative compilation of autobiographical and doctrinal statements is *Contemporary Indian Philosophy*, edited by S. Radhakrishnan and J. Muirhead, first published in 1936.[9] While this first volume still largely acknowledges the precedence of Advaita Vedānta, the second volume of this anthology ("Series II"), edited by M. Chatterjee and published in 1974, possesses a quite different character; it deals primarily with the theory of science, linguistic analysis, and logic, and documents the impact of current Anglo-Saxon philosophy.[10] Other compilations include K. Bhattacharya, *Recent Indian Philosophy* (Calcutta, 1963); N.K. Devaraja, *Indian Philosophy Today* (Delhi, 1975); and the anthology edited by K. Satchidananda Murty and K. Ramakrishna Rao, *Current Trends in Indian Philosophy* (Waltair, 1972) which is distinguished by a very critical and thoughtful introduction by K.S. Murty ("Modern India and Philosophy").[11]

Presentations and surveys may be found in the following works: V.S. Naravane, *Modern Indian Thought — A Philosophical Survey* (London, 1964); R.S. Srivastava, *Contemporary Indian Philosophy* (Delhi, 1965); P. Nagaraja Rao, *Contemporary Indian Philosophy* (Bombay, 1970); N. Sharma, *Twentieth Century Indian Philosophy* (Benares, 1972); B.K. Lal, *Contemporary Indian Philosophy* (Delhi, second ed., 1978); R.P. Srivastana, *Contemporary Indian Idealism* (Delhi, 1973, which presents Vivekananda, Aurobindo, and Radhakrishnan as "idealists"). In addition to such comprehensive surveys and anthologies, individual monographs dealing with particular thinkers and representatives of modern Indian intellectual life (portrayed as "philosophers") have also appeared. Here again, the versions in Hindi as well as in other Indian languages tend to use the word *darśana* in their titles.[12]

As could be expected, independent presentations of the history of Western philosophy are not as numerous, although they are not completely lacking.[13] In contrast, comparative and parallelizing presentations of Indina and Western philosophy as a whole or of particular Western and Indian teachings are quite common.

5. The literature on "modern" or "contemporary" Indian philosophy shows a remarkable conformity in design. It tends to present essentially uniform lists of names and to portray its subjects in a glorifying and apologetic manner. Most surveys begin with Rammohan Roy, describing him as the "Father of Modern India" and especially of modern Indian philosophy. As a rule, they also discuss Vivekananda (together with Ramakrishna), R. Tagore, Gandhi, Aurobindo, and Radhakrishnan; not infrequently, Tilak, Iqbal, and K.C. Bhattacharya are also included, as are such figures as Nehru and Vinoba Bhave.

As this list reveals, the tendency is to use the word "philosophy" in a broad sense which goes far beyond its academic usage. With the exception of K.C. Bhattacharya, those thinkers who represent philosophy as an academic or methodologically defined discipline are almost completely ignored. Also disregarded are the traditionalist pandits who have continued the tradition of the classical systems into the present through their Sanskrit commentaries and similar works. As we have already indicated, there is little continuity between the presentations of traditional Indian philosophy and those concerning "modern" Indian thought. Instead, visionaries, reformers, and national founding figures – and in general personalities who stand for the cultural and national identity and the international resonance of modern India – are depicted as "philosophers," while philosophy itself is claimed as a domain for cultural and national self-affirmation and apologetics. The development of philosophy as a particular discipline or branch of intellectual life is not the only concern of such works, nor is it even the primary one. Rather, modern India is portrayed as a country whose national and cultural identity bears the stamp of "philosophy," with philosophy itself being assigned important tasks for the future shaping of national and international life.

In this context, we would do well to remember that some of the central figures in these presentations of "modern Indian philosophy," for example, Gandhi, never expressed any interest in "philosophy," or even expressly refused the title of "philosopher."[14]

6. If we turn away now from the manner in which "modern Indian philosophy" is portrayed in the secondary literature, and instead turn to the philosophical authors themselves, in particular the academic representatives of philosophy, we also notice much talking *about* philosophy. Instead of pursuing particular philosophical questions, these authors often discuss what philosophy is or should be; definitions of philosophy, programs for and demands upon philosophy, and comparative observations about the

concept of philosophy in the Indian and the European traditions play a striking and symptomatic role.

In the following, we shall exemplify the development and characteristics of this discussion *about* philosophy, this explicit thematic treatment of the word and concept of "philosophy," using testimony from a number of sources. Some of these involve formal definitions, while others present programmatic statements, personal creeds, or simply exemplary ways of using the word "philosophy." It is not our intention to provide a precise analysis of the conceptual implications of these definitions and usages; nor do we intend to discuss or evaluate the philosophical doctrines or positions advocated by each of these authors. Instead, our primary concern is again the fundamental hermeneutic constellation of modern Indian thought: What is the role of the *alien* concept of philosophy in modern Indain *self*-understanding? How does it reflect the encounter between India and Europe?

In India, questions about philosophy and the concept of philosophy, about philosophy's present and future, and about its Indian and universal character, have been raised especially during the twentieth century. They have retained their programmatic and symptomatic importance, which is often linked with the national self-awareness of India, since independence was attained in 1947.[15] This notwithstanding, our discussion shall begin with several of the aforementioned founders and early representatives of modern Indian thought and Neo-Hinduism.

7. With Rammohan Roy, the so-called "father" of modern Indian thought, the word and concept of "philosophy" do not have any great role to play. He utilizes the words "philosopher" and "philosophy" only in a casual and unreflected sense. He does not refer in such usages to the relationship between religion and philosophy, a question which would later come to occupy such a central position.[16]

Similarly, Rammohan's successors among the leadership of the Brāhma Samāj attach no major thematic role to the concept of philosophy; they do, however, make use of it from time to time in a manner which is both characteristic and illuminating. For example, in the speech referred to above,[17] Keshab Chandra Sen contrasts with "spirit of true philosophy" – which the English offer the Indians – with the Indian "spirit of heavenly bliss," of religious and poetic emotion and inspiration. In his eyes, philosophy, an essentially European intellectual attitude, is aligned entirely with science and "hard facts," and is opposed to "sweet poetry and sentiment." In the *nava vidhāna*, the "New Dispensation," both shall be joined within the true and harmonious religion of the future. As we have seen, the model of a complementing between Western science and Indian religious inspiration which lies behind this view had a substantial part to play in Neo-Hinduism.

We found an especially poignant expression of this model in Vivekananda's thought; there, however, philosophy and religion appear in a more differentiated and more clearly thematized relationship than was the case with Keshab.

8. Vivekananda associated philosophy with "reason," "intellect," and "clear language," as well as with "professors from the colleges" and with "scientific men and physicists."[18] He contrasted this with the "beautiful expressions of poetry," with the mythical, the mystic, and the emotional.[19] Addressing "philosophers," he declared: "You may reason it out and understand it intellectually, but there is a long way between intellectual understanding and the practical realisation of it."[20] However, his concept of philosophy received its fullest thematic expression in a scheme in which philosohy is one of three "parts" of religion — or rather, one of three levels — as well as its very "essence": "In every religion there are three parts: philosophy, mythology, and ritual. Philosophy of course is the essence of every religion; mythology explains and illustrates it by means of the more or less legendary lives of great men, stories and fables of wonderful things, and so on; ritual gives to that philosophy a still more concrete form, so that every one may grasp it - ritual is in fact concretised philosophy."[21] This scheme appears more or less explicitly throughout Vivekananda's work, and is occasionally expressed in a modified form; thus, he also makes a fourfold division of religion into "Symbology," "History/Mythology," "Philosophy," and "Mysticism."[22] What is being presented here as the "essence" or decisive part of religion clearly corresponds to a normative concept of philosophy, which may be contrasted with Vivekananda's critical comments about the one-sided intellectualness of philosophy mentioned above. His basic view is: "Religion without philosophy runs into superstition; philosophy without religion becomes dry atheism."[23]

The successors and followers of Vivekananda adhered to the views of their master while re-expressing them in more or less independent variations: for instance, Svami Abhedananda, Vivekananda's friend and his successor in America, declared: "Religion is nothing but the practical side of philosophy, philosophy is the theoretical side of religion."[24] Ultimately, however, the distinction between philosophy and religion, along with the determination of their mutual relationship, is irrelevant, for both are considered to be emcompassed within the superordinated wisdom of the Advaita Vedānta, which overcomes this and similar dichotomies. Therein, "all sciences, philosophies, and religions of the world" are contained with respect to their ultimate meaning; and the Vedānta, it is said, is both the "universal religion" and the "true philosophy."[25]

9. Formulas which are familiar from the works of Vivekananda and the Ramakrishna movement are echoed in an article by Aurobindo:

> Philosophy is the intellectual search for the fundamental truth of things, religion is the attempt to make the truth dynamic in the soul of man. They are essential to each other; a religion that is not the expression of philosophic truth degenerates into superstition and obscurantism, and a philosophy which does not dynamise itself with the religious spirit is a barren light . . .[26]

Of course, the voluminous and somewhat chaotic work of Aurobindo also contains other statements about philosophy which are more directly associated with his own mystic and syncretistic world view. Here, the primary tendency is to affiliate this concept with the concept of "realization" or subordinate philosophy to "realization" as a kind of auxiliary discipline: philosophy thus appears as an "intellectual canaliser of spiritual knowledge and experience."[27] For those who have already attained realization, philosophy is essentially only an instrument for communication, to be used in the attempt to bring others to that path which will eventually lead them beyond philosophy. For Aurobindo, this transcendence of philosophy, bound as it is to the intellect and its concepts, does not just involve the spiritual progression of the individual; it also has cosmic and historical implications. His adoption and reinterpretation of modern Western evolutionary thought also has consequences in this context, for philosophy is seen as something which is not just appropriate to a particular degree of individual, personal maturity, but also to a particular cosmic and historical stage of development. Consequently, it may be superseded by the further development of humanity. Philosophy corresponds to the level of "mental intelligence" in Aurobindo's hierarchy of modes of consciousness, and its relevance is limited to this stage. For those who have gone beyond this, "philosophy, intellectual expression of the Truth may remain, but mainly as a means of expressing this greater discovery and as much of its contents as can at all be expressed in mental terms to those who still live in the mental intelligence."[28] Aurobindo is obviously convinced that India, through its yogic tradition, is closer to surmounting philosophy and the concomitant mode of consciousness than is Europe.

10. The authors we have spoken of up till now were neither representatives of the field of philosophy in an academic sense nor in general from academic circles at all. In India, philosophy as an academic subject was initially a largely British affair, not only in terms of the curriculum and teaching methods, but also with respect to the academic teachers themselves. Calcutta University became the first major center of academic philosophical study in the Western sense. Yet even there, the large-scale participation of native academic teachers of philosophy did not begin until the end of the nineteenth and the beginning of the twentieth centuries. Brajendranath Seal (1864–1938) played a significant part in shaping and institu-

tionalizing academic philosophical instruction and in the development of independent curricula for the study of philosophy and other subjects; the "King George V. Chair" of philosophy in Calcutta, which he occupied, was later renamed in his honor.[29]

Hiralal Haldar, who was almost exactly the same age as B.N. Seal and was also "King George V. Professor" for philosophy in Calcutta for a time, wrote in looking back upon the 1880s and his own time of study in Calcutta:

> More than fifty years ago, when I entered Calcutta University as an undergraduate, there was very little of what can rightly be called philosophical teaching in the University. Certain textbooks, mainly on psychology and ethics, were prescribed and all that the Professors generally did was to expound them and to dictate to the students short summaries of them.[30]

The advance of British Hegelianism or "Neo-Hegelianism" (whose historian Haldar emerged to be) resulted in a greater and more lastingly effective resonance on the part of the Indians.[31] Until most recently, F.H. Bradley has enjoyed much esteem in India, where he is considered one of the exemplary exponents of European philosophy. Kant has also been increasingly drawn into the philosophical discussion and self-exploration, having received particular emphasis in the work of another teacher of philosophy at Calcutta University, Krishna Chandra Bhattacharya (1875-1949). Bhattacharya was one of the most important and influential academic representatives of the subject of philosophy in India. What makes him especially important within the present context is his intense, almost passionate, yet highly reserved philosophizing about the *concept* of philosophy.

11. Speaking programmatically, K.C. Bhattacharya stated: "An explication of the concept of philosophy appears to me more important than the discussion of any specific problem of philosophy."[32] Determining the domain of activity and knowledge intrinsic to philosophy, i.e., its self-demarcation and self-exploration vis-à-vis the empirical sciences on the one hand and certain non-communicable modes of presence and "experience" on the other, is one of the essential and primary tasks of philosophy. Here, the reflective determination of the position of philosophy takes precedence over the clarification of systematic philosophical problems.[33]

"Philosophy starts in reflective consciousness. Reflection is the awareness of a content *as to* a mode of consciousness."[34] "Philosophy deals with the object that is intelligible only in reference to the subject."[35] This is what distinguishes it from science, which is concerned with objects per se — or more precisely: with objectively knowable and determinable, theoretically available, usable occurrences, i.e., with facts which are correlates of judgements in a complete and proper sense.

Science alone speaks in genuine judgements, the content of which is fact intelligible without reference to speaking and is alone actually known and literally thought. Philosophy deals with contents that are not literally thinkable and are not actually known, but are believed as demanding to be known without being thought. Such contents are understood as self-subsistent object, real subject and transcendental truth.[36]

These three "contents" correspond to the three stages or levels of philosophy: "philosophy of the object"; "philosophy of the subject"; "philosophy of truth." In reflective philosophical consciousness, the Absolute itself is presented in a threefold manifestation: as "truth," "value," and "freedom,"[37] corresponding to the trinity of knowing, feeling, and volition.

Philosophy has no actual judgements about the "contents" which it assigns itself. It uses language in a more or less indirect manner; its forms of expression are symbolic, and their variability is inescapable and irreducible. "There is no question of philosophy progressing towards a single unanimously acceptable solution. All philosophy is systematic symbolism and symbolism necessarily admits of alternatives."[38]

12. K.C. Bhattacharya's quest for the concept of philosophy is not just talk *about* philosophy, and he is far from drawing up a placative program *for* philosophy; his statements articulate his reflection upon the actuality of his own philosophizing, his recognition of the rank of science in the modern world, and his attempt to provide a definition of philosophy that is simultaneously a self-delimitation and self-proclamation of philosophy itself. Reflection upon the concept of philosophy is a philosophical effort to clarify the conditions and limits of theoretical thought. A philosophy which understands itself in this fashion and which conceives of and explicates its limits and the limits of science is, in essence, transcendental philosophy; of all the Western philosophical systems, that of Kant was the one which attained the greatest importance for Bhattacharya.

Philosophical reflection is both reflection upon the conditions and limits of science and the self-demarcation of philosophy against science. At the same time, however, it is also a self-delimitation vis-à-vis domains to which philosophy has no access: by defining itself, by recognizing and internalizing its limits, philosophy makes room for what is beyond its reach -something it may acknowledge in its possibility without being able to determine it theoretically. There can be little doubt that Bhattacharya's ultimate concern is with the truth of the Vedānta. He explicitly confesses to a "drive towards advaitism" in his argumentation;[39] however, the Advaita Vedānta describes only the direction which his philosophizing takes, not its professed source or its unquestioned contents and possessions. "His philosophy does not give the impression as if all the answers were known in advance and as if the philosophizing activity were only a question of showing the most convenient and most convincing way of arriving at those answers."[40]

Bhattacharya's orientation towards the Vedānta is undogmatic and non-rhetorical. The Vedānta is not utilized as a national emblem, and he does not presuppose that the truth it possesses is inviolable. He pleads his case for the Vedānta in an indirect manner, not by affirming its truth or appealing to the venerability of its tradition, but rather by reflecting upon the conditions and limits of modern scientific and philosophical thought and thus providing room for its potential acceptance. K.C. Bhattacharya does not present any explicit cultural apologetics; yet he is deeply concerned about regaining for India a lost dignity and autonomy of thought, a "svaraj in ideas" which avoids hasty imitation and "hybridization."[41]

13. The relationship between Advaita Vedānta and philosophy is often the focal point for those modern Indian authors who make efforts to define the concept of philosophy, although they usually lack the rigor and subtleness of thought typical of K.C. Bhattacharya. Often, they simply presuppose that all philosophy is in reality Vedānta, that the Vedānta is the fulfillment of all philosophical doctrines, or that it is nothing less than philosophy itself. Instead of Bhattacharya's cautious yet intensive efforts to come to grips intellectually with this relationship, we often find a placative and apologetic treatment of both concepts: "Philosophy" is usurped in the name of the Vedānta, while cultural and national identity is asserted in the name of "philosophy." Not infrequently, this even occurs with those authors who make reference to K.C. Bhattacharya, e.g., G.R. Malkani, whose repeated attempts to arrive at a definition of philosophy have been pointed out by P. Schreiner: "Malkani tried to defend where Bhattacharya's task was that of the interpreter and constructor."[42] Malkani declared: "If philosophy is understood as the search for Truth or the highest form of wisdom, then philosophy serves a religious purpose and becomes in fact the best form of religion . . . The motto of all real philosophy should be: Truth alone can make us free."[43] "Philosophical truth . . . is eternal truth – or truth that was, is, and shall ever be hereafter."[44] In the face of this definition of "philosophy," it can come as no surprise when Malkani assures us: "We may conclude by saying that the Advaitic concept of philosophy is superior to all other concepts suggested here."[45] While he does refer to K.C. Bhattacharya, he adds that he has further developed the former's ideas in his own manner and "from the standpoint of the Advaita Vedānta,"[46] claiming in turn to have completely "re-vedanticized" the concept of philosophy.

Another author who makes repeated reference to K.C. Bhattacharya is T.R.V. Murti, yet his adherence to the Advaita Vedānta is also much more explicit and avowed. For him, the "spirituality" of the Vedānta is what defines the concept of philosophy, it constitutes its norm and ultimately supersedes it:

Philosophy is the discovery of the Spirit (*adhyātmavidyā*). The actual progression towards this goal as well as its symbolic formulations may be comprised in the concept of philosophy . . . The realisation of Spirit is not necessarily by philosophy alone. Religion, too, has the same aim. The Spiritual is the genus of which the philosophical and the religious consciousnesses are the species.[47]

14. Krishna Chandra Bhattacharya's son Kalidas Bhattacharya systematically developed the doctrine about the inescapable variability of philosophical thought. His main work, *Alternative Standpoints in Philosophy* (Calcutta, 1953), opens with the characteristic words: "In modern times the first business of Philosophy should be to justify its own existence." This book, in which he exemplifies his scheme of "alternative standpoints" with numerous doxographic references, closes with some observations about the relationship between "reality itself" and philosophy which in itself is a subject of metaphysics: "The relation between reality itself, on the one hand, and Philosophy as the final grasp, on the other, has been studied nowhere except in Buddhism, Jainism, the Upaniṣads, and partly in Hegel."[48] Kalidas Bhattacharya has also written a comprehensive presentation of his father's philosophy.[49]

R.V. Das, a student of K.C. Bhattacharya, follows him in a very independent and critical manner. His style of reflecting upon the concept of philosophy provides a good example of this. In his considerations of the philosophy concept, he is concerned with an empiricism of philosophical acts, a grasping of that which de facto occurs in philosophizing and in the history of philosophy. His basic demand is: "I) that our definition of philosophy should hold good of the work of all recognized philosophers, and II) that it should be borne out by our own experience as philosophers."[50]

This demand, together with the definition of philosophy as "critical reflection," stands in sharp contrast to the prevailing style of speaking *about* philosophy, the familiar programmatic statements, and the Vedāntic idealizations that may be exemplified by the following statement:

Philosophy is what seeks, as the *end* of all thinking, the truth that admits of no difference of views and of no doubts whatever . . . Philosophy rises above distinctions of creed, caste, colour, race, calling, age or school of thought. . . In India, Philosophy is sought for the sake of the one and only lesson it teaches man: How to attain and live the life in which is realised the all as himself and himself as the all.[51]

15. Such and similar statements about philosophy – about its "true" Indian sense and its mission in the world of today, about what it is, can be, or should be (and the distinction between the "is" and the "ought" is often neglected) – are very numerous and may be found both within and without academic circles. Often, they are contained within special studies, anthologies, and monographs on the concept of philosophy,[52] yet they may also be found in discussions of various other themes, many of a social or

political nature. In numerous variations, we hear of "philosophical synthesis" and "synthetic philosophy," of "comparative philosophy" and "world philosophy."[53] Let us quote some further examples:

I believed then, as I feel convinced now, that the characteristic attitude of philosophy is synoptic, which duly considers all the aspects and levels of reality in their interrelations, all forming together a unified spiritual whole. Analysis and criticism play an important role in philosophical investigation, but they cannot usurp the place of construction; and the construction of a world-view is the main task of philosophy.[54]

"Indian philosophy was a weapon. Its business was to secure human fulfilment and to give meaning and significance to human existence."[55] — "Indian philosophy is essentially a philosophy of values."[56] — "Philosophy has to show that man is embodied spirit . . ." "Philosophy should be made socially useful, and the strong individualism of our traditional spiritual philosophies has to be modified."[57] "Philosophy was ever man's guide for finding the truths of physics and metaphysics; it should now help him in the equally valuable sphere of international understanding."[58]

16. Once again, S. Radhakrishnan is exemplary in this regard. A great number of "definitions" and programmatic statements, interpretive and evaluating comments arė scattered throughout his extensive work, and these lend the Neo-Hindu discussion about the concept of philosophy some of its most memorable formulations.

"Philosophy in India is essentially spiritual."[59] — "To the Indian mind, philosophy is essentially practical, dealing as it does with the fundamental anxieties of human beings, which are more insistent than abstract speculations."[60] "Philosophy of religion is religion come to an understanding of itself . . . If philosophy of religion is to become scientific, it must become empirical and found itself on religious experience."[61] — "The Hindu philosophy of religion starts from and returns to an experimental basis."[62] — "Every philosophy is the exposition and justification of an experience."[63] — "Political insights, agreements and differences are on the secondary level of man's thinking. Social and political conditions in the several areas depend, in the final analysis, upon the philosophical and spiritual thought . . . ."[64]

"Though India has impressive achievements to her credit in art and architecture, literature and morals, science and medicine, all these derive their inspiration from philosophy as love of wisdom or the life of spirit."[65]

The following motifs are both exemplary and conspicuous: the tendency to place philosophy entirely at the center of the Indian tradition; the orientation around the relationship between philosophy and religion; the blurring of the distinction between what should be and what is; the inclination to present both Indian philosophy and philosophy per se on the basis of invoked ideal definitions; the emphasis upon the practical implications of philosophy ranging from the ethical orientation of the individual to global politics;[66] the tendency to present "experience" and "intuition" as the foundations of religion and philosophy and to allow the two to merge together upon this basis; the use of the idea of philosophy as a vehicle for the universalistic and inclusivist claims of modern Hinduism.[67]

17. In order to further illustrate and clarify the modern Hindu adoption and critique of the concept of philosophy, it is important that we also discuss the function and interpretation of *darśana* and in particular consider how *darśana* and "philosophy" have been related to one another. We shall begin by referring once more to Radhakrishnan, who draws upon the Sanskrit word *darśana* to articulate both his view of philosophy and his understanding of religion.

"A system of thought is called a *darśana* from the root *dṛś*, to see. It is a vision of truth."[68] "Religion is not the acceptance of academic abstractions or the celebration of ceremonies, but a kind of life or experience. It is insight into the nature of reality (*darśana*), or experience of reality (*anubhava*)."[69]

> *Darśana* is a word which is conveniently vague, as it stands for a dialectical defence of extreme monism as well as the intuitional truth on which it is based. Philosophically *darśana* is putting the intuition to proof and propagating it logically . . . It is the one word that stands for all the complex inspiration of philosophy by its beautiful vagueness. A *darśana* is a spiritual perception, a whole view revealed to the soul sense. This soul sight, which is possible only when and where philosophy is lived, is the distinguishing mark of a true philosopher.[70]

Here, "philosophy" and *darsána* are neither simply equated, nor is *darśana* played directly off against "philosophy." Instead, we are faced with a hermeneutic interplay, within which *darśana* expresses a normative and idealizing concept of philosophy, an *Indian* idea and ideal which is capable of showing philosophy its true basis and meaning. At the same time, Radhakrishnan is convinced that he can anchor the unity of philosophy and religion which he continually calls for in the concept of *darśana*. In his view, both are founded in the "intuitive experience" which is expressed by *darśana*.[71] This understanding of *darśana* as the common root and basis of religion and philosophy is thus simultaneously an Indian answer to the European understanding of philosophy as distinct from religion; it appears, in fact, as its neutralization and fulfillment.

18. The view that *darśana* represents the traditional Indian equivalent of "philosophy" and yet also provides testimony of a genuinely Indian philosophical self-understanding based upon "experience" and "intuition" has become almost canonical in the modern Indian presentations of Indian philosophy. The following quotes may help to exemplify this.[72]

"The systems of Indian Philosophy are called darśanas. This word significantly distinguishes Indian philosophy from the European. Darśana is perception, apprehension, experience. Our philosophy is a philosophy of experience."[73]

"As philosophy aims at knowledge of truth it is termed in Indian literature 'the vision of truth' (darśana)."[74]

"That is why the term for 'Philosophy' in India is 'Darśana' – a supremely appropriate term which definitely shows that Philosophical Knowledge must be a direct, immediate, perceptual knowledge."[75]

". . . what does 'philosophy' mean in India? The meaning of the term 'philosophy' is quite clear from the very use of the word *Darśana* for it."[76]

"The word 'darshana' means 'vision' and also the 'instrument of vision.' It stands for the direct, immediate and intuitive vision of Reality . . . 'See the Self' (*ātmā vā are draṣṭavyaḥ*) is the keynote of all schools of Indian philosophy."[77]

"The term Darśana is very significant linguistically, etymologically, conventionally and technically. Anubhūti (experience) or Sākṣātkāra (realization) is the basic characteristic of the Bhāratīya-Darśana . . "[78]

Closely related to this, frequent references are made to the experiences of the "seers" (*ṛṣi*), which are considered to be the original source of the Indian philosophical tradition. "The term 'Indian Philosophy' covers a comprehensive group of philosophical systems that originated in the soil of ancient India some three thousand years ago, and have developed from the primary and plenary spiritual insights of India's sages and seers."[79] From time to time, the expressions "philosopher" and "seer" are used synonymously.[80]

What we have said about the Indian presentations of Indian philosophy in English is also basically true with respect to the analogous works in Hindi and other Indian languages.[81] To be sure, a certain weakening in the terminological and conceptual confrontation does result from the fact that in these works, *darśana*, and not "philosophy," serves as the basic terminological and conceptual category; here, *darśana* does not just designate that which is specifically Indian, it also functions as a more generic concept which may be applied to both Western and Indian "philosophy" (*pāścātya* and *bhāratīya darśana*, respectively). Baladeva Upādhyāya's juxtaposition of *darśana* and "philosophy" (transliterated as *philāsaphī*) as two different species of *one* genus, the neutral, more general category *vicāraśāstra*, "doctrine of thought," "doctrine of reflection," forms an exception rather than the rule.[82] The situation is, of course, somewhat different in works written in Marathi, Gujarati, etc., which use *tattvajñāna* or *tattvavidyā* instead of *darśana*.

19. As the preceding chapter has already shown, the Neo-Hindu interpretation and use of *darśana* does not accord with the traditional dox-

ographic understanding of the word, i.e., its use in the sense of "viewpoint" or "world-view," or simply as a synonym of *mata*, "opinion, doctrine." The etymologizing interpretation which ascribes the meanings "intuition," "realization," "direct experience" to this doxographic use is foreign to the tradition. Even the actual "phenomena" presented under the title of *darśana*, i.e., the teachings and methods of the traditional philosophical systems, do not really justify this interpretation. Certainly, "experience" and "intuition" do play an important role in the Indian tradition; yet this role is much more ambivalent than it appears, for example, in Radhakrishnan's presentation. This may be exemplified by referring to Śaṅkara, who has often been invoked as a prime witness for the importance of "experience" in Hindu thought.

In his exposition of the Advaita Vedānta, Śaṅkara does not refer to his own "experiences," nor does he trace the authority of the Vedas and Upaniṣads to the "experiences" of "seers" (*ṛṣi*); in accordance with the principle of *apauruṣeyatva* adopted from the Pūrvamīmaṃsā, he considers the Vedic texts to be "authorless." Nevertheless, "experience," the direct awareness (*anubhava, anubhūti, sākṣātkāra*) of truth, remains central to his thought — although as a goal to strive for, to which the Vedic "revelation" is capable of leading, and not as the foundation and legitimation of philosophical and religious doctrine. "Revelation" (*śruti*) is the criterion and basis for legitimate experiences; it cannot in turn be measured against the standard of experience, nor can *human* experiences and insights serve as independent and equal sources of authority *alongside* these superhuman sources of knowledge. Śaṅkara emphatically rejects the notion that the experiences and insights of such teachers as Kapila possess a binding force of their own.[83]

It appears that Śaṅkara was quite consciously concerned with neutralizing and channeling the persuasive power and weight of "experiences," subjecting them to the authority of the sacred tradition, and ruling out the possibility of their becoming a source of critique of the tradition and the starting point for possibly "heterodox" innovations.[84]

20. This indicates Śaṅkara's proximity to the traditionalistic Pūrvamīmāṃsā, which radically withdraws the contents of the Veda from all human possibilities of verification, thereby negating "yogic perception" (*yogipratyakṣa*) and similar modes of awareness as well. Obviously, such a restrictive treatment of "experiences" is a response to the challenge posed by Buddhism and other movements which refer back to the enlightenment experiences of their individual founders. More directly and explicitly, the argumentation of the Pūrvamīmāṃsā is directed at the Nyāya doctrine that God (*īśvara*) is the author of the Vedic revelation, and in general, it rejects all references to the insights of omniscient "seers" (*ṛṣi*).[85]

Although there are "more liberal" positions than that of Śaṅkara, and although they recognize *anubhūti* and *svasamvedana* ("experience," "self-experience") as sources of sacred knowledge *alongside* of "revelation" (*śruti* or *āgama*), this does not amount to Radhakrishnan's approach. Radhakrishnan continues a development which first began in this form with the new orientation of Neo-Hinduism in the nineteenth century, specifically in the thought of Debendranath Tagore and Keshab Chandra Sen, and which is part of India's response to the West.[86]

To be sure, metaphors of "seeing" and "experiencing" already played a great role within the Vedic literature, and Yāska associated the words *ṛṣi* and *darśana*.[87] By claiming to be able to measure the Vedic texts against the standard of experience of his "own heart," however, Debendranath took up a position clearly incompatible with the traditional way of dealing with these texts. Other more recent attempts, such as that of "Ṛṣi Daivarāta," to realize Vedic processes of intuition and experience in the present and to "visualize" new Vedic hymns also have to be understood in connection with modern developments.[88] As for Radhakrishnan's use of the concept of "religious experience," we should recall that he was following a linguistic usage that was becoming increasingly widespread in the West, appearing around 1900 in the works of W. James and others.[89]

21. While *darśana* may have become the most conspicuous Indian translation of, and response to, the concept of philosophy, it is not the only Indian expression that has been used in this context. Quite apart from the mere transliteration of "philosophy" into Indian scripts, *darśana* has also had to assert itself against rival expressions, some of which still have a role to play and which were, moreover, suggested by Europeans as possible translations of "philosophy." While European authors did indeed take note of *darśana* in the sense of "doctrine" or "philosophical system" at an early date, they seldom thought of it as a possible equivalent to "philosophy" itself.

One of the first Western authors to refer to *darśana* – written as "dirsen" – was A. Dow: "Neadirsen (i.e., *nyāyadarśana*) is a compound from Nea, signifying right, and Dirsen, to teach or to explain . . . ."[90] Paulinus a S. Bartholomaeo spoke of a "Patanjala dershana" (i.e, *pātañjaladarśana*) as well as of "darshana" with the meaning "visus, aspectus, visio."[91] W. Ward presented the "six durshunus" (i.e., *darśana*) of Hinduism as the "six Systems of Philosophy."[92] H.Th. Colebrooke referred to the "six grand systems of doctrine (*darśana*) in Indian philosophy" or simply to the "six systems of philosophy."[93] E.B. Cowell and A.E. Gough presented the *Sarvadarśanasaṃgraha* of Mādhava-Vidyāraṇya as a "Review of the different systems of Hindu philosophy." In these and in similar cases, the concept of philosophy was being applied to that which the Indian doxographic literature terms *darśana*; however, this does not imply a more precise and thematically explicit terminological or conceptual association.[94]

The older Sanskrit lexica provide additional insight. In F. Bopp's *Glossarium sanscritum* (Berlin, 1830) and in his *Glossarium comparativum linguae sanscritae* (Berlin, third ed., 1867), the word *darśana* is not assigned the meaning of a "philosophical doctrine, system," not to mention that of "philosophy." In H.H. Wilson's *Dictionary in Sanscrit and English* (Calcutta, 1832), one of the fourteen definitions is "a śāstra, one of the six religious or philosophical systems."[95] Especially interesting is the fact that M. Monier-Williams, in his *Dictionary, English and Sanskrit* (London, 1851) lists a large number of terms for "philosophy" – *tattvajñāna, tattvavidyā, jñāna, tattvaśāstra, jñānaśāstra, pāṇḍitya* – while excluding *darśana*; moreover, the terms *tattvajñāna* and *tattvavidyā* are also listed under "theology."[96]

22. In contrast, it is striking that "philosophy" and *darśana* are lexicographically related by the two nineteenth-century Indian authors of English-Sanskrit dictionaries. In his three-volume *English-Sanskrit Dictionary*,[97] published in 1877–1880, A.R. Borooah presents both *darśana* and *darśanaśāstra* as analogues to "philosophy"; in *The Student's English-Sanskrit Dictionary*[98] of V.S. Apte, which was published in 1884, *darśana* appears in the first position, followed by *tattvajñāna, vijñāna*, and *tattvavidyāśāstra*.

Of course, presenting the actual English usage in Sanskrit, or listing the lexicographic equivalents already available in classical Sanskrit usage, cannot be the only, perhaps not even the primary concern in such dictionaries, irrespective of whether they are compiled by Indians or Europeans. Another major concern is to have an effect upon Sanskrit, to "modernize" it, to prepare it for the semantic possibilities of English, and, one might say, to actively create terminological points of contact. The same applies to the attempts to Sanskritize "philosophy." Monier-Williams experimented more or less freely with suggestions for translations. Borooah's citation of *darśana* and *darśanaśāstra* may hardly be considered a reflection of a linguistic practice that had already become standard or binding in his time, although it certainly corresponds more closely to the terminological associations that had already been made than do the suggestions put forth by Monier-Williams.[99]

The testimony of Bankim Chandra Chatterji, who exhibited an especial interest in questions of terminological correspondence, helps to shed light upon this question. In his Bengali article *Jñāna* ("Cognition"), which appeared at almost the same time as Borooah's dictionary and specifically discusses epistemological problems, with references to Kant and J. St. Mill, the author associates "philosophy" (*filasafi*) with *darśana* while simultaneously pointing out the important differences in the meanings of the two. In particular, he emphasizes that the knowledge intended by *darśana* has a practical and soteriological aim and is simply a means (*sādhana*), while philosophy considers knowledge itself as its aim (*sādhanīya*).[100] He also states that *darśana* is far less divided into special branches of knowledge than philosophy. This notwithstanding, Bankim also characterizes Western philosophical doctrines, e.g., Comte's "Positive Philosophy," as *darśanaśāstra*.[101] It seems obvious that Bankim's discussion of the relationship between *darśana* and "philosophy" articulates ideas which had already gained a certain familiarity in his day.

23. The lexicographic problems indicated above must also be taken into consideration when consulting English-Hindi dictionaries, and corresponding presentations of other Indian languages. Hindi is not simply a factually "existing" language, it is also a linguistic program, goal, and ideal - as the national and cultural language of *modern* India which is still in the process of being developed, "enriched," and "purified." In addition to providing inventories of the actual linguistic usage, the Hindi lexicographers have contributed to this development by including both their own suggestions as well as more or less official terminological guidelines and norms. Efforts "to promote the spread of the Hindi language, to develop it . . . , and to secure its enrichment" are called for in the Indian constitution itself. The lexicographer must be ready to adopt the motto "make words," as suggested in S.S. Das' introduction to his *Hindi Scientific Glossary* (Benares, 1906). Thus, terminological unanimity for such a word as "philosophy" cannot be expected from these sources; nor do they provide reliable information as to the actual usage of its alleged Hindi equivalents. The great range of variation, occasionally bordering on confusion, which some lexica exhibit in this regard and which far exceeds anything found in actual linguistic usage, becomes understandable when seen in this light.[102]

The *Comprehensive English-Hindi Dictionary of Governmental and Educational Words and Phrases*, which was prepared by Raghuvīra in connection with the official language policy, and which is characterized by its puristic Sanskritizing tendencies, lists *darśana* as the only terminological equivalent of "philosophy"; but this is quite unusual, and certainly not representative.[103] One of the most widely used lexica, *Bhargava's Standard Illustrated Dictionary*, includes *tattvajñāna* along with the etymologizing paraphrase *vidyā kā prema* ("love of wisdom").[104] A striking list is found in Haradeva Bāharī's *Bṛhat aṃgrejī-hindī kośa* (*Comprehensive English-Hindi Dictionary*, Benares, 1960), where, in addition to *darśana* and *darśanaśāstra, śāstra, tattva, vidyā, brahmajñāna, tattvajñāna*, and *dārśanika siddhānta* are also given. The *New English-Hindi Dictionary* by Sūrya Kānta (Delhi/Allahabad, 1962) does not even list *darśana* as an analogue to "philosophy," but only such terms as *jñānavijñāna, tarkaśāstra,* and *vidyā.*

We have to abstain here from pursuing these lexicographic and terminological developments in other Indian languages. Urdu is a special case insofar as it adopts the original Greek term through its Arabic-Persian intermediary *falsafa.*[105] In south India, the developments in Tamil have been markedly different not only from those in North Indian languages, but also from those in the other Dravidian languages. Most conspicuously, Tamil often uses the Sanskrit term *vedānta* as an equivalent of "philosophy."[106] We shall also refrain from comparing the Indian developments with those in other Asian traditions. Here, Japan would provide the most significant and most exemplary case. It introduced and adopted European philosophical thought without colonial subjugation. Much of the terminological groundwork was laid by Amane Nishi (1829–1897). The word *tetsugaku*, with which he tried to capture the etymological meaning "love of wisdom," became the standard term for "philosophy" in Japan.[107]

24. Apart from *darśana*, the most frequent word in the Hindi dictionaries is *tattvajñāna*. And in fact, this word, together with other compounds using *tattva* (i.e., "truth," "reality"; e.g., *tattvavidyā; tattvajijñāsā; tattvamīmāṃsā*; and *tattvadarśana*), continues to play a significant role in modern Indian literature on philosophical subjects. As we have already mentioned, it is used instead of *darśana* in several Indian languages, specifically in Marathi.

The expressions *tattvajñāna, tattvavidyā, tattvadarśana,* or *tattvamīmāṃsā* appear also in the sense of "metaphysics," and as terms for a special discipline of philosophy existing alongside such domains as *nīti* ("ethics"), *jñānamīmāṃsā* and *pramāṇamīmāmsā* ("epistemology"), *tarkaśāstra* ("logic"), etc.[108] On the other hand, several of the above-named English-Hindi dictionaries give *ātmavidyā* and *adhyātmavidyā* ("science of the absolute self") as lexicographic analogues to "metaphysics." Prior to this, various other translations had also been suggested. Thus, for example, A. Govinda Pillai gave his Sanskrit translation of P. Deussen's *Elemente der Metaphysik* the title *Atītaprakṛtiśāstram* (Trivandrum, 1912), thereby attempting to precisely and literally duplicate the expression "metaphysics" – the doctrine about that which "goes beyond nature" – in Sanskrit.[109]

Similarly, a unified and generally accepted Indian terminology has not yet been attained for the other philosophical disciplines. For instance, besides being rendered as *nīti* or *nītiśāstra*, "ethics" is also occasionally translated as *kartavyaśāstra* ("doctrine of that which is to be done," "doctrine of duty"). Neither Raghuvīra's extensive lexicographic projects, nor the comprehensive and systematic efforts of the "Marathi Encyclopaedia of

Philosophy" (*Tattvajñāna mahākoṣa*) have produced a definitive terminological clarification and agreement.[110]

Regardless of all terminological discrepancies and uncertainties, *darśana* is the most significant and symptomatic Indian response to European "philosophy." It is not simply a lexicographic equivalent to "philosophy," but a reflection of Neo-Hindu self-understanding and self-assertion. It expresses the modern Indian adoption of, and self-demarcation against, "philosophy" in its European sense. *Darśana* corresponds to "philosophy", but it is also supposed to be something more profound. In its Neo-Hindu, specifically Neo-Vedānta usage and interpretation, it represents vision and realization instead of analysis and discursive thought – and a deeper dimension of that same intellectual and spiritual enterprise which Europeans call "philosophy."

25. We have already referred to the symptomatic tendency of modern Hinduism to speak *about* philosophy and to advance definitions of or programs for philosophy. In the same sense, "Comparative Philosophy" has attained a symptomatic meaning in India – as a field of cultural and national self-assertion. Brajendranath Seal (1864–1938) may have been the first to have used the expression "Comparative Philosophy." In the introduction to his *Comparative Studies in Vaishnavism and Christianity* (Calcutta, 1899; "with an examination of the Mahabharata legend about Narada's pilgrimage to Svetadvipa and an introduction on the historico-comparative method"), he pleads for a scientific "comparison" which assigns equal rank to that which it compares. Such "comparison" and "coordination" should rectify and overcome the historical subordination of non-European cultures which Hegel exemplifies. In the place of "European side-views of Humanity," an understanding of history that is truly universal and encompasses all of mankind should emerge.

The comparative sciences, including "Comparative Jurisprudence, Politics, Religion and Mythology", should aid in discovering the "general laws of the social organism," and "Comparative Philosophy" should be established as the "most sovereign of the sciences of the sociological group." The influence of the ideas of A. Comte and his followers in obvious in Seal's statements. Yet these ideas are fitted into a context which is different from that of the European "Positivists"; moreover, they also serve for Hindu self-assertion and self-defense. The synthesis and universality which is strived for in such "comparing" is supposed to lead to a "new European Renaissance," but one which differs from the old:

> A new European Renaissance, if it is to come, must not . . . look to Greece for inspiration . . . The speculative ardour, the metaphysical genius, the science of the Absolute of the Hindus are exactly fitted to infuse a new blood into European philosophy, and to rouse its dormant activity.[111]

What is especially noteworthy is that B.N. Seal tries to demonstrate the value of Hinduism through its potential for a *European* Renaissance. He does not speak of a Renaissance of Hinduism per se. European culture is "undeniably the main stream of the world's Civilisation"; it is here that the new and greater Renaissance is to occur. Hinduism can maintain itself within the historical framework created by Europe through its universalistic potential. B.N. Seal finds the power of "comparing," the potential for universality, in works as early as Yāska's *Nirukta* (fifth century B.C.), as well as in Rammohan Roy, whom he celebrates as the founder of "Comparative Religion" and, in another context, as a "universal man."[112] The *Comparative Studies in Vaishnavism and Christianity* have received only little attention and their direct impact has been very limited. However, Seal also formulated his program of "Comparative Philosophy" in a work that did receive more recognition, *The Positive Sciences of the Ancient Hindus* (1915); this may have led P. Masson-Oursel to his use of "philosophie comparée," or "comparative philosophy."[113]

26. Irrespective of how we evaluate the influence and the historical role of B.N. Seal, the literature on comparative philosophy that currently issues from India is very extensive. In particular, the Advaita Vedānta is often invoked as the goal and standard of "comparison." In this sense, Kant and Hegel, Spinoza and Bradley have been "compared" with Śaṅkara.[114]

> If only Bradley had realized what his own premises pushed to their logical conclusions lead to, he would have come to this very conclusion and joined hand with Śaṅkara . . . If existentialism had carried its discrimination of Dasein from what is not Dasein still further . . . then certainly existentialism would have come to the position of Śaṅkara.[115]20

It is obvious that such comparisons which try to demonstrate the superiority of the Vedānta by measuring it against foreign, Western standards also testify to the continuing authority of these standards.[116]

In an apologetic reference to the tendency to assimilate and compare that is so predominant within modern Hindu thought, D.M. Datta, one of the best-known representatives of academic philosophy in India, has remarked:

> Unlike their Western brethren Indians feel it their duty now to understand and assimilate the Eastern and the Western before making any new contribution. This is one of the reasons why India's original contribution has been so meager in present times. The other reason is, of course, the loss of confidence caused by long political subjugation.[117]

In another passage, the same author expressly relates his patriotism and his work as a philosopher and historian of philosophy:

> When four years of social work, disturbed by bitter political controversies made me physically and morally sick, my frustrated patriotism sought expression in this more

congenial cultural and academic field . . . The motive behind all this was of course the defence of Indian thought and culture (slighted and disgraced by the West) with the help of the up-to-date logical and philosophical weapons forged by the West.[118]

At the close of this chapter, as a kind of question mark, we quote the judgement of an Indian historian who has looked at European domination and the Indian reaction thereto with equally critical eyes and who has concentrated his critique upon the field of philosophy, the domain to which so many other Indian authors have attached so much hope:

There is one field of intellectual activity in which the Indian mind has been particularly barren during the last 100 years, and that is in philosophical thinking. Until quite recently philosophical thinking in the Indian universities was confined to the systems of Western thinkers, and when Indian systems came again to be taught the categories had become confused. The translations of Indian philosophical systems into English added to the confusion, for these tried to express Indian thinking in terms of Western philosophy. Thus Western education in this field has been altogether sterile and may be said to have helped to dry up the roots of philosophical thinking in India – except among classes among whom this education had not penetrated.[119]

Other Indian authors have voiced similar sentiments, though perhaps less eloquently. They have deplored the continuing "confusion" and "alienation" of modern Indian thought; and they have expressed their disappointment that the liberation from the British, and the promotion of Hindi and other Indian languages, have not been accompanied by a new sovereignty of self-understanding and philosophical thinking.[120]

17. *Dharma* in the Self-Understanding of Traditional Hinduism

1. As we have seen, the relationship between philosophy and religion was decisive for the Neo-Hindu assimilation of philosophy. The inseparability of religion and philosophy was presented as a constituent element of the Hindu tradition and used to confront a European tradition in which philosophy had acquired an increasingly autonomous nature. To this extent, the self-assertion of Indian philosophy is simultaneously a self-representation in the name of religion; and the concept of religion stands at the very center of Neo-Hindu thought.

Just as there is no traditional Indian word which precisely corresponds to "philosophy," there is also no exact equivalent for "religion." In modern Indian linguistic usage, specifically in modern Sanskrit[1] and in the languages of North India, the word *dharma* has largely assumed this role; *dharma* appears as the designation of religion in general as well as in the titles of particular religions, e.g., *khṛṣṭadharma* (also *kraiṣṭavadharma*, etc., "Christianity," "Christian religion") or *bauddhadharma* ("Buddhism"). The correlation of *dharma* and *darśana* reflects the contrast between religion and philosophy; discussions of this may be found in some of the modern Indian presentations of Indian philosophy listed in the previous chapter; and monographs are also available on this subject.[2] *Dharmadarśana* has been used as the equivalent of "philosophy of religion." While such terms as *īśvarabhakti* or *īśvaropāsana*, which stress the element of being bound to a personal God, occasionally appear as analogues of "religion" in both the lexicography and actual linguistic usage, and while the more general term *mata* is widely used in South India, it can nevertheless be stated that the lexical association of *dharma* and religion is even more consistent than that of *darśana* and philosophy. *Dharma* also serves as the "official" term for "religion" in the Indian constitution[3] and in the constitutional definition of the Indian Republic as a "secular state" (*dharmanirapekṣa rājya*).

M. Monier-Williams, who does not offer *darśana* as an Indian expression for philosophy, lists *dharma* first in his entry "religion," followed by *īśvarabhakti*, etc.; A. R. Borooah gives only *dharma*. In the English dictionaries for North Indian vernaculars, *dharma*, when not given alone, usually appears in the first position. *Bhargava's Standard Illustrated Dictionary*, which places *īśvarabhakti* before *dharma*,[4] is among the few exceptions.

2. We have seen how *darśana* is not only a translation and indigenous linguistic receptacle for the Western concept of philosophy, but also an Indian answer to and a means of self-assertion against European philosophy and science. Insofar as *dharma* is much more central to traditional Hindu self-understanding and is also a more complex concept than *darśana*, we can expect even less that the modern function of this term would remain limited to that of a mere vehicle of translation and reception; and the greater diversity of its traditional usages is reflected in the greater hermeneutic complexity of its modern appropriation and reinterpretation.

There is probably no better exemplification for the basic orientation of modern Hindu thought than the concept of *dharma*: "This is perhaps the most instructive instance of a reinterpretation in Hindu modernism."[5] The Neo-Hindus themselves emphasize time and again the importance of this concept: "Next to the category of reality, that of dharma is the most important concept in Indian thought."[6]

We have already discussed *dharma* as the main concept of traditional Hindu xenology, as the standard used to demarcate the Aryan from the *mleccha*.[7] This core concept of a rigorous ethnocentric self-assertion became a catalyst for the encounter between foreign and Neo-Hindu thought, at first primarily with the Christian missionaries, who used the concept of *dharma* in order to transmit the Christian message and attempted to adopt it for the terminology of Indian Christianity. The basic positions of modern Hindu thought and the basic motives of self-assertion and receptivity, of exclusivism and universalism, are mirrored in the various ways in which this concept was used.

3. The following discussion will not be concerned with presenting a comprehensive history of the *dharma* concept. For any such presentation, even if limited to Hinduism, would also have to deal with the historically and systematically important relationships between the Hindu usage and the ways in which the Buddhists and Jainas utilized *dharma*. In the present context, we shall content ourselves with a discussion of basic ways in which this concept has been used within traditional Hinduism, and with providing a general background for the modern reinterpretations and, in particular, the Neo-Hindu appropriation of the concept of religion.

In view of the central and generally recognized importance which the concept of *dharma* possesses for any understanding of the Hindu tradition, it may appear surprising that a comprehensive monograph on the concept has yet to appear. There is not even a philological or lexical survey like that which M. and W. Geiger have made for the use of *dhamma* in the Buddhist Pali canon.[8] Special studies on particular aspects of the dharma theme are also relatively rare.[9] While the concept is usually discussed in some detail in the more general works on Hinduism, in particular in those on the history of Indian religion and law, this can be no replacement for a thorough monographic treatment of the subject.

Numerous statements have emphasized the fullness of meaning and the complexity of *dharma*, as well as the difficulty of translating it or of even adequately paraphrasing it. "The term *dharma* seems to be one impossible to reduce even to a few basic definitions. It is ubiquitous throughout the texts of the Indian tradition, ancient and modern, and has been used in a bewildering variety of ways."[10] Let us now look at a few exemplary attempts from modern Indological research to clarify this "bewildering variety" and to define some basic conditions for its understanding.

4. Originally referring to the principle of universal stability, the power which sustains, upholds, and maintains, the firmly established order, this term . . . in general means the lawfulness and regularity, the harmony, the fundamental equilibrium, the norm which reigns in the cosmos, nature, society, and individual existence. *Dharma* is the basis for the norms of individual conduct, it sustains the structure of the community and regulates the continuity in all the manifestations of reality. The person who follows the Dharma realizes the ideal of his own character and manifests the eternal lawfulness in himself. As long as a phenomenon is normal, as long as a person (or animal) adheres to his normal behavior, his individual destiny and task, and possesses undiminished the individuality and appropriate properties which come to him through the power of his nature, as long as his doing and his omissions are in agreement with the normal, traditional, and personally approved actions, goals, and livelihood of his position, his gender, his family, his age-group, so long does he adhere to the Dharma. Here, stability and regularity in the cosmos and nature on the one hand and order and correct behavior of a moral, social and legal type on the other do not fundamentally differ. The events in nature and in the world of humans must occur in accordance with their Dharma . . .[11]

"The Veda and Smṛti teach what Dharma is, in particular the Dharma books whose actual and original purpose lay in teaching the correct, salutary behavior in its religious, moral, and social aspects (*Ācāra*)."[12] "*Dharma, Karman* and *Saṃsāra* constitute one complex, *one* ideological system."[13]

"Dharma is propriety, socially approved conduct, in relation to one's fellow men or to other living beings (animals, or superhuman powers). Law, social usage, morality, and most of what we ordinarily mean by religion, all fall under this head."[14]

5. It has been repeatedly emphasized that the concept of *dharma* is so difficult to define because it ignores or transcends differences which are essen-

tial or irreducible for Western understanding - differences between fact and norm, cosmos and society, physics and ethics, etc. Thus, R. Lingat states:

Le *dharma* est une notion qu'il est malaisé de définir, parce qu'elle méconnaît, – ou transcende, – des distinctions qui nour paraissent essentielles et parce qu'elle se fonde sur des croyances qui nous sont aussi étrangères qu'elles sont familières aux Hindous . . . Le sens général est donné par la racine *dhṛ*, qui exprime l'action de maintenir, soutenir, entretenir, et qui a donné en latin *fre* (fretus, appuyé sur, fort de) et *fir* (firmus, ferme au sens physique et moral, d'où solide, fort, durable). Le dharma, c'est ce qui est ferme et durable, ce qui soutient et maintient, ce qui empêche de défaillir et de choir. – Appliqué à l'universe, le dharma désigne les lois éternelles qui maintiennent le monde.[15]

R. Lingat also notes that in Vedic times, the cosmic order expressed by *dharma* was identified with the "laws of sacrifice," and that "dharma par excellence" was "the sacrificial act which maintains and even conditions the cosmic order." This meaning remained present, but was included in a wider usage:

. . . la notion de dharma s'est élargie, elle englobe le monde moral aussi bien que le monde physique; la norme rituelle devient une norme de conduite . . . De là on passe aisément au sens que prend dharma le plus souvent dans nos textes: ensemble des devoirs qui incombent à chacun suivant sa condition (*varṇa*) et le stade de son existence (*āśrama*), ensemble des règles sur lesquelles il doit conformer sa conduite s'il ne veut pas déchoir . . .[16]

Following this, reference is made to the position of this religio-social norm and duty alongside the principles of the useful ("utile," *artha*) and the sensually agreeable ("agréable," *kāma*), i.e., to the classical three-fold schema (*trivarga*) of human aims (*puruṣārtha*), to which, as is well known, "salvation" (*mokṣa*) was added as the fourth aim which transcends all the other values of life.

6. Against attempts to derive *dharma* from general ethical, metaphysical, or religious principles, P. Hacker maintains:

The Hindu concept of dharma is radically empirical. In order to know what dharma is, one must go to the Ārya in India, if possible to Āryāvarta, and observe what those among them who are advanced in years, experienced, well-mannered, and respectable all consider as dharma . . . Dharma, whose meaning concerns the castes and the stages of life, which encompasses the entire field of morals, cult, law, and custom, and whose fulfillment effects one's welfare in the world beyond, is not derivable from a philosophical principle or a religious origin, but can only be determined empirically, whether from the Veda, or from the consensus of the good under consideration of geographical location.[17]

What is expressed in the concept of dharma is a self-awareness of Aryanism, which was initially the self-awareness of a particular epoch of intellectual history . . . As an expression of the self-awareness of Aryanism, the concept of dharma, with certain adjustments to more advanced viewpoints, yet with few changes at its core, has been retained through the ages. It was, in all its vagueness and in its empiricism, the unifying band of Aryanism, the one factor which somehow held together the complexity of Hinduism.[18]

In another context, P. Hacker says:

First of all, dharma is the *religious law* or the *religious order*. Yet this does not just comprise the cultic and the moral, but beyond this the entire legal order as well as an abundance of conventional customs and habits . . . Secondly, dharma is also *order in performance*. All activity which corresponds to the order of dharma is dharma. Thirdly, dharma is also *order after performance*, i.e., that which is called 'good karma.'[19]

In keeping with the associational wealth of *dharma*, the range of the Western expressions which have been utilized to translate this word (which is often called untranslatable) is wide indeed: it reaches from "norm," "duty," and "command" to "religion" and "faith," from "justice," "custom," and "law" to "piety," "moral fitness," "virtue," "good work," and "religious merit."[20]

In the following discussion, we shall return to these citations, adopting, criticizing, or modifying them. With respect to the above-cited remarks of J. Gonda (§ 4), it may be said that they should not be judged as historical and philosophical theses alone: insofar as they reflect the Neo-Hindu reinterpretation of the dharma concept, they are themselves part and symptom of the hermeneutic interplay between India and Europe.

7. As to the earliest determinable meaning of *dharma* and the role of *dharma/dharman* in the Vedic literature, we shall merely provide a few general comments and reminders.

There are approximately sixty occurrences of the *nomen actionis dhárman* (neuter) in the *Ṛgveda*, in addition to numerous verb forms and other derivatives of the root *dhṛ* (including several instances of the *nomen agentis dharmán*). According to P.V. Kane, the meaning is in most cases "religious ordinances or rites." H. Grassmann gives such meanings as "law, established order or custom." K.F. Geldner's translation has twenty different German expressions. A. Bergaigne, on the other hand, consistently uses "loi" ("law").[21] *Dharman* usually appears explicitly in the plural or possesses an at least potentially plural function and meaning. In particular, the references to the "first dharmas" (*dharmāṇi prathamāni, prathamā dharmā*[22]) should be emphasized. Only later did an essentially singular use as a "complex" or "totality of binding norms" gain in prominence.[23]

In its plural function and as *nomen actionis, dharman* differs significantly from a fundamental Vedic concept of norm and order with which it has often been associated - the essentially singular concept of *ṛta*. The Vedic texts themselves do not establish an explicit and thematic relationship between the two concepts; associations or linkages between the two words are casual and rare. The connection between *ṛta* and *dharma* is certainly much more elusive and problematic than it appears in numerous attempts to derive *dharma* from *ṛta*, or to explain it as its later "equivalent."[24] The plural use of *dharma* remained important and common in post-Vedic works, e.g., in the *Bhagavadgītā*, which refers among other things to the "venerable norms (or statutes) for the families" (*kuladharmāḥ*).[25] Yet even in the later use of the concept, when the singular prevailed, a plurality of precisely established "rules" remained a determining and constitutive factor of *dharma*. This plurality that is immanent in *dharma* should, of course, be distinguished from that plurality in which *dharma* is understood when used in the sense of juxtaposable "religions" or forms of belief.

8. The association between *ṛta* and *dharma*, which Neo-Hinduism emphasizes, usually presupposes that the concept of *dharma* involves universal cosmic laws. This interpretation has also gained a certain popularity among Western authors, and lies, for example, behind the above-cited statements of J. Gonda. Yet the idea of an objective natural order effective in the world, specifically in inanimate things, i.e., of something like a natural law, has little importance for the ancient and traditional usage of *dharma*. To be sure, the activities characterized as *dharma*, at first ritualistic and then more general, also have cosmic implications and affect the course of nature. But this does not mean that *dharma* functions in the "natural" and "objective" world as such. There is no such "objective" world in Vedic ritualism. Instead, there is a framework of mythical, magical reciprocity, which correlates the ritual and socio-religious activities of certain privileged groups of actors with cosmic and "natural" phenomena. If the sun does not rise with regularity, or if a river overflows its banks, then this may indeed indicate a violation of the *dharma*; but it does not imply that the sun or the river has violated its own *dharma*. Similarly, the fact that the sun does rise with regularity does not mean that the sun is following or fulfilling its own *dharma*. In this context, we should consider what S. Schayer has termed the "structure of the magical view of the world" in the *Brāhmaṇa* texts — a view which must be distinguished from the conception of a natural or supernatural order which exists "in itself":

> This simultaneously suggests the fundamental contrast between the ancient Vedic ṛta and the ideal of the magical order in the Brāhmaṇas: while ṛta forms a kind of supernatural sphere and 'determines from without' the behavior of men, the magical man is himself a gopā ṛtasya, the agent and fulfiller of the law.[26]

Dharma, from this "magical" point of view, is neither a "natural" order immanent in the subsistence of the world nor an "objective" transcendental order and lawfulness. Instead, it is the continuous *maintaining* of the social and cosmic order and norm which is achieved by the Aryan through the performance of his Vedic rites and traditional duties.

The *dharma* can only be violated and protected by the members of the Aryan community who are subject to its provisions. By nurturing and preserving the *dharma*, they do not just preserve the identity and continuity of their own tradition and society, but also the order and regularity of the cosmos, of the physical world in which they live. The sacred tradition, and the behavior of the Aryan which accords with it, are important for the balance and order of the physical world as well, and to this extent, cosmos and society, ethics and physics do indeed merge; and in this sense, the *dharma* and the Veda which teaches it represent a power to maintain and preserve that is of universal importance.[27] The idea of a mythico-magical correspondence between human behavior and the physical world is certainly important as a backdrop to the dharma literature; J.J. Meyer's description of these works as books of magic and sorcery ("Zauberbücher") is, however, too one-sided.[28]

9. Citations intended to support a universal cosmological interpretation of *dharma* are often taken out of context; and the extent to which Vedic texts, especially *Brāhmaṇas*, employ repeatable and interchangeable formulas remains unconsidered. This is true of the frequently cited passage *Taittirīya Āraṇyaka* X,79, which gives *dharma* as part of a listing of twelve factors or principles of human order, including *satya* ("truth"), *tapas* ("asceticism"), *dama* ("self-control"), and *prajana* ("procreation"). Sāyaṇa explains that this is a list of the means (*sādhana*) or causes (*hetu*) for achieving human goals, in particular salvation.[29] If we view the formula *dharme sarvaṃ pratiṣṭhitam, tasmād dharmaṃ paramaṃ vadanti* ("Everything has its support in dharma; this is why it is said that dharma is the highest") within this context as a stereotyped recurrent phrase, then it is hardly possible to derive a definition of *dharma* as a universal cosmic lawfulness. Sāyaṇa is far from suggesting such an interpretation; in order to explain the "supportive," "maintaining" function of dharma, he instead refers to the installation of such essential facilities as wells and water reservoirs.[30] This may also be questionable; yet it demonstrates that the idea of a cosmic lawfulness present in the nature of things is far removed from the traditional Hindu understanding of the concept of *dharma*.[31]

Likewise, the etymologizing interpretation which explains *dharma* through *dhāraṇa*, "supporting," "maintenance," does not warrant R. Lingat's assertion that *dharma*, when applied to the universe, refers to "the eternal laws which maintain the world" ("les lois éternelles qui maintiennent le monde").[31] In the verse of the *Mahābhārata* to which Lingat is referring, *dhāraṇa* does not mean a supporting principle that is inherent in things, but rather a "maintenance" and "preservation" which is incumbent to man. In particular, this involves the ideal of *ahiṃsā*, of "non-injury," or "the sparing" of living beings, which is here presented as the core and essence of *dharma*; the expressions *dhāraṇasaṃyukta* and *ahiṃsāsaṃyukta* ("connected with preservation" and "connected with non-injury," respectively) are used here as virtual synonyms.[32]

10. Whatever the most appropriate translation of *dharma(n)* in any given context may be, its derivation from the root *dhṛ*, "to support," "to uphold," is significant not only with regard to its Vedic usages. The meaning "upholding," "maintenance" can certainly not account for all specific usages, and for the historical changes and ramifications associated with the concept of *dharma*. But if there is a source of meaning, or a semantic focus towards which the various usages converge, then it is the "etymological" meaning of "upholding." This basis also accounts for a certain elusive coherence of the various functions of *dharma* in such different areas as cosmogony and ethics, ritualism and ontology, and in the different traditions of Hinduism, Buddhism, and Jainism. Once again, we have to go back to the *Ṛgveda*, and in addition to the noun *dharman*, we have to consider the usages of the verb *dhṛ* itself. In numerous statements, we hear about Gods "supporting" (*dhṛ, dhāray-*) the world and its creatures, and "holding apart" (*vi-dhṛ*) heaven and earth, and the different beings. Verbs such as "to stem" (*stabh, skabh*), "measure" (*mā*) and "spread" (*prath*) sometimes play a related or analogous role. For instance, Varuṇa "measured the first abode" (*dhāma pūrvyam mame*) and "held the two worlds apart" (*vi rodasī . . . adhārayat*).[33]

The idea of a primeval opening, separation, holding apart is of extraordinary importance in Vedic cosmogony, and it remains a significant, though often forgotten presupposition in later developments of Indian thought. It is clearly present in, or associated with, some of the earliest usages of the noun *dharman*. According to *Ṛgveda* VI,70,1, *dharman* is the means of separating heaven and earth (*dyāvāpṛthivī*); and in I,22,18, it is itself the inner object of acts of upholding (*dharmāṇi dhārayan*).[34] Other passages mention the "holding apart" not just of heaven and earth, but of more ordinary entities, such as plants and rivers, *within* the primeval opening. Sometimes, the intermediate space between heaven and earth, which was created by the cosmogonic act of separation, is itself called *vidharman*.[35]

The ritual *dharma* is the reactualization and earthly analogue of the original cosmogonic acts of "upholding" and "holding apart." Whatever the functions of the ritual in Indian history may have been — its fundamental, though forgotten connection with cosmogony, and its commitment to "upholding" the space of the world, and to keeping the entities in it apart from each other and in their appropriate identities, is beyond question. Two of the most famous hymns of the *Ṛgveda*, I,164 (*Asya vāmasya*) and X,90 (*Puruṣasūkta*),[36] refer to divine acts of sacrificial cosmogony and state that these were the first ritual statutes or laws (*tāni dharmāṇi prathamāny āsan*). In the *Puruṣasūkta*, this is associated with the primeval separation and institutionalization of the four main castes, i.e., the establishment of that structure of society which later came to dominate the meaning of *dharma*. Other texts refer to ritual actions, such as the kindling of the fire (*agni*), which happen "in accordance with the first dharmas" (*prathamā-anu dharmā*).[37]

11. Already in the *Ṛgveda* itself, *dharma(n)* is used not only in cosmogonic and "strictly" ritualistic contexts, but also in the wider sense of ethical and social "norms," "statutes," or "laws."[38] In the *Atharvaveda*, the meanings "law" and "(authoritative) custom" become more prominent. At the same time, there is an important morphological change: *dharman* becomes *dharma*; the old *nomen actionis*, with its strong verbal and dynamic connotations, is replaced by the much more abstract noun *dharma*, which does not refer to "upholding" as an action or event, but to the result of such action, the stable norm, the established order. Already the *Atharvaveda* refers to the *dharma purāṇa*, the "ancient law."[39]

It might seem that the old meaning "supporting," "upholding" is irrelevant and obsolete in these new contexts and usages. Yet the etymological affiliation with *dhṛ* is never completely forgotten, and from time to time, it is explicitly invoked. We have already referred to the theory that *ahiṃsā*, "non-violence," is the core and essence of *dharma*, and the "etymological" argument that *ahiṃsā* is a form of *dhāraṇa*, "upholding," "preservation." The great epic *Mahābhārata*, which articulates this theory, also reminds us that "the creatures are kept apart, i.e., upheld in their respective identities, by dharma" (*dharmeṇa vidhṛtāḥ prajāḥ*).[40] According to Manu, ritual performances and social norms uphold and support "both the movable and the immovable creation," society as well as the physical world. Elsewhere, Manu says that *dharma* itself preserves, if it is preserved, and destroys, if it is violated.[41] The "reciprocity of upholding" and "causal ambivalence" which is indicated by this famous verse is highly significant. *Dharma* itself is that upholding which is incumbent on qualified men; but it is also the condition under which such upholding is possible. It protects its protectors. Only the original cosmogonic *dharman* is "upholding" and "establishing" per se, i.e, upholding of the world itself and establishment of order and tradition. All subsequent human *dharma* is perpetuation and renewal of the primeval upholding, is upholding of the original *dharma*, i.e., of those primordial cosmic and social divisions and polarizations which are the very condition of ritual and ethics. In this sense, *dharma* is "upholding" (*dhāraṇa*) as well as that which "has to be upheld" (*dhārya*). Those who fulfill the *dharma* uphold the condition which upholds them. Such reciprocity of upholding, such linkage and balance of cosmogony and ethics, "human action" and "natural events," is obviously different from any world-view which leaves the cosmos to its own immanent, "natural" and "objective" laws.

The association of *dharma* with keeping entities apart, and in their particularity, is essential in the philosophy of Śaṅkara, even if it is not very conspicuous. Here, the realm of *dharma*, of ritual and other "works" (*karman*), is coextensive with that of *māyā*, "cosmic illusion." On the other hand, Madhva, Śaṅkara's great dualist opponent, characterizes the Lord Viṣṇu as the personified *dharma*, since he is the upholder of the fundamental distinctions in the world (*dhārakatvād dharmo bhagavān*).[42] We cannot discuss the role which the connotation of "upholding" plays in the Buddhist understanding of *dharma/dhamma*. It is by no means negligible.[43]

12. In addition to the ritual and normative usages of *dharma*, this word may also be used in the general and neutral sense of "essential quality," "characteristic attribute," or simply "predicate." Such usages are attested since the time of the Brāhmaṇas, for instance in the *Śatapatha Brāhmaṇa*,[44] and they are very conspicuous in the Nyāya and Vaiśeṣika systems. This meaning is sometimes associated with the passive voice of *dhṛ* (*dhriyate*) and explained as something that "is supported" by the entity in which it inheres as a qualifying factor.[45] Yet even in this function, *dharma* contributes "actively" to the identity and particularity of its substratum. Moreover, the normative connotation is not necessarily excluded from the meaning "attribute." This is demonstrated by a number of interesting usages of the word *dharma* in Jaimini's *Mīmāṃsāsūtras*. In these instances, *dharma* refers to attributes or characteristics which are appropriate for ingredients of a sacrificial performance, and which substances, acting persons or actions should possess in order to function properly in the normative context of the ritual. It refers to what is right and proper, not just to empirically ascertainable qualities.[46]

Although this meaning of *dharma* is present in the great majority of its usages in the *Mīmāṃsāsūtras*, it became more or less obsolete in later Mīmāṃsā literature which emphasized the sense of active ritual duty, of a *dharma* which has to be "done" (*kārya*) or performed, which is never simply there. However, we cannot further discuss the relationship between "active" and "passive" *dharma*, or between the meanings "norm" or "duty" and "attribute." Instead, we have to focus on the role which *dharma* came to play in the self-understanding and the xenology of classical and later Hinduism.

13. Regardless of its original Vedic or etymological meaning, in traditional and "orthodox" Hinduism, *dharma* appears as an essentially anthropocentric, sociocentric, and, moreover, Indocentric and Brahmanocen-

tric concept. *Dharma* is the differentiated "custom" and "propriety" which constitutes the Aryan form of life, which upholds the identity of the *ārya* and distinguishes him from the *mleccha*, and which also legitimizes the privileged position of the Brahmins as the teachers and guardians of the *dharma*.

The *Dharmaśāstra* literature which explicates the rules of the *dharma* in detail is an essentially brahmanic literature: its authors were Brahmins, and Brahmins are its focus, even if some texts, primarily from without the *dharma* literature in the special sense, assign the office of the king and the *rājadharma* a privileged and central position.[47] The *dharma* in its ritual core is not a universal lawfulness which applies to the Hindu society as well as other societies; instead, it is the unique and exclusive norm and order of this society, and as such, it is the framework and prototype of "righteousness" and order per se.[48] It is the framework and context in which the Aryan is an Aryan, and from which the *mleccha* is by definition excluded. Likewise, the *mleccha* stands apart from the one real and correct language - Sanskrit. In general, there are important connections between the orthodox Hindu conceptions of language and *dharma*. Sanskrit is the language par excellence, of prototypical correctness, firmly established by its grammar and the linguistic usages of authoritative speakers, a domain of "normative empiricism," an exemplary structure of rules and exceptions, complex and infinitely differentiated, yet irreducibly one and unique. All this provides a most significant model and analogue for the "orthodox" understanding of *dharma*. For Bhartṛhari, grammar is the *dharma* science par excellence: Kumārila also recognizes it as an important domain of *dharma*.[49] We may also refer to the use of the word *sādhu*, "good," "correct," which signifies both the grammatically "correct" forms of words and persons who are "good" insofar as their behavior conforms to the norms of *dharma*.[50]

Here again, we may recall our observations concerning traditional Hindu xenology: in large and important parts of its historical function, the concept of *dharma* can only be understood when it is viewed in close proximity to the complex xenology and the introverted traditionalism of Hinduism. To a remarkable degree, the history of the *dharma* concept reflects the history of Hindu xenology; and even when modern Hinduism universalizes *dharma*, it still looks therein for its identity, continuity, and exclusivity.

14. In traditional Hinduism, *dharma* is primarily and essentially the *varṇāśramadharma*, the "order of the castes and the stages of life" which breaks down into countless specific rules and cannot at all be derived from a general principle of behavior. The *varnāśramadharma* allocates each of the various castes and stages of life "duties" (*svadharma*) and "qualifications" or "mandates" (*adhikāra*); it links them to certain roles and ways of life and excludes them from the ways of life of others; it controls their access to

ritual performance, to the sources of sacred knowledge, and to the means of salvation. Beyond this, it also contains provisions for exceptional situations (*āpaddharma*), and provides norms and legitimation for deviations from the norm.[51] A further important element of variability and flexibility arises through the fact that the four ages of the world (*yuga*) are each assigned their own particular mode of realizing *dharma*, i.e., a successively declining portion of the *dharma*.[52]

This inner variety and flexibility does not affect the fundamental unity of *dharma: Dharma*, in its full and proper sense, is the *one* system that is differentiated within itself and which assigns specific norms to specific groups of Hindus and excludes the *mleccha* by definition. Admittedly, there is also another, more neutral use of the word *dharma*: it applies to "customs" and forms of behavior which are not necessarily associated with this system of norms. Thus, for example, the *dharma* literature speaks of "regional customs" (*deśadharma*) which the rulers were later able to add to, or include in, the framework of the one "correct" *dharma*.[53] Moreover, in a pejorative sense, one may also speak of an "animal *dharma*" (*paśudharma*) or the "*dharma* of cows" (*godharma*).[54] All this does not imply that the *dharma* literature opened itself to a functional use of *dharma*, in the sense of the νομος of the Greek Sophists, or to a relativistic concept of religion. The notion of a plurality of essentially equal systems of *dharma* remained completely alien to this literature.

15. Of course, the fact that the Buddhists and Jainas also availed themselves of the *dharma* concept did lead to a plurality and rivalry of usages. Yet this plurality, i.e., the fact that Buddhism and other movements laid claim to a *dharma* of their own, was hardly reflected within Hindu thought and did not lead to universalistic or relativistic reinterpretations. To be sure, the Buddhist understanding of *dharma* has had its effects upon Hindu thought. Yet the orthodox efforts to exclude Buddhism from the domain of the true and real *dharma* were predominant and ultimately prevailed, and the restorative philosophy of *dharma* contained in the Mīmāṃsā is to a large degree an answer to the Buddhist challenge. At the beginning of the eleventh century, the Jaina author Amitagati wrote a work entitled *Dharmaparīkṣā* (rendered by N. Mironov as "Kritik der Glaubensformen," "Critique of Forms of Belief"[55]) which contrasted Jainism with Brahmanism and Buddhism. In Kṛṣṇamiśra's *Prabodhacandrodaya*, a *Vaiṣṇava* philosophical drama from the late eleventh century, the doctrines and customs of the various religious groups are discussed under the title of *dharma/dhamma*. Yet it is a telling fact that most of these statements come from a Jaina – here called *kṣapaṇaka*.[56]

The co-existence of the various Hindu sects also implies a certain coexistence of *dharma* systems as well as the beginnings of an opening up and functionalizing of the *dharma* concept. In this context, attention is merited by the *Nārāyaṇīya* section of the *Mahābhārata*, which provides important early testimony on the history of the Hindu sects. This section deals with the *dharma* of the *ekāntin*, i.e., the "exclusive," "single-minded" worshippers of Viṣṇu-Nārāyaṇa; their *dharma*, whose focus is monotheistic devotion, is also described as "venerable," "eternal *dharma*" (*dharmaḥ sanātanaḥ*). In this presentation, which is replete with cosmological and mythological references - including some pertaining to the four ages of the world - we notice a clear challenge to the orthodox Vedic view of *dharma*.[57] Such expressions as *śaivadharma, kauladharma*, etc., which were used to describe the soteriologies and ways of life of particular sects, may be found frequently in the later literature of the various sects. In a usage probably inspired by Buddhism, the word *yogadharma* appeared around 500 in Vyāsa's commentary on Patañjali's *Yogasūtra* II,33. Similarly, we have already referred to the Bengali *Vaiṣṇava* use of the term *hindudharma*. We also hear about the "dharma of heretics" (*pākhaṇḍadharma*) and about specific regional *dharmas* (*mahārāṣṭradharma*).[58] On the other hand, it is symptomatic that the *Vāyupurāṇa*, which at first refers to the "many norms" or "statutes" (*bahavo dharmāḥ*) that are taught in the Purāṇas, afterwards lists the sectarian forms of belief (*brāhma, śaiva, vaiṣṇava*, etc.) under the heading of *darśana*, and not *dharma*.[59] There is no need to discuss here the curious ways in which the *Bhaviṣyapurāṇa* speaks of the forms of *dharma* that may be found among the *mleccha*.

16. J. Gonda's observation that "*Dharma, Karman,* and *Saṃsāra* constitute *one* complex, *one* ideological system"[60] is certainly incontrovertible; and yet the relationship between the concept of *dharma* and the doctrines of karma and rebirth is by no means unproblematic; while *dharma* and *karman* may indeed complement one another and merge together in some ways, they do not constitute an original unity. For the *dharma* concept stems from a time in which the doctrines of *karman* and *saṃsāra* were not yet fully developed, and it was initially associated with explanatory and causal models of a different type.

While *dharma*, in its very essence, is subdivided into a countless number of individual obligations and may, in keeping with the original pluralistic use of the word, be characterized as the very sum or system of such rules, the doctrine of karma develops *one* central and universal principle – the principle of the causality of retribution, which fundamentally binds the actor to the results of his action. In its inseparability from the identity and continuity of the individual actor or subject (which extends over many lives), karmic causality differs significantly form the mythical and magical causality of correspondence which provided the earlier background for *dharma*. Cosmos and society increasingly come to appear as the stage and machinery of individual reward and retribution. The context of *karman* rationalizes and legitimizes the differentiations of *varṇāśramadharma*, which may now be seen as forms of karmic retribution as well as stations on the way to final liberation. To this extent, the karma doctrine appears to offer a universalistic context for the positivistic and exclusivistic order of *dharma*. However, in the history of traditional Hinduism, the connections between and mutual interpretation of *dharma* and *karman* have limited the potential universalism of the karma principle and restricted it in an ethnocentric sense: Only in Bhārata, or India, the region of the *varṇāśramadharma*, the "land of works" (*karmabhūmi*), is it possible to produce, to control, and to transcend karma. Everywhere else, all that occurs is an automatic ripening and manifestation of the results of actions.

17. The relationship between *dharma* and *artha* ("success") and *kāma* ("sensual pleasure") on the one hand and between *dharma* and *mokṣa* ("final liberation") on the other may also be understood within the context of karma and rebirth. *Kāma* and *artha* are more narrow horizons of motivation which are limited to goals within *this* life. In contrast, the domain of *dharma* exceeds the limits of *this* life and refers to goals within the wider compass of *saṃsāra*, to the attainment of religious and ethical merit which can have its effect during later existences; insofar, it implies a suppression of immediate desires and an overcoming of a merely secular egocentrism. At the same time, however, *dharma* remains oriented towards actions and their results, towards the purposes of the individual, and thus towards an egocentric structure in a wider sense. In contrast, *mokṣa* refers (at least in the more radical soteriologies) to the overcoming of all attitudes that are oriented towards personal goals and merit, and thus of egocentrism itself.

Śaṅkara has laid especial emphasis upon the fundamental differences in these two attitudes: *dharma* implies an active effort to obtain "results" (*phala*) in the broadest sense and is thus not suited for freeing oneself from *saṃsāra*, i.e., from the domain of karmic works and results. And thus, the "discarding of the dharmas" which is, for example, referred to in the *Bhagavadgītā*, amounts to an abandonment of all selfish, goal-oriented efforts.[61] The multifarious and occasionally very complex manners in which *dharma* and *mokṣa*, or "action" and "knowledge," have been related to one another, do not need to concern us here.[62] We should, however, recall the historically significant tendency to include "renunciation" and "liberation" in the system of *dharma* and to expand the concept of *dharma* in such a way that it also regulates and legitimizes the discarding of the social and, ultimately, goal-oriented norms or rules. In this way, "final liberation" may also be assigned its own *dharma* (*mokṣadharma*), and the *dharma* of action (*pravṛttidharma*) can be contrasted with the *dharma* of detachment (*nivṛttidharma*). Even Śaṅkara, who laid such stress upon the difference between *dharma* and *mokṣa*, expressed this in another context as a distinction within the concept of *dharma* itself.[63] In this sense, *dharma* may even regulate its own transcendence; and it is not simply an "upholding" of the worldly order per se, but also an upholding of the proper correlation and balance between the world and its transcendence.

18. The sources of the knowledge of *dharma* are essential for both its specific contents and its fundamental meaning. We have already mentioned the fact that *śruti* and *smṛti*, and in particular the dharmasastra literature, are held to be the sources of *dharma*. Beyond this, the "behavior of the good" and, in certain cases, "one's own inner inclination" (*ātmatuṣṭi*) may also be consulted.[64] P. Hacker has laid particular emphasis upon the constitutive importance of the "behavior of the good," referring in this connection to such passages as the following from the law book of Āpastamba (I,7,20):

> . . . that which the Aryas praise, when it is done, that is dharma; that which they censure, that is adharma. A person should orient his behavior around that behavior which is unanimously recognized by the well-mannered, elderly, the self-restraining, and the Aryas of all countries who are free of possessiveness and hypocrisy.[65]

In a quote referred to above, he adds that the Hindu concept of *dharma* is "radically empirical,"[66] and he also assumes that the empiricism of the actual modes of behavior has historical priority over the references to sacred texts.

The conviction that what is "in itself correct" can be inferred from certain forms of society and rules of behavior that are de facto given, empirically determinable, and sanctioned by tradition, is indeed crucial to the traditional Hindu understanding of *dharma*. Here, there is no place for such an idea as that of a natural law which is contrasted to actual social conventions and may serve as a basis for criticizing them.[67] Similarly, there is no "philosophy of *dharma*" in the sense of a systematically developed legal and social philosophy aimed at providing it with a rational justification.

This notwithstanding, A.B. Creel's comment: "For philosophers to talk about *dharma* is thoroughly modern, and reflects the breakdown of the traditional *dharma*,"[68] is only true to a limited degree. For what is new and modern is not the fact *that* Neo-Hindu thinkers speak about *dharma*, but rather *how* they do this. There can be no denying that the Hindu philosophical systems (*darśana*) show a lack of critical reflection upon the specific contents of *dharma*; yet the concept of *dharma* has been taken up in a variety of ways in theoretical and philosophical discourse. It has become the object and catalyst of philosophical reflection, and it has had its history of conceptualizations. There have indeed been explicit attempts to account for it within the framework of cosmological, metaphysical, and "categoriological" doctrines, and it would thus be incorrect to view this concept as a mere "proto-philosophical" premise of Hindu thought.

19. In the ninth century, the Nyāya author Jayanta, possibly following Kumārila, presented a list of explanations of the *dharma* concept which included Buddhism and Jainism as well as the Sāṃkhya and Mīmāṃsā; within the Mīmāṃsā, a distinction was made between three varying views. These explanations were contrasted to the Nyāya view (which is in basic agreement with the Vaiśeṣika) that *dharma* (along with its negative counterpart *adharma*) is to be understood as a property or "disposition" inherent in the soul.[69]

Absent from the list of seventeen *guṇa* in the *Vaiśeṣikasūtras*, *dharma/adharma* (encompassed under the title *adṛṣṭa*, "invisible result of actions"), appeared in Praśastapāda's presentation of the Vaiśeṣika (fifth-sixth century) and its expanded list of twenty-four "qualities" (*guṇa*). Here, *dharma*, defined as *puruṣaguṇa* ("property of the soul"), is understood as "resulting dharma;" as the "good karma" or "merit" which results from acting in accordance with *dharma*. *Dharma* in this sense, which corresponds to P. Hacker's "order after the performance," has thus attained a clearly defined position within the Vaiśeṣika system of categories.[70] Older views which interpret *dharma* as a substance or leave its ontological status unspecified have been rejected by a number of Nyāya and Vaiśeṣika commentators.[71] What is usually described as *dharma*, i.e., the rules of the *varṇāśramadharma* which form the object of the *Dharmaśāstras*, appears within Praśastapāda's work as *dharmasādhana*, the "means to generate good karma." There are no attempts to clarify, criticize, or justify these means; Praśastapāda limits himself to pointing out the rules of the *varṇāśramadharma* which are taught in the *śruti* and *smṛti*. He also avoids any form of universalizing: his concern is exclusively with the members of the Hindu society, for whom the rules of *dharma* (or *dharmasādhana*) are in part generally valid and in part refer to caste status and stage of life.[72] No association of any kind is made to the other and much more general meaning (i.e., "attribute") which *dharma* also possesses in the Vaiśeṣika.

20. The treatment of *dharma* in the Pūrvamīmāmsā is more significant and has had a greater historical impact. Here, "orthodox" Hinduism found its most uncompromising expression. In a sense, its major "philosophical" achievement is its method of shielding the Vedic *dharma* from the claims of philosophical, i.e., argumentative and universalizing thought, its demonstration that it cannot be rationalized or universalized within the framework of argumentative and epistemologically oriented thought, and its uncompromising linkage of *dharma* to the sources of the sacred tradition and the identity of the Aryan.

Essentially, *dharma* is that which can only be learned from the Veda and justified through the Veda; there are no other means for knowing it, and no other sources for legitimizing it: to be sure, this "rooting in the Veda" (*vedamūlatva*) should itself be secured by reason and argumentation (*yukti, nyāya*). The *dharma* is *vedamūla*; yet the insight that this is so is considered as *nyāyamūla*, as being based upon reason. *Dharma* is *codanālakṣaṇa*, is bound to Vedic "injunctions."[73] In particular, the Vedic revelation shows the aims of ritual actions which lie beyond this life; it can also make reference to mundane and empirical goals and motives and affect worldly life in, so to speak, an other-worldly manner.[74] In any case, it is the Veda itself which is ultimately decisive for the establishment of *dharma*, and not the mere absence of worldly motives and empirical means of verification. Still, it may be said that everything which is accessible to the regular, worldly, and universally available means of knowledge, i.e., sense perception, inference, etc., and included in the worldly "context of experience," belongs to the domain of worldly existence and cannot be considered *dharma*. The *dharma* is "Vedic" (*vaidika*), and the Vedic is demarcated from the merely "worldly" (*laukika*): The rigidity of this demarcation is sometimes combined (especially by Kumārila) with a remarkable freedom for the "secular," with an openness for reasoning and common sense in areas which are *not* regulated by *dharma*. Such practical and empirical concerns as agriculture, trade, etc., are not subject to the Vedic injunctions; activities in these domains are universal among all peoples, and no strict delimitation is made here between the Aryan and the *mleccha*.[75]

21. In the atmosphere of systematic philosophizing within which the Mīmāṃsā was expounded, it was unavoidable that attempts would be made to conceptually clarify *dharma* more precisely. One the one hand, these attempts were primarily concerned with more closely defining the "injunctive," imperative character of the Vedic injunctions in which *dharma* is formulated; on the other, they aimed at a "categorial" and ontological classification of *dharma*. In the latter regard, the Mīmāṃsā followed the models provided by the Nyāya and the Vaiśeṣika; in contrast, it developed great originality and subtlety in the "deontological" domain.

Kumārila explained the efficacy of the Vedic sacrificial acts that make up the *dharma* by means of the *apūrva* which is deposited and stored in the soul of the sacrificer as a result of his ritual deeds. This *apūrva*, which shows the influence of the Nyāya and Vaiśeṣika,[76] accounts for the causal connection between ritual performance and the results of such activity, which often lie in the distant future, beyond the limits of this life.

Kumārila assumes that the Vedic injunctions motivate the sacrificer by appealing to his self-interest, and by showing ritual means to reach desired ends. In contrast, Prabhākara, his great rival, found an "unconditional" sense of obligation, a kind of "categorical imperative" for the Aryan, associated with the Vedic commands (*vidhi*). They are simply binding "duty" (*kārya*), and not a mere means to an end (*sādhana*);[77] the constitutive meaning which they possess for the identity of the Aryan is only realized when they are followed unconditionally. For Prabhākara, the concept of *apūrva*, like that of *dharma*, was inseparable from the unconditional imperative power of the Vedic injunctions; in contrast to Kumārila, he avoided hypostasizing it as one factor in the processes of ritual causality and classifying it as a "disposition" (*saṃskāra*) of the soul.

The third great systematizer of the Mīmāṃsā, Maṇḍanamiśra, dealt with the problems associated with the Vedic injunctions and their motivating power in monographic form.[78]

22. For Kumārila, the behavior of the "good" and "respectable" (*sādhu, sat*), or the "cultured" and "learned" (*śiṣṭa*), whose significance Hacker has correctly emphasized, is an important basis for the knowledge of *dharma*; yet in keeping with the basic definition of *dharma* as *codanālakṣaṇa*, it cannot in any way compete with the Veda as an additional and possibly independent means of knowledge. The "good" are "good" and "respectable" and suitable as a source of legitimation for the knowledge of *dharma* to the extent that they in turn are legitimized by the Veda. Only a person whose behavior conforms consistently with Vedic norms in all cases for which the Veda provides explicit advice can be considered exemplary and authoritative in cases where the Veda does not tell us what to do.[79] Moreover, Kumārila considers it possible that some Vedic texts were lost or forgotten, and that they are no longer available as direct and explicit sources for ascertaining *dharma*.

In his discussion of the "behavior of the good," Kumārila is concerned with averting any suspicion of conventionalism or appeal to mere human consensus. In no place does he attempt to base the authority of the Veda itself upon its acceptance by the "good" and the "educated." He rejects such attempts, which were made by several Nyāya and Vaiśeṣika authors: These authors argue that the Veda must be authoritative since it is recognized as such by those whose conduct is faultless and exemplary. "Faultless behavior," in turn, is usually measured against the standard of the *varṇāśramadharma*.[80] At the same time, the plea is made that the great majority of the (sc. Indian) population accepts the Veda and the social order based upon it. The word *mahājana* which is used in this context possesses an ambivalence that is significant, for it can refer to both a great number and to a special qualification of persons. As opposed to the tendency to appeal to the majority which may be found, for example, with Jayanta,[81] other authors stress the fact that what is accepted by the "great" (*mahājana*) is not necessarily that which is accepted by the "many" (*bahujana*).[82]

Kumārila knows of and names several anti-Vedic attempts to reduce the criteria of "good behavior" to conventions and to relativize the concept of the "good"; he knows and reflects upon the argument that practices which are considered to be good in different countries may be completely incompatible.[83] In the face of all attempts to derive legitimacy from consensus, however, he maintains that the Veda alone can bear witness to its own validity and to the authority of the *dharma* which it teaches.

23. The fourth source for determining *dharma* that was named by Manu and other *Dharmaśāstra* teachers, the "inner tendency" (*ātmatuṣṭi*), also draws its legitimacy exclusively from the Veda. For only those persons possess a dependable "inner voice" whose thought and feeling is completely penetrated by the Veda and who are so committed to the Vedic *dharma* that even when explicit injunctions are lacking, they will automatically act in accordance with this *dharma*.[84]

The radicalization of the *vedamūlatva* principle that occurs in the Mīmāṃsā, i.e., the assertion that the *dharma* is justified by the Veda alone, has had distinct effects upon the development of the *Dharmaśāstra* literature. This is exemplified by the commentaries on Manu II,6. Medhātithi already emphasized that *ātmatuṣṭi* refers to the inner feelings of a "knower of the Veda" (*vedavid*) alone;[85] but unlike his successors, he still exhibited a certain openness in the discussion of this matter.

Kumārila's rigorous denial of what the Nyāya and other systems recognized as "yogic perception" (*yogipratyakṣa*), and of the idea of a "direct experience" (*sākṣātkāra*) of *dharma*, also has to be seen in this light. In the oldest extant work of the Vedic auxiliary science of "etymology," Yāska's *Nirukta* (probably fifth century B.C.), the Vedic "seers" (*ṛṣi*) are described as having attained a direct experience of *dharma* (*sākṣātkṛtadharman*). In the *Vākyapadīya* of Bhartṛhari, who lived more than a century before Kumārila, reference is made to this passage from the *Nirukta* (I,20); at the same time, however, it is asserted that the seer's ability to receive the Vedic texts in turn presupposes an adherence (perhaps in a previous life) to the rules of *dharma* taught by the Veda.[86] In full conformance with the orthodox view represented by the Mīmāṃsā, Durga's commentary to the *Nirukta* states that the expression *sākṣātkṛtadharman* must be understood figuratively, for in truth *dharma* cannot be "seen."[87]

The influence of the Mīmāṃsā is obvious in Medhātithi's view that references to seers, whether "supermen" (*puruṣātiśaya*) or "special gods" (*devatāviśeṣa*), are nothing less than a symptom of that heterodoxy which may be found among the Buddhists, *Bhojaka* (i.e., priests of the sun), followers of *Pāñcarātra*, and other outsiders (*bāhya*).[88] "Seers" come and go; only the eternal and authorless Veda can, according to this view, guarantee the identity and continuity of the Aryan *dharma*.

24. According to Kumārila, the sacrificial specialist, the *Mīmāṃsaka* who

explicates the ritual instructions, is the prototype of the knower of *dharma*, and he is "characterized by *dharma*" (*dhārmika*). *Dharma* is primarily that which is enjoined by precise rules and, moreover, specified in a temporal sense. Those Brahmins who excel through their familiarity with this central domain of *dharma*, who carry out and monitor the sacrificial rites, and who are thus "penetrated" by *dharma*, also set binding standards for what is good and correct through their behavior (*ācāra*) and their "inner tendency" (*ātmatuṣṭi*) in other areas which are not as strictly and directly regulated by the Veda.[89]

The Mīmāṃsā teachers before Kumārila had already reaffirmed the linkage between *dharma* and the ritual domain. In his commentary on *Mīmāṃsāsūtra* I,1,2, Śabara stated that those persons may be characterized as *dhārmika* who perform sacrificial acts (*yāga*); and he referred to the above-mentioned passage in *Ṛgveda* X,90, which speaks of the "first sacrificial norms" or "statutes" (*dharmāṇi prathamāni*). Clearly, it was not a matter of course in the time of Śabara (ca. 500 A.D.) to understand *dharma* in the sense of "sacrifice." This usage of the word had to be explicitly recalled and restored through a recourse to the most ancient sources. The decisive motive behind such a restoration, which is again especially obvious with Kumārila, is self-assertion in the face of Buddhism and other threats to the tradition; for only when it is linked again to the rites that define the Aryan community can *dharma* be effective as a constituent of its religious and social identity.

The essential *dharma* is not what the "good" and "respectable" who are experienced in the Veda share with other men and with living beings in general, but what distinguishes them.[90] Kumārila objected forcefully to the attempts to trace the *dharma* back to rationally justified and universally valid utilitarian rules of behavior. If *dharma* consisted of helping others or increasing their well-being (*anugraha*) and *adharma* in hurting or tormenting (*pīḍā*) them, then would, e.g., having sexual intercourse with the wife of one's own teacher (one of the most severe transgressions of the *dharmaśāstra*) not be an act of *dharma*? And would *dharma* not then be found among the *mleccha* as well as among the Aryans? Moreover, if "non-injury" or "non-killing" (*āhiṃsā*) may be postulated as a principle of *dharma*, could it not in turn be claimed that killing (*hiṃsā*, allegedly among the so-called *saṃsāramocaka*), insofar as it may be jusitified as liberation from a condition of suffering, is also *dharma*? It is perilous to leave *dharma* to reason or worldly usage (*lokaprasiddhi*). In Kumārila's eyes, such rationalization and universalization of *dharma* would be tantamount to its destruction and to a self-betrayal of the Aryan: the identity and uniqueness of the "Aryan" is inseparable from the sacred Vedic tradition (*na ca āryāṇām viśeṣo 'sti yāvac chāstram anāśritam*).[91]

25. In this context, Kumārila takes explicit exception to Buddhism. The fact that self-control, generosity, etc. have a role to play in Buddhism does not in any way imply that the Buddha should be recognized as a teacher of *dharma*. Instead, Kumārila characterizes the extreme altruism which is expressed in the willingness of the *Bodhisattva* to take the suffering of all beings upon himself as a violation of *dharma*. And how can the Buddha, who was born as a *kṣatriya* and who disregarded the *dharma* of his own caste by presumptuously assuming the brahmanic authority to teach and ignored the caste status of his audience when teaching, be seriously considered a teacher of *dharma*?[92]

The most memorable testimony of an ethical and universalistic concept of *dharma* that also serves to reconcile various forms of belief and ethnic communities is offered by the famous edicts of Emperor Aśoka (third century B.C.). Yet this tendency to ethicize and universalize which Kumārila so objected to may also be found within Hindu literature, for instance in the *Mahābhārata* and in such popular texts as the *Pañcatantra*. Here, we find attempts to derive *dharma* from the principle of *ahiṃsā* ("non-injury") and from the "golden rule." As we have already seen, *ahiṃsā* has been presented as the principle of *dharma* in etymologizing references to *dhāraṇa*, "maintenance," "preservation"; and it has also been stated that *ahiṃsā* is the "highest dharma" (*paramo dharmaḥ*) and that *dharma* is "characterized by ahiṃsā" (*ahiṃsālakṣaṇa*). For centuries, the defense of the Vedic *dharma* against such universalistic claims of the ideal of *ahiṃsā* has been a symptomatic phenomenon of Hindu intellectual life; in addition to the Mīmāṃsā, the Nyāya and other schools have also taken part in this.[93] The golden rule of not doing to others what one hopes and wishes not to be done to oneself has been variously described as "summarized dharma" (*saṃgraheṇa, saṃkṣepataś*) and as the "totality of dharma" (*dharmasarvasva*). Even closer to the view which Kumārila rejected are such formulations as those in the *Pañcatantra*, in the *Vikramacarita*, and in the *Vetālapañcaviṃśatika* which reduce all of *dharma* to the maxim that it is good to be helpful to others (*paropakāra*) and bad to hurt them (*parapīḍana*).[94]

The orthodoxy represented by Kumārila also refuted other attempts to identify *dharma* with *ācāra* (i.e., ethical behavior per se), or to explain it as "characterized by ethical behavior" (*ācāralakṣaṇa*).[95] Kumārila considered the "general" or "generally binding" *dharma* (*sādhāraṇadharma*) that is the center and basis of the ethicizing view of *ācāra* to be a peripheral phenomenon.

A number of soteriological and theological attempts to re-define the concept of *dharma* and to loosen its close ties to the caste system may be found in the theistic movements, especially in the definition of the love of God (*bhakti*) as the "highest dharma" (*paramo dharmaḥ*) that was advanced by the Caitanya school and other movements affiliated with the *Bhāgavata-purāṇa*.[96] In the present context, we do not need to concern ourselves any further with these developments.

26. To conclude this chapter, we have to emphasize again the xenological implications of the "orthodox" notion of *dharma*, as found in the *Mīmāṃsā* and *Dharmaśāstra*: It is *dharma* which distinguishes the castes from one another and draws a line between the "Aryan" and the "non-Aryan"; *dharma* is the principle behind the hierarchical ordering of society (at whose peak stands the Brahmin), the concentric arrangement around a center, the increasing distancing or "alienation," which implies that those who "have less dharma," the *dharmahīna*, are "farther away." The Aryan owes his identity and singularity to *dharma*, just as the Brahmin owes his privileged social and ritual position to *dharma*.

He who is born as an Aryan, and in particular as a Brahmin, has thus achieved a "dharmic" potential which is essentially inaccessible to others. The *dharma* which constitutes the identity of the Aryan is not the *svadharma* of the Aryan, it is not one "appropriate norm" among many. Rather, as *varṇāśramadharma*, it is the system in which *svadharma* first attains its significance and its function.

The "non-Aryans" are not only – not even primarily – distinguished from the "Aryans" because they factually fail to "hold *dharma* in honor,"[97] but rather because they have no right or mandate to honor it. Similarly, they cannot *violate* it in the same manner as Aryans can, for they stand outside the sphere of dharmically relevant action.

The "orthodox" exposition of *dharma* is essentially restorative. Here, the universalization of *dharma* is refuted in the same way as the ethical interpretation of the differences between the Aryan and the *mleccha* is refuted. The fundamentally hereditary definition of this difference accords with the understanding of the four principal castes (*varṇa*), which, in Kumārila's view, differ from one another in the same way that biological species do.

27. This fundamental differentiation within the human race is an indispensable prerequisite of the "orthodox" concept of *dharma*: It must always

> be presumed that the brahmins, etc. are already defined in their being so that the rules of behavior that are given for them are even capable of being applied to them . . . Only when someone *is* a brahmin, kṣatriya, etc., can he be told what he has to do as one.[98]

The same is true of the distinction between the Aryan and the *mleccha*: a person must already *be* an Aryan, must have been born as one, in order to be able and obliged to behave as an Aryan. According to the doctrine of karma and rebirth, any possibility of rising up to the status of the Aryan must be left to a later life. On the other hand, the ethical and religious norm is by no means fulfilled merely by being born as an Aryan: a person can fall short of it, can fall into the "Mleccha state" (*mlecchabhāva*), can lose his hereditary qualification (*adhikāra*) and his identity as an Aryan.

As we noted in our survey of traditional Hindu xenology, there are also myths of origin which explain the rise of hereditary "non-Aryan" *groups* and *peoples* through a similar fall from *dharma* – due to the neglect of caste duties (*kriyālopa*), but especially as a result of inadmissible caste mixing (*varṇasaṃkara*), thus tracing such groups genetically back to the Aryan. The implications of this, however, are not completely clear, and the application of the theory of mixed castes remains usually limited to the groups living in India.[99]

One curious and symptomatic passage occurs in the conversation between Bhṛgu and Bharadvāja which is contained in the *Śāntiparvan* of the *Mahābhārata*. This discussion begins by asserting that the differences between the castes were not originally present and that the existence of the three lower castes may be explained through their neglect of *dharma* and fall from the brahmanic state. Following this, reference is made to monsters and spirits (*piśāca, rākṣasa, preta*), while "barbaric tribes" (*mlecchajāti*) are named whose knowledge and reason was lost and whose behavior was governed solely by their desires (*svacchandācāraceṣṭita*).[100] For the orthodoxy represented by the Mīmāṃsā, however, the original unity and affinity which such models insinuate played no role.

28. In the history of traditional Hinduism, *dharma* is one of the most pivotal, most symptomatic concepts. It is the key-term of "Aryan" self-understanding. Its uses exemplify the basic orientation, but also major changes, reinterpretations, and tensions in the tradition. The term refers to the primeval cosmogonic "upholding" and opening of the world and its fundamental divisions, and then to the repetition and human analogues of the cosmogonic acts in the ritual, as well as the extension of the ritual into the sphere of social and ethical norms. Subsequently, there is increasing emphasis on the "upholding" of the social and religious status quo, of the distinction between hereditary groups and levels of qualification (i.e., the *varṇāśramadharma*), and on the demarcation of the *ārya* against the *mleccha*. The rituals and social norms which were once associated with the upholding of the universe are now primarily a means of upholding the identity and continuity of the Aryan tradition. An ancient cosmogonic term becomes a vehicle of traditionalism and ethnocentrism.

The *varṇāśramadharma*, as understood by the "orthodox" (*smārta*) core of the tradition and articulated in the Mīmāṃsā and Dharmaśāstra literature, is "positive" law and "radically empirical" in the sense of P.

Hacker. But such "empiricism" is at the same time normative, since it implies reliance on sacred texts and groups of people whose actual behavior is supposed to be exemplary and normative. This leaves little room for rational ethical critique, or for the contrast between "natural" and "positive law." Attempts from various directions (which are sometimes accompanied by references to the etymological meaning "upholding") to ethicize and universalize *dharma* and to base it on such principles as *ahiṃsā*, compassion, or the "golden rule," are rejected or disregarded by the tradition.

The *varṇāśramadharma* is not the peculiar *dharma* of the Hindus, is not one system of orientation among others, but it is the framework of *dharma* per se, an absolute, comprehensive structure which includes many specific group *dharmas* (*svadharma*) and excludes other groups entirely. The distinction between the "common norm" (*sādhāraṇadharma*) and specific group duties does not normally extend beyond this structure; what is "common" to mankind at large is of no real concern. References to "absolute" and "relative" duties are quite misleading in this context.[101]

We cannot reduce the meanings of *dharma* to one general principle; nor is there one single translation which would cover all its usages. Nevertheless, there is coherence in this variety; it reflects the elusive, yet undeniable coherence of Hinduism itself, its peculiar unity-in-diversity. There is no *one* system of understanding *dharma*, but a complex network of interactions and tensions between different usages. Various groups and movements have laid claim to this fundamental term. They have reinterpreted it in different ways, and they have used it in order to challenge the "orthodox" core of the tradition. Yet these reinterpretations and competing usages were in most cases indebted to, and oriented around, the "orthodox" brahmanocentric usages.[102] It is easy to argue that *Mīmāṃsā* and *Dharmaśāstra* do not represent the totality of the Hindu tradition; but it is also easy to underestimate their central and paradigmatic role.

18. Reinterpretations of *Dharma* in Modern Hinduism

1. Since ancient times *dharma* has also possessed a meaning which may be rendered as "property," "characteristic attribute," "essential feature," or more generally as "defining factor" or "predicate." Evidence of this is available since the time of the *Śatapatha Brāhmaṇa*.[1] In classical Hindu philosophy, and most clearly in the Nyāya and Vaiśeṣika, *dharma* functions as "attribute" or "property" in the broadest sense and is used to characterize anything that is inherent in, or predicable of, an identifiable substratum (*dharmin*).[2]

Traditional Hindu literature, specifically the *dharma* literature, does not use the meaning "property" to explain or justify the religious, social, and normative sense of *dharma*; insofar as this meaning was made explicit at all, it was obviously understood in the sense of a semantic alternative without explanatory value.[3] As for the root *dhṛ*, "to hold," "support," or "maintain," which lies behind both meanings of *dharma*, we may observe that *dharma* as "property" is obviously used in the sense of a passive derivation, with the implication of "being supported," "being maintained" (*dhriyate*) and without the active, "maintaining" function which is postulated for the normative, i.e., religious or ritual, *dharma*.[4] Of course, the situation is different in the case of Buddhism.[5]

P. Hacker sees the deliberate conspectus and combination of the two meanings as a constitutive element in the Neo-Hindu usage of *dharma* which he – following the lead of R. Antoine – first finds explicitly developed with Bankim Chandra Chatterji.[6] This new interpretation postulated a fundamental linkage between being and obligation, essence and norm. *Dharma*, as the "essential property" of an entity, or as the "essence" (*svabhāva*) by which it is defined, is simultaneously seen as the norm against which it must be measured, as the duty which it is obliged to fulfill. In particular, this concerns the "essence of man," "humanity" (*manuṣyatva*) as the norm of human behavior, as the religious duty which is fulfilled through human self-perfection.

> In this way, through an ingenious play with the various meanings of the word *dharma*, Bankim arrives, apparently without leaving Indian ground, at the result which he obviously first learned from John Stuart Mill and Auguste Comte: the religion of man is humanness, l'humanité, manushyatva![7]

2. Bankim himself realized that his interpretation of the *dharma* concept, which has achieved an "almost canonical"[8] status in Neo-Hinduism, was a major reinterpretation which could hardly be reconciled with the older views of the Mīmāṃsā and the Dharmaśāstra, and at times he very explicitly distanced himself from these traditions. On the other hand, he found his concept of *dharma* anticipated and at least implicitly contained in the "teachings of Kṛṣṇa," in the *Mahābhārata*, specifically in the *Bhagavadgītā*, and in the *Bhāgavatapurāṇa*. Here, he felt he had found an openness which was not bound to the rules and limits of the caste system, to the *varṇāśramadharma* and the legalistic, hereditary *svadharma* which it contains:

> Most people stand outside of the caste system, do they have no Svadharma? Has the Lord of the World established no Dharma for them? He has created millions and millions of people; did he establish a Dharma for the Indians alone, while creating all of the others without Dharma? . . . – No, the religion of the Bhagavān (bhāgavata dharma) is not so narrow-minded.[9]

Hacker has correctly emphasized the fact that the passages from the *Bhagavadgītā* to which Bankim -- who occasionally spoke of "European Hindus" (*iuropīya hindu*) – refers do not at all justify his position:

> The old meaning is replaced by modern, individualistic ideas: the dharma of man is the appropriate exercise or practice (*vihita anuśīlana*) of his mental and physical dispositions (*vṛtti*) or powers (*śakti*). Bankim thus arrives at a viewpoint which states exactly the opposite of what . . . is implied in the Gītā verse 3,35, namely that *dharma* is not dependent upon individual aptitude or inclination.[10]

Verse III,35, which states that it is better to fulfill one's own *dharma* poorly than to fulfill another's well, leaves no doubt whatsoever that the *svadharma* is linked completely to the *varṇāśramadharma*, the hereditary order of the castes and stages of life, and that one should not yield to any inclination to become involved in the behavior of another caste. The passages in the eighteenth chapter which refer to the various *svabhāva*[11] also must be understood in this context: it must always be remembered that all human existence and experience is conditioned by past actions, is karmic result or even "metaphysically congealed act,"[12] and that there is no purely factual, empirically ascertainable human "reality" from which an "ought," an obligation, could be derived. The karmic result which is manifested as caste membership and hereditary social role must be accepted and upheld against all temptations posed by the inclinations and dispositions of the individual. This is the core of the doctrine of *svadharma*, and it also applies to the rare cases in which this notion is extrapolated beyond the caste system, as, for instance, in Vanamālimiśra's assertion that the weaving of straw mats, etc. is an appropriate *svadharma* for such groups as the *yavana*, who are even lower than the *caṇḍāla.*[13]

3. However, the classical commentaries on the Gītā already reveal a certain range of variation in the interpretation of the concepts of *dharma* and *svadharma*, and the Gītā itself contains (as Hacker noted) elements which go beyond the caste system. In spite of its basic orientation around the caste system, it leaves room for ethical and characterological points of view, while its soteriology of devotion avoids all exclusivism and restrictive legalism.

The explication of the Gītā given by Bhāskara, who links his concept of *svadharma* with an exclusivistic and legalistic *adhikāra*, is especially conservative.[14] Śaṅkara may also be considered conservative, or at least cautious. In contrast, in his explication of the exemplary Gītā verse XVIII,66, Rāmānuja assigns the concept of *dharma/svadharma* a soteriological function and relates it to the "methods of liberation" of knowledge (*jñānayoga*), action (*karmayoga*), and devotion (*bhaktiyoga*).[15]

We have already referred to the fact that the *Bhāgavatapurāṇa*, of which Bankim so often spoke, presents *bhakti* as the "highest dharma" (*paramo dharmaḥ*). Since it is taken for granted that the true essence of the soul (*jīva*), freed of its outward distortions, is made manifest in devotion, this implies that the "highest dharma" is concerned with bringing out the intrinsic, true character of the soul, i.e., its divine nature. The "ethical norm" of pious devotion concerns the "intrinsic essence" of the soul, and it is clear that the two primary meanings of the word *dharma* converge at this point. Modern representatives of Vaiṣṇavism, e.g., Thakur Bhaktivinode (1838–1914), who was born in the same year as Bankim and later founded a modern Kṛṣṇaitic revival movement that is still internationally active today, have also proclaimed the linkage of the two meanings as the basis of a universal concept of religion. They were apparently not under Bankim's direct influence.[16]

Instances of a casual overlap and non-thematic interplay of the two meanings are not unusual in the Hindu literature. For instance, the *Vāmanapurāṇa* presents a twelve-fold list of "races" (*yoni*) which ranges from the gods, over various types of supernatural beings, to humans and finally to inferior demons (*rākṣasa, piśāca*). Each of these categories is assigned a *dharma* of its own. Under this title, various capabilities, customs, and characteristics are presented alongside of ethical and religious norms. Thus, it is stated that the *gāndharva* possess a knowledge of music and that the *pitṛ* are able to move completely as they wish (*kāmacāritva*). The case of the *rākṣasa* and the *piśāca* is most conspicuous: Their *dharma* is coveting the women and possessions of others (*paradārāvamarśitva, pārakye 'rthe lolupā*) as well as confusion (*aviveka*) and impurity (*śaucahāni*). Finally, the "twelve *dharma*" are described as "eternal" and "everlasting" (*śāśvata, avyaya*).[17]

In any case, it must be kept in mind that a systematic and explicit correlation of the two meanings of "property" and "social and religious norm" is not only lacking in this passage, but generally plays no part in the traditional Hindu usage of the word *dharma*

4. The opening up and universalizing of the concept of *dharma/svadharma* postulated by Bankim has remained one of the key points of the Neo-Hindu program. As with Bankim, the concept of man and his humanity lies at the center of this opening; for it involves the "dharma of human beings," the idea of a universal human order.[18] The caste system has been similarly idealized and universalized. Radhakrishnan has expressed this in an exemplary fashion: "The caste scheme is meant to apply to all mankind."[19] Viewed thus, the system of the four *varṇa* is not a hereditary and legalistic order, but rather an arrangement in accordance with natural dispositions of character and capabilities and the reflection of a universal lawfulness encompassing both the "is" and the "ought": "The basis of the varṇa dharma is that every human being must try to fulfill the law of his development."[20] ". . . each individual has his inborn nature, *svabhāva*, and to make it effective in his life is his duty, *svadharma*."[21]

Radhakrishnan maintains that dharma ". . . is the norm which sustains the universe, the principle of a thing by virtue of which it is what it is."[22] Such formulations recall J. Gonda's explication, in which he defined *dharma* as "lawfulness and regularity . . . in the cosmos, nature, society, and individual existence," explaining: "The person who follows the *dharma* realizes the ideal of his own character and manifests the eternal lawfulness in himself."[23] The following statements by Western authors reflect the Neo-Hindu understanding of *dharma* even more clearly: "Everything by being what it is, and not being something else, has its *dharma*, its distinctive character and therefore its special function."[24] — ". . . to realize their natures, all beings must act in accord with *dharma*."[25]

Whereas traditional Hinduism considered India — and India alone — as the "region of dharma" (*dharmakṣetra*) and the "land of works," i.e., of the active determination of karma (*karmabhūmi*), Neo-Hindu thinkers reinterpreted these concepts in a global and universal sense. Vivekananda stated:

"This earth is called the Karma-Bhumi, the sphere of Karma. Here alone man makes his good or bad Karma."[26] According to Radhakrishnan, the Indian tradition had indeed begun with the ethnocentric world view of the "Vedic Aryans"; yet it soon "developed an ethical code applicable to the whole of humanity," a "dharma of humanity," "mānava dharma."[27] With this term, Radhakrishnan obviously alludes to the title of the law book of Manu (*Mānavadharmaśāstra*), which is, however, entirely Indocentric and hardly compatible with such universalistic claims.

5. Besides the universality or universalizability of *dharma*, the Neo-Hindus also emphasize its historical flexibility, and its openness to the discoveries of science and contemporary conditions in the modern world:

> The rules of dharma are the mortal flesh of immortal ideas, and so are mutable . . . Though dharma is absolute, it has no absolute and timeless content . . . We should introduce changes today, and make the content of Hindu dharma relevant to modern conditions . . . Dharma is an elastic tissue which clothes the growing body.[28]

What is important is that the "principle of dharma" not be lost sight of: "The basic principle of dharma is the realisation of the dignity of the human spirit."[29] The extent to which Radhakrishnan's reinterpretation of *dharma* also takes the Buddhist concept of *dharma/dhamma* into regard is remarkable.[30] However, attempts to fully secularize the *dharma* concept are rare among Neo-Hindu authors; while *dharma* should indeed be related to the modern world, it was not meant to be a merely temporal, worldly principle. We have already spoken of Bankim's older contemporary Aksay Kumar Datta (1820–1886), whose secularization or "naturalization" of the *dharma* concept was even more pronounced than that of Bankim. For Datta, *dharma* was ultimately nothing but conformance to the "laws of nature"; and he considered the natural universe itself, the very world of *saṃsāra*, to be "dharmaśāstra."[31]

As for Bankim, it would be inappropriate to reduce his programmatic and consequential new interpretation of the *dharma* concept to a mere confusion of its various meanings. In an appendix to the *Dharmatattva*, his main philosophical work, he distinguished six meanings of *dharma*. To clarify them, he inserted a number of English terms into his Bengali text: 1) Religion; 2) Morality (*nīti*); 3) Virtue; 4) The "sanctioned behavior" (*anumodita kārya*) allowed by religion or morality (*nīti*); 5) Property (*guṇa*); e.g., the peculiar ability (*dharma*) of the magnet to attract iron; 6) Behavior, Custom (*ācāra, vyavahāra*). Bankim criticized the confusion (*golaghoga*) of these meanings which reigned within the Indian tradition, especially within the *dharmaśāstra* literature, describing it as one of the causes behind the degeneration of modern Hinduism.[32]

6. Bankim discusses in particular detail the problems involved in the relationship between *dharma* and "religion." In the second appendix of the *Dharmatattva,* he cites a number of attempts by Western thinkers (including Kant, Fichte, Schleiermacher, E.B. Tylor, J.St. Mill, J.R. Seeley, and Comte) to define the concept of religion. In keeping with his own conviction that the essence of religion is "culture," he gives precedence to Comte's interpretation, which identifies the meaning of religion with its regulation of human affairs. He also finds "religion" in this sense in the *Mahābhārata* and the *Bhāgavatapurāṇa,* texts in which he sees Kṛṣṇa as the teacher of an ethical *dharma* oriented around the concept of humanity and opposed to the legalism and ritualism of the Mīmāṃsā.[33]

In the same context, he cites one of his own "letters on Hinduism" (which he wrote in English).[34] This particular "letter" contains Bankim's most memorable and articulate statements on the relationship between *dharma* and religion, the applicability of the concept of religion to Hinduism, and the unity and self-definition of Hinduism.

> Search through all the vast written literature of India, and you will not, except in modern writings where the Hindu has sought obsequiously to translate the phraseology of his conquerors, meet with any mention of such a thing as the *Hindu religion*. Search through all the vast records of pre-Mohamedan India, nowhere will you meet with even such a word as *Hindu,* let alone Hindu religion. Nay more. Search through the whole of that record, and nowhere will you meet with such a word as *religion*. The word *Dharma,* which is used in the modern vernaculars as its equivalent, was never used in pre-Mohamedan India in the same sense as *Religion* . . . The pre-Mohamedan Hindu called himself *Arya,* disdaining to include under the denomination the Indian whom he had conquered. For religion he had no name, because he never entertained any conception to which such a name would have been applicable. With other peoples, religion is only a part of life; there are things religious, and there are things lay and secular. To the Hindu, his whole life was religion.[35]

7. As the following discussion will show, Bankim's evaluation of this situation was quite ambivalent. On the one hand, he asserted that a pan-religious orientation has an advantage over traditions which consider religion merely as one part of human existence and more or less isolate it. Yet at the same time, he wanted to overcome what he saw as a fatal confusion in the understanding of *dharma*; the "truly" religious elements of Hinduism had to be isolated as such and separated from the multifarious forms of "superstition," from local and popular cults, and from "social polity or domestic morality."[36] Such a "purified" Hinduism – i.e., in Bankim's eyes, an idealized Kṛṣṇaism – could, as a more and perfect religion, then be contrasted with, and placed above, Islam and Christianity.

Bankim's remarks about the self-characterization of Hinduism and the use of *dharma* as "religion" are linked with problems in traditional Hindu xenology which we discussed earlier: We first observed the self-definition of Hinduism as *hindudharma* among the Bengali Vaiṣṇavas of the Caitanya School, as a self-demarcation against Islam and as an answer to the Islamic challenge. At that time, this was a relatively isolated phenomenon. More significant and pervasive changes in the traditional self-representation and the traditional use of the concept of *dharma* have taken place since about 1800 as a result of the missionary activities and the European presence in general (especially in Bengal). The self-definition of Hinduism as a "religion," as a *dharma* which confronts and asserts itself against the *dharma* of the Christians, and more generally the use of *dharma* as an analogue or answer to "religion," is largely due to the fact that the missionaries in Bengal laid claim to the concept and term *dharma*, using it to proclaim Christianity as the "true dharma" (*satyadharma*). In contrast, the use of the Islamic concept of religion *dīn* as an Arabic-Persian analogue to *dharma* had no comparable consequences.[37]

8. In the translations of Christian texts that have been made in South India since the close of the sixteenth century, *veda* and *mata* are the most common terms for the Christian religion and for "religion" in general. The first edition of the "Tranquebar Bible" in Tamil (1714) was entitled *Vedapustagam*, "Veda Book."[38] In a sense, this continued a Tamil tradition of extending the use of the word *veda* by applying it to authoritative Tamil works, specifically the *Tiruvāymoli* by Nammālvār (the so-called *drāviḍaveda*). The pioneer of the Protestant mission in South India, B. Ziegenbalg, described both the Bible and the "true" (i.e., Christian) religion as the "true Veda" (*satyavedam*). The word *veda*—and *vedāgama*—continued to be used in South Indian (and particularly Tamil) translations of the Bible up until modern times.[39] A Sanskrit catechism written by the Jesuit priest Calmette during the first half of the eighteenth century received the title *Satyavedasārasaṃgraha*.[40] Paulinus a S. Bartholomaeo utilized such expressions as *vedapāla* ("protector of the Veda") as the Sanskrit equivalent for "Bishop" ("episcopus"), and *vedapustaka* for "Holy Scripture."[41] Besides these, the more neutral term *mata* (*matam*, "doctrine") has also been widely used and has, moreover, retained its meaning up to the present time in the languages of South India, for example in Malayalam.[42]

In contrast, the Baptist missionaries active in Serampore (Bengal) since the end of the eighteenth century chose *dharma* as the key word for their translations into Bengali and Sanskrit (*dharmapustaka* for the Bible; also *nūtanadharmaniyama* for "New Testament").[43] In the translations of the Bible into North Indian languages, *dharma* has gained wide acceptance, especially in Hindi, in which *Dharmaśāstra* (Allahabad, 1939) and *Dharmagrantha* (Allahabad, 1963) have been used as titles. Both *dharma* and *mata* appear in J.R. Ballantyne's *Christianity Contrasted with Hindu Philosophy (English and Sanskrit)* (London, 1859); here, the author refers, e.g., to *khṛṣṭadharma, khṛṣṭamata*, and *khṛṣṭīyadharma.*[44] The English-Sanskrit dictionary by Monier-Williams (1851) lists *dharma* as the first and most obvious equivalent to "religion"; in addition, it gives *īśvarabhakti* and *devabhakti* ("devotion"), while offering *mata* as well as *dharma* for the qualified meaning of "system of faith." Monier-Williams also presented compounds with *dharma* as translations of "mission" and "missionary" (e.g., *dharmasandeśahara*). In modern Hindi, *dharmapracāra* has become the usual translation for "mission" and *dharmapracāraka* for "missionary."[45] It is symptomatic that the term *dharma*, which is the expression par excellence of Hindu self-assertion, should also be applied in this way to a foreign message and its promulgators.

9. The fact that this concept, which has been traditionally used to characterize what is most intrinsic to Hinduism, should be adopted by the Christian missionaries as the key concept of *their* alien message that was directed against Hinduism, is a clear and momentous challenge to Hindu self-awareness. In order to meet this challenge, new ways of using *dharma* were developed whose ambivalence is a characteristic facet of modern Hinduism. The concept of *dharma* was asserted against the Christian missionaries, and their message was refuted or "neutralized" within the greater context of the Hindu *dharma*; at the same time, the ways in which the missionaries presented their message had far-reaching effects upon the ways in which Hinduism conceived of and represented its *own* tradition, which is anchored in the very concept of *dharma*.

One initial effect of this was that attempts were made (in a manner foreign to the Hindu tradition) to commit Hinduism to certain articles of faith, to a "creed" which could be used to confront the Christian message. Here, we may recall, e.g., the "confession of faith" published by Debendranath Tagore in his *Tattvabodhinī Patrikā* (1857).[46] Bankim Chandra Chatterji, B.G. Tilak, M.K. Gandhi and a number of other spokesmen for Neo-Hinduism also made efforts to express the "essence" of Hinduism in a few concise statements of faith and to thus make it comprehensible for the Europeans as well as for the Hindus themselves. Several authors published full-fledged catechisms of the "Hindu Dharma" or the "Sanātana Dharma."[47]

However, it has not been typical of Neo-Hinduism to demarcate itself *against* Christianity, or to confront it in accordance with Christian standards, i.e., as a well-defined "positive" religion with a different, yet equally specific creed. Instead, Neo-Hindus tend to claim that their tradition accepts, includes, and transcends all religions, by providing them with a limited and preliminary legitimacy. In this sense, the "Hindu Dharma" does not compete with the special *dharma* of the Christian missionaries. In the Hindu self-understanding, it does not even share a common border, and no area of potential conflict, with Christianity. Instead, it claims to represent the *dharma* per se, a higher unity of all specific religions: Unlike the religions, and regardless of all differences in interpretation, *dharma* itself is one (*dharma eka*).[48]

10. What led the European missionaries in Bengal to present the Christian message under the title of *dharma*? In what sense did they use the word *dharma*, and how did they understand it? And how did the Indians in turn understand the missionaries' use of *dharma*? The answers to these questions do not have to do with the success or the failure of the Christian missions in India alone, but also more generally with the hermeneutic situation of modern Hinduism.

Through their use of the term *dharma*, the missionaries appealed to the binding norm of life, the principle which legitimizes the religious and social orientation of the Hindus. At the same time, however, they used the word in a sense which was alien to the Hindu "orthodoxy" and yet, as we have seen, enjoyed a certain degree of popularity in particular in Bengal. This usage juxtaposed and distinguished a variety of sectarian forms of life and belief under the title of *dharma* and, as a result of the demarcation against Islam, also led to the occasional formation of the word *hindudharma*. On the other hand, it cannot be completely ruled out that Western usages were already reflected in the *Mahānirvāṇatantra*, whose age and origins are rather uncertain and which presents the Śaivite *kauladharma* as "true dharma" (*satyadharma*).[49] The missionaries did not concern themselves with the differences between the two meanings, nor did they explicitly reflect upon the ambivalence of *dharma*.

The missionaries invoked a concept which stands for the principle of ethnocentric Indian self-representation. They referred to the most intrinsic element in Hindu self-awareness in order to introduce the Hindus to the foreign. It was the missionaries' intention to supersede and replace the principle of Hindu identity. By trying to deprive the Hindus of their *dharma*, which they expounded as a false "religion," and trying to convert them to another religion, they channeled the Hindu reaction in two directions: first, to a self-definition and a new interpretation of the Hindu tradition in the name of "religion," and second, to a reassertion of the *dharma* concept *against* the concept of religion. On the one hand, Hinduism was now shown in a new way to be *one* religion, *one* dharma which is distinct from and opposed to other religions; on the other hand, *dharma* was considered as a principle superior to and, moreover, encompassing the "mere religions." Whereas *dharma* became an indigenous, Indian receptacle for alien, European concepts, and for the assimilation not only of the concept of religion as such, but also the European reinterpretations of the concept of religion, this concept was also utilized to assert what was most intrinsically Hindu and to claim for it a global and universal validity.

11. Rammohan Roy spoke in passing of the *dharma* which the Christian missionaries brought to the Hindus (and Moslems), i.e., of the religion to which they desired to convert them.[50] While Rammohan's reaction may have initially been one of deistic openness and a syncretistic will to reform, the universalist claims of modern Hinduism became apparent in his later idea of a "universal religion" derivable from the sources of Hinduism. Yet it was not just primarily the reaction against Christianity, but also the opposition to Rammohan and his reforms, which led the term *dharma* to become the central concept of Hindu self-assertion. In 1822, Kāśīnātha Tarkapañcānana (who described himself as "one who is concerned with defending dharma" - *dharmasaṃsthāpanākāṅkṣī*), presented four polemic questions to Rammohan in the Bengali journal *Samācāra Darpaṇa*; Rammohan answered in his "Reply to the Four Questions" (*Cāri praśner uttara*). Therein, he made a somewhat inaccurate reference to the "venerable dharma" (*dharmaḥ sanātanaḥ*) spoken of in the *Mahānirvāṇatantra*.[51] In 1830, Rammohan's critic Radhakant Deb (Rādhākanta Deva) founded an association named *Dharma Sabhā*; and a number of journals, pamphlets, etc. used the word *dharma* in their titles.[52] The Dharma Sabhā, which did not have many Brahmin members, shows that the defense of the traditional *dharma* was by no means exclusively in the hands of Brahmins. Next to Bengal, Maharashtra played the most active part in these earlier developments. A great many other *dharma* societies arose during the second half of the nineteenth century, often explicitly opposed to the Brāhma Samāj and other reform movements, in particular the Ārya Samāj of Dayānanda Sarasvatī. The expression *sanātanadharma* became increasingly important as a programmatic expression of traditionalist self-assertion. Hinduism, as *sanātanadharma*, as the "venerable," "eternal religion," has no temporal beginning, no historical founding figure comparable to Jesus Christ, and requires no innovations and reforms.[53] What is more, this "eternalness," as some authors added, is simultaneously an all-encompassing universality and inclusivity which in itself essentially anticipates all innovations: the *sanātanadharma* is at the same time an "all-encompassing," "inclusive" (*sarvavyāpaka*) *dharma*. "Why is the Sanatan Hinduism of the Indians undecaying, immortal and complete, in all conditions? Because it is the wide, all-embracing, all-merciful religion, open for all kinds of sādhana and to all classes of seekers."[54] Hinduism offered itself as the primeval fulfillment of what European authors, including A. Comte, called "universal religion." In the *Tattvabodhinī Patrikā* of 1855, Debendranath Tagore (Devendranātha Ṭhākura) stated that his *brāhmadharma* was ready for,

and somehow anticipated, all future developments: "Whatever has been already known about religion, whatever will be known in subsequent times, will all fall within the scope of our Brahmoism (*brāhmadharma*)."[55]

12. To be sure, the expression *sanātanadharma* (*dharmaḥ sanātanaḥ*) and related expressions (e.g., *śāśvatadharma*) are by no means foreign to traditional Hinduism. Before the encounter with the West, however, they were not used as self-descriptions of Hinduism in the face of other religions or to characterize Hinduism as *one* religious tradition among many. Instead, they characterized the "unshakable, venerable order" and the particular rules and norms of life which have been ever valid and are hallowed by tradition. In the *Mahābhārata*, the expression "this is a venerable rule" or "norm" (*eṣa dharmaḥ sanātanaḥ*) often appears as a sanctioning formula intended to emphasize the obligatory nature of social and religious rules.[56] The occurrence of this expression in the *Nārāyaṇīya* section is less exemplary; and references to the "venerable root of the venerable dharma" (*sanātanasya dharmasya mūlam etat sanātanam*) are infrequent and somewhat atypical.[57] Often, *sanātana dharma* and similar expressions appear in the plural. For example, the *Bhagavadgītā* refers to the "venerable norms for the families" (*kuladharmāḥ sanātanāḥ*).[58] When Kṛṣṇa is described in Gītā verse XI,18 as *śāśvatadharmagoptā sanātanaḥ*, he is not being presented as the "defender of Hinduism," but rather as the "protector of the established norms." Manu also uses *sanātanadharma* to refer to particular statutes or norms, e.g., for the king or the warrior, and even explicitly uses the plural when speaking of the unshakable (i.e., traditionally established) "customs and statutes of the countries, castes, and families."[59] This use still largely prevailed in very late texts up to the *Mahānirvāṇatantra*. The words *vyavahāra* ("custom," "habitual practice") and *vidhi* ("injunction") were also occasionally associated with *sanātana*.[60] As late as the *Śāstratattvavinirṇaya* of Nīlakaṇṭha Śāstrī Gore (1844), who later converted to Christianity, we may still as a rule find the old use or even the plural form.[61]

When, in contrast, modern pandits describe themselves as "members" or "followers of the *sanātanadharma*" (*sanātanadharmīya, sanātanadharmāvalambin*), then this exemplifies a way of using *sanātanadharma* which exhibits the influence of the European concept of religion.[62]

13. "Sanātana Dharma is a universal religion."[63] We have already spoken of the forms in which this claim to universality was expressed in the work of Debendranath Tagore, Keshab Chandra Sen, and especially of Vivekananda and Aurobindo.[64] What is remarkable is the manner in which the new self-representation of Hinduism which grew out of its encounter with the West was in turn taken up by the West. Here, particular mention should be made of Annie Besant, the leader of the Theosophical movement, who went to In-

dia in 1893 (the same year in which Vivekananda attended the "World Parliament of Religions" in Chicago) and played a decisive part in the founding of the nationalist Central Hindu College in Benares. In this connection, she also gained great influence in shaping the "sanatana-dharma text-books" which later spread throughout India. All of the previous attempts to catechetically fix and systematically teach the *sanātanadharma* were surpassed by the practical and organizational efficiency of this undertaking. Cooperating with Indian scholars, Annie Besant herself drew up the basic version of a "textbook" of the *sanātanadharma* intended primarily for Central Hindu College. This was concerned with presenting "an outline of the basic principles of religion, which all Hindus, of whatever special sect, will be glad to see in the heads and the hearts of their children."[65] Later, this textbook was divided into a series of three works - a catechism, an elementary textbook, and a textbook for advanced students; the catechism was also translated into a number of Indian languages. Annie Besant's closest collaborator was Bhagavan Das, whose main work, *The Essential Unity of All Religions*, evokes the unity of all religions from the spirit of Hinduism. The Sanskrit *Sanātanadharmadīpikā* (Madras 1917) of Haṃsayogin, who also wrote a commentary on the *Bhagavadgītā*, also bears the mark of the Theosophical movement.[66]

An impressive example of the *sanātanadharma* literature, entitled *The World's Eternal Religion*, appeared shortly after the close of the First World War and made reference to this event;[67] J. Abs published a German translation of this work entitled *Indiens Religion: Der Sanātana-Dharma* (Bonn and Leipzig, 1923). In this work, an interpretation and classification of dharma is made which combines the traditional concept of *dharma* with the Neo-Hindu reinterpretation and universalization: the *sanatanadharma*, as the "eternal Vedic dharma," the "all-encompassing Indian religion," was to bring about the reconciliation of all religions and ways of life in the "Dharma-Samanvaya."[68] Ganga Prasad's *The Fountainhead of Religion* (1909; fifth ed.: 1932), which was inspired by the Ārya Samāj as well as the Theosophists, presents the Veda as the source of all historical religions, and of religion per se.

14. A great variety of representatives of modern Hindu thought have laid claim to the concept of *sanātanadharma*, traditional pandits as well as Vivekananda, Radhakrishnan, and other "Neo-Hindus," the founders and followers of reform movements as well as their orthodox opponents. A plethora of positions have been defended and propagated under this title: at first, *sanātanadharma* was a concept of self-assertion against Christianity, a religion which had a temporal beginning and an historical founding figure; in this sense, *sanātanadharma* was synonymous with *vaidikadharma* and had a restorative and apologetic function. Later, the expression

sanāta[illegible] increasingly became associated with such Western concepts as the *philosophia perennis*, the "universal religion" or "eternal religion,"[69] appearing as a program of deistic openness and a search for common denominators of all religions. Yet even in this context, *sanātanadharma* still remained a concept of self-assertion, for Hinduism alone was supposed to provide the framework for the fulfillment of the universal potential inherent in the various religions. Accordingly, it was not considered merely as one religion among many, but rather as a comprehensive and transcending context for these other religions.

The traditional relationship of the "totality" of Hinduism to the Hindu sects became the model for the relationship between Hinduism and the world's religions: "Hinduism has evolved out of itself a multitude of *religions*, each of which bears perfect analogy to Christianity and Mohammedanism so far as the application of this term is concerned . . . We commit an obvious logical fallacy when we put Hinduism by the side of Christianity, Mohammedanism, Buddhism etc., to signify that it is one of the sectarian religions of the world."[70]

The harmonizing and "spiritualizing" of sects and local cults by including them in the "unity" of Hinduism or by subordinating them to its highest stage, the Vedānta, was considered to be the prototype and basis for a global harmonizing. Radhakrishnan spoke of the acceptance and neutralization of local Indian cults within Hinduism, adding: "Hinduism is not limited in scope to the geographical area which is described as India . . . There is nothing which prevents it from extending to the uttermost parts of the world."[71] Even before Radhakrishnan, the Marathi scholar and writer S.V. Ketkar (1884–1937), the editor of a multi-volume Marathi encyclopedia, stated that Hinduism had in fact begun to expand the processes of synthesis and assimilation which had been going on within India to the whole world, but it was prevented from carrying out its mission by Islam and Christianity. "Once the entire Hindu civilization was in process of spreading itself over the whole world, and was going to accomplish a unification of civilizations in the world. But this course was arrested by the rise of 'religions,' the great dividers of mankind."[72] In one of the most acute and impressive Neo-Hindu discussions of the European concept of religion, Ketkar rejected the application of this term to the Indian tradition and the concept of *dharma*; in his eyes, the concept of religion was a culture-specific and purely European phenomenon. "Such a term would be useful in studying the European civilization, just as the term 'Obeah' could be of use in interpreting the civilization of the West Indian negroes."[73] If this concept corresponded to anything at all in India, then this would be the concept of *saṃpradāya*, the "sectarian" tradition. Referring to the idea of a future world civilization, Ketkar said: "The religions will take the same place in this cosmopolitanism as the sampradāyas have taken under Hinduism."[74] Ketkar lived and studied in America from 1906 until 1911, also serving as the president of the "Society of Comparative Theology and Philosophy" at Cornell University.[75]

It is a somewhat unusual phenomenon in modern Hinduism when a learned critic of the stature of L.S. Joshi, editor of the monumental *Dharmakośa*, denies the potential of unity and the synthetic power of Hinduism. Rejecting the claims of Radhakrishnan, he maintains that various forms of religious life and thought simply coexist within Hinduism, as within a "mosaic" or a "museum," and that such passive coexistence should not be confused with deliberate synthesis and tolerance.[76]

15. The term *dharma* was essential not only in dealing with the concept of religion, but also in responding to the European notion of ethics; the *hindudharma* had to assert and prove itself not only as a religious universalism, but also as an ethical one. We have already discussed the program of the "practical Vedānta" and the Neo-Hindu attempts to ground ethics and social practice in the Vedāntic metaphysics of unity.[77]

In particular, the idea of *ahiṃsā*, of "non-injury," has been presented as the core of the *hindudharma* and as India's ethical message to the world. As is well known, M.K. Gandhi has been the most effective propagator of this message. Moreover, through this, Buddhism (especially in its ethicized form as, e.g., with Aśoka or in the Dhammapada) has also been recognized by and reclaimed for Hinduism. Here again, we should mention Bankim Chandra Chatterji, who presented *ahiṃsā* as the central and original message of Vaiṣṇavism, as the "daughter of the Vaiṣṇavas" (*vaiṣṇava kanyā*) which did not enter the "house of the Buddhists" (*bauddhaghara*) until a later date. Bankim rejected the identification of *ahiṃsā* with vegetarianism, etc.; it was ultimately nothing other than a "non-differentiating view" (*samadarśitā*) which respects the other self exactly as one's own, does not recognize any kind of sectarian barriers, and thus provides the basis for human harmony.[78] As our survey has shown, the ethical interpretation of *dharma*, and especially its linkage to the principle of *ahiṃsā*, has been expressly refuted by the orthodoxy of the Mīmāṃsā.

Neo-Hinduism claims that ethics and religion, social order and soteriological orientation, are fully integrated within the concept of *dharma*, which appears as the "unity of all ideal ends,"[79] an idealized structure capable of reconciling the multitude of human modes of life and providing a model and framework of orientation for the non-Indian world as well. Neo-Hindus have generally no doubt that the concept of *dharma* is flexible enough to be applied to the modern technological world, specifically to the social and political sphere, and to problems of international understanding.[80] Even in its modern reinterpretation and universalization, the concept of *dharma* has remained the expression of the Hindu sense of identity and continuity. The Western experiences of historicism, relativism, and radical secularization remain excluded from this self-understanding; insofar, and regardless of all innovations and reinterpretations, no radical break with tradition has taken place.

19. The Sanskrit Doxographies and the Structure of Hindu Traditionalism

1. Like the absence of a developed historiography in general, the Indian tradition's lack of any historiography of philosophy has been commented upon frequently and been the object of some speculation. The Indian tradition has not brought forth any independent historical presentations of philosophy, not even chronologically arranged surveys of philosophical doctrines and the lives and works of philosophers such as have been passed on by the Greek tradition. With the exception of the genealogies of teachers and disciples (which usually begin in the mythical past) and the legendary hagiographies of individual shapers of Indian thought, in particular Śaṅkara,[1] the literature of India offers nothing apart from entirely nonhistorical and as a rule completely impersonal doxographic surveys of the various philosophical traditions.

The doxographic style, along with the tendency to present the philosophical systems as structures essentially complete for all time, is also a distinctive feature of many of the more recent treatments of Indian philosophy, especially those written by Indians. Here, it is sufficient to recall the well-known presentations by S.C. Chatterjee & D.M. Datta, M. Hiriyanna, J. Sinha, and U. Mishra. Moreover, while chronological and "historical" topics have indeed gained in interest, Indian authors continue to emphasize that it would be inappropriate to apply Western historical and chronological methods to the presentation of the Indian material.

> In the history of Western philosophy we usually find the different schools coming into existence successively. Each school predominates till another comes in and replaces it. In India, on the other hand, we find that the different schools . . . flourish together during many centuries, and pursue parallel courses of growth.[2]

It is therefore not possible to write any history of successive philosophies of India, but it is necessary that each system should be studied and interpreted in all the growth it has acquired through the successive ages of history . . .[3]

Of course, the image of a nonhistorical and static India which has "always been what it is now," and which has found its classical expression in the work of Hegel,[4] has been criticized from many sides as an ethnocentric distortion. Yet at the same time, many Indians have also exhibited a tendency to appropriate this view as an aspect of Indian self-assertion and self-assurance; for the nonhistorical perspective and the lack of interest in "historical records" has often been seen as a strength and not a weakness - as commitment to a living tradition, and a focus upon the timeless and continuous as opposed to the rootlessness of the West and its historical discontinuity, its dispersal into the temporal and the temporary.[5] This view has also received occasional expression by Western authors; P. Deussen, for example, who agreed with the pejorative concept of history of his master Schopenhauer, admonished Western historians to realize that the Indians "stood too high" for the usual type of historiographic interest.[6]

2. Deussen's presentation of classical Indian philosophy owes a considerable debt to one of the traditional Indian doxographies: a German translation of nine chapters from the most significant of these works, the fourteenth-century *Sarvadarśanasaṃgraha* ("Summary of All Systems") by the Vedanta author Mādhava-Vidyāraṇya, was incorporated into his *Allgemeine Geschichte der Philosophie*. Before Deussen, H.H. Wilson had drawn upon this work, which was also translated into English by E.B. Cowell and A.E. Gough. While the interest in this work has decreased as the primary sources have become increasingly available, it has still attracted the interest of more recent scholars.[7]

The *Ṣaḍdarśanasamuccaya* ("Compendium of the Six Systems") of the Jaina author Haribhadra (eighth century) has also become relatively well-known in the West; several commentaries are available on this work, the oldest of the known doxographies.[8] Other doxographic works, difficult to date but in any case all written after the first millennium, include: the *Sarvasiddhāntasaṃgraha*, which has been falsely ascribed to Śaṅkara and published a number of times;[9] the anonymously transmitted *Sarvamatasaṃgraha*, perhaps the work of Rāghavānanda (edited by T. Gaṇapati Śāstrī, Trivandrum, 1918; this obviously not very old work first provides a survey of doctrines concerning the means of knowledge, *pramāṇa*, and then utilizes the number of the means of knowledge which each of the particular philosophical schools recognize as a guideline for its doxographic discussion; here it follows a model which we find first documented around 500 A.D., in Cāttanār's Tamil verse epic *Maṇimekhalai*[10]); Mādhava Sarasvatī, *Sar-*

vadarśanakaumudī (edited by K. Sāmbasiva Śāstrī, Trivandrum, 1938); Rājaśekhara, *Ṣaḍdarśanasamuccaya* (edited by Haragovindadāsa and Becaradāsa, Benares, 1912; indebted to Haribhadra's work of the same name); Merutuṅga, Ṣaḍdarśananirnaya (in: *Jaina Philosophical Tracts — Jainadārśanikaprakaraṇasaṃgraha*, edited by N.J. Shah, Ahmedabad, 1973); Rāmabhandra Dīkṣita et al., *Ṣaḍdarśanīsiddhāntasaṃgraha* (partially printed in: A Descriptive Catalogue of Sanskrit Manuscripts in the Tanjore Mahārāja Serfoji's Sarasvatī Mahāl Library, XIII, Srirangam, 1931, Nr. 7631 ff.; complete edition: Thanjavur 1985). The *Sarvasiddhāntapraveśaka*, compiled by an anonymous Jaina author, consists primarily of quotes and is intended as an introductory work (edited by Jambuvijaya, Bombay, 1964). The *Sarvadarśanakaumudī* by Dāmodara Mahāpātraśāstrin (Bhuvaneshvar, 1975) is a twentieth-century curiosity which includes a chapter on Western philosophy.[11]

Most of these works, whose titles indicate that they offer a survey of "all" or "six" systems or doctrines, have met with little recognition in the West. And considering their tendency to schematize and stereotype, the knowledge which they provide about the doctrines they discuss is quite limited indeed. In the present context, however, we shall not be concerning ourselves with their value as sources, but instead with their role as expressions of Indian self-awareness and as indicators of the Indian view of tradition and traditional knowledge. For in this role, they merit a consideration which they have generally not been accorded up till now.

3. One of the first things which strikes us is that the Indian doxographic literature is largely the work of two religious-philosophical groups - the Jainas and the Advaita Vedāntins. Almost all of the aforementioned titles are the work of members of one of these two traditions: Haribhadra and his commentators, Rājaśekhara, Merutuṅga, and the author of the *Sarvasiddhāntapraveśaka* are all Jainas; while Mādhava-Vidyāraṇya, Mādhava Sarasvatī, Ps.-Śaṅkara, and the authors of the *Ṣaḍdarśanīsiddhāntaatsaṃgraha* and the *Sarvamatasaṃgraha* are representatives of a more or less strictly understood Advaita Vedānta. Whereas the Jaina doxographies do not follow any recognizable schema in their presentation of the six systems, the Advaita Vedānta doxographic texts are usually based upon a hierarchical classification at whose apex stands the Vedānta. Here, the first (and lowest) system is materialism, which is presented as the school of Cārvāka or Lokāyata, or — when only "orthodox" teachings are discussed (i.e., those which do not deny the authority of the Veda) — the Vaiśeṣika or the Nyāya. The arrangement used in the *Sarvasiddhāntasaṃgraha* of Ps.-Śaṅkara is: Lokāyata, Ārhata (i.e., Jainism), Bauddha (Buddhism, divided into four sub-types), Vaiśeṣika, Nyāya, the Mīmāṃsa of the schools of Prabhākara and Kumārila, Sāṃkhya, Yoga, the doctrine of "Vedavyāsa"

(essentially that of the *Mahābhārata*), and Advaita Vedānta. In the *Sarvadarśanasaṃgraha*, we find: Cārvāka, Bauddha, Ārhata, Rāmānuja, Pūrnaprajña (i.e., the philosophy of Madhva), Nakulīśa-Pāśupata, Saiva (following the South Indian Śaivasiddhānta), Pratyabhijña (i.e., the Śaivite non-dualism of Kashmir), Raseśvara, Vaiśeṣika, Nyāya, Jaiminīya (i.e., Mīmāṃsā), Pāṇinīya (i.e., grammar and the philosophy of grammar), Sāṃkhya, Yoga, and Advaita Vedānta. The *Ṣaḍdarśanīsiddhāntasaṃgraha* begins with the Nyāya and Vaiśeṣika, then discusses the Mīmāṃsa (Prabhākara and Kumārila), Sāṃkhya, Yoga, and Advaita Vedānta. In addition, a closing chapter deals with *vyākaraṇa*, or grammar. The arrangement and especially the importance assigned to particular schools in Mādhava Sarasvatī's *Sarvadarśanakaumudī* is quite unusual: the work first addresses the Vaiśeṣika and the Nyāya in great detail (here, the philosophy of the Jainas is curiously treated in the *viparyaya* section of the Vaiśeṣika chapter), then very briefly discusses the Sāṃkhya, Yoga, etc., finally going into detail again in the closing chapter dealing with the Advaita Vedānta. While Śaṅkara is referred to with respect, no mention is made of his followers, e.g., Sureśvara. The *Sarvamatasaṃgraha* begins with the "heterodox" doctrines of the Buddhists, Jainas, and Materialists, following which it discusses the Vedic- "orthodox" systems, ranging from the Vaiśeṣika to the Vedānta. This work, which uses the number of the recognized means of knowledge as its guideline, concludes its discussion with the "Purāṇic" form of the Vedānta (*paurāṇikamata*).[12]

As we have noted, the Jaina doxographies do not make use of any comparable hierarchical arrangement, Jaina philosophy instead appearing amidst the other systems. In both Haribhadra's and Rājaśekhara's *Ṣaḍdarśanasamuccaya* as well as in the *Sarvasiddhāntapraveśaka*, the closing chapter (which is more or less an appendix) is devoted to the Materialists. Only in Merutuṅga's *Ṣaḍdarśananirṇaya* are the Jainas discussed in the closing chapter. None of these four Jaina doxographies presents the Vedānta as a separate doctrinal system.

4. These works also differ in the number of doctrines they discuss. The *Sarvadarśanasaṃgraha* examines sixteen doctrines (including the Advaita Vedānta), the *Sarvasiddhāntasaṃgraha* ten (disregarding the sub-divisions of Buddhism and the Mīmāṃsā). Most of the doxographies are oriented around the number six, which also serves as a guideline even when a greater number of systems are actually treated. The number six also figures in other classifications of traditional branches of learning, for instance in the six Vedic auxiliary sciences (*vedāṅga*) and in the six medical schools.[13] Typically, the Jaina doxographies include the number six in their titles, while Materialism may be appended as a seventh system.[14] Many of the Hindu-Vedāntic doxographies arrange the systems they treat into two groups of

three, the "non-Vedic" or "heterodox" (*avaidika, nāstika*), and the "Vedic" or "orthodox" (*vaidika, āstika*) traditions; for example, the *Sarvamatasaṃgraha* contrasts the Buddhists, Jainas and Materialists to the orthodox trinity of the Mīmāṃsā, Sāṃkhya, and Tarka, while the *Sarvadarśanakaumudī* juxtaposes the former group to the Tarka, Tantra (i.e., here: Mīmāṃsā), and Sāṃkhya. By dividing Buddhism into four schools, the number six is then obtained for the heterodox side, while the division of the Mīmāṃsā into the Pūrvamīmāṃsā and the Uttaramīmāṃsa. the Sāṃkhya into Kapila's Sāṃkhya and Patañjali's Yoga, and the Tarka into the Nyāya and the Vaiśeṣika in turn yields the six orthodox systems.[15] Various other six-fold groupings of philosophical systems may also be found outside of the doxographic literature.[16]

During the last centuries, the six-fold group of Vaiśeṣika, Nyāya, Sāṃkhya, Yoga, Mīmāṃsā, and Vedānta (which were also contained in some of the older doxographies) has gained increasing recognition in presentations of Indian philosophy, and this scheme of the systems is generally accepted today. In this model, the theistic teachings of Rāmānuja, Madhva, etc. are usually more or less explicitly assigned or subordinated to the Vedānta. In the *Sarvamatasaṃgraha*, however, the works of Brahmadatta, Bhāskara, Rāmānuja, Ānandatīrtha (i.e., Madhva), etc. are considered to be "pseudo-commentaries" (*bhāṣyābhāsa*) not belonging to the Vedānta.[17]

For this reason, it is all the more remarkable that the *Sarvadarśanasaṃgraha* steers clear of the six-fold (as well as any other numerical) scheme, and also includes several doctrines that were considered quite modern at the time it was written. It is also interesting that this work makes a clear distinction between sectarian philosophies and the classical systems, setting the former alongside the latter as something new. In contrast, the two Jaina doxographies entitled *Ṣaḍdarśanasamuccaya* present in the Nyāya and the Vaiśeṣika as sectarian, Śaivite philosophies. In the introduction to his Sanskrit commentary to the *Sarvadarśanasaṃgraha*, the modern pandit V.S. Abhyaṅkara has attempted to provide a systematic framework and justification for Mādhava's factual enumeration by supplying a diheretical scheme of possible viewpoints.[18]

5. Several of these doxographies do not limit themselves to presenting and classifying the traditional philosophical doctrines (*darśana*), but also attempt to place them within the greater context of the traditional branches of knowledge. In doing so, they refer to traditional lists which speak of either fourteen or eighteen "sciences" (*vidyā*). The older fourteen-fold list encompasses: four Vedas, six "Vedic limbs" or auxiliary sciences (*vedāṅga*), i.e., grammar, etc., and four "additional limbs" (*upāṅga*), viz., *mīmāṃsā, nyāya, purāṇa, smṛti*. In the eighteen-fold list, the four "additional Vedas"

(*upaveda*), e.g., medicine (*āyurveda*) etc., are added to this list. The longer list may be found in the *Sarvasiddhāntasaṃgraha* of Ps.-Śaṅkara;[19] there is no discussion, however, of the way in which the philosophical systems then discussed fit into this scheme. The *Sarvamatasaṃgraha* deals with the classification of the sciences in a chapter on *āgama*, "authoritative tradition," which is part of its introductory discussion concerning the means of knowledge (*pramāṇa*). Here, a distinction is made between two types of tradition: that which is of human origin and that which is not: *āgamo dvividhaḥ pauruṣeyāpauruṣeyabhedāt.*[20] The Vedas and their auxiliary sciences (*vedāṅga*) are considered to be of "non-human origin," while the "fifth Veda," i.e., the *Mahābhārata* and the Purāṇas, the "additional Vedas," and the Smṛti (i.e., Dharmaśāstra) are of "human origin." The philosophical systems are then connected with this schema in such a way that they are either assigned to the *pūrvakāṇḍa*, the "earlier" portions of the Veda which refer to "works," or to the *uttarakāṇḍa*, the "knowledge section" of the Veda. In a direct and obvious manner, this applies only to the positions of the Mīmāṃsā and the Vedānta. But insofar as they are suited to defend against anti-Vedic attacks, the Nyāya and the Vaiśeṣika, as "additional limbs" (*vedopāṅga*), are also, though more indirectly, related to the Veda. The Sāṃkhya and Yoga are described as parts of the "fifth Veda," i.e., of the *Mahābhārata* and the Purāṇas (*itihāsapurāṇe 'ntarbhūtam*).[21]

In the "additional limbs" section of the *Prasthānabheda* of Madhusūdana Sarasvatī (the most representative presentation of the eighteen-fold classification of the sciences), the Nyāya and Vaiśeṣika are (as could be expected) placed under the heading of *nyāya* and the Vedānta and the Mimāṃsā under the heading of *mīmāṃsā*; in the section on the Smṛti and Dharmaśāstra, we are then told that the Sāṃkhya (together with the other systems) is a part of the Dharmaśāstra. Finally, Madhusūdana divides the basic cosmological viewpoints into the doctrines of "production," "transformation," and "apparent evolution" (*ārambhavāda, pariṇāmavāda*, and *vivartavāda*). He assigns the Nyāya, Vaiśeṣika, and Mīmāṃsā to the first, Sāṃkhya, Yoga, and the theistic philosophies to the second, and the Advaita Vedānta to the third of these basic views.[22]

6. As we have noted, most doxographies are connected with either Jainism or the Advaita Vedānta. All the same, this should not suggest that the other systems and schools were not interested in the doctrines of their rivals. Since ancient times, references to outside teachings and their more or less careful consideration in the presentation of a school's own position has been a part of Indian thought; this is documented since the period of the early Upaniṣads. Presenting one's own teachings as answers (*uttarapakṣa*) to competing views (*pūrvapakṣa*) is a common procedure in Indian philosophical literature. As

an indication of the richness of doxographic information which this style of thought and presentation may yield, it is sufficient to recall the Buddhist *Madhyamakahṛdayakārikā* by Bhavya (or Bhāvaviveka, sixth century, with his autocommentary, the *Tarkajvālā*), Śāntarakṣita's *Tattvasaṃgraha* (with the commentary by Kamalaśīla, eighth century), and the *Nyāyamañjarī* by the Naiyāyika Jayanta (ninth century).

Since early times, there have been a number of modalities for dealing with other doctrines which were by no means limited to their mere refutation or rebuttal. In our discussion of the concept of *darśana*, we noticed a tendency which Buddhism manifested at an early date, viz., to list and to classify the different philosophical doctrines or viewpoints in order to refute them *as* doctrines, as mere theories (*dṛṣṭi, diṭṭhi*). We have also spoken of the Jaina practice of presenting non-Jaina points of view in such a way that they appear as partial truths within a context of comprehensive perspectivism.[23] It would be inappropriate to draw a sharp line between the doxographies and the other forms of dealing with competing doctrines. Especially in Jainism, as our discussion of the concept of *naya* has shown the treatment of "other" doctrines has been integrated into "one's own" philosophizing, so that the claim to understand and master them has become a constituent element of Jainism's own philosophical standards. It is characteristic that Haribhadra, the author of the doxography *Ṣaḍdarśanasamuccaya*, also discusses the other systems in a different yet pertinent form, e.g., in a work entitled *Anekāntajayapatākā*, the "Victory Flag of Perspectivism."[24] As we have seen, the doxographic presentations of other doctrines by the Vedāntins — in which these were viewed as stages on the way to the absolute truth attained in the Advaita Vedānta — was tantamount to their subordination to the Vedānta. To be sure, precisely because of the claim that the Vedānta transcends all other teachings, it was essential to refer to them. Jaina perspectivism and the Vedāntic hierarchical form of treating other doctrines have, moreover, often been combined in both traditional and modern Hinduism; in Jainism, Kundakunda developed an analogous connection by linking the conception of the "two truths" (which was developed within Madhyamaka Buddhism) with the doctrine of *naya*.[25] In no case, however, does a presentation of the opinions of others imply a relativizing or abandoning of one's own position. Instead, the own position is explicated and justified precisely through the discussion of other positions — by demarcating one's own teachings against them, or by claiming to encompass and transcend them.

7. The doxographies may be a not very impressive by-product of the Indian philosophical tradition, and they have certainly not evolved into an independent form of literature or a scientific discipline with an importance that could place them alongside of the Western literature on the history of

philosophy. Yet they are also more than merely incidental, for they provide symptomatic testimony of a contextuality that is essential to Indian thought, a deeply rooted tendency to articulate one's own position by referring to, and trying to dispose of, other points of view, as well as by integrating one's own views into the entire framework of the tradition. Indeed, we may say that classical Indian philosophy has developed as a historical network of mutually related concepts and problems which is much closer and more coherent than the history of European philosophy.

The recapitulation of philosophical doctrines within doxographies is more than a merely extrinsic addition to these doctrines; rather, it reflects their own style of presentation; it supplements and illustrates them. For this reason, it is no accident that the doxographic literature developed within Jainism and Advaita Vedānta. Here, the references to other systems and their synopsis, comprehension, and neutralization had particular importance for the philosophical self-representation. The two traditions claim to include and fulfill other doctrines - as a perspectivistic or a hierarchically subsuming inclusivism. They claim that in their ultimate and perhaps hidden meaning these doctrines converge in what is clearly and explicitly taught in Advaita Vedānta (or in Jainism according to the Jainas). This is expressly stated in the introductory verse of the *Sarvasiddhāntasaṃgraha* of Ps.-Śaṅkara: that which, in a variety of forms, all philosophical doctrines express, is the *one* Brahman which is taught by the Upaniṣadic Vedānta.[26]

Even the great Śaṅkarācārya himself explained that what the Vedānta regards as the goal of its desire to know (*jijñāsā*), the *one* Brahman, the *one* Ātman, is also the ultimate intention of the other philosophies, including Materialism. The differences in the clarity in which this *one* reality was conceived of and the exclusive derivation of its full realization from the Vedic revelation admittedly led Śaṅkara to sharp polemics when distinguishing his view of the Vedānta from other philosophies.[27] The *Brahmasūtrabhāṣya* did not attempt a comprehensive concordance (*samanvaya*) of the philosophical systems, and the potential for concordance which results from the ultimately common reference to the Ātman was never carried out. The explicit program of harmonizing which Śaṅkara implemented following Bādarāyaṇa was much more narrow and specific, for it aimed at demonstrating the concordance of the authoritative texts — i.e., essentially the Upaniṣads — in the sense that all, without exception, teach the unity and absoluteness of Brahman.[28]

8. The inclusivistic model of reducing foreign doctrines and concepts to key concepts of one's own system has an extensive and varied tradition in India, both prior to and after Śaṅkara, and both within and without the Vedānta. Neo-Hinduism, as we have noted, has applied and reinterpreted it in different ways. It has claimed the *Ṛgvedic* formula that there are many

names for that which in truth is only *one* as early testimony of this inclusivism which it identified with universal tolerance.[29]

In a variety of ways, the idea of the manifold designations of the One has been linked in Indian religious and philosophical thought with attempts at neutralizing competing and asserting one's own doctrines. This is not only exemplified by Vedāntins, but also by the great Nyāya teacher Udayana, who, in an impressive use of the hierarchical, inclusivistic model, subordinates in his *Ātmatattvaviveka* the remaining systems to the Nyāya, which he calls the "ultimate, final Vedānta" (*caramavedānta*); in the *Nyāyakusumāñjali*, he presents a list of what he considers to be many names and implicit ways of understanding the personal God (*īśvara*) of the Nyāya theology.[30] The fact that the same inclusivistic model could be claimed by and utilized for quite differing positions obviously limits its dialectical effectiveness. This is certainly one reason why Śaṅkara did not actually realize the possibilities which he appears to suggest through his allusion to Brahman/Ātman as the universal focus for all philosophical systems, and why he did not try to work out a general concordance of philosophies within the framework of Advaita Vedānta. For conversely, the Buddhists, whom Śaṅkara so vehemently opposed, also utilized the inclusivistic model in their argumentation against other schools, including the Vedānta. As the Madhyamaka philosopher Bhavya stated, the ultimate concern of the Vedānta, although misunderstood by the Vedāntins themselves, is the principle of absolute "emptiness" and freedom taught by the Buddhists; the concept of Brahman ultimately amounts to the Buddhist notions of *nirvāṇa* and *śūnya*. On the other hand, Bhavya countered the Buddhist thinkers who tended to interpret the principle of "suchness" (*tathatā*) as a real entity with the argument that this would amount to adopting the Vedāntic *ātman*.[31] In his strict adherence to the authority of the Vedas, Śaṅkara could not admit that there were indeed affinities to Buddhist doctrines and concepts. Such affinities or concordances were not infrequently polemically asserted by the opponents of his Advaita Vedānta; thus, for instance, Madhva stated that the "emptiness" (*śūnya*) of Madhyamaka Buddhism corresponds to the Brahman of Advaita Vedānta.[32]

9. The "special" *samanvaya*, the concordance which Śaṅkara (following Bādarāyaṇa) wished to secure among the authoritative Vedic/Upaniṣadic texts, clearly differs from the inclusivistic and reductive treatment of rival systems which asserts that because of their reference to the *one* Ātman (however distorted this reference may be), *all* systems ultimately agree. Nevertheless, the two approaches were often conjoined, and the concordance of sacred texts also attained a model character for the efforts towards more far-reaching harmonizing of the philosophical systems and the traditional sciences in general.

In Śaṅkara's view, agreement within the Vedic revelation could be secured by assigning its statements to two levels: the level of empirical, conventional (*vyāvahārika*) truth, and the level of absolute (*pāramārthika*) truth. Supposed contradictions could be resolved by considering the forms of statements and the meanings of words appropriate to each particular level.[33] Later authors, especially the representatives of the Vedānta, extrapolated this assignment to different levels or stages of instruction in a number of ways and applied it to the totality of Hindu and, more generally, Indian philosophical systems. Modern Indian presentations of Indian philosophy have emphasized that the differences between the systems may be attributed to pedagogical aspects, to a consideration of the different levels of qualification (*adhikārabheda*) of the disciples: "Though the different schools were opposed to one another, a sort of harmony among them was also conceived by the Indian thinkers. They believed that all persons were not fit for all things and that in religious, philosophical and social matters we should take into consideration these differences and recognize consequent distinctions of natural aptitudes (*adhikārabheda*)."[34]

The "agreement of all philosophical systems" (*sarvadarśanasamanvaya, sarvardarśanaikavākyatā*)[35] is a motif which appeared primarily during the later period of traditional Indian philosophy, for instance, in the work of the sixteenth century authors Vijñānabhikṣu, Madhusūdana Sarasvatī, and Appaya Dīkṣita, Vijñānabhikṣu stated that all orthodox systems, specifically Vedānta and Sāṃkhya, teach true knowledge and are ultimately without contradiction.[36] Appaya Dīkṣita's exposition primarily considered the Vedānta and the schools which developed within it.[37] Madhusūdana Sarasvatī did the same in his *Vedāntakalpalatikā*, in which he stated that he had "shaken off" (*nirdhūya*) the other systems, i.e., left them behind on his soteriological path. He applied a wider framework in his classical *Prasthānabheda*, in which he assumed that all orthodox teachers, i.e., Kapila, Jaimini, etc., were omniscient teachers of one and the same truth. However, they had adapted their teachings to the different capabilities of their disciples, trying to prepare them for the ultimate truth, and to protect them from lapsing into anti-Vedic heterodoxy (*nāstikya*).[38]

10. However, it is significant that Madhusūdana rejected any extension of his method of concordance to the Buddhists and other heterodoxies (not to mention the *mlecchas*). Their teachings were not even credited with a preliminary and pedagogical value. Such traditional Hindu programs of harmonization thus differ fundamentally from the Neo-Hindu universalizing of the concepts of *samanvaya* and *adhikārabheda*.

It is clear that the idea of a didactic adjustment of philosophical teachings to the qualification of the students is indebted to the Buddhist ideal of "skillfulness in the means (of teaching)" (*upāyakauśalya*). In his own way,

Śaṅkara (who did not carry out a harmonizing of the Hindu philosophical systems based upon the *adhikārabheda*) also bears witness to the exemplary nature of the Buddhist model: referring to the variety of Buddhist philosophical systems, namely the *Sarvāstivāda*, the *Vijñānavāda*, and the *Śūnyavāda*, he mentions and criticizes the claim that the Buddha himself offered these alternatives because he took the differing abilities of his students into consideration.[39] Śaṅkara's commentator Vācaspati explains that the direct and full statement of the *Śūnyavāda*, the "doctrine of emptiness," is a form of Buddhist instruction reserved for the especially capable (*prakṛṣṭamati*), while the other systems may be considered indirect forms leading to the *Śūnyavāda*. It is noteworthy that Vācaspati also presents a Buddhist citation in this context — from the *Bodhicittavivaraṇa*, attributed to Nāgārjuna.[40]

Apart from its regard for the pedagogical dimension, Madhusūdana's harmonizing presentation of the branches of traditional Hindu knowledge also provides an especially clear example of a motif effective within Hinduism since ancient times: the effort to establish not just the sources and bases of tradition, but also its framework and context, and to define once and for all its developmental possibilities. Not only the Vedic basis of the true and liberating knowledge, but also the forms of its explication and supplementation and the ways and stages of its attainment, should be established and validated. And in general, all true and legitimate knowledge should be anchored once and for all in authoritative tradition. The authoritative texts of the *Śruti* and *Smṛti* themselves provide a starting point: the *Bṛhadāraṇyaka Upaniṣad* explains that not only the Vedas themselves, but also the Upaniṣads, verses, *Sūtras*, explications (*anuvyākhyāna*), explanations (*vyākhyāna*), etc. are "exhalations of the great Being" (*mahato bhūtasya . . . niḥśvasitāni*).[41] The *Mahābhārata* also credits various doctrines and sciences with a status of originality and eternity comparable to that of the Veda.[42]

11. The extent to which other traditions and branches of knowledge possess an authoritative status of their own alongside or independently of the Veda or the degree to which their authority is merely secondary, derivative, and dependent upon the Veda, has remained the subject of controversy. The extent of the Vedic *śruti* itself has been debated a number of times, especially with respect to the inclusion of the *Atharvaveda*, but also concerning the status of certain explanatory and supplementary texts (*arthavāda*) within the Vedic collections themselves. Following the principle of "anchoring in the Veda" (*vedamūlatva*) that was developed in the Pūrvamīmāṃsā, this concern is not with a *mutual* relationship of concordance, but solely with a confirmation (or refutation) of other traditions through the Veda. With Śaṅkara, who conforms to the Pūrvamīmāṃsā in this

respect, the domain of strict (i.e., mutual) concordance and thus of autonomous textual authority remains limited to the Vedic texts. As a rule, however, this domain was greatly expanded by the later theistic commentators of the *Brahmasūtra*. The variety of ways in which the Pāñcarātra has been treated is symptomatic of this; the independent authority which Śaṅkara denied this religious tradition has usually been conceded by the representatives of the theistic and sectarian Vedānta, especially Vaiṣṇava Vedānta.[43]

Madhva remarked that in addition to the Vedic texts, the Pāñcarātra, the *Mahābhārata*, the "original Rāmāyaṇa" (*mūlarāmāyaṇa*) and the *Brahmasūtra* were recognized as independently authoritative sources of knowledge (*mānaṃ svataḥ smṛtam*); here, the Vaiṣṇava Purāṇas are encompassed under the heading *Pāñcarātra*. In the school of Madhva, the *Brahmasūtra* (as well as the authoritative systematizing tradition which follows it), as an "explicit," "definite," and hermeneutically determinative tradition (*nirṇītaśāstra*, also *nirṇāyakaśāstra*), is set apart from the "implicit," "not fully specified" (*nirṇeya*, *nirṇetavya*) message contained in the remaining texts.[44] We do not need to concern ourselves in more detail with questions pertaining to the authority of tradition within Hinduism or the determination of its extent and its justification. Modern research has treated this subject a number of times. At the present, however, we are still far from an adequate documentation and understanding of these developments, and of the possible connections between Hinduism and the rich and complex theories of tradition and exegesis within Mahāyāna Buddhism and Buddhist Tantrism.[45] We shall merely mention an exemplary chapter in Jayanta's *Nyāyamañjarī*. Here, a doctrine is discussed which asserts that all religious traditions (*āgama*) issue from the same divine author (*īśvara*), who appeared, e.g., as Kapila, Jina, and Buddha in order to teach beings according to their particular state of maturity; thus, these traditions each possess an authoritative status which is essentially equivalent to that of the others.[46] In his philosophical drama *Āgamaḍambara*, Jayanta himself advocates a very open attitude towards the question of the legitimacy of traditions; he does, however, stress that such legitimacy requires a certain antiquity, continuity, and respect for the fundamental ethical and religious norms of the Indian tradition. In essence, this represents an attempt at stabilizing and legitimizing the social and religious status quo which may have been influenced by political motives,[47] but which was also linked to motifs of Kashmiri Śaivism that received their most memorable expression a century later in the thirty-fifth chapter of Abhinavagupta's *Tantrāloka*. This chapter invokes the "union of the traditions" (*śāstrāṇāṃ melanam*) and presents the manifold religious and philosophical traditions of the country as fragments of *one* divine original and universal revelation.

12. To be sure, the authorship of God which Jayanta and the theistic Nyāya in general claimed as the basis for validating "revelations" and religious traditions was not always conceived of in such a positive sense. Parallel to this, there was also the idea of the divine seducer and deceiver, which is most commonly associated with the Vaiṣṇava Purāṇas, but which Madhva, for example, also adopted. In this view, Viṣṇu manifests himself as the Buddha or another deceiving teacher in order to disseminate "teachings of delusion" (*mohanaśāstra*). He uses these in order to confuse and ruin such demonic and infamous beings as the Asura and Daitya. Or he may advise Śiva, or such teachers as Jaimini, to advance and propagate Śaivite or atheist heresies.[48] This too is an application of the *adhikārabheda*, of the "differentiation of qualification," and it is also a (albeit negative) form of appropriation and inclusivistic neutralization of foreign and rival doctrines.

This model also excludes non-Indian religious and philosophical traditions from its horizon. The fundamental theoretical framework of the tradition remains intact; the extrapolation and universalization of the inclusivistic schemes and frameworks of concordance is reserved for modern Hinduism. The understanding of tradition, the theoretical reflection upon the meaning of tradition, and the forms of debate and encounter first develop – apart from a few inconsequential exceptions[49] – within the indigenous Indian context which was related to the Veda in a positive or negative way. This context comprises not only what was recognized as true or relevant for salvation in a positive sense, but also various forms of critique, deviation, and aberration. To be sure, Madhusūdana Sarasvatī held that the teachings of the Materialists, Buddhists, etc. were, like those of the *mlecchas*, to be excluded from the compass of his consideration; and they were not incorporated into the lists of legitimate teaching traditions and sciences (*vidyā*). Nevertheless, as we have seen, they were usually included in the Jaina as well as the Hindu doxographies, and although they were rejected, they were part of traditional Hindu self-understanding.

13. While the orthodox Mīmāṃsā view is that only the Veda itself may be considered eternal in a strict and complete sense, we have seen that there is also a tendency to consider other legitimate "sciences" (*vidyā*) as equally eternal constituents of a timeless structure of traditional learning. There is no research in the sense of a desire to know, which keeps itself methodically open for future answers and possibilities of solution; unanswered questions and problems are not recognized as such. There is no concept of a future in which currently open questions and problems might be expected to be answered and solved; the present has to live up to the potential of the past. There is no commitment to what has not yet been, has not yet been known. There are no notions of method, of progress, or of the accumulation of knowledge which keep the present explicitly open for the future. The pre-

sent is not seen as the starting point on a path leading into the future - except perhaps in a soteriological regard, as the practical starting point for the process of liberation from time and space.

It would be wrong, however, to see this as an a priori given and invariably valid difference between Indian and European thought. Historical differentiation is also required in this case. Just as the empirical attitude and the consciousness of progress and method has not been present during the entire history of Western thought, the absence of such an orientation is not a timeless presupposition of Indian thought. As we have seen, India has also displayed theoretical curiosity and empirical openness. However, this has been overshadowed by soteriological interests and the consolidation of the theory of *karman*.[50] As for the general readiness to ask questions and explicitly formulate what is not yet known, the more ancient (especially the late Vedic and Upaniṣadic) texts present us with a picture that is different from that of the later works. Here, questions are still posed as such and in a manner that their answer does not always appear to be presupposed; and interrogative words play a much more noticeable and important role in these texts than in the later literature.[51] When, however, interrogative conversations are presented in the Upaniṣads, it is usually presumed that at least one of the participants is in the possession of the complete and ultimate truth; the systematic and deliberate openness for questions and problems which may be found in the Platonic dialogues is lacking here. Questions play a noticeable role in the older Buddhist texts, although primarily in the critique of the theoretical desire to know. Thus, for example, numerous theoretical questions are formulated in the instruction of Māluṅkyāputta (*Majjhimanikāya* 63) solely for the purpose of demonstrating their irrelevance and soteriological harmfulness. In this connection, we may also refer to Śaṅkara's response to the question "whose is *avidyā*?" – a question which was raised by the opponents of his Advaita Vedānta. Śaṅkara says that as long as the questioner considers it necessary to pose such a question, he himself is the subject or substrate of a fundamental misconception (*avidyā*).[52]

14. What possibilities does the non-historical self-understanding of classical Indian philosophy, with its apparent rejection of the ideas of progress and innovation, leave for the self-assessment of the individual thinker? What importance does it attach to the addition of new works to the old, whose validity is beyond dispute?

In his *Nyāyamañjarī*, Jayanta assures his readers that he is in no position to expound new ideas or doctrines of his own (*na vayaṃ ātmīyām abhinavāṃ kām api kalpanām utpādayituṃ kṣamāḥ*); his imperfect insight is not even capable of discovering a single blade of grass that may have been overlooked by the astute sages of the past.[53] In his introduction, he states that he is not in a position to offer any new material (*nūtanaṃ vastu*); for this reason, when evaluating his work, one should only consider the variety and novelty of his manner of presentation (*vacovinyāsavaicitryamātra*), as if, for example, it were a new type of floral arrangement.[54] The truth may indeed stand fast for ever, and the tradition may indeed have already anticipated the substance of all true insights. Yet there still remains the possibility of introducing variety and novelty into its presentation. The more or less successful summary, the greater or lesser degree of detail, the degree of success in the defense against misunderstanding, attacks, rival doctrines; all these reflect the capabilities of the individual author. And it is in precisely this sense that Jayanta defines the role of the scientific and philosophial "author" (*kartṛ*): since such sciences as grammar, Mīmāṃsā, and Nyāya have, like the Veda itself, existed since the world was created (*ādisargāt prabhṛti*), speaking of "authors" or "creators" can only refer to the facets of "condensation or explication" (*saṃkṣepavistaravivakṣā*).[55]

As characteristic as Jayanta's remarks on the role of originality and novelty may be, in their extent and explicitness they are unusual. They also demonstrate that Jayanta was not concerned with an entirely undisputed issue. His disclaimer of any ideas of his "own" (*ātmīya*) was made in response to the critical question of an opponent.[56] There is also occasional evidence of a much more pronounced sense of achievement and originality, for instance, in the work of the great Buddhist epistemologist Dharmakīrti, or the great Śaivite Abhinavagupta.[57] An awareness of having gone a "new way" (*mārgo navaḥ*), of doctrinal innovation, etc., may be found both in the self-assessment of philosophers and in the evaluations of philosophical doctrines made by others. Probably the most frequent occurrence of this concerns the description of the later Nyāya as "New Nyāya" (*navyanyāya*); it also may be found, for instance, in occasional references to "Neo-Mīmāṃsakas" (*navyamīmāṃsaka*); here, "novelty" is by no means always measured using only the criteria of "condensation and explication" to which Jayanta had referred.[58]

15. Jayanta's philosophical and literary self-assessment accords with the form of the works which predominated in the Indian philosophical tradition during classical and later times, viz., commentaries, sub-commentaries, introductions, compendia, and polemic and dialectic works. Common to all is the fact that they do not present their subject matter as such or choose their own points of reference, but instead adhere to the medium of commenting and explicating, and link up with the given stock of tradition. We do not need to concern ourselves further with the actual extent of freedom and "originality" which this manner of presentation allowed authors, or the manifold reinterpretations, developments, and innovations for which it left room. It will suffice to recall that the varieties in the form of the commen-

taries permitted the commentator considerable freedom, and that the aphoristic brevity and ambivalence of some of the basic texts were almost tantamount to an invitation to speculative and free interpretation. What is more, a great deal of openness also remained with respect to the choice of one's commentarial and spiritual affiliation.

An author's personal ambition, to the extent that it became manifest at all, usually concerned aspects of clarity, distinctness, and succinctness of presentation, pedagogical and dialectical qualities, and the successful defense against rival positions. In this regard, many authors were quite aware of their own personal achievements, and it is obvious that disclaimers concerning doctrinal innovations did not eo ipso imply personal modesty or a willingness to remain anonymous.[59]

The Hindu philosophical authors found the underlying legitimation for their new presentations and explanations of supposedly eternal truths in the fact that the tradition had to be reclaimed; it had to be rearticulated and made intelligible for the present. In the Indian world-view, the present is not merely "later" than the past; there are fundamental qualitative differences between the two as well. Among the basic presuppositions of classical Indian thought, the doctrine of the cosmic cycles, i.e., of periodically recurring destructions and regenerations of the universe, has special significance. Within each major world-period, there are repeated successions of four ages (*yuga*), each involving a degeneration from the "golden age" (*kṛtayuga*) into the dark *kaliyuga*, in which law and order, wisdom, the love of truth, and intellectual capacity reaches its nadir.[60] Just as this cyclical view appears to generally exclude a linear view of progress, the scheme of decay and regression expressed in the *yuga* theory also seems to imply that the present lags behind the past, and therewith the direct opposite of "progress." At the same time, there is a clear relationship between this scheme and the tendency to dispense with all claims to new discoveries and ideas and to project all insights back into the basic texts and into the most ancient past, crediting the teachers of earlier times with greater abilities and deeper insights than could be found in the later ages. In a characteristic passage in the *Brahmasūtrabhāṣya*, for example, Śaṅkara thus attributes a greater yogic and mental potential to the humans of the far distant past, emphasizing that the abilities of the Vedic "seers" (*ṛṣi*) cannot be judged using the standard of our own current capabilities.[61]

16. In the Purāṇas, the appearance of erroneous and corruptive texts and deceptive traditions opposed to the Veda (*mohanaśāstra*) is often seen as a symptom of the emerging *Kaliyuga*.[62] On the other hand, we find the claim that texts have to possess superior qualities in order to fulfill the special needs and difficulties of the worst of the ages of the world. In this sense, the association of a text with the *Kaliyuga* may be considered a mark of special

merit. The Vaiṣṇava school of Caitanya, for example, made such a claim for the *Bhāgavatapurāṇa*.[63] The coordination of texts and layers of tradition with the ages of the world, which also occurs in the *Dharmaśāstra* literature is finalized in Tantrism: the Veda is assigned to the *Kṛtayuga*, the *Smṛti* to the *Tretāyuga*, the Purāṇas to the *Dvāparayuga*, and the Tantras to the worst and most difficult of the ages of the world, the *Kaliyuga*.[64]

This classificatory scheme was explicated and applied in a number of different ways; the manner in which references were made to the Veda was particularly ambivalent. On the one hand, it was asserted that the Tantra was autonomous, even superior to the Veda; on the other, repeated attempts were made to trace the Tantric teachings back to the Veda, thereby providing them with legitimation.[65] In spite of the emphasis placed upon the special status of the Tantric texts, it was still largely assumed that the truth expressed in the Veda had been presented in the Tantra merely in a form more appropriate to its time – a form in which it could best work upon our own present. At the same time, this meant that the Tantric orientation could be claimed to be more authentic, offering a vision of the Vedic truth that was more fitting for the present than the mere archival preservation of Vedic formulae and rites. Here we find a dynamic concept of tradition opposing a static view, not infrequently in open rivalry. The mere preservation of Vedic texts was contrasted with the retrieval and actualization of living truth. At the same time, the doctrine of general historical decay was linked to a new principle of progress – in which progress was viewed as an adaptation to continually worsening times: the special and in a certain sense superior status of the Tantras arises from the fact that they are able to accomplish in difficult times what the Vedas accomplished in better times. Such a view of "progress" implies and is based upon decline; it offers the prospect of a future in which the distance to the original sources (which retain their validity as idealized points of reference) continually widens. Moreover, this is not a "progress" which humans shape. The fact that the Tantras are able to achieve what they do is due to the fact that they, like the Vedas themselves, are of divine origin.

17. The inclusivistic models, the ideas of harmonizing (*samanvaya*), and the differentiation of qualification (*adhikārabheda*) which we have discussed in the preceding sections[66] are part of a largely non-historical and timeless horizon of understanding, and there is no concern with a historical integration of the earlier into the later. In connection with the doctrine of the ages of the world and the layers of tradition appropriate to each, however, these models acquire a certain temporal and dynamic dimension. The effects of this are not limited to the claim that the "superiority" of the Purāṇas or Tantras vis-à-vis the Veda is justified because the former are better adapted to the current age of the world; the more far-reaching claim that these are

simply superior and more comprehensive teachings which encompass and supersede the teachings of the Veda may also be made, and the view of the Veda as a fundamentally insurmountable source of authority has at times yielded to the view that it is merely a preliminary stage which could and had to be surpassed. Buddhism offers a significant and impressive model - in the way the Mahāyāna presents itself in the face of the older Hīnayāna. Yet there are also examples of this within Hinduism, as, e.g., when Kṛṣṇa appears in the *Bhagavadgītā* as the proclaimer of a doctrine which transcends and supersedes the Vedic/Upaniṣadic orientations towards ritual activity (*karmayoga*) and knowledge (*jñānayoga*).[67] In this context, the *Nārāyaṇīya* section of the *Mahābhārata* is also significant: here, the Pāñcarātra system is presented as a higher and more inclusive unity within which the Vedas and the Āraṇyakas, Sāṃkhya and Yoga appear as mutually complementary parts (*parasparāṅgāni*).[68] In theistic philosophical thought, these motifs are linked to the idea that God appears, as it were, as his own commentator, capable of fulfilling and justifying his own "earlier" statements within the "later" layers of tradition; this model has been especially effective since the *Āgamaprāmāṇya* of the South Indian Vaiṣṇava Yāmuna, which was written around 1000 A.D. Here, God does not secure the sacred tradition merely by creating its pristine foundations, but also by supplementing and renewing it through his own clarifications and explications.

Subsequently, it was above all the *Bhāgavatapurāṇa* which was said to have transcended and superseded the Vedas. Following suggestions by Kṛṣṇa Caitanya (ca. 1500), the founder of the *Gauḍīya Vaiṣṇava* school, Jīva Gosvāmin's *Tattvasandarbha* (one of the main philosophical works of the school) provides an exemplary expression of this view. Jīva denies that the *Bhāgavatapurāṇa* is dependent upon the Vedas at all (i.e., its *vedasāpekṣatva*), explaining that the teachings of the Veda are contained in it in a more perfect and comprehensive manner. Moreover, this work is considered to be a genuine and organic "commentary" (*bhāṣya*) on the *Brahmasūtra* that was not the result of human exegesis and approximation.[69] The Mīmāṃsā doctrine of the *vedamūlatva* of all the legitimate traditions, i.e., the theory that they are "rooted" in, and derived from, the Veda, and dependent upon its authority, is here confronted with a model which maintains that the Veda is established and confirmed (*pratiṣṭhita*), fulfilled and strengthened (*paribṛṃhita*), explained and secured (*nirṇīta*) by the subsequent layers of tradition.[70]

In accordance with this model of "progressive" inclusion, the *Mahānirvāṇatantra* declares that all of the other religious traditions are encompassed by and disappear within the Śaivite Tantric *kuladharma*, just as the tracks of all other animals disappear within the tracks of the elephant.[71] It is, however, an unusual phenomenon in the Indian context when a successor of Madhva states that the work of his master has definitively exhausted the sacred tradition, and when he justifies this in a temporal sense by claiming that it is the final and unsurpassed system of philosophical and theological thought.[72] On the other hand, because the ages of the world continually repeat themselves, the temporal and "historical" model of fulfillment and development is in turn completely absorbed within the timeless and cyclical view: in the last analysis, everything is equally primordial and eternal; it is only the specific "manifestation and concealment" which is distributed within time.[73]

18. The Indian tradition has brought forth a number of surveys of the religious and philosophical teachings which have developed within it. It has developed a variety of ways of reflecting upon the meaning and the authority of tradition as such and upon the meaning of and the relationships between particular traditions. It has developed models of concordance which also consider temporal matters, the mutual relations between various layers of tradition, and the assignment of these layers to the different ages of the world. This notwithstanding, an explicit interest in the historical actuality and genesis of philosophical ideas has not arisen. And this brings us back to the starting point of this chapter: the Indian tradition has not brought forth historical accounts or inventories of developments, changes, and chronological sequences of ideas. Innovations and reorientations have not been documented as such. The "progress" of thought (whatever its extent) is seldom visible at the surface of explicit reflection and documentation; instead, it seems to be covered and canceled by it.

The systems and schools of Indian and in particular Hindu philosophy have, to the extent that they achieved an established status, functioned as channels of continuity which have regulated the developments over the centuries, neutralized innovations and change, and presented these as the organic outgrowth of what went before. Even the fundamental changes which occurred within the Indian tradition during the pre-systematic time of the Upaniṣads and then in response to the Buddhist challenge have, in retrospect, been concealed beneath the all-encompassing sense of continuity. This continuity has been claimed and maintained with such determination that this in itself testifies to the seriousness with which it had been called into question. Classical Hindu thought has indeed committed itself to a "non-historical" traditionalism; however, this was not a condition simply intrinsic to it, but rather itself a historically conditioned mode of self-presentation and self-understanding.

As we have seen, the non-historical mode of self-presentation is still significant in modern Hindu thought and self-awareness. India has responded to the historical, future-oriented challenge posed by Europe with its schemes of timeless concordance and inclusivism. But in this process, the old schemes did not remain unchanged. They were universalized and extrapolated beyond the Indian sphere for which they had been developed, and within which they had been applied. And they did not preclude the Indian mind from a new fascination with "progress."

The doxographic models and the concepts of tradition which we have considered in the present chapter have ambiguous social and xenological implications. The hierarchical arrangement of the systems implies a soteriological gradation which assigns the followers of the lower (i.e., heterodox) doctrines an ethically and socially inferior status. The rules of purity, and the restrictions on human interaction which apply vis-à-vis the lower castes and the *mlecchas*, also pertain to the intercourse with Materialists, Buddhists, etc. And, like the *mlecchas*, the Materialists and other heretics are presented as threats to the *dharma* and portents of the darkest age of the world, the *Kaliyuga*. Yet there are also significant differences. The Cārvākas, Buddhists, etc. are, in a fundamentally different way, part of the intellectual horizon of the tradition. They are partners in a theoretical debate which has played a constitutive part in the history of Indian philosophy, and the fact that a human and social distance has been maintained towards such groups does not imply that their doctrines have not been the subject of close inspection. In general, it is not their theoretical views per se which caused offense, but rather the disregard for proper dharmic behavior, for the rules of ritual and social purity, which frequently accompanied such views. Moreover, Bṛhaspati and other legendary Materialist teachers were usually considered to be Brahmins; they were by no means *eo ipso* excluded from the domain of ritual and social legitimacy.

While the mutual relations as well as the conflicts between religious and philosophical doctrines may not have moved beyond the Indian context, they nevertheless contained a potential for a greater encounter which differs starkly from the factual tendency towards isolationism. Those foreigners who have tried to assimilate the traditional Indian context and framework of thought and debate, and to penetrate the Indian horizon of self-understanding by using the traditional linguistic medium of Sanskrit may indeed have been viewed as *mlecchas*; yet they have still attained a notice and recognition which has had an important part to play in intellectually opening India up to Europe.

20. Epilogue

1. India has not reached out for Europe, has not searched for it, has not historically prepared the encounter with it. It has been the object of European interests of political domination, economic exploitation, religious proselytism, scientific research and historical understanding, but also the goal and referent of Utopian projections, of searching for the identity and the origins of Europe, of European self-questioning and self-criticism. The conditions and perspectives on the two sides of the encounter are fundamentally different; the relationship is an asymmetrical one. Europe has brought about the historical situation within which India and Europe came to face each other, and to speak and listen to one another. This is a basic condition of modern Indian self-understanding and self-articulation. Even in their rejection of, or their self-affirmation against, European ideas and orientations, modern Indian thinkers are not free from such ideas. Explicit or implicit reference to the West, and membership in a Westernized world, is an irreversible premise of modern Indian thought.

Does this mean that Europe simply dominates the "dialogue" with India, that it has once and for all determined its medium and conditions, and that it has thus deprived India of the possibility to speak for itself? Does it mean that the horizon of the encounter is simply a European one?

India has been surprised and overpowered by the encounter with Europe; and yet in its own way, it has been ready and prepared for it. The Hindu tradition has disregarded the non-Indian world, has enclosed and isolated itself in its own immanent structures; yet within this framework, it has produced an extremely rich heritage of forms of spiritual interaction, of dealing with religious plurality and the divergence of human orientations; through its self-centered and xenophobic traditionalism, it has created a remarkable potential of openness and universality. In a sense, this dormant potential was awakened and historically actualized by the encounter with the modern

West. Did the rupture in the tradition, the destruction of its petrified schemes of self-understanding, break the ethnocentric dams to which the inherent universality of the Indian tradition had been artificially confined? Did it release powers of thought which may now in turn overwhelm the West? Neo-Vedāntins like Vivekananda have indeed made this claim: Europe has not truly overpowered India; it has only created the historical opportunity for the full actualization of the inherent universality of the Hindu tradition; it has, through its science and technology, created the channels through which Indian thought can flow.[1] It has, through its political and technological victories, created the condition for its spiritual defeat. Its thought may have been more successful in determining the current historical situation; but ultimately, it will be, and has always been, included in the universality of the Vedānta.

2. P. Hacker has characterized Indian thought, and the Indian way of dealing with divergent and competing religious and philosophical views as "inclusivistic." "Inclusivism" in this sense is a "typically Indian" method of debate and of the promotion of ideas, "a form of religious self-assertion which is particularly appropriate to the Indian mind" ("eine dem indischen Geist besonders gemässe Form der religiösen Selbstbehauptung").[2] Hacker insists that what Europeans tend to see as Indian tolerance is "almost always inclusivism": "Was dem Europäer Toleranz zu sein scheint, ist fast immer Inklusivismus."[3] It is an attitude which credits foreign systems with a relative, preliminary validity, by considering them as "lower stages of one's own system, thus included in it."[4] It does not recognize other systems in their otherness, as genuine alternatives. Inclusivistic recognition is ultimately a form of devaluation and subordination. By being affiliated with, and included in one's own system, the foreign systems are used to enhance its glory. In particular, the "supreme" non-dualism of the Advaita Vedānta tends to reflect itself in the other systems which it thus recognizes and transcends.[5]

Hacker's notion of inclusivism is obviously open to critical questions. Yet it refers to a phenomenon which has indeed been significant in the history of Indian thought in general, and specifically for the modern Indian response to Christianity.[6]

To the missionary attempts to convert and to subordinate them, the Hindus responded with their notion of a timeless, non-historical inclusion of Christianity and other religions in Advaita Vedānta, or in a universalized Vaiṣṇavism. Testimony for this response, which often thwarted the efforts of the missionaries, goes back to the period before Rammohan Roy. At the beginning of the eighteenth century, B. Ziegenbalg reported that the Indians were indeed willing to "accept" Jesus Christ, but only as one incarnation or manifestation of God among many others, side by side with Viṣṇu and his *avatāras*.[7] "Tolerant" in this sense were also the pandits who worked for W.

Hastings and N.B. Halhed, and whose views are recorded in the "Preliminary Discourse" of Halhed's *Code of Gentoo Laws.*[8] Considering the inclusivistic "tolerance" of the Hindus, W. Jones was convinced that the missionary activities in India would be more or less futile.[9]

3. Neo-Vedāntins as well as Neo-Vaiṣṇavas, followers of the Brāhma Samāj, and others argue that their traditions provide comprehensive frameworks which are a priori ready for encounters with, and challenges from, other traditions and developments, including the challenge of Western science and technology. According to Bhudeb Mukherji (Bhūdeva Mukhopādhyāya, 1827–1894), the Hindu *dharma* is "all-encompassing" (*sarvavyāpaka*).[10] Vivekananda declares that the tradition of Śaṅkara is ready to include all other religions and world-views "in the infinite arms of the religion of the Vedānta."[11] No actual conversion, no historical and ephemeral event can reverse this timeless order, which relegates other positions to "preliminary stages" (*pūrvabhūmi*) on the way to the ultimate truth of Advaita Vedānta.[12]

The fundamental alternative and the basic line of defense seem to be clear: the strength and patience of the Hindu tradition faces the ephemeral claims of the Europeans; the commitment to a timeless, transhistorical truth is upheld against their future-oriented zeal. Yet the Neo-Vedānta position is more ambiguous than this; and its self-affirmation is more precarious than it appears at first sight. Regardless of the underlying postulate that the quiet transhistorical inclusiveness of the Vedānta is superior to the historical restlessness of European thought—the Vedānta is supposed to prove itself, to actualize its potential, in the current historical situation, and by responding to ethical, social and political problems. In a sense, the Neo-Vedāntins want to translate the timeless, transhistorical schemes of their tradition into concrete historical events, solutions to current, actual problems. Once again, the Neo-Hindu self-assertion against the West is also a concession to it.

It is this concession to "actuality" and modernity which critics like A.K. Coomaraswamy and R. Guénon have held against the Neo-Vedānta. In their view, such accomodation not only implies a surrender of the Orient to the Occident, but it also deprives the Occident of the possibility to rediscover its own inherent, though forgotten traditionality; and it destroys the basis on which a true meeting and dialogue of East and West would have been possible.[13] That the East did not find the way to modernity on its own, appears as a fundamental strength; the encounter between East and West, India and Europe seems to amount to the encounter between traditionality and modernity per se. There is, however, virtually no historical and hermeneutical reflection on the implications of such an encounter, and on the conditions of the historical situation in which it takes place.

4. In its attempts to define itself and to assert its identity and continuity against the West, modern Indian thought does not find itself on neutral ground: instead, it finds itself in a Westernized world. In responding to the West, it exposes itself to an "actuality" and universality which European philosophy and science have brought about. Regardless of the ultimate metaphysical truth and potential of the Indian doctrines—Indian thought is not in the same sense *historically* actual and present as European philosophy. It does not "live" and articulate itself in a present which it has actively shaped and helped to bring about. Even when it confronts, challenges and questions Western thought—it reflects and presupposes its global actuality, and it not only responds to, but also participates in, the global predicament of Westernization. European science and philosophy have not simply "met," or come into contact with, Indian thought: They have also created the global openness and the channels of communication which are the conditions of any "dialogue" between East and West. They have provided Indian thought with the opportunity to speak to the world, to be questioned and interpreted in new ways, and to question and challenge Western science and philosophy themselves. They have thus set the stage for the mutual access between India and the West, for a mutual understanding as well as for misunderstandings and failures which would be much deeper than anything that could occur between traditional cultures.

Several modern Indian thinkers have clearly and explicitly recognized their dependence upon the actuality and global presence of European thought, for instance D.N. Shastri:

> I have strongly felt that Indian Philosophy can be properly studied only by those who have studied and are fully conversant with Western philosophy. The obvious reason is that the latter has got a living tradition, while the former, i.e. Indian Philosophy has come to us, specially during the later period, through a sort of dead and blind tradition.[14]

A century earlier, Bankim Chandra Chatterji, one of the founders of Neo-Hinduism and of modern Indian nationalism, observed: "Natives who have fitted themselves for the work by that wider culture which a complete acquaintance with European science alone can impart, are in a position peculiarly suited for giving to Hindu philosophy its proper position in the history of human achievements."[15]

On the other hand, modern Indian authors deplore that the exposure to Western thought has caused paralysis, sterility and the loss of traditional substance in Indian philosophical thinking; this, too, illustrates the deep ambiguities of modern Indian self-understanding.[16]

5. Christian theologians, for instance H. Bürkle, have argued that the universality of the modern world, its sense of history, and the world-historical openness in which a "dialogue" between India and Europe is

possible, are genuinely Christian phenomena. The "universality" of modern Hinduism is, according to this view, only a derivative and secondary one, made possible and conditioned by the historical and universal message of Christianity. More specifically, the opening for the "dialogue," the Indian participation in it, appears itself as a result of the Christian missionary initiatives.

> Hinduism is about to occupy a horizon, within which the other religions have a preliminary character. In this process, the Christian hope and the underlying significance of the event which is Jesus Christ serve as a model. The framework is adopted which God, with the event of Christ, has laid out for the history of the world, and with it for the domain of the religions.[17]

Insofar as Hinduism on its part lays claim to historical actuality and universality, it has already prepared itself for the dialogue with Christianity; and the missionary debate has a "common subject-matter."[18] The self-assertion against Christianity, i.e. the assertion of a dimension of universality in Hinduism itself, would thus be an important first step towards Christianity, which appears as the religion of universality par excellence.

It is evident that such arguments are themselves part and symptom of a historical interplay between India and Europe. It is not just the "dialogue" between Christianity and the Indian tradition which is at stake in Bürkle's conception of a "dialogue with the East," but also the debate between "Neo-Hinduism" and what might be termed "Neo-Christianity." His invocation of "universality" is an attempt to neutralize and subordinate the universalistic claims of Neo-Hinduism; but in a sense, it also echoes them. There has been reinterpretation and retrospective adjustment on both sides. Most significantly, Bürkle tries to reclaim the openness and universality of the modern secular world for Christianity. He tries to explain and vindicate it as a genuinely Christian event, and to use it for missionary purposes and for the self-assertion of Christianity. — Christian missionaries have certainly done much to initiate the modern Indian rediscovery and reinterpretation of the Hindu tradition. In significant cases, their arguments have served as catalysts for the universalistic self-presentation and self-assertion of Neo-Hinduism. But this can hardly justify Bürkle's far-reaching theological and historical claims.[19]

6. A century after Hegel and in the face of historicism and cultural relativism, E. Troeltsch proclaimed once again what he considered to be the irrevocable universalism of Europe. But this proclamation was no longer an expression of Hegelian self-confidence; instead, it was a somewhat melancholy epilogue.

> For us, there is only the universal history of European culture, which requires comparative references to foreign cultures in a practical and theoretical sense, in order to

understand itself and its relationship to the others,—but which cannot thereby, together with the others, merge into a general history and development of mankind.[20]

It may be "useful and necessary to write histories of India, China, Japan, etc.": "But then, this is no historical context and no development, but it belongs in the domain of the bookbinder's synthesis ('Buchbindersynthese'), or the learned factory and cooperation, which are so common today."[21] "For us, there is only a world-history of European-ness" ("eine Weltgeschiche des Europäertums"),[22] i.e. the "relationship of the planet with Europeanism and its fate" ("Beziehung des Planeten auf den Europäismus und sein Schicksal").[23]

Troeltsch evokes the idea of Europe against the spirits which Europe itself has summoned. He evokes it in the name of, but also against a European universalism which has turned against Europe itself. Whether there will ever be a truly global culture or civilization is very doubtful. It is, however, certain that the globality and universality which Europe has brought about is no longer Europe's "own" universality. The "world-history of European-ness," the "universal history of Europeanism"[24] has also been a pervasive tradition of self-questioning, self-criticism and self-alienation. The historical unfolding of this tradition has seen the Europeans as discoverers and conquerors of the non-European world; but it has also made them distrustful of themselves. It has led them into doubts and questions concerning their fundamental goals and presuppositions, into a sense of loss and insufficiency, and to the search for alternatives and correctives.

In the unfolding of its "universality," Europe has awakened forces which have turned against itself. Its "superiority" has become the cause of its predicament.

7. Is there a philosophy today which is nourished by an equal, and equally committed, familiarity with Indian and European sources? Has the encounter between India and Europe, and the "comparison" of Indian and European philosophies, opened new prospects for philosophy itself? To what extent have we gone beyond the projection of speculative images of India on the one hand, and the accumulation of historical and philological information on the other? To what extent have the Indians gone beyond apologetics, reinterpretation, and the combination and interplay of Indian and European concepts? Will Indian and European thought come together in a "truly cosmopolitan world-philosophy" ("*wahrhaft kosmopolitische Weltphilosophie*")?[25] Will there ever be a "global philosophy"[26] and a genuine "fusion of horizons" ("*Horizontverschmelzung*"),[27] i.e. a new context of orientation and self-understanding which would be fundamentally different from what Troeltsch called "bookbinder's synthesis"[28] or from a merely additive accumulation of data about foreign traditions, and a non-

committal recognition and "understanding" of alternative world-views? In what sense can the "dialogue" between India and Europe affect our way of asking fundamental questions, as well as our reflection upon the meaning and limits of philosophy itself? Is there hope for a philosophically significant "comparative philosophy" which would imply the freedom to transcend philosophy in its European sense?

These questions may remain open. The temptation to answer and discard questions of this nature by presenting general and programmatic declarations has itself contributed greatly to the abstract rhetoric which continues to dominate wide areas of "comparative philosophy."

The preceding chapters have emphasized the historical and hermeneutical preeminence of Europe. Modern Indian thought finds itself in a historical context created by Europe, and it has difficulties speaking for itself. Even in its self-representation and self-assertion, it speaks to a large extent in a European idiom. This does not, however, mean that the dialogue and debate between India and Europe has been decided in favor of Europe, or that India has been superseded by Europe. The power of the Indian tradition has not exhausted itself in the self-representation and self-interpretation of modern India. The dialogic situation is still open.[29]

III

Appendices: Illustrations and Reflections

21. The Concept of Experience in the Encounter Between India and the West

1. "Experience" is one of the most significant, but also most ambiguous and evasive terms in the recent literature on comparative religion, philosophy and theology. It is perhaps most conspicuous in works on Indian religion and philosophy, and in the so-called dialogue between India and the West. Furthermore, recent fascination with popularized Eastern cults, sects and methods of meditation reveals a veritable "hunger for experience."[1] Referring to these phenomena H. Cox speaks about a "gluttony of experience."[2]

Already in 1926, Dean W.R. Inge, quoted approvingly by S. Radhakrishnan, stated: "The centre of gravity in religion has shifted from authority to experience."[3] In 1938, J.M. Moore observed: "No term has been more frequently employed in recent religious discussion than the phrase 'religious experience.'"[4] And again more recently, in 1968, J.E. Smith claimed: "The major intellectual task of the present is the recovery of experience from the distortions to which it has been subjected."[5] According to W. Kasper, it is one of the decisive tasks of contemporary theology to recover and rediscover the "foundation of experience" which makes it "meaningful and intelligible to speak of God;" however, Kasper adds that the concept of experience is one of the "most obscure of all philosophical concepts."[6] And the elder statesman of European philosophy, H.-G. Gadamer, declares in his *Truth and Method*: "It seems to me that the concept of experience is among the least clarified concepts which we have."[7]

The word used in the original German versions of Kasper's and Gadamer's statements is, of course, not experience, but "Erfahrung." "Erfahrung" covers only part of the semantic field of "experience"; besides "Erfahrung," there is the German word "Erlebnis,"[8] which corresponds to the more subjective and emotional connotations or implications of "experience"—experience as a state of mind, being affected by an event, etc. So if Kasper and Gadamer found "Erfahrung" obscure and ambivalent enough—what can we say about "experience," which is even more multi-faceted and ambiguous? Of course, one can neatly classify the different roles and functions of the *word* "experience"—this is done quite well and convincingly by the *Oxford English Dictionary.*[9] It distinguishes, among other meanings: "putting to the test"; "trial"; experiment;" "actual observation of facts or events, considered as a source of knowledge"; "the fact of . . . being consciously affected by an event"; "a state or condition viewed subjectively"; "a state of mind or feeling forming part of the inner religious life"; "what has been experienced; the events that have taken place within the knowledge of an individual, a community, mankind at large"; "knowledge resulting from actual observation or from what one has undergone"; "the state of having been occupied in any department of study or practice, in affairs generally, or in the intercourse of life"; "the aptitudes, skill, judgement, etc., thereby acquired."

2. Let us try to bring this variety to a higher level of philosophical reflection and into closer connection with current usages and what may be more specifically relevant for understanding its role in the "East-West dialogue." We are talking about experience in the context of scientific research, philosophy of science, etc., on the one hand, and in the field of religious emotions on the other. We are talking about experience as a process of accumulation, mutual confirmation, coherence, as something that is gradually acquired—and as something that breaks into our lives as a sudden event; we speak of experience as related to our world of practical, empirical acquaintance—the Kantian context of experience, but also of experiences which transcend this realm and open new prospects. We speak of experience in more or less veridical usages, referring to subjective states of awareness, but also to a standard of truth in an objective sense. Experience on the one hand is what man seems to possess, what he cultivates and accumulates in order to take charge of his own affairs; and on the other hand, it overcomes, overwhelms him. On the one hand, it is associated with the methodically conducted experiment, and on the other hand, it is something that escapes and transcends all methods and frameworks of human planning.

Is this just a plurality or variety of usages? Are there any meaningful and instructive connections, interrelations and perhaps tensions between these usages? How did such variety affect the "dialogue" between India and the West and the thought and phraseology of Neo-Hinduism? What is the kind of experience Westerners are expecting from India? What is the kind of experience Indians are ready to supply? In what sense do Indians and Westerners participating in the "dialogue" use the word "experience?" Has its ambiguity created misunderstanding and confusion, or has it opened new perspectives of understanding and mutual challenges? Why has the word "experience" become so conspicuous and important in the encounter between India and the West? With which Indian concepts has it been associated, and how do these concepts correspond to the ambiguities of "experience?" Is the popularity of "experience" in the interreligious and cross-cultural dialogue only a symptom of what is questionable about this dialogue, or does it hold the promise of future insights and of new horizons of philosophical, religious and scientific orientation?

3. Let us prepare the possibility of an answer to these questions by recalling some of the basic features of the encounter and dialogue between India and the West, and, more specifically, the Neo-Hindu attitude and response to Western thought, as they were outlined in the preceding chapters. As we have noticed, the encounter and relationship is, at least as far as its historical origins and conditions are concerned, an uneven and asymmetrical one. Europe has been in search of India in a variety of ways for many centuries: It has looked for analogies, origins, alternatives or correctives; it has tried to define its own identity by demarcating it against, and reflecting it in, the otherness of India; it has confronted and tried to subordinate India to its claims and interests of political domination, religious conversion, philosophical and scientific superiority. Traditional Hinduism, on the other hand, has not tried to find European or other non-Indian origins or alternatives; it has not taken any initiatives in trying to teach, convert or understand Europeans on its own. India has discovered the West and started responding to it while being discovered, subdued and objectified by it. The encounter with the West was not the result of developments initiated and carried on in India itself, but of changes and breaks imposed from the outside; and the response was often, and almost inevitably, a somewhat hasty accomodation or apologetics.

In what Paul Hacker has described and critically analysed as Neo-Hinduism, the Hindu tradition is reinterpreted and transformed by applying Western concepts and responding to Western expectations and presuppositions. Fundamental notions of traditional religious and philosophical self-understanding and self-articulation function as vehicles of translation or as receptacles for the adoption of Western ideas and perspectives, but also as devices of apologetics and self-affirmation.

This is well-exemplified by the Neo-Hindu use and reinterpretation of the traditional key concept of Hindu self-understanding, *dharma*, in response to the Western notion of religion.[10] A different, yet analogous case of response, reinterpretation and hermeneutic interplay is provided by the ambiguous manner in which the concepts of philosophy and *darśana* have been correlated in modern Hinduism:[11] *Darśana*, while serving as a vehicle of translation and as an alleged original Indian equivalent of "philosophy," functions also as a device of apologetics and cultural self-affirmation, an emblem of what distinguishes Indian thought from what is called "philosophy" in the West. As we have noticed, the etymological derivation of *darśana* from the root *dṛś*, "to see," is given special significance by Neo-Hindu authors. It is interpreted as indicating a priority of "seeing" and "direct experience" in the Indian tradition and associated with the idea of a "direct immediate and intuitive vision of Reality;"[12] and accordingly, it is contrasted with the analytic and discursive preoccupations of Western philosophy. In this connection, the "experiences" of the ancient "seers" (*ṛṣi*) are frequently referred to and presented as the fountainhead of the Indian religious and philosophical tradition; and "experience" is invoked as something genuinely and characteristically Indian: Philosophy and religion ought to be rooted in experience, and the Indian tradition has, more than other traditions, preserved and respected this association.

4. The case of *darśana*/philosophy indicates how significant the concept of "experience" has become in modern Indian thought. The works of the leading and most widely known representatives of Neo-Hindu thought, for instance, S. Radhakrishnan, provide many other illustrations for this general significance. P. Hacker has called Radhakrishnan the "most typical Neo-Hindu,"[13] and he was without question one of the most effective spokesmen of the Neo-Hindu ideology of experience, providing us with some of the most memorable formulations concerning experience and trying to derive a program of harmony and concordance (*samanvaya*) from what he considers a proper evaluation of the role of experience.

"If philosophy of religion is to become scientific, it must become empirical and found itself on religious experience."[14] "The Hindu philosophy of religion starts from and returns to an experimental basis."[15] – "Every philosophy is the exposition and justification of an experience."[16] – "Religion is not the acceptance of academic abstractions or the celebration of ceremonies, but a kind of life or experience. It is insight into the nature of reality (*darśana*) or experience of reality (*anubhava*)."[17] Radhakrishnan also speaks about "experts in the field of religion," "re-experiencing," "experimenting," . . . "intuitions," "the experimental basis" of religion, and so forth;[18] and he says: "While philosophy cannot take anything for granted it cannot ignore the testimony of religious experience to the nature of ultimate reality which it also seeks to apprehend."[19]

"Religious," "spiritual," even poetic experiences, scientific "experiments," "intuition" as an epistemological term, indicating a direct mode of awareness – while Radhakrishnan does occasionally distinguish between these ideas, the manner in which he blurs the distinctions and combines the different connotations is much more typical of his approach.

According to Radhakrishnan, all genuine religious (or religious-philosophical) documents have their origin in authoritative personal experiences of "seers," experiences of indubitable, unquestionable immediacy; they are records of "intuitions," of "experiences of the experts in the field of religion."[20] "Experience" is "the soul of religion,"—the one ground of legitimacy for all forms and expressions of religious life, the one ultimate source which is often hidden under thick and manifold layers of ritualism, symbolism and interpretation.

5. But while experience may be invoked as the common ground of *all* religions, it is also, and perhaps even more so, a means of Hindu self-affirmation. It may be true that all religions have their roots in experience, but it is Hinduism which is the religion of experience par excellence, the religion which has not disavowed or concealed its experimental basis, which keeps itself open for experience and will not accept its truncation or petrification by dogmas and theoretical structures. "Intellect is subordinated to intuition, dogma to experience."[21]

Radhakrishnan contrasts the Asian, specifically Indian "religions of experience" with the prophetic and dogmatic religions of the West, which in his view give objective truth and objectified theoretical and institutional structures priority over the living dynamism of experience. Hinduism, in particular Vedānta, as understood by Radhakrishnan, remains open for what is underneath all symbols—their living source, direct, transymbolic experience—while other religions tend to lose touch with this source, leaving it buried under dogmas and petrified institutions.[22]

The Vedic revelation, *śruti*, provides the most original, most immediate documentation of religious experience. "The experience is recorded as a pure and direct intellectual intuition in *śruti*."[23] The experiences recorded by the Vedic seers can and ought to be re-experienced, re-examined, reconfirmed in everybody's own inner awareness. "The truths revealed in the Vedas are capable of being re-experienced. . . . By experimenting with different religious conceptions and relating them with the rest of our life, we can know the sound from the unsound";[24] ". . . the ultimate basis of religious trust must be found in personal experience."[25] In general, Radhakrishnan sees the Indian religious tradition as a tradition of inner experimentation or psychological empiricism. In his words, Indian religious thought is "experimental and provisional in its nature, attempting to keep pace with the progress of thought . . . the facts of mind or consciousness were studied by the Indian thinkers with as much care and attention as the facts of the outer world are studied by our modern scientists. The philosophical conclusions of Advaitic monism are based on the data of psychological observation."[26] Experience is, at least potentially, universal, and it is universally accessible. The different religions ought to respect each other in recognizing experience as their common ground. They should see their differences and disagreements as representing a variety of interpretations of experiences which are multi-faceted in themselves, yet indicators of an ultimately identical source of experience. "As the experiences themselves are of varied character, so their records are many-sided (*viśvatomukham*) or suggestive of many interpretations (*anekārthatām*)."[27]

6. According to Radhakrishnan, tolerance and universality accompany any true commitment to experience; and accordingly, he sees Hinduism, the religion of experience, also as the religion of tolerance and universality and as capable of reminding other religions of their own universalistic potential, and of reviving in them what they share with other religions, the *philosophia perennis*. He who understands the fundamental, irreducible unity of the absolute from his own personal experience, also understands and respects the plurality and variety of its interpretations and approximations: He sees them as indirect references to what he has experienced directly. "The true seer is gifted with a universality of outlook."[28] – "The intuitive seer understands the variety of theological doctrines and codes. They are but attempts to express the inexpressible, to translate into human words the music of the divine."[29] Understanding and concordance which are rooted in religious experience will also lead to understanding and harmony in the social and political sphere. The fact that Hinduism is the religion of experience par excellence implies, in Radhakrishnan's view, that it is conducive to democracy and international reconciliation. In a characteristic sequence of his *The Hindu View of Life*, perhaps the most concise and eloquent statement of his Neo-Hindu ideology, he associates the experiential "Hindu solution" in religion with "the spirit of democracy," "conferences and congresses of liberal thinkers," and again with "mysticism" and "experience."[30]

Radhakrishnan speaks about the significance of experience in general, about religious documents which are records of experience, and, more specifically, about Vedic and Vedāntic experiences in the Indian tradition. He speaks about the experiences of others and does not place any veridical claims on specific experiences of his own; apart from a casual and general remark concerning the significance of "spiritual experience" for his own thought,[31] he does not even refer to his own experiences. The same can be said about most other advocates of experience in modern Indian thought. Among them, we may mention Radhakrishnan's slightly elder contemporary R.D. Ranade (1886–1957); his learning and personal enthusiasm revived the mystical and experiential tradition of the "poet saints" of Maharashtra, yet towards the end of his life he stated explicitly "that he had never yet enjoyed the 'unitive experience' described by the great mystics."[32] Even recognized Yogins of contemporary India do not normally claim such higher states as *turīya*, "the fourth (state of consciousness)," for themselves.[33]

7. There are, however, some representatives of modern Hindu thought and life who have become living symbols of the idea of religious experience, and of Hinduism as the religion of experience. Outstanding among these are Sri Ramakrishna (Rāmakṛṣṇa Paramahaṃsa; i.e., Gadādhara Caṭṭopādhyāya, 1836–1886) and Ramaṇa Maharṣi (i.e., Venkaṭaramaṇa Ayyār, 1879–1950). The actual utterances of these two men are certainly very significant and by no means negligible; yet they are only one, and possibly not the most important, aspect of the phenomenon which they represent.

Ramakrishna did not leave behind any written teachings; and his lack of scholastic interests is itself a part of his personal message. Ramaṇa Maharṣi did produce some written works, in addition to his oral teachings; but his often long and sustained silence was at least as important as what he did say. Neither of them took any initiative in spreading their message. Both were claimed and stylized by their followers as sources of authentication and validation of Hinduism in the modern world. For Ramakrishna, we have to mention Keshab Chandra Sen and, of course, the Svami Vivekananda; for Ramaṇa Maharṣi, we may refer to Gaṇapati Śāstrī and T.M.P. Mahadevan:[34] They found in these two masters, or projected into them, what they considered essential for the identity and vitality of Hinduism—the living presence of authoritative experience, the fullness and immediacy of realization.

Compared to the inclusivistic exuberance of Ramakrishna's Tantric Vaiṣṇavism, Ramaṇa Maharṣi represents a more austere type of "pure" Advaita Vedānta. His written and oral statements reflect the "straight Advaitic monism"[35] of the Śaṅkara school, as found, for instance, in the *Vivekacūḍāmaṇi*, which Ramaṇa translated into Tamil. There are virtually no expressions of personal experiences or feelings in these teachings; nor are there attempts to apply Vedānta to the problems of the modern world, or of a concordance of religions. This does, of course, not mean that there is no connection between Ramaṇa Maharṣi and his historical situation.[36]

8. A very different type of modern Vedāntin was Sri Aurobindo (Aurobindo Ghose, Aravinda Ghoṣa; 1878–1950), whose life-time coincides almost exactly with that of Ramaṇa Maharṣi. He was a theoretician and systematizer as well as a practitioner of experience, combining in a unique way speaking about experience with his own inner experimentation; and moreover, he responded very explicitly and extensively to his historical situation and the Western challenge.[37]

Aurobindo has been called a "mystic empiricist in that he would count particular extraordinary experiences as providing important data for his metaphysical theory-building."[38] It is indeed obvious that Aurobindo is trying to respond to the Western achievements in the natural sciences, i.e., experimentation in the external world by revitalizing an Indian tradition of inner "experimentation," i.e., experimentation with modes of awareness. Experience in the inner world should supplement and complete that in the outer world, and the results of both should ultimately coincide. Aurobindo interprets the Upaniṣads and other Indian texts as records of experience, which ought to be verified by the reader's or the hearer's own experience.[39] Experience in general, including religious experience, must be "verifiable" by similar experiences. In this sense, it is proclaimed as the common ground for a meeting or merger of religion and science. Yet, inner experience has its own rules and standards. That it should be verifiable cannot mean that it should be accessible to public scrutiny by the "average" mind. It requires experiencers who are willing and able to acquire the necessary capacity, to be transformed as subjects of experience, to ascend to higher levels of awareness and being. The following passage from *The Life Divine* illustrates Aurobindo's usage, or usages, of "experience," and his ambiguous attitude towards Western science:

> The greatest inner discoveries, the experience of self-being, the cosmic consciousness, the inner calm of the liberated spirit, the direct effect of mind upon mind, the knowledge of things by consciousness in direct contact with other consciousness or with its objects, most spiritual experiences of any value, cannot be brought before the tribunal of the common mentality which has no experience of these things and takes its own absence or incapacity of experience as a proof of their invalidity or their non-existence. Physical truth of formulas, generalisations, discoveries founded upon physical observation can be so referred, but even there a training of capacity is needed before one can truly understand and judge; it is not every untrained mind that can follow the mathematics of relativity or other difficult scientific truths or judge of the validity either of their result or their process. All reality, all experience must indeed, to be held as true, be capable of verification by a same or similar experience; so, in fact, all men can have a spiritual experience and can follow it out and verify it in themselves, but only when they have acquired the capacity or can follow the inner methods by which that experience and verification are made possible.[40]

9. The reconciliation of Eastern mysticism and Western science, of meditation and scientific experimentation, the spiritualization of science and the scientific verification of religion—such and similar ideas have often been articulated, or at least tacitly accepted, in the history of the encounter and dialogue between India and the West, by Indians as well as by Westerners. And as the success of such publications as F. Capra's *The Tao of Physics*, recent developments in Maharishi Mahesh Yogi's "Transcendental Meditation" and numerous related phenomena indicate, they are currently more popular than ever.

How does all this relate to or compare with traditional Indian thought? What was the role of "experience" in the Indian tradition prior to its encounter with the West? Are there original Indian concepts corresponding to the breadth and ambiguity of "experience?"

There can be no doubt that India has produced an extremely rich and complex legacy of ideas, doctrines, methods and practices related to religious, meditational, and in general inner experience. There has been much fascination—expressed at different levels of discourse—with phenomena of immediate awareness, modes of consciousness, and the transformative potential of knowledge and realization, i.e., with the possibility of changing or transforming the subject of cognition instead of merely clarifying and mastering its objects.

The "vision" of the Vedic poets, the Upaniṣads, the traditions of Yoga and Buddhism, *turīya* speculations, Kashmir Śaivism (specifically the Pratyabhijñā school), Gauḍīya Vaiṣṇavism, the declarations of the so-called poet-saints of Maharashtra—all this illustrates the role of "experience," "awareness" and so forth in Indian thought. The Upaniṣads show an early interest in the states or levels of awareness—waking, dreaming, sleeping and beyond. The very title of the Buddha, the former Siddhārtha Gautama, indicates an event of awakening, a radical transformation of awareness. The Gauḍīya Vaiṣṇavas combine modes of religious realization with aesthetic feelings and emotions. The Śaivites of Kashmir, in particular Utpaladeva and Abhinavagupta, glorify consciousness and internality; and in various ways, the absolute or divine itself is identified with the pure immediacy of awareness.

The Buddhist and other traditions have been legitimized by referring to "experiences" and "visions" of their founders. The Buddha was credited with personal accounts of what happened to him during the night of his enlightenment on the banks of the river Nairañjanā; his teaching was characterized as "description of the path seen by himself" (*svadṛṣṭamārgokti*)[41] and contrasted with the traditionalism of the followers of the Veda. Other religious groups interpreted their sacred and authoritative texts as expressions of higher states of awareness, of realization and experience of divine teachers, in particular Viṣṇu. For instance, the *Bhāgavatapurāṇa* was often interpreted as Viṣṇu's *samādhibhāṣā*, a text coming out of God's deep concentration.[42]

10. Indeed, this is a rich tradition of "religious" and "inner experience." But does it support the more specific claims of such modern Hindu thinkers as Radhakrishnan? And is it really a tradition of "mystical empiricism?" Which are the original Indian terms and concepts with which such claims have been associated? The Neo-Hindu advocates of experience mention several original Sanskrit terms as corresponding to what they call "ex-

perience," in particular *anubhava, anubhūti* and *sākṣātkāra*; as we have seen, *darśana* is also a familiar term in this connection. In a more general sense, the whole vocabulary of immediate awareness and manifestation (*prakāśa, svaprakāśa, cit, saṃvit, svasaṃvedana*, and so forth) may be referred to.—On the other hand, M. Monier-Williams had characteristic difficulties with his entry "experience" in his *Dictionary, English and Sanskrit* (1851). In addition to *anubhava*, he lists another set of terms which are obviously supposed to correspond to the modern scientific usages of "experience," as well as the connotations of expertise and so on (*parīkṣā, abhyāsa, pūrvābhyāsa*, as "knowledge derived from trials;" even *ācāra*, "experience as practice"). Monier-Williams' article illustrates once again the wide semantic scope and the peculiar ambiguities of "experience."

How do such terms as *anubhava, anubhūti* or *sākṣātkāra*, which modern authors frequently invoke as equivalents of "experience," function in traditional Indian literature? Are there differences between the traditional and the modern applications? Are there significant variations in the traditoinal usage itself?

Most of the leading spokesmen of Neo-Hinduism, among them Radhakrishnan, are advocates of Vedānta, specifically Advaita Vedānta. Śaṅkara is its central figure, and his thought is very frequently presented as the philosophical culmination of Hinduism, the religion of experience. And explicitly or implicitly, the concept of experience appears as the key to his thought. Western authors, too, often try to interpret Śaṅkara's Advaita Vedānta as a philosophy of experience, although few go as far as Eliot Deutsch in his book *Advaita Vedanta: A Philosophical Reconstruction* (Honolulu, 1969).

How does Śaṅkara himself deal with experience? How does he use the terms *anubhava, anubhūti, sākṣātkāra, darśana*, and so on?

11. K.S. Murty, whose interpretation of Advaita Vedānta is conspicuously different from that of Neo-Vedānta, states: "Śaṇkara nowhere claims that his doctrine is the fruit of the experimental science of mysticism."[43] The *Brahmasūtrabhāṣya*, the great Upaniṣad commentaries, and the *Upadeśasāhasrī* confirm this statement: Śaṅkara does not base any veridical claims upon personal experiences of his own; he does not even speak about them. Does he refer to the experiences of others in order to support the truth of non-dualism? Śaṅkara's ultimate authority in matters of metaphysical and soteriological significance is the Veda, specifically the Upaniṣads. Radhakrishnan and the Neo-Vedāntins see these texts as primeval documents of experience, the recorded experiences of the "seers" (*ṛṣi*). Does Śaṅkara's reliance on the Vedic revelation (*śruti*) mean that he, too, recognizes the personal experiences of the Vedic "seers" as the

validating ground, the ultimate source of legitimacy for his tradition of non-dualism?

Śaṅkara, the great *Uttaramīmāṃsaka*, accepts the principle of *apauruṣeyatva*, i.e., the authorlessness of the Veda, as developed by his Pūrvamīmāṃsā predecessors. The Veda and the Upaniṣads, Śaṅkara's main source of inspiration, do not record anybody's personal experiences. They are an eternal, impersonal structure of soteriologically meaningful discourse.

Śaṅkara uses such terms as *anubhava* rarely and cautiously. But this does not mean that experience is not very significant for his thinking and his interpretation of the Veda. On the contrary—the Upaniṣads are texts which teach or indicate the knowledge of *brahman* (*brahmajñāna*), and that means ultimate experience. Śaṅkara uses the example of sense perception, of the sheer perceptual, experiential givenness of something, in order to illustrate the nature of *brahmajñāna* and to distinguish it from anything that can be produced or pursued by human action. However, that experience which the Veda itself teaches as a transcendent soteriological goal, the sheer undisguised presence of *brahman*, should not be confused with "personal experiences" or "observations" which one might use as evidence for or against the Veda. The Veda reveals *brahman* and its modes of presence; and it legitimizes *anubhava* as a mode of access to it.

12. Instead of being a documentation of subjective experience, the Veda is an objective structure which guides, controls and gives room to legitimate experience, as well as legitimate argumentation. Śaṅkara compares the Veda to a sun which shines into the world of appearance, orienting man towards what transcends such appearance and making true seeing possible. It is an objective, transpersonal epiphany, an authorless, yet didactically well-organized body of soteriological instruction, which distinguishes between different levels of qualification, eligibility or mandate (*adhikāra*). It adjusts its message, in its work and knowledge portions, accordingly. Although its ultimate message is that of the unity and identity of *ātman* and *brahman*, it carefully structures the path towards such unity through the multiplicity of appearance.[44]

Acceptance of and commitment to the objective structure of Vedic revelation are central for Śaṅkara and certainly more than a concession to historical and cultural circumstances. It is within such acceptance that he finds room for reasoning and argumentation, as well as for meditation and the veridical use of personal, subjective experiences. As a follower of Uttaramīmāṃsā, Śaṅkara inherited and continued the critical attitude toward extraordinary experiences, yogic states of awareness, and so forth, which had been developed in Pūrvamīmāṃsā, particularly by Kumārila. Kumārila's rejection of "yogic perception" (*yogipratyakṣa*) is well-known.

Perhaps less familiar is his critique of such "inner" principles of orientation as "inner consent" or the "voice of the heart or conscience" (*ātmatuṣṭi, hṛdayakrośaṇa*).[45] It is a fundamental presupposition of Pūrvamīmāṃsā that its subject matter, *dharma*, "ritual duty," cannot be experienced or ascertained by any faculty of the human mind. It has to be derived from the Veda.[46] The claims of independent personal experience in this area are inevitably spurious and conducive to heterodoxy. Śaṇkara does not deal with *dharma*; in his view, the Vedic revelation relates ultimately to what *is and always has been*, the non-dual reality of *brahman*. For him, this is very significant insofar as the applicability of reasoning and the appropriateness of experience are concerned.

13. In Śaṅkara's words, the Veda itself, in its "knowledge portion," indicates its "alliance with human cognition" (*puruṣabuddhisāhāyya*), and this leaves room for experience, *anubhava*, as well. Śaṅkara adds:

> In the inquiry into *brahman*, Vedic and other authoritative texts are not, as in the inquiry into *dharma*, the only source of knowledge; but rather, it is the Veda and so on, and also, as far as possible, *anubhava* and so forth, since the knowledge of *brahman* culminates in *anubhava* and deals with an already existing entity (*na dharmajijñāsāyām iva śrutyādaya eva pramāṇam brahmajijñāsāyām, kiṃ tu śrutyādayo 'nubhavādayaś ca yathāsaṃbhavam iha pramāṇam, anubhavāvasānatvād bhūtavastuviṣayatvāc ca brahmajñānasya*).

This passage from the *Brahmasūtrabhāṣya* 1, 1,2 is as significant as it is ambiguous and elusive. How does Śaṅkara use the word *anubhava*? Does he invoke a special "intuition" or "mystical experience" of *brahman*? Does the word have the same meaning in both usages? Śaṅkara resumes this topic in the second *adhyāya*, first by introducing an opponent in II, 1,4, who claims that reasoning (*yukti*) should be more appropriate for the knowledge of *brahman* than scriptural instruction, since it is closer to *anubhava*; in an obvious reference to I 1,2, the *pūrvapakṣin*, too, characterizes the knowledge of *brahman* as "culminating in *anubhava*" (*anubhavāvasāna*), and he adds that the Veda itself encourages reasoning. In II, 1,6, Śaṅkara responds by emphasizing that the Veda does not legitimate independent "dry reasoning" (*śuṣkatarka*), and that only such reasoning which supports the Veda can be relied on as being conducive to *anubhava* (*anubhavāṅgatvena-āśriyate*).

Again, what is the meaning of *anubhava* in these statements? How does Śaṅkara use it elsewhere?

Anubhava and corresponding verb forms appear in statements about "experiencing" pain, "being in" states of consciousness, such as waking and dreaming,[47] "realizing" or "comprehending" the meanings of words and sentences,[48] but also in the compound *ātmānubhava*, "experience of the self," which is said to be *free* from all pain (*sarvaduḥkhavinirmukta*).[49] On the other hand, *anubhava* is used in an absolute sense, as "experience," "immediate awareness," "self-presencing" *per se*; we hear about a "seeing" (*dṛśi*) which has the "nature of immediate awareness" (*anubhavātman*),[50] about the absolute or *brahman* as *anubhavātmaka*,[51] or simply about *anubhava* as such in a sense which commentators unanimously paraphrase as *sākṣin*, "absolute witness" or "self."[52]

It is obvious that Śaṅkara uses the word *anubhava* at different levels of reflection and in accordance with his hierarchy of "conventional" and "absolute" truth. There is "wrong" and "right,"[53] provisional and absolute experience. Yet, there is a common denominator; even false *anubhava*, which implies superimposition and false identification of self and non-self, is still *anubhava*, containing the element of immediate presence, in which being and knowing, subject and object coincide.[54] Insofar, any act of perception or awareness can remind us of, and help us to approach, that absolute and ultimate experience which according to the Upaniṣads coincides with the being of *brahman* itself.

In all this, Śaṅkara does not invoke any extraordinary "psychological events," and he does not try to validate the truth of non-dualism by referring to "visionary" or "mystical" experiences of extraordinary persons. Instead, he reflects on the nature of self-awareness and immediacy, as it is present even in ordinary life, and he tries to find in it what the Upaniṣads teach explicitly. However, he insists that without the guidance of revelation such reflection would not be able to uncover the true, i.e., non-dual nature of "experience" and the self.[55] He projects absolute *anubhava*, i.e., *brahmānubhava* or *brahmabhāva* as a soteriological goal, which is by definition transpersonal and transworldly. He never refers to such "experience" as an actual worldly occurrence which could be used as empirical evidence for the truth of non-dualism. There are no worldly "empirical data" for what transcends the horizon of worldly cognition.[56]

14. Does the fact that Śaṅkara does not report any personal "mystical experiences" imply that he did not have such experiences? Or should we assume that they remained unmentioned because of the impersonal style of Indian *śāstra* literature? Could there still be an unacknowledged reliance on personal experiences and an "unofficial mystical empiricism" which was only superficially covered by the professed Vedic orthodoxy? "Is it likely that Śaṅkara would have put forth the view he has if he had not felt drawn to such a view because of personal experience?"[57]

This may or may not be the case. We do not know; nor do we have to know in order to appreciate Śaṅkara's systematic and historical achievements. There is no need to question Śaṅkara's deep existential commitment to experience as transcendence; but such experience is not a subjective state of mind which could be brought about by mental, meditational acts (*mānasī kriyā*); and it is not opposed to accepting the Veda as an objective epiphany, i.e., as self-revelation of that very reality which is supposed to be the content of the culminating experience.[58] The historically and philosophically significant question is not whether or how Śaṅkara privately valued "personal experience," but why and how he tried to anchor it in a text, the Veda, and how he experienced this text itself as an objective revelation or epiphany which guides and anticipates all legitimate "personal" experiences, but also transcends itself by relegating itself to the world of appearance and teaching its own ultimate irrelevance.[59] And whatever he may have owed to "experiences"—he certainly did not advocate an "empiricism," a systematic openness for the accumulation of empirical observations; nor did he collect "psychological data" to establish the "theory" of Advaita Vedānta.[60]

Śaṅkara's disciple and commentator Padmapāda pursues the phenomenology of immediate awareness (*anubhava*) further than his master; and he comes closer to seeking in its immediacy independent, extra-scriptural confirmation for the absolute unity of the self: Immediacy or self-evidence (*aparokṣatā*) as such is always one and the same in different acts of awareness and perception; and the immediacy which is attached to objects (in sense-perception) is not different from inner immediate experience, since the same character of self-evidence is manifest in them (. . . *antaraparokṣānubhavāt na viṣayasthā-aparokṣatā bhidyate, ekarūpaprakāśanāt*).[61] Accordingly, experience (*anubhava*) itself, which is of the nature of immedicay, is one and the same with regard to all individuals (. . . *anubhavo 'parokṣatayā sarvān praty aviśiṣṭo 'pi*);[62] and it must ultimately be identical with the self-luminous (*svayaṃjyotis*) "witness" or self (*ātman*).[63]

Padmapāda's argumentation, which is based upon a phenomenology of immediacy and deals with the nature of experiencing as such, is obviously different from any mystical reliance on extraordinary experiences. As a matter of fact, Padmapāda never refers to such special experiences. And Śaṅkara's other great disciple, Sureśvara, reminds us once more of the ambiguity and unreliability of experiences: *Anubhava* which is not guided by scripture does not speak for its own truth, as the experience of the conch-shell as silver exemplifies; it can be valid or invalid, depending on its agreement or non-agreement with its object.[64]

15. "Personal experiences," whether occurring in one's own mind or reported by others, are variable, open to different interpretations and easily misunderstood by those who are still in ignorance. The Buddhists, Jainas, Pāñcarātrins and many others have been led into heterodoxy and confusion by the false claims of "personal experience."[65] Only the authorless, impersonal Veda itself has absolute epistemic authority (*svātantrya, svataḥprāmāṇya*)[66] and can provide unambiguous soteriological guidance.

Śaṅkara's commentator Vācaspati Miśra tries to explain in more detail how and why the testimony of the Veda is epistemologically superior to merely human, personal modes of awareness, such as *anubhava* or *pratyakṣa*, and why it is, in a sense, even more direct and immediate. Any person that has an experience or direct awareness of objects or meanings (*artha*) has to verbalize or articulate what he knows, and must commit and entrust such knowledge to his memory. As Śaṅkara himself says in the passage commented upon by Vācaspati: the authority of teachings which have their origin and basis in human experiences would be "separated" from their source, i.e., the moment of actual experiencing, by the "recollection of the speaker," i.e., the person who articulates them (*vaktṛsmṛtivyavahita*). In the Veda, on the other hand, the verbalization of soteriologically relevant contents is direct and primary, not based upon or mediated by perception and recollection.

Human experience and recollection are subject to the conditions of temporality. *Anubhava* as a state of awareness is only temporarily present. It slips into the past and has to be recalled as recollection and preserved as tradition; and it may be susceptible to questioning and reexamination. The Vedic revelation, on the other hand, speaks in the mode of timeless presence. Its words are not articulations of experiences, and they are not subsequent and subordinate to an awareness of meanings, but prior to such awareness—not only insofar as their validity is concerned, but even from a temporal and psychological angle: The words of the Veda are words per se, not utterances or expressions, and they can speak to those whose minds are open and free for them more directly, and will convince them more quickly, than any statement that articulates an experience and is transmitted by recollection and tradition (*smṛti*). While recollection and experience (*smṛtyanubhavau*) have to be brought in to support and substantiate their verbal expressions, the Vedic statements, which do not need such support, testify immediately and with greater speed to their own truth.

Accordingly, the message of *smṛti*, i.e. of traditional teachings based upon experience and recollection, "is set aside by *śruti* which functions more quickly, immediately" (*śīghratarapravṛttayā śrutyā smṛtyartho bādhyata iti*).[67]

16. The Mīmāṃsā attitude towards experience and, more specifically, the views of Śaṅkara or Vācaspati do not represent the Indian tradition as such. The fact alone that *Pūrva* and *Uttara Mīmāṃsā* are so concerned about channeling "experience" in the proper fashion, about showing its limits and possible misuses, about subordinating it to the authority of the Veda, indicates how controversial and problematic this issue was in the Indian tradition. Even some of the writings traditionally included in the corpus of Śaṅkara's works, though most probably not produced by the author of the

Brahmasūtrabhāṣya, show a different approach. For instance, in the Vedāntic hymns attributed to Śaṅkara, and even the *Vivekacūḍāmaṇi*,[68] personal emotions and visions are more significant and prominent than in the *Brahmasūtrabhāṣya*. This is even more so in numerous theistic traditions of thought, although actual "reports" about personal experiences in the first person singular are not very common. The glorification of personalized *anubhava* which we find among the "poet-saints" of Maharashtra, most conspicuously in Tukārāma,does not have many parallels;[69] if it occurs, it is usually expressed in poetry and not in prose discourses. The theistic philosophers, such as Rāmānuja or Madhva, are generally more cautious than the religious poets (including the poets of the *Ṛgveda*). Rāmānuja states categorically that not only ordinary perception, but also Yogic perception cannot provide access to *brahman*: "Nor again, perception based on Yoga; for although such perception — which springs from intense imagination — implies a vivid presentation of things, it is, after all, nothing more than a reproduction of objects perceived previously, and does not therefore rank as an instrument of knowledge . . ."[70]

The Buddhists themselves, the greatest and most consistent champions of personal experience in the history of Indian philosophy, are acutely aware of the hazards of experience. Dharmakīrti and others discuss in detail the potential deceptiveness of states of awareness, including Yogic states, and they try to determine criteria such as *sphuṭatva*, "clarity," which can help distinguish true Yogic perception from mere hallucinations.[71] — Concerning the concept of *anubhava*, the great Madhyamaka commentator, Candrakīrti states that "experience" is no basis for valid argumentation; it may be false, simply because it is experience (*anubhavatvāt*), just like the illusory experiences of those whose visual organs are not functioning properly.[72]

17. Buddhism and other traditions which are built upon the insights and experiences of personal founders encourage their followers to aim at the same experiential goals, at re-living, re-experiencing the original insights. However, this does not imply that they ask them to re-examine or test the claims of the founders in an experimental fashion and to pursue their own independent consciousness research. Following the experiential path of the Buddha does not mean to continue a process of open-ended experimentation and inquiry. There is no "empiricist" openness for future additions or corrections; there is nothing to be added to the discoveries of the Buddha and other "omniscient" founders of soteriological traditions. In the understanding of their followers, their experiences provide objective standards and frameworks and anticipate all future experiences of their followers. This understanding reflects the traditional and traditionalistic Indian pattern of timeless, eternally complete "branches of learning" (*vidyā*) which leave no room for future-oriented research.[73] There is no programmatic and

systematic accumulation of "psychological" data or observations, no pursuit of fact-finding in the realm of consciousness. Contrary to what Radhakrishnan and others claim, there is no more "inner experimentation" in these traditions, than there is experimentation relating to the "outer" sphere of nature. This does, of course, not at all exclude the possibility of insights and discoveries at least as momentous as anything the modern "scientific method" can provide us with.

Some philosophical teachers and schools claim that the absolute, or the true nature of reality, is revealed in immediate, pre-predicative perception (*nirvikalpakapratyakṣa*). But what is this true and absolute reality? Is it the one absolute being, the "great universal" (*mahāsāmānya*) of the Advaita Vedāntins? Is it the Buddhist universe of momentary particulars (*svalakṣaṇa*)? Is it the world as divided according to the Vaiśeṣika "categories," substance, quality and so forth? Jayanta Bhaṭṭa, the Kashmirian Nyāya philosopher of the ninth century, exposes the fundamental problem implied in such controversies. It is nice to postulate that disagreements ought to be resolved by referring to what is immediately given in pre-predicative perception. But who decides which awareness is truly immediate? In situations where they cannot agree whether something is manifest or not manifest in awareness, people have to resort to swearing (*śapatha*) while trying to convince their opponents.[74] The "dignity of perception" (*pratyakṣasya māhātmyam*) has its limits.[75]

In general, the Naiyāyikas use the term *anubhava* to define perception in its immediacy and, beyond that, to characterize any kind of cognition or insight that is direct and different from memory or recollection (*smṛtibhinnaṃ jñānam*).[76] The difficulties inherent in the Nyāya notion of *anubhava* or *sākṣātkāra*, and the ideas of "directness" and "immediacy," have been exposed in the great masterpiece of polemical, reductive Advaita Vedānta, Śriharṣa's *Khaṇḍanakhaṇḍakhādya*.[77]

The Nyāya-Vaiśeṣika tradition itself has not failed to distinguish very clearly between psychological factuality and epistemological validity. A state of mind or mode of awareness merely as such is neither valid nor invalid. The Nyāya-Vaiśeṣika terms for "cognition" and "experience"—*jñāna, buddhi, pratyaya* and also *anubhava*—refer to an attribute (*guṇa*) of the soul, which is epistemologically or verdically neutral. The question of truth and validity cannot be answered by referring to a mental event as such and in isolation; coherence, practical efficiency, and so forth have also to be taken into consideration in order to determine its truth-value.

All this exemplifies the extent of critical reflection upon experiences and phenomena of immediate awareness in the Indian tradition. India has not simply been fascinated with experiences and visions. It has also produced much analytical thought about their veridical status, and about the nature of experiencing and the immediacy of awareness as such.

18. The role of the concept of experience in Neo-Hinduism is not a mere continuation or extension of that of *anubhava* and similar notions in traditional Hinduism. The changes are not only a matter of emphasis; they reflect a radically new situation—the encounter of the Indian tradition with Western science and philosophy; and they represent one of the most exemplary cases of reinterpretation and revision of the tradition in response to Western ideas and perspectives.

It is evident that Radhakrishnan's conspicuous references to "spiritual experience" find little support in the works of Śaṅkara or others whose authority he invokes. Why then did he give so much prominence to "experience?" Which were the sources of his peculiar understanding of "religious experience," and of his interpretation of the tradition?

Paul Hacker has suggested that Radhakrishnan's inspiration and information concerning "spiritual experience" came not so much from Hindu sources, but from contemporary Western literature, specifically *The Varieties of Religious Experience* by William James, from which Hacker quotes the statement that "personal religious experience has its root and centre in mystical states of consciousness."[78] Hacker has not dealt with the implications of his equally casual and provocative suggestion, and he has made no attempt to investigate in detail the background of Radhakrishnan's use of "experience" and to answer such questions as the following ones: Did Radhakrishnan have predecessors among modern Hindu thinkers? Which specific Western sources, apart from W. James, were important for him? When and how did the concepts of "religious" and "spiritual" experience emerge in the "dialogue" between India and the West?

And in general, very little has been done to document and clarify the history of the concept of experience in modern Hindu thought and its encounter with the West.

19. It has become customary to present Rammohan Roy (1772–1833) as the "father of modern Indian thought;" his work is, indeed, the first fully explicit Hindu response to the challenges of Western thought and Christian religion. Rammohan tries to meet these challenges by rediscovering the "original" spirit of Hinduism and by revitalizing a forgotten potential of Hindu universalism. In doing so, he does not pay much attention to "experience." It is obviously not very significant for him in his attempt to articulate Hinduism, and in particular Vedānta, for the modern world.[79]

Rammohan does not refer to his own personal experiences, nor does he interpret the Upaniṣads (whose pioneer translator he was) as documenting the experiences of "seers." This is, however, different when we turn to the second major figure in the history of the Brāhma Samāj, its most effective reorganizer and, in a sense, its second founder: Debendranath Tagore (Devendranātha Ṭhākura, 1817–1905), father of the poet Rabindranath Tagore.[80] He poses the question of the authority and legitimacy of the sacred Hindu texts, the Upaniṣads in particular, in a new sense, and much more sharply than Rammohan, and he tries to determine which traditional texts deserve recognition as authoritative sources of the "religion of the devotees of *brahman*" (*brāhma dharma*). He rejects Śaṅkara's commentaries on the Upaniṣads, as well as other texts which had been accepted as authoritative by Rammohan. The texts themselves do not provide us with a criterion of their legitimacy: Debendranath finds this criterion in his own "pure heart, filled with the light of intuitive knowledge" (*ātmapratyayasiddhajñānojjvalita viśuddha hṛdaya*).[81]

Only those texts deserve to be recognized as authoritative which are confirmed by the testimony of the heart, i.e., one's own inner experience. The Upaniṣads are documents of what the ancient seers (*ṛṣi*) have experienced as well as examined (*parīkṣita*), and they invite and challenge us to perform our own "examinations of the heart" (*hṛdayer parīkṣā*) or "inner experiments."[82] Accordingly, Debendranath tried to place himself in the position of a *ṛṣi* and to re-experience and examine what is authentic and verifiable in the Upaniṣads, thus effectively substituting his own "intuition" for scriptural authority.[83] Whatever inspiration Debendranath may have received from Indian sources, specifically from medieval Bengali mysticism[84], it is evident that European epistemological concepts and motivations have also played their role in his search for personal experience. In its own way, this search reflects the modern European commitment to certainty, self-evidence and personal authentication of accepted truths. More specifically, Debendranath seems to have been influenced by the concepts of self-evident truths, intuitive certainty and common sense which we find in the works of Th. Reid, Dugald Stewart, W. Hamilton and other proponents of the so-called Scottish School of Common Sense.[85] He tried to prove that these principles can be applied in the area of religion, and that they were not unknown to the teachers of the Upaniṣads. *Ātmapratyaya*,[86] used in the sense of "intuitive certainty" and associated with the Western concept of "self-evidence," is Debendranath's central epistemological concept. Since 1855, he distinguished between two modes of *ātmapratyaya* or "self-evidence:" 1. *svataḥsiddha ātmapratyaya*, i.e., immediately convincing and "uncriticized" self-evidence; 2. *vijñānamūlaka ātmapratyaya*, i.e., "criticized" self-evidence which has been subjected to critical examination and reflection. *Ātmapratyaya* as such is the immediate testimony of our consciousness or self-awareness (*ātmacaitanyer pramāṇa*); in accordance with the principles of the "School of Common Sense", and unlike the Cartesian "Cogito," it provides certainty not only with reference to one's own consciousness, but also with reference to the existence of the world, religious truths, etc.[87]

20. All "criticized," "examined" self-evidence is ultimately based upon certainty and self-evidence which is "uncriticized" and "natural" (*svābhāvika*). Debendranath also uses the expression *sahaja jñāna*, "innate cognition," to characterize the immediate certainty associated with the "intuitions" of "common sense."

Keshab Chandra Sen later on used *sahaja jñāna* as a Bengali equivalent of "intuition" and defined it as the "basis of Brahmoism:" "Intuition denotes those cognitions which our nature immediately apprehends—those truths which we perceive independently of reflection."[88]

Debendranath's approach to the Upaniṣads foreshadows Aurobindo's "mystical empiricism" which requires experimental verification of Upaniṣadic statements and "does not accept everything in the Upaniṣads as well-founded in mystic experience."[89]

In his *Brāhmadharmagrantha*, which was meant as a religious source book for the Brāhma Samāj, Debendranath collected what he considered authentic documents of religious experience almost exclusively from Hindu sources. It was Debendranath's partner and counterpart in the history of the Brāhma Samāj, Keshab Chandra Sen (1838–1884), who came to represent the transcultural, universalistic and syncretistic potential of the movement.[90] Keshab was ready to find genuinely inspired sources and documents of intuition and experience in all religious traditions. In his contemporary Gadādhara Caṭṭopādhyāya, better known as Sri Ramakrishna, or Rāmakṛṣṇa Paramahaṃsa (1838–1886), he saw a modern incarnation of the inclusivistic and harmonizing power of religious experience.

Although the contributions of Bengal were most conspicuous in this period of modern Hindu thought, there were other advocates of "religious experience" and "immediacy" in other parts of India. In Maharashtra, Viṣṇu Bhikājī Gokhale, known as Viṣṇubāvā Brahmacārī (1825–1892) played an important role. "Rāmakṛṣṇa Paramahaṃsa became prominent only after 1870. Before him Viṣṇubāvā Brahmacārī explained that religious experience, immediate experience of God or visionary experience is the basis of religion."[91] In South India, Appaya Dīkṣita the Younger (second half of nineteenth century), wrote a series of Sanskrit treatises on the "non-dualism of experience" (*Anubhavādvaitaprakaraṇa, Anubhūtimīmāṃsāsūtra* with *Bhāṣya*, etc.), which give the concept of *anubhava* much more prominence than traditional Advaita Vedānta.[92]

21. In the meantime, the concept of experience was gaining significance and becoming more conspicuous in European religious thought. A. Schopenhauer referred to the "inner experiences" ("innere Erfahrungen") of religious seers and mystics which he found to be homogeneous or even identical "in spite of the greatest variety of their historical periods, countries and

religions."[93] In the later nineteenth and earlier twentieth century, an increasing number of Western authors used the term "experience" in a sense which was compatible with, and in several cases directly influential upon, the thought and terminology of Radhakrishnan and other Neo-Hindus.

We already cited Hacker's reference to W. James, whose highly successful book *The Varieties of Religious Experience* was first published in 1902 and reached its twenty-fourth edition as early as 1913. James had some major disagreements with a British thinker who gained special fame and recognition in India and whom Radhakrishnan mentions as one of his major influences:[94] F.H. Bradley. Bradley introduced some very peculiar usages of the word "experience." Without ever referring to Indian thought, Bradley spoke about "immediate experience," "absolute experience," and so forth,[95] in a manner which was very appealing to the Neo-Vedāntins, although it was criticized by S.N. Dasgupta.[96] Not surprisingly, Bradley's thought has often been compared with that of Śaṅkara.[97] Radhakrishnan also mentions H. Bergson as a thinker who impressed him; and it is obvious that Bergson's concept of "intuition" is relevant in the present context. Radhakrishnan discusses it in some detail in his book *The Reign of Religion in Contemporary Philosophy* (1920).[98] Another name which has to be mentioned is that of the Baron F. von Hügel, a German nobleman who lived in England and wrote mostly in English. Von Hügel may be less famous than James and Bradley, but he represents a remarkable attempt within liberal Catholicism to come to terms with Non-Christian religions by utilizing the concept of experience.[99] Radhakrishnan cites him repeatedly.[100] Generally, von Hügel did not say or know much about Indian religions. But he wrote an article on the Sādhu Sundar Singh, a Sikh who converted to Christianity[101] and whose accounts of religious experiences made him famous in Europe for some time around 1920. Von Hügel's friend, F. Heiler wrote a monograph on Sundar Singh in which he praised his "experimental theology" ("theologia experimentalis") as a genuine and precious gift which Western Christianity should gratefully accept from the Indian tradition.[102]

Liberal Christian missionaries in India have expressed similar views: Christians should learn from the Indian orientation towards inner experience and the inner life, in order to appreciate neglected areas of Christianity itself. They should learn from the Vedānta those "terms and modes of expression" which will enable them "to express the more immanental aspects of Christianity."[103] Few, however, went as far as the Benedictine monk H. Le Saux (1910–1973), who immersed himself into Upaniṣadic "experience," became an admirer of Ramaṇa Maharṣi and lived the life of a Hindu *saṃnyāsin* under the name Abhiṣiktānanda.

22. As we have noticed, the Neo-Hindu appeal to religious or mystical experience often involves the claim that religion can and should be scientific,

and that Hinduism, and Vedānta in particular, has a scientific and experimental basis. The concept of experience has thus become one of the most significant devices for presenting and interpreting the Hindu tradition to a world dominated by science and technology. Westerners, too, have been attracted by this idea: "Experience," with its suggestive ambiguity and its broad range of connotations, seems to indicate a possible reconciliation or merger of science and religion, providing religion with a new measure of certainty and science with a new dimension of meaning.

For the Hindu tradition, the encounter with modern science and technology was the most momentous part of its encounter with the West. Since India opened itself to European ideas, i.e., since the beginning of the nineteenth century, at least three basic models have been developed and variously utilized in order to cope with the fundamental challenge of science and technology:

1. There is a model of mutual supplementation or even exchange, which was prepared by Rammohan Roy and developed and popularized by Keshab Chandra Sen, Vivekananda and others. It postulates that India should accept the superiority of Western science and technology, but that it might well reciprocate with higher religious and spiritual insights. In the words of Vivekananda, "spiritual adjustment" should come from the Orient, and expertise in "machine-making" from the Occident.[104]

2. A related, yet different model recognizes the Europeans as superior explorers of the external, physical world, but presents the Indians as greater and equally scientific experts of the inner, mental sphere, the realm of consciousness and the self. This was advocated, for instance, by Aurobindo and S. Radhakrishnan, but also by Vivekananda.[105] – In this connection, we may also refer to the recent attempts to find "external" experimental confirmation for "inner" meditational experiences and to prove the concordance of both approaches – as, for instance, among the advocates of "Transcendental Meditation."

3. There is the claim that India is the original homeland of science and technology, and that Westerners ultimately owe their expertise in this field to Indian sources. By opening itself to scientific progress, India – according to this model – only rediscovers its own forgotton roots. Most explicitly and conspicuously, this has been advocated by Dayānda Sarasvatī and his followers in the Ārya Samāj.

23. For some time, the founders of the Theosophical Society, Mme. H.P. Blavatsky and Col. H.S. Olcott, tried to affiliate their movement with the Ārya Samāj. These attempts did not have lasting success. Still, the Theosophists were among the most persistent advocates of a meeting or merger of ancient Eastern wisdom and modern science, or of the idea of an original, primeval, primarily Eastern wisdom and experience in which science and religion are one. The movement of G. Gurdjieff and P.D. Ouspensky, which had various personal and doctrinal ties with Theosophy,

went further in propagating the agreement between ancient mystical and meditative experiences and the results of modern mathematics ("transfinite mathematics"), "metageometry" and theoretical physics. "We have seen that *mathematics* has already found a way into this higher order of things. Penetrating there, it first of all renounces its *fundamental axioms* of identity and difference. . . . Before Bacon and before Aristotle, in ancient Indian scriptures there were given formulae of that higher logic which unlocked the doors of the mysteries."[106]

Much more serious and significant was the work of Sir John Woodroffe (alias Arthur Avalon), Chief Justice in Bengal and, in a sense, a British Neo-Hindu. In the first decades of the twentieth century, he was one of the most vigorous advocates of the experiential and experimental nature of Indian religious thought, specifically Tantric thought and methodology; and he proclaimed its ultimate coincidence with modern science. According to Avalon, the Indian religious teachers based their philosophy upon "experiments;" and he states that Vedāntic and Tantric thought "is in conformity with the most advanced scientific and philosophical thought of the West, and that where this is not so, it is science which will go to Vedānta and not the reverse."[107] Speaking about the Tantric non-dual absolute, Avalon frequently invokes the concepts of "pure experience" and "perfect experience" in a sense which reminds us of F.H. Bradley's use of "experience."[108]

Some recent programmatic statements by followers of Maharishi Mahesh Yogi sound like applications of Avalon's ideas. They proclaim a "unified field" as the common datum of deep meditation and experimental science. The meditator should verify the laboratory experiments of the physicist through his "personal experience of the unified field in the self-referral state of consciousness."[109] Maharishi's "technology of experience" is supposed to ensure the coincidence of "inner" realization and external, object-oriented experimentation, of "ancient wisdom" and "modern science." Whatever the value of these claims may be—they pursue a certain line of thinking to its end.

The thesis of a deep affinity between "Eastern mysticism" and "modern science" gained new and unprecedented publicity with F. Capra's *The Tao of Physics* (1975). The book has been successful in India as well as in the West; and it exemplifies some of the basic problems of the movement which it has helped to popularize. Capra summarizes the argument of his book "by saying that modern physics leads us to a view of the world which is very similar to the views held by mystics of all ages and traditions."[110] Later on, he explicates this as follows: "In modern physics, the universe is thus experienced as a dynamic, inseparable whole which always includes the observer in an essential way. In this experience, the traditional concepts of time and space, of isolated objects, and of cause and effect, lose their meaning. Such an experience, however, is very similar to that of the Eastern mystics."[111]

24. What does such "similarity" amount to? How can modern physics and Eastern mysticism in general, correspond to, or converge with, one another? Occasionally, Capra suggests that mysticism and science should just supplement "one another for a fuller understanding of the world."[112] But more frequently and conspicuously, he claims that modern science has returned to the views of the ancient Eastern mystics: "This time, however, it is not only based on intuition, but also on experiments of great precision and sophistication, and on a rigorous and consistent mathematical formalism."[113]

Does this mean that the ancient mystics have anticipated modern physics as such, including its more specific results, and that their discoveries have been rediscovered through laboratory experiments? Or does it only mean that there is a general convergence of metaphysical implications? Has what is most modern finally caught up with what is most ancient? Has Western science transcended itself, its own historical roots and conditions, its inherent tendency to dissect and objectify nature and to subject it to technology and human domination? Has it returned to a unity and totality which its own previous developments had denied? Has the restlessness of experimental research merged with the quiet experience and self-manifestation of an undivided absolute?

Capra's scheme of a meeting and merger of modern science and Eastern mysticism is as grand as it is vague and elusive. It disregards the fundamental differences between what the "mystic" and the "modern scientist" do; and it does not recognize the concrete historical situation of which the scientist is an active part. In spite of what Capra suggests, even the so-called "New Physics" remains deeply committed to and dependent upon technology, and it implies and requires that kind of open-ended research and unfulfilled progress which we found to be incompatible with the traditional Indian ideas of knowledge and soteriological experience.

In our introductory remarks, we asked: "Why has the word 'experience' become so conspicuous and important in the encounter between India and the West?" Some of the reasons have become evident in our preceding survey: "Experience" seems to refer to a category transcending the dichotomies of science and religion, the rational and the irrational. It promises a reconciliation of the ancient and the modern. It appeals to the modern fascination with science, but rejects its commitment to objectification and quantification. It is a device of reinterpretation and cultural self-affirmation, which serves to defend the Indian tradition against charges of mysticism and irrationalism.

We also asked the following question concerning the use of "experience" in the encounter between India and the West: "Has its ambiguity created misunderstanding and confusion, or has it opened new perspectives of understanding and mutual challenges?"[114] It is evident that there has been much vague rhetoric and more or less deliberate blurring of conceptual distinctions in the use of "experience." Is this the final word? Is the conclusion of this survey a negative one?

It is easy and tempting to criticize much of what has been going on in Neo-Hindu thought and in the so-called East-West dialogue by invoking conceptual clarity and historical accuracy. But while such criticism may have correctness and precision on its side, it may also be more shallow and parochial than its target. In its eagerness to provide historical corrections and conceptual differentiations it will easily forget what is at stake in the East-West dialogue – its unfulfilled potential, its deeper, though still hidden aspirations.

Historical and hermeneutical criticism and conceptual clarification are indispensable, but they cannot be more than a preface.

22. "Inclusivism" and "Tolerance" in the Encounter Between India and the West

1. "Inclusivism" ("*Inklusivismus*") is the title of a posthumous article by Paul Hacker (1913–1979), and it is a theme which accompanied the Indological research as well as the theological and philosophical thinking of this important scholar for several decades.[1] It gained its greatest and most conspicuous significance during the final years of his life, when he presented this concept as a pervasive, specifically Indian way of dealing with foreign religions and world-views, and when he argued that what appeared to be Indian tolerance was "almost always inclusivism."[2] Hacker's treatment of "inclusivism," together with his penetrating critique of the idea of "tolerance" in the Indian context, exemplifies his personally committed and often provocative approach to classical as well as modern Hinduism and, moreover, his intense critical reflection on the history and the fallacies of the "dialogue" between India and Europe. But in a wider sense, it also illustrates fundamental conceptual and hermeneutical problems, questions concerning the relationship between categories of analysis and devices of self-assertion or critique, and in general between Indological research and the participation in the cultural and religious debate between India and Europe. What has been said about the concept of syncretism—that it "not only describes the encounter of religions, but *is* itself a part of that encounter"[3]—certainly applies to Hacker's concept of inclusivism.

2. Hacker first used the term "inclusivism" and related terms, such as "inclusivistic" ("*inklusivistisch*"), in an article on "tolerance" and "intolerance" in Hinduism which appeared in 1957 and which was based on a lecture delivered in 1956—in a somewhat casual and tentative manner which he criticized in some of his later statements.[4] In this article, Hacker distinguished between "practical tolerance" ("*praktische Toleranz*"), which is a way of human interaction with members of different religious groups, and "doctrinal tolerance" ("*doktrinäre Toleranz*"), which is a manner of

recognizing other religious teachings. Within the domain of "practical tolerance," he distinguished again between the tolerance instituted by a ruler or state, and the "private tolerance" practiced by the individual. Merely factual processes of absorption and assimilation, which are not accompanied by explicit reflection, should not be accepted as cases of "tolerance."[5] Referring to the religious and philosophical literature, Hacker discussed examples often cited as evidence for the "doctrinal tolerance" of Hindusim, such as the identification of the highest principles of different religious and philosophical traditions with the absolute of Vedāntic monism, or the recognition of foreign traditions as preliminary stages. Again, this should not be called "tolerance." Instead, it is "a peculiar mixture of doctrinal tolerance and intolerance" and a "form of religious self-assertion" which seems to be particularly appropriate to the Indian way of thinking[6] Hacker found it exemplified by the "inclusivistic" Vaiṣṇavism of Tulsīdās, who saw Śiva himself as a worshipper of Viṣṇu's incarnation Rāma, and by the even more comprehensive Śākta inclusivism, which presents itself as an all-encompassing ocean of doctrines and traditions. Concerning the concept of tolerance which came to be used by modern Hindu thinkers, Hacker believed that it had its origins in eighteenth-century European Deism, and that its distinguishing feature was a peculiar alliance with the notion of "religious experience." At the same time, inclusivism was still alive among these modern authors. In conclusion, Hacker suggested that the terms "tolerance" and "intolerance" might be useless "slogans" ("*Schlagworte*"), and inappropriate for the description of Hinduism.[7]

3. In a series of subsequent statements, Hacker reiterated, supplemented and modified the observations presented in 1957. In a review article published in 1964, his statements concerning the relationship between "inclusivism" and "tolerance" became more pronounced. He now said that it was one of the functions of the modern uses of the concept of tolerance "to maintain the fiction of a unity of Hinduism," that the practice of inclusivism was "in its essence" ("ihrem Wesen nach") different from tolerance, and that it was a "typically Indian" method of debate and of the promotion of ideas. He found it graphically illustrated by the myth of Śiva-Śarabha who devoured Viṣṇu-Nṛsiṃha, thus bringing about the "unity" of Śaivism and Vaiṣṇavism.[8] Hacker did not entirely exclude the occurrence of "non-inclusivistic" doctrinal tolerance in India, for instance in the work of Jayanta Bhaṭṭa; but it was the exception rather than the rule. In particular, he suggested that the powerful tradition of Vedāntic non-dualism was essentially inclusivistic.[9]

In his lecture on "Aspects of Neo-Hinduism as Contrasted with Surviving Traditional Hinduism" which was delivered in 1970 and published in 1978, Hacker summarizes his views on inclusivism as follows: "It consists in claiming for, and thus including in, one's own religion what really belongs to an alien sect. The most outstanding example of such behavior is perhaps Tulsīdās . . . It seems that this method was employed especially by such religious groups as felt themselves inferior to their environment. — The same method has often been practiced by Neo-Hindus, notably Vivekānanda and Rādhākrishnan."[10] Referring specifically to the inclusivism of Radhakrishnan, Hacker adds:

> Now we must remember that Rādhākrishnan, like more or less all Hindus today, affirms that all religions are equal in their worth or essence or aim. If, however, the hidden goal or centre or essence of all religions is the Vedānta which primarily constitutes the spiritual unity of Hinduism, then all religions are in a way included in Hinduism. This is the most comprehensive application which the principle of inclusivism has ever found. Incidentally, it would perhaps be more accurate to speak of inclusivism in many cases where we are inclined to see Hindu tolerance.[11]

Towards the end of his career, Hacker returned to the theme of "inclusivism" with renewed and even greater intensity. In his last lecture course at the University of Münster (held in 1978 and published posthumously in 1985), he referred to the combination of inclusivism and "gradualism" ("*Gradualismus*," i.e. hierarchization) in Indian thought and suggested that it was a device to cope with the "teeming variety which is the predominant trait of Hinduism."[12] The most significant late statement is, of course, the posthumous article which we mentioned in the introduction to this appendix; it is the published version of a lecture delivered in 1977.

4. A chronological review of Hacker's statements on inclusivism, and a comparison between his earlier observations and the posthumous article, demonstrate a development in which his views became more sweeping and radical. Although he suggests as early as 1957 that the concepts of "tolerance" and "intolerance" might be out of place in dealing with Hinduism, he nevertheless refers in a variety of ways to factual occurrences of tolerance in the history of Hinduism. He characterizes "doctrinal tolerance" as "the most interesting manifestation of toleration in Hinduism,"[13] and he cites several exemplary cases. He does not consider the inclusivistic "practice of affiliating the foreign with what is one's own by way of subordination," this "attitude of inclusive recognition" ("Haltung des inklusiven Geltenlassens")[14] to be utterly incompatible with tolerance; he only characterizes it as a "peculiar mixture of doctrinal tolerance and intolerance." In the review article of 1964, Hacker's depiction of the contrast between inclusivism and tolerance, and of the specific affinity of inclusivism to the Indian mind, becomes more intransigent. And in the preface, which he added in 1978 to the collection of his *Kleine Schriften*, he simply says: "What seems to be tolerance to the European, is almost always inclusivism."[15] The most radical expression of the claim that inclusivism is

an essentially, even exclusively, Indian phenomenomen is found in the posthumous article on "*Inklusivismus*"; unlike earlier contributions, this article gives full consideration to Buddhism as well as Hinduism. Hacker now describes inclusivism as a specifically Indian way of thinking, which he recognized a such "only in the course of two or three decades;" he claims that it is a mental and spiritual attitude which is characteristic of, and exclusive to, "the Indian cultural domain" ("*Kulturkreis*"), and that it is to be found only in this cultural domain, "but not elsewhere" ("anderswo aber nicht").[16] In his concluding remarks, Hacker raises the question whether inclusivism is perhaps a "general human possibility, or whether it is really confined to India." He refrains from an explicit discussion of this question, but suggests once more than inclusivism is, indeed, "confined to India" ("auf Indien beschränkt").[17]

5. From the outset, Hacker's conception of inclusivism has been inseparable from his critique of common and stereotyped ideas of Indian "tolerance," as well as of certain Neo-Hindu views concerning the unity of Hinduism. It was a conception destined to be controversial.

In a monograph published in 1961, J.W. Hauer rejected Hacker's characterization of "tolerance" and "intolerance" as "slogans," and he stated: "When Hacker assumes that the notion of tolerance among the modern Hindu thinkers took its origin from European Deism, then this assertion has to be positively rejected."[18] Hauer treats passages from the *Bhagavadgītā* (especially IX, 22f.), which Hacker cites as examples of inclusivism, as cases of a "hierarchical universal tolerance;" he finds this type of tolerance comparable to the attitude of Western authors like E. Troeltsch, R. Otto, F. Heiler, G. Mensching and J.N. Farquhar.[19] G. Mensching himself, whose name appears in this list, called Hacker's article of 1957 "an essay written not without a certain bias."[20] H. von Glasenapp responded more favorably; although he emphasized the dimension of tolerance in the Indian tradition, he missed "genuine toleration" ("*echte Duldsamkeit*") in Neo-Hindu thought, and he paraphrased Hacker's "inclusivism" as "non-violent fanaticism" ("*gewaltloser Fanatismus*").[21] Other authors have adopted the term "inclusivism" without committing themselves to its more radical implications.[22]

It is evident that Hacker's concept of inclusivism is not merely a descriptive category or a device of "objective" research, and it cannot be measured by the standards of factual, i.e. philological or historical, "correctness" alone. It is also an instrument of the critique of Indian, specifically Neo-Hindu thought, and of an implicit defense of the Christian-European tradition against certain claims and temptations posed by the Indian tradition. It exemplifies a kind of research which is at the same time participation in a living debate, and it has its proper position not only in the history of Indology, but also in the wider historical context of the encounter and dialogue between India and Europe. By setting "inclusivism" against "tolerance," Hacker also responds to a European tradition of perceiving India, and of a concomitant self-understanding and self-critique. The European application of the idea of tolerance to India, and its reception by the Indians, is itself part of a hermeneutic interplay between India and Europe; and it provides the indispensable wider context for the role which "inclusivism" plays in Hacker's work.

6. For a number of centuries, and long before the beginning of modern Indology, Europeans have associated India with ideas of "religious toleration" and "pluralism." Among the missionaries of the early eighteenth century, B. Ziegenbalg made exemplary statements of this kind.[23] In his influential work on India, F. Bernier, one of the best-known travelers of the seventeenth century, presented a Brahmin who declared that the Hindus

> did not claim that their law is universal, that God had made it only for them, and that therefore they could not receive a foreigner into their religion; and moreover, that they did not claim that ours is false, that it was quite possible that it was good for us, and that God could have made several different paths in order to reach heaven; but they did not want to hear that while our religion was universal for the whole earth, theirs could only be fiction and pure invention.[24]

In accordance with Bernier's presentation, I. Kant said about the Hindus:

> They say that their religion is confined to their race and that the Indian is subject to his religion by virtue of his birth . . . They do not hate the other religions, but they believe that they are also right . . . It is a principle of the Indians that every nation has a religion for itself. Hence they force nobody to adopt theirs. When Christian missionaries tell them about Christ, his teachings, his life, and so on, they listen politely and object nothing. But when they begin afterwards to talk about their religion, and when the missionaries get angry at them and object to them as to how they could believe such falsehoods, then the Indians take offence at them and say that they had believed everything, without the missionaries being able to prove their stories, and ask why the missionaries did not likewise believe them.[25]

On the other hand, Kant thought that the Hindu religion gave its followers "the character of pusillanimity" ("den Charakter der Kleinmütigkeit").[26] Some memorable and influential depictions of the "mild" and "tolerant" Hindus are found in the works of J.G. Herder, the forerunner of the Romantic glorification of India.[27]

In 1786, W. Jones, one of the pioneers of modern Indology, observed:

> The Hindus . . . would readily admit the truth of the Gospel; but they contend that it is perfectly consistent with their Sastras: the deity, they say, has appeared innumerable times, in many parts of this world and of all worlds, for the salvation of his creatures; and though we adore him in one appearance, and they in others, yet we

adore, they say, the same God, to whom our several worships, though different in form, are equally acceptable, if they be sincere in substance.[28]

Jones and others contrast this attitude with that of the Muslims. Some of the authors who invoked the tolerance and religious flexibility of the Hindus were personally inclined towards deism, for instance A. Dow, who declared that "whatever the external ceremonies of religion may be, the self-same infinite being is the object of universal adoration."[29]

7. Rammohan Roy, the so-called "father of modern India," rejected the liberal interpretation of Hinduism represented by Jones and others, and he believed that it could be used as a "plausible apology for idolatry."[30]

However, his successors fully endorsed this interpretation, and they combined traditional schemes of concordance (*samanvaya*) with the Western concept of tolerance. The terms "tolerance" and "toleration" became increasingly conspicuous in Neo-Hindu usage, for instance in the works of Vivekananda.

Vivekananda saw his master Ramakrishna, whose religious devotion included Jesus and Mohammed, as the incarnation of the comprehensive openness and toleration of Hinduism; and he proclaimed the non-dualistic "spirituality" of Vedānta as the metaphysical root and basis of universal tolerance and brotherhood, as well as of India's national identity.

India alone was to be, of all lands, the land of toleration and of spirituality . . . in that distant time the sage arose and declared, *ekaṃ sad viprā bahudhā vadanti* (He who exists is one; the sages call him variously). This is one of the most memorable sentences that was ever uttered, one of the grandest truths that was ever discovered. And for us Hindus this truth has been the very backbone of our national existence . . . our country has become the glorious land of religious toleration. . . . The world is waiting for this grand idea of universal toleration. . . . The other great idea that the world wants from us today . . . is that eternal grand idea of the spiritual oneness of the whole universe . . . This is the dictate of Indian philosophy. This oneness is the rationale of all ethics and all spirituality.[31]

Such toleration is at the same time the power to include and absorb other religions. Buddhism, this "gigantic child" of Hinduism, "was absorbed, in the long run, by the mother that gave it birth."[32] Likewise, all other religions and world-views are ultimately included in Vedāntic Hinduism; no external and artificial methods of conversion are needed. In such contexts, Vivekananda used images of inclusion, as well as the word "inclusive" itself: "Ours is the universal religion. It is inclusive enough, it is broad enough to include all the ideals. All the ideals of religion that already exist in the world can be immediately included, and we can patiently wait for all the ideals that are to come in the future to be taken in the same fashion, embraced in the infinite arms of the religion of the Vedānta."[33] – Universal inclusiveness of a somewhat different type was also proclaimed by several spokesmen of modern Vaiṣṇavism: ". . . the concept of Viṣṇu or Kṛṣṇa is so very rich in character and content that while retaining its own uniqueness it includes the various concepts of the object of worship in the other religious sects prevailing here and abroad."[34]

"The Vedānta is not a religion, but religion itself in its most universal and deepest significance." This formula by S. Radhakrishnan,[35] which echoes earlier statements of Neo-Hinduism as well as Madame H. Blavatsky's definition of Theosophy,[36] summarizes his attempts to derive the "tolerance" and "inclusiveness" of Hinduism from the metaphysics of Advaita Vedānta. It also epitomizes his comprehensive universalization and globalization of the traditional, fundamentally Indocentric schemes of concordance and inclusion. As we have noted earlier, Hacker called this "the most comprehensive application which the principle of inclusivism has ever found."[37]

8. The question whether and to what extent there has been "tolerance" in India can obviously have different implications. It can refer to peaceful coexistence and mutual toleration of various forms of religious life as a factual, social phenomenon; or it can refer to an "ideological" phenomenon, the conception and articulation of an idea with normative connotations as well as with specifically modern implications. Inclusivism, on the other hand, is characterized by Hacker as an intellectual "practice," but increasingly also as a "*Denkform*" or "*Denkschema*," i.e. a "form" or "scheme of thought" which is neither a mode of social behavior nor necessarily an explicit and programmatic idea. The article of 1957 already suggests that neither "tolerance" nor "intolerance" should be used in dealing with this phenomenon. Yet Hacker still described in subtle detail what he himself called factual cases of tolerance and intolerance in India, and he did not interpret the relationship between inclusivism and tolerance as an exclusive alternative. But this is what some of his later statements imply. Abandoning his own earlier differentiations, Hacker now suggests that the Indians had inclusivism *instead* of tolerance, that they could not have had both, and that inclusivism has its place only in the Indian tradition and in no other "cultural domain of the world."[38] This polemical radicalization of the notion of inclusivism has caused some understandable confusion and indignation, and it has in general not been conducive to a sober and serious analysis of the phenomenon of inclusivism.[39]

Tolerance as a modern European idea or ideology obviously has implications and ramifications which we do not find in traditional India, and it is important to recall the peculiar historical context in which tolerance in this sense had its origin. The modern European idea of tolerance has gained its special significance in connection with the tensions between different Christian denominations since the period of the Reformation. It has been conceived and articulated in response to religious strife and persecution, i.e. to manifestations of intolerance. Non-Christian religions, which were originally less significant in this context, also came to be included into the debate. The subsequent development of the idea of tolerance culminates in the works of Spinoza, Locke and Voltaire.[40] It is inseparable from modern European secularism, from the separation of church and state, as well as of the private and public spheres, from the ideas of personal freedom and human rights, but also from the growth of relativism and indifferentism.[41] This is something we have to keep in mind when we apply the concept of tolerance to the pre-modern or non-European world. On the other hand, it does not justify the conclusion that such applications should be avoided altogether.

9. After characterizing the specific circumstances of the emergence of "tolerance" in its modern sense, the historian B. Kötting emphasizes: "The problem of the coexistence of followers of different religious views is, however, much older than the modern attempt to circumscribe it by means of the word 'tolerance.'"[42] Kötting deals with European antiquity; but his statement is equally applicable to India. In both cases, the modern concept of tolerance is absent; yet there are not only factual forms of coexistence, but also modes of reflection upon such coexistence, models of reconciliation, and deliberate perspectives of toleration. It would hardly be appropriate in these cases to discard the word "tolerance" as a mere "slogan" ("Schlagwort"). Even if there is no fully explicit conceptualization of tolerance, there can be "lived tolerance" ("gelebte Toleranz") and the "creation of the spiritual presuppositions of tolerance" ("Schaffen der geistigen Voraussetzungen der Toleranz").[43] Regardless of all conceptual ambiguities—there is rich documentation that this has, indeed, been the case in classical India. Hacker himself mentions the religious policy of Aśoka (third century B.C.) as one of the most memorable cases of officially instituted, administrative tolerance; he also refers to Jayanta and his ruler Śaṅkaravarman, and other instances of deliberate programs of coexistence and tolerance.[44]—"Inclusivism" is not "tolerance." But there can certainly be tolerant behavior and "lived tolerance" on the basis of, or in connection with, "inclusivistic" thought. On the other hand, inclusivistic thought does not by itself exclude intolerant actions.

What makes the application of the concept of tolerance to the Indian, specifically the Hindu tradition problematic, is not the presence of inclusivism per se. More important is the fact that traditional Hinduism does not recognize the ideas of man, and of human freedom and equality, which constitute the background of the modern concept of tolerance. Traditional Hinduism presupposes an irreducible, cosmologically established inequality of human beings, and a fundamentally hierarchical structure of society which leaves little room for the mutual recognition of free persons and their individual rights and choices. Divergent and foreign forms of religious behavior and orientation, and religious plurality in general, are recognized and tolerated not as legitimate expressions of personal choice and human autonomy, but as manifestations of different levels of soteriological development.

Tolerance in this context is certainly a tolerance sui generis, but it may still be tolerance. "Hierarchical" or "inclusivistic tolerance" is not a contradiction in terms. Hacker himself did not explore the undeniable connections between "inclusivism" and the pervasive hierarchization of Hindu society. L. Dumont, on the other hand, who gave the classic description of the "homo hierarchicus," referred somewhat casually to the theme of tolerance, noting that the heterogeneity which excludes one group from other groups is the very basis for its integration into the total hierarchical system, i.e. its qualified recognition and toleration.[45]

10. The central and pervasive element in Hacker's definitions and exemplifications of "inclusivism" is the practice of "claiming for, and thus including in, one's own religion" or world-view what belongs in reality to another, foreign or competing system.[46] It is a subordinating identification of the other, the foreign with parts or preliminary stages of one's own sphere. It is not considered to be a process of additive annexation; nor is it a form of syncretism or eclecticism. The other, the foreign is not seen as something that could be added to, or combined with, one's own system; instead, it is something a priori contained in it. Hacker provides a variety of examples which show that there are various types and modificiations of inclusivism. Time and again, he refers to Tulsīdās, the *Bhagavadgītā*, and Radhakrishnan's universalized inclusivism, and he suggests a deep affinity between non-dualism and inclusivism. But he also mentions the Buddhist incorporation of the Vedic pantheon, the Pāñcarātra tradition, and, he invokes the Śaivite Śarabha myth as a graphic illustration of the "practice" of inclusivism. He does, however, not explicitly pursue the systematic ambiguities in the relationship between "one's own" and "the other," "the foreign" system or doctrinal sphere. What is the "intrinsic" sphere, the horizon of identity, for which the other, the foreign is claimed, in which it is supposedly contained and included? "Intrinsic" and "extrinsic" are concepts which can be filled with fundamentally different contents, and which can be utilized at very different levels of reflection.

"One's own sphere" may be a simple theistic faith or a complex theological doctrine; it may represent a specific and well-defined metaphysical and soteriological system, or the attachment to a particular personal God, but also an open, abstract absolutism which avoids or transcends, and thus leaves room for, everything that is definite and particular. What is more, one's "own," the "intrinsic," the horizon and receptacle for any inclusion, is nothing static. It grows and changes in the historical processes of dealing with the other, of trying to supersede it, etc., and it may reflect within itself in a more or less significant manner the relationship to the other. It may itself be the result of dialectics, debate, interaction with other systems, and reflection upon such interaction. The perspectivistic coordination of other views in Mallavādin's version of Jainism is part of its own identity. Nāgārjuna's Madhyamaka Buddhism, and Śaṅkara's or Śrīharṣa's Advaita Vedānta, are what they are insofar as they reflect upon, and transcend and supersede, other systems or viewpoints. When they refer to other systems in an "inclusivistic" fashion, it is certainly not in the sense of that pre-reflexive doctrinal possessiveness for which the Śarabha myth seems to provide an appropriate illustration. In general, Hacker does not discuss the relationship between "inclusivism" and the deliberate transcendence of other doctrines, or of views and doctrines *per se*.

11. The examples which Hacker cites are taken primarily from the religious mythology and poetry of traditional Hinduism, as well as from Neo-Hinduism. References to classical Indian philosophy are less frequent and conspicuous. Occasionally, Hacker even contrasts the procedures of the "great theologians and philosophers of Hinduism and Buddhism," who took conceptual distinctions very seriously, to the inclusivism of the Purāṇas and similar texts on the one hand, and of Neo-Hinduism on the other hand.[47] Yet Śaṅkara, who "included" theism in his own system by subordinating it to his absolutistic non-dualism, is also referred to as an example of inclusivism; and Hacker even suggests a very special affinity between monism and inclusivism.[48]

The differences between classical thinkers, such as Śaṅkara, and Neo-Hindus like Radhakrishnan are, indeed, unmistakable. Śaṅkara draws clear borderlines between what he considers to be true and soteriologically legitimate, and the views of other systems; he discards and excludes what he considers to be false. He explicitly rejects an inclusivistic and hierarchical model used by the Madhyamaka Buddhists, i.e. the view that the *Sarvāstivādins* and *Vijñānavādins* ultimately taught the same truth as the *Śūnyavādins*, but in a didactically adjusted fashion, and that they represent preliminary stages which are ultimately encompassed and fulfilled by the *Śūnyavāda*. Śaṅkara, who is obviously aware that such inclusivistic schemes of didactic gradation can be used to propagate very different doctrines, argues that the diversity of Buddhist teachings only testifies to the Buddha's "incoherent loquacity" (*asambaddhapralāpitva*), or even to a deliberate plan to lead people into confusion.[49]

Unlike later Vedāntins, Śaṅkara himself does not try to construe a didactic hierarchy which would demonstrate the ultimate concordance between the Advaita Vedānta and other systems of thought. In his view, the Veda teaches not only ultimate truth itself, but also the principles of soteriologically relevant didactic gradation. The Vedic instructions are adjusted to different levels of understanding, as well as to different types of motivation and interest. Strict concordance (*samanvaya*) should only be attempted within the exegesis of the Vedic-Upaniṣadic "revelation" (*śruti*), by subordinating all apparently divergent teachings to the doctrine of the absolute unity of *brahman*. In the area of human views and aberrations, no such concordance can be achieved; what is false and soteriologically harmful has to be refuted and discarded.

Yet from another angle, Śaṅkara assumes that even those who do not accept the authority of the Veda and whose views he attacks, are ultimately referring to the reality of the absolute self which is revealed in the Veda. Even the most radical opponents of the Veda and of the Vedāntic notion of the *ātman*, i.e. the Buddhists and the Materialists, somehow "mean" and recognize, though in a highly distorted fashion, what they try to refute in their explicit argumentation. The absolute *ātman* is, after all, the one and only (and everybody's own) reality, and nobody can avoid "meaning" and implicitly recognizing it.[50] In this ultimate sense, Śaṅkara and other Vedāntins subordinate to, and "include" in, their own system what they reject and exclude at another level of thought and argumentation.

12. Hacker himself suggests that the practice of inclusivism can be traced back to the late Vedic hymns, as well as to the Brāhmaṇas and Upaniṣads; he does, however, not explain all instances of "identification" in the Brāhmaṇas and early Upaniṣads as inclusivistic. As one very significant case, which prepares or anticipates later non-dualistic inclusivism, he mentions the *tat tvam asi* and the doctrine of being (*sat*) in the sixth chapter of the *Chāndogya Upaniṣad*. The advocates of the one absolute *sat* claim that all other speculations concerning the self (*ātman*), truth (*satya*), etc., are ultimately included in the doctrine of *sat; ātman* and *satya* themselves are "comprised within being" ("einbegriffen in das Seiende").[51]

It is, however, obvious that the inclusion and subordination of earlier speculations and of competing concepts is only one side of the "inclusivism" which we find in the *Chāndogya Upaniṣad*. What seems to be more important is the subordinating and reductive "identification" of cosmic and physical phenomena, or occurrences of everyday life. The sun, the moon, fire, and so forth, are traced back to being itself; they are explained as being contained in it, as emanating from it, and as ultimately identical with it. The inclusivistic neutralization of all doctrines and concepts by subordinating them to the doctrine of pure, absolute being, and the reductive explanation of all phenomena by tracing them back to this one being cannot be separated. He who knows being (*sat*) as the one substance and principle of all phenomena, also knows the principle of all teaching and understanding; he knows the instruction (*ādeśa*; i.e. method of substitution) "whereby what has not been heard of becomes heard of, what has not been thought of becomes thought of, what has not been understood becomes understood,"[52] i.e. that teaching which includes, neutralizes and anticipates all other teachings. The "form" or pattern of thought is basically identical: The phenomena are traced back to the fundamental cosmological principle *sat* in the same manner in which all specific concepts and teachings are reduced to the all-encompassing doctrine of pure being.

In the present context, there is no need to elaborate on the formal analogies between the reductive explanation of phenomena and the inclusivistic subordination and neutralization of concepts and doctrines. Instead, we will now return to the later and "classical" manifestations of inclusivism in Indian religious and philosophical literature.

13. In addition to the "vertical," hierarchical model of inclusivism, there is also a "horizontal" model, which is typified by the Jaina doxographies. The Jainas present their own system not as the transcending culmination of lower stages of truth, but as the complete and comprehensive context, the full panorama which comprises other doctrines as partial truths or limited perspectives. Although these two models are not always kept apart in doxographic practice, they represent clearly different types of inclusion. The subordination of other views to the Vedāntic idea of *brahman* or the Madhyamaka viewpoint of "emptiness" (*śūnyatā*) postulates an ascent which is at the same time a discarding and transcendence of doctrinal distinctions; the inclusion and neutralization of other views is not a subordinating identification of specific foreign concepts with specific aspects of one's own system, but an attempt to supersede and transcend specific concepts and conceptual and doctrinal dichotomies in general. The Jaina perspectivism, on the other hand, represents a horizontally coordinating inclusivism which recognizes other views as parts and aspects of its own totality.[53] Of course, the Jainas, too, claim a superior vantage point, and a higher level of reflection.

Among the familiar inclusivistic images, we find the metaphor of the many rivers which are united in the one ocean, and that of the footprints of the elephant which obliterate the footprints of all other animals. Adopting a formula which the *Mahābhārata* had used to glorify the ethics of *ahiṃsā*, several Tantric texts declare that the various religious traditions are contained and disappear in the Tantric tradition, specifically in the *kauladharma*, in the same manner in which the footprints of other creatures disappear in those of the elephant.[54] Vijñānabhikṣu, the leading representative of the revival of classical Sāṃkhya and Yoga in the sixteenth century, states that the other systems are contained in the Yoga of Patañjali and Vyāsa just as rivers are preserved and absorbed by the ocean.[55] Both metaphors illustrate the idea of inclusion, but with a significant difference. The ocean extinguishes the individuality of the rivers, but it also preserves them and needs them for its own fullness. The footprints of the elephant simply obliterate the other footprints. This ambiguity is a pervasive and symptomatic phenomenon in the history of inclusivism, and it recalls the fundamental ambiguity in the Hegelian concept of "*Aufhebung*."

14. Hacker claims that inclusivism is a typically, even exclusively Indian phenomenon. To what extent, if at all, can this claim be justified? Hacker himself asks the question whether the use and assimilation of Greek concepts in early Christian thought provides an analogue. In this particular case, we may accept his negative answer.[56] There are, however, other phenomena in late antiquity which seem to be much closer to what Hacker describes, for example the belief of the devotees of Isis that all nations and religious groups ultimately worship Isis, the one universal deity which has many different shapes and names (πολυμορφος; πολυωνυμος, μυριωνυμος).[57] This is obviously an inclusivistic procedure: Whatever others may regard as divine, is identified with and subordinated to Isis. We may also recall the declarations of Stoic philosophers that other forms of religious devotion are only different approaches to the one universalized Zeus.[58] Another relevant phenomenon, which may be compared as well as contrasted with the cases described by Hacker, is the doctrine of the "unknown God," or the "unknown gods," which various religious movements invoke with more or less "inclusivistic" implications. Its most famous version is found in the New Testament. In the Acts of the Apostles, Paul refers the Athenians to the altar which they have dedicated to the "unknown God," and tells them that unknowingly they already worship that God whom he proclaims to them.[59] In this case, the gods of the Greek pantheon are not in toto subordinated to, or absorbed by, Christianity; instead, Paul claims that a certain "blank spot" within the Greek pantheon belongs, and has always belonged, to the Christian faith. The inclusivistic potential of the formula of the "unknown God" is, nevertheless, very significant; among the missionaries in India, de Nobili has explicitly referred to Paul's invocaton of the "unknown God."[60]

In general, "tolerance" within Christianity has often been inclusivistic, although it is clearly different from its Indian counterpart by virtue of its historical and "kerygmatic" orientation. The pagan religions are "tolerated" as preliminary stages, unfulfilled promises, implicit steps towards the fullness of the Christian revelation; the missionaries, most conspicuously the Jesuits, have often appealed to such implicit "inclusion" of pagan ideas in Christianity.[61] In the fifteenth century, Nicolaus Cusanus (Nicholas of Cusa) claimed that all other kinds of true religious faith were "included" in the faith in Jesus Christ.[62]

15. In a thoughtful discussion of the relationship between Christianity and tolerance, the theologian U. Mann defines the potential of tolerance which he finds in early Christianity as "kerygmatic inclusivity," i.e. as inclusivism in a positive, dynamic sense. "Early Christianity understands itself as the 'religion of fullness' ('Religion der Fülle'). In its self-understanding and in its understanding of religion, it is inclusive."[63] According to Mann, such "kerygmatic inclusivity" exemplifies tolerance in its fullest sense; and he claims that this kind of tolerance is to be found only in religions "which have risen to the self-understanding of the absolute religion." Mann recognizes that this applies not only to Christianity but also to other religions, in particular to Buddhism.[64] Indeed, we may say that any kind of tolerance which is allied with, and committed to, religious absolutism, and which keeps itself free from relativism, scepticism or indifferentism, is by definition inclusivistic.

In this connection, we should also recall the traditional Islamic way of dealing with the Biblical Prophets and Jesus: "The doctrine preached is essentially one and the same, although in matters of detail there has been a gradual evolution in their messages towards the final and perfect revelation . . . the Koran in particular not only confirms earlier scriptures, but, as the final revelation, clears up all uncertainties and is the repository of perfect Truth."[65] The relatively isolated attempts within Indian Islam to assimilate Hinduism, in particular Dārā Shukōh's "Mingling of the Oceans" (*Majma 'al-baḥrain*), are clearly indebted to this way of thinking, which they extend, however, beyond its traditionally accepted domain. On the other hand, the so-called *Allah Upaniṣad* which subsumes Indian deities under the name of Allah and seems to postulate their identity, shows the influence of Indian inclusivistic models. It was apparently composed during the period of Akbar and designed to support his program of religions reconciliation.[66]

We cannot discuss here the numerous manifestations of inclusivistic thought in East Asia, for instance in the encounter between Taoism and Buddhism in China, or between Buddhism and Shintoism in Japan.[67]

As we have seen, Hacker found "the most comprehensive application" of the "principle of inclusivism" in Neo-Vedānta, and he associated it with Radhakrishnan's claim that "the Vedānta is not *a* religion, but religion itself in its most universal and deepest significance."[68] In 1901, at a time when Radhakrishnan was receiving his Christian education, the great church historian A. Harnack declared that Christianity represented "the second level in the history of religions" which contained all earlier manifestations in an enhanced manner, and that "in its pure form it was not a religion side by side with others, but *the* religion," i.e. religion per se ("nicht eine Religion neben anderen, sondern *die* Religion"). In the history of Christianity, the genuine possibilities of religious thought and life were fully and most clearly contained. There was no need for the church historian "to take to the Babylonians, Indians and Chinese, or even to the Negroes or Papuas."[69]

We may also refer again to the theology of "fulfilment," which was advocated by Indologists like M. Müller and M. Monier-Williams, and missionaries like T.E. Slater and, above all, J.N. Farquhar. Farquhar presented Jesus Christ as the "Crown of Hinduism" and stated: "This is the attitude of Jesus to all other religions also. Each contains a partial revelation of God's will, but each is incomplete; and He comes to fulfil them all."[70] Such "inclusivistic" accomodation was criticized sharply by the Barthian theologian H. Kraemer; likewise, he condemned the inclusivistic tolerance of Neo-Hinduism as syncretism, indifferentism, naturalism, and even as "ultimate intolerance."[71]

16. The most monumental example of an all-encompassing dynamic "inclusivism" in the West is provided by Hegel's system of universal historical inclusion and "suspension" ("*Aufhebung*"). How does this systematic and historical "superseding" relate to Indian inclusivism? All other doctrines and traditions appear as preliminary and subordinate stages, to be included in, and superseded by, the context of European thought and specifically Hegel's own system. Nothing remains "outside"; here, everything finds its *historical* completion and fulfilment. It is the historical dimension which distinguishes Hegel's system most significantly from the Indian schemes of inclusion in which time and history seem to be priori discarded or superseded. This remains true in spite of the fact that one very important manifestation of inclusivistic thought in India is the "retrospective" inclusion of earlier layers of the tradition by its later developments; we find this, for instance in the Vaiṣṇava doctrine that the *Bhāgavatapurāṇa* encompasses and somehow supersedes the Vedas. However, as we have noted in our discussion of the "structure of Hindu traditionalism," even such temporal perspectives are ultimately subsumed under cyclical and transhistorical schemes of thought.[72]

Hegel himself has evoked the grossly simplified, but highly influential image of an essentially ahistorical and static Indian tradition. He has combined this with the claim that Indian thought is dominated by "substantialism," i.e. by the idea of an absolute abstract substance in which all concrete individuality is lost. There are some curious analogies between Hegel's notion of "substantialism" (or "substantiality") and Hacker's inclusivism.

Hacker cites the *Bhagavadgītā*, its presentation of Kṛṣṇa as the hidden and implicit goal of all forms of religious devotion, and the ultimate identification of all other deities with Kṛṣṇa, as an exemplary case of inclusivism.[73] For Hegel, on the other hand, this represents "substantialism," i.e. the absorption of all individual differences and all particularity by the one indefinite absolute, the substance which is pure being-in-itself and "the night in which all cows are black"[74] In making such statements, Hegel asserts the historical superiority of Europe, and its commitment to being-for-itself, individuality and historical development.

Unlike Hegel, Hacker was not a systematic philosopher; and unlike Hegel's "substantiality," his concept of inclusivism does not carry the claims of a Eurocentric metaphysics of history. Hacker never referred to Hegel, and in general, he despised German idealism. He considered his concept of inclusivism to be the result as well as a useful instrument of Indological, basically philological, research. Yet this concept, too, is the reflection and expression of systematic philosophical and theological premises and of a specific Christian and European standpoint. In using this concept, Hacker responds to the Indian tradition, and to Neo-Hinduism in particular. He asserts his own tradition against the Neo-Hindu claims to universality and comprehensive "tolerance." He is not a "pure Indologist," and he does not speak solely in the language of "objective" research. He is also a personally and systematically committed participant in the continuing encounter and dialogue between India and Europe.

23. India and the Comparative Method

1. The title of this appendix[1] is open to several interpretations, and it suggests at least the following different questions: How was the "comparative method," whatever it may be, applied to India and the Indian tradition? How does it contribute to our understanding of India (and perhaps ourselves)? On the other hand, how was this so-called method applied *in* India, *by* the Indians? How did they use it to understand the West and to reinterpret their own tradition? To these questions, we may add the following ones: How do the European and the Indian usages of comparison relate to one another? How does mutual comparison and, in general, the openness for foreign traditions, relate to the European tradition on the one hand and to traditional Indian thought on the other? Might comparison itself be a suitable topic for comparative studies?

It is a well-known and conspicuous fact that the development of comparative studies in the humanities has a special affinity with the development of Indian studies, and that later on the Indians themselves took a very active part in the business of comparison. The discovery of Indian materials stimulated the comparative instinct of European scholars from the end of the eighteenth century. Some sort of comparison is, of course, a more or less natural ingredient of many kinds of intellectual activity, and it had in fact been practiced, even with occasional cross-cultural applications, in many previous centuries. In the days of their early historians like Herodotus, the Greeks compared their own traditions with those of the Orient; al-Bīrūnī and others compared the Hindus with the Greeks and with their own Muslim tradition; and deists like Herbert of Cherbury compared various religious traditions in order to determine their universally valid common denominators.[2] Yet in all these approaches comparison as such does not appear as an explicit, consciously utilized method; its concept is not posited and proclaimed as a programmatic idea. This is what happened towards the end of the eighteenth century: At this time, the word and the concept of comparison itself ("comparative," *comparé, vergleichend*, and so forth) became much more explicit and conspicuous than it had ever been before, and by the end of the nineteenth century, the "comparative method" had found at least a few advocates in most scholarly disciplines.[3]

2. Some of the best-known advocates of such fully explicit comparison in the nineteenth century were themselves active Indologists or at least clearly aware of the newly discovered Indian materials. F. Bopp, one of the pioneers of Sanskrit and Indo-European studies, and other early Indologists are associated with the inauguration of "comparative linguistics" as a scholarly discipline. W. von Humboldt, a student and admirer of Sanskrit literature, presented the project of a "comparative anthropology." F. Schlegel, himself one of the advocates of "comparative linguistics," regretted in his famous book of 1808, *Über die Sprache und Weisheit der Indier* ("On the Language and Wisdom of the Indians"), that the comparative study of mythology and philosophy could not yet be pursued in a similar fashion. Th. Benfey, the first full-fledged Indologist at the University of Göttingen, propagated the comparative study of fairy tales, folklore, and so forth.[4] The best-known advocate of comparison among Indologists of the nineteenth century is, of course, Max Müller, with his projects of the "comparative science of religion," "comparative theology," and "comparative mythology." In his address at the International Congress of Orientalists in 1874, Müller said: "The comparative spirit is the truly scientific spirit of our age, nay of all ages."[5] We should not forget, however, that Müller also warned against uncautious applications of the "comparative method;" for example, he criticized in detail what he called the "false analogies in comparative theology" in the works of William Jones.[6]

Moreover, Müller never spoke of "comparative philosophy." This term became popular in the West only after the publication in 1923 of P. Masson-Oursel's book *La philosophie comparée*, an English translation of which appeared in 1926 under the title *Comparative Philosophy*. Without the use of this term, there have certainly been earlier applications of the "comparative method" to the study of philosophy and its history. Some conspicuous cases of cross-cultural comparison, parallelization, and even equalization are found in A.H. Anquetil Duperron's *Oupnek'hat* (Strasbourg, 1801–1802; that is, his Latin translation of a Persian translation of fifty Upaniṣads), specifically in the appendix "De Kantismo."[7] This discussion of the ultimate convergence of Kantian and Vedāntic thought anticipated some basic ideas and suggestions of A. Schopenhauer, P. Deussen, and numerous Neo-Vedāntins. In 1804, J.M. Degérando published his *Histoire comparée des systèmes de philosophie* ("Comparative History of the Systems of Philosophy").[8] This work, however, contains very few references to non-European thought, and it represents an orientation which is quite different from that of Anquetil Dupperon. Around the middle of the nineteenth century, the philosopher and Orientalist E. Röth recommended the "comparative way" ("vergleichender Weg") for the historiography of philosophy, referring to the successful applications of this "way" or method in the natural sciences.[9] Max Müller's expression "comparative theology," by the way, had a lonely and merely terminological forerunner in J. Garden's *Theologia pacifica seu comparativa* (London, 1699), an English version of which appeared in 1700 under the title *Comparative Theology, or the True and Solid Grounds of Peaceable Theology.*

3. Of course, there were numerous "comparisons" made by Christian missionaries and theologians which were meant to demonstrate the uniqueness and superiority of Christianity. This is exemplified by several writings of the chemist and theologian J. Priestley (1733–1804), who was not only a contemporary of the early Indologists, but also a keen student of their reports on Indian religion. The preface of Priestley's *A Comparison of the Institutions of Moses with those of the Hindoos and Other Ancient Nations* (Northumberland, 1799) begins as follows:

> It has long appeared to me that a fair comparison of the ancient Heathen religions with the system of Revelation would contribute in an eminent degree to establish the evidences of the latter. Its superiority in sentiment and practice to anything that the most enlightened of mankind have ever devised is so great, that it cannot be rationally accounted for, but by supposing it to have had a truly divine origin.[10]

"Comparison" in this sense often amounts to "opposition" and "contrast" and to the attempt to demonstrate the incomparability of Christianity; insofar, it is not an application of the "comparative method." Later on, Christian theologians have often referred to comparison, and to "comparative religion" in particular, with mistrust. They have even rejected it in general. In their view, Christianity is the absolute and therefore "incomparable" religion, which fulfills and transcends the other, merely "comparable" religions. In this sense, A. von Harnack argued against the claims of a general and comparative "history of religions," for instance in a famous speech on "*Die Aufgabe der theologischen Fakultäten und die allgemeine Religionsgeschichte*" ("The Task of the Theological Faculties and the General History of Religions") which he delivered in 1901. Subsequently, K.Barth and his followers were among the most radical advocates of the "incomparability" of Christianity.[11]

Since Masson-Oursel's *La philosophie comparée*, much has been written or said on "comparative philosophy." In India, the program and the phraseology of the comparative disciplines were received with great interest or even enthusiasm. Max Müller, the high priest of comparison, became the most celebrated Western Indologist in India. With the possible exception of the United States, there is now probably more literature on "comparative philosophy" being produced in India than in any other country in the world.[12] Great representatives of the Indian philosophical tradition, specifically Śaṅkara, but also Rāmānuja and others, are frequently compared with the real or alleged leading figures of the Western tradition--Hegel, Kant, Spinoza, and still F.H. Bradley, for a long time one of the most respected Western philosophers in India. There are numerous publications with titles like *Spinoza in the Light of Vedānta*, by R.K. Tripathi (Benares, 1957); *Rāmānuja and Bowne*, by F.K. Lazarus (Bombay, 1962); *Śaṅkara and Bradley*, by S.N.L. Shrivastava (Delhi, 1968); *Rāmānuja and Hegel*, by R. Prasad (New Delhi, 1983), and *The Idealistic Philosophy of Śaṅkara and Spinoza*, by A.N. Bhattacharya (Delhi, 1985).

In addition to such comparative studies of specific figures, movements, teachings, or concepts of Indian and Western thought, there are also more general and comprehensive essays in "comparative philosopy" and, for example, an *Introduction to Comparative Philosophy* (second edition, Carbondale, Illinois, 1970), by P.T. Raju, a follower and friend of S. Radhakrishnan. While a good deal of this literature is in English and often seems primarily addressed to Western readers, there are also numerous products of this kind in Indian languages. The most common term for "comparison" is *tulanā* (verbal root *tul*, "to lift," "to weigh"; compare *tulā*, "balance," and *tulya*, "equal").[13]

4. While most of the Indian literature on "comparative philosophy" has been produced since India attained independence in 1947, the term and project as such were familiar in India much earlier. As a matter of fact, it seems that the very expression "comparative philosophy" was first introduced by Indian authors. Long before the foundation of the Society for Asian and Comparative Philosophy in 1967, an Indian doctoral candidate at Cornell University, S.V. Ketkar, organized a Society of Comparative Theology and Philosophy. After his return to India, Ketkar — who had been in America from 1906 to 1911—became a leading intellectual figure in Maharashtra, above all as editor and principal author of the great Marathi encyclopedia.[14] However, the first Indian author (and quite possibly the first author altogether) to present the term and project of "comparative philosophy" in a published work was the Bengali philosopher and educator B.N. Seal, in his *Comparative Studies in Vaishnavism and Christianity* (Calcutta, 1899).[15]

Introducing this appendix, we referred to the possibility of a comparative study of comparisons. How and why did the Europeans compare? How and why did the Indians compare? What are the standards, goals, and methods of comparison? Are there any significant differences in this respect between Indian and Western authors? What is the framework and the historical background of comparison in India and the West? How were the Indians and how were the Europeans historically prepared and conditioned for their mutual encounter and for juxtaposing and comparing their traditions? Trying to clarify these questions means attempting to clarify some major hermeneutic presuppositions of the philosophical encounter and the so-called dialogue between India and the West.

Let us start by looking more closely at the author who may have introduced the expression "comparative philosophy" and who was an important figure in the academic and philosophical life of modern India--Brajendranath Seal (1864–1938).

Seal's *Comparative Studies in Vaishnavism and Christianity* (Calcutta, 1899), in which he developed his ideas about the "comparative method" and about "comparative philosophy" in particular, received very little immediate attention and has also been overlooked by most modern scholars. However, Seal referred again to his project of "comparative philosophy" in his much better-known book on *The Positive Sciences of the Ancient Hindus* (London, 1915).[16] P. Masson-Oursel used this book, and it may in fact have been the source of his term and concept "philosophie comparée."[17]

5. In his *Comparative Studies*, Seal advocates a "historico-comparative method" which is supposed to rectify the shortcomings and the one-sidedness of the subordinating method exemplified by Hegel's philosophy of history. "Historical comparison, such as is here proposed, implies that the objects compared are of co-ordinate rank" (p.i.). Further on in his introduction, Seal says: "The same correction and extension of the historical method is a crying necessity of our age, if it is to lay the foundation of a true philosophy of Universal History, and not to give us mere European side-views of Humanity for the world's panorama" (p.v.). Accordingly, he proclaims the systematic study of "Comparative Jurisprudence, Politics, Religion and Mythology"—and finally "the science of Comparative Philosophy, most sovereign of the sciences of the sociological group"—and adds the following programmatic statements:

> Chinese, Hindoo, Mohamedan culture-histories, therefore, require to be worked out on a general historic plan, and in obedience to a general law of progress...this will furnish new and comprehensive material for more correct generalisations, — for the discovery of general laws of the social organism... It will bring new influences, new inspirations, new cultures to Europe. It will infuse new blood, the blood of Humanity, and bring on the greater European Renaissance of the coming century. (p. vii)

In Seal's view, the new, more universal Renaissance would take place on the basis and within the framework of modern European thought and culture. However, it is Hinduism, with its potential of universality, synthesis, synopsis, and comparison, which is supposed to initiate and guide this regeneration and universalization of European thought. As a matter of fact, Seal claims that the principles of modern comparative grammar, as well as of comparative mythology, are found in the works of ancient Indian authors, specifically Yāska, Pāṇini, and Kumārila Bhaṭṭa. Rammohan Roy, the so-called father of modern India, is presented as the founder of comparative religion (p. 83).

It is obvious that B.N. Seal's proclamation of comparative studies has an apologetic function. It is a device for defending the dignity of the Indian tradition against the challenges of Western thought and its claims of superiority and domination. More specifically and explicitly, Seal argues against Hegel's scheme of historically *sub*ordinating the Indian and other Oriental traditions to the European standpoint, emphasizing that comparison in the proper sense requires objects which are of "*co*-ordinate rank."

The apologetic motivation becomes even more conspicuous in some later developments of comparative thought and studies in India. India's own tradition is measured against and reinterpreted in terms of Western concepts and teachings; and such comparison, synopsis, or reinterpretation often serves the purpose of proclaiming the superiority, or at least equality, of the Indian tradition. This can be done in a direct and straightforward manner, or in a more refined and implicit way, as, for example, in the writings of S. Radhakrishnan. Radhakrishnan and others are advocates of a *philosophia perennis*, or of a universal religion, in or behind all particular religions, which is supposed to emerge as the result of comparative studies in religion and philosophy. While the potential for such universality is recognized in all traditions, it is Hinduism in particular, as culminating in Advaita Vedānta, which is credited with a higher degree of actualization of this ideal than other traditions. In Radhakrishnan's interpretation, it is that tradition in which the ultimate convergence of all central religious and philosophical teachings becomes most manifest and which thus provides an exemplary framework and basis for comparative or synthetic studies in religion and philosophy.

6. Some of the underlying premises of such an approach have already been criticized by Hegel himself. In his view, the idea of a *philosophia perennis* and the attempt to identify or amalgamate the ultimate meaning of Eastern and Western teachings is utterly ahistorical and hence naive and abstract. Indian thought is basically a matter of the past. It is--in Hegel's suggestive and ambiguous terminology—*aufgehoben*, that is cancelled, preserved, and exalted all at once in Western, Occidental thought. There is *one Weltgeist* and *one* world-historical process. There is no plurality of independent or parallel streams of historical, cultural, or spiritual developments.

The way of development, which is the way of the "world spirit" ("Weltgeist"), leads from the more simple and abstract to the more differentiated and determined; and by the same token, it leads, according to Hegel, from the East to the West. European thought, as Hegel sees it, cannot return to Oriental or Indian thought, and they cannot be equated or paralleled with one another. They are not on the same level and cannot be *compared* in the full sense of the word "comparison."

With regard to such ahistorical and abstract categories as the One, unity, or pure being, it is, of course, not difficult to find parallels or similarities everywhere and to equate, for example, "Chinese, Indian, Eleatic, Pythagorean, Spinozistic, or even all modern metaphysics . . . Such equating, however, proves that it knows only of abstract unity, and in judging thus of philosophies is ignorant of what constitutes the interest of philosophy."[18] This is, as Hegel says in his *Phänomenologie des Geistes* ("Phenomenology of the Spirit"), only the "night in which all cows are black";[19] and in a remarkable passage in his *Logik* ("Logic"), he criticizes comparison as such, as an utterly abstract, mechanical, and extrinsic activity of thought, which never gets to the inner essence of what it deals with.[20]

Hegel's sharpest critic was A. Schopenhauer (1788-1860), whose name is much more automatically associated with India than that of Hegel. Schopenhauer did not accept the directedness of history in the Hegelian sense. He did not have a historical and conceptual scheme which would allow him somehow to construe the succession and interrelation of cultural traditions and philosophical systems. There is no doubt that he saw his own philosophy as true fulfillment of philosophical thought. But since he did not see the history of philosophy in terms of growth and progress, he was free and open to recognize not only preliminary stages in the more distant past and in foreign traditions, but ideas and insights which were genuinely at the same level as his own thought. And he was fascinated with Indian thought because it seemed to him to have reached the same basic truths which he himself claimed to have discovered. Schopenhauer's procedure of rediscovering one basic truth in different traditions and different historical periods was put into scholarly, that is, historiographic and Indological, practice by his apostle P. Deussen. Deussen, who became well known in India, somehow set the scene for much of what has become promising as well as questionable in "comparative philosophy." He compared Plato, Śaṅkara, and Kant and found the same basic truth concerning the merely phenomenal nature of the causal, spatio-temporal world in each of them—although he then left no doubt that in his view this one truth was explicated much more fully and clearly in the philosophy of his own master, A. Schopenhauer.[21]

7. Yet it is not at all the tradition of Schopenhauer and Deussen in which B.N. Seal's project of "comparative philosophy" has to be understood. In-

stead, we have now to mention the name of a philosopher who is hardly ever associated with India, but whose programmatic ideas are clearly behind the comparative approach advocated by B.N. Seal as well as by P. Masson-Oursel: I refer to A. Comte (1798–1857). Comte may not have been a very original or subtle thinker; but his writings are among the most symptomatic and influential expressions of nineteenth-century thought. Among his ideas which are relevant for our present context let me mention the following ones: the "law of three stages" ("loi des trois états"), that is, of the ascent of mankind from theological and metaphysical systems of belief to a "positive," that is, empirical, scientific and technological orientation; his attempt to apply the basic methods of the natural sciences in the study of human affairs and to transform philosophy into sociology and anthropology; and his propagation of a comprehensive study of the "totality of the human evolution" ("l'ensemble de l'évolution humaine") as a condition for successful self-mastery of the human species. Naturally, Comte's "positive philosophy" has been most influential in France, for example, in the sociology of É. Durkheim, who has written that the "comparative method" is the instrument par excellence of sociological research, and that the relation between sociology and history corresponds to that between comparative grammar or linguistics and the particular grammars of individual languages.[22] The famous ethnologist L. Lévy-Bruhl, who was actually a professor of philosophy, published a book on the philosophy of A. Comte in 1900. Lévy-Bruhl was one of the teachers of P. Masson-Oursel, the author of *La philosophie comparée*, together with the great Indologist and Buddhologist S. Lévi, who also at times reflects the "anthropological" orientation of Comte.[23]

8. For Masson-Oursel, "philosophie comparée," i.e. "compared" as well as "comparing philosophy, is a contribution to "positive philosophy;" in fact, it constitutes the indispensable prerequisite for philosophy itself to attain to the "positivity" expounded by Comte and his followers ("la condition même de l'avènement de la philosophie á la positivité").[24] There is no "positivity" without "comparison." In order to become as "positive," "scientific," and "comparative" as other sciences, philosophy has to have its own "facts," "phenomena," and realities. These may be found within philosophy's own history, which must be construed as universally as possible. "The basic principle of any positive philosophy must be then that of resolute intention to take the facts of philosophy from history, and from history alone." ("...de saisir dans l'histoire, et exclusivement dans l'histoire, les faits philosophiques").[25] This helps in guaranteeing genuine scientific "disinterest"—"le désintéressement de la véritable science"[26]—which was lacking in the previous treatments of alien traditions of thought, insofar as they were concerned with self-confirmation, self-critique, exotic curiosity, etc. Philosophy thus attains the positivistic stage through the radical objec-

tification of its own legacy, thereby transforming it into data that are accessible to scientific research and avoiding questions concerning the truth and meaning intended in these earlier philosophies. "L'important est ici d'envisager les philosophies comme des matériaux aussi réels que n'importe quelles autres données" ("What is important here is to regard philosophies as materials no less real than other data, no matter what").[27]

Thus "philosophie positive," which ultimately amounts to "philosophie comparée," differs from historical research and understanding in that it is not concerned with individual historical phenomena and events, but rather with more general findings—not with laws in the strict sense, and yet with the constancy of certain conditions, structural relationships, etc. Of fundamental importance to positive philosophy is the comparison of and confrontation between traditions and types of thought which are completely foreign to one another and have no genetic connection. In Masson-Oursel's eyes, as many of the various types of human thought should be taken into consideration as possible, although he actually concentrated on the three great traditions of Europe, India, and China. At any rate, "philosophy cannot achieve positivity so long as its investigations are restricted to the thought of our own civilization." It "must be comparative philosophy."[28]

9. Masson-Oursel regarded "analogy," which corresponds to what in mathematics is called the proportion, i.e., the equality of two relations, as the principle of his "comparative philosophy." According to this principle, it is possible to state that Confucius had been for China what Socrates had been for Greece:[29]

$$\frac{\text{Socrates}}{\text{Sophistique grecque}} = \frac{\text{Confucius}}{\text{Sophistique chinoise}}$$

Masson-Oursel uses four examples to illustrate the comparative method: 1) *Chronologie comparée*; 2) *Logique comparée*; 3) *Métaphysique comparée*; 4) *Psychologie comparée*. Within each of these domains, developmental schemas and repeatable structural relationships should be worked out, while the specific contents are of secondary importance. The basic premise is that comparisons are more worthwhile the greater the differences among the traditions in question. In conjunction with other comparative disciplines, "comparative philosophy" should help to cartographically encompass, as it were, "l'ensemble du donné humain" ("the human datum in its entirety"),[30] thereby making its relationships and fundamental conditions more intelligible. Here, both philosophy and history of philosophy converge with universal anthropology and are, as with Comte, actually superseded by it. The concept of the *philosophia perennis* which Degérando had invoked in his *Histoire comparée*[31] is here excluded.

What appears as a "positive," objective, and completely neutral self-study of man in all of the historical forms of his thought nevertheless follows *one* very special line of development which came to dominate the European tradition, viz., that of anthropocentrism, one of whose spokesmen was Comte. That this fact was largely ignored in the later uses of "comparative philosophy," which gained an especially wide following in India, is a symptomatic phenomenon. Of course, the "comparative" program implies a claim to theoretical objectification which does not associate itself with any particular tradition of philosophy, and represents instead the idea of a "meta-philosophy" which transcends and supersedes all traditions, and the very idea of tradition. But this itself is a European phenomenon.

In England, John Stuart Mill pursued Comte's positivist program in his own manner. A more orthodox British apostle of Comte was W. Congreve, who actually sent out positivist "missionaries" to India, specifically to Bengal. "Positivism" and the "religion of humanity," as advocated by Comte and his followers, were in fashion among Bengali intellectuals for several decades of the nineteenth century;[32] and among these Bengali positivists, we find Brajendranath Seal's father, Mohendranath. Concerning Brajendranath Seal himself: Some of his statements quoted earlier–for example, his references to "a general law of progress" and to "new and comprehensive material for more correct generalisations–for the discovery of general laws of the social organism"–obviously reflect Comtian spirit and phraseology.

10. In Germany, W. Dilthey sharply criticized Comte (as well as Mill) for not recognizing the peculiar character and methodic requirements of the historical disciplines and of what he calls *Geisteswissenschaften*–a term which has often been falsely traced back to the first edition of Schiele's German translation of Mill's *Logic*, where it stands for "moral sciences;" Schiele's second edition, by the way, replaces *Geisteswissenschaften* with *moralische Wissenschaften*.[33] Dilthey criticized the manner in which Comte superimposes methods and basic orientations of the natural sciences upon the historical disciplines.[34] However, if we look at Dilthey's own work and his lifelong attempts to establish the historical disciplines, the *Geisteswissenschaften*, in their own right, it is clear that he himself was under the spell of the natural sciences. It is specifically obvious in how he advocates and explicates the usage of the "comparative method" in historical research. And this leads us to the more general question of how his so-called "comparative method" is related to the natural sciences on the one hand and to history on the other. Dilthey himself presented a number of historical observations concerning this question.

He wrote that Aristotle had already developed "comparative methods" in biology, and that these were subsequently applied in the humanities, in politics, and so forth. This was resumed in modern times, and the "comparative method," which Dilthey also called a "morphological method" (since it focuses on the comparison of organic structures), became the only method which the "historical school" could accept in order to arrive at higher levels of generality and regularity.[35] This is, indeed, the fascination of the "comparative method" ("die vergleichende Methode, das vergleichende Verfahren") in the historical disciplines, that it is expected to turn the description and accumulation of individual historical data into more ordered schemes, that it might help us to reach higher levels of scientific order and abstraction in these disciplines, that it might turn history itself into something more scientific, more structural and "nomothetic," that is, into a truly theoretical science. In this sense, Dilthey advocated the study of "comparative humanities" ("vergleichende Geisteswissenschaften"), and specifically of "comparative psychology" ("vergleichende Psychologie"). "Comparative psychology" deals with mankind in terms of the "homogeneity of constituents" ("Gleichartigkeit von Bestandteilen") and the "uniformity of processes" ("Gleichförmigkeit von Prozessen"). It is thus a kind of structural anthropology.[36] We may assume that Dilthey would have given even more room and credit to the "comparative method" if it had not been for the warnings of is friend P. Yorck von Wartenburg, who argued that comparison was quite unsuitable as a general method in the historical disciplines, the "Geisteswissenschaften," that it was a reflection of the natural sciences and could not do justice to the peculiar nature and demands of historical understanding.[37] Without looking for structural similarities or dissimilarities, Yorck himself discussed the Indian "disposition of awareness" ("Bewusstseinsstellung") in his posthumous fragment *Bewusstseinsstellung und Geschichte*.[38]

11. As a matter of fact, the explosion of comparative studies in the humanities in the early nineteenth century was preceded by the appearance of important comparative investigations in the biological sciences, such as comparative physiology, anatomy, or embryology. The first book of this kind was *The Comparative Anatomy of Truncks*, by Nehemiah Grew, originally presented to the Royal Society in London and published in 1675; this was followed by another work by the same author, *The Comparative Anatomy of Stomachs and Guts*, presented to the Royal Society in 1676 and published in 1681. A much more famous and influential work appeared more than a century later: G. Cuvier's *Anatomie comparée* (Paris, 1800–1805). Immediately after this, we have a series of comparative studies, or projects of comparison—not just in the biological sciences, but also in the humanities; there is, for example, "comparative mythology" ("mythologie comparée;" M. de Tressan) or "comparative grammar" ("grammaire comparée," F. Raynouard). In general, biological or morphological comparison played an exemplary role in these developments, and its impact upon other areas of comparison in nineteenth-century thought is unquestionable.

Baron Eckstein stated the connection between various types of comparison in the natural sciences and the humanities: "Just as men like Cuvier and (Alexander von) Humboldt are discovering the mysteries of structure in the bowels of the earth, so men like Rémusat, Saint-Martin, Sacy, Bopp, the Grimms, and Wilhelm Schlegel are pursuing the recognition of the inmost structure and the original grounds of human thought in the words of language."[39] Dilthey himself left no doubt that the structural, morphological perspective was most significant in his own work on the history of philosophy. His explicit or implicit goal was a universal typology of human world views and the discovery of pervasive rules or even laws in the formation of such world views; and he clearly followed the model of the biological and morphological sciences:

> Just as the botanist divides the plants into classes and investigates the laws of their development, so the analytic investigator of philosophy has to search for the types of world views and recognize the lawful nature of their formation. Such a comparative approach raises the human mind above the confidence (a confidence rooted in its own limiting conditions) to have grasped in any of these world views truth itself. ("Wie der Botaniker die Pflanzen in Klassen ordnet und das Gesetz ihres Wachstums erforscht, so muss der Zergliederer der Philosophie die Typen der Weltanschauung aufsuchen und die Gesetzmässigkeit in ihrer Bildung erkennen. Eine solche vergleichende Betrachtungsweise erhebt den menschlichen Geist über die in seiner Bedingtheit gegründete Zuversicht, in einer dieser Weltanschauungen die Wahrheit selber ergriffen zu haben").[40]

12. In Dilthey's statements on the uses of comparison in the historiography of philosophy or the study of world views, the references to non-European traditions, such as India and China, are rare and casual.[41] However, his disciple and son-in-law G. Misch (1878–1965), trying to actualize the cross-cultural potential of Dilthey's thought, wrote a comparative analysis of the origins of philosophy in Europe, India, and China, *Der Weg in die Philosophie* (1926; second edition, 1950), which also appeared in an English edition under the title *The Dawn of Philosophy* (London, 1950).[42]

Dilthey has been associated with "historicism" and historical relativism. Indeed, his use of the "comparative method" is an expression of his historicism, as well as an attempt to overcome it. In one of his posthumous fragments, Dilthey's contemporary, F. Nietzsche, called his own time, the late nineteenth century, the "age of comparison" ("*Zeitalter der Vergleichung*"). This implies that it is an age of historical "understanding," of rapidly growing amounts of information, and of relativity; in this situation, comparison is "our most instinctive activity" ("unsere instinktivste Tätigkeit").[43] A few decades later, O. Spengler, author of *Der Untergang des Abendlandes* (1918; revised in 1923; English translation: *The Decline of the West*, London, 1932), presented "comparative" thinking as the final phase of European philosophy, and as analogous to ancient scepticism, and he claimed that his own method of comparative historical and cross-cultural morphology was a historical necessity.[44]

We may now return to B.N. Seal's project of "comparative" studies, and to the Indian approach to comparison in general. We mentioned the "positivistic" associations of Seal's thought. But his background is, of course, by no means exclusively, or even primarily, positivistic, nor is it exclusively European. Seal himself emphasized the traditional Indian roots of comparative thought, claiming, as we have seen, historical priority for India in such areas as comparative linguistics and comparative mythology. To what extent are his claims justified? No doubt, they cannot be accepted in the form in which they have been presented; yet they are not completely unfounded. There is, indeed, a very rich and complex tradition of synopsis and classification of linguistic, religious, and philosophical phenomena in classical India, but it remains almost exclusively *within* the Indian sphere.

13. To refer to other standpoints and, moreover, to understand and articulate one's own standpoint by relating it to other views—this is an essential, integral ingredient of religious and philosophical thinking in classical India. There is a wide-ranging readiness to accept other views as partial or preliminary approaches to that same truth which has found its definitive and comprehensive expression in one's own teachings. That means, other views are credited with a relative, limited validity either in a perspectivistic context or in terms of a vertical, hierarchic arrangement. These are the two main varieties of what P. Hacker has called "inclusivism"—a phenomenon which is certainly not exclusively Indian, but more conspicuous in India than elsewhere.[45] Inclusivism of the hierarchic, subordinating type is still clearly present in numerous works produced by representatives of modern Hinduism, specifically the so-called Neo-Vedāntins, such as Vivekananda or Radhakrishnan; and it characterizes and conditions their approach to the comparative study of religion and philosophy. Explicitly or implicitly, Advaita Vedānta appears as the standpoint from which a certain relative value and truth is assigned to other religions and philosophies, or as the horizon and context in which they are supposed to be coexisting, reconcilable and accessible to "comparative" and harmonizing studies.

Problems of understanding and interpretation, hermeneutic questions concerning the access to other traditions, are not taken into serious consideration by the Neo-Vedāntins. The encounter with the West is not conceived of in a historical context, as a historical event; and the Western ways of thinking are not seen in their genuine otherness, as something foreign and possibly requiring its own categories of understanding. The Vedāntic standpoint of nondualism appears as that standpoint which guarantees an impartial access to all traditions, a standpoint from which all doctrines can be understood, juxtaposed, compared, and recognized in their relative and limited truth. Comparison remains included, embedded in an unquestioned religious and metaphysical framework, while at the same time serving as a device for apologetics and cultural self-affirmation. Religions and philosophies do not constitute mere data for comparative historical or anthropological research, as in the works of Dilthey or Masson-Oursel. The notion of an absolute, ultimate truth to which they are supposed to refer is never seriously questioned, and there is hardly any awareness of the dangers of relativism and historicism which have often been associated with the development of the comparative study of religion and philosophy in the West.

14. Comparison means different things to different people; this is obvious when we compare its applications in India and Europe. It is done for different reasons, based upon different cultural and historical conditions, and pursued with different methods. P. Masson-Oursel's positivistic, anthropocentric style of comparison is quite different from the Neo-Vedāntic approach, and it is Eurocentric to a degree of which its author was hardly aware. B.N. Seal was indebted to the Comtian ideology, but he added an apologetic touch which is typical of many of the "comparative" efforts of modern Hindu thinkers. W. Dilthey's historicism has never had any counterpart in India. Furthermore, the extent to which the development of comparative studies in India and the West has been influenced by the patterns and theoretical ideals of the natural, specifically biological, sciences is obviously different in both traditions. And modern Hindu thought has hardly ever felt the relativistic implications of cross-cultural comparison. In Neo-Vedānta in particular, "comparison" remains covered by an inclusivistic absolutism; it tries to reconcile or identify different religions or philosophies by extrapolating and universalizing traditional, and fundamentally metaphysical, Vedāntic schemes of "concordance" (*samanvaya*).

Just as Masson-Oursel and the "positivists," Neo-Vedāntic proponents of "comparative philosophy" often invoke man as their central theme. But this does not mean that they are advocates of Comtian anthropocentrism, or of the transformation of philosophy into empirical, secularized anthropology. Their idea of man is embedded in a metaphysics of unity and associated with very unpositivistic notions of spiritual concordance and integration. This may be illustrated by quoting from P.T. Raju's *Introduction to Comparative Philosophy*: "It is the author's conviction and conclusion that, for the comparison of philosophical traditions, philosophy should start with man. . . . Why not start with man, for whom philosophy is meant as a guide to life and for whom life, mind and Spirit have meaning and significance? In man all have met and been integrated. Philosophy has to clarify this integrality and give man a picture of what he is."[46]

15. "Comparative philosophy," if it is possible at all,[47] is still in a nascent stage, and it requires much critical reflection and hermeneutic awareness. Western partners in the comparative enterprise and the East-West "dialogue" have to be aware of their historical background and of some long-standing biases in the European approach to non-European traditions—as well as of an inherent bias and one-sidedness in the "comparative" approach as such: They have to recognize that their allegedly neutral, purely theoretical, and objective approach is itself the result and expression of peculiar historical and cultural developments, and that the very openness of comparative, cross-cultural "research" is conditioned by an implicit European parochialism, by one peculiar, almost idiosyncratic manner of understanding reality. On the other hand, Indians in many cases still have to find the necessary freedom for a kind of comparison which is not primarily apologetics and cultural self-defense against the Western challenge, which does not amount to hastily reinterpreting or readjusting their own traditional concepts and ways of thinking, and which at the same time does not simply extrapolate and perpetuate the traditional schemes of inclusivism by subordinating all other world views to Advaita Vedānta.

The expression "comparative philosophy" itself is ambiguous. It does not make it clear whether philosophy is the subject or the object of comparing. Do we philosophize while we are comparing, i.e. in and through comparison, or do we just deal with philosophy or philosophies as objects of comparative historical or anthropological research? If "comparative philosophy" is supposed to be *philosophy*, it cannot just be the comparison of *philosophies*. It cannot be the objectifying, juxtaposing, synoptic, comparative investigation of historical, anthropological or doxographic data. Comparative philosophy is philosophy insofar as it aims at self-understanding. It has to be ready to bring its own standpoint, and the conditions and the horizon of comparison itself, into the process of comparison which thus assumes the reflexive, self-referring dimension which constitutes philosophy. And, of course, in applying the term and concept of philosophy cross-culturally and beyond the sphere in which it was created and originally used, we cannot be sure whether we are indeed comparing philosophies, or whether we are comparing the Western tradition of philosophy with other traditions which, in spite of all analogies, are ultimately not philosophical traditions. But this might be a deeper challenge to self-understanding than merely dealing with what is explicitly referred to as philosophy, i.e. with the history of philosophy under the secure and thoughtless guidance of the word "philosophy."

24. In Lieu of a Summary and Conclusion: Europe, India, and the "Europeanization of the Earth"[1]

1. We opened this study by referring to Hegel, whose philosophy epitomizes the European claims to "understand" and supersede India and the Orient. According to Hegel, the Indian tradition is a matter of the past. It has never reached the level of philosophy, science, and the autonomy of the human individual, which is a genuinely and uniquely European achievement.

Is this scheme of historical subordination entirely obsolete? To what extent does it reflect earlier attitudes, and to what extent has it influenced or anticipated subsequent developments? Has it finally been superseded by the progress of Indian studies and by the self-articulation of modern India? How has the encounter with India affected the European self-understanding and sense of identity? Has it affected the meaning of religion and philosophy itself? How and why did Europeans become interested in Indian thought? Which questions and expectations did they have concerning India and themselves? How did the Indians respond? How did their interest in Europe develop? How did they receive European thought, how did they redefine their own identity in the encounter? What does the European interest in India, and the Indian reception of, and response to, European thought and attitudes tell us about Europe?

Modern Indological research and the systematic exploration of India's religious and philosophical tradition began in Hegel's own time, with the foundation of the Asiatic Society of Bengal, and the works of W. Jones, Ch. Wilkins, and H. Th. Colebrooke. But the encounter between Europe and India, as well as the development of interest in, attitudes towards, and images of Indian life and wisdom began much earlier, and can be traced back to classical antiquity. There is certainly no coherent history of European search for India. Yet, there is an identifiable historical path leading to the situation of modern Indological research and of intercultural communication. It is a process which accompanies and reflects the development of European thought in general—a process in which Europe has defined and questioned itself, and in which misunderstandings and prejudices may be as significant as the accumulation of factual truth and correct information.

The most ancient Greek accounts associate India with the miraculous and the fabulous. A new era began with the Indian campaign of Alexander the Great (327–325 B.C.). The subsequent, usually vague and speculative, interest in India was guided by various perspectives. It was an interest in one's own origins, i.e., the background and prehistory of the Greek tradition, or a search for alternatives and correctives, or a projection of completeness and fulfillment. The Stoics saw in the Indian gymnosophists the practical fulfillment of their theoretical aspirations concerning immunity towards pleasure and pain. Others suggested that philosophy itself, the Hellenic reliance on reason, might have its origin among the "barbarians" of India and Egypt: However, in accordance with the classical Greek view, Diogenes Laertius (third cent. A.D.) insisted that in the ultimate analysis philosophy was something fundamentally and uniquely Greek, and that there was no Oriental equivalent for the word and concept "philosophy."

The Portuguese explorers who reopened the seaway to India around 1500 were not interested in ancient Indian wisdom. Instead, they were looking for "Christians and spices." And the missionaries who accompanied the conquerors and merchants were not interested in learning, but in teaching and persuading. Yet, it was this very intention of delivering a message which forced them to listen and learn and explore the linguistic and contextual conditions for successful teaching and preaching. It is therefore not surprising that missionaries became the Western pioneers in the study of Indian languages including Sanskrit, and that they gave the first knowledgeable accounts of Indian thought.

The motivations and perspectives for the study of India, and Asia in general, were again quite different for the representatives of Deism and the Enlightenment, whose factual information depended largely on the reports of the missionaries. The search for alternatives and correctives assumed a new significance, and in a peculiar, frequently anti-Christian fashion, it was combined with the old motif of Oriental "origins." The idea of God and the fundamental principles of religion were said to be older, more original and less deformed in the ancient cultures of Asia, specifically India, than in the Christian Occident. The glorification of India as the country of origins, of primeval revelations, of unadulterated childhood, assumed mythical proportions in the German Romantic movement. India was not seen as a foreign, alien tradition, but as the forgotten basis and hidden depth of our own, European identity, and it was invoked against materialism, rationalism, and other aberrations of modern Europe.

Hegel was one of the heirs, but also the most rigorous critic of the Romantic conception of India. What distinguishes his approach above all from that of the Romantics is his commitment to the present, and his sense of an irreversible direction of history; he does not glorify origins and early stages. Hegel sees India from the peak of his own time and his philosophical system which is meant to summarize and consummate the history of European thought. In his view, his European horizon transcends all Asian horizons. Asian thought is comprehensible and interpretable within European thought, but not vice versa. The question of an adequate standpoint for the evaluation and comparison of different cultural traditions has been decided by the course of history itself, and it has been decided in favor of Europe. European thought has to provide the context and the categories for the exploration of all traditions of thought.

Among the representative European philosophers of the nineteenth century, A. Schopenhauer is associated much more commonly with India than Hegel. No other major Western philosopher so signalizes the turn towards India, combined with a disenchantment with the European-Christian tradition and its key concepts of history, reason, the human individual, the personal God, etc. The notorious incompatibility between Hegel and Schopenhauer is clearly reflected in their attitudes towards India. While Schopenhauer proclaimed the concordance of his philosophy with the teachings of Vedānta and Buddhism, he also recognized, although less conspicuously, its factual inseparability from the history of European thought. His critique of European tradition shows us the other side of the nineteenth century. It negates but also supplements the Hegelian consummation of European thought. Schopenhauer, too, was a "son of his time." Yet he showed an unprecedented readiness to integrate Indian ideas into his own European thinking and to utilize them for his artiluation of the doctrine of the "will" and its "negation" which implies a critique of the European confidence in representational and rational thinking, in calculation and planning, science and technology.

Schopenhauer's contribution to the propagation and popularization of Indian concepts has been considerable. His impact upon academic studies of Indian philosophy has been less significant. And the new Renaissance which he predicted has not taken place. In the nineteenth and early twentieth centuries, historians of philosophy generally followed Hegel's example and excluded India from the history of philosophy, and they continued to proclaim philosophy, "pure theory" and "value-free" science as genuinely and uniquely Greek and European phenomena. They denied that the autonomy of thought and the freedom from dogma, myth and tradition which they considered to be the prerequisite of "true" philosophy and science were to be found in India or any other Asian tradition.

Towards the end of his life, and a few years before the beginning of the Second World War, E. Husserl once again invoked the spirit of "philosophy," "science," "pure theory": According to Husserl, Europe alone can provide other traditions with a universal framework of meaning and understanding. They will have to "Europeanize themselves, whereas we, if we understand ourselves properly, will never, for example, Indianize ourselves." The "Europeanization of all foreign parts of mankind" ("Europäisierung aller fremden Menschheiten") is the destiny of the earth.[2]

Of course, there were those who proclaimed the end of philosophy itself, or its transformation into sociology, anthropology, and so forth. This happened, for instance, in the wake of Comte's "positivism"; and claims and programs of a totally open-minded exploration of the "human phenomenon" were presented which were meant to replace Hegel's historical subordination of non-European traditions with a more objective "coordination" and "comparison" of different cultures. However, in their attempt to "objectify" other traditions, and to explore and understand them in an utterly "positive" and neutral fashion, these programs remain committed to a specifically European orientation; and in their own way, they continue and reinforce a Eurocentric and anthropocentric tradition.

2. The changing attitudes towards India and the various manifestations of interest in the Indian tradition are also expressions of European self-understanding, self-affirmation and self-criticism. They accompany and reflect basic developments in European thought and life. There is no parallel or analogous development of Indian interest in or speculation about Europe. There can be no symmetry in the historical presentation of the encounter between Europe and India and their mutual approaches in the areas of religion and philosophy.

Traditional Hinduism has not reached out for the West. It has not been driven by the zeal of proselytization and discovery, and by the urge to understand and master foreign cultures. India has discovered Europe and begun to respond to it in being overrun and objectified by it. It was not the course of Indian history, nor the inner dynamism of the Hindu tradition that led to the encounter. In traditional Hindu thought and literature, there has been virtually no interest in foreign countries, societies, cultures or religions. There has been no accumulation of information about the non-Indian world, no differentiation of xenological understanding. Even with reference to the foreigners in India—the Muslims and other invaders—Hindu literature, specifically the literature in Sanskrit, presents us for the most part with a tradition of silence and evasion. There is no sign of active theoretical interest, no attempt to respond to the foreign challenge, to enter into a "dialogue"--up to the period around 1800.

This period, which saw the full establishment of European power and presence in India, also saw the beginnings of modern Indology, i.e., the scientific exploration and objectification of India's past. The combination of these two events, which is more than a temporal coincidence, had a fundamental impact upon Indian attitudes towards themselves and the "other." The Indians began presenting themselves to the world in a new fashion. They took more distinctive initiatives to interpret their identity for the Europeans, and to defend and affirm it against them. They began to demarcate themselves against the foreign and to recognize the other in a new sense; but they also tried to comprehend and assimilate the Western ideas within the framework of their own tradition. They responded to the universalistic claims of Western thought with a universalism of their own. They opened, even exposed themselves to the West. But this very openness appeared as a confirmation and consummation of their own tradition, its potential of universality and inclusiveness. Yet the presence of European ideas in Indian thought is far more pervasive than the presence of Indian ideas in the West. What is the meaning of the "Westernization," this apparent intellectual subjugation of India by the West? Is it sheer alienation, or does it conceal an underlying strength and flexibility of the Indian tradition?

The Indians reinterpreted key concepts of their traditional self-understanding (such as the concept of *dharma*), adjusting them to Western modes of understanding. Did they rediscover and reinvigorate their identity in this unprecedented exposure to the other? Did they expose and reveal inherent limitations and weaknesses in the Western tradition? What did they find, what did they miss in European thought and life? What was new and unprecedented in the encounter with the West, specifically the British, as it occurred around 1800?

Hegel's lifetime (1770–1831) coincides with that of a man who, like no other, has been celebrated as the herald of modernization in India: Rammohan Roy (1772–1833). Rammohan's role has often been exaggerated. Yet his life and work represent more than just a chronological starting-point for the development of modern Hindu thought. Like nobody else before him, he tried to guide India and Hinduism into the open arena of the "great wide world." He exposed his own tradition to comparisons and contrasts with other religious and cultural traditions, and he invoked Western rationality and science and Christian ethics against what he considered the aberrations of Hinduism. On the other hand, he invoked what he called "the pure spirit" of the Vedas and Upaniṣads against Christianity.

The hermeneutic situation which is reflected in Rammohan Roy's use of English, together with his native Bengali and Sanskrit, his cross-cultural horizon of self-understanding, his position between receptivity and self-assertion, "Westernization" and "Hindu revivalism," forms the background and basic condition of modern Hindu thinking and self-definition. Since Rammohan's time, it has become increasingly obvious that the European, i.e., primarily British presence in India was not just another case of foreign invasion and domination, or of cross-cultural, interreligious "encounter." Instead, it was an encounter between tradition and modernity, i.e., an exposure to new forms of organization and administration, to unprecedented claims of universality and globalization, to the ideas of history and progress and human mastery of the earth, to rationalization, technology and a comprehensive objectification of the world. It also meant the advent of a new type of objectification of the Indian tradition itself, an unprecedented exposure to theoretical curiosity and historical "understanding," and to the interests of research and intellectual mastery. It was a presence which was much more pervasive, much more penetrating than any previous domination. It affected the very self-understanding of the tradition and turned out to be inescapable even when it was rejected or discarded. For it began to provide the means even for its rejection, and for the Hindu self-affirmation against it. In the words of J.L. Mehta:

> The coming of modernity to India signified not merely the impingement of an alien world of knowledge, ideas, and ideals upon the Indian consciousness, but of a world which was itself rapidly reaching out toward a newly conceived future, as well as spreading out its tentacles to encompass the whole world. Under the colonial origins of his modernization, the Indian encountered 'philosophy' and 'religion' and began forthwith the long journey of reinterpreting his tradition in terms of these Western categories. Most importantly, he began thinking about it in the English language, not just to expound it to English scholars, but as the principal medium of his own self-understanding.[3]

3. The conditions of the encounter and "dialogue" between India and Europe have changed drastically during the twentieth century. European self-questioning and self-destruction have progressed rapidly. There has been an unprecedented multiplication of channels of international communication and interaction, and an explosion of easily accessible information. Academic research is only one mode of presence of the Indian tradition in the modern Western world. In addition, we have its presence in the arts, literature, popular cults, methods of meditation, sectarian movements, "transpersonal psychology," the syndrome of "ancient wisdom and modern science," and so forth. Western scientists are turning towards Eastern metaphysics of awareness. Are the boundaries finally dissolving? Has there been a genuine "fusion of horizons?"

What has happened to Hegel's verdict that the Orient has been superseded by the Occident, that India is a matter of the past? What has happened to

Husserl's claim that the "Europeanization" of mankind is the destiny of the earth? Are the Europeans abandoning their global mission of philosophy, science, "pure theory"? Or have they discovered the limits of this mission and its "universality"? Was the expansion of European ways of understanding the world and mastering nature, was the globalization of European science and technology only an episode? Will the "Europeanization" of the earth be reversed? Are other cultures and traditions, and India in particular, ready to provide alternatives? In the modern planetary situation, Eastern and Western "cultures" can no longer meet one another as equal partners. They meet *in* a Westernized world, under conditions shaped by Western ways of thinking. The medium, the framework of any "dialogue" seems to be an irreducibly Western one. But is this factually inescapable "universality" the true *telos* of mankind? Could it be that the global openness of modernity is still a parochially Western, European horizon? Or was Europe itself somehow left behind by the universality which it had inaugurated? Did it help others to gain freedom and distance from their traditional foundations and limitations, while it remained committed to its own historical roots and—paradoxically—within its "traditional" horizon? Is the alienation, the loss of an authentic "traditional" self-understanding which Europe has inflicted upon non-European cultures, perhaps something enviable?

In a sense, Europe itself has been "superseded" and left behind by the modern Westernized world. It is certainly no longer the master and protagonist of the process of "Europeanization." The direction of this process, the meaning of progress, the significance of science and technology have become thoroughly questionable. The doubts and questions which had already been raised by the Romantics, Schopenhauer and others and which determined their interest in India have become much more urgent. The search for alternatives now appears as a matter of life or death.

Europe is turning towards those non-European traditions which it tried to master, supersede, "understand" and "explain"; it tries to enlist them as allies against developments initiated by itself. The West is turning towards the East for new inspiration, or even for therapy. Can it expect help from those ways of orientation, those modes of awareness of which it tried to deprive others? Can it retrieve and adopt for its own future what it once tried to supersede and relegate to the past? How would this differ from, or relate to, the Neo-Hindu attempts to "actualize" ancient Indian teachings for the present? The Neo-Hindus tried to appeal to the modern West; they tried to validate traditional Indian ideas by reinterpreting them, and by adjusting them to the needs and expectations of the modern Westernized world, to the ideas of social and scientific progress, and so forth. Should this be avoided? Should we focus instead on what is not appealing to modernity, and on dimensions of the tradition which have been disavowed or disregarded by its modern advocates and "actualizers"? Should we, can we abrogate an orientation which has come to dominate the Westernized world as well as Europe itself?

Whatever the nature of the current crisis may be – we cannot *return* to the past, and we cannot escape into foreign traditions and ways of orientation. The teachings and methods of the past and of Eastern traditions cannot speak and function in the modern Westernized world as they did in the past or in their own traditional contexts. It does not help to invoke Eastern methods of meditation, or the cultivation of inner awareness, against objectification, instrumentalization, consumerization, if these methods are supposed to function, and be useful within, the basic constellation of the modern world, if they are supposed to be part of those developments against which they are invoked. No calculated importation and application of Eastern ways of thinking, or methods of meditation, will enable us to reverse history, or to change the basic conditions of a world which is dominated by science and technology, driven by blind rationality, and overpowered by mechanisms of mastery and calculation. The recent history of Indian spiritual movements in the West illustrates this simple truth: In their application within the modern Western world, the Indian methods and teachings become parts and manifestations of this world, and the constellation of science and technology. And for the foreseeable future, we may have to live with this tantalizing paradox: The globalization of the world coincides with its parochialization; the meeting and "dialogue" of the cultures and religions of this world coincides with their trivialization.

Just as E. Husserl, M. Heidegger has referred to the "complete Europeanization of the earth and of mankind" ("vollständige Europäisierung der Erde und des Menschen"). But unlike Husserl, Heidegger does not present such "Europeanization" as a proud and unambiguous achievement. Philosophy, science and technology may have become dominant in Europe, and through the expansion of European forms of knowledge and organization, they may have begun their factual domination of the earth. But this in itself implies that they remain parochial. They may have overrun other traditions, but they have not been the own inner *telos* and fulfilment of these traditions. They do not provide the medium in which the Indian tradition can reveal its full potential; nor do they constitute the unquestionable basis, or the definitive meaning and purpose, for any future "dialogue" between India and the West. Neither the language of "science," nor that of "metaphysics," nor that of "historical understanding," can provide the proper foundation for a dialogue in which all these ideas themselves will have to be questioned. We have to transcend "what is European" ("das Europäische"); we have to reach "beyond Occident and Orient." Yet for the time being there is no escape from the global network of

"Europeanization," and no way to avoid the conceptual and technological ways and means of communication and interaction which the European tradition has produced.[4]

To conclude this presentation, I want to refer once more to an Indian thinker whom I have quoted before—J.L. Mehta. In a remarkable response to Heidegger's notion of the "Europeanization of the earth," he accepts the challenge of "belonging, irretrievably and inescapably, to this 'one world' of the *Ge-stell*," i.e., of the global presence of Western science and technology, and he adds:". . . there is no other way open, to us in the East, but to go along with this Europeanization and to go *through* it. Only through this voyage into the foreign and the strange can we win back our own self-hood; here as elsewhere, the way to what is closest to us is the longest way back."[5]

For Indians as well as Europeans, the "Europeanization of the earth" continues to be inescapable and irreversible. For this very reason, ancient Indian thought, in its unassimilable, non-actualizable, yet intensely meaningful distance and otherness, is *not* obsolete.

Abbreviations; frequently cited works

Abh.	Abhandlung(en).
ABORI	*Annals of the Bhandarkar Oriental Research Institute.*
AGPh	P. Deussen, *Allgemeine Geschichte der Philosophie,* 6 vols., Leipzig, 1894–1917 (several reprints).
AKM	Abhandlungen für die Kunde des Morgenlandes.
Ak.Wiss.(Lit.)	Akademie der Wissenschaften (und der Literatur).
ALB	*Adyar Library Bulletin.*
ASS	Ānandāśrama Sanskrit Series.
Bankim Chandra Chatterji	(*Baṅkimcandra Caṭṭopādhyāya*), *Racanāvalī*, 3 vols. (vol.3: *English Works*), ed. J.C. Bāgala, Calcutta, fourth ed., 1969f.
Berl.Schr.	G.W.F. Hegel, *Berliner Schriften*, 1818–1831, Frankfurt, 1970 (Werke, vol.11; based upon the edition 1832–1845).
Breloer-Bömer	*Fontes historiae religionum Indicarum,* collegerunt B. Breloer et F. Bömer, Bonn, 1939 (Fontes historiae religionum, fasc.7).

BS — *Brahmasūtra.*

BSOAS — *Bulletin of the School of Oriental and African Studies.*

ChSS — Chowkhamba Sanskrit Series.

Contemporary Indian Philosophy, — ed. S. Radhakrishnan and J.H. Muirhead, London, fourth ed., 1966 (first ed.: 1936).

Dasgupta I–V — S.N. Dasgupta, *A History of Indian Philosophy,* 5 vols., Cambridge 1922–1955 (several reprints).

Diss. — doctoral dissertation.

E. Frauwallner, — *Geschichte der indischen Philosophie,* 2 vols., Salzburg 1953–1956 (trans. V.M. Bedekar: *History of Indian Philosophy,* Delhi 1973).

G.d.Ph.I — G.W.F. Hegel, *Vorlesungen über die Geschichte der Philosophie,* ed. J. Hoffmeister, Leipzig, second ed., 1944 (the sections on Oriental philosophy are missing in the new and revised edition of this volume by F. Nicolin, Hamburg, 1959).

L. Geldsetzer, — *Die Philosophie der Philosophiegeschichte im 19. Jahrhundert,* Meisenheim, 1968.

H. von Glasenapp, — *Das Indienbild deutscher Denker,* Stuttgart, 1960.

Gonda I–II — J. Gonda, *Die Religionen Indiens,* 2 vols., Stuttgart, 1960–1963.

GOS — Gaekwad's Oriental Series.

Grundriss — *Grundriss der indo-arischen Philologie und Altertumskunde,* begun by G. Bühler.

P. Hacker, — *Kleine Schriften,* ed. L. Schmithausen, Wiesbaden, 1978 (Glasenapp-Stiftung 15).

W. Halbfass,	*Zur Theorie der Kastenordnung in der indischen Philosophie,* Göttingen, 1976 (NAWG, Phil. hist.Kl., 1975/9).
id.,	*Studies in Kumārila and Śaṅkara,* Reinbek, 1983.
Hist.Wb.Phil.	*Historisches Wörterbuch der Philosophie,* ed. J. Ritter and K. Gründer, Basel, 1971ff.
HN	A. Schopenhauer, *Handschriftlicher Nachlass.*
IHQ	*Indian Historical Quarterly.*
IIJ	*Indo-Iranian Journal.*
Indienbild	see H. von Glasenapp.
JA	*Journal Asiatique.*
JAOS	*Journal of the American Oriental Society.*
JAS Bengal	*Journal of the Asiatic Society of Bengal.*
JIPh	*Journal of Indian Philosophy.*
JOI	*Journal of the Oriental Institute* (Baroda).
JRAS	*Journal of the Royal Asiatic Society of Great Britain (and Ireland).*
Kane I–V	P.V. Kane, *History of Dharmaśāstra,* 5 vols., Poona, 1930–1962 (vol.I/2: second ed., 1968).
W. Kirfel,	*Die Kosmographie der Inder,* Bonn, 1920 (reprint Hildesheim, 1967).
KLL	*Kindlers Literatur Lexikon,* 8 vols., Zurich, 1965–1974.
Kl.Schr.	see P. Hacker.
Lach I/1ff.	D.F. Lach, *Asia in the Making of Europe,* Chicago, 1965ff. (in progress; published so far: I/1-2; II/1-3).
H. de Lubac,	*La rencontre du bouddhisme et de l'occident,* Paris, 1952.

Manu, ed. J.H. Dave	*Manusmṛti with Nine Commentaries*, ed. J.H. Dave, Bombay, 1972ff. (in progress).
P.J. Marshall (ed.),	*The British Discovery of Hinduism in the 18th Century*, Cambridge, 1970.
J.L. Mehta,	*India and the West. The Problem of Understanding*, Chico, Cal., 1985.
MS	*Mīmāṃsāsūtra*.
Muir I–V	J. Muir, *Original Sanskrit Texts on the Origin and History of the People of India*, 5 vols., New Delhi, 1976 (reprints of the partly revised and enlarged editions, London, 1870-1874).
S. Murr,	"Les conditions d'émergence du discours sur l'Inde au Siècle des Lumières." *Puruṣārtha* 7 (1983), 233-284.
NAWG	*Nachrichten der Akademie der Wissenschaften in Göttingen.*
NBh	*Nyāyabhāṣya* by Vātsyāyana; cf. ND.
ND	*Nyāyadarśana*, ed. G. Jhā, Benares, 1925 (ChSS; contains NS; NBh; *Khadyota* by G. Jhā; *Bhāṣyacandra* by Raghūttama).
Neill	S. Neill, *A History of Christianity in India*, vol.1: *The Beginnings to AD 1707*, Cambridge, 1984; vol.2: 1707-1858, Cambridge, 1985.
F. Nietzsche,	*Werke in drei Bänden*, ed. K. Schlechta, Munich, 1966.
id.,	*Sämtliche Werke.* Kritische Studienausgabe in 15 Bänden, ed. G. Colli and M. Montinari, Munich/Berlin, 1980.
NM	*The Nyāyamañjarī of Jayanta Bhaṭṭa*, ed. S.N. Śukla, Benares, 1934-1936 (Kashi Sanskrit Series).

NS — *Nyāyasūtra.*

NV; NVT — *Nyāyavārttika* by Uddyotakara; *Nyāyavārttikatātparyaṭīkā* by Vācaspati; as far as possible *(i.e., Adhyāya I)*, quoted from: *Nyāyadarśana* of Gautama I, ed. A. Thakur, Darbhanga, 1967; for the remaining parts, cf. NV, ed. V.P. Dvivedin, Calcutta, 1914 (Bibliotheca Indica); NVT, ed. R.S. Drāviḍa, Benares, 1925–1926 (Kashi Sanskrit Series).

OLZ — *Orientalistische Literaturzeitung.*

PAIOC — *Proceedings of the All-India Oriental Conference.*

PB — *The Bhāṣya of Praśastapāda, together with the Nyāyakandalī of Śrīdhara*, ed. V.P. Dvivedin, Benares, 1895 (Vizianagram Sanskrit Series).

PEW — *Philosophy East and West.*

Ph.d.W. I–III — G.W.F. Hegel, *Vorlesungen über die Philosophie der Weltgeschichte I: Die Vernunft in der Geschichte*, ed. J. Hoffmeister, Hamburg, fifth ed., 1955; II-III: *Die orientalische Welt; Die griechische und die römische Welt*, ed. G. Lasson, Hamburg, third ed., 1968.

Phil.d.Rel. — G.W.F. Hegel, *Vorlesungen über die Philosophie der Religion*, ed. G. Lasson, Hamburg, second ed., 1966 (first ed.: Leipzig, 1925–1929).

PP — A. Schopenhauer, *Parerga und Paralipomena*; quoted from the edition of Schopenhauer's works begun by P. Deussen, Munich, 1911–1942; with additional references to the edition by A. Hübscher, Wiesbaden, 1946–1950.

PW — "Petersburger Wörterbuch"; i.e. O. Böhtlingk and R. Roth, *Sanskrit-*

Wörterbuch, 7 vols., Petersburg, 1855–1875 (reprint Osnabrück, 1966).

S. Radhakrishnan, *The Hindu View of Life*, London, 1968 (first ed.: 1927).

Ramakrishna *The Gospel of Sri Ramakrishna,* trans. Nikhilananda, Madras, fifth ed., 1969.

Rammohan Roy, *Veds:* *Translation of Several Principal Books, Passages and Texts of the Veds,* London, 1832.

id., *Rāmamohana-Granthāvalī,* ed. B.N. Bandyopādhyāya and S.K. Dāsa, Calcutta, n.d. (1959).

RE *Realenzyklopädie der klassischen Altertumswissenschaft* (new ed. by K. Ziegler et. al.).

Sachau I–II *Alberuni's India*, trans. E.C. Sachau, 2 vols., London, 1888 (several reprints).

Sb. Sitzungsberichte.

R. Schwab, *La Renaissance orientale*, Paris, 1950 (trans. G. Patterson-Black and V. Reinking: *The Oriental Renaissance*, New York, 1984).

Sources of Indian Tradition, 2 vols., ed. W.Th. de Bary, New York, 1970 (first ed.: 1958).

ŚV *Ślokavārttika* by Kumārila; quoted from: *Mīmāṃsāślokavārttika* with Nyāyaratnākara by Pārthasārathimiśra, ed. R.S. Tailaṅga, Benares, 1899 (ChSS).

S.W. F.W.J. Schelling, *Sämmtliche Werke*, ed. K.F.A. Schelling, 14 vols., Stuttgart and Augsburg, 1856–1861.

TV *Tantravārttika* by Kumārila; quoted from: *Mīmāṃsādarśana*, ed. K.V. Abhyaṅkara and G.S. Jośī, vol. 1, Poona, second ed., 1970 (ASS; this

	volume contains the section on MS 1,2,1-II,1,49).
Überweg	F. Überweg, *Grundriss der Geschichte der Philosophie*.
v.	verse.
Vivekananda	*Complete Works*, 8 vols., Calcutta 1970-1973 (Mayavati Memorial Edition); in ch. 13, Roman numerals without further characterization refer to this edition).
VP	*Vākyapadīya* by Bhartṛhari.
VS	*Vaiśeṣikasūtra*.
Windisch I–II	E. Windisch, *Geschichte der Sanskrit-Philologie und indischen Altertumskunde*, 2 vols., Strasbourg, 1917-1920 (Grundriss I/1b).
WWV I–II	A. Schopenhauer, *Die Welt als Wille und Vorstellung*; quoted from the edition of Schopenhauer's works begun by P. Deussen, Munich, 1911-1942; with additional references to the edition by A. Hübscher, Wiesbaden, 1946-1950.
WZKM	*Wiener Zeitschrift für die Kunde des Morgenlandes*.
WZKS(O)	*Wiener Zeitschrift für die Kunde Südasiens* (formerly: *Süd- und Ostasiens*).
YS	*Yogasūtra*.
ZDMG	*Zeitschrift der Deutschen Morgenländischen Gesellschaft*.
ZMR	*Zeitschrift für Missionswissenschaft und Religionswissenschaft*.

Quotes and references without indication of specific editions follow generally accepted divisions into chapters, verses, etc. The *Mahābhārata* is quoted according to the critical edition begun by V.S. Sukthankar and published in Poona, the *Rāmāyaṇa* according to the Baroda edition prepared by G.H. Bhatt and others. Otherwise, all references are page references.

Notes

1. The Philosophical View of India in Classical Antiquity

1. *Ph.d. W.* II, 344.

2. *G. d. Ph.* I, 232; for Hegel's understanding of India, see below, ch. 6.

3. Diogenes Laërtius 1, 7: also, for example, IX, 61(on Pyrrho).

4. *Stromateis* I, 15(§71).

5. Sotion's work is indebted to the doxography of Theophrastus.

6. Cf. E. Schwartz, "Diogenes Laertios," *RE* 5(1905), 738–763; also in *Griechische Geschichtsschreiber*. Leipzig 1957, 453–491.

7. I, 4: *και ωδε μεν αφ* Ελληνων *ηϱξε·φιλοσοφια ης και αυτο το ονομα την βαϱβαϱον απεστϱαπται πϱοσηγοϱιαν.*
In the preceding section, I, 3, we are even told that mankind itself had its origin with the Greeks.

8. On the concept of "spontaneous development" ("Selbstentfaltung") cf., for example, W. Nestle, *Vom Mythos zum Logos. Die Selbstentfaltung des griechischen Denkens von Homer bis auf die Sophistik und Sokrates*. Stuttgart, second ed., 1942.

9. Cf. R. Garbe's exemplary and balanced survey, *Indien und das Christentum*. Tübingen, 1914. (Eng. trans.: *India and Christendom*. LaSalle, Ill., 1959).

10. Cf., for example, *Éléments orientaux dans la religion grecque ancienne* (Colloque de Strasbourg, 1958). Paris, 1960; especially the contributions of O. Eissfeldt and H. Schwabl; furthermore U. Hölscher, "Anaximander und die Anfänge der Philosophie," *Hermes* 81 (1953), 257–277; 385–418 (also in: *Um die Begriffswelt der Vorsokratiker*, ed. H.-G. Gadamer, Darmstadt, 1968, 95–176); M.L. West, *Early Greek Philosophy and the Orient*. Oxford, 1971 (for the possibility that Indian influences were transmitted by the Persian Magi). F.M. Cornford's works are also relevant in this connection. A useful, but uncritical, work based on secondary sources is J. Sedlar, *India and the Greek World*. Totowa, N.J., 1980. We are not dealing with the question of the common Indo-European background of the Greek, Iranian and In-

dian traditions here, nor with the problems of the relations which may have existed between the ancient Harappan civilization, Babylonia and the Mediterranean world; on this, see *Ancient Cities of the Indus*, ed. G. Possehl. New Delhi, 1979.

11. See below, ch. 9.

12. E. Zeller, *Die Philosophie der Griechen in ihrer geschichtlichen Entwicklung*, vol. 1. Darmstadt, fifth ed., 1963, 20f.; cf. also Überweg I (twelfth edition), 27.

13. Schäfer, 3; 50.

14. If we may trust the testimonies, especially that of Clement of Alexandria, Megasthenes, approximately 300 B.C., had already advocated the opinion that the essential concepts of Greek philosophy had been anticipated by the Indian Brahmins as well as the Syrian Jews; see Clement, *Stromateis* I, 15 (§72) (Breloer-Bömer, 30).

15. See below, §6. The allegedly Aristotelian *Magikos*, which Diogenes cites, is not authentic.

16. H. Schwabl, "Das Bild der fremden Welt bei den frühen Griechen," *Grecs et Barbares*. Geneva, 1962 (Entretiens sur l'antiquité classique 8), 23.

17. Cf. F. Heinimann, *Nomos und Physis*. Basel, 1945 (reprint, Darmstadt, 1972).

18. Cf. H. Diller, "Die Hellenen-Barbaren-Antithese im Zeitalter der Perserkriege"; *Grecs et Barbares* (see above, note 16), 63. On this issue, for example, Herodotus I, 131ff.

19. Herodotus I, 30 (Croesus to Solon): . . . *ως φιλοσοφεων γην πολλην θεωρις εινεκεν επεληλυθας*; for the earliest ascertainable use of φιλοσοφος cf. Heraclitus, B35. The ideal of knowledge for its own sake is also exemplified by the statement attributed to Democritus (B118), that he would prefer one single causal explanation over the possession of the whole Persian empire.

20. Cf. Cicero, *Tusculanae disputationes* V, 3, 8-9 ("*qui nec plausum nec lucrum quaererent sed visendi causa venirent*"); Diogenes Laërtius, VII, 8; 1, 12; cf. also, W. Jaeger, "Über Ursprung und Kreislauf des philosophischen Lebensideals." *Sb. Preuss. Ak. Wiss., Phil.-Hist. Kl.*, Jg. 1928, 390–421. Heraclitus (B40) accuses Pythagoras of πολυμαθιη, i.e., "much learning" without real understanding.

21. Diogenes Laërtius I, 12.

22. Cf. E. Zeller (see above, n.12), 303ff. Cf., also, Herodotus, who already claims that (II, 123) the Pythagorean doctrine of the transmigration of souls had its origin in Egypt.

23. For the emergence of the Greek-European sense of distinctness vis-à-vis the Orient in general see K. Goldammer, *Der Mythus von Ost und West*. München, 1962. Also J. Jüthner, *Hellenen und Barbaren*. Leipzig, 1923.

24. Cf., for example, Herodotus I, 60: *῎Επει γε απεκριθη εκ παλαιτερου του βαρβαρου εθνεος το Ελληνικον εον και δεξιωτερον και ευηθιης ηλιθιου απηλλαγμενον μαλλον* . . .

25. Cf. *Politeia* IV, 435, e7ff., "love of knowledge" (το φιλομαθες) is ascribed to the Greeks and "love of what is useful" (το φιλοχρησιμον) to the Orientals, specifically the Egyptians and Phoenicians.

26. *Metaphysics* I, 983b 20: Thales as της τοιαυτης αρχηγος φιλοσοφιας.

27. *Epinomis*, 987d: . . . λαβωμεν δε ως οτιπερ αν Ελληνες βαρβαρων παραλαβωσι, καλλιον τουτο εις τελος απεργαζονται.

28. *Ph. d. W.* III, 566.

29. Überweg I (twelfth edition), 27.

30. Marcus Aurelius, IV, 4: 'Ο κοσμος ωσανει πολις εστι; cf. also the Stoic concepts of οικειωσις, κοιναι εννοιαι,etc. Occasionally, the idea of the "cosmopolitan" is attributed to Socrates; for example, Cicero, *Tusculanae disputationes* V, 108. On the idea of the unity of mankind, see also M. Landmann, *Philosophische Anthropologie*. Berlin, 1955, 19–39.

31. Cf. especially Plutarch's work on Isis and Osiris; see also the testimonies in *The Oxyrhynchus Papyri*, particularly XI, ed. by B.P. Grenfell/A.S. Hunt. London, 1915, N. 1380. This section contains a reference to India on p. 198: . . . εν 'Ινδοις Μαιαν. However, the relationship of this Μαια, who is also known as the mother of Hermes, to the Indian *māyā* is questionable.

32. Apuleius, *Metamorphoses* XI, 3ff. For a general survey see *Hellenistic Religions. The Age of Syncretism*, ed. F.C. Grant, New York, 1953.

33. Cf. H.A. Wolfson, *Philo* I. Cambridge, Mass., second ed., 1948, 1ff. Concerning Aristobulus, who is supposed to have preceded Philo on this path in the second century B.C., we know very little.

34. *Praep. evang.* XI, 3; in F. Wehrli, *Die Schule des Aristoteles II: Aristoxenos*, Basel, 1945, 24 (fr.53). According to Diogenes Laërtius II, 45, a Magian from Syria visited Socrates and predicted a violent death for him.

35. See H.A. Wolfson (see above, note 33), 1ff.; 138ff. Occasionally, Philo depicts Heraclitus as a plagiarist, who acquired his teachings from Moses (loc. cit. 141); however, Philo also works with a model which implies a conception of "two truths."

36. See *Stromateis* I, 15 (§71ff.); VI, 4–5 (§37ff.).

37. Μωυσης αττικιζων (fr. 13 in the edition by F. Thedinga. Bonn, 1875. A new collection of fragments with a French translation has been edited by E. des Places. Paris, 1973).

38. For the *Life of Apollonius* of Philostratus see below, §17; see also his association of older type of Greek "Sophists" with Oriental "Manticism," *Vita sophist.* I, 2 (Olearius 480ff.).

39. *Vita Plot.* 3 (§15ff.); see below, §17. For a biography of Plotinus, see H. Oppermann, *Plotins Leben*. Heidelberg, 1929.

40. Diodorus II, 30; also G. Murray, *Five Stages of Greek Religion*. Garden City, N.Y., 1955, 138. On Claudius Aelianus, see Breloer-Bömer, 143 (from Var. hist. II, 31).

41. See A.-J. Festugiere, *La Révélation d'Hermes Trismégiste*, 4 vols. Paris, 1942ff. See esp. I (third edition, 1950), 6ff.

42. See *Leben und Taten Alexanders von Makedonien. Der griechische Alexanderroman nach der Handschrift L.*, ed./trans. H. van Thiel. Darmstadt, 1974. Also R. Merkelbach, *Die Quellen des griechischen Alexanderromans*. München, 1954.

43. See W. Reese, *Die griechischen Nachrichten über Indien bis zum Feldzuge Alexanders des Grossen*. Leipzig, 1914. The article "India," *RE* 9 (1916), 1264–1325 (by Wecker) is still very useful for an overview of the Greco-Roman knowledge of India. See also F.F. Schwarz, "Neue Perspektiven in den griechisch-indischen Beziehungen." *OLZ* 67 (1972), 5-26 (a good survey of recent studies); and J. Sedlar, *India and the Greek World* (see above, note 10).

44. See above, note 10. On the role of Egypt, see S. Morenz, *Die Begegnung Europas mit Ägypten*. Stuttgart, 1969.

45. See K. Goldammer (see above, note. 23), 1ff.

46. See H.W.A.M. Sancisi-Weerdenburg, *Yauna en Persai. Grieken en Perzen in een ander perspectief*. Diss. Leiden, 1980. This is one of the few attempts to study the very scarcely documented Persian views of their Greek enemies and partners. For a good survey of the mutual relations between Greeks and Persians, see G. Walser, *Hellas und Iran*. Darmstadt, 1984.

47. W. Reese (see above, note 43), 92.

48. The *Mahābhārata*, the *Purāṇas* and Varāhamihira's *Bṛhatsaṃhitā* are the most important Indian sources. The correspondences, some of which had already been noticed by Chr. Lassen in his *Indische Altertumskunde* (1847-1858), have recently been investigated by K. Karttunen; see, for instance: "Κυνοκέφαλοι and κυναμολγοί in Classical Ethnography," *Arctos. Acta Philologica Fennica* 18 (1984), 31–36; "The Reliability of the Indika of Ktesias," *Studia Orientalia* 50 (1981; Proceedings of the Nordic South Asia Conference), 105–107.

49. For a collection of these fragments, see Breloer-Bömer, as well as F. Jacoby, *Die Fragmente der griechischen Historiker*. Berlin/Leiden, 1923–1958 (Documents concerning India: Vol. III C, 1958, 587-666).

50. See W. Reese (see above, note 43), 66f.; for "cannibalism," see Breloer-Bömer, Index, s.v. "caro." Cannibalism and vegetarianism are placed side by side by Eusebius, *Praep. evang.* VI, 10 (Breloer-Bömer, 130).

51. In addition, see the compilations of classical documents in English translations in the publications of J.W. McCrindle. For Arrian, see the new edition and translation by P.A. Brunt: Arrian, *History of Alexander and Indica*. 2 vols., Cambridge, Mass./London, 1976-1983 (vol. 2, 443–474: "Indian Questions").

52. See Diogenes Laërtius IX, 61.

53. See F. Pfister, "Das Nachleben der Überlieferung von Alexander und den Brahmanen," *Hermes* 76 (1941), 143–169; U. Wilcken, "Alexander der Grosse und die indischen Gymnosophisten," *Sb. Preuss. Ak. Wiss., Phil.-hist. Kl., Jg.* 1923/24, 150–183; J. Seibert, *Alexander der Grosse*. Darmstadt, 1972.

54. Βραχμανες (also Βραγμανες, Βραχμαναι etc.) and Γυμνοσοφισται. The term "gymnosophist" does not appear in the extant fragments of Megasthenes; Strabo XV, 1,70 has the term "gymnes".

55. XV, 1, 66 (Breloer-Bömer, 10); the "Brahmins" are depicted as political advisors. The relation of "Brahmins" and "gymnosophists", etc., is not always clear and unambiguous. Megasthenes and others contrast the *Σαρμαναι* with the "Brahmins"; in Clement they are also different from *Σαμαναιοι*. See below, n. 72.

56. See Breloer-Bömer, 10 (Chares of Mytilene); 12 (Onesicritus); 75f. (Plutarch, the best known description).

57. See Diodorus XII, 107 (Breloer-Bömer, 40); on the one side, it appears as an expression of *μανια* and *κενοδοξια* (madness and vanity), on the other, of *ευψυχια* and *θανατου καταφρονησις* (good courage and contempt of death).

58. Breloer-Bömer, 14; on Kalanos, see the article by W. Kroll, *RE* 10 (1919), 1544–1546.

59. *Tusculanae disputationes* V, 77; see also Flavius Josephus, *De bello Iudaico* VII, 352ff. (Breloer-Bömer, 64); Cicero, loc. cit., II, 17; 22.

60. See Breloer-Bömer, 40f.; 76; 54; 60. In spite of the stereotypes, this seems to indicate that the practice of widow-burning, which became known as *satī* and was passionately debated at the beginning of the nineteenth century, has an old tradition. For general observations concerning the history and geographic diffusion of this custom see O. Schrader, *Totenhochzeit*. Jena, 1904. Also, A. Hillebrandt, "Der freiwillige Feuertod in Indien und die Somaweihe," *Sb. Bayer. Ak. Wiss., Phil.-hist. Kl., Jg.* 1917, Nr. 8; Th.Zachariae, "Zur indischen Witwenverbrennung." *Opera minora*, ed. C. Vogel, Wiesbaden 1977, 545–599.

61. Cf. Breloer-Bömer, 13: . . . *νομον πρo της φυσεως τιθεμενους* (as in Strabo XV, 1,65); see also the works cited in note 51.

62. Cf. Strabo XV, 1, 64; on Onesicritus in general, see T.S. Brown, *Onesicritus. A Study in Hellenistic Historiography*. Berkeley, 1949.

63. See Breloer-Bömer, 75 (Plutarch, *Vita Alexandri*); also J.W. de Jong, "The Discovery of India by the Greeks," *Asiatische Studien* (Bern), 27 (1973), 115–142; specifically 119f.

64. The fragments have been collected by Chr. Lassen's disciple E.A. Schwanbeck, *Megasthenis Indica*. Bonn, 1846 (repr. Amsterdam, 1966). For an English translation, see J.W. McCrindle, *Ancient India as Described by Megasthenes and Arrian*. London, 1877 (several reprints). For general information on Megasthenes, see the relevant articles in *RE* (by O. Stein) and *Der Kleine Pauly* (by J.D.M. Derrett). Cf. also B.C.J. Timmer, *Megasthenes en de Indische Maatschappij*. Amsterdam, 1930. In 305–304 B.C., Seleucus and Candragupta agreed on a "matrimonial alliance" (*κηδος*), which authorized mixed marriages between Greeks and Indians.

65. J.H. Mordtmann, "Mythologische Miszellen," *ZDMG* 32 (1878), 552.

66. See A. Dahlquist, *Megasthenes and Indian Religion*. Stockholm, 1962 (repr. Delhi, 1977), esp. 69ff. (Heracles); 175ff (Dionysus).

67. This connection is already documented for the Alexander historian Cleitarchus; see Breloer-Bömer, 14. Euripides, *Bakchai* 13ff., already associates Dionysus with Asia.

68. See Dahlquist (see above, note 66; partly speculative); for a more recent discussion: S.R. Goyal, *Kauṭilya and Megasthenes*. Delhi, 1986.

69. See Schwanbeck, fr. 1; 33; 41–43 ("Brahmins" and "Sarmans" are contrasted).

70. *Stromateis* I, 17, 3ff.

71. *De abstinentia* IV, 17ff (ed. Nauck, [second edition] 1886, 256ff.). Porphyry quotes the Gnostic Bardesanes.

72. See A. Dihle, "Indische Philosophen bei Clemens Alexandrinus," *Mullus. Festschrift Th. Klauser*. Münster, 1964, 60–70. Also "The Conception of India in Hellenistic and Roman Literature," *Proceedings of the Cambridge Philological Society* 1964, 15–23 (esp. 21ff.). In addition to the Bactrian Σαμαναιοι, Clement mentions other Indian followers of the Buddha (Βουττα). On the various names applied to the Indian "philosophers," see already Chr. Lassen, "De nominibus quibus a veteribus appellantur Indorum philosophi." *Rheinisches Museum* 1(1833), 171–190 (180ff.: on the Bactrian Σαμαναιοι). The important investigations by A. Dihle have now been collected in: *Antike und Orient*. Heidelberg 1984.

73. See Schwanbeck, fr.42 (Breloer-Bömer, 30; following Clement).

74. See Flavius Josephus, *Contra Apionem* I, 178f.

75. See Schwanbeck, fr. 41 (esp. pp. 137; 139).

76. See along with E.H. Warmington, *The Commerce between the Roman Empire and India*. Cambridge, 1928 (repr. 1951). Also M. Wheeler, *Rome beyond the Imperial Frontiers*. London, 1954.

77. A. Dihle, "The Conception of India" (see above, note 72), 20.

78. A. Dihle, op. cit., 21ff.

79. See above, note 34. The classical study of Aristoxenus' story is R. Hirzel, "Aristoxenos und Platons erster Alkibiades," *Rheinisches Museum*, N.S. 45 (1890) 419–435. See also A.-J. Festugière, "Grecs et sages orientaux." *Revue de l'histoire des religions* 130 (1945), 29–41; especially 34ff.; this supplements Festugière's earlier discussion of legendary encounters between Greeks and Indians: "Trois rencontres entre la Grèce et l'Inde," *Revue de l'histoire des religions* 125 (1943), 32–57.

80. See the study by F. Pfister mentioned in note 53, 147f.; also H. Gregor, *Das Indienbild des Abendlandes bis zum Ende des 13.Jh.* Diss. Wien, 1963, 39.

81. H. Gregor, loc. cit.; see Lach II/2, 91ff.

82. *The Brahman Episode. St. Ambrose's Version of the Colloquy between Alexander the Great and the Brahmins of India*, ed. and trans. by S.V. Yankowski. Ansbach, 1962, p.47. The Latin original reads:

Tu vero, si vera vis sapere, ad Indiam veni, habita in solitudinibus ipsis nudus, omnes tamen, omnes quas diligis, et quibus videris ornari, proiciens dignitates; nam aliter non susciperis a nobis. Et tunc amabis ea, quaecumque ante paulo vidisti, quaeque miratus es. Neque ullus contra te ulterius dimicabit, aut quicquam mox tibi auferre quis poterit; neque aliena collatione, neque aliorum sudore pasceris; eris enim in omnibus dives.

83. See Flavius Josephus in Breloer-Bömer, 64.

84. See Clement, *Stromateis* IV, 4 (§17); shown in a positive light vis-à-vis Alexander: IV, 7 (§50), as already in Philo; see Breloer-Bömer, 55.

85. See Breloer-Bömer, 95 (Pausanias; on the doctrine of immortality of the soul); 103 (Apuleius; Plato allegedly tried in vain to make contact with the Indians and Magi); 190 (Claudianus Mamertus).

86. Cf. Diogenes Laërtius, IX, 35.

87. Breloer-Bömer, 159 (Eusebius Pamphilus, ca. 300A.D.).

88. Breloer-Bömer, 102 (Apuleius, Florid. 15).

89. This is seen above all in the *Life of Apollonius* of Philostratus. When Clement, *Stromateis* III, 7 (§60), refers to the belief of the Brahmins in "palingenesis," it is not necessary to assume that reincarnation is meant. The modern discussion of this topic began with L. von Schröder, *Pythagoras und die Inder*. Leipzig, 1884, 5–31. The arguments of von Schröder, which had been received more favorably by R. Garbe, E.W. Hopkins and A.A. Macdonell, were criticized and rejected by A.B. Keith, "Pythagoras and the Doctrine of Transmigration," *JRAS* 1909, 569–606. On the development of the doctrine among the Greeks see H.S. Long, *A Study of the Doctrine of Metempsychosis in Greece from Pythagoras to Plato*. Princeton, 1948.

90. As an example of the lively interest taken in this theme during the nineteenth century we may mention: O. de Beauvoir Priaulx, *The Indian Travels of Apollonius of Tyana and the Indian Embassies to Rome*. London, 1873 (originally in *JRAS* 17, 1860, 70–105. Later, for example, R. Goossens, "Un texte grec relatif a l'aśvamedha," *JA* 217 (1930), 280–285; J. Charpentier, *The Indian Travels of Apollonius of Tyana*. Uppsala, 1934.

91. See É. Bréhier, *La philosophie de Plotin*. Paris, 1928, 107; Bréhier later complained that his suggestion was not adopted by the Indological camp; see "Images plotiniennes, images bergsonniennes," *Études Bergsonniennes* 2 (1949), 105–128; 215–222; remarks in conversation with J. Baruzi, ibid. 223. Bréhier's thesis was decisively rejected by the classical scholar A.H. Armstrong, "Plotinus and India," *Classical Quarterly* 30 (1936), 22–28; an overview of the newer literature pertaining to this theme is to be found in J.F. Staal, *Advaita and Neoplatonism*. Madras, 1961, 235ff.

92. For one of the most penetrating comparative studies, see P. Hacker, "Cit and Nous, or the Concept of Spirit in Vedāntism and in Neoplatonism," *Kleine Schriften*, ed. L. Schmithausen. Wiesbaden, 1978, 320–337.

93. The conclusions drawn by E. Benz are premature. See E. Benz, "Indische Einflüsse auf die frühchristliche Theologie," *Ak. Wiss. Lit. Mainz. Abh. d. geistes- und sozialwiss. Kl. Jg.* 1951, Nr. 3 (Wiesbaden, 1951), esp. 197ff.,

94. See already I.J. Schmidt, *Über die Verwandtschaft der gnostisch-theosophischen Lehren mit den Religionssystemen des Orients, vorzüglich des Buddhismus*. Leipzig, 1828. Later, for example, J. Kennedy, "Buddhist Gnosticism, the System of Basilides," *JRAS* 1902, 377–415; E. Conze, "Buddhism and Gnosis," *Further Buddhist Studies*. Oxford, 1975, 15–32 (originally in *Le origine dello gnosticismo*, 1967, 651–667).

95. On Bardesanes, see H.J.W. Drijvers, *Bardaisan of Edessa*. Assen, 1966.

96. See G. Messina, *Christianesimo, Buddhismo, Manicheismo nell' Asia antica*. Rome, 1947. In Mani's time, there were also Buddhists living in the eastern parts of the Persian Empire. On Nestorian and Manichean encounters with Buddhism in Central Asia see H.J. Klimkeit, "Gottes- und Selbsterfahrung in der gnostisch-buddhistischen Religionsbegegnung Zentralasiens," *Zeitschrift für Religions- und Geistesgeschichte* 35 (1983), 236–247.

97. *Fugitivi* 6f. (Breloer-Bömer, 100f.). H. von Glasenapp *Die Philosophie der inder*. Stuttgart, 1949, 436, seems to assume that this is a serious contribution to the debate on the problem of the origin of philosophy, comparable to that of Diogenes, but this is very unlikely.

98. See *The Moral Edicts of King Aśoka*, ed. P.H.L. Eggermont/J. Hoftijzer. Leiden, 1962, 42ff; É. Lamotte, *Histoire du bouddhisme indien*. Louvain, 1958, 789ff. (on the Greek-Aramaic edict of Kandahar).

99. According to the testimony of Porphyry, *De abstinentia* IV, 17ff (ed. Nauck, second edition, 1886, 256ff.; in Breloer-Bömer, 131ff.; see also ibid., 131ff., after a fragment preserved by Stobaeus).

100. See Dion of Prusa (usually called Chrysostomos), *Orationes* 32 (Ad Alexandrinos), 40 (ed. G. de Budé, Leipzig, 1916, I, 355); see also 35, 22ff (Budé I, 430f; Breloer-Bömer, 67): Speaking in the Phrygian city of Celaenae, Dion refers to "Brahmins" who gave up the wonders and pleasures of India in order to do trade in foreign countries, and who were criticized for this by other Indians (*αφιχνουνται δε ου πολλοι τινες εμποριας ενεχεν . . . οι τε αλλοι ψεγουσιν αυτους*).

101. See "La doctrine brahmanique à Rome au IIIe siècle" (originally 1945); in: J. Filliozat, *Les Relations extérieures de l'Inde I*, Pondicherry, 1956, esp. 48. Against Filliozat, L.C. Ruggini argues that Hippolytus got his information from a source close to Megasthenes, or even Megasthenes himself. In her view, the same source was also available to Clement, Bardesanes and the author of the *Commonitorium Palladii*; see "Sulla christianizzazione della cultura pagana," *Athenæum* (Pavia) 43 (1965), 3–80; esp 38: "Sicché appare molto probabile che entrambi i testi seguano dappresso una fonte commune vicinissima a Megastene (se non Megastene stesso). . ."

102. W.W. Tarn, *The Greeks in Bactria and India*. Cambridge, second edition, 1951, 387.

103. See below, ch. 11, §18.

104. For a good survey of the many versions of the *Alexander Romance*, see the article "Alexanderroman," *KLL* I, 389ff. A very learned, but occasionally speculative, attempt to find traces of the *Alexander Romance* in Indian literature is J.D.M. Derrett, "Greece and India again: the Jaimini-Aśvamedha, the Alexander-Romance and the Gospels," *Zeitschrift für Religions- und Geistesgeschichte* 22 (1970), 19–44. In this article, Derrett also tries to revive suggestions by A. Weber concerning Christian influences in the Kṛṣṇa literature and the *bhakti* traditions of the Indians. We cannot discuss the validity of these suggestions here, nor of the various attempts to find Greek influences in Indian dramatic literature and so forth.

105. The attempt of W.W. Tarn (see above, note 102), 414–436 to infer an originally Greek version of the *Milindapañha* is not convincing. Concerning the relation between Buddhism and the Mediterranean world see also S. Lévi, "Le bouddhisme et les Grecs," *Revue de l'Histoire des Religions* 23 (1891), 36–41; R. Garbe, *Indien und das Christentum*. Tübingen, 1914; H. de Lubac, *La rencontre du bouddhisme et de l'occident*. Paris, 1952; J.D.M. Derrett, "Greece and India: The Milindapanha, the Alexanderromance and the Gospels," *Zeitschrift für Religions- und Geistesgeschichte* 19 (1967), 33–63.

106. U. Hölscher, "Anaximander und die Anfänge der Philosophie" (see above, note 10), 167.

107. See A. Momigliano, *Alien Wisdom. The Limits of Hellenization*. Cambridge, 1975, 8: "But the Greeks were seldom in a position to check what the natives told them: they did not know the languages. The natives, on the other hand, being bilingual, had a shrewd idea of what the Greeks wanted to hear and spoke accordingly. This reciprocal position did not make for sincerity and real understanding."—149: "Once again we have come up against the dilemma of Hellenistic civilization. It had all the instruments of knowing other civilizations—except concerning languages."

108. See below, ch. 4.

109. Documents of a more relaxed and, in a sense, "comparative" approach to other religions, for instance *Contra Sarracenos*, a refutation of Islam by Petrus Venerabilis (twelfth century), are more exceptional in Christianity than Islam. A unique document of "tolerance" in the fifteenth century is the treatise *De pace fidei* by Nicolaus Cusanus (Nicholas of Cusa). It was written after the Muslim conquest of Constantinople in 1453 and interprets the "variety of rites" ("varietas rituum") as a natural God-given phenomenon, which does not justify persecution. There is even an Indian appearing in this work who states that, just like the Romans and so forth, the Indians are "reasonable people" ("sapientes") who might be willing to abandon idolatry, but still find it difficult to accept the Christian trinity. See B. Kuhn-Emmerich, *Die Toleranz bei Nikolaus von Cues*. Diss. Bonn, 1968, 31ff.

110. For the historical tradition and geographical diffusion of these materials, see *KLL*, articles "Barlaam and Josaphat"; "Kalīla wa-Dimna" (following the title of the Syrian version of the *Pañcatantra*).

111. See H. Gregor (see above, note 80), 37ff. On the connection of India with the conception of Paradise (the Ganges as the river in the Garden of Eden) see S. Darian, *The Ganges in Myth and History*. Honolulu, 1978, 172ff. (uncritical). Cf. also E. Bloch, *Das Prinzip Hoffnung*. Frankfurt, 1959, 889ff.

112. See Breloer-Bömer, 208; furthermore 201 (Isidor); 175 (Augustine, *De civ. Dei* XIV, 17): "adhibent tamen genitalibus tegmina, quibus per cetera membrorum carent." The "Brahmins" of Alexandria, first referred to by Dion of Prusa (see above, note 100), were still mentioned by Damascius around 500 A.D. in his *Vita Isidori* (Breloer-Bömer 194f.; according to the testimony of the Byzantine scholar Photius, ninth century). Damascius attributed to them a noble, reserved and simple mode of life.

113. H. Gregor, loc. cit., 7. For numerous additional references, see Th. Hahn, "The Indian Tradition in Western Medieval Intellectual History." *Viator* 9 (1978), 213-234; for later references to "virtuous" brahmins, cf. Th. Hahn, *Upright Lives*. Los Angeles, 1981.

114. See Lach I, 25; V. Slessarev, *Prester John,* Minneapolis, 1959; J. Dahlmann, *Die Thomas-Legende*, Freiburg, 1912; A. Dihle, "Neues zur Thomas-Tradition," *Antike und Christentum* 6 (1963), 54-70; S. Neill, *A History of Christianity in India: The Beginnings to AD 1707*. Cambridge, 1984.

115. See, for example, Lach I, 59ff (on Niccolo de'Conti); as also K.A. Nilakantha Sastri, *Foreign Notices of South India from Megasthenes to Ma Huan*. Madras, 1939; second edition, 1972; F.M. Rogers, *The Quest for Eastern Christians*. Minneapolis, 1962; P. Winter-Wirz, *Die Reise des russischen Kaufmannes A. Nikitin*. Heidelberg, 1960 (Diss. Basel).

116. On the origin of philosophy and along with it a connected interest in the Orient, see, for example, Pico della Mirandola, *Heptaplus* (1489) I, Prooemium; also in this connection R.W. Meyer, "Pico della Mirandola und der Orient," *Asiatische Studien* 18/19 (1965), 308-336. A good overview of the early doxographic and historical interest in the philosophy of the Orient, and India in particular, is found in F.A. Carus, *Ideen zur Geschichte der Philosophie*. Leipzig, 1809; on Carus, see below, ch. 9, §3.

2. Islamic Encounters With Indian Philosophy

1. See M. Steinschneider, *Die europäischen Übersetzungen aus dem Arabischen bis Mitte des 17. Jh.* Graz, second edition, 1956 (originally *Sb. Ak. Wiss.* Wien, 1905); R. Walzer, "Arabische Übersetzungen aus dem Griechischen," *Misc. mediaevalia I* (Berlin, 1962), 179-195.

2. See the relevant sections of M. Ullmann, *Die Natur- und Geheimwissenschaften im Islam*. Leiden/Köln, 1972. Also his *Die Medizin im Islam*. Leiden/Köln, 1970, 130ff. On the decimal system, see also A.L. Basham, *The Wonder That Was India*. New York, 1959, 495f. (Appendix IV).

3. See B.B. Lawrence, *Shahrastānī on the Indian Religions*. The Hague/Paris, 1976, 17ff. For bibliographical references: 279ff. Pioneering work on this literature was done by V. Minorsky; see in particular: "Sharaf al-Zamān Ṭāhir Marvazī on China, the Turks and India," *BSOAS* 12 (1948), 625-640; for Idrīsī, see: *India and the Neighbouring Territories in the Kitāb nuzhat al-mushtāq fī'khtirāq al-ᶜāfāq of al-Sharīf al-Idrīsī*, trans. with commentary by S. Maqbul Ahmad. Leiden, 1960.

4. For a survey of his numerous writings see M. Horten, *Die Philosophie des Islam*, München, 1924, 325ff.; also 171ff.

5. Still authoritative is the English translation by E.C. Sachau, *Alberuni's India*. 2 vols. London, 1888 (numerous reprints and abbreviated editions, e.g., A.T. Embree, New York, 1971); Sachau brought out the Arabic text in London, 1887. See further, A. Jeffery, "Al-Bīrūnī's Contribution to Comparative Religion," *Al-Bīrūnī*

Commemoration Volume. Calcutta, 1951, 125–160; B.B. Lawrence, "Al-Bīrūnī's Approach to the Comparative Study of Indian Culture," *Bīrūnī Symposium* (Persian Studies Ser. 7), ed. E. Yarshater. New York, 1976, 27–47. The recent monograph by A. Sharma, *Studies in "Alberuni's India."* Wiesbaden, 1983, which deals with such topics as "al-Bīrūnī and the Bhagavadgītā," is inadequate. A. Schimmel calls al-Bīrūnī's work "the first objective study ever made of a foreign culture" (*Islam in the Indian Subcontinent*. Leiden, 1980, 7). Al-Bīrūnī himself prepared a list of his works; for those dealing with Indian topics, see F. Mujtabai, *Aspects of Hindu Muslim Cultural Relations*. New Delhi, 1978, 15ff.

6. See Sachau I, 5; 7; 24.

7. We cannot deal with the development of hermeneutics on the Eastern side; on Chinese reflections concerning the problem of translation from Sanskrit see, for example, A. Held, *Der buddhistische Mönch Yen-Ts'ung (557–610) und seine Übersetzungstheorie*. Diss. Köln, 1972.

8. See Sachau I, XXXIXf.

9. See Sachau I, 125ff.; 130f.: Lists of *Purāṇas*.

10. E.g. I, 132: a text assigned to Kapila, *Nyāyabhāṣā*.

11. See Sachau I, XL; II, 264ff.; on Bīrūnī's style of quoting in general, see J. Gonda, "Remarks on al-Bīrūnī's Quotations from Sanskrit Texts," *Al-Bīrūnī Commemoration Volume*. Calcutta, 1951, 111–118 (also in: *Selected Studies* IV. Leiden, 1975, 515–522); on his knowledge of Sanskrit and his cooperation with Indian scholars also S.K. Chatterji, "Al-Bīrūnī and Sanskrit," loc. cit., 83–100; B.B. Lawrence, *Bīrūnī Symposium* (see above, n.5), 33f.

12. On al-Bīrūnī's translation of the *Yogasūtras*, see J.W. Hauer, "Das neugefundene arabische Manuskript von al-Bīrūnī's Übersetzung des Pātañjala," *OLZ* 33 (1930), 273–282. The Arabic text was edited by H. Ritter, "Al-Bīrūnī's Übersetzung des Yoga-Sūtra," *Oriens* 9 (1956), 165–200; the first three chapters are available in English translation by S. Pines and T. Gelblum: "Al-Bīrūnī's Arabic Version of Patañjali's Yogasūtra," I–III. *BSOAS* 29 (1960), 302–325; 40 (1977), 522–549; 46 (1983), 258–304. Concerning *Sāṃkhya*, see Sachau I, 89ff.; 132; 321.

13. Sachau I, 6f.: his work is nevertheless a major source for Bīrūnī's views on Buddhism.

14. Sachau I, 24.

15. Sachau I, 24f.; to be sure, Bīrūnī believed that the Greeks had an influence on the Indian sciences, which was later forgotten; on his efforts to translate Greek-Arabic scientific works into Sanskrit see Sachau's introduction to the Arabic text, XIXf.

16. Sachau I, 19f.

17. Sachau I, 17ff.; 25.

18. Sachau I, 7.

19. See Sachau I, 179: "The strangeness of a thing rests on the fact that it occurs but rarely, and that we seldom have the opportunity of witnessing it."

20. See above, ch.1, §5.

21. Sachau I, 22f.

22. Sachau I, 27ff.; 39.

23. On Sūfism see Sachau I, 8; 33f.; concerning Abū Yazīd: 88; Plato: 35f.; Ammonius, Pythagoras: 85.

24. On Arabic renderings of *Sāṃkhya* terminology see L. Massignon, *Essai sur les origines du lexique technique de la mystique musulmane*. Paris, 1954, 92ff. Bīrūnī is, however, relatively independent of Sūfī terminology.

25. Ed. W. Cureton, London, 1846; German transl. Th. Haarbrücker, *Abu-'l-Fath' Muhammad asch-Schahrastāni's Religionsparteien und Philosophen-Schulen*, 2 Teile, Halle, 1850. Concerning the portions relating to India see B.B. Lawrence, in the work cited in note 3.

26. See B.B. Lawrence (see above, note 3), 275: "The inescapable truth is that, aside from the unique essay on 'the Followers of the Buddhas,' Shahrastānī makes no substantive contribution to medieval Indian history which could not be found in similar, and usually superior, detail in one or more parallel Muslim sources."

27. See Th. Haarbrücker (see above, note 25) II, 372ff.; B.B. Lawrence, 253ff.; on the problem of the connection between the Brahmins and the aforementioned Barhām: 266. As one might expect in such a case, Lawrence's identifications of Indian sects leave a number of questions open.

28. See Th, Haarbrücker II, 356ff.; B.B. Lawrence, 77ff.

29. See M. Schreiner, "Zur Geschichte der Polemik zwischen Juden und Mohammedanern," *ZDMG* 42 (1888), 591-675; esp. 605ff; W. Engelkemper, *Die religionsphilosophische Lehre Saadja Gaons über die Hl. Schrift*. Münster, 1903, 66f.

30. S. Stroumsa, "The Barāhima in Early Kalām," *Jerusalem Studies in Arabic and Islam* 6 (1985), 229-241; specifically 229. It was P. Kraus in particular who questioned the identity of the Barāhima with the Brahmins.

31. Ibid., 241. The notion of prophecy as a unique personal message and an unrepeatable historical event would obviously have been objectionable or even incomprehensible to the representatives of traditional Hindu thought.

32. See K. Jahn, *Rashīd al-Dīn's History of India*. The Hague, 1965, X. For Rashīd's role in the larger context of universal historiography, see *Mensch und Weltgeschichte*, ed. A. Randa, Salzburg/München, 1969, esp. 145ff. (the contribution by K. Jahn).

33. See K. Jahn, loc. cit. XIV; XXXIff.

34. See D. Gimaret, "Bouddha et les bouddhistes dans la tradition musulmane," JA 257 (1969), 273-316; J.L. Smith, "Early Muslim Accounts of Buddhism in India," *Studies in Islam* 10 (1973), 87-100.

35. See K. Jahn, loc. cit., LXXVII.

36. *A History of Muslim Historiography*. Leiden, 1952 (second edition, 1968), 130.

37. In general, see Gonda II, 97ff; rich in data, but to be used with caution is T. Chand, *The Influence of Islam on Indian Culture*. Allahabad, 1954.

38. Gonda II, 97.

39. Ibid., 100.

40. A. Schimmel, *Islam in the Indian Subcontinent*. Leiden, 1980, 10.

41. See R. Nath and Faiyaz 'Gwaliari,' *India as Seen by Amir Khusrau*. Jaipur, 1981; specifically chs. 4 & 5.

42. See Gonda II, 107; also, for instance, Y. Husain, *L'Inde mystique au moyen age, hindous et musulmans*. Paris, 1929; A. Ahmad, *Studies in Islamic Culture in the Indian Environment*. London, 1964 (esp. 140ff.); A. Roy, *The Islamic Syncretistic Tradition in Bengal*. Princeton, 1983. On Dādū Dayāl, see K.M. Sen, *Medieval Mysticism of India*, trans. from the Bengali by M.M. Ghosh. London, 1936 (reprint New Delhi, 1974), 173-202; also W.G. Orr, *A Sixteenth-Century Indian Mystic*. London, 1947.

43. See, for instance, W.H. McLeod, *Guru Nānak and the Sikh Religion*. Oxford, 1968.

44. See R.C. Zaehner, *Hindu and Muslim Mysticism*. New York, 1969 (originally London, 1960), 93ff.; 105; M. Horten, *Indische Strömungen in der islamischen Mystik*, 2 vols. Leipzig/Heidelberg, 1927-1928 (unreliable).

45. See above, §5.

46. For a survey of the Sūfī contributions, see S.A.A. Rizvi, *A History of Sufism in India*. New Delhi, 1978. Rizvi has also dealt with the intellectual climate of the Akbar period: *Religious and Intellectual History of the Muslims in Akbar's Reign*. New Delhi, 1975.

47. Gonda II, 106.

48. See B.J. Hasrat, *Dārā Shikuh*. Calcutta, 1953, 187ff.; 191.

49. For an overview, see N.S. Shukla, "Persian Translations of Sanskrit Works," *Indological Studies* (Delhi) 3 (1974), 175-191; F. Mujtabai, *Aspects of Hindu Muslim Cultural Relations*. New Delhi, 1978, 60-91: "Persian Hindu Writings" (see the reference to a Persian translation of Śaṅkara's *Brahmasūtrabhāṣya*, 84, note 69; and the survey of *Yogavāsiṣṭha* translations, 81ff.).

50. See *Ain-i-Akbari of Abdul Fazl-i-Allami*, III. Trans. by H.S. Jarrett, revised by J.N. Sarkar.Calcutta, 1948 (Bibliotheca Indica). See already J.G. Schweighaeuser, "Sur les sectes philosophiques de l'Inde," *Archives littéraires de l'Europe* 16 (1807), 193-206.

51. Loc. cit., 229-253; for a presentation of the classical philosophical systems, see 143-228. Madhusūdana is mentioned alongside numerous other Hindu and Islamic scholars from the time of Akbar; cf., for instance, D.C. Bhattacharyya, "Sanskrit Scholars of Akbar's Time," *IHQ* 13 (1937), 31-36; also P.C. Divanji, Intro. to: *Siddhāntabindu of Madhusūdana*. Baroda, 1933 (GOS), XXI (Madhusūdana as a guest at the court of Akbar).

52. Abu'l Faḍl's brother Faiḍī is credited with a work which dealt, among other topics, with Vedāntic thought and was titled *Shāriq al-ma'rifat*; see Hasrat (see above, note 48), 206f.

53. Ed. T. Chand and J. Naini, Teheran, 1957; for Anquetil Duperron's translation, see below, ch. 4. For an overview of Dārā Shukoh's writings, see A. Schimmel, *Islamic Literatures of India*. Wiesbaden, 1973, 39ff.

54. Cf. E. Göbel-Gross, *Sirr-i Akbar*. Diss. Marburg, 1962.

55. See C. Huart and L. Massignon, "Les entretiens de Lahore," *JA* 209 (1926), 285-334 (includes the Persian text with a French translation); Hasrat (see above, note 48), 239-254; K.R. Qanungo, *Dara Shukoh*. Calcutta, second edition, 1952, 240-251.

56. English transl. D. Shea/A. Troyer, Paris, 1843 (repr. New York, 1937; Lahore, 1973); already partially translated by F. Gladwin, a contemporary of W. Jones, who also worked on Abu'l Faḍl.

57. *Majma' ul-Bahrain or The Mingling of the Two Oceans*, by Prince Dārā Shikūh. Ed. in the orig. Persian with Engl. transl. by M. Mahfuz-ul-Haq. Calcutta, 1929 (Bibliotheca Indica).

58. See, for instance, Haq, 72; 74f.

59. Haq, loc. cit., 13.

60. E. Göbel-Gross, loc. cit. (see above, note 54), 14.

61. Göbel-Gross, loc. cit., 23.

62. See Qanungo (see above, note 55), 228ff.

63. See Y. Friedman, *Shaykh Aḥmad Sirhindī*. Montreal/London, 1971, 23; 59ff. Worth noting in this connection are the reminiscences of M. Buber on the experience of "Zweitlosigkeit" ("non-duality") out of which he returned to the personal I-Thou; see "Zwiesprache" (1929); in *Werke* I. Heidelberg, 1962, esp. 197ff.

64. See A. Schimmel (see above, note 40), 276.

65. See M. ᶜAbdu'l Walī, "Hinduism according to Muslim Sūfīs," *JAS Bengal*, N.S. 19 (1923), 238-252; esp. 238f.; also Y. Friedman, "Medieval Muslim Views of Indian Religions," *JAOS* 95 (1975), 214-221.

66. See below, ch. 4, §12ff.; aside from Schopenhauer, Görres, Krause, Rixner and others were fascinated by Anquetil's *Oupnek'hat*.

67. See *Sechzig Upanishad's des Veda*. Darmstadt, fourth edition, 1963, 829. The Sanskrit version of the *Praṇava Upaniṣad* ("Pranou"), which Deussen had originally translated from its version in the *Oupnek'hat*, was subsequently discovered in the *Gopatha Brāhmaṇa*.—"Reflections from the famous Oupnek'hat" (by M.C. von Krempelhuber) appeared in 1869 in Munich under the title of *Mahabak* (i.e. Sanskrit *mahāvākya*). Deussen's German version of the Upaniṣads was translated into English by V.M. Bedekar and G.B. Palsule, Delhi, 1980.

68. On N.B. Halhed's English translation of the *Sirr-i-Akbar* (completed in 1787) and on Jones' unfavorable assessment of the Persian text, see below, ch.4.

3. The Missionary Approach to Indian Thought

1. On the formula "Christians and spices," see Neill I, 91.

2. Lach I, 337.

3. Cf. Neill I, 191ff.; see also Lach I, 157.

4. On the speculations about Indian Christians who had lost their faith, see, for instance, *Monumenta Ignatiana* I/5, 415 (letter by Polanco, dated 1553). Francisco Xavier himself was reluctant to believe these rumors and speculations; see H. de Lubac, *Rencontre*, 79f. In 1552, G. Postel published his work *Des merveilles du monde*, probably the most remarkable document propagating the rediscovery and "retrieval" of forgotten forms of Christianity in the religious traditions of Asia, specifically Buddhism; in this connection, he refers to the efforts of the Jesuits to "bring back the spiritual unity of the world" ("refaire l'unité spirituelle du monde"); cf. de Lubac, 55f.

5. See Lach I, 401 (on Duarte Barbosa).

6. Lach I, 426.

7. See below, ch. 4, §3.

8. Cf. Lach I, 360. On Sassetti, see also *Lettere inedite di Filippo Sassetti*, ed. E. Marcucci. Florence, 1855; and Lach II/2, 520f.

9. See J. Wicki, "Die ältere katholische Mission in der Begegnung mit Indien," *Saeculum* 6 (1955), 345–367; specifically 349f.

10. See Neill I, 237; 476; also Lach I, 280; 438; and the original reports by L. Frois (1559 and 1560) in: *Documenta Indica* IV, ed. J. Wicki (Monumenta Historica Soc. Iesu, vol. 78). Rome, 1956, 334ff.; 802f. (with Wicki's notes).

11. Neill I, 240.

12. Cf. Neill I, 241f.; S.G. Tulpule, *Classical Marāṭhī Literature*. Wiesbaden, 1979, 380ff.; G. Schurhammer, *Gesammelte Studien II: Orientalia*. Rome/Lisbon, 1963, 367–391.

13. Cf. Neill I, 240; since 1556, there was a printing press in Goa.

14. Cf. Lach I, 436ff.; J.H. Hein, "Father Henriques' Grammar of Spoken Tamil, 1548," *Indian Church History Review* 11 (1977), 127–157.

15. Although the form "de' Nobili" has become more familiar, our missionary normally referred to himself simply as "Roberto Nobili"; cf. Neill I, 484, note 4 (referring to the investigations of J. Wicki).

16. See S. Rajamanickam, *The First Oriental Scholar*, Tirunelveli, 1972, 159ff.; also 85 (with reference to M. Müller); P.R. Bachmann, *Roberto Nobili*. Rome, 1972. Among the earlier studies, cf. W. Caland, "Roberto de' Nobili and the Sanskrit Language and Literature," *Acta Orientalia* (Leiden) 3 (1924), 38–51; P. Dahmen, *Un Jésuite Brahme: Robert de Nobili*. Bruges, 1924.

17. See S. Rajamanickam, op. cit., 260ff.: "Nobili's Technical Terms in Āttuma Nirṇayam"; and in general on terminological problems in the missionary traditions of South India: B. Tiliander, *Christian and Hindu Terminology*. Uppsala, 1974.

18. Both works were edited by S. Rajamanickam: *Adaptation* (i.e. *Narratio fundamentorum quibus Madurensis Missionis institutum caeptum est et hucusque consistit*, with English translation by J. Pujo). Palayamkottai, 1971; *On Indian Customs* (i.e. *Informatio de quibusdam moribus nationis Indicae*, with English translation by the editor). Palayamkottai, 1972. For a survey of Nobili's writings, see Neill I, 415f.

19. On the preservation of caste distinctions among the Christian converts, see P.R. Bachmann (above, n.16), 109f.

20. *Informatio*, 69 (§7.2).

21. *Informatio*. 34: "nomen Dei communissimum."

22. *Informatio*, 35; for the Sanskrit citations presented in this passage, cf. *Taittirīya Upaniṣad* II, 1,1: *brahmavid āpnoti param*.

23. *Informatio*, 9 (§2.1); in this connection, Nobili refers to Thomas Aquinas, *Summa theol.* I, 2, q.3 and II, 2, q.180.

24. Cf. *Informatio*, 15f. (§3.0).

25. Cf. *Informatio*, chapter 5 (on the "priesthood" of the Indians: "De sacerdotio huius gentis").

26. See *Informatio*, chapter 7 (64–79) and the essay "De linea Brahmanorum," which Rajamanickam added as Appendix I (175–193) to his edition of the *Narratio* (*Adaptation*, 1971).

27. See *Informatio*, I (§0.1; introduction), which emphasizes that the purpose of wearing the thread is a merely "political" one (". . . finemque impositionis in linea mere politicum esse").

28. See also the reference to "Bardeseres" (i.e. Bardesanes): according to Eusebius, he described the Brahmins as a hereditary group of "wise men" ("sapientes"; *Informatio* 6; §2.0).

29. *Informatio*. 114: "Discamus scilicet, feramus quae humana sunt, ut tradamus et firmemus divina."

30. A refutation of this doctrine is found in his Tamil work *Punarjanma-ākṣepam*, ed. S. Rajamanickam. Tuticorin, 1963.

31. *Narratio*, 6 (§1.1).

32. *Narratio*, 14 (§1.1.2.3). In this connection, the Indians appear as comparable to patients, and we may feel reminded of the Buddhist ideal of "skill in means" (*upāyakauśalya*). Matteo Ricci (1552–1610), who became known as Hsi-t'ai, had set a precedent in China. Another Jesuit, Ippolito Desideri (1684–1733), tried to achieve the same in Tibet; see his *Opere Tibetane*, ed. and trans. (into Italian) G. Toscano, 2 vols. Rome, 1981–1982.

33. *Narratio*, 23 (§1.1.3.6); cf. *Acts of the Apostles* 17.16ff. Nobili's missionary efforts focused originally on Brahmins, and he was convinced that the lower castes required a special and different type of missionaries. However, Nobili's attitude

towards lower castes changed after 1626.

34. See P.R. Bachmann, *Roberto Nobili*. Rome, 1972, 78.

35. P.R. Bachmann, 80f.; on the use of the word *veda* in the missionary literature of South India, see B. Tiliander, *Christian and Hindu Terminology*. Uppsala, 1974.

36. See *Ezourvedam. A French Veda of the Eighteenth Century*, ed. L. Rocher. Amsterdam/Philadelphia, 1984, 30–42 (on speculations and refutations concerning Nobili's authorship of the Ezourvedam).

37. See Neill I, 417ff.; R. Hauschild, *Der Missionar P. Heinrich Roth aus Dillingen und die erste europäische Sanskrit-Grammatik*. Berlin, 1972 (Sb. Sächs. Ak. Wiss., Phil.-hist. Klasse, 115/6). In the final decades of the sixteenth century, the religious policy of Akbar had raised high, but unfulfilled, hopes among the missionaries; during this period, three Jesuit delegations visited the court of Akbar (1580–1583; 1591; 1595–1605).

38. Cf. in this connection the claim of the Cartesian writer P.S. Regis that Christianity is basically free from conflicts with civil and secular institutions and therefore generally acceptable as "universal religion"; see *L'usage de la raison et de la foi*. Paris, 1704, 309f.

39. On this issue, see, for instance, D. Yeshudas, "Indigenization or Adaptation?" *Bangalore Theological Forum* I (1967), 39–52; especially 51.

40. Nobili himself initiated a tradition of debates between missionaries and Indian scholars; such debates, if not conducted by missionaries of the highest level of qualification, often turned out to be counterproductive. On the history of public disputations with Buddhist scholars in Ceylon, see the article "Pānadurē vādaya," in *KLL* (supplementary volume); for a survey of the "Bombay debates" between J. Wilson and Hindu pandits in the 1830's , see R.F. Young, *Resistant Hinduism*. Vienna, 1981, 25ff.

41. First published in 1743 (*Lettres édifiantes et curieuses, Recueil* XXVI); quoted from: *Lettres édifiantes et curieses concernant l'Asie, l'Afrique et l'Amérique*, publ. sous la dir. de M.L. Aimé-Martin, II, Paris, 1840. For a series of valuable reviews of missionary literature on India (including the important *Breve Noticia dos erros*), cf. Th. Zachariae, *Opera minora*, ed. C. Vogel. Wiesbaden, 1977, 660–783.

42. Aimé-Martin II, 644; on the critique of *Advaita* Vedānta, see also 647. Other authors, too, warn against this doctrine, which appears to them as self-deification; cf., e.g., Marshall, 41, on the *Mémoires sur les anciens philosophes de l'Inde* by the Abbé Mignot.

43. Aimé-Martin II, 645.

44. Aimé-Martin II, 642b; 644b; 645a.

45. Aimé-Martin II, 344–353; Bouchet argued for a derivation of Indian ideas from those of the Jews.

46. See S. Murr, *Conditions*, 268 (from a letter to Huet on metempsychosis, dated 1718; first published in *Lettres édifiantes et curieuses, Recueil* XIII).

47. Aimé-Martin II, 621 (letter to Delmas, dated 1735).

48. Aimé-Martin II, 628.

49. Paulinus wrote the first grammar of the Sanskrit language ever to be published in Europe: *Sidharubam seu Grammatica Samscradamica*. Rome, 1790; a reprint and English translation of the introduction to this work was published by L. Rocher under the title: *Dissertation on the Sanskrit language*. Amsterdam, 1977. This contains a good survey and evaluation of Paulinus' achievements. Paulinus' other writings include: *Systema brahmanicum*. Rome, 1791 (German translation: Gotha, 1797); *Vyacarana*. Rome, 1804. On the eighteenth century in general, see R. Streit, *Bibliotheca Missionum* VI: *Missionsliteratur Indiens. . . 1700–1791*. Aachen, 1931. On Hanxleden, see Neill II, 88f.

50. For a survey, see H. de Lubac, *Rencontre*.

51. P.-S. Filliozat, "The French Institute of Indology in Pondicherry," *WZKS* 28 (1984), 133. See also the investigations of G. Dharampal on the connections between missionary literature and Indology: *La Religion des Malabars. Tessier de Quéralay et la contribution des missionaires européens à la naissance de l'Indianisme*. Immensee, 1982 (249–285: on the Indological evaluation of Tessier's work, with special reference to E. Jacquet).

52. See R. Schwab, *La Renaissance orientale*, 37ff. (Engl. trans.: 29ff); in general on this period: S. Murr, *Conditions*.

53. Cf. P.-S. Filliozat, *WZKS* 28 (above, n.51), 135f.; L. Rocher, *The Purāṇas*. Wiesbaden, 1986, 150.

54. The work of Coeurdoux, who died in 1779, and his younger contemporary N.-J. Desvaulx has been brought to light again by S. Murr: *Moeurs et coutumes des Indiens* (1777). Paris, 1986 (part 2: *L'Indologie du Père Coeurdoux*). See also "Nicolas-Jacques Desvaulx (1745–1823), véritable auteur des Moeurs, Institutions et Cérémonies des peuples de l'Inde de l'Abbé Dubois," *Puruṣārtha* 3 (1977), 245–267; for some revisions concerning this article, see S. Murr, *Conditions* (especially 270, n. 14).

55. Cf. F.W. Ellis, "An Account of a Discovery of a Modern Imitation of the Vedas," *Asiatic Researches* 14 (1822) 1–59). On the history of the *Ezourvedam* controversy, see the introduction by L. Rocher to his edition of: *Ezourvedam. A French Veda of the Eighteenth Century*. Amsterdam/Philadelphia, 1984. Jesuit scholars still tend to believe that the Pondicherry Jesuits were victims rather than perpetrators of a deception.

56. The Dutch text of the work was published in Leiden in 1651, i.e., after Roger's death (1649); a new edition by W. Caland was published in The Hague in 1915. Speculations on an original Latin version are unfounded. Chapter 1/3 gives a survey of six "sects" of the Brahmins, including the "Schaerwacka" (i.e. Cārvāka, "materialists"; see the reference in: J.F. Reimmann, *Historia universalis atheismi et atheorum*. Hildesheim, 1725, 92).

57. La Grue also discusses the possibility of influences of the Thomas Christians upon Hinduism.

58. Cf. Neill I, 421ff.; for Dubois' use of the work of Coeurdoux, see above, n.54; even P. Sonnerat's famous travel book seems to be indebted to an older manuscript.

59. See A. Lehmann, *Es begann in Tranquebar*. Berlin, second edition, 1956 (English translation: Madras, 1955). For a survey of Bible translations, see J.S.M. Hooper, *Bible Translation in India, Pakistan and Ceylon*. London, second edition, 1963. On terminological problems, see J.S.M. Hooper, *Greek New Testament Terms in Indian Languages*. Bangalore, 1957.

60. Cf. W. Germann, preface to his edition of the *Genealogie*. Madras, 1867, VII. An English version of the *Genealogie* was published under the title: *Genealogy of the South Indian Gods*. Madras, 1869 (reprint 1984). On textual problems of both versions, see Neill II, 435.

61. Letters and reports from Tranquebar were published in Halle since 1708; since 1718, these publications included letters of "Malabarian priests," i.e. Tamil brahmins; cf. H. Grafe, "Hindu Apologetics at the Beginning of the Protestant Missionary Era in India," *Indian Church History Review* 6 (1972). See also *Thirty-Four Conferences Between the Danish Missionaries and the Malabarian Brahmans. . .* trans. J.T. Philipps, London, 1719; J.L. Niekamp, *Kurzgefasste Missionsgeschichte oder Historischer Auszug der evangelischen Missionsberichte aus Ostindien*, Halle, 1740 (the authoritative contemporary account).

62. *Genealogie der malabarischen Götter*, ed. W. Germann. Madras, 1867, 15.

63. *Malabarisches Heidentum*, ed. W. Caland. Amsterdam, 1926, 43. For the expression "Barabarawastu"—*parāvaravastu* is actually more common than *parāparavastu*—see, e.g., 39. The doctrine of rebirth and transmigration is among those Indian teachings which Ziegenbalg attributes to the influence of the devil; see 167ff.

64. *Genealogie der malabarischen Götter*. Madras, 1867, 18.

65. Cf. P.J. Marshall, 24. In India itself, the controversies were often bitter; the Jesuit C. Beschi even wrote a Tamil treatise against the Protestants (cf. Neill II, 88).

66. Windisch I, 6 (with reference to M. V. de La Croze, *Histoire du Christianisme des Indes*. The Hague, 1724, 425; 457).

67. See Windisch I, 4f.; 17ff.

68. Cf. Marshall, 22ff.

69. See, for instance, Th. Burnet, *Archaeologiae philosophicae*, London, 1692, 358: "Faxit Deus, ut easdem non subeamus vices, neque retrahat iratus id luminis quo gaudemus in Occidente" (also in: P. Bayle, *Dictionnaire historique et critique*, article "Brachmanes").

70. Cf. W. Koppers, "Das Schicksal des Gottesgedankens in den Religionen Indiens"; in: *Christus und die Religionen der Erde*, ed. F. König. Freiburg, 1951, II, 672ff.

71. A. Hübner, *Mächte der Finsternis. Die indischen Götter und ihre Anbetung*. Zwickau, 1921 (as quoted in H. von Glasenapp, *Indienbild*, 167).

72. Cf. Marshall, 15.

73. Cf. S.K. De, *Bengali Literature in the Nineteenth Century (1757–1857)*. Calcutta, second edition, 1962, 85; 221; 442ff. Also E.D. Potts, *British Baptist Missionaries in India, 1793–1837*. Cambridge, 1957.

74. *A Dictionary, English and Sanskrit.* London, 1851 (reprint Delhi, 1971). *A Sanskrit-English Dictionary*, Oxford, 1972 (revised edition 1899; numerous reprints; on the missionary connections of this work and the Boden Chair for Sanskrit at Oxford, see Preface, IXf.). H.H. Wilson, Monier-Williams' predecessor, had been associated with Bishop W.H. Mill in Calcutta.

75. Cf. W. Ward, *An Account of the Writings, Religion and Manners of the Hindoos.* 4 vols. Serampore, 1811. On Carey and his successors, see R.F. Young, "Church Sanskrit: An Approach of Christian Scholars to Hinduism in the Nineteenth Century," *WZKS* 23 (1979), 205–231.

76. See below, chapters 13f.; 19.

77. See *Christianity Contrasted with Hindu Philosophy.* London, 1859, Xf. G. Mundy, *Christianity and Hinduism Contrasted*, Serampore, second edition 1834, is an earlier example of this genre of "contrastive" literature.

78. *Christianity Contrasted with Hindu Philosophy.* Vf.; 194. See also the appendix "Translation into the Languages of India" (195–236).

79. A much less generous approach is found in numerous publications, e.g., *Vedānta Examined*, compiled by J. Murdoch, London/Madras, 1902; or the series "Sacred Books of the East Described and Examined" (see specifically Hindu Series II: Philosophic and Law Books, London/Madras, 1898), which was published in response to M. Müller's series "Sacred Books of the East" and the World Parliament of Religions, held in Chicago in 1893.

80. See J. Muir, "St. Paul a Model for the Missionary," *Calcutta Christian Observer* 7 (1838), 63–73; also R.F. Young, "Church Sanskrit" (see above, n.75.), 222ff. Muir even expressed his appreciation of the so-called Pseudo-Vedas, including the discredited *Ezourvedam*, of the Pondicherry Jesuits; see L. Rocher, *Ezourvedam* (above, n.55), 26f.

81. See the thorough and comprehensive study of this episode by R.F. Young, *Resistant Hinduism: Sanskrit Sources on Anti-Christian Apologetics in Early Nineteenth-Century India.* Vienna, 1981.

82. Cf. K.M. Banerjea, *Dialogues on the Hindu Philosophy.* London/Edinburgh, 1861; N. Nīlakaṇṭha Śāstrī Gore, *Ṣaḍdarśanadarpaṇa: Hindu Philosophy Examined by a Benares Pandit.* Calcutta, 1860 (in Hindi; English translation by Fitz-Edward Hall, *A Rational Refutation of the Hindu Philosophical Systems*, Calcutta, 1862; second edition 1895). His earlier, anti-Christian Sanskrit treatise *Śāstratattvavinirṇaya* was published posthumously (Ujjain 1951; ed. S.S. Katre).

83. Cf. E. Sharpe, *Not to Destroy but to Fulfil*, Uppsala, 1965, 53 (with reference to M. Monier-Williams, *The Bible and the Sacred Books of the East.* London, 1887; Monier-Williams now sees a "bridgeless chasm" between Christianity and the non-Christian religions).

84. E. Sharpe, *Not to Destroy but to Fulfil*, 52.

85. Cf. E. Sharpe, 102.

86. Cf. E. Sharpe, 260 (from: *The College St. Matthew.* Madras, 1909, 106f).

87. T.E. Slater, *Studies in the Upanishads*. Madras, 1897, 15. See also P. Johanns, *Vers le Christ par le Vedānta*, trans. M. Ledrus. Louvain, 1932; G. Dandoy, *L'ontologie du Vedānta*, trans. L.-M. Gauthier. Paris, 1932.

88. W.S. Urquart, *The Vedānta and Modern Man*. London, 1928, 247f.; 250. See also R. Panikkar, *The Unknown Christ of Hinduism*. London, 1964 (on the problems of an encounter of Hindu and Christian universalism).

89. See *Krishna Mohan Banerjea: Christian Apologist*, intr. by T.V. Philip. Madras, 1982 (especially 116ff.: Jesus as fulfilment of the Vedic Prajāpati).

90. R.G. Milburn, "Christian Vedantism," *The Indian Interpeter* (Madras) 7/4 (1913), 153–160; especially 155; 158f.

91. See, for instance, R.H.S. Boyd, *Khristadvaita: A Theology for India*. Madras, 1977. We may also refer to the radical approach of H. Le Saux (Abhiṣiktānanda).

92. See, for instance, K. Hutten and S. von Kortzfleisch, *Asien missioniert im Abendland*. Stuttgart, 1962; F. Melzer, *Indien greift nach uns*. Stuttgart, 1962.

93. Cf. R. Otto, *Vishnu-Nārāyaṇa. Texte zur indischen Gottesmystik*. Jena, 1917, 141ff.; *Indiens Gnadenreligionen und das Christentum*, Gotha, 1930; *Mysticism East and West*, New York, 1970 (originally Haskell Lectures at Oberlin College, 1924; first published 1932).

94. Cf. P. Knauer, "Das Verhāltnis des Neuen Testaments zum Alten als historisches Paradigma für das Verhältnis der christlichen Botschaft zu anderen Religionen und Weltanschauungen," in: *Offenbarung, geistige Realität des Menschen*. Vienna, 1974, 153–170. Also E.C. Dewick, *The Christian Attitude to Other Religions*. Cambridge, 1953.

95. The literature on the Christian "encounter" and "dialogue" with India is immense; see, e.g., E. Sharpe, *Faith Meets Faith*. London, 1977. Also the reviews by P. Hacker, Kl. Schr., 780ff.; 805ff. On Indian theology and Christology, see, e.g., M.M. Thomas, *The Acknowledged Christ of the Indian Renaissance*. London, 1969; R.H.S. Boyd, *An Introduction to Indian Christian Theology*. Madras, 1965; S.J. Samartha, *Hindus vor dem universalen Christus*, Stuttgart, 1970 (English version Madras, 1974).

4. Deism, the Enlightenment, and the Early History of Indology

1. See *Hist. Wb. Phil.*, art. "Deismus"; specifically the quote from G. Arnold (1699): "God likes all religions." ("Gott mag alle Religionen.").

2. H. Scholz, *Die Religionsphilosophie des Herbert von Cherbury*. Giessen, 1914, 20f. Herbert is quite familiar with the classical reports and speculations about India, specifically in connection with Apollonius of Tyana. His examples are, however, usually taken from Greek and Roman polytheism.

3. See Augustinus Steuchus (Eugubinus), *De perenni philosophia* (1540), ed. Ch. B. Schmitt. New York/London, 1972. Th. More's *Utopia* contains certain Indian references; cf. Lach II/2, 99 (on the word "gymnosophaon"); 363ff.(Utopia and the

gymnosophists); 530f. (possible Indian elements in the alphabet of the Utopians). Th. Campanella associates his Utopian "Sun State"(*Civitas solis*. Frankfurt, 1623) with the island of Taprobana(i.e., Ceylon).

4. See W.J. Bouwsma, *Concordia Mundi: The Career and Thought of Guillaume Postel(1501–1581)*. Cambridge, Mass., 1957. Cf. also Lach II/2, 268: "Through his travels and reading, Postel found evidence of true religion and human understanding in every corner of the earth. Christianity, like the primitive language, was universal before the dispersal of Babel. The vestiges that remain of a primitive, universal Christianity are particularly impressive in the East."

5. *The History of Hindostan* I, London, 1768; cf. Marshall, 139.

6. Cf. Marshall, 27 (quoted from *The History of Hindostan* I, LXXVI). Cf. in this connection the masonic hymn by F.H. Ziegenhagen, set to music by W.A. Mozart in 1791, which equates "Jehova," "Brahma" etc. as mere names of God.

7. Marshall, 26f.

8. Marshall, 130ff.

9. On Rammohan Roy's "deistic" tendencies, see below, ch. 12.

10. Cf. S.N. Mukherjee, *Sir William Jones*. Cambridge, 1968, 78.

11. Cf. D. Kopf, *British Orientalism and the Bengal Renaissance*. Berkeley/Los Angeles, 1969, 139. On the reaction against the "deistic" openness of some Orientalists, see Marshall, 41ff.

12. Holwell's work appeared 1767 in German and 1768 in French translation; a French version of Dow's *History of Hindostan* was published in 1769.

13. Cf. G.W. Leibniz, *Novissima Sinica historiam nostri temporis illustratura* (1697; English trans. of the preface by D.F. Lach, Honolulu, 1957); *Discourse on the Natural Theology of the Chinese*, trans. H. Rosemont and D.J. Cook. Honolulu, 1977; D.E. Mungello, *Leibniz and Confucianism: The Search for Accord*. Honolulu, 1977.

14. Cf. O. Franke, "Leibniz und China," *ZDMG* 82 (1928), 155–178; especially 165; V. Pinot, *La Chine et la formation de l'esprit philosophique en France*. Paris, 1932. The superiority of Chinese social and political thought has been invoked since the sixteenth century, for instance by G. Botero (cf. Lach II/2, 235ff.; especially 252).

15. Cf. J.H. Brumfitt in: *Voltaire, La philosophie de l'histoire*. Geneva, 1963, 54; Marshall, 31.

16. Marshall, 23ff.; 28ff.

17. Cf. D.S. Hawley, "L'Inde de Voltaire," *Studies on Voltaire and the Eighteenth Century*, vol. 120, Banbury, 1974, 139–178; specifically 166f.

18. Cf. D.S. Hawley, loc. cit. 149ff.; J. Castets, *L'Ezourvédam de Voltaire et les pseudo-védams de Pondichéry*. Pondicherry, 1935.

19. Voltaire, *Les oeuvres complètes*, vol. 126, Banbury, 1975, 299 (*Correspondence*, definitive ed. by Th. Besterman, vol. 41, no. 19806).

20. Cf. D.S. Hawley, loc. cit. (n. 17), 139.

21. D.S. Hawley, loc. cit.; "...que Voltaire se sert de l'Inde plus qu'il ne l'étudie."

22. *Fables et contes indiens*. Paris, 1790, Xff. Cf. Marshall, 33.

23. Cf. e.g., F. Nork (i.e. F.A. Korn), *Braminen und Rabbinen*. Meissen, 1836; A. Lillie, *Buddhism in Christendom*. London, 1887 (reprint New Delhi 1984); L. Jacolliot, *Occult Science in India*, trans. W.L. Felt, London, n.d. Jacolliot's writings were often referred to by M. Ludendorff and F. Nietzsche. See also R. Schwab, *Renaissance orientale*, 250ff. (*Oriental Renaissance*, 235ff.; on "India and the Occult").

24. Cf. R. Garbe, *Indian und das Christentum*. Tübingen, 1914 (trans. L.G. Robinson: *India and Christendom*, La Salle, Ill., 1959).

25. Cf. S. Murr, *Conditions*, 252; see also N. Fréret, *Défense de la chronologie contre Newton*. Paris, 1758.

26. Cf. Marshall, 32f.; also Dugald Stewart, *Elements of the Philosophy of the Human Mind* III. Edinburgh, 1854 (Coll. Works, ed. W. Hamilton, vol. 4), 102.

27. Voltaire, *Les oeuvres complètes*, vol. 124. Banbury, 1975, 92(*Correspondence*, definitive ed. by Th. Besterman, vol. 40, no. 18511).

28. See G.S. Bayer, *Historia regni Graecorum Bactriani*. Petersburg, 1738. E. Gibbon and Dugald Stewart accept the views of Bayer; cf. Stewart (see above, n.26), 78–115. According to Chr. Meiners, the Indians had no science and philosophy at all before Alexander (cf. Stewart, 102). We hear even about Greek influences on the Sanskrit language.

29. See the articles "Brachmanes"; "Bramines"; "Gymnosophistes"; "Indiens, Philosophie des"; "Malabares."

30. Fo, the Chinese name of the Buddha, is used in the missionary reports from East Asia. Diderot incorporates the information found in Bayle's *Dictionnaire* without mentioning his source. The article "Indiens, Philosophie des" relies primarily on Philostratus.

31. See G.W. Leibniz, *Essais de théodicée* I (Discours de la conformité de la foi avec la raison), 10 ("quiétisme de Foë"). Among Leibniz' sources, we find F. Bernier, who published a "Mémoire sur le quiétisme des Indes" (*Histoire des savants*, 1688).

32. Cf. *Ph. d. W.* II, 355.

33. On Schopenhauer, see below, ch. 7.

34. *Encyclopédie*, art. "Bramines."

35. Cf. Th. Burnet, *Archaeologiae philosophicae*. London, 1692, 358: "Miseret me quidem terrarum orientalium, primae sapientium sedis, florentissimi olim bonarum literarum emporii, a multis retro saeculis in foedam barbariem conversarum."

36. Cf. *Dictionnaire historique et critique*, art. "Spinoza." Burnet's statement(*Archaelogiae philosophicae*, 354) on the Indian "world spider" which periodically retracts the cosmic "web" it has spun and reabsorbs everything into itself is quoted in the article "Brachmanes"(n.L): "Fingunt enim immensam quandam araneam esse

primam rerum causam... Tandem, cum satis lusit in sua tela adornanda et contemplanda, retrahit, quae evolverat, fila, atque ita omnia resorbet in seipsam." On the simile of the spider, see the following *Upaniṣads: Bṛhadāraṇyaka* II,1,20; *Muṇḍaka* I, 1,7; *Śvetāśvatara* VI, 10.

37. Cf. H. von Glasenapp, *Kant und die Religionen des Ostens*. Würzburg, second ed., 1954, 32f. Also *Indienbild*, 7f. (from the transcripts of a lecture). On similar statements in the reports of French travelers in India, see Z. Bamboat, *Les voyageurs français aux Indes aux XVIIe et XVIIIe siècles*. Diss. Paris, 1933, 156ff.

38. See M. Mendelssohn, *Jerusalem oder über religiöse Macht und Judentum*. Berlin, 1783, 84ff.(*Sämtliche Werke*, Vienna, 1838, 272ff.).

39. M. Mendelssohn, loc. cit. (*Sämtliche Werke*, 273). According to Mendelssohn, "script" or writing ("Schrift") itself, i.e., the use of symbols, contains the potential of degeneration into "idolatry" ("Abgötterei"). On the "elephant" and the "tortoise," cf. J. Locke, *An Essay Concerning Human Understanding* II, 13, 19; for a comprehensive survey concerning this metaphor, see D. Henrich, "Die 'wahrhafte Schildkröte.'" *Hegel-Studien* 2 (1963), 281–291.

40. See the comprehensive survey of this literary genre in W. Weisshaupt, *Europa sieht sich mit fremdem Blick*. Frankfurt/Bern, 1979.

41. N.B. Halhed and A.H. Anquetil Duperron were the main representatives of the "Persian interlude" of early Indology. W. Jones and several others, including F. Schlegel, studied Persian before they turned to Sanskrit.

42. Cf. S.N. Mukherjee, *Sir William Jones*. Cambridge, 1968, 79.

43. S.N. Mukherjee, *Sir William Jones*, 83. For a survey of Jones' work, see also G. Cannon, "Sir William Jones' Indian Studies," *JAOS* 91(1971), 418–425; and numerous other contributions by Cannon, e.g.: *Oriental Jones: A Biography*, Bombay, 1964; *Sir William Jones: A Bibliography of Primary and Secondary Sources*. Amsterdam, 1979.

44. See the relevant sections in Windisch I.

45. W. Jones, *On the Hindus* (cf. Marshall, 254); however, Jones suggests Indian influences on Greek logic; cf. *Asiatic Researches* 4 (reprint London, 1799), 163.

46. Cf. Marshall, 260; 253.

47. Marshall, 252. However, Halhed tries to derive Greek and Latin from Sanskrit.

48. Cf. Th. Benfey, *Geschichte der Sprachwissenschaft*. Munich, 1869, 336ff.; Lach II/2, 518 ff.

49. Cf. Windisch I, 24.

50. See W. Jones, *Works*, vol.6. London, 1799, 423–425. The same volume contains other "extracts from the Vedas." An interesting comparative reference to the Christian confession of faith ("First Article of our Church") is found on p. 422. Jones did not see the Hindus as promising targets of Christian proselytism:

"The Hindus...would readily admit the truth of the Gospel; but they contend that it is perfectly consistent with their *Sastras*: the deity, they say, has appeared innumerable times, in many parts of this world and of all worlds, for the salvation of his creatures; and though we adore him in one appearance, and they in others, yet we adore, they say, the same God..."

(On the Gods of Greece, Italy, and India; cf. Marshall, 245).

51. *Works*, vol.6. London, 1799, 415.

52. Cf. R. Rocher, "Nathaniel Brassey Halhed on the Upaniṣads (1787)," *ABORI(Poona), Diamond Jubilee Volume(1977–78)*. 279–289. Halhed believed that the *Upaniṣads* were commentaries on the Vedic *Saṃhitās*, of which he had no specific knowledge. For a comprehensive and detailed study of Halhed's life and works, see R. Rocher, *Orientalism, Poetry, and the Millenium: The Checkered Life of Nathaniel Brassey Halhed, 1751–1830*. Delhi, 1983.

53. Cf. R. Rocher, *Alexander Hamilton (1762–1824)*. New Haven, 1968, 24f. Hamilton was the Sanskrit teacher of Friedrich Schlegel.

54. See below, ch. 7; on Anquetil's life and achievements in general, cf. R. Schwab, *Vie d'Anquetil Duperron*. Paris, 1934. *Oupnek'hat* is a modification of *upaniṣad*, which results from transliteration into the Arabic-Persian script, in conjunction with a regional variety of pronouncing the retroflex ṣ.

55. Cf. *Zend-Avesta*, 3 parts. Riga, 1776–1777. This was followed by an "appendix" ("Anhang") in two volumes, Riga 1781–1783 (second ed. of vol. 1: 1786). Kleuker also translated Holwell's *Interesting Historical Events*, as well as various other works.

56. A.H. Anquetil Duperron, *Zend-Avesta*. vol. 1, p. III.

57. Cf. A.H. Anquetil Duperron, *Législation orientale*. Paris, 1778, 21; 244f.

58. See *Recherches historiques et géographiques sur l'Inde*, ed. J. Bernoulli (i.e. vol.2 of: *Description historique et géographique de l'Inde*), part 2, Berlin, 1781, 297–344 (translated into German in: *Sammlung asiatischer Originalschriften*, Zürich, 1791). Part 1 of the *Recherches* (Berlin, 1786) contains references to the "4 Vedams ou Beids" (p.193).

59. On the copies of Sanskrit texts, specifically dictionaries, which he acquired in India, see *Zend-Avesta*, vol. 1, p.CCCLXVIII; on the Veda: CCCLXVI. After his return from India, Anquetil remained very interested in Sanskrit; cf. J. Filliozat, "Une grammaire sanscrite du XVIIIe siècle et les débuts de l'indianisme en France," *JA* 1937, 275–284; especially 282ff. (also in: *Laghu-Prabandhāḥ. Choix d'articles d'Indologie*. Leiden, 1974, 303–312).

60. *Recherches historiques et géographiques* (see above, n.58), 296 (quoted by R. Schwab, *Renaissance orientale*, 172f.; the translation in *Oriental Renaissance*, 160: "...and to then confer, book in hand, with the scholars of the country which the materials treat" is inaccurate).

61. *Recherches historiques et géographiques*, Appendix (cf. R. Schwab, *Renaissance orientale*, 173).

62. Not only Schopenhauer, but also Schelling, Krause, Rixner, Görres and other German philosophers studied the *Oupnek'hat*.

63. *Oupnek'hat* I, 792.

64. *Oupnek'hat* I, 562ff.; 568ff.

65. *Oupnek'hat* I, XXIII-CXI.

66. On Synesius and his time, see above, ch.I.

67. *Oupnek'hat* II, 659; 665.

68. See the appendix "De Kantismo," *Oupnek'hat* I, 711–724.

69. *Oupnek'hat* I, 711.

70. Th. A. Rixner, *Versuch einer neuen Darstellung der uralten indischen All-Eins-Lehre.* Nürnberg, 1808, 5; 8.

71. Cf. F.W.J. Schelling, *Philosophie der Mythologie*, S.W. II/2, 476f.

72. *Oupnek'hat* II, 658f.

73. Cf. *L'Inde en rapport avec l'Europe* I, Paris 7 (French Republican Era), XXI. Anquetil writes "MAL-AISE européen."

74. Cf. D. Kopf, *British Orientalism and the Bengal Renaissance.* Berkeley, 1969, 215ff.: "Macaulayism and the Decline and Fall of the Orientalist Movement, 1828–1835"; also Marshall, 41ff.

75. "Minute on Indian Education (1835)"; in: Th.B. Macaulay, *Prose and Poetry*, ed. G.M. Young. London, 1952; especially 722; 728.

5. India and the Romantic Critique of the Present

1. See H. Schanze, *Romantik und Aufklärung. Untersuchungen zu F. Schlegel und Novalis.* Nürnberg, 1966; especially 1–10. J.J. Rousseau, F. Hemsterhuis and even J.G. Herder exemplify the connections and transitions between Enlightenment and Romanticism.

2. See P. Th. Hoffmann, *Der indische und der deutsche Geist von Herder bis zur Romantik.* Diss. Tübingen, 1915; R. Gérard, *L'Orient et la pensée romantique allemande.* Paris, 1963; also H. von Glasenapp, *Indienbild*, 14–24. On Herder's philosophy of culture and history, cf. M. Rouché, *La philosophie de l'histoire de Herder.* Paris, 1940; I. Berlin, *Vico and Herder.* London, 1976.

3. On Herder's idea of humanity, cf. E. Adler, *Herder und die deutsche Aufklärung.* Vienna, 1969, especially 287ff.

4. *Auch eine Philosophie der Geschichte, Sämtliche Werke*, ed. B. Suphan. Berlin, 1877–1913 (reprint Hildesheim 1967–1969), vol.5, 511.

5. *Sämtliche Werke*, vol. 5, 529.

6. *Ideen zur Philosophie der Geschichte der Menschheit, Sämtliche Werke*, vol. 13, 406.

7. *Älteste Urkunde des Menschengeschlechts, Sämtliche Werke*, vol. 6, 321.

8. On Kleuker, see above, ch. 4. Kleuker's *Das brahmanische Religionssystem* (Riga, 1797) is an adaptation of the *Systema brahmanicum* by Paulinus a S. Bartholomaeo.

9. *Ideen zur Philosophie der Geschichte der Menschheit, Sämtliche Werke*, vol. 13, 416. See also J. Grundmann, *Die geographischen und völkerkundlichen Quellen und Anschauungen in Herders Ideen...*, Diss. Berlin, 1900, 64ff.

10. *Sämtliche Werke*, vol. 13, 222.

11. *Sämtliche Werke*, vol. 26, 420; also vol. 29, 145 ("Die Entzauberung. Lehre der Braminen"). Herder used W. Jones' English version of the *Mohamudgara.*

12. Cf. in this connection Herder's position in the controversy over Spinoza's system ("Spinozismus-Streit")' *Gott. Einige Gespräche*. Gotha, 1787.

13. *See Ideen zur Philosophie der Geschichte der Menschheit, Sämtliche Werke*, vol. 14, 25ff.

14. *Sämtliche Werke*, vol. 14, 25ff. On the other hand, Herder develops his own version of the doctrine of metempsychosis, which excludes the possibility of a relapse to lower stages; cf. *Über die Seelenwanderung, Sämtliche Werke*, vol. 15; also M. Rouché, *La philosophie de l'histoire de Herder*. Paris, 1940, 209ff.

15. *Briefe zur Beförderung der Humanität, Sämtliche Werke*, vol. 18, 301.

16. Cf. R. Gérard, *L'Orient et la pensée romantique allemande*. Paris, 1963, 64: "Bien que née en Asie, notre humanité n'aurait atteint l'âge adulte que sur les bords grecs de la Méditerranée."

17. *Adrastea*, part 5; *Sämtliche Werke*, vol. 23, 498ff. Herder has also criticized the missionary activities in other parts of the world.

18. *Sämtliche Werke*, vol. 18, 246ff; especially 249.

19. Cf. W. Halbfass, "Indien und die Geschichtsschreibung der Philosophie." *Philosophische Rundschau* 23 (1976), 104–131; ib., 107.

20. See in this connection H. Hesse, *Die Morgenlandfahrt*. Berlin, 1932. This work by Hesse reflects very clearly the Romantic orientation.

21. See the studies by P. Th. Hoffmann and R. Gérard (see above, n.2); also A.L. Willson, *A Mythical Image: The Ideal of India in German Romanticism*. Durham, N.C., 1964; E. Behler, "Das Indienbild der deutschen Romantik," *Germanisch-Romanische Monatsschrift* 49 (1968), 21–37.

22. Cf. R.F. Merkel, "Schopenhauers Indien-Lehrer," *Jahrbuch der Schopenhauer-Gesellschaft* 32 (1945–1948), 158–181.

23. See *Brahma oder über die Religion der Indier als Brahmaismus*. Leipzig, 1818, 215 (quoted in R.F. Merkel, "Schopenhauers Indien-Lehrer," 180); cf. also *Allgemeines Mythologisches Lexikon*, 2 volumes, Weimar, 1803-1804; especially VIIf.

24. J. Görres, *Glauben und Wissen* (Munich, 1805); *Gesammelte Schriften*, vol.3, Cologne, 1936, 8; 10. See also *Mythengeschichte der asiatischen Welt* (Heidelberg, 1810); *Gesammelte Schriften*, vol.5, Cologne, 1935, 21: "There was *one* service and *one* myth in primeval times, there was *one* church and *one* state and *one* language." ("*Ein* Dienst und *eine* Mythe war in uralter Zeit, es war *eine* Kirche und auch ein Staat und *eine* Sprache.") On p.5, Görres expresses his firm conviction that of all documents of mankind none can compare-- "as regards antiquity and faithful sense of nature" ("in Rücksicht auf Altertümlichkeit und Treue des Natursinns")-- to the

Indian Vedas. He celebrates Anquetil Duperron as the one to whom we owe the "enjoyment of this milk of ancient Oriental wisdom" ("Genuss dieser Milch alter orientalischer Weisheit"): "Anquetil Duperron drew it from that Indian sacred ocean, from which also the seven gems were produced"(*Gesammelte Schriften*, vol. 5, 310; from a review of the *Oupnek'hat*).

25. N. Müller, *Glauben, Wissen und Kunst der alten Hindus in ursprünglicher Gestalt und im Gewande der Symbolik*. Mainz, 1822 (reprint Leipzig, 1968), III; XVIIff.

26. Novalis (i.e., F. von Hardenberg), "Die Christenheit oder Europa," *Schriften*, ed. P. Kluckhohn and R. Samuel, Stuttgart, second ed., 1960–1975, vol.2, 80; see also A.L. Willson, *A Mythical Image: The Ideal of India in German Romanticism*. Durham, N.C., 1964, 137; 158.

27. Letter to Just, *Schriften*, ed. P. Kluckhohn and R. Samuel, second ed., vol.4, 341f.: "Religion ist der grosse Orient in uns, der selten getrübt wird." A chapter on the Orient, which Novalis planned to include in his *Heinrich von Ofterdingen*, was not completed.

28. Cf. K. Goldammer, *Novalis und die Welt des Ostens*. Stuttgart, 1948; see also H.-J. Mähl, *Die Idee des goldenen Zeitalters im Werk des Novalis*. Heidelberg, 1965 (without specific references to India). In the correspondence between Novalis and F. Schlegel, India does not play a significant role; cf. *F. Schlegel und Novalis*, ed. M. Preitz. Darmstadt, 1957.

29. *Europa* 1 (1803), 35.

30. Cf. *Europa* 1 (1803), 35.

31. *Athenäum* 3 (1800), 103f.

32. Cf. *L. Tieck und die Brüder Schlegel*, ed. H. Lüdeke. Frankfurt, 1930, 140.

33. *Kritische Friedrich-Schlegel-Ausgabe*, vol. 14/2, ed J.-J. Anstett. Munich, 1960, 19.

34. Cf. R. Rocher, *Alexander Hamilton (1762–1824)*. New Haven, 1968.

35. Cf. U. Oppenberg, *Quellenstudien zu F. Schlegels Übersetzungen aus dem Sanskrit*. Marburg, 1965. For a more general survey see the same (U. Struc-Oppenberg), "Zu F. Schlegels orientalistischen Studien," *Zeitschrift für deutsche Philologie* 88 (1969), 114–131.

36. New edition in: *Kritische Friedrich-Schlegel-Ausgabe*, vol.8, ed. E. Behler and U. Struc-Oppenberg. Munich, 1976 (with detailed introduction).

37. E. Behler, art. "Über die Sprache und Weisheit der Indier," *KLL* VII, 40; Behler also provides information on reviews and other responses to the book.

38. Cf. *Kritische Friedrich-Schlegel-Ausgabe*, vol.9, ed. J.-J. Anstett. Munich, 1971, especially 127ff.; 82ff.

39. Cf. R. Gérard, *L'Orient et la pensée romantique allemande*. Paris, 1963, 121ff.

40. *Sprache und Weisheit*, 307.

41. *Sprache und Weisheit*, 203.

42. *Sprache und Weisheit*, 193. The "original revelation" is not to be understood as an "instruction by the father in pictures and explicit words" ("Unterricht des Vaters in Bild und ausrücklichem Wort"), but an "unfolding of inner feeling" ("Aufgehen des inneren Gefühls," p.207).

43. The Sanskrit language keeps its role as the oldest Indo-European language (115); Indian mythology is presented as the "source of so many other" mythologies (193); on philosophy, see specifically 301ff.

44. *Sprache und Weisheit*, 301.

45. *Sprache und Weisheit*, 193; 297.

46. *Sprache und Weisheit*, 205; 207.

47. *Sprache und Weisheit*, 209.

48. *Sprache und Weisheit*, 253; on the distinction between the doctrine of emanation and pantheism, see 199ff.

49. *Sprache und Weisheit*, 243; see also E. Behler, "Das Indienbild der deutschen Romantik," *Germanisch-Romanische Monatsschrift* 49 (1968), 21–37; especially 35.

50. *Sprache und Weisheit*, 243.

51. *Sprache und Weisheit*, 243; see also *Krisenjahre der Romantik*, ed. J. Körner, vol. 1, Bern/Munich, second ed., 1969, 604 (Schelling's remarks concerning Jacobi's response to Schlegel's book). On Schlegel's critique of "idealism," see E. Behler's introduction to *Sprache und Weisheit*, CXXXff; on "revelation": CXLIVff.

52. See E. Behler, introduction to *Sprache und Weisheit*, CXXXIXff. (from a letter to Schubert).

53. Cf. S. Sommerfeld, *Indienbild und Indiendeutung romantischer Philosophen*. Diss. Zürich, 1943, 39.

54. See below, ch.7.

55. See below, ch.8. Rixner was one of the most enthusiastic readers of the *Oupnek'hat* before Schopenhauer knew of its existence. Later on, he became more critical and was closer to Hegel.

56. See E. Behler, "Friedrich Schlegel und Hegel," *Hegel-Studien* 2 (1963), 203–250.

57. Cf. *Sprache und Weisheit*, 193ff. (on mythology); 299 (on the relationship between Christianity and Buddhism).

58. Cf. *Ph. d. W.* I, 158ff.

59. See above, §10.

60. *Sprache und Weisheit*, 305.

61. *Sprache und Weisheit*, 303.

62. A French translation of Schlegel's book (by A. Mazure) was published in Paris in 1837.

63. On Eckstein, see R. Schwab, *Renaissance orientale*, 277ff. (*Oriental Renaissance*, 259ff.).

64. Cf. especially *Ph.d. W.* I, 158ff.; also *G.d. Ph.* I, 263; in this presentation, the vacuous speculation on "origins" appears almost as a symptom of Catholicism. On Lamennais and the association between India and the "occult," see also R. Schwab, *Renaissance orientale*, 250ff. (*Oriental Renaissance*, 235ff.).

65. Although there may be more continuity in F. Schlegel's attitude towards India than is apparent at first sight, U. Struc-Oppenberg's critique of the "disillusionment" thesis seems to be somewhat exaggerated; see introduction to *Sprache und Weisheit*, CCXIIff.

66. Cf. E. Behler, introduction to *Sprache und Weisheit*, CXXXIff.

67. In this connection, we may refer to the translation samples which Schlegel has appended to his presentation.

68. *Sprache und Weisheit*, 377.

69. *Sprache und Weisheit*, 381.

70. These lectures were first published in: *Europa* 2 (1803).

71. *Europa* 2 (1803), 40ff.

72. Cf. R. Gérard, *L'Orient et la pensée romantique allemande*. Paris, 1963, 130ff. A third Schlegel brother, Karl August, actually went to India (although not for scholarly reasons) and died in Madras. Friedrich refers to him in the preface of *Sprache und Weisheit*.

73. The first European chair for Sanskrit was established at the University of Paris in 1814; since 1815, it was occupied by A.L. de Chézy.

74. See below, ch.6.

75. F.M. Müller, *India – What Can It Teach Us?* London, 1883, 29ff.

76. *India – What Can It Teach Us?*, 29.

77. *India – What Can It Teach Us?*, 112f.; cf. also 254.

78. See below, ch.8. Bunsen himself wrote *Gott in der Geschichte*, 3 vols. Leipzig, 1857. For a critical discussion of Indian "pantheism," see vol.2, 97–190; vol. 3, 405–432.

79. See "Discours d'ouverture: De la langue et de la littérature sanscrite," *Revue des Deux Mondes* 1/2 (1833), 264–278.

80. Cf. D. Riepe, *The Philosophy of India and Its Impact on American Thought*. Springfield, 1970, especially 25ff.; J.P. Rao Rayapati, *Early American Interest in Vedānta*. New York, 1973; A.K.B. Pillai, *Transcendental Self: A Comparative Study of Thoreau and the Psycho-Philosophy of Hinduism and Buddhism*. Lanham, 1985 (interesting, but speculative); still useful as a survey: A. Christy, *The Orient in American Transcendentalism*. New York, 1932.

81. Among the numerous writings of R. Guénon, who was personally committed to Sūfism, cf. *Introduction générale à l'étude des doctrines hindoues*. Paris, 1921 (trans. by M. Pallis: *Introduction to the Study of Hindu Doctrines*. London, 1945). *L'homme et son devenir selon le Vedānta*. Paris, 1925 (trans. by R.C. Nicholson: *Man and His Becoming according to the Vedānta*. London, 1945). See also A. Désilets, *René Guénon: index-bibliographie*. Quebec, 1977.

6. Hegel

1. Colebrooke's essays on Indian philosophy were republished in: *Miscellaneous Essays*. Vol. I. London, 1837 (several reprints).

2. The following presentation uses sections of W. Halbfass, "Hegel on the Philosophy of the Hindus," in: *German Scholars on India*. Vol. I, ed. by the Embassy of the Federal Republic of Germany (New Delhi). Benares, 1973, 107–122. Some passages (specifically §9) are borrowed from: W. Halbfass, "Hegel on Meditation and Yoga," in: *Zen Buddhism Today. Annual Report of the Kyoto Zen Symposium* 3 (Kyoto, 1985), 72–84.

3. See H. von Glasenapp, *Indienbild,* 39f.; 59. A more favorable assessment is found in H. Zimmer, *Philosophies of India*. New York, 1951. See also, for instance, the references to Hegel in L. Dumont, *Homo Hierarchicus*. Paris, 1966, 63 (cf. revised English translation, Chicago 1980, 42; 355: Hegel on the caste system).

4. See his critique of the "platitude . . . to face the facts without bias" (*G. d. Ph.* I, 8).

5. For Hegel's criticism of the speculations on "origins" by F. Schlegel and other catholic (or "catholicizing") Orientalists, cf. *Ph. d. W.* I, 158ff.; *G. d. Ph.* I, 263f.

6. On Hegel's interest in the Orient in general, see E. Schulin, *Die weltgeschichtliche Erschliessung des Orients bei Hegel und Ranke*. Göttingen, 1958; M. Hulin, *Hegel et l'Orient*. Paris, 1979. On non-Christian religions: R. Leuze, *Die ausserchristlichen Religionen bei Hegel*. Göttingen, 1975 (not always adequate; see the review by H. Schneider, *Hegel-Studien* 13, 1978, 319–323). On India: F. Kreis, "Hegel's Interpretation der indischen Geisteswelt," *Zeitschrift für deutsche Kulturphilosophie* 7/2 (1941), 133–145 (inadequate); on Indian philosophy: W. Ruben, "Hegel über die Philosophie der Inder," in: *Asiatica, Festschrift F. Weller*, Leipzig, 1954, 553–569 (very superficial); I. Viyagappa, *G.W.F. Hegel's Concept of Indian Philosophy*. Rome, 1980.

7. On an early essay on the "Spirit of the Orientals" ("Geist der Orientalen," probably written in 1797), see E. Schulin (see above, note 6), 18.

8. See J. Hoffmeister, "Hegel und Creuzer," *Deutsche Vierteljahrsschrift für Literaturwissenschaft und Geistesgeschichte* 8 (1930), 260–282; esp. 262f.

9. See E. Schulin (note 6), 40; on Hegel's treatment of Chinese philosophy, cf. Young Kun Kim, "Hegel's Criticism of Chinese Philosophy," *PEW* 28 (1978), 173–180.

10. See I. Viyagappa (note 6), 57ff.

11. A special section on Indian and Oriental philosophy was first added to the *Lectures on the History of Philosophy* in the version of 1825/26; cf. J. Hoffmeister, Introduction to *G. d. Ph.* I, XXXII.

12. *Transactions of the Royal Asiatic Society* 1 (1824), 19–43 (part I, read June 21, 1823); 92–118 (part II, read February 21, 1824).

13. Cf. *G.d.Ph.* I, 293ff.

14. *Asiatic Researches 6* (1801), 163-308; on *nirvāṇa* ("nieban"), cf. 180; 266ff.; Buchanan used Latin translations of Burmese texts by the Italian missionary V. Sangermano. See also I. Viyagappa (see above, note 6), 229ff.

15. However, it would have been theoretically possible for him to consult Burnouf's early "Sketch of Buddhism Derived from the Bauddha Scriptures of Nipal," *Transactions of the Royal Asiatic Society* 2 (1829), 222–257.

16. This review has not found the attention which it deserves. It was never translated into English. A French translation is found in M. Hulin, *Hegel et l'Orient*. Paris, 1979.

17. See *Berl. Schr.*, 193: a reference to *Oupnek'hat* IX (i.e. the *Atharvaśiras Upaniṣad*, which is dedicated to Rudra-Śiva); Hegel may be following Th. A. Rixner in this reference. On Hegel and the *Oupnek'hat*, see also I. Viyagappa (note 6), 24ff.

18. See *Ph. d. W.* II, 420. Hegel read Anquetil's *Zend Avesta* in Kleuker's German version. For an indirect quote from Anquetil, see *G.d. Ph.* I, 264 (following Abel Rémusat and added to the version of 1829/30).

19. See H. Schneider, "Unveröffentlichte Vorlesungsmanuskripte Hegels," *Hegel-Studien* 7 (1972), 28; I. Viyagappa (note 6), 28ff. H.J. Schoeps, "Die ausserchristlichen Religionen bei Hegel," *Zeitschrift für Religions- und Geistesgeschichte* I (1955), 1–34.

20. *G.d.Ph.* I, 14 (following the Heidelberg version). Apart from the translation of the *Lectures on the History of Philosophy* by E.S. Haldane and F.H. Simson (London, 1892; many reprints), there are two recent translations of the "Introduction" to these *Lectures* (both more or less abridged): Q. Lauer, *Hegel's Idea of Philosophy*, New York, 1971; *Introduction to the Lectures on the History of Philosophy*, trans. T.M. Knox and A.V. Miller, Oxford, 1985.

21. *G.d.Ph.* I, 34f.

22. *G.d.Ph.* I, 71f.: "Wie nun im logischen System des Denkens jede Gestaltung desselben seine Stelle hat, auf der es allein Gültigkeit hat. . ., so ist auch jede Philosophie im Ganzen des Ganges eine besondere Entwicklungsstufe und hat ihre bestimmte Stelle, auf der sie ihren wahrhaften Wert und Bedeutung hat."

23. *G.d.Ph.* I, 72.

24. Cf. *G.d.Ph.* I, 74; see also 69: "What is in the beginning, is the most abstract, because it is in the beginning" ("Das Anfängliche ist das Abstrakteste, weil es das Anfängliche ist").

25. Cf. *G.d.Ph.* I, 124: "The history of philosophy considers only *one* philosophy, *one* process, which is, however, divided into different stages" ("Die Geschichte der Philosophie betrachtet nur *eine* Philosophie, nur *eine* Handlung, die aber in verschiedene Stufen abgeteilt ist").

26. On "substantiality" and "pantheism," cf. *Phil.d.Rel.* I/1, 195ff.

27. See specifically *Phil.d.Rel.* I/2, 119ff.

28. Cf. I. Viyagappa (note 6), 121f.

29. Hegel prefers "Brahm" for the neuter and "Brahma" for the masculine, but he also speaks in general about "Brahman."

30. See *G.d.Ph.* I, 289f.; but see his later qualification (below, §16).

31. Cf. *Berl. Schr.*, 185–188; according to Hegel's *Logic*, "pure being" coincides with "pure nothingness."

32. *Phil.d.Rel.* I/2, 149.

33. *Ph.d.W.* II, 398.

34. *Berl. Schr.*, 190.

35. W.T. Stace, *The Philosophy of Hegel*. London, 1924, 496.

36. See *Ph.d.W.* II, 400; *Berl. Schr.*, 193.

37. Cf. *Phil.d.Rel.* I/2, 137ff.; 149ff.; also *G.d.Ph.* I, 289ff.; 335.

38. See *Vorlesungen über die Ästhetik* I (*Jubiläumsausgabe*, ed. H. Glockner, vol. 12), 445ff.

39. *Vorlesungen über die Ästhetik* I, 451: The Indian "religion of fantasy" does not distinguish between symbolic reference and identity. The "ape, the cow, the individual brahmin, etc. . . . are not a related symbol of the divine, but the divine itself."

40. *Berl. Schr.*, 190; "being" in this sense is so abstract that it includes even "nonentities."

41. Cf. *Berl. Schr.*, 158; 184f.; 190ff.

42. *G.d.Ph.* I, 335; see also 332ff.

43. *Ph.d.W.* I, 167: "Die Weltgeschichte stellt . . . die Entwicklung des Bewusstseins des Geistes von seiner Freiheit und der von solchem Bewusstsein hervorgebrachten Verwirklichung dar."

44. *Ph.d.W.* II, 399; cf. also *G.d.Ph.* I,267.

45. W.T. Stace, *The Philosophy of Hegel*, London, 1924, 497.

46. *Ph.d.W.* II, 407: "Die Erhebung zum Brahm wird durch höchste Abgestumpftheit und Bewusstlosigkeit bewirkt." See also *Ph.d.W.* I, 176; *G.D.Ph.* I, 286 (associating the cynics and the gymnosophists); 293; 331.

47. *Ph.d.W.* II, 406; see also *Berl. Schr.*, 151, on the "contentlessness of the subject" ("Inhaltslosigkeit des Subjekts").

48. *Phil.d.Rel.* I/2, 166.

49. *Berl. Schr.*, 148: "Wir dürfen daher mit Recht das, was Joga heisst, für den allgemeinen Mittelpunkt indischer Religion und Philosophie betrachten."

50. See *Berl. Schr.*, 150f. See also W. von Humboldt, *Gesammelte Schriften* (Akademie-Ausgabe) I/5 (Berlin, 1906; reprint 1968), 221: *yoga* as "Vertiefung"; 164: *samādhi* as "contemplation" (defending Schlegel's Latin "contemplatio").

51. *Berl. Schr.*, 157.

52. *Berl. Schr.*, 163.

53. *Enzyklopädie der philosophischen Wissenschaften* (1830), ed. F. Nicolin and O. Pöggeler. Hamburg, 1959, §573(p.455) The long note (pp.451–461) in which this phrase ("reine Einheit des Gedankens in sich selbst") occurs is an addition to the revised third edition of 1830; the first edition was published in 1817.

54. The word "Meditation" does not appear at all in H. Glockner's *Hegel-Lexikon*. But cf. *Berl. Schr.*, 195ff.

55. *Ph.d.W.* II, 403; see the parallel passage, *Phil.d.Rel.* II/1, 165.

56. See the introduction by G. Lasson, *Ph.d.W.* II, XI. Lasson refers to the testimony of E. Gans.

57. *Phil.d.Rel.* I/2. 124.

58. *Ph.d.W.* II, 334f. See also *Phil.d.Rel.* I/2, 134: After mentioning the Buddhist "Nirwana," Hegel refers to meditation and paraphrases it as "going back into oneself" ("Zurückgehen in sich").

59. See above, ch. 4, §6; also H. de Lubac, *La rencontre du bouddhisme et de l'occident*. Paris, 1952, 86ff. A.E. Gough, *The Philosophy of the Upanishads*, London, 1882 (third ed.: 1903), claims: "The Indian sages seek for participation in the divine life . . . by the crushing out of every feeling and every thought, by vacuity, apathy, inertia and ecstasy."

60. *G.d.Ph.* I,232; but see below, §16.

61. *Phil.d.Rel.* II/2, 172, has the expression "present spirit" ("präsenter Geist"); "präsenter Gott" is found in the corresponding passage of the *Jubiläumsausgabe*, ed. H. Glockner, vol. 15, 307; see also *Werke, Vollständige Ausgabe*, vol. 12, Berlin 1832, 253: "der Mensch" instead of "das Menschliche."

62. *Grundlinien der Philosophie des Rechts*, ed. J. Hoffmeister. Hamburg, fourth edition, 1955, 16.

63. *Ph.d.W.* I,175.

64. *G.d.Ph.* I, 264 (addition to the version of 1829/30).

65. See *Wissenschaft der Logik*, ed. G. Lasson. Leipzig, 1951, II, 36f.

66. *G.d.Ph.* I, 287.

67. *G.d.Ph.* I, 287; 334. The metaphor of "bathing" the spirit in the "ether of the one substance" is also used with reference to Spinoza, whom Hegel calls an "echo of the Orient" ("Nachklang des Morgenlandes"); see *G.d.Ph.* III, 368; 376.

68. See O. Pöggeler, *Hegels Kritik der Romantik*. Bonn, 1956, 66ff; 263ff. Also E. Behler, "Friedrich Schlegel und Hegel," *Hegel-Studien* 2 (1963), 203–250; specifically 208ff. (on Hegel's criticism of "Romantic irony") and 212ff. (criticism of Schlegel's "irony").

69. See E. Behler (note 68),210.

70. *Phil.d.Rel.* I/2, 168.

71. See above, ch. 5, §10f.

72. See E. Behler (note 68), 241ff; esp. 249: "Ebenso wie Schlegels frühromantische Ironie Hegel als 'unendliche absolute Negativität' erschienen war, wird also Hegels

Dialektik von Schlegel als 'böser Geist der Verneinung und des Widerspruchs' empfunden."

73. *Phänomenologie des Geistes*, ed. J. Hoffmeister. Hamburg, sixth edition, 1952, 19. Quoted from the translation by J.B. Baillie, *The Phenomenology of Mind*(1910). New York, 1967, 79. On Hegel's notion of "Orientalism," which seems to be implied in this passage, see *Dokumente zu Hegels Entwicklung*, ed. J. Hoffmeister. Stuttgart, 1936, 338.

74. See, for instance, *Ph.d.W.* II, 365.

75. *Grundlinien der Philosophie des Rechts*, ed. J. Hoffmeister. Hamburg, fourth edition, 1955, 16.

76. Cf. *G.d.Ph.* I, 330ff.; 312ff.

77. *Berl. Schr.*, 133; 203. Hegel concurs with W. von Humboldt's postulate that a detailed study of the sources should precede all further activities of interpretation, comparison, and so forth.

78. This applies, above all, to the versions of the *Lectures on the History of Philosophy* since 1825/26 and the *Bhagavadgītā* review (1827).

79. See *G.d.Ph.* I, 232.

80. *G.d.Ph.* I, 293ff. (" . . . der Weg, das Gehen durch den entwickelten, durch den bestimmten Gedanken . . . "); these are additions to the versions since 1825/26; see also 288 (1827/28): "abstract philosophies." The aforementioned references to "real philosophy" in India are not found in the edition of the *Lectures* by H. Glockner (*Jubiläumsausgabe*, vol. 17), which reproduces the first edition of the text by K.L. Michelet, published in 1833. Michelet's abbreviated second edition (1840-1844) was used for the English translation by E.S. Haldane and F.H. Simson (1892). But even here, we hear about "wirklich philosophische Werke" in India (*Jubiläumsausgabe*, vol. 17, 163; cf. Haldane/Simson, 127; "real philosophic writings").

81. *Berl. Schr.*, 144.

82. *Phil.d.Rel.* I, 29.

83. G.d.Ph. I, 331ff. We need not discuss the factual accuracy of Hegel's statements; a somewhat naive and superficial attempt to assess such accuracy is made by R. Leuze, *Die ausserchristlichen Religionen bei Hegel*. Göttingen, 1975, 112ff.

84. *G.d.Ph.* I, 373f. (appendix; additions to the version of 1829/30). On further Hegelian reflections concerning the applicability of the concept of philosophy to Indian thought see below, ch.9, §7.

85. *Differenz des Fichteschen und Schellingschen Systems der Philosophie*. Hamburg, 1962, 1f. Hegel associates such accumulation of information with the "collection of mummies."

86. *Berl. Schr.*, 203 (" . . . weil sie in die höchsten Begriffe unseres Bewusstseins eingreift . . . ").

87. M. Hulin, *Hegel et l'Orient*, Paris, 1979, 139, calls Hegel's interpretation of the Orient "a unique enterprise in the history of ideas" ("une enterprise unique dans l'histoire des idées").

88. See below, ch. 9.

89. Among Hegel's direct disciples and successors, only E. Gans and K. Rosenkranz showed a noteworthy interest in India.

90. See, e.g., H. Haldar, *Neo-Hegelianism*. London, 1928; P.T. Raju, *Thought and Reality*. London, 1937; L. Saxena, *Neo-Hegelian and Neo-Advaitic Monism*. Delhi, 1980; and numerous references in *Contemporary Indian Philosophy*, ed. S. Radhakrishnan and J.H. Muirhead. London, 1936 (fourth edition, 1966).

7. Schelling and Schopenhauer

1. The great poet F. Hölderlin was the third member of this group of friends.

2. They were published as volumes 1 and 2 of the "second division" of Schelling's collected works, in the edition of his son, K.F.A. Schelling (i.e., *Sämmtliche Werke*, II/1-2, Stuttgart and Augsburg 1856–1857).

3. See, for instance, *Briefe und Dokumente*, ed. H. Fuhrmans, vol.2, Bonn 1962, 414. (letter to A.W. Schlegel); supporting the idea of "a complete Oriental academy" ("eine ganze orientalische Akademie").

4. These lectures were first published in 1803; see also H. von Glasenapp, *Indienbild*, 34f.

5. See *Briefe und Dokumente*, ed. H. Fuhrmans, vol. 3, Bonn 1975, 616f. (letter to Windischmann). See also J.W. Sedlar, *India in the Mind of Germany: Schelling, Schopenhauer and Their Times*. Washington, D.C., 1982.

6. Cf. *S.W.* II/1, 23, note 1; also II/2, 431ff. (criticism of the notion of an Indian "Urvolk," or "original," "primeval nation," and specifically of the speculations of P. von Bohlen and A.H.L. Heeren concerning Indian influences on Egypt).

7. See below, ch.8.

8. *Propädeutik der Philosophie* (1804); S.W. 1/6,78 (in the translation by F. de W. Bolman; see his introduction to: Schelling, *The Ages of the World*. New York, 1942, repr. 1967, 18. See also Bolman's notes on Schelling's evaluation of "traditional and mystical empiricism," 41ff.).

9. See *S.W.* I/4,113.

10. *S.W.* I/4, 128; as translated by F. de W. Bolman (see above, n.8), 16.

11. *Bruno oder über das göttliche und natürliche Princip der Dinge* (1802); *S.W.* I/4, 258.

12. See above, ch. 6, §13; cf. also *Wissenschaft der Logik*, ed. G. Lasson, I. Leipzig, 1951, 59.

13. Cf. *Briefe von und an Hegel*, ed. J. Hoffmeister, vol. I. Hamburg, 1952, 194 (Schelling's response to the preface).

14. *S.W.* 1/6, 38. Cf. Hegel, *Enzyklopädie der philosophischen Wissenschaften* (1830), ed. F. Nicolin and O. Pöggeler. Hamburg, sixth ed., 1959, §248 (p.201). Although Hegel uses the expression "Abfall der Idee von sich selbst" ("secession of

the idea from itself"), he does not accept the implications which this concept has in Schelling's thought.

15. *S.W.* II/2, 482.

16. See *S.W.* II/2, 148ff. Cf. Gauḍapāda, *Kārikā* II, 19, on divine "self-delusion": *māyā-eṣā tasya devasya yayā saṃmohitaḥ svayam.*

17. *S.W..* II/2,482.

18. *S.W.* II/2, 480. However, Max Müller claims that he translated several Upaniṣads for Schelling in 1845, and that Schelling considered the Upaniṣads as "the original wisdom of the Indians and mankind" ("die Urweisheit der Inder und der Menschheit"; see "Damals und jetzt," *Deutsche Rundschau* 41, 1884, 416; quoted by H. von Glasenapp, *Indienbild*, 35). This is hardly compatible with the statements in the *Philosophy of Mythology.*

19. J.W. Sedlar states in her aforementioned study (see above, n.5), 130: "A list of Schelling's errors on the subject of India—avoidable errors, for the most part—makes painful reading." Unfortunately, Sedlar's own understanding of Schelling and his contemporaries is as superficial as her knowledge of the Indian tradition, and she does not even attempt to explore Schelling's hermeneutical situation and the philosophical and theological background of his statements on India. It is obvious that Schelling's approach to India and the Orient in general deserves a more competent and sympathetic exploration. W. Heinrich, *Verklärung und Erlösung im Vedānta, bei Meister Eckhart und bei Schelling*, München, 1961, is an unsatisfactory "comparative" study.

20. V. Nuovo, Introduction to his translation of: P. Tillich, *The Construction of the History of Religion in Schelling's Positive Philosophy*. Lewisburg, 1974, 22. This is a translation of Tillich's first doctoral dissertation (*Die religionsgeschichtliche Konstruktion in Schellings positiver Philosophie*, Breslau, 1910), which continues to be one of the most valuable studies of Schelling's lectures on the *Philosophy of Mythology* and the *Philosophy of Revelation*. Tillich's philosophical dissertation was followed by a theological dissertation on Schelling: *Mystik und Schuldbewusstsein in Schellings philosophischer Entwicklung*. Halle, 1912 (published Gütersloh, 1912). On Schelling's interpretation of mythology and revelation, paganism and Christianity see also: C.M. Schröder, *Das Verhältnis von Heidentum und Christentum in Schellings Philosophie der Mythologie und Offenbarung*. München, 1936. On Schelling's later philosophy in general: W. Schulz, *Die Vollendung des deutschen Idealismus in der Spätphilosophie Schellings*. Stuttgart, 1955.

21. *S.W.* II/2, 577.

22. *S.W.* II/2, 509.

23. *S.W.* II/2, 441.

24. *S.W.* II/2, 472; according to Schelling, indications of a genuine sense of religious unity are not specifically Indian, but a heritage of mankind in general, of which India was a part (431ff.).

25. P. Tillich, *The Construction of the History of Religion* (see above, n.20), 86; cf also *S.W.* II/2, 444f.

26. Cf. *S.W.* II/2, 447: "das Nachempfundene einer Philosophie . . . ." Schelling does not trust the reports of Paulinus a S. Bartholomaeo concerning a "highest God," *parabrahma*, in Indian religion; he suspects that this could be an *ad hoc* invention of a modern "brahmin or pandit."

27. *S.W.* II/2, 476.

28. *S.W.* II/2, 24.

29. *S.W.* II/2, 40, note 1; on Spinoza and pantheism, see also 68ff.

30. *S.W.* II/2, 26; elsewhere (S.W. II/1, 568), Schelling says that there cannot be any "rational religion" ("Vernunftreligion"), since this would be a contradiction in terms.

31. *S.W.* II/2, 179; see also 574, on the meaning of *mokṣa*, "final liberation."

32. Cf. S.W. II/2, 488: "Einheit ist auf jeden Fall das Vorherrschende im Begriff." In this passage, Schelling discusses various attempts to translate the word *yoga*; without mentioning Hegel's name, he refers to his *Bhagavadgītā* review.

33. *S.W.* II/2, 457.

34. *S.W.* II/2, 466.

35. Cf. *S.W.* II/2, 519.

36. *S.W.* II/2, 455.

37. See above, notes 17; 28f.

38. Cf. *Zur Geschichte der neueren Philosophie* (Münchener Vorlesungen). *S.W.* I/10, 137f.; also 127f.: God himself as "concept" ("Begriff").

39. *S.W.* I/10, 141.

40. *S.W.* I/10, 144f. Schelling introduces the dwarf, generally known as the fifth *avatāra*, as Viṣṇu's "third incarnation."

41. See, for instance, *PP* I; Deussen IV, 32–42 (Hübscher V, 22–32). There is an English translation of *PP* by E.F.J. Payne; *WWV* is available in two English versions (by R.B. Haldane/J. Kemp and E.F.J. Payne).

42. See *PP* I, "Über die Universitäts-Philosophie," Deussen IV, 159–221, specifically 188; 190, 201 (Hübscher V, 178; 180; 191); also S. Hochfeld, *Das Künstlerische in der Sprache Schopenhauers*. Leipzig, 1912, for an inventory of Schopenhauer's terminology of abuse.

43. Cf., for instance, F. Mockrauer, "Schopenhauer und Indien," *Jahrbuch der Schopenhauer-Gesellschaft* 15 (1928), 3–26; M.F. Hecker, *Schopenhauer und die indische Philosophie*. Köln, 1897; H. von Glasenapp, *Indienbild*, 68–101; P. Wörner, *Der Idealismus und das Ding an sich bei Schopenhauer und den Indern*. Diss. Erlangen, 1914; D.W. Dauer, *Schopenhauer as Transmitter of Buddhist Ideas*. Bern, 1969 (inadequate); A. Hübscher, "Schopenhauer und die Religionen Asiens," *Jahrbuch der Schopenhauer-Gesellschaft* 60 (1979), 1–16 (unreliable); see below, n.101.

44. On Majer, see R.F. Merkel, "Schopenhauers Indien-Lehrer," *Jahrbuch der Schopenhauer-Gesellschaft* 32 (1945/48), 158–181.

45. Cf. *PP* II, §179 (Deussen V, 415; Hübscher VI, 406); §184 (Deussen V, 431f.; Hübscher VI, 421f.).

46. On Dārā Shukōh, see above, ch. 2: on Anquetil Duperron, ch. 4.

47. *PP* II, §184 (Deussen V 432; Hübscher VI, 422): "Es ist die belohnendste und erhebendste Lektüre, die (den Urtext ausgenommen) auf der Welt möglich ist: sie ist der Trost meines Lebens gewesen und wird der meines Sterbens sein."

48. *PP* II, §184; *HN*, ed. A. Hübscher, vol.5, 324; 341ff. Schopenhauer does not tolerate any attempt to interpret the *Upaniṣads* in a theistic sense.

49. See *PP* II, ch. 16 (§183–190); the following statement introduces this chapter: "Regardless of my admiration for the religious and philosophical works of Sanskrit literature – I have rarely been able to appreciate its poetical works; at times it has even appeared to me that they are as tasteless and monstrous as the sculpture of the same peoples." He adds, however, that this may be due to the problems of translating poetry.

50. *PP* II, §185 (Deussen V, 434; Hübscher VI, 423f.).

51. He deals somewhat more explicitly with the Sāṃkhya system, for which he relies not only on H. Th. Colebrooke, but also on F.H.H. Windischmann and Ch. Lassen; see *HN*, ed. A. Hübscher, vol.5, 331ff; *PP* II, §187 (criticizing the fundamental dualism of the system).

52. For a survey of Oriental materials in Schopenhauer's library and a reproduction of his marginal notes, see *HN*, ed. A. Hübscher, vol. 5, 319–352.

53. *Briefe*, Deussen XV, 470.

54. *HN*, Deussen XI, 459.

55. *WWV* II, ch.48 (Deussen II, 696; Hübscher III, 698): "Die Buddhaisten aber bezeichnen, mit voller Redlichkeit, die Sache bloss negativ, durch Nirwana, welches die Negation dieser Welt, oder des Sansara ist. Wenn Nirwana als das Nichts definiert wird, so will dies nur sagen, dass der Sansara kein einziges Element enthält, welches zur Definition oder Konstruktion des Nirwana dienen könnte." The translation follows E.F.J. Payne.

56. See *WWV* II, ch.35: "Über Geschichte" ("On History"). Schopenhauer argues against the "Hegelians, who consider history as the main purpose of all philosophy"; in his view, they have not grasped the fundamental truth that "at all times there is one and the same, that all becoming and origination are only apparent, ideas alone are permanent, time is ideal" (" . . . dass nämlich zu aller Zeit das Selbe ist, alles Werden und Entstehen nur scheinbar, die Ideen allein bleibend, die Zeit ideal").

57. *PP* II, §187: "How wise is, by contrast, the assumption of the thousand Buddhas in Buddhism."

58. *WWV* I, §1. In the second edition (1844), Schopenhauer added to his opening statements a reference to a "fundamental proposition" ("Fundamentalsatz") of the Vedānta system, which he had found in W. Jones' article "On the Philosophy of the Asiatics" (*Asiatic Researches* 4, 164) and in which he recognized his own doctrine of transcendental ideality.

59. Cf. Schopenhauer's doctoral dissertation of 1813: *Über die vierfache Wurzel des Satzes vom zureichenden Grunde* ("On the Fourfold Root of the Principle of Sufficient Reason").

60. We borrow the expression "wiedererkennende Philosophiegeschichte" from G. Teichmüller without adopting its systematic implications.

61. Cf. *WWV* I, §68; 65; on the "metaphysical urge" ("metaphysisches Bedürfnis"), cf. *WWV* II, ch.17.

62. Cf. *HN*, Deussen XI, 410.

63. *HN*, Deussen XI, 323.

64. *HN*, Deussen XI, 46.

65. *PP* II, §115 (Deussen V, 240; Hübscher VI, 233); *Preisschrift über die Grundlage der Moral*, §22 (Deussen III, 741; Hübscher IV, 271); *WWV* I, §66 (Deussen I, Hübscher II, 440ff.). See also P. Hacker, "Schopenhauer und die Ethik des Hinduismus," *Saeculum* 12 (1961), 366–399 (*Kl. Schr.*, 531–564).

66. CF. *WWV* II, ch.48 (Deussen II, 696; Hübscher III, 698); PP II, §189 (Deussen V, 436f.; Hübscher VI, 426f.); on the etymology of *nirvāṇa*, *WWV* II, ch.41 (Deussen II, 581; Hübscher III, 583); *WWV* I, §71 (Deussen I, Hübscher II, 487) is more critical.

67. Cf. *PP* II, §189 (Deussen V, 436f.; Hübscher VI, 426f.).

68. See H. von Glasenapp, *Indienbild*, 85; *Briefe* II (Deussen XV), 522; 563.

69. *Briefe* II (Deussen XV), 359.

70. *Briefe* II (Deussen XV), 46 (letter to A. von Doss, Febr. 27, 1856).

71. *PP* I, Deussen IV, 348 (Hübscher V, 334).

72. *Senilia* (1858); see *HN*, ed. A. Hübscher, vol. 4/2, 29; cf. also *WWV* II, ch. 48 (Deussen II, 703; Hübscher III, 705).

73. *HN*, Deussen IX, 89.

74. *WWV* II, ch. 17 (Deussen II, Hübscher III, 186); also *Über die vierfache Wurzel des Satzes vom zureichenden Grunde* (revised version of 1847), §34 (Deussen III, 233; Hübscher I, 125); *Gespräche*, ed. A. Hübscher, Stuttgart 1971, 244 (conversation with C.J. Bähr).

75. *WWV* II, ch. 48 (Deussen II, 702; Hübscher III, 705).

76. *Prolegomena zu einer jeden künftigen Metaphysik*, preface (1783).

77. *Über die vierfache Wurzel des Satzes vom zureichenden Grunde* (847), §34 (Deussen III, 236; Hübscher I, 128): "Denn das Christentum . . . hat indisches Blut im Leibe und daher einen beständigen Hang, vom Judentume los zu kommen."

78. *PP* II, §179 (Deussen V, 413; Hübscher VI, 404).

79. *PP* II, §163 (Deussen V, 341; Hübscher VI, 334).

80. Cf. *PP* II, §179 (Deussen V, 415; Hübscher VI, 406); §190 (connections with Egypt, etc.). For contemporary speculations concerning India and Egypt, see P. von Bohlen, *Das alte Indien, mit besonderer Rücksicht auf Ägypten*. Königsberg, 1830.

81. *WWV* I, §63 (Deussen I, Hübscher II, 421).

82. *PP* II, §115 (Deussen V, 246; Hübscher VI, 239); *HN*, Deussen IX, 89.

83. *PP* II, §115 (Deussen V, 243; Hübscher VI, 236). Schopenhauer criticizes the activities of Christian missionaries in Asia, predicts their failure, and would like to see "Buddhist priests" in Europe (Deussen V, 247f.; Hübscher VI, 240f.).

84. *PP* II, §115 (Deussen V, 248; Hübscher VI, 241).

85. See, e.g., *PP* II, §189 (Deussen V, 437; Hübscher VI, 427). His judgement on Islam is in general very harsh.

86. *WWV* I, §63 (Deussen I, Hübscher II, 419); II, ch. 17 (Deussen II, Hübscher III, 178); II, ch.41 (Deussen II, 542, Hübscher III, 543).

87. *WV* II, ch. 41 (Deussen II, 542; Hübscher III, 544); see also ch. 17 (Deussen II, Hübscher III, 178), where Schopenhauer refers to the "greater energy of the intuitive cognitive powers" ("grössere Energie der intuitiven Erkenntniskräfte") of the ancient Vedic teachers.

88. *WWV* I, preface to the first edition (1818; Deussen I, XXIVf.; Hübscher II, XIIf.); cf. R. Schwab, *Oriental Renaissance*, 13 (on Anquetil Duperron's earlier reference to the Renaissance).

89. *HN*, Deussen IX, 89f.

90. *WWV* I, preface to the first edition (Deussen I, XXV; Hübscher II, XIII).

91. *WWV* I, §71 (Deussen I, Hübscher II, 487).

92. PP II, §187 (Deussen V, 435; Hübscher VI, 425; referring to the Sāṃkhya dualism).

93. *HN*, Deussen XI, 459; this passage is, however, not without a sense of irony.

94. See above, n.72.

95. *Briefe*, Deussen XIV, 221 (letter to his publisher, F.A. Brockhaus; 1818). On the other hand, Schopenhauer often acknowledges his indebtedness to Kant.

96. *De Kantismo; Oupnek'hat* I, 711–724; see above, ch. 4.

97. HN, Deussen IX, 90f (from Schopenhauer's unsuccessful lectures at the University of Berlin, 1820; new edition by V. Spierling; *Theorie des gesammten Vorstellens, Denkens und Erkennens*. München, 1986, 106).

98. See F. Mockrauer, "Schopenhauer und Indien," *Jahrbuch der Schopenhauer-Gesellschaft* 15 (1928), 6; 26.

99. See R. Gérard, *L'Orient et la pensée romantique allemande*, Paris, 1963, 220: "Orient et Occident se rejoignent dans la pensée Schopenhauerienne."

100. See M. Scheler, *Liebe und Erkenntnis*. München, 1955, 55.

101. Cf. H. von Glasenapp, Indienbild, 68–101; I. Vecchiotti, *La dottrina di Schopenhauer. Le teorie schopenhaueriane considerate nello loro genesi e nei loro rapporti con la filosofia indiana*. Rome, 1969; J.W. Sedlar, *India in the Mind of Germany: Schelling, Schopenhauer and Their Times*. Washington, D.C., 1982.

102. Cf. *Materialien zu Schopenhauers 'Die Welt als Wille und Vorstellung,'* ed. V. Spierling. Frankfurt, 1984, 328.

103. Letter to J. Frauenstädt, August 21, 1852; *Briefe*, Deussen XV, 155f.

104. *WWV I*, §29 (Deussen I, Hübscher II, 193).

105. *WWV* II, ch. 28 (Deussen II, 401; Hübscher III, 400).

106. See, for instance, *WWV* I, §7 (Deussen I, Hübscher II, 30f.); *WWV*. Appendix (Deussen I, Hübscher II, 574); *WWV* II, ch. 4 (Deussen II, Hübscher III, 50).

107. *PP* II, §161 (Deussen V, 338; Hübscher VI, 331).

108. *Metaphysik der Sitten*, ed. V. Spierling, München, 1985, 272 (based upon *HN*, Deussen X, 364–584).

109. Cf. H. von Glasenapp, *Indienbild*, 85. Schopenhauer uses the form "Brahm" to refer to *brahman/brahma* as neuter.

110. *WWV* I, Appendix (Deussen I, Hübscher II, 574).

111. *Über den Willen in der Natur*; Deussen III, 322; Hübscher IV, 30f.

112. *Briefe* II (Deussen XV), 46 (a letter to A. von Doss, Febr. 27, 1856).

113. PP II, §187 (Deussen V, 435; Hübscher VI, 425). WWV II, ch. 19 (Deussen II, Hübscher III, 233) uses the simile of the blind and the lame, which is familiar in Sāṃkhya (e.g., *Sāṃkhyakārikā*, v.21).

114. *HN*, Deussen XI, 323 (§441; a note written in 1815).

115. See above, n.68.

116. Cf. *PP* I, §9 (Deussen IV, 73f.; HübscherV, 66).

117. Cf. *Indienbild*, 84.

118. Cf. *Metaphysik der Sitten*, ed. V. Spierling. München, 1985, 39 (introduction).

119. Cf. *WWV*, §68 (Deussen I, Hübscher II, 448; 452f.; 460).

120. *PP* II, §189 (Deussen V, 436f.; Hübscher VI, 426f.). On "quietism" in its connection with mysticism and asceticism, see also *WWV* II, ch.48 (Deussen II, 702ff.; Hübscher III, 704ff.)

121. Cf. A. Diemer, "Schopenhauer und die moderne Existenzphilosophie," *Schopenhauer*, ed. J. Salaquarda, Darmstadt, 1985, 125, n.3; M. Heidegger, *Nietzsche* I. Pfullingen, 1961, 44. See, on the other hand, Heidegger's remarks on the relationship between "will" and "releasement" ("Gelassenheit") in: *Gelassenheit*. Pfullingen, 1959, 30ff.; 57ff. (tr. J.M. Anderson and E.H. Freund: *Discourse on Thinking*. New York, 1969, 59ff.; 79ff.).

122. Cf. I. Vecchiotti, "Schopenhauer im Urteil der modernen Inder," *Schopenhauer*, ed. J. Salaquarda. Darmstadt, 1985, 185ff. (Italian original in I. Vecchiotti, *A. Schopenhauer*. Florence, 1976, 108–117).

123. See R.L. Mitra's preface to: *The Yoga Aphorisms of Patañjali with the Commentary of Bhoja Rājā*. Calcutta, 1883.

8. Developments in the Interpretation of India Following Hegel and Schopenhauer

1. We may disregard here the contributions of Schopenhauer's earliest devotees, such as J. Frauenstädt and D. Asher, or the variations of "pessimism" in the works of J. Bahnsen and others. For a discussion of the relation between German "pessimism" (including the thought of O. Spengler and J. Gebser) and Indian thought, see J.J. Gestering, *German Pessimism and Indian Philosophy: A Hermeneutic Reading*. Delhi, 1986.

2. E. von Hartmann, *Zur Geschichte und Begründung des Pessimismus*. Berlin, 1880, presents Kant, not Schopenhauer, as "father of pessimism."

3. See *Philosophie der Erlösung*. Berlin, 1876, 326f. See also 334: "everything in the world is will to death" ("Wille zum Tode"), which appears in the guise of "will to life" ("Wille zum Leben"). The historical process of civilization is a "movement from life into absolute death" ("Bewegung aus dem Leben in den absoluten Tod," 312). On Buddhism, specifically the Buddhist karma theory, see, e.g., 613–620. In accordance with his philosophy, Mainländer committed suicide immediately after the publication of his work; cf. R. Gebhard, "Ein Jünger Schopenhauers: Ph. Mainländer." *Jahrbuch der Schopenhauer-Gesellschaft* 18 (1931), 220–228.

4. See *Religionsphilosophie* I. Leipzig, second ed., 1888 ("Das religiöse Bewusstsein der Menschheit"). In his presentation of "naturalism," Hartmann frequently uses the concept of "henotheism."

5. *Schellings positive Philosophie als Einheit von Hegel und Schopenhauer*. Berlin, 1869. Although different from Mainländer's scheme, this synthesis also implies a reverse teleology, a "reasonable" development towards the annihilation of the world.

6. *Philosophie des Unbewussten* I. Leipzig, twelfth ed., 1923, XIV f.

7. "Persönliches und Sachliches." In: *Deutschland*, ed. P. von Hoensbroech, I (1902), 79.

8. Although von Hartmann praises the "religious and ethical autonomy of Buddhism," he also associates it with illusionism, indifferentism, and quietism. He even invokes the old opium metaphor; cf. *Religionsphilosophie* I. Leipzig, second ed., 1888, 350.

9. Loc. cit., 626ff.

10. *Geschichte der Metaphysik* I. Leipzig, 1899, I.

11. Cf. L. Ziegler, *Der ewige Buddho*. Darmstadt, 1922; *Das Lehrgespräch vom allgemeinen Menschen*. Hamburg, 1956 (cf. 163ff: Eastern introspection versus Western "mastery of nature"); see also *Das Weltbild Hartmanns*. Leipzig, 1910.

12. See Neumann's notes to his translation of the Dhammapada: *Der Wahrheitpfad*. Munich, second ed., 1921, 133ff.

13. Grimm's major work, *Die Lehre des Buddha*. Munich, 1915, has the characteristic subtitle *Die Religion der Vernunft* ("The Religion of Reason").

14. Cf. M. Scheler, *Die Stellung des Menschen im Kosmos*. Munich, 1949 (first ed.: 1927), 58ff. Scheler finds a direct connection between Freud's "death urge," "Todestrieb," and the teachings of the Buddha. On Scheler's comparison of Schopenhauer and the Buddha, see above, ch. 7, §22.

15. Cf. H. von Glasenapp, *Indienbild*, 131ff.; especially 133.

16. On Wagner's attitudes towards Indian thought, see G. Lanczkowski, *Die Bedeutung des indischen Denkens für R. Wagner und seinen Freundeskreis*. Diss. Marburg, 1947; C. Suneson, *R. Wagner och den indiska tankevärlden*. Stockholm 1985. Wagner's brother-in-law H. Brockhaus, son of the publisher of Schopenhauer's *Die Welt als Wille und Vorstellung*, was a professor of Indology at the University of Leipzig.

17. Wagner had found this story in E. Burnouf, *Introduction à l'histoire du buddhisme indien*. Paris, 1844.

18. Letter to E. Rohde, November 9, 1868 (Schlechta III, 999). In *Die fröhliche Wissenschaft*, §99 (Schlechta II, 106), Nietzsche refers to Wagner's Schopenhauerian "attempt to understand Christianity as a scattered grain of Buddhism" and to "prepare a Buddhist era."

19. Windisch became the successor of H. Brockhaus at the University of Leipzig.

20. See F. Mistry, "An Aspect of Nietzsche's Perspectivism in 'Die Geburt der Tragödie.'" *Nietzsche-Studien* 8 (1979), 245–269; especially 246ff. On Nietzsche and India in general, see Ch. Andler, *Nietzsche, sa vie et sa penseé*. Paris, sixth ed., 1958, II, 412 ff.; 459ff.

21. Schlechta I, 362: "Das indische Altertum eröffnet seine Tore, und seine Kenner haben zu den unvergänglichen Werken der Inder, zu ihren Philosophien, kaum ein anderes Verhältnis als ein Tier zur Lyra."

22. Cf. L. Andreas-Salomé, *Friedrich Nietzsche in seinen Werken*. Vienna, 1911, 242.

23. Cf. A. Riehl, *Zur Einführung in die Philosophie der Gegenwart*. Leipzig, third ed., 1908, 240.

24. Cf. F. Mistry, *Nietzsche and Buddhism. Prolegomenon to a Comparative Study*. Berlin, 1981; Mistry's rejection of popular images of Nietzsche and the Buddha, as advocates of "power" and "resignation" respectively, is, of course, fully justified. For a more critical assessment, see J. Stambaugh, *Nietzsche's Thought of Eternal Return*. Baltimore, 1972.

25. Cf. G. Welbon, *The Buddhist Nirvāṇa and its Western Interpreters*. Chicago, 1968; 188;190. Even the later "identifications . . . of *śunyatā* and *saṃsāra*" to which Welbon refers and of which Nietzsche himself was totally unaware cannot justify the association of *nirvāṇa* with "triumph and creativity in this world."

26. Cf. *Nachlass*; Schlechta III, 701 (Colli/Montinari XIII, 380).

27. *Der Antichrist*, §56 (Schlechta II, 1224).

28. *Nachgelassene Fragmente*, Colli/Montinari XIII, 378: "Der offizielle Begriff des Tschandala ist genau der eines Auswurfs und Excrements der vornehmen Classen . . . " This passage is not found in K. Schlechta's edition.

29. *Nachlass*, Schlechta III, 815f. (Colli/Montinari XIII, 439f.; also *Der Antichrist*, §55 (Schlechta II, 1222ff.). Nietzsche's assessment of Manu was strongly influenced by J. Jacolliot, *Les législateurs religieux. Manou-Moïse-Mahomet*. Paris, 1876. Cf. his letter to P. Gast, May 31, 1888 (Schlechta III, 1296f.)

30. Cf. *Nachlass*, Schlechta III, 639 (Colli/Montinari XIII, 167); *Der Antichrist*, §20 (Schlechta II, 1179); *Die fröhliche Wissenschaft*, §347 (Schlechta II,213: "in einer ungeheuren Erkrankung des Willens").

31. *Nachlass*, Schlechta III, 770 (Colli/Montinari XIII, 267); *Der Antichrist*, §22 (Schlechta II, 1182): "Der Buddhismus ist eine Religion für späte Menschen, für gütige, sanfte, übergeistig gewordene Rassen, die zu leicht Schmerz empfinden . . . Der Buddhismus ist eine Religion für den Schluss und die Müdigkeit der Zivilisation . . . "). Europe and Christianity are far less "mature" than Buddhism.

32. Cf. *Nachlass*, Schlechta II, 649f. (Colli/Montinari XIII, 125f.).

33. Cf. *Nachlass*, Schlechta III, 712 (Colli/Montinari XIII, 381); Schlechta III, 569 (Colli/Montinari XII, 569).

34. *Der Antichrist*, §20 (Schlechta II, 1179); cf. *Ecce homo* I, §6 (Schlechta II, 1077): the Buddha as "deep physiologist" ("tiefer Physiolog"), who is free from the Christian ways of moralizing.

35. Morgenröte, §96 (Schlechta I, 1074).

36. Cf. *Nachlass*, Schlechta III, 488 (Colli/Montinari XII, 138): ". . . weshalb im stillen überall der Buddhismus in Europa Fortschritte macht"; Schlechta III, 450 (Colli/Montinari XI, 512): "ein europäischer Buddhismus könnte vielleicht nicht zu entbehren sein." See also Schlechta III, 546 (Colli/Montinari XII, 377), and F. Mistry, *Nietzsche and Buddhism*, Berlin, 1981, 119, on the "second Buddhism"; A.M. Frazier, *A European Buddhism*, PEW 25 (1975), 145–160, is inadequate.

37. Cf. H. Wein, *Positives Antichristentum*. The Hague, 1962.

38. *Nachlass*, Schlechta III, 550 (Colli/Montinari XII, 367): " . . . bevor die Kraft da ist, die Werte umzuwenden und das Werdende, die scheinbare Welt als die einzige zu vergöttlichen und gutzuheissen."

39. Cf. *Nachlass*, Schlechta III, 557f. (Colli/Montinari XII, 350f.). *Die fröhliche Wissenschaft*, §134 (Schlechta II, 131) associates the spread of Buddhism among the Indians with the "debility" caused by their "rice nutriment."

40. *Nachlass*, Schlechta III, 634 (Colli/Montinari XIII, 190): "der erste vollkommene Nihilist Europas, der aber den Nihilismus selbst schon in sich zu Ende gelebt hat, — der ihn hinter sich, unter sich, ausser sich hat."

41. *Jenseits von Gut und Böse*, §56 (Schlechta II, 617).

42. *Nachgelassene Fragmente*, Colli/Montinari X, 109 (not included in the edition by K. Schlechta).

43. Cf. *Nachlass*, Schlechta III, 661 (Colli/Montinari XIII, 89).

44. Letter to Deussen, March 16, 1886 (Schlechta III, 1203f.); the "manifesto" referred to by Nietzsche is *Also sprach Zarathustra* (parts 1 and 2, 1883); on

Vedānta, see also *Jenseits von Gut und Böse*, §54 (Schlechta II, 616). Nietzsche's marginal notes in his copies, which are preserved in the Nietzsche Archive at Weimar, do not indicate a careful study of Deussen's Vedānta books (private communication of M. Sprung).

45. H. Scholz, "Paul Deussen†". *Kant-Studien 24 (1920), 304*–317; ib., 317. See also the contributions by F. Mockrauer and others in: *Jahrbuch der Schopenhauer-Gesellschaft* 9 (1920).

46. H. Scholz, loc. cit., 316f.

47. Cf. Windisch I, 63ff.; among Frank's contributions to Indian philosophy, we may mention his edition and translation of Sadānanda's *Vedāntasāra* (1835).

48. Röer's dissertation is entitled: *De notione absolute infinitae substantiae in Spinozae Ethice constituta*. Berlin, 1833; other philosophical works are: *Über Herbarts Methode der Beziehungen*. Braunschweig, 1833; *Das spekulative Denken in seiner Fortbewegung zur Idee*. Berlin, 1837. Cf. also L. Geldsetzer, *Die Philosophie der Philosophiegeschichte*, 117.

49. P. Deussen, *Mein Leben*. Leipzig, 1922, 165.

50. Letter to P. Gast, September 8, 1887 (Schlechta III, 1262).

51. Cf. B. Heimann, "Paul Deussen und die heutige Indologie." *Jahrbuch der Schopenhauer-Gesellschaft* 18 (1931), 246–254.

52. Cf. *AGPh* I/1, 1.

53. *AGPh* I/1, 4ff.

54. *Vedānta, Platon und Kant*. Vienna, 1917, 41.

55. *AGPh* I/1, 31.

56. *AGPh* I/1, 31.

57. Cf. *AGPh* I/1, 30;32.

58. *Vedānta, Platon und Kant*. Vienna, 1917, 41. Cf. 15: "immediate experience" ("unmittelbare Anschauung," "Schauen," "Innewerden") as their common source.

59. Cf. *AGPh* I/1, 32.

60. *AGPh* I/1, 35f. (=*Die Sūtras des Vedānta*. Leipzig, 1887, Vf.).

61. See above, ch. 8, §15.

62. *AGPh* I/1, 36.

63. *AGPh* II/3, 586; Deussen treats Hegel as a mere interlude between Kant and Schopenhauer (loc. cit., 340–366).

64. *Mein Leben*. Leipzig, 1922, 21. See Schopenhauer's own claim to Christianity, *PP* II, §163 (Hübscher VI, 334).

65. Cf. *AGPh* II/3, 574ff.

66. A Sanskrit translation of Deussen's *Elemente der Metaphysik* ("Elements of Metaphysics," 1877) by A. Govinda Pillai, which was based upon a prior English translation, was published under the title *Atītaprakṛtiśāstram* (Trivandrum, 1912).

67. See above, ch. 6, §11; also below, ch. 13, on Vivekananda and Deussen.

68. Cf. F.M. Müller, *My Autobiography*. New York, 1901, 289: ". . . I had talked with Schelling and Schopenhauer."

69. Cf. G.A. Müller, *The Life and Letters of the Right Hon. F.M. Müller*, 2 vols. London, 1902; N.C. Chaudhuri, *Scholar Extraordinary: The Life of the Right Hon. F.M. Müller*. London, 1974; also Windisch II, 270–304; and above, ch. 5, §14f. Müller moved to England in 1846, became Deputy Professor in 1851, and Professor at Oxford in 1854.

70. Cf. J.H. Voigt, *Max Müller-The Man and His Ideas*. Calcutta, 1967. The great series Sacred Books of the East, which Müller edited, was meant to be a demonstration of "impartial inquiry into all religions" (see the motto by Bishop Beveridge, vol. 1).

71. *Critique of Pure Reason*, Introduction; cf. G.M. Müller, *Life and Religion. An Aftermath from the Writings of F.M. Müller*. New York, 1905, 100.

72. Cf. *Life and Religion*, 221; 167.

73. *Life and Religion*, 221; 175.

74. *Life and Religion*, 160f.; 48.

75. *Life and Religion*, 182; see also J.H. Voigt, *Max Müller*. Calcutta 1967, 21.

76. Cf. G.A. Müller, *The Life and Letters of the Right Hon. F.M. Müller*. London, 1902, I, 198 (letter to Bunsen).

77. Cf. *The Six Systems of Indian Philosophy*, London, 1899, 93; *Three Lectures on the Vedānta Philosophy*, London, 1894, 8; *Upanishads* I (Sacred Books of the East, vol. 1), LIX-LXII; on Rammohan Roy: LXIII.

78. Cf. J.H. Voigt, *Max Müller*. Calcutta, 1967, 28ff; 31ff.

79. See above, ch. 5, §14f. On the other hand, *The Six Systems of Indian Philosophy*, London, 1899, 386ff., focuses on a transhistorical concordance of ideas. In one of his early studies (*ZDMG* 6, 1852, 22), Müller criticized the practice of comparison of which he later became a leading advocate.

80. See, for instance, the enthusiastic statements by Svami Vivekananda in *M. Müller-I Point to India*, ed. N. Mookerjee. Bombay, 1970, 171. Also L. Rocher, Max Müller and the Veda. *Mélanges Armand Abel*, vol.3. Leiden, 1978, 221-235.

81. Cf. Th. Stcherbatsky, *Buddhist Logic*, 2 vols., Leningrad. 1930–1932 (several reprints); St. Schayer, "Über die Methode der Nyāya-Forschung." *Festschrift M. Winternitz*, Leipzig, 1933, 247–257.

82. See N. Hartmann, "Der philosophische Gedanke und seine Geschichte." *Kleinere Schriften*, vol. 2. Berlin, second ed., 1957, 11. B.K. Matilal, *Epistemology, Logic and Grammar in Indian Philosophical Analysis*. The Hague, 1971, 14, refers to "rethinking."

83. See above, ch. 6.

84. Cf. K. Rosenkranz, *Die Poesie und ihre Geschichte*. Königsberg, 1855, 58–109. Among the students of Rosenkranz, we find the Indologist Th. Goldstücker; Rosen-

kranz added a preface to Goldstücker's anonymous translation of Kṛṣṇamiśra's philosophical drama *Prabodhacandrodaya* (1842).

85. Three of the four sections ("Abteilungen") of the work, which comprises more than 2000 pages, deal with India; the first section deals with China.

86. Cf. A. Schopenhauer, *Der handschriftliche Nachlass*, ed. A. Hübscher, vol. 5. Frankfurt, 1968, 186f. On Windischmann, see also A. Dyroff, *C.J. Windischmann und sein Kreis*. Köln, 1916.

87. See *Die Philosophie im Fortgang der Weltgeschichte*, 81f.

88. The younger Windischmann did pioneering work on Vedānta; cf. his dissertation *Sancara sive de theologumenis Vedanticorum* (Bonn, 1833; partly published already in 1832; this includes the text and a translation of the *Bālabodhinī*).

89. The impact of Hegel's understanding of India is obvious in K. Braniss, *Geschichte der Philosophie seit Kant*. Breslau, 1842, 34ff.

90. See specifically Leçons V and VI, presented in 1828; in: V. Cousin, *Cours de l'histoire de la philosophie I*. Paris, 1829.

91. Cf. V. Cousin, *Cours de l'histoire de la philosophie moderne* I/2. Paris, 1846, 12f.

92. *Histoire générale de la philosophie*. Paris, fourth ed., 1861, 118.

93. Cf., e.g., L. Feuerbach, *Das Geheimnis des Opfers oder Der Mensch ist was er isst*. Sämtliche Werke, vol. 10, Stuttgart, second ed. 1960, 41–67 (refers to Manu, the *soma* ritual, etc.). See also E. Benz, "Hegel's Religionsphilosophie und die Linkshegelianer." *Zeitschrift für Religions-und Geistesgeschichte* 3 (1955), 247ff.

94. Cf. F. Engels, *Dialektik der Natur*. Berlin, 1952, 237.

95. Cf. W. Ruben, *Geschichte der indischen Philosophie*. Berlin, 1954, 1–12; "Hegel über die Philosophie der Inder." *Asiatica, Festschrift F. Weller*, Leipzig, 1954, 553–569; see also H. von Glasenapp, *Indienbild*, 181.

96. Cf. specifically vol. 4: *Die Entwicklung der Philosophie*. Berlin, 1971.

97. Cf. N.P. Anikeev, *Modern Ideological Struggle for the Ancient Philosophical Heritage of India*, Calcutta n.d. (*Indian Studies Past and Present*).

98. Cf. H. von Glasenapp, *Indienbild*, 181; see also T. Ling, *Karl Marx and Religion in Europe and India*, London, 1960, 68ff.: "Marx's studies of India."

99. The article appeared on August 8, 1853, under the title "The Future Results of British Rule in India;" see *Karl Marx on Colonialism and Modernization*, ed. S. Avineri. Garden City, N.Y., 1969, 132–139.

100. See specifically vol. 2, 101–237; among Gobineau's most important sources, we find the works of Chr. Lassen and E. Burnouf.

101. Philadelphia, 1856 (trans. H. Hotz; reprinted New York, 1984); London, 1915 (trans. A. Collins; reprinted New York, 1967). On the reception of Gobineau's work, see L. Schemann, *Gobineaus Rassenwerk*. Stuttgart, 1910 (157f.: Gobineau and Nietzsche).

102. H.V. White, art. "Gobineau." *The Encyclopedia of Philosophy*, ed. P. Edwards, vol. 3. New York, 1967, 343.

103. *The Inequality of Human Races*, trans. A. Collins. New York, 1967, 34.

104. E. de Michelis, *L'origine degli Indo-Europei*. Turin, 1903 (quoted by L. Wilser, "Indogermanische Probleme." *Politisch-Anthropologische Revue* 3, 1904/1905, 45. In India, B.G. Tilak was an advocate of the "polar" hypothesis (cf. *The Arctic Home in the Vedas*. Bombay, 1903) which had first been proposed by W.F. Warren, *Paradise Found*. London, 1885. For much valuable information on these and related developments, see the contributions by M. Sieferle and J. Lütt in: *Zeitschrift für Kulturaustausch* 37/3 (1987; "Utopie-Projektion-Gegenbild: Indien in Deutschland").

105. On Georg (Jörg) Lanz (von) Liebenfels (originally: Adolph Lanz), see W. Daim, *Der Mann, der Hitler die Ideen gab*. Munich, 1958. Cf. specifically 70 ff., on the history of the *svastika*; 116f.: Lanz on Manu; 173: Lanz as "one of the historically most powerful figures of the European underground" ("eine der geschichtsmächtigsten Figuren des europäischen Untergrundes").

106. See *Der Mythus des 20. Jahrhunderts*. Munich, 1934, 28ff.; 390ff.; 660ff. References to India are also frequent in the works of the race theorist H.F.K. Günther. On "Jisnu Krischna" and his "influence" on Biblical teachings see, for instance, M. Ludendorff, *Triumph des Unsterblichkeitswillens*. Pähl, 1959 (first ed.: 1921), 115ff.

107. Cf. B.F. Campbell, *Ancient Wisdom Revived. A History of the Theosophical Movement*. Berkeley, 1980; J. Wichmann, "Das theosophische Menschenbild und seine indischen Wurzeln." *Zeitschrift für Religions-und Geistesgeschichte* 35 (1983), 12–33.

108. Cf. A. Comte, *Cours de philosophie positive*, 6 vols., Paris, 1830–1842; specifically the introduction to vol. 1.

109. See *Catéchisme positiviste, ou sommaire exposition de la religion universelle*. Paris, 1874 (first ed.: 1852), 73ff.

110. See below, ch. 9, §11. On the attitudes towards India taken by J.St. Mill and other British contemporaries and followers of Comte, see G.D. Bearce, *British Attitudes towards India, 1784–1858*. London, 1961.

111. See R. Schwab, *Renaissance orientale*, 267f. (*Oriental Renaissance*, 251).

112. R. Schwab, *Renaissance orientale*, 269 (*Oriental Renaissance*, 252; from Littré's preface to his new edition of Comte's *Cours de philosophie positive*).

113. See R. Schwab, *Renaissance orientale*, 259f. (*Oriental Renaissance*, 243f.).

114. On Durkheim's views on Indian social phenomena, see G.R. Madan, *Western Sociologists on Indian Society*. London, 1979, 252–284. Unlike Durkheim and Mauss, Lévy-Bruhl did not show any noticeable interest in India.

115. *La philosophie comparée* is dedicated to L. Lévy-Bruhl. On Masson-Oursel and the history and background of "comparative philosophy," see also below, Appendix III.

116. See, for instance *Esquisse d'une histoire de la philosophie indienne*. Paris, 1923; *La philosophie en Orient*. Paris, 1938 (supplement to E. Bréhier, *Histoire de la philosophie*); *Le Yoga*. Paris, 1941; also *Le fait métaphysique*. Paris, 1941.

117. See *La philosophie comparée*, 43; "l'ensemble du donné humain" (*Comparative Philosophy*, 62: "the human datum in its entirety"); Comte himself had talked about "l'ensemble de l'évolution humaine;" see above, §26.

118. See *La philosophie comparée*, 26–34 (*Comparative Philosophy*, 44–51).

119. Cf. *La philosophie comparée*, 11: "L'important est ici d'envisager les philosophies comme des matériaux aussi réels que n'importe quelles autres données." (*Comparative Philosophy*, 29: "What is important here is to regard philosophies as materials no less real than other data, not matter what.")

120. Cf. W. Schluchter, *The Rise of Western Rationalism*, trans. G. Roth. Berkeley, 1981, 25. See also R. Bendix, *Max Weber. An Intellectual Portrait*. Garden City, N.Y. 1960; G.R. Madan, *Western Sociologists on Indian Society*.London, 1979, 64–251.

121. Weber's major study of Indian religion and society was published after his death: *Gesammelte Aufsätze zur Religionssoziologie, vol.2: Hinduismus und Buddhismus*. Tübingen, 1921. The translation by H.H. Gerth and D. Martindale (*The Religion of India*. New York, 1958) is in many places inadequate.

122. See the contributions in: *Max Webers Studie über Hinduismus und Buddhismus-Interpretation und Kritik*, ed. W. Schluchter. Frankfurt, 1984. For a highly inadequate, yet symptomatic Weber critique, see J. Rösel, *Die Hinduismusthese Max Webers*. Munich, 1982; Rösel argues that Weber does not deal with Indian social realities, but with "self-fulfilling prophecies" of the British colonialists.

123. See K. Jaspers, *Max Weber*. Munich, 1958, 65.

124. Cf. D. Rothermund, *The German Intellectual Quest for India*. New Delhi, 1986, 15.

125. G. Roth and W. Schluchter, *M. Weber's Vision of History*. Berkeley, 1979, 21f.

126. See K. Jaspers, *Max Weber*. Munich, 1958, 48: "Die weitere, umfassendere Frage ist daher die nach dem Ursprung und den Folgen der Rationalisierung des menschlichen Geistes überhaupt."

127. For a critical discussion of Indian responses to Weber see D. Kantowsky, "Max Weber on India and Indian Interpretations of Weber." *Contributions to Indian Sociology* 16 (1982), 141–174.

9. On the Exclusion of India from the History of Philosophy

1. See H. Hess, "Das romantische Bild der Philosophiegeschichte," *Kant-Studien* 31 (1926), 251–285.

2. Cf. L. Geldsetzer, *Philosophie der Philosophiegeschichte*, 93.

3. *Grundriss der Geschichte der Philosophie*. Leipzig, 1887, 6; on Krause's view of India, cf. Glasenapp, *Indienbild*, 61 ff.

4. Three volumes, Mannheim, 1846–1858 (second ed., 1862); on Röth, cf. Geldsetzer, *Philosophie der Philosophiegeschichte*, 96 ff.

5. See above, ch. 6. The lack of interest which greeted these remarks was partially the result of the way in which Hegel's lectures were initially edited.

6. See above, ch. 1.

7. F.A. Carus, *Ideen*, 38 f., speaks of the "long thoughtless repetition and satisfaction with excerpts from the only Diogenes" during the fifteenth and sixteenth centuries. Of course, these "excerpts" were frequently enhanced by references to events specific to the times.

8. *The History of Philosophy*. London, 1655 ff. (second ed. 1687, third ed. 1701).

9. *De scriptoribus historiae philosophicae*. Jena, second ed., 1716.

10. *Ideen zur Geschichte der Philosophie*, Leipzig, 1809 (*Nachgel. Werke*, Part 4), 21–90: "Geschichte der Geschichte der Philosophie."

11. "Universal histories" were especially popular during the eighteenth century; cf. also J. Freyer, *Geschichte der Geschichte der Philosophie im 18. Jh.* Leipzig, 1912.

12. On Adam as "philosopher," cf. L. Geldsetzer, *Philosophie der Philosophiegeschichte*, 184.

13. Cf. the comprehensive definition of the history of philosophy given by J. Gurlitt, *Abriss der Geschichte der Philosophie*. Leipzig, 1786, 1.

14. F.A. Carus, *Ideen*, 106 f.

15. *Kritik der reinen Vernunft*, B 864; cf. also W.E. Ehrhardt, *Philosophiegeschichte und geschichtlicher Skeptizismus*. Bern/Munich, 1967, 44 ff.

16. Cf. W.E. Ehrhardt, 46 (from Akademie-Ausg. XX, 340 ff.).

17. Loc. cit., 101 f.; and W.E. Ehrhardt, loc. cit., 49 ff.

18. De facto, this "universality" usually remained within the horizon of the Biblical tradition.

19. J. Brucker, *Historia critica* I, 50; I, 8 defined philosophy as the "scientia veri et boni, quatenus ex rationis humanae principiis cognosci atque demonstrari potest."

20. F.A. Carus, *Ideen*, 143 ff.

21. Loc. cit., 146.

22. *Grundriss der Geschichte der Philosophie*. Leipzig, third ed. 1820, 11,n. Tennemann also spoke of the theory and methodology of the history of philosophy in: *Geschichte der Philosophie I*. Leipzig, 1798, I ff.

23. *Dissertatio philosophica de peccatis Tennemanni in historia philosophica*. Jena, 1814.

24. Cf. *Griechenlands erste Philosophen*. Leipzig, 1780, 12; see also *Geist der spekulativen Philosophie I*, Marburg, 1791, XVIII:

Nun wird allgemein zugestanden, dass alle Lehren der Chaldäer, Perser, Indier und selbst der Ägyptier, so weit sie uns bekannt sind, entweder blosse Dichtungen halb roher Zeiten enthalten oder auf religiöse Vorstellungen hinausgehen. Keine zuverlässige Nachricht wenigstens gedenkt irgend einiger Beweise aus Begriffen oder Erfahrungen. Von der Philosophie dieser Völker haben wir demnach kein Recht zu reden noch in einer Geschichte der Philosophie solche Lehren aufzustellen.

This passage is cited in E. Reinhold, *Handbuch der allgemeinen Geschichte der Philosophie I.* Gotha, 1828, XXVIII. In this connection, Reinhold himself stressed that the "Oriental doctrines" were to be excluded from the history of philosophy (XXVII); in a different context, he termed the teachings of the Indians "lückenhaft, trübe, unreif und ungründlich" (*Lehrbuch der Geschichte der Philosophie.* Jena, 1849, 6).

25. *Grundriss der Geschichte der Philosophie.* Leipzig, third ed., 1820, 10. Tennemann thought that "eine beschränkte Denkart, das Prinzip der Faulheit, sowie Verwechslung der Philosophien und Philosopheme" lay behind the assumption of a "philosophical Urvolk" in the ancient Orient; F. Schlegel is referred to in this connection (8).

26. Loc, cit.; nevertheless, Tennemann also presented a "kurze Übersicht" of the religio-philosophical views of the Oriental peoples (37 ff.).

27. Cf. *Lehrbuch der Geschichte der Philosophie I.* Göttingen, 1796; 13; 92.

28. An exemplary statement may be found in Descartes' *Discours de la méthode*; cf. the introductory statement about the "bon sens."

29. *Specimina philosophiae veteris.* Franeker, 1672; *Historia philosophica,* ib. 1674.

30. *Discursus philosophicus in quo historia philosophiae antiquae et recentioris recensetur.* No city, 1705. For Regis, the Orient possessed only "theologia superstitione imbuta," and no rational philosophizing (11); cf. also Chr. Garve, who only recognized certain "incunabula philosophiae" in the Orient. Cf. *De ratione scribendi historiam philosophiae,* Leipzig, 1768; reprinted in *Beiträge zur Geschichte der Philosophie,* edited by G.G. Fülleborn, XI/XII. Jena, 1799, 88 ff.; ib. 125.

31. On Hegel, see above, ch. 6; cf. also H. Schneider, *Das Verhältnis von System und Geschichte der Philosophie als Methodenproblem,* Diss. Munich, 1968.

32. *G.d.Ph. I,* 10 f.; see also L. Geldsetzer, *Philosophie der Philosophiegeschichte,* 120 ff., for a discussion of the circular problems involved in Schleiermacher's and Zeller's thought.

33. *G.d.Ph. I,* 266.

34. *G.d.Ph. I,* 372 (from the introduction to the edition of 1829–30); this involves a clear demarcation vis-à-vis the school of Schelling.

35. Tennemann (see above, n. 22): "Nur Tiedemann ist für die Ausschliessung der morgenländischen Völker."

36. *Versuch einer neuen Darstellung der uralten indischen All-Eins-Lehre.* Nuremberg, 1808, 5.

37. Sulzbach, 1822; second ed., 1829.

38. Loc. cit., I, 21 ff.

39. A. Schwegler, *Geschichte der Philosophie im Umriss*. Stuttgart, fifth ed., 1863, 4 (first ed., 1848; 16th ed., 1905).

40. J.F. Fries, *Die Geschichte der Philosophie dargestellt nach den Fortschritten ihrer wissenschaftlichen Entwicklung I*. Halle, 1837, 67 f. (reprinted Aalen 1969; *Sämtliche Schriften* XVIII).

41. E. Zeller, *Die Philosophie der Griechen in ihrer geschichtlichen Entwicklung I*. Leipzig, fifth ed., 1892, 41 (first ed., 1844; seventh ed., Darmstadt 1963). Similarly, H.C.W. Sigwart, *Die Propädeutik der Geschichte der Philosophie*. Tübingen, 1840, 116. In *Geschichte der Philosophie I*, Stuttgart/Tübingen, 1844, 27ff., Sigwart admittedly recognized the high conceptual level of Indian philosophy and developed a chain of thought reminiscent of Jaspers' "Achsenzeit" ("axial age").

42. F. Michelis, *Geschichte der Philosophie von Thales bis auf unsere Zeit*. Braunsberg, 1865, 2.

43. J.E. Erdmann, *Grundriss der Geschichte der Philosophie I*. Berlin, 1866, 11 (fourth ed., 1896).

44. E. Dühring, *Kritische Geschichte der Philosophie von ihren Anfängen bis zur Gegenwart*. Leipzig, third ed., 1878, 12 (first ed., 1869; fourth ed., 1894).

45. F. Überweg, *Grundriss der Geschichte der Philosophie I*. Berlin, eighth ed., 1894 (M. Heinze, editor), 16 f. (first ed. 1862).

46. Twelfth ed., 1926 (K. Praechter, editor), reprinted Basel, 1967, 8; on the philosophy of the Indians, cf. 27.

47. E. von Hartmann, *Geschichte der Metaphysik I*. Leipzig, 1899, I (*Ausgewählte Werke* XI); von Hartmann devoted more attention to Oriental and especially Indian thought in his philosophy of religion.

48. W. Windelband, *Lehrbuch der Geschichte der Philosophie*. Tübingen, fifteenth ed., 1967 (H. Heimsoeth, editor), 22, n. 1 (first ed., 1892); in the same note, Windelband speaks of the "Oriental prehistory" of philosophy.

49. J. Bergmann, *Geschichte der Philosophie I*. Berlin, 1892, 8. In the Italian language, see, for instance, the representative *Grande Antologia Filosofica*, ed. U.A. Padovani, I. Milan, 1954, XV. However, the *Storia della Filosofia*, ed. M. Dal Pra, has a volume on India by G. Scalabrino Borsani.

50. G.H. Lewes, *The History of Philosophy from Thales to Comte I*. London, fourth ed., 1871, 1 (first published in 1845–46 under the title *The Biographical History of Philosophy*).

51. S.G. Martin et al., *A History of Philosophy*, New York, 1941, 9.

52. J. Burnet, *Early Greek Philosophy*. London, 1908, 21 (originally 1892; numerous new editions and translations; e.g., in German, Berlin, 1913). Cf. also J. Burnet, *Greek Philosophy I*. London, 1914, 9.

53. F. Thilly, *A History of Philosophy*. New York, 1914, Introduction.

54. New York, 1957 (several reprints), 7.

55. B. Russell, *A History of Western Philosophy*. New York, 1945, 3.

56. See above, ch. 4, for the treatment of Indian philosophy in several older lexica, specifically the *Encyclopédie*.

57. Leipzig, second ed., 1832–1838; see especially II (1833), 520–524; as well as such articles as "Menu," "Budda," and "Ram Mohun Roy." It is symptomatic that Krug also listed the *Lebensweisheit der Hindus* (the translation of *The Economy of Human Life*. London, 1750), an occasionally very popular albeit completely nonauthentic work which he ascribed to the Earl of Chesterfield, among his sources.

58. It encompasses pages 233–252 of vol. III (Paris, 1847).

59. See above, ch. 8.

60. Leipzig, 1858.

61. Krotoschin, 1859.

62. *Einleitung in das Verständnis der Weltgeschichte*, Part 2: *Die Eleaten und die Indier*. Posen, 1844.

63. Such an increasing "scholarly" distancing from Hegel may be found, e.g., with Zeller.

64. A. Weber, *Indische Streifen* 3 (1879), 253 (review of Schlüter's book).

65. "Eine indische Ästhetik," *Archiv für Philosophie*, New Series 11 (1905), 113–134. B. Croce refers to another work by H. Jacobi in his remarks on Indian logic, *Logica come scienza del concetto puro*. Bari, seventh ed., 1947, 376 (Indian logic as "immune dall' errore formalistico").

66. Berlin/Leipzig, 1909.

67. Paris, 1938.

68. By Garbe, see especially *Die Sāṃkhya-Philosophie*, Leipzig, 1894, 85–105 (second ed., 1917); and *Indien und das Christentum*. Tübingen, 1914 (*India and Christendom*, trans. L.G. Robinson. La Salle, Ill., 1959).

69. C.A. Brandis, *Handbuch der Geschichte der griechisch-römischen Philosophie I*, Berlin, 1835, 7 speaks in contrast to the Greek "Trieb zu wissen" of the Oriental motivation to knowledge based upon mere "Bedürfnisse des physischen Wohlseins"; here, he makes reference to the self-understanding of Plato and Aristotle. The motif of a closed and homogeneous context of research which we mentioned earlier appears very clearly in Brandis' work; cf. loc. cit., 4; 23.

70. Cf., e.g., the cited passages from Dühring (n. 44) and Überweg (n. 45).

71. See above, ch. 1; also Plato, *Politeia* 435e 7 ff.: the Greek φιλομαϑές as compared to the Oriental φιλοχρησιμον.

72. See above, n. 29 f. Some authors, e.g., A. Schwegler (see above, n. 39), excluded the European Middle Ages as completely and fundamentally as they did the Orient. The inauguration of modern philosophy by F. Bacon, Descartes, etc., is seen as a kind of renewed step from myth to logos; Hegel, *Geschichte der Philosophie* III (*Jubiläums-Ausgabe* XIX), 329, speaks of a "Wiederaufgang der Philosophie."

73. See especially "Die Krisis des europäischen Menschentums und die Philosophie" (lecture, 1935); *Die Krisis der europäischen Wissenschaften und die transzendentale Phänomenologie*, ed. W. Biemel, The Hague, 1954 (*Husserliana* VI), 314–348 (on the "Orient," 325 ff.). See also D. Sinha, "Theory and Practice in Indian Thought: Husserl's Observations," *PEW* 21 (1971), 255–264 (a discussion of the posthumous manuscript BL 21, which contrasts the Indian emphasis on soteriological practice and world-renunciation with the "pure theory" of the Greeks).

74. E. Husserl, loc. cit., 321; 348. In contrast to Hegel, Husserl's discussions of Oriental thought and culture are vague and casual.

75. "Vita contemplativa" (Academic Address, Heidelberg, 1920); *Kleine Schriften zur Sternenkunde des Altertums*. Leipzig, 1950, 303–331. Boll was of the opinion "dass erst mit den Griechen das Bedürfnis nach objektiver Kenntnisnahme der Welt beginnt, indes alle anderen Völker im wesentlichen nur 'für ihre eigenen Königsburgen, Tempel und Götter' Augen hatten."

76. See below, ch. 15.

77. Cf. "Über den arischen Anteil an der indischen Philosophie," *WZKM* 46 (1939), 267–292; as well as *Gesch. d. ind. Philos.* (*History of Indian Philosophy*), vol. 1, Introduction.

78. Cf. *Epistemology, Logic and Grammar in Indian Philosophical Analysis*. The Hague/Paris, 1971, 9 ff.

79. Cf. J. Habermas, *Erkenntnis und Interesse*. Frankfurt, 1968. W. Jaeger, "Über Ursprung und Kreislauf des philosophischen Lebensideals," *Sb. Preuss Ak. Wiss., Phil.-hist. Kl.*, 1928, 390–421; Jaeger finds the first conscious formulation of the "theoretical" life-ideal in Plato's thought.

80. See below, ch. 15.

81. In contrast to the historians of philosophy, leading historians of mathematics prior to and around 1900, especially M. Cantor and H. Hankel, were much less reluctant to include India in their discussions.

10. Preliminary Postscript: The Hermeneutic Situation in the Twentieth Century

1. Among the many works dealing with the role of "the West" in the global context of the modern world see, for instance, A. Toynbee, *The World and the West*. London, 1953.

2. See the preface by J. Ritter, *Hist. Wb. Phil.* I. Basel/Stuttgart, 1971, VII.

3. W. Totok, *Handbuch der Geschichte der Philosophie*, vol. 1 (Altertum). Frankfurt, 1964, 13.

4. See above, ch. 9, §10. An English translation of F. Überweg's *Grundriss* by G.S. Morris was published in 1888: *History of Philosophy* (New York; reprint Freeport, 1972).

5. See also Jaspers' references to India in connection with his theory of an "axial age" ("Achsenzeit"): *Vom Ursprung und Ziel der Geschichte*. Munich, 1949 (trans. M. Bullock: *The Origin and Goal of History*. New Haven, 1953).

6. In accordance with Aurobindo, Gebser predicts that Asia, specifically India, and Europe together will reach a new level of suprarational "integral" awareness; for references to Aurobindo see, e.g., *Asienfibel*. Frankfurt, 1962, 165. Gebser's most important work is: *Ursprung und Gegenwart*. Stuttgart, 1966 (first published 1949-1953; trans. N. Barstad and A. Mickunas; *The Ever-Present Origin*. Athens, Ohio, 1985). Religious thinkers, psychologists, etc., have referred more frequently to Indian thought than "philosophers" in the strict sense. See, for instance, M. Friedman, "Martin Buber and Oriental Religions," *Buddhist and Western Philosophy*, ed. N. Katz, New Delhi, 1981, 149-171; H.G. Coward, *Jung and Eastern Thought*. Albany, 1984.

7. See D. Riepe, *The Philosophy of India and Its Impact on American Thought*. Springfield, 1970, 77ff.

8. D. Riepe, 82ff.; 103ff.; 93ff. As a young man, Hocking attended the "World Parliament of Religions" in Chicago and heard the famous address by Vivekananda, who also delivered some lectures at Harvard University.

9. D. Riepe, 91ff.

10. See R. Nozick, *Philosophical Explanations*. Cambridge, Mass., 1981.

11. See *Encyclopedia of Indian Philosophies*, vol. 2 (*Indian Metaphysics and Epistemology*), ed. K.H. Potter, Princeton, 1977, XII: "It is to be stressed that the work is addressed to philosophers primarily, and Indologists secondarily."

12. As examples, we may mention the names of J.N. Mohanty, D. Sinha and K.N. Upadhyaya.

13. See above, ch. 8, §18.

14. Cf. F.S.C. Northrop, *The Meeting of East and West*. New York, 1946 (several new editions and reprints). This book contrasts Eastern holistic "intuition" with Western analysis.

15. W.E. Hocking, "Value of the Comparative Study of Philosophy", in: *Philosophy—East and West*, ed. Ch.A. Moore. Princeton, 1944 (reprint 1946), 1-11; specifically 11.

16. Cf. D. Riepe (above, n.7), 210ff.

17. On Moore's assessment of the value of "personal representatives," see his preface to: *The Indian Mind*. Honolulu, 1967, VIIIf. Among the American philosophers who have taken a special interest in modern "spiritual" groups and other manifestations of the Orient in America, J. Needleman has to be mentioned; see, e.g., *The New Religions*. Garden City, 1970; *A Sense of Cosmos: The Encounter of Modern Science and Ancient Truth*. Garden City, 1975.

18. Cf. E. Frauwallner, *Geschichte der indischen Philosophie*, vol. 1. Salzburg, 1953, 3ff. (trans. V.M. Bedekar: *History of Indian Philosophy*. Delhi, 1973, XLVIIIf. Bedekar's translation is often awkward and unreliable).

19. H.-G. Gadamer, Preface to: W. Dilthey, *Grundriss der allgemeinen Geschichte der Philosophie*. Frankfurt, 1949, 18 (note). More than twenty years later, he still referred to the Asian, specifically Indian systems of thought as "enigmatic expressions of spiritual depth and wisdom" ("rätselhafte Aussageformen von Tiefsinn und Weisheit"); cf. "Begriffsgeschichte als Philosophie," *Archiv für Begriffsgeschichte* 14 (1970), 137. More recently, his attitude seems to have changed to some extent, perhaps in connection with his teaching in North America: see, for instance, his contribution to the "comparative" volume *The Question of Being: East-West Perspectives*, ed. M. Sprung. University Park/London, 1978.

20. Cf. H.-G. Gadamer, *Truth and Method*. New York, 1985, 245ff. (original German edition: *Wahrheit und Methode*. Tübingen, 1960, 261ff.).

21. Cf. S. Schayer, "Indische Philosophie als Problem der Gegenwart," *Jahrbuch der Schopenhauer-Gesellschaft* 15 (1928), 46–69; especially 59: "philosophische εποχη", "philosophical abstention" from one's own tradition, as condition of understanding foreign cultures.

22. Cf. H.-G. Gadamer, *Truth and Method*, 271 (*Wahrheit und Methode*, 288).

23. B. Heimann, *Studien zur Eigenart indischen Denkens*. Tübingen, 1930, IV.

24. H.-G. Gadamer, *Truth and Method*, 238 (*Wahrheit und Methode*, 253f.).

25. *Truth and Method*, 273 (*Wahrheit und Methode*, 289).

26. *Truth and Method*, 349 (*Wahrheit und Methode*, 365: ". . . bedeutet nur einen gesteigerten Fall von hermeneutischer Schwierigkeit, d.h. von Fremdheit und Überwindung derselben").

27. *Truth and Method*, 271 (*Wahrheit und Methode*, 288).

28. *Truth and Method*, 251 (*Wahrheit und Methode*, 267); understanding itself is "a kind of effect" (305; "eine Weise von Wirkung," 323) of the past.

29. *Truth and Method*, 253 (*Wahrheit und Methode*, 268).

30. Gadamer's presentation focuses on the "historical school" of the nineteenth century.

31. See J.L. Mehta, *India and the West*. Chico, 1985, 121; 185.

32. E. Husserl, *Die Krisis der europäischen Wissenschaften und die transzendentale Phänomenologie*, ed. W. Biemel. The Hague, 1954, 14.

33. E. Husserl, *Die Krisis*, 320 (Appendix).

34. E. Husserl, *Die Krisis*, 14; see below, ch. 20, §6. (on E. Troeltsch).

35. M. Heidegger, *Unterwegs zur Sprache*. Pfullingen, 1959 (reprint 1960), 103.

36. On Heidegger and the East, see the proceedings of a symposium on "Heidegger and Eastern Thought," *PEW* 20 (1970), 221–321; especially E.F. Hirsch, "Martin Heidegger and the East" (247–263) and J.L. Mehta, "Heidegger and the Comparison of Indian and Western Philosophy" (303-317). In general, Heidegger refers more frequently and explicitly to East Asia than to India, and he does not show any acquaintance with details of Indian thought.

37. *Truth and Method*, 251f. (*Wahrheit und Methode*, 267f.).

38. *Truth and Method*, 8f. (*Wahrheit und Methode*, 4f).

39. M. Heidegger, *Holzwege*. Frankfurt, third edition, 1957, 80.

40. Cf. M. Heidegger, *Was heisst Denken*? Tübingen, 1954, 136.

41. Cf. M. Heidegger, *Was ist das – die Philosophie?* Pfullingen, 1956, 13; 15 (as translated by J. L. Mehta, *India and the West*, 138f).

42. Cf. J. L. Mehta, *Martin Heidegger. The Way and the Vision*. Honolulu, 1976, 463.

43. M. Heidegger, *Vorträge und Aufsätze*. Pfullingen, second edition, 1959, 77: ". . . ein einziges, aber vielleicht auch das notwendige Verhängnis des Abendlandes und die Voraussetzung seiner planetarischen Herrschaft."

44. M. Heidegger, *Vorträge und Aufsätze*, 47.

45. J.L. Mehta, *Martin Heidegger* (see above, n.42),. 462f.

46. Cf. the preface by K. Nishitani in: H. Waldenfels, *Absolutes Nichts*. Freiburg, 1976, 12.

47. M. Heidegger, *Wegmarken*. Frankfurt, 1967, 194: "Das künftige Denken ist nicht mehr Philosophie, weil es ursprünglicher denkt als die Metaphysik, welcher Name das gleiche sagt."

48. Cf. H. Heidegger, *Holzwege*. Frankfurt, third edition, 1957, 300.

49. Cf. M. Heidegger, *Wegmarken*. Frankfurt, 1967, 252. See also *Unterwegs zur Sprache*. Pfullingen, second edition, 1960, 93f.

50. See M. Heidegger, *Gelassenheit*. Pfullingen, 1959. Also *Vorträge und Aufsätze*. Pfullingen, second edition, 1959, 45–70 ("Wissenschaft und Besinnung"). For an analysis of Heidegger's concept of "Gelassenheit," see R. Ohashi, *Ekstase und Gelassenheit*. Munich, 1975.

11. Traditional Indian Xenology

1. J.L. Mehta, *India and the West*, 117.

2. I borrow the word "xenology," as a term for attitudes towards, and conceptualizations of, foreigners, from: M. Duala-M' bedy, *Xenologie. Die Wissenschaft vom Fremden und die Verdrängung der Humanität in der Anthropologie*. Freiburg/München, 1977. I do not accept certain claims of this book; see my review in: *Philosophischer Literaturanzeiger* 31 (1978), 126–129.

3. Cf. Muir I, 162ff.

4. Later on, the experience of *being conquered* and *invaded* became more typical.

5. See Manu VIII, 66 (with commentaries); V, 131 (*dasyu* as generic term, comprising *caṇḍāla*, etc.). The ethnic connotation seems to precede meanings such as "demon." Cf. Muir II, 358ff.; P. Thieme, *Der Fremdling im Ṛgveda*. Leipzig, 1938 (AKM 23), 145ff. On *asura* and its relation to *dasyu/dāsa*, cf. W.E. Hale, *Asura in Early Vedic Religion*. Delhi, 1986, 173ff.; 181f.

6. P. Thieme, *loc. cit.*. 154; on hospitality in Vedic times: 152ff.

7. Cf. Muir I, 176ff.; see also the speculative elaborations by R.C. Jain, *Ethnology of Ancient India*. Benares, 1970, 70ff.

8. *Nirukta* III, 8; also the "Illustrations" by R. Roth (quoted in Muir I, 177); *Aitareya Brāhmaṇa* III, 31; Muir I, 162.

9. See Manu X, 45; regardless of linguistic criteria, *dasyu* refers to all those who are not committed to the norms of dharma. On the linguistic aspect, cf. *Mahābhārata* VIII, 30, 80; Vācaspati, *Tattvavaiśāradī* on YS II, 30. According to the Jaina *Ācārāṅgasūtra* II,3,1,8, the *mleccha* (*milakkhu*) are jungle tribes and other groups of outsiders.

10. On the word *mleccha* see V. Pisani, "Ai. *mlecchaḥ*, pāli *milakkha-*," *Indogermanische Forschungen* 57 (1939), 56–58. On the possibility of Sumerian connections, see A. and S. Parpola, "On the Relationship of the Sumerian Toponym *Meluhha* and Sanskrit *mleccha*," *Studia Orientalia* 46 (1975; Festschrift A. Salonen), 205–238.

11. It occurs, for instance, in the *Mahābhārata*. Greek *βαρβαρος* is already found in Homer. These forms, as well as Babylonian-Semitic *barbaru*, may go back to Sumerian *barbar*.

12. See Cs. Töttössy, "The Name of the Greeks in Ancient India," *Acta Antiqua Academiae Scientiarum Hungaricae* (Budapest) 3/4 (1955), 301–319. For further references to epigraphic materials, cf. Kane I, 383f.

13. Cf. *Mahābhārata* XIII, 33, 19ff.; 35, 17ff. (degeneration into *vṛṣalatva*); see also *Viṣṇupurāṇa* IV, 3, 48 (ed. Gītā Press). We may also refer to the concept of *vrātya*; e.g. Manu X, 20; for a somewhat speculative study of this group of outsiders, see J.W. Hauer, *Der Vrātya*. Stuttgart, 1927.

14. For references to the *yavana* as travellers, artisans, etc., see P. Meile, "Les yavanas dans l'Inde tamoule," *JA* 232 (1940/41; *Mélanges Asiatiques*), 85–123.

15. See Gautama IV, 17. According to this explanation, the *yavana* rank higher than the *caṇḍāla*, who are regarded as descendents of *śūdra* fathers and Brahmin mothers, the worst kind of *pratiloma* combination. On mixed castes in general, see H. Brinkhaus, *Die altindischen Mischkastensysteme*. Hamburg, 1978.

16. Cf. Kane I, 19; but also H. Brinkhaus, loc. cit. 97ff.

17. Cf. Kane II, 92.

18. See L. de La Vallée Poussin, *L'Inde aux temps des Mauryas et des Barbares*. Paris, 1930, 201f.; 239ff; S. Konow, "Professor Poussin on Śakayavanam." *Indian Culture* 3 (1936), 1–7. For further references and a concise survey of the debate, cf. G. Cardona, *Pāṇini. A Survey of Research*. Delhi, 1980, 265f. Cf. also 261, on the implications of *yavana/yavanānī* in Pāṇini IV, 49 (and Kātyāyana's *vārttika* 3),

19. Cf. Kane II, 169; 384.

20. *Bṛhatsaṃhitā* II, 15: *mlecchā hi yavanās* . . . (quote from Garga). On the ethnographic information found in the *Bṛhatsaṃhitā*, see A.M. Shastri, *India as Seen in the Bṛhatsaṃhitā of Varāhamihira*. Delhi, 1969, 65–107; specifically 71f. (*barbara*); 90 (*mleccha*).

21. See Manu II, 17ff.; somewhat differently Vasiṣṭha I, 8ff. For a long time, South Indian regions, such as Āndhra, were regarded as unfit for the performance of rituals; see, e.g., Govindarāja on Manu II, 23 (Kane, I, 311); visits to "problematic" regions, such as Saurāṣṭra and Sindhu, may require expiations (*prāyaścitta*; cf. Kane II, 15). However, already Śabara rejects the argument that the inhabitants of Āryāvarta have greater linguistic authority than those of Āndhra; cf. Bhāṣya on MS II, 3, 3. A "pan-Indian" geographical awareness, extending from the Himālayas to Cape Comorin, is common in later texts; see, e.g., Jayanta (ninth century), NM, 390.

22. See W. Kirfel, *Kosmographie*, 58; id., *Bhāratavarṣa*. Stuttgart, 1931; Muir I, 495f.

23. Cf. Manu II, 24.

24. Cf. Manu II, 23 (with commentaries).

25. Cf. Kirfel, *Kosmographie*, 70; *Bhāratavarṣa* (see above, n.22), 25; 32: *mlecchas* among the "regular" inhabitants of Bhārata.

26. Medhātithi on Manu II, 22f.: *āryā vartante tatra punaḥ punar udbhavanty, ākramya-ākramya-api na ciraṃ tatra mlecchāḥ sthātāro bhavanti*. See also Kane II, 16.

27. *bhūmir na svato duṣṭā, saṃsargād dhi duṣyati*. On a mythical campaign against the "Persians" (*pārasīka*) etc., cf. Kālidāsa, *Raghuvaṃśa* IV, 60ff.

28. The recommendation of Manu II, 20 that "all men on earth" (*pṛthivyāṃ sarvamānavāḥ*) should learn from the Brahmin does not imply a global concept of "the earth," nor does it mean that all men should have access to *the same* teaching. The picture is, however, somewhat different in the *Mahābhārata*, which has a less rigid hereditary orientation and a more open, "teachable" concept of *dharma*; XII, 65, 13ff. suggests that all foreign residents (*viṣayavāsin*) under the jurisdiction of a king, such as the *yavana, cīna* and *pahlava*, be taught the basic rules of *dharma*.

29. *Mahābhāṣya*, introd. (ed. Kielhorn/Abhyankar I, third ed., Poona, 1962, 2).

30. *Śatapatha Brāhmaṇa* III, 2, 1, 23f.

31. See *Kathāsaritsāgara*, ch. 99; 120 (trans. C.H. Tawney/N.M. Penzer, VII, 124; IX, 2f.).

32. *Bṛhadāraṇyaka Upaniṣad* 1, 3, 10: *tasmān na janam iyān na-antam iyān net pāpmānaṃ mṛtyum anvayāyānīti*.

33. Kumārila, TV, 190 (on 1, 3, 24) quotes this as a *smṛti*. See also Kane I, 54 (on Vasiṣṭha VI, 41); I, 126 (Bharadvāja). In *Mahābhārata* I, 135, Vidura and Yudhiṣṭhira converse with each other in a *mleccha* language.

34. Viṣṇu 71, 59; 84, 2; Gautama IX, 17; cf. Kane I, 67.

35. The *Pārasīprakāśa* by Kṛṣṇadāsa (sixteenth century) tries to apply this method to the Persian language; cf. A. Weber, *Über den zweiten, grammatischen, Pārasīprakāśa des Kṛṣṇadāsa*. Berlin, 1889 (Abh. Preuss. Ak. Wiss.); H. Scharfe, *Grammatical Literature*. Wiesbaden, 1977, 196f. Kṛṣṇadāsa also wrote a work on the

sun priests (he may have been one of them); cf. A. Weber, "Über die Magavakti des Kṛṣṇadāsa," *Monatsberichte der Königl. Preuss. Ak. Wiss.*, Berlin, 1879, 446–488 (468: the Vedānta philosopher Śrīharṣa as *maga*).

36. Cf. Śabara and Kumārila on MS I, 3, 10.

37. *Ṛgveda* III, 34, 9: *hatvī dasyūn pra āryaṃ varṇam āvat.*

38. Cf. Muir II, 366 (on *Atharvaveda* IV, 20, 4; 8; XIX, 62, 1).

39. Cf. Kane II, 48: ". . . that the śūdras were the dasyus so subjugated and made subservient."

40. Cf. Kane II, 48: ". . . the spirit of exclusiveness and pride of superiority existing among the āryas with reference to dasyus soon extended to groups among the āryas themselves." R.S. Betai, "Are the Sūdras Anāryas according to Manu?" *JOI* (Baroda) 10 (1960/61), 53–60 does not do justice to the ambiguities of this issue.

41. See Bhāruci on Manu X, 45 (ed. Derrett, 214): *na kevalaṃ kṣatriyāṇāṃ, kiṃ tarhi sarvavarṇānām eva kriyālopād bāhyatvaṃ brāhmaṇādarśanena ca-ity.* However, P. Deussen's statement that "all foreigners are śūdras according to the brahminical system" (cf. *Erinnerungen an Indien.* Kiel/Leipzig, 1904, 74) is too general. See also *Mahābhārata* XII, 181, 10ff. (lower castes, *mlecchas* etc. as products of degeneration); XIII, 33, 19ff.; 35, 17ff. (degeneration into *vṛṣalatva*, condition of a *śūdra* or outcaste); *Viṣṇupurāṇa* IV, 3, 48 (ed. Gītā Press): *ete ca-ātmadharmaparityāgād brāhmaṇaiḥ parityaktā mlecchatāṃ yayuḥ.* Vāsudeva Śāstrin Abhyaṅkara, *Dharmatattvanirṇaya*, Poona, 1929, 35f., exemplifies the modern pandit approach to the problem of *mlecchabhāva.*

42. On the blurring of the concept of man in the context of *saṃsāra*, see W. Halbfass, "Anthropological Problems in Classical Indian Philosophy," *Beiträge zur Indienforschung, E. Waldschmidt zum 80. Geburtstag gewidmet.* Berlin, 1977, 225–236.

43. See W. Halbfass, *Kastenordnung*; cf. Kullūka on Manu X, 4: on "biological" bastardization among castes: *saṃkīrṇajātīnāṃ tv aśvataravan mātāpitṛjātivyatiriktajātyantaratvān na varṇatvam*; also Medhātithi on Manu I, 2.

44. Cf. Kane II, 183; IV, 378.

45. Cf. e.g., *Mahābhārata* I, 79, 13, on sexual (*gurudāraprasakta, tiryagyonigata*) and other perversions of the *mlecchas*. Works on erotics (*kāmaśāstra*) such as the *Anaṅgaraṅga* and the *Pañcasāyaka*, find the *mleccha* women malodorous (*durgandha*) and lacking in erotic culture. Cf. R. Schmidt, *Beiträge zur indischen Erotik.* Berlin, second ed. 1911, 244ff.; 248ff. The dictionary *Medinīkoṣa* simply defines *mleccha* as *pāparakta*, "fond of evil"; cf. PW, art. *mleccha.*

46. See above, n. 18.

47. *Kl. Schr.*, 380.

48. Cf. Kauṭilya, *Arthaśāstra* (ed. R.P. Kangle) VII, 14, 27; see also III, 13, 3, on *mleccha* practices of selling or pawning the own children (*mlecchānām adoṣaḥ prajāṃ vikretum ādhātuṃ vā*)

49. See, for instance, *Dhammapada*, ch.26.

50. Cf. Umāsvāti, *Tattvārthasūtra* III, 36 (or 15): *āryā mlecchāś ca*; Akalaṅka divides the *mlecchas* into those "born in other continents" (*antaradvīpaja*) and those born in India, the "land of works" (*karmabhūmija*); cf. *Tattvārthavārttika*, ed. M.K. Jain. Benares, 1953, vol. 1, 204. See also *Pt. Sukhlalji's Commentary on Tattvārtha Sūtra*, trans. K.K. Dixit. Ahmedabad, 1974, 147f.

51. For a recent study of Indian responses to European innovations in shipbuilding, architecture, etc., see A.J. Qaisar, *The Indian Response to European Technology and Culture* (A.D. 1498–1707). Delhi, 1982. Even in this practical area, the readiness for foreign methods was half-hearted—though by no means entirely absent.

52. See S. Lévi, "Alexander and Alexandria in Indian Literature," *IHQ* 12 (1936), 121–133; E. Lamotte, "Les premières relations entre l'Inde et l'Occident," *La Nouvelle Clio* 5 (1953), 83–118; especially 111ff.: "Témoignages indiens"; but see above, ch. I, notes 104f., for the attempts of J.D.M. Derrett to find traces of the Alexander Romance in India. For epigraphic and literary references to invaders and other foreigners, see also D.R. Bhandarkar, "Foreign Elements in the Hindu Population," *Indian Antiquary* 40 (1911), 7-37.

53. On vernacular references to Islam, see P. Gaeffke, "Muslims in the Hindi Literature," *Beiträge zur Indienforschung, E. Waldschmidt zum 80. Geburtstag gewidmet*. Berlin, 1977, 119–126. Akbar was referred to as a mleccha who had been a Brahmin ascetic in his immediately preceding life; cf. K.E. Bryant, *Poems to the Child-God*. Berkeley, 1976, 1f.

54. The *Bhāvaprakāśa* of Bhāvamiśra, a medical text of the sixteenth century, already mentions the syphilis which was brought in by the Europeans; it also contains other references to the "Franks" (*phiraṅga*).

55. See M. Hiriyanna, "The First Commentary on the Mahābhāṣya," *IHQ* 2 (1926), 415–16; also V. Bhattacharya, *The Āgamaśāstra of Gauḍapāda*. Calcutta, 1943, LXXIIff.

56. Cf. Muir I, 497ff.; Kirfel, *Kosmographie*, 70ff.; 173ff. (on geography according to astronomical texts). On Śākadvīpa and Śvetadvīpa see W.E. Clark, "Śākadvīpa and Śvetadvīpa," *JAOS* 39 (1919), 209–242; K. Rönnow, "Some Remarks on Śvetadvīpa," *BSOAS* 5 (1928–1930), 253–284; and especially H. von Stietencron, *Indische Sonnenpriester*. Wiesbaden, 1966 (Śākadvīpa in the *Sāmba*- and *Bhaviṣyapurāṇa*).

57. Kumārila, TV, 150 (on 1,3,10): *anantamlecchadeśāṃs ca kaḥ sarvān upalapsyate* (in the *pūrvapakṣa*, yet in accordance with Kumārila's view; the correct reading, instead of the absurd *sarvo 'nūpalapsyate*, appears in the footnote).

58. The significance of this section was already noticed by H. Th. Colebrooke in his third essay "On the Philosophy of the Hindus," published in the *Transactions of the Royal Asiatic Society* (1826), 439–461.

59. *TV*, 153: *tasmād yathā-eva sevādau gṛhādiṣu ca kauśalam/mlecchānām adhikam* . . . ; on *patrorṇa* etc., as well as the Sanskritizing interpretation of Dravidian words: 151. The catching and rearing of birds is, however, traditionally associated with persons of lower status.

60. Cf. *NBh* on *NS* I, 1,7: *sākṣātkaraṇam arthasya-āptiḥ, tayā pravartata ity āptaḥ, ṛṣyāryamlecchānām samānaṃ lakṣaṇam.* Raghūttama, *Bhāṣyacandra* (ND, ed. G. Jha), 86, distinguishes three levels of reliability, from the *ṛṣi* down to the *mleccha*. Vācaspati, NVT, 202, notes that highwaymen, too, are potentially reliable sources of information.

61. However, Kumārila seems to accept certain premises of this *pūrvapakṣa*, specifically the idea that the sharp division between *ārya* and *mleccha* with regard to the transempirical *dharma* does not apply, as far as empirical, worldly objects are concerned (TV, 143: . . . *dṛṣṭārtheṣu tu tulyatvam āryamlecchaprayoginām*); in the *mleccha* countries, too, smoke indicates fire (. . . *mlecchadeśe 'pi dhūmo 'gner avabodhakaḥ*). Kumārila himself subsequently asserts such "equality" (*tulyatā*) with reference to empirical transactions (*dṛṣṭārthavyavahāra*). On the special semantic status of Sanskrit, cf. K. Kunjunni Raja, *Indian Theories of Meaning*. Adyar, 1963, 67ff.

62. *TV*, 152: *pikanemādi . . . mlecchair avadhṛtaṃ paścād āryair dvaibhāṣikaiḥ kvacit/tādṛśam tu pratīyeta prāmāṇyena-iti niścitam.* Cf. P.T. Srinivas Iyengar, "Kumārila's Acquaintance with Tamil," *IA* 42 (1913), 200–201 (referring to A.C. Burnell, "An Interesting Passage in Kumārila's Tantravārttika," *IA* I, 1872, 309–311); K. Kunjunni Raja, "Kumārilabhaṭṭa on the Dravidian Languages," *Annals of Oriental Research* (Madras) 28/1 (1978), Sanskrit Section, 1–7. The corresponding passages in Prabhākara's *Bṛhatī* are very brief, but confirm the basic thesis: *tasmād apratipakṣamlecchavyavahārasiddham api nimittam eva vedārthāvagatau* (*Bṛhatī* on MS I, 3, 10).

63. Cf. Sachau I, 23; this corresponds to *Bṛhatsaṃhitā* II, 15: *mlecchā hi yavanās, teṣu samyak śāstram idaṃ sthitam/ṛṣivat te 'pi pūjyante, kiṃ punar daivavid dvijaḥ.*

64. See D. Pingree, *Jyotiḥśāstra. Astral and Mathematical Literature*. Wiesbaden, 1981, 10ff. Cf. also Kane V, 515f.; 563; 600f.; G.N. Banerjee, *Hellenism in Ancient India*. Delhi, third ed. 1961, 134ff.; 150.

65. D. Pingree, *loc. cit.*, 10f.; the edition and translation appeared in two volumes, Cambridge, Mass., 1978 (Harvard Oriental Series); Pingree also edited the *Vṛddhayavanajātaka*. Baroda, 1976ff.

66. Cf. A.K. Narain, *The Indo-Greeks*. Oxford, 1957 (reprint Delhi, 1980), 165ff.

67. Cf. Kumārila, *ŚV* II, v. 247f.; *TV*, 75; Vācaspati, *NVT*, 432; *Tattvakaumudī* on *Sāṃkhyakārikā* 5 (see below, n.82). Vanamālimiśra, a follower of the school of Nimbārka, explicitly assigns a position to the *mlecchas* which is lower than that of the *caṇḍālas* and represents that point in the hierarchy of *saṃsāra* where the transition from the animal kingdom to "mankind" (*mānuṣya*) takes place; cf. *Vedāntasiddhāntasaṃgraha* I, 60f. (ed. D.P. Śarmakavi, Benares, 1912ff., 12).

68. *Prasthānabheda*, introduction: *vedabāhyatvāt teṣāṃ* (i.e., of the Buddhists etc.) *mlecchādiprasthānavat paramparayā-api puruṣārthānupayogitvād upekṣanīyatvam eva*; the phrase *paramparayā-api* excludes even an indirect soteriological contribution.

69. Cf. Appaya Dīkṣita, *Siddhāntaleśasaṃgraha*, ed./trans. S.S. Suryanarayana Sastri, Madras, 1935, I, I, 154: *vedārthe brahmaṇi mokṣāya jñātavye bhāṣāprabandhādīnām aprāpteś ca.*

70. Cf. J. Jüthner, *Hellenen und Barbaren*. Leipzig, 1923 (idealization of barbarians: 42ff.); G. Walser, *Hellas und Iran*. Darmstadt, 1984, 1–8.

71. On "ethnocentrism" in general, see R.A. LeVine and D.T. Campbell, *Ethnocentrism*. New York, 1972.

72. See É. Lamotte, *Histoire du bouddhisme indien*. Louvain, 1958, 789ff.; *The Moral Edicts of King Aśoka*, ed. P.H.L. Eggermont/J. Hoftijzer. Leiden, 1962, 42ff. Greek names appear in Rock Edict 13 (ib., 17f.). Cf. also D.A. Scott, "Ashokan Missionary Expansion among the Greeks." *Religion* 15 (1985), 131–141.

73. Cf. Rock Edict 12; Pillar Edicts 2;7.

74. Cf. É. Lamotte, *Histoire du bouddhisme indien*. Louvain, 1958, 607ff.

75. *Catuḥśataka* VII, 19 (quoted by Candrakīrti, *Prasannapadā* on *Madhyamakakārikā* XVIII, 8): *na-anyayā bhāṣayā mlecchaḥ śakyo grāhayitum yathā/na laukikam ṛte lokaḥ śakyo grāhayituṃ tathā.* The Jaina teacher Kundakunda echoes this verse in *Samayasāra* I, 8: *jaha ṇa vi sakkam aṇajjo aṇajjabhāsaṃ vinā du gāhedum . . .*

76. Cf. Majjhimanikāya 93 (*Assalāyanasutta*); ed. V. Trenckner/R. Chalmers, London, 1888ff., II, 149.

77. See *Pramāṇavārttika* I, 245 ed. R. Gnoli): *mlecchādivyavahārāṇāṃ nāstikyavacasām api/ anāditvāt tathābhāvaḥ pūrvasaṃskārasaṃtateḥ.*

78. See, for instance, Bhāsarvajña, *Nyāyabhūṣaṇa*, ed. Yogīndrānanda. Benares, 1968, 406 (on *mātṛvivāha* and other types of *mlecchavyavahāra*); Jayanta, *NM*, 224. See also Vācaspati; *NVT*, 432 (on the question how *mleccha* parents can produce offspring without performing the *putrakāmeṣṭi* or *putreṣṭi* ceremony normally required for the birth of sons). On *pārasīka* and incest, cf. Kane III, 859.

79. For a more detailed presentation and discussion of the Buddhist references to the "Persians" (*pārasīka, maga*) and their alleged practices of ritual killing and incest, see W. Halbfass, *Studies in Kumārila and Śaṅkara*, 13ff.; 24f. In addition to Dharmakīrti, Vasubandhu, Bhavya/Bhāvaviveka, Śāntarakṣita, Kamalaśīla, Prajñākaragupta, Durvekamiśra and others have contributed to this debate. On Bhavya (sixth century), see S. Kawasaki, "A Reference to Maga in the Tibetan Translation of the Tarkajvālā," *Journal of Indian and Buddhist Studies* (Tokyo) 23 (1975), 14–20.

80. Cf. Bhāvasena, *Viśvatattvaprakāśa*, ed. V.P. Johrapurkar. Sholapur, 1964, 80ff., 98ff. (polemical references to parallels between the Vedas and the "sacred texts of the Turks," *turuṣkaśāstra*). Another typically "barbarian" group of foreigners are the *hūṇa*, "Huns."

81. Cf. W. Geiger, *Pāli Literatur und Sprache*. Strasbourg, 1916 (Grundriss I/7),5; and the contributions by J. Brough and K.R. Norman in: *Die Sprache der ältesten buddhistischen Überlieferung/ The Language of the Earliest Buddhist Tradition*, ed.

H. Bechert. Göttingen, 1980 (Abh. Ak. Wiss. Göttingen). The Jainas proclaimed their Ardhamāgadhī as the original language (cf. R. Pischel, *A Grammar of the Prākrit Languages*, trans. S. Jha. Delhi, second ed., 1981, 16f.); yet Sanskrit became increasingly significant in their tradition.

82. *NVT*, 432; also *Tattvakaumudī* on *Sāṃkhyakārikā* 5(ed. S.A. Srinivasan, Hamburg, 1967, 86).

83. G. Coedès, *The Indianized States of Southeast Asia*, ed. W.F. Vella; trans. S.B. Cowing. Honolulu, 1968, XVIf.

84. G. Coedès, loc. cit., 25f.

85. Cf. J.C. van Leur, *Indonesian Trade and Society*. The Hague, 1955, 103f.

86. Cf. H.B. Sarkar, *Cultural Relations between India and Southeast Asian Countries*. Delhi, 1985. See also U.N. Ghoshal, *Progress of Greater India Research (1917-42)*. Calcutta, 1943; Candragupta Vedālaṃkāra, *Bṛhattara bhārata*. New Delhi, second ed., 1969 (first ed.: 1939). An extreme, yet symptomatic proclamation of Indian expansionism is A. Kalyanaraman, *Aryatarangini. The Saga of the Indo-Aryans*, 2 vols. Bombay, 1960-1970.

87. Quoted by H.B. Sarkar, loc. cit., 76. Cf. also B.K. Sarkar, *Creative India*. Lahore, 1937; and *India's Contribution to World Thought and Culture* (Vivekananda Commemoration Volume). Madras, 1970, for impressive celebrations of Hindu dynamism.

88. Cf., for instance, H.B. Sarkar, loc. cit., 68.

89. See below, ch. 18.

90. On the question of "sectarianism" in the South Asian context, cf. *Identity and Division in Cults and Sects in South Asia*, ed. P. Gaeffke/D.A. Utz. Philadelphia, 1984 (Proceedings of the South Asia Seminar, I).

91. A.T. Dev, *Student's Favourite Dictionary (Bengali to English)*, Calcutta, 24th ed., 1969, gives "atheistic," "godless," "immoral," etc. Already in Manu (e.g. IX, 225) and the *Mahābhārata*, the connotation is pejorative; it is more neutral in Kauṭilya's *Arthaśāstra* III, 16, 33 (*āśramiṇaḥ pāṣaṇḍā vā*). On the etymology, see M. Mayrhofer, *Kurzgefasstes etymologisches Wörterbuch des Altindischen*, vol. 2, Heidelberg, 1963, art. *pāṣaṇḍaḥ* (connection with *parṣad / pariṣad*, "assembly;" *pārṣada*, "associate," "attendant"). The form *pākhaṇḍa* results from a variant pronunciation of the retroflex ṣ.

92. Cf. T.K. Raychaudhuri, *Bengal under Akbar and Jahangir*. Calcutta, 1953, 117f. See also R. Cohen, "Sectarian Vaishnavism: the Vallabha Sampradāya," *Identity and Division in Cults and Sects* (see above, n.90), 65-72. On *pāṣaṇḍa/pākhaṇḍa* in the *Purāṇas*, see R. Choudhary, "Heretical Sects in the Purāṇas," *ABORI* 37 (1956), 234-257.

93. See J.T. O'Connell, "The Word 'Hindu' in Gauḍīya Vaiṣṇava Texts," *JAOS* 93 (1973), 340-343.

94. O'Connell, loc. cit., 340.

95. See Gonda II, 185f.; J. Sarkar, *Shivājī and His Times*. Calcutta, 1952. Cf. also B.K. Sarkar, *Introduction to Indian Positivism* (The Positive Background of Hindu Sociology, I). Allahabad, 1937 (reprint New York, 1974), 500ff.; 560ff (565ff.: on *mahārāṣṭradharma*).

96. Both encyclopedias also mention the "etymology" *hīnaṃ dūṣayati*, which implies that the Hindu "spoils" what is "inferior" (*hīna*).

97. Cf. M.S. Golwalkar, *Bunch of Thoughts*, Bangalore, 1966, 98f.; V.D. Savarkar, *Hindutva*, Bombay, fifth ed., 1969 (first ed. 1923). The Ārya Samāj tried to replace the word "Hindu" with the ancient term "Ārya." R.N. Suryanarayana calls "Hindu" a "detestable term . . . of which we should be ashamed." Cf. "Brāhmaṇa Dharma, the Universal Religion," *Poona Orientalist* 4 (1939/40), 63–78; 121–133; ib., 63.

98. See, for instance, *Bhāgavatapurāṇa* II, 4, 18: "purification," i.e. inclusion in Vaiṣṇavism, of *mleccha* tribes; cf. also S. Sinha, "Vaiṣṇava Influence on a Tribal Culture," *Krishna, Myths, Rites and Attitudes*, ed. M. Singer. Chicago, second ed., 1971, 64–89.

99. Cf. *Mahānirvāṇatantra* XIV, 187; also XIV, 177; 184. The authenticity of this Tantra has been called into question by J.D.M. Derrett, "A Juridical Fabrication of Early British India: The Mahānirvāṇa-Tantra," *Zeitschrift für vergleichende Rechtswissenschaft* 69 (1968), 138–183. His approach is probably too radical.

100. Cf. P.C. Bagchi, "On Foreign Element in the Trantra," *IHQ* (1931), 1–16; T. Goudriaan and S. Gupta, *Hindu Tantric and Śākta Literature*. Wiesbaden, 1981, 44f.; 52f.

101. T. Goudriaan and S. Gupta, loc. cit., 89.

102. See below, ch. 12.

103. *The Sarva-Deva-Vilāsa*, ed. V. Raghavan, Adyar n.d. (reprint from *Adyar Library Bulletin* 21/22, 1957–58).

104. *Sarva-Deva-Vilāsa*, 80f.

105. *Sarva-Deva-Vilāsa*, 2; 90; and 50; 78; 93; 97.

106. Cf. F.E. Pargiter, *The Purāṇa Text of the Dynasties of the Kali Age*. London, 1913 (reprint Benares, 1961), XVIII, n. 1; Th. Aufrecht, "Über das Bhaviṣyapurāṇa. Ein literarischer Betrug." *ZDMG* 57 (1903), 276–284; J.J. Meyer, "Moses and Zarathustra, Jesus und Muhammad in einem Purāṇa." *WZKM* 43 (1904), 9–18. G. Bonazzoli, "Christ in the Bhaviṣya Purāṇa," *Purāṇa* 21 (1979), 23–39, finds influences of the "Indian Renaissance."

107. *Bhaviṣyapurāṇa* III, 4, 23, 108ff.; cf. A. Hohenberger, *Das Bhaviṣyapurāna*. Wiesbaden, 1967, 29.

108. Cf. H. Hoffmann, introduction to A. Hohenberger (see n.107), IX.

109. III, 4, 22, 70; *nandinyā goś ca ruṇḍād vai jātā mlecchā bhayānakāḥ*. In older literature, we find occasional references to barbarian *muruṇḍa*; cf. S. Chattopadhyaya, *The Śakas in India*. Santiniketan, 1955, 8ff.; P.H.L. Eggermont, "The Murundas", *Journ. Ec. Soc. Hist. Orient* 9 (1966), 257–296 (speculative).

110. III, 4, 22, 72.

111. III, 1, 5, 37; see also H. Hoffmann, (above, n.108), VIII. On the attitudes of modern Hindu pandits to foreigners, see below, ch. 14, §10ff.

112. See, for instance, Manu I, 844ff. On the invasions of the yavanas in the *Kaliyuga* and the obliteration of the distinction between *ārya* and *anārya*, cf. Kane V, 827f. (according to the *Yugapurāṇa*); on the *Yugapurāṇa*, see also D.C. Sircar, *Studies in the Yugapurāṇa and other Texts*. Delhi, 1974, 1-16. The connection between *Kaliyuga* and *mleccha* rule appears also in the *Sagāthaka* appendix (ca. 500A.D.?) of the Buddhist *Laṅkāvatāra Sūtra* (v.784ff.; ed. B. Ṇanjio, Kyoto, 1923, 362f.).

113. Cf. Kane III, 923. On the *Kalkipurāṇa*, see L. Rocher, *The Purāṇas*. Wiesbaden, 1986, 183.

114. See above, ch. 2.

115. See above, ch. 3; 4.

116. See *The Private Diary of Ananda Ranga Pillai*, trans. from the Tamil by F. Price and K. Rangachari. Madras, 1904 (reprint New Delhi, 1985). Also G.K. Mookerjee, *The Indian Image of Nineteenth-Century Europe*. Bombay, 1967, 15ff. We may also mention the Marathi *Ājñāpatra*, written in 1716 and attributed to Rāmacandrapanta Amātya; it contains references to different European nationalities; for an English translation by S.V. Puntambekar, see *Journal of Indian History* 8 (1929), 81-105; 207-233 (especially 212f.).

117. On the Indian students at Leiden, see S.A. Wolf, *Grosses Wörterbuch der Zigeunersprache*. Mannheim, 1960, 18. For an account of Mirza Abū Tālib Khān, see *The Travels of Mirza Abū Tāleb Khān in Asia, Africa and Europe during the years 1799 to 1803*. Trans. from the Persian by Ch. Stewart. New Delhi, 1972 (originally 1814). Cf. also B. Lewis, *The Muslim Discovery of Europe*. New York, 1982, 131; 198f.; 215f.

118. Cf. H. Bechert, *Zum Ursprung der Geschichtsschreibung im indischen Kulturbereich*. Göttingen, 1969 (NAWG, Phil.-hist. Kl., 1969, 2), especially 16f. (on the case of Ceylon).

12. Rammohan Roy and His Hermeneutic Situation

1. For the views of Marx on modernization, see *K. Marx on Colonialism and Modernization*, ed. S. Avineri. Garden City, N.Y., 1969.

2. Cf. the reference by H.H. Wilson in the introduction to his Sanskrit dictionary (1819), XVI; on Schelling and Schopenhauer, see below, n. 8; 13.

3. Cf. M. Carpenter, *The Last Days in England of the Raja Rammohan Roy*. London, second ed., 1875; A. Moore, *Rammohan Roy and America*. Calcutta, 1942; S. Lavan, *Unitarians and India*. Boston, 1977.

4. Cf. W.T. Krug, *Allgemeines Handwörterbuch*, III. Leipzig, second ed., 1833; V, 1838.

5. W.T. Krug, V, 203.

6. Cf. M. Björnstjerna, *Die Theogonie, Philosophie und Kosmogonie der Hindus*. Stockholm, 1843, 77. Björnstjerna suggested that only "a new *avatāra*" would be able to accomplish the task which Rammohan had set for himself: "Ram-Mohun Roy machte den Versuch; aber dieser misslang, und keinem wird es glücken, der nicht die Gestalt einer neuen *Avatare* annimmt; denn mit natürlichen Mitteln macht man keine Proselyten in Asien."

7. See, for instance, J. Bentham, *Works*, ed. J. Bowring, Edinburgh, 1838–1843, X, 570: "Rammohun Roy has cast off thirty-five millions of gods, and has learnt from us to embrace reason in the all important field of religion." Cf. also E. Stokes, *The English Utilitarians and India*. Oxford, 1959.

8. See F.W.J. Schelling, *S.W.* II/2, 476.

9. C.J.H. Windischmann, *Die Philosophie im Fortgang der Weltgeschichte* IV. Bonn, 1834, 1794.

10. F.M. Müller, *Biographical Essays*. London, 1884, 13.

11. M. Monier-Williams, *Religious Thought and Life in India*. London, 1883, 479.

12. See, for instance, Müller's introduction to: *The Upanishads I*, Oxford, 1879 (*Sacred Books of the East*), LXIII (Rammohan's *Upaniṣad* translations as basis for the Christianization of India).

13. See A. Schopenhauer, *HN*, ed. A. Hübscher, Vol. 5, 341f.; cf. also E. Burnouf in: *Journal des Savants*, Dec. 1832, 705–712.

14. See, for instance, *The Father of Modern India*. Commemoration Vol. of the Rammohan Roy Centenary Celebrations, 1933, ed. S.C. Chakravarti, Calcutta, 1935; J. Das, *Rammohan Roy - The Modernizer*. Calcutta, 1958; N.S. Bose, *The Indian Awakening and Bengal*. Calcutta, 1960, 10: "In the midst of the darkness that prevailed all over the country the first man who saw the vision of a new India was Rammohan Roy."

15. Cf. B.N. Seal, *Rammohan Roy - The Universal Man*. Calcutta n.d. (ca. 1933); Rammohan himself suggests the idea of an "awakening" in the introduction to his *Abridgement of the Vedant*.

16. See D. Kopf, *British Orientalism and the Bengal Renaissance*. Berkeley, 1969; as well as various other contributions by the same author, e.g., "Rammohan Roy's Quest for an Identity in the Modern World", *Bengal Regional Identity*, ed. D. Kopf. East Lansing, Mich., 1969, 51–59; especially 52.

17. See S. Hay, *Asian Ideas of East and West*. Cambridge, Mass., 1970, 14 f.

18. J.T.F. Jordens, "Hindu Religious and Social Reform in India," *A Cultural History of India*, ed. A.L. Basham, Oxford, 1975, 365–382; especially 367.

19. Cf. A.K. Ray, *The Religious Ideas of Rammohan Roy*. New Delhi, 1976, 20 ff.; and the preface by A.L. Basham to this work. See also A. Ghazi, "Raja Rammohun Roy's Response to Muslim India," *Studies in Islam* 13 (1976), 1–38.

20. Cf. R.C. Majumdar, *On Rammohan Roy*. Calcutta, 1972, 40. Majumdar has done much to "demythologize" Rammohan.

21. S.D. Collet, *The Life and Letters of Raja Rammohan Roy*. Calcutta, third ed., 1962 (first ed.: 1900). The additions by D.K. Biswas and P.C. Ganguli to the third edition are not very reliable. An important contribution in Bengali is: B.N. Bandyopādhyāya, *Rāmamohana Rāya*. Calcutta, fifth ed., 1960.

22. R.C. Majumdar, *On Rammohan Roy*, Calcutta, 1972, 3 ff., argues that 1774 is a more likely date of birth. At any rate, 1772 has been "officially" accepted for Rammohan Roy memorial celebrations, etc.

23. Cf. M. Lederle, *Philosophical Trends in Modern Mahārāṣṭra*. Bombay, 1976, 51.

24. The work was translated into English by Obaidullah el Obaid, Calcutta, 1884 (several new editions and reprints, e.g. Calcutta 1975). See also A.K. Ray, *The Religious Ideas of Rammohan Roy*. New Delhi, 1976, 20 ff.

25. The complete title is: *Translation of an Abridgement of the Vedant or Resolution of all the Veds, the most celebrated and revered work of Brahminical theology, establishing the unity of the Supreme Being, and that He alone is the object of propitiation and worship*. As early as 1817, the work appeared in London (together with the English translation of the *Kena Upaniṣad*); in the same year, a German translation (*Auflösung des Wedant . . .*) was published in Jena.

26. On the controversy over the *Precepts*, cf. M.M. Thomas, *The Acknowledged Christ of the Indian Renaissance*. London, 1969, 1–37. Rammohan usually distributed his publications at his own expense.

27. For an edition of Rammohan's Bengali writings, see *Rāmamohana-Granthāvalī*, ed. B.N. Bandyopādhyāya and S.K. Dāsa. Calcutta n.d. (1959). A few selections from these writings (introductions to *Vedāntagrantha* and *Māṇḍūkya Upaniṣad*, replies to Utsavānanda and a Gosvāmin) are available in English translation by D.H. Killingley: *The Only True God. Works on Religion by Rammohan Roy*. Newcastle upon Tyne, 1982. The English works were edited by J.C. Ghose, Calcutta, 1885–1887 (published again in a one-volume adaptation, Allahabad, 1906; reprinted New York, 1978); also by K. Nag and D. Burman, 3 vols., Calcutta, 1958 (first ed.: 1945–1947). The most important collection published during Rammohan's lifetime: *Translation of Several Principal Books, Passages und Texts of the Veds*. London, 1832 (quoted as: *Veds*.).

28. Cf. J.N. Farquhar, *Modern Religious Movements in India*. London, 1915; S.N. Sastri, *History of the Brahmo Samaj*. Calcutta, second ed., 1974 (first ed. 1911–1912; often uncritical and unreliable); D. Kopf, *The Brahmo Samaj and the Shaping of the Modern Indian Mind*. Princeton, 1979.

29. See *Veds*, 3 f.

30. Cf. *Defence of Hindu Theism*. Calcutta, 1827 (*Veds*, 138 f.): "I must remark, however, that there is no translation of the Vedas into any of the modern languages of Hindoostan with which I am acquainted, and it is for that reason that I have translated into Bengali the Vedanta, the Cenopanishad of the Sama Veda, Ishopanishad of the Yojur Veda, etc."

31. Cf. *Abridgement*, *Veds*, 6.

32. Cf. *Abridgement, Veds*, 4: " . . . that the superstitious practices which deform the Hindoo religion have nothing to do with the pure spirit of its dictates."

33. *Veds*, 84 (introduction to *Īśā Upaniad*). On the other hand, H.Th. Colebrooke states in the concluding section of his essay "On the Vedas," *Asiatic Researches* 8 (1805), 369–476 (*Miscellaneous Essays* I. London, 1937, 9–113): "Rituals founded on the Puranas and observances borrowed from a worse source, the Tantras, have, in great measure, antiquated the institutions of the Veda." Colebrooke finds the "unity of the deity" *only* in the Veda. In *Gosvāmīr sahita vicāra*, Rammohan rejects the special status which the Gauḍīya Vaiṣṇavas attribute to the *Bhāgavatapurāṇa*. In general, he pays respect to the *Purāṇas*, but warns of sectarian reinterpretations, interpolations, and falsifications and emphasizes the superior authority of the Veda (cf. D.H. Killingley, *The Only True God*. Newcastle upon Tyne 1982, 33 ff.).

34. The date of the *Mahānirvāṇatantra* is so questionable that J.D.M. Derrett suggested that it might have been produced under the actual influence of Western ideas; cf. "A Juridical Fabrication of Early British India: The Mahānirvāṇa-Tantra," *Essays in Classical and Modern Hindu Law*, Vol. 2. Leiden, 1977, 197–242 (originally 1968; see above, ch.11, n.99).

35. Cf. the introduction to the *Kaṭha Upaniṣad* (*Veds*, 57), which contrasts *Purāṇas* and *Upaniṣads* with explicit reference to the "European community." The Bengali *Cāri praśner uttara*, as well as the introduction to the *Māṇḍūkya Upaniṣad*, treat the Tantras with respect and find at least a pedagogical value in their teachings.

36. Cf. *Defence of Hindoo Theism, Veds*, 138; on Raghunandana as "modern": *Veds*, 264; 114.

37. *Second Defence of the Monotheistical System, Veds*, 1269 (adopted from the introduction to the *Īśā Upaniṣad*); cf. *Veds*, 58 (introduction to the *Kaṭha Upaniṣad*): " . . .prefer custom and fashion to the authorities of their scriptures."

38. Cf. *Veds*, 92; 84 (*Īśā Upaniṣad*); 162 f. (*Second Defence*); 44 f. (*Kena Upaniṣad*).

39. Cf. *Veds*, 26 (*Muṇḍaka Upaniṣad*): "natural inclinations of the ignorant towards the worship of objects resembling their own nature . . . joined to the self-interested motives of their pretended guides." On the other hand, the sacred texts are "confirmed by the dictates of common sense" (*Veds*, 92; *Īśā Upaniṣad*).

40. Cf. *Vedāntagrantha*, Bhūmikā; *Granthāvalī* I, 4.

41. See, for instance, *Veds*, 167 (*Second Defence of the Monotheistical System*); 195 (*Apology*).

42. Cf. Śaṅkara on BS I, 3, 34 ff.

43. *Defence of Hindoo Theism, Veds*, 146.

44. Cf. *Vedāntagrantha*, Anuṣṭhāna (D.H. Killingley, *The Only True God*, 13).

45. Cf. *Veds*, 255; 266.

46. Cf. *Vedāntagrantha*, Bhūmikā (*Granthāvalī* I, 5); *paśujātīyer dharma*.

47. *Veds*, 46 (*Kena Upaniṣad*).

48. Letter to A. Duff (quoted by S.D. Collet, *The Life and Letters of Raja Rammohan Roy*. Calcutta, 1962, 280).

49. Cf. *Veds*, 58 (*Kaṭha Upaniṣad*).

50. In an unpublished M.A. thesis presented to the University of Pennsylvania, Philadelphia, in 1976, L. Katz has made a detailed comparison of the Bengali and English versions of the *Kena Upaniṣad*.

51. See above, § 3.

52. See, for instance, *Veds*, 119 (*Abridgement*).

53. See, for instance, the different treatment of *Kena Upaniṣad* IV, 8; 28; II, 5; 13 in the Bengali and English versions; on *adhikāriviśeṣa*, see the introduction to the *Māṇḍūkya Upaniṣad* (only Bengali).

54. Cf. *Kena Upaniṣad* I, 2; II, 4; IV, 9 (in Bengali and English); see also *An Apology for the Pursuit of Final Beatitude*. Calcutta, 1820 (*Veds*, 191 ff.).

55. Cf. *Veds*, 15 (*Abridgement*): "all the desired consequences." See also *Vedāntagrantha*, Bhūmikā.

56. See above, ch. 3.

57. The reaction of Deocar Schmid is exemplary; he first seeks Rammohan's friendship, then later rejects him as a "heathen" and an enemy of the truth; cf. *Dialogue between a Theist and an Idolator . . . An 1820 Tract probably by Rammohan Roy*, ed. S.N. Hay. Calcutta, 1963, 4 ff. The ascription of this "Dialogue" to Rammohan is highly questionable.

58. Cf. "Vedantism - What Is It?" *Calcutta Review* 4 (1845), 43–61 (anonymous; probably by A. Duff).

59. Cf. the documents of the so-called Tytler Controversy (published in the editions of Rammohan's English works).

60. Cf. M.M. Ali, *The Bengali Reaction to Christian Missionary Activities, 1833–1857*. Chittagong, 1965.

61. *The Precepts of Jesus*. New York, 1825, XVIII.

62. Cf. A.K. Ray, *The Religious Ideas of Rammohan Roy*. New Delhi, 1976, 51.

63. The Bengali version has been republished in *Rāmamohana-Granthāvalī*, part I; on its attribution to Mṛtyuṃjaya, cf. *Calcutta Review* 4 (see above, n. 58), 44. Rammohan responded in the same year (1817), also in Bengali and English (*Bhaṭṭācāryer sahita vicāra* and *A Second Defence of the Monotheistical System of the Veds*).

64. See, for instance, *Granthāvalī*, 129; 132 (*Apology*, 1 ff.).

65. Cf. *Apology*, 2.

66. The English *Apology* (1 f.) speaks simply of "honourable men."

67. Cf. *Apology*, 35 (*Granthāvalī*, 146).

68. *Apology*, 28 (*Granthāvalī*, 142).

69. See *Apology*, 14: "Many authorities prove this, therefore God is worshipped by any person who worships any thing in any of the prescribed forms and in whatever point of view."

70. *Veds*, 95 (*Īśā Upaniṣad*); cf. also *Vedāntagrantha*, Bhūmikā (specifically *Granthāvalī* I, 5, which refers to the foreigners as *yavana*).

71. Cf. D.H. Killingley, *The Only True God* (see above, n. 27), 10 f.; 27; 44.

72. *Veds*, 88 f. (*Īśā Upaniṣad*); see also 91f.

73. W. Jones, *On the Gods . . .*; P.J. Marshall, 245. On the other hand, Rammohan has much praise for Jones; cf. *Veds*, 117 (*Gāyatrī*).

74. See P.J. Marshall, 194.

75. See A.K. Ray, *The Religious Ideas of Rammohan Roy*. New Delhi, 1976, 22.

76. See J.A. Dubois, *Letters on the State of Christianity in India*, ed. S. Paul. New Delhi, 1977, 87 ff.

77. The *Purāṇaprakāśa* (or *Purāṇārthaprakāśa*) is a summary of Purāṇic teachings. The *Code of Gentoo Laws* (London, 1776) is B.N. Halhed's translation of an intermediate Persian version of the *Vivādārṇavasetu*, a Sanskrit compilation of law texts commissioned by W. Hastings; cf. R. Rocher, "The Vivādārṇavasetu, Chapters 1 and 2," ALB 44/45 (1980-1981; K. Kunjunni Raja Felicitation Volume), 63-73; also *Orientalism, Poetry, and the Millenium: The Checkered Life of N.B. Halhed*, 1751-1830. New Delhi, 1983, 48 ff.

78. Cf. P.R. Sen, *Western Influence in Bengali Literature*. Calcutta, 1932, 78ff. (third ed. 1966, 39ff). On the Hindu College, cf. R.C. Majumdar, *On Rammohan Roy*. Calcutta, 1972, 20 ff.

79. Cf. S.K. De, *Bengali Literature in the 19th Century (1757-1857)*. Calcutta, second ed., 1962, 457 ff.; 478 ff.

80.Cf. M.C. Kotnala, *Raja Ram Mohun Roy and Indian Awakening*. New Delhi, 1975, 41 ff.

81. Even Ramram Basu, whose association with the British began around 1780 and who started working for W. Carey and other missionaries in 1793, can hardly be called a forerunner of Rammohan, even though he developed a certain critical distance from his tradition. D. Kopf, *British Orientalism and the Bengal Renaissance*, Berkeley, 1969, 121-126, tends to overrate the significance of Ramram Basu.

82. See *Veds*, 43; 45 (*Kena Upaniṣad*); 3 f. (*Abridgement*): "affirmed to be coeval with the creation"; "most highly revered by all Hindoos."

83. For a survey of Sanskrit studies and philosophical learning in Bengal around 1800, see W. Ward, *Account of the Writings, Religion and Manners of the Hindoos*, Vol. 1. Serampore, 1811, 191 ff. Cf. also P.J. Marshall, 120 (on A. Dow; Dow's "Bedang" confounds *vedāṅga* and *vedānta*).

84. This sense of authority is confirmed by the fact that the Bengali Vaiṣṇava Baladeva Vidyābhūṣaṇa composed a *Brahmasūtra* commentary around 1750. Jones and his successors were also aware of the significance of the Vedānta.

85. On this question, see Y. Sahae, *Brāhma Samāj und Ārya Samāj*. Diss. Bonn 1964, 110 ff. On Rammohan as a Vedānta commentator and the discrepancies between him and Śaṅkara, see D.H. Killingley, "Rammohan Roy on the Vedānta Sūtras," *Religion* 11 (1981), 151–169.

86. See *English Works*. Allahabad, 1906 (reprint New York, 1978), 906 ff. In response to his Christian critics, Rammohan emphasizes that Jesus Christ himself was Asian.

87. See above, ch. 11, § 30 f.

88. *Veds*, 196 (*An Apology for the Pursuit of Final Beatitude*). A different, much less Westernized ethical and social "reform" was initiated by Rammohan's contemporary Sahajānanda (1781–1830), who became known as Svāminārāyaṇa. This movement in Gujarat was inspired by Vaiṣṇava sources and encouraged by the British; cf. R.B. Williams, *A New Face of Hinduism: the Swaminarayan Religion*. Cambridge, 1984.

13. Neo-Hinduism, Modern Indian Traditionalism, and the Presence of Europe

1. See F.W. Thomas, *History and Prospects of British Education in India*. Cambridge, 1981; G. Hertz, *Das britische Erziehungswesen in Indien*. Berlin, 1932; B. Bhattacharya, *Bengal Renaissance: A Study in the Progress of English Education, 1800–1858*. Calcutta, 1963; M.A. Laird, *Missionaries and Education in Bengal, 1793–1837*. London, 1972 (especially 263 ff.: on the dissemination of secular knowledge by the missionaries). On Islam in modern India, see, for instance, A. Ahmad, *Islamic Modernism in India and Pakistan, 1857–1964*. London, 1967; *Muslim Self-Statement in India and Pakistan: 1857–1968*, ed. A. Ahmad and G.E. von Grunebaum. Wiesbaden, 1970; Chr. W. Troll, *Sayyid Ahmad Khan: A Reinterpretation of Muslim Theology*. New Delhi, 1978; *Islam in India: Studies and Commentaries*, ed. Chr. W. Troll. New Delhi, 1982 ff. (a series).

2. P. Hacker, "Aspects of Neo-Hinduism as Contrasted with Surviving Traditional Hinduism," *Kl. Schr.*, 580–608; but see 581: " . . . the interesting coincidence of a reform oriented towards European patterns with a Hindu renaissance offers a preview of what Neo-Hinduism is." Exemplary older surveys are found in: J.N. Farquhar, *Modern Religious Movements in India*. London, 1915; D.S. Sarma, *Studies in the Renaissance of Hinduism*. Benares, 1944.

3. *Kl. Schr.*, 608 ("onslaught of Marxism").

4. *Kl. Schr.*, 583.

5. Cf. ib.: " . . . maintains a living continuity with the past."

6. *Kl. Schr.*, 587.

7. *Kl. Schr.*, 582.

8. Cf. *Kl. Schr.*, 589, on the reinterpretation and re-evaluation of *sevā*, "service," as an element of *dharma*.

9. *Kl. Schr.*, 608.

10. *Kl. Schr.*, 583.

11. Hacker finds "surviving traditional Hinduism" exemplified by the Hindi publications of the Gītā Press in Gorakhpur.

12. *Kl. Schr.*, 581.

13. Cf. *Kl. Schr.*, 581 f.; also 609: " . . . modernization, though amounting to Westernization, is an outcome of nationalism, which is the chief impulse of Neo-Hindu thinking." On the relationship between "modernization" and "Westernization," see A. Toynbee, *The Present Experiment in Western Civilization*. London, 1962, 24 ff.; D. Kopf, *British Orientalism and the Bengal Renaissance*. Berkeley, 1969, 275 ff. On the meaning of "Westernization" in the Indian context, see M.N. Srinivas, *Social Change in Modern India*. Berkeley, 1966, 46–88. In spite of various attempts to dissociate the two concepts, and regardless of the understandable resentments against the idea of "Westernization" in "non-Western" countries, "modernization" and "Westernization" are fundamentally inseparable. This remains true even at a time when the geographical "West," and Europe in particular, are no longer leading the process of modernization, and when geographical categories in general seem to become obsolete.

14. Letter to J. Crawford, August 8, 1828; quoted by S.D. Collet, *The Life and Letters of Raja Rammohan Roy*. Calcutta, third ed., 1962, 267. It is symptomatic that modern Indian patriotism and nationalism found one of their earliest expressions in the writings and lectures of H. Derozio, the famous and controversial teacher at the Hindu College who was partly of European descent.

15. Cf. S.N. Hay, "Western and Indigenous Elements in Modern Indian Thought: The Case of Rammohan Roy." *Changing Japanese Attitudes toward Modernization*, ed. M.B. Jansen. Princeton, 1965, 326.

16. See above, ch. 12.

17. In traditional Sanskrit literature, we find expressions like *navyanyāya* and *navyamīmāṃsā*

18. Cf. *Calcutta Review* 2 (1844), 267 (under "Miscellaneous Notices"); also 17 (1852), 281 ("Vedantism and Christianity"); XVI f.: "Modern Vedantists" as deists and rationalists; 3 (1845), 133: Rammohan's "New Vedantism."

19. Hacker does not explore the different levels and connotations of "traditionalism" in modern India, and the great variety of its popular and scholastic expressions.

20. He was the son of Rammohan Roy's contemporary and friend, Dvarkanath Tagore, and the father of the great poet Rabindranath Tagore.

21. See *The Autobiography of Maharshi Devendranath Tagore*, trans. Satyendranath Tagore/Indira Devi. London, 1914 (reprint 1916), 72 f. (Bengali original: *Ātmajīvanī*, ed. Satīśacandra Cakravarttī. Calcutta, fourth ed., 1962, 34 f.). The translators refer to the "experiences" of Western mystics, such as Mme. Guyon, Suso, Teresa of Avila. G. Fox (IX ff.) and J. Böhme (XXVII f.). See also Y. Sahae, *Brāhma Samāj und Ārya Samāj*. Diss. Bonn, 1964, 26 ff., 119 ff.

22. *Autobiography*, 161 (*Ātmajīvanī*, 124).

23. *Autobiography*, 162 (*Ātmajīvanī*, 124; referring to *Muṇḍaka Upaniṣad* III,1,8).

24. *Autobiography*, 167, 169.

25. See D. Kopf, *The Brahmo Samaj and the Shaping of the Modern Indian Mind*. Princeton, 1979, 50 f. (Kopf uses the spelling Akkhoy Kumar Dutt). See also M. Chaudhuri, *Maharshi Devendranath Tagore*. Delhi, 1973; A.K. Cakravarttī, *Maharṣi Devendranātha Ṭhākura*. Allahabad, 1916 (reprint Calcutta, 1971; in Bengali; the major reference work on Debendranath).

26. Cf. S.N. Tattvabhushan, *The Philosophy of Brāhmaism*. Madras, 1909, 93 ff.

27. Tenth edition: Calcutta, 1949.

28. See below, ch. 14; 21.

29. Cf. P.K. Sen, *Biography of a New Faith*, vol. 1, 184 (quoted by Y. Sahae, *Brāhma Samāj und Ārya Samāj*, Diss. Bonn, 1964, 42).

30. Y. Sahae, loc. cit., 128.

31. On Keshab, see M. Borthwick, *Keshub Chunder Sen. A Search for Cultural Synthesis*. Calcutta, 1977; D. Kopf, *The Brahmo Samaj and the Shaping of the Modern Indian Mind*. Princeton, 1979, 294 ff.

32. On the idea of a "new, Indian kind of Christianity which should embrace all religions in the name of Jesus Christ" among Keshab's followers, cf. Chr. Isherwood, *Ramakrishna and His Disciples*. New York, 1970, 157 f.

33. Cf. Y. Sahae (see above, n. 29), 56 f.

34. Cf. M.M. Thomas, *The Acknowledged Christ of the Indian Renaissance*. London, 1969, 64. Keshab as well as Bankim Chandra Chatterji were influenced by J.R. Seeley, *Ecce homo* (1866), which emphasizes the "humanistic" aspects of Christianity.

35. Cf. *Jeevan Veda or Life, Its Divine Dynamics*, trans. J.K. Koar. Calcutta, second ed., 1955, 140 f.

36. Cf. S.N. Tattvabhushan (see above, n. 26), 78 ff.; Y. Sahae, (see above, n. 29), 130 f.

37. See *Lectures in India*. London 1901-1904, I, 325. India and England appear as "parted cousins, the descendants of two different families of the ancient Aryan race."

38. *Lectures in India* II, 115.

39. Cf. M.N. Sen (Manonīta Sena), *Bhāi Pratāpacandra Majumadāra*. Calcutta, 1971 (in Bengali; contains the English text of P.C. Majumdar's presentation in Chicago, "The World's Religious Debt to Asia").

40. Cf. *Lectures in India* I, 466.

41. Cf. *Sources of Indian Tradition* II, 180 ff.; *The Political Awakening in India*, ed. J.R. McLane. Englewood Cliffs, N.J. 1970, 59 ff.

42. See also F.M. Müller, *Ramakrishna, His Life and Sayings*. New York, 1899.

43. Cf. *The Gospel of Sri Ramakrishna*. Madras, fifth ed., 1969; Index, s.v. "Keshab."

44. Cf. Y. Sahae (see above, n. 21), 51; see also G.C. Banerji, *Keshub Chandra and Ramakrishna*. Allahabad, 1931.

45. See above, ch. 12; on Ramakrishna, see also C.A. Stark, *God of All. Sri Ramakrishna's Approach to Religious Plurality*. Cape Cod, Mass., 1974 (uncritical).

46. Cf. *The Gospel*, 1023 (criticism of Keshab: 326).

47. *The Gospel*, 326.

48. *The Gospel*, 1023; see also 374 f.; 204: the different names of the *one* God, the *one* truth; for a reversal of the water metaphor, cf. 9.

49. Among Western authors, see, for instance, R. Rolland and S. Lemaître.

50. P. Hacker, "Der religiöse Nationalismus Vivekanandas", *Evangelische Missionszeitschrift* 28 (1971), 4 f. (*Kl. Schr.*, 568 f.).

51. See, for instance, G.C. Dev, *The Philosophy of Vivekananda and the Future of Man*. Dacca, 1963, 96 f.; 100 ff.

52. See R. Rolland, *La vie de Vivekananda et l'évangile universelle*, Paris, 1930; F. Heiler, "Vivekananda, der Verkünder der Harmonie der Religionen." *Religion und Religionen*, Festschrift G. Mensching. Bonn, 1967, 35–49.

53. Even the otherwise useful studies by G.M. Williams do not provide much critical hermeneutic analysis; cf. *The Quest for Meaning of Svami Vivekananda*, Chico, Cal., 1974; also the contributions by Williams in: *Religion in Modern India*, ed. R.D. Baird. New Delhi, 1981, 55–80; 197–226.

54. See "Schopenhauer und die Ethik des Hinduismus." *Saeculum* 12 (1961), 366–399) (*Kl. Schr.*, 531–561), as well as other contributions reprinted in *Kl. Schr.*

55. Cf. Gambhirananda, *History of the Ramakrishna Math and Mission*. Calcutta, 1957, 100: " . . . the value of foreign appreciation is in rousing India up." In his paper "My Plan of Campaign" (III, 226), Vivekananda himself states: "I travelled twelve years all over India, finding no way to work for my countrymen, and that is why I went to America." Cf. in this connection A. Bharati's notion of the "pizza-effect"; e.g. "The Hindu Renaissance and Its Apologetic Patterns." *Journal of Asian Studies* 29 (1970), 267–287; especially 273.

56. On Vivekananda's activities and reception in America, see M.L. Burke, *Swami Vivekananda in America*. Calcutta, 1958. Also *Swami Vivekananda: His Second Visit to the West*, Calcutta, 1973.

57. Cf. *Complete Works* III, 211 ff. See also S.N. Dhar, *A Comprehensive Biography of Swami Vivekananda*. Madras, 1975–1976, vol. 1, 22 ff.

58. Cf. *The Life of Swami Vivekananda, by his Eastern and Western Disciples*. Almora, seventh ed., 1965.

59. Cf. P. Hacker, *Kl. Schr.*, 567 (see above, n. 50).

60. III, 267 f.

61. P. Hacker, *Kl. Schr.*, 567.

62. III, 148 (from a speech in India).

63. III, 186 f.

64. III, 187; cf. III, 126: "brotherhood of universal life."

65. III, 189.

66. III, 148 f. Very sharp criticism of the West is found in the treatise *The East and the West* which was originally published in Bengali in the journal *Udbodhan* and appeared subsequently as an independent publication in English (Madras, 1909).

67. Cf. VIII, 325 ff.

68. See, for instance, VII, 181 ff.; III, 443; V, 288 (on the achievements of the Japanese).

69. III, 190.

70. Cf. H. Rüstau, "Swami Vivekananda und Lokamanya Bal Gangadhar Tilak." *Neue Indienkunde/New Indology*, Festschrift W. Ruben, Berlin, 1970, 539–549; especially 542. We may recall here Vivekananda's "deification" of the poor in the concept of *daridranārāyaṇa*, which was later adopted by Vinoba Bhave. In V, 110, Vivekananda postulates the establishment of equal and fair conditions for everybody.

71. Cf. IV, 156.

72. Cf. I, 20: " . . . the crying evil in the East is not religion - they have religion enough . . . It is an insult to a starving people to offer them religion"; IV, 318: "We Hindus . . . have no need or desire to import religion from the West." See also VIII, 208–213 ("Hindus and Christians"; "Criticism of Christian Missionaries").

73. Cf. IV, 426 f. (from a report on a presentation in Paris).

74. Under the title "Practical Vedanta," Vivekananda gave four lectures in London; see II, 291–358. Ultimately, Vivekananda tries to minimize the need to learn from the West: "Have we to learn anything else, have we to learn anything from the world? We have, perhaps, to gain a little in material knowledge, in power of organisation . . . " (III,149).

75. III, 190 f.; cf. above, § 18. Vivekananda often encouraged his listeners to see themselves "as God."

76. Cf. III, 265.

77. Cf. III, 457: "But nowadays we have put the Puranas on even a higher pedestal than the Vedas! The study of the Vedas has almost disappeared from Bengal." However, there are also positive references to the *Purāṇas*, as well as to such texts as the *Mahānirvāṇatantra* (see *Karmayoga*, ch. 2).

78. Cf. III, 264 f.: "Little do they know that Buddhism created Brahminism and idolatry in India . . . The most hideous ceremonies, the most horrible, the most obscene books that human hands ever wrote or the human brain ever conceived, the most bestial forms that ever passed under the name of religion, have all been the creation of degraded Buddhism" (also quoted by Kane V, 1030). See also VI, 224 f.; III, 216 f.

79. I, 23 (1893 in Chicago); Buddhism even appears as the fulfilment of Hinduism, and their relationship is compared to that between Christianity and Judaism (I, 21).

80. See, for instance, II, 494 ff.; II, 507: "What Buddha taught, the Hindu believes, but what the Buddhists teach, we do not accept." IV, 135 ff. ("On Lord Buddha") praises the "heart" of the Buddha; in III, 528 f., the Buddha is called "the sanest philosopher the world ever saw." Ramakrishna himself referred repeatedly to the Buddha, but he understood him in terms of the Hindu mythology of "incarnations" (*avatāra*); see *The Gospel*, 382; 940 f.

81. See III, 264: "I smile when I read books written by some modern people who ought to have known better, that the Buddha was the destroyer of Brahminical idolatry."

82. III, 512.

83. III, 511: "from Lapland on the one side to the Philippine islands on the other."

84. III, 536: "Buddhism was the first sect in India." One the other hand, J.N. Farquhar, a Christian advocate of the idea of "fulfilment," claimed that early Christianity had superseded an opposition "which in many respects closely resembled Hinduism" (*The Future of Christianity in India*, Madras, 1904, 6; quoted by E. Sharpe, *Not to Destroy but to Fulfil*. Upsala, 1965, 204).

85. See, for instance, II, 510 ff. (followed by a reference to Schopenhauer).

86. See *Dharmatattva*, ch. 17 (*Racanāvalī* II, 634); see also Dayananda Sarasvati, *Satyārthaprakāśa*, ch. 12; and above, n. 80.

87. See below, ch. 14.

88. III, 461.

89. III, 340.

90. See III, 253; 456. This can only refer to Bhāṣya on NS I,1,7; a similar misinterpretation of this passage is found in S. Radhakrishnan, *Recovery of Faith*. London, 1956, 190.

91. I, 506.

92. IV, 259.

93. Cf. IV, 301 (from a speech in South India); according to this passage, *Śūdras* are "Aryas in novitiate".

94. III, 126; on the other hand, the categories of "race" and "blood" appear in III, 534 ff.

95. See, for instance, III, 276 f.; see also the patriotic statements in: *Our Motherland*, compiled by P. Sankaranarayan. Bombay, 1963.

96. Cf. V, 163 (from an interview, given in 1899).

97. III, 251 f. (from a speech in India). Speaking in Chicago in 1893, Vivekananda refers to the "infinite arms" of an all-comprehensive "universal religion" without identifying this religion with Hinduism; see I, 19.

98. "Modern India"; IV, 408 ff. (originally in Bengali, 1899).

99. "Schopenhauer und die Ethik des Hinduismus." *Saeculum* 12 (1961), 366–399 (*Kl. Schr.*, 531–564).

100. Loc. cit., 389 (*Kl. Schr.*, 554); Hacker claims that B.G. Tilak, too, was strongly influenced by this speech.

101. See *Prahlāda. Werden und Wandlungen einer Idealgestalt.* Abh. Ak. Wiss. Mainz, 1959.

102. "Der religiöse Nationalismus Vivekanandas". *Evangelische Missionszeitschrift* 28 (1971), 13 (*Kl. Schr.*, 577).

103. See, for instance, *Karmayoga*, ch. 5 (conclusion): "In helping the world we really help ourselves" (referring to Ramakrishna's metaphor of the "dog's tail").

104. *Kl. Schr.*, 532 (see above, n. 99).

105. *WWV* I, § 53.

106. See *Mein Leben*. Leipzig, 1922, 121; 124 f. Deussen himself sent a printed version of his Bombay speech to his Indian friends; the text was reprinted as an appendix to: *Erinnerungen an Indien*. Kiel/Leipzig, 1904. See also *AGPh* I/2, 45 f.

107. *Calcutta Review* 27 (1852), 271 (from an anonymous contribution: "Vedantism and Christianity").

108. See the references to the "practical success" following from the adoption of Christianity: *Calcutta Review* 17 (1852), 281; also 3 (1845), 136: the Indians should accept the Christian faith, the true basis of Western strength and superiority, and not only the worldly ingredients of Western civilization.

109. See M. Lederle, *Philosophical Trends in Modern Mahārāṣṭra*. Bombay, 1976, 191 ff.; 261 ff. Lederle mentions and cautiously criticizes Hacker's thesis. Cf. also S. Mayeda, "Śaṅkara and Nārāyaṇa Guru." ALB 50 (1987), 138–164.

110. "My Plan of Campaign"; III, 223; Vivekananda also refers to earlier examples of India's "spiritual" influence on the world. For other manifestations of Vivekananda's sense of "history," see G. Stephenson, "Ansätze zum geschichtlichen Denken im Reformwerk Swami Vivekanandas." *Saeculum 23 (1972), 90*–108.

111. Cf. R. Guénon, *Introduction to the Study of the Hindu Doctrines*, trans. M. Pallis. London, 1945, 322 ff.; P. Hacker, *Kl. Schr.*, 398. Deussen's judgement is reserved; cf. *Mein Leben*. Leipzig, 1922, 305. On the other hand, Vivekananda's references to Deussen are very friendly; cf. IV, 272 ff.

112. Hegel appears as the major advocate of *saṃsāra* and secularism: "Fortunately for us, Hegelianism was nipped in the bud and not allowed to sprout and cast its baneful shoots over this motherland of ours" (III, 342). Vivekananda obviously preferred Hegel's antipode, Schopenhauer.

113. Cf. H. Maheshwari, *The Philosophy of Swami Rama Tirtha*. Agra, 1969, 169.

114. See *The Gospel*, 636–647; 770.

115. See below, ch. 18; on Comte and Bengal, see G.H. Forbes, *Positivism in Bengal*. Calcutta, 1975.

116. Cf. *Dharmatattva*, ch. 4; English translation by M. Ghosh; *Essentials of Dharma*. Calcutta, 1977. Although an advocate of the Bengali language, Bankim Chandra also wrote several works in English; see *Racanāvalī*, vol. 3: *English Works*.

117. Cf. T.W. Clark, "The Role of Bankimcandra in the Development of Nationalism." *Historical Writings on the Peoples of Asia* I, ed. C.H. Philips, London, 1961, 429–445; especially 441 f. (referring to the final chapter in Bankim's novel *Anandamaṭh*).

118. The English terms "religion," "culture," "duty," etc., often appear in Bengali contexts; on *darśana* and "philosophy," see below , ch. 16.

119. In particular, he criticizes the treatment of Kṛṣṇa in the writings of Western scholars, specifically A. Weber.

120. *Dharmatattva*, ch. 24 (*svadeśaprīti*; cf. *Racanāvalī*, II, 600 f.).

121. See *Racanāvalī* II, 241; also T.W. Clark (see above, n. 117), 442.

122. Cf. specifically his *Kṛṣṇacaritra* and his unfinished commentary on the *Bhagavadgītā*; in his Gītā commentary, he refers to Kṛṣṇaism as the "Catholic" and "only religion" (see *Racanāvalī* II, 746: *ekamātra dharma*).

123. The interpretation of Jesus Christ by J.R. Seeley (*Ecce homo*, 1866) provided the most important model.

124. *The Gospel*, 770; the *gopīs*, "cowherdesses," are Kṛṣṇa's female companions.

125. On Aksay Kumar Datta (Akkhoy Kumar Dutt), see D. Kopf, *The Brahmo Samaj and the Shaping of the Modern Indian Mind*. Princeton, 1979, 49 ff.

126. Cf. Y. Sahae, *Brāhma Samāj und Ārya Samāj*. Diss. Bonn, 1964, 133f.

127. See *Satyārthaprakāśa* ch. 13 (English translation by Durga Prasad: *Light of Truth*, second ed., New Delhi, 1970). The discrepancies between the original edition (Benares, 1875) and the revised edition of 1883 (Allahabad, 1884) have lead to controversies concerning vegetarianism and other issues; cf. H.B. Sarda, *Works of Maharshi Dayanand and Paropkarini Sabha*. Ajmer, 1942. For a clear and convincing discussion of the problems concerning the *Satyārthaprakāśa* and Dayananda's development, see J.T. F. Jordens, *Dayānanda Sarasvatī. His Life and Ideas*. Delhi, 1978, especially 99 ff. The most reliable edition of the *Satyārthaprakasa* is by Yudhiṣṭhira Mīmāṃsaka, Sonipat, 1972.

128. Cf. K.W. Jones, *Arya Dharm*. Berkeley, 1976, 166.

129. See *Autobiography of Swami Dayanand Sarasvati*, ed. K.C. Yadav, New Delhi, 1976, 61; Y. Sahae, *Brāhma Samāj und Ārya Samāj*. Diss. Bonn, 1964, 64; on the contrast of "Hindu" and "Arya," cf. K.W. Jones, *Arya Dharm*, 186.

130. For a critique of other "reform" movements, such as the Brāhma Samāj and the Prārthanā Samāj, see *Satyārthaprakāśa*, ch. 11.

131. Cf. K.W. Jones, *Arya Dharm*, 108 ff. Apart from all doctrinal differences, it was "a sound, common-sense pragmatism" (J.T.F. Jordens, *Dayānanda Sarasvatī*, 292) that distinguished Dayananda and his followers from other groups.

132. See *Ṛgvedabhāṣya* I, ed. Yudhiṣṭhira Mīmāṃsaka. Karnal, 1973, 160 ff.; 234 ff.; 255 ff. The introduction (*bhūmikā*) was edited and translated by Parmanand. New Delhi, 1981.

133. *Ṛgvedabhāṣya* I, 316 ff. Accordingly, Dayananda presented a purified version of the *Manusmṛti*, which reduces the text to its allegedly true and Vedic dimensions; see *Vaidikamanusmṛti*, Delhi, fourth ed., 1968.

134. See above, n. 108 f.; J.R. Ballantyne was a leading advocate of this idea. For the older period, see also M.A. Laird, *Missionaries and Education in Bengal, 1793–1837*. London, 1972, 263 ff. On the dissemination of European science in general, see B.V. Subbarayappa, "Western Science in India to the End of the Nineteenth Century A.D." *A Concise History of Science in India*, ed. D.M. Bose et al. New Delhi, 1971, 434–567.

14. Supplementary Observations on Modern Indian Thought

1. Cf. G.K. Mookerjee, *The Indian Image of Nineteenth-Century Europe*. Bombay, 1967, 24ff.

2. G.K. Mookerjee, 30ff.

3. G.K. Mookerjee, 30.

4. Cf. H.-J. Klimkeit, "Bipin Chandra Pal-Der Künder eines indischen Humanismus." *Zeitschrift für Religions-und Geistesgeschichte* 32 (1980), 241–254; id., *Der politische Hinduismus*. Wiesbaden, 1981.

5. The development of "modernism" in Indian Islam will remain excluded from our presentation; on this, see, for instance, Z.A. Hanfi, *Die modernistische Denkbewegung im indischen Islam (1858–1940)*. Freiburg, 1964; A. Ahmad, *Islamic Modernism in India and Pakistan, 1857–1964*. London, 1967; as well as the recent studies by Chr. Troll. On Buddhist "modernism" in Ceylon (Sri Lanka) see H. Bechert, *Buddhismus, Staat und Gesellschaft in den Ländern des Theravāda-Buddhismus*, vol. 1. Frankfurt, 1966, 37ff.

6. On Aurobindo's life, see A.B. Purani, *The Life of Sri Aurobindo (1872–1926)*. Pondicherry, second ed., 1960; K. Singh, *Prophet of Indian Nationalism*. London, 1963. For bibliographical information, cf. H.K. Kaul, *Sri Aurobindo. A Descriptive Bibliography*. New Delhi, 1972.

7. Cf. *Sri Aurobindo and His Ashram*. Pondicherry, 1964 (first ed.: 1951), 35f.: ". . . I was hearing constantly the voice of Vivekananda speaking to me for a fortnight in the jail."

8. Cf. K. Singh, *Prophet of Indian Nationalism*. London, 1963, 73ff.

9. Cf. *Sources of Indian Tradition*, vol. 2, 179ff.

10. See *Speeches*, Pondicherry, third ed., 1952,56; in Bengali: *Dharma o jātīyatā* ("Religion and Nationalism"), Calcutta, 1920 (fourth ed.: 1946).

11. "On Original Thinking." *The Harmony of Virtue. Early Cultural Writings* (Centenary Edition, vol.3, 1970), 111ff.

12. See A.M.G. van Dijk, *Europese invloeden op het denken van Sri Aurobindo*. Diss. Utrecht, 1977, 302f. For a philosophical evaluation of Aurobindo, see S.H. Phillips, *Aurobindo's Philosophy of Brahman*. Leiden, 1986.

13. Cf. A.M.G. van Dijk, op. cit.; V.P. Varma, *The Political Philosophy of Sri Aurobindo*. Bombay, 1960, 30ff.

14. The speculative and "occultist" tendencies of Aurobindo's later writings indicate the increasing influence of "the Mother." See also R.S. Srivastava, *Sri Aurobindo and the Theories of Evolution*. Benares, 1968 (uncritical presentation of rich materials). Aurobindo's views on evolution have often been compared with the philosophy of P. Teilhard de Chardin.

15. On Aurobindo's interpretation of authoritative Sanskrit texts, see K. Dockhorn, *Tradition und Evolution. Untersuchungen zu Sri Aurobindos Auslegung autoritativer Sanskritschriften*. Gütersloh, n.d. (ca. 1968).

16. P. Hacker, *Kl. Schr.*, 599.

17. The literature on Radhakrishnan is vast; but examples of critical hermeneutical analysis are very rare. Among these few exceptions, see P. Hacker, "Ein Prasthānatraya-Kommentar des Neuhinduismus. Bemerkungen zum Werk Radhakrishnans." *OLZ* 56 (1961), 565–576 (*Kl. Schr.*, 525–530).

18. See R.N. Minor, *Radhakrishnan: A Religious Biography*. Albany, 1987.

19. See, for instance, *The Philosophy of S. Radhakrishnan*, ed. P.A. Schilpp, New York, 1952 (e.g., 282); *Dr. S. Radhakrishnan Souvenir Volume*, ed. B.L. Atreya and others. Moradabad, 1964.

20. See the contribution by M.N. Roy in: *The Philosophy of S. Radhakrishnan*, ed. P.A. Schilpp. New York, 1952. On A.K. Coomaraswamy see below,§9.

21. Cf. R.N. Minor, *Radhakrishnan: A Religious Biography*. Albany, 1978. The title of the master's thesis is programmatic: *The Ethics of the Vedānta and Its Metaphysical Presuppositions*. Madras, 1908. See also Radhakrishnan's response to A. Schweitzer in: *Eastern Religious and Western Thought*. London, second ed., 1940, 64ff.; as well as M.D. Hunnex, "Mysticism and Ethics: Radhakrishnan and Schweitzer." *PEW* 8 (1958/59), 121–136.

22. *The Brahma Sūtra*. London, 1960, 7. Cf. *The Principal Upaniṣads*. London, 1953, 9: "For us Indians, a study of the Upaniṣads is essential if we are to preserve our national being and character."

23. The introductions to *The Principal Upaniṣads* and *The Brahma Sūtra* also contain numerous references to Western, primarily Christian, sources.

24. *The Brahma Sūtra*. London, 1960, 249. Cf. also 11: "Any system of thought should satisfy two basic requirements; it should state the truth and interpret it for each new generation."

25. To his annotated translations of the Hindu *prasthānatraya* (*Upaniṣads, Bhagavadgītā, Brahmasūtra*), Radhakrishnan added his version of one of the most popular Buddhist texts: *The Dhammapada*. London, 1950 (several reprints).

26. See, for instance, the statement on *ṛṣi* and *mleccha* in: *Recovery of Faith*. London, 1956, 190. It is based upon a misinterpretation of *NBh*I,1,7 which is also found in the works of Vivekananda (see above, ch.13, n. 90). See also *The Hindu View of Life*, 28f.

27. Notes on *Bhagavadgīta* IV, 11; Radhakrishnan proposes the following Sanskrit supplement to his quotation of the *Vaiṣṇava* verse: *kraistvāḥ kristur iti kriyāpararatāḥ, allā-iti māhammadāḥ*. He seems to confuse this verse with the prose passage on *Kusumāñjali* I,2; as usual in the traditions of Nyāya and Vaiśeṣika, Udayana was a *Śaivite*, not a *Vaiṣṇava*.

28. We should also recall his universalistic and ethicizing reinterpretation of the hereditary caste system; cf. *The Hindu View of Life*, 67ff. See also *Religion and Society*. London, second ed., 1948, 130f. This work, which is based upon notes of lectures delivered at the Universities of Calcutta and Benares, records Radhakrishnan's assessment of the "actualities" of the Second World War.

29. Cf. *An Idealist View of Life*. London, fifth ed., 1957, 84ff.; 127ff.; *The Brahma Sūtra*. London, 1960, 111ff. On the role of "experience" in Neo-Hinduism, see below, Appendix 1.

30. Cf. *The Hindu View of Life*, 16: "The Hindu philosophy of religion starts from and returns to an experimental basis."

31. Cf. *The Hindu View of Life*, 43f.; this section refers, in a sequence of associations, to "the Hindu solution," "the spirit of democracy," "conferences and congresses of liberal thinkers," "mysticism" and "experience."

32. Cf. *The Bhagavadgītā*. London, sixth ed., 1960, 12: "It represents not any sect of Hinduism, but Hinduism as a whole, not merely Hinduism, but religion as such, in its universality, without limits of time or space, embracing within its synthesis the whole gamut of the human spirit, from the crude fetishism of the savage to the creative affirmations of the saint." On Vivekananda, see above, ch. 13, §25 (n.97).

33. *The Hindu View of Life*, 18; in contrast to such universality, Radhakrishnan criticizes the Christian "servitude to one historic fact" (*The Bhagavadgītā*, 157).

34. Cf. H. Bürkle, *Dialog mit dem Osten*. Stuttgart, 1965, 247; Th.P. Urumpackal, *Organized Religion According to Dr. S. Radhakrishnan*. Rome, 1972; two uncritical studies of Radhakrishnan's "universalism": W. Cremer, *Die universale Religion des Geistes*. Diss. Munich, 1966; I.C. Harris, *Radhakrishnan: The Profile of a Universalist*. Calcutta, 1982.

35. Radhakrishnan tends to idealize "the Hindu," as opposed to the "majority of the Hindus"; cf. *The Hindu View of Life*, 24f.; also 66.

36. For another example of "political Vedānta," see C. Rajagopalachari, *Hinduism. Doctrine and Way of Life*. Bombay, 1959. For a general survey, cf. S.K. Malhotra, *Social and Political Orientations of Neo-Vedantism*. Delhi, 1970.

37. Cf. K.R. Stunkel, "The Meeting of East and West in Coomaraswamy and Radhakrishnan." *PEW* 23 (1973), 517–524.

38. On Coomaraswamy and Guénon, see R.W. Lipsey, *Signature and Significance:*

A Study of the Life and Writings of A.K. Coomaraswamy. Diss. New York, 1974, 489ff. Lipsey has edited Coomaraswamy's *Selected Papers*, 2 vols. Princeton, 1977 (vol.3: *Coomaraswamy, His Life and Work*). For a compilation of reviews on Coomaraswamy, see R. Guénon, *Études sur l'Hindouisme*. Paris, 1968.

39. Cf.H. Rau, *Mahatma Gandhi*. Reinbek, 1970, 59ff. See also *Gandhi, India and the World*, ed. S. Ray. Philadelphia, 1970; M. Chatterjee, *Gandhi's Religious Thought*. Notre Dame, 1983.

40. Lincoln, 1962 (second ed.: Carbondale, 1970); together with R.W. Inge, Raju has edited a felicitation volume for Radhakrishnan: *Comparative Studies in Philosophy*. London, 1951.

41. On "comparison," see below, Appendix III.

42. See below, ch. 16, §12 (n. 41).

43. See below, Appendix IV.

44. See above, ch. 13, n. 1; also D.P. Sinha, *The Educational Policy of the East India Company in Bengal to 1854*. Calcutta, 1964.

45. Cf. P.R. Sen, *Western Influence in Bengali Literature*. Calcutta, 1932, 153. A thousand copies of the original English text were shipped to Calcutta; see also 78ff. (on the Hindu College).

46. Cf. G.H. Forbes, *Positivism in Bengal*. Calcutta, 1975. See also Bankim Chandra Chatterji, *Racanāvalī* II, 676ff. (on H. Spencer, etc.).

47. See P.C. Joshi and K. Damodaran, *Marx Comes to India*. Delhi, 1975.

48. Cf. *Contemporary Indian Philosophy*, vol.2, ed. M. Chatterjee. London, 1974.

49. Some useful references are given by Satyavrat Shastri, "Modern Sanskrit Poetry." *Saṃskṛtasaṃskṛtiḥ-Cultura Sánscrita*, Mexico, 1984, 141-149.

50. Cf. R.F. Young, *Resistant Hinduism*. Vienna, 1981.

51. In their responses, the pandits defend the *adhikārabheda* ("differentiation of qualification"), which the missionaries criticized as exclusivistic, as a superior universalism; cf. Nīlakaṇṭha Śāstrī Gore, *Śāstratattvavinirṇaya*, ed. S.L. Katre. Ujjain, 1951.

52. Cf. K. Bhattacharya, "Ananta Kumar Bhattacharya." *Indian Studies. Past and Present* 4 (1962/63), 111-112.

53. Cf. Upendradatta Pāṇḍeya, *Upendravijñānasūtra*, ed. M.D. Shastri. Benares, 1936.

54. Sanskrit translations of Western philosophy are found in *The Pandit - Old Series*. Cf. G. Jha, "Autobiographical Notes," ed. H. Jha. *Journal of the Ganganatha Jha Kendriya Sanskrit Vidyapeetha* (Allahabad) 30 (1976); *Life and Philosophy of Mahamahopadhyaya Gopinath Kaviraj. Papers Presented at the Seminar* (Nov. 1978). Calcutta, n.d. Such scholars as Rajendralal Mitra and R.G. Bhandarkar were pandits as well as pioneering Indologists in the Western sense. Lax-

man Shastri Joshi (Jośī; born 1901), editor of the monumental *Dharmakośa*, was a pandit who joined Gandhi and became a "leftist" critic of Radhakrishnan and Neo-Vedānta; cf. *A Critique of Hinduism*. Bombay, 1948 (originally in Marathi, 1941).

55. H.-G. Gadamer, *Truth and Method*. New York, 1985 (translation of *Wahrheit und Methode*), 250.

56. Cf. F.M. Müller, *Auld Lang Syne* II, New York, 1899, 35: ". . . who will ere long rise to the rank of a Veda-Vyāsa . . . of the Kaliyuga." A reprint of the *Śabdakalpadruma* was published in Delhi (1961; 5 vols.).

57. Cf. B.K. Cakravartī, *Taḍer rājasthāna o bāṅgālā sāhitya*, Calcutta, 1981; and the review by R.P. Das. *ZDMG* (1985), 148–150).

58. Cf. Bhagawad Dutt, "Western Indologists: A Study in Motives." *A Review of 'Beef in Ancient India.'* Gorakhpur, 1971, 17–38 (on Müller: 23ff.). Already Bankim Chandra Chatterji was a critic of European Indology. On the glorification of Müller in India, see L. Rocher, "Max Müller and the Veda." *Mélanges Armand Abel* III. Leiden, 1978, 221–235.

59. We may also refer here to the Indian activities and influences of the Theosophical Society, which was, however, rejected by Dayānanda Sarasvatī and Vivekananda.

60. Poona, 1929 (*ASS*, vol. 98).

61. *Dharmatattvanirṇaya*, 39 (there is no *sanātanadharmaprāpti*).

62. *Dharmatattvanirṇaya*, 35: *mlecchasaṃsargiṇo mlecchānnabhakṣādidoṣaduṣṭā yāvatkālaparyantaṃ mlecchabhāvaṃ prāptās tāvat prāyaścittena pūtā bhavanti. tadbhāvaṃ āpannānāṃ tu na prāyaścittam . . .*

63. Cf. *Dharmatattvanirṇaya*, 40.

64. The *Advaitāmoda* was translated into English by M.J. Comans, Diss. Canberra, 1986 publ. Delhi 1988).

65. Calcutta, n.d. (the preface is dated Dec. 15, 1937).

66. Cf. *Dharmapradīpa*, 189ff.: *Śuddhitattvaprakāśa*; especially 219: *atra kevalaṃ balād eva mlecchadharmaṃ svīkāritānāṃ hindūnām . . . vividhāḥ prāyaścittavidhayo nirdiṣṭā dṛśyante.*

67. Cf. *Dharmapradīpa*, 64: *śāstrasamājādiparivartanena hi na sanātanadharmasaṃrakṣaṇaṃ, kiṃ tu nūtanasampradāyapravartanam eva phalati.* The expression *nūtanasampradāya* ("new sectarian tradition," "new doctrine") was already used by the *Vedāntacandrikā* in its critique of Rammohan Roy; cf. *Rāmamohana-Granthāvalī*, 146.

68. See, for instance, *Dharmapradīpa*, 207; 219; *Dharmatattvanirṇaya*, 39ff.

69. N. Varmā, *Śabda aur smṛti*. Delhi, 1976, 67. A German translation of *Atīta* was published by L. Lutze: "Die Vergangenheit: Eine Selbstbesinnung." *Internationales Asienforum* 11 (1980), 319–330 (cf. ib., 324).

70. Loc. cit., 72f. (cf. L. Lutze, 329).

71. J.L. Mehta, *India and the West*, 159 (originally published as: "Understanding and Tradition." *Anvīkṣikī* 2, 1969, 117–136).

72. *India and the West*, 163 (originally published as: "The Problem of Philosophical Reconception in the Thought of K.C. Bhattacharya." *PEW* 24, 1974, 59–70). Cf. also "Heidegger and the Comparison of Indian and Western Philosophy." *PEW* 20 (1970), 303–318; also Mehta's conference contribution in: *PEW* 21 (1971), 491

15. *Darśana, Ānvīkṣikī*, Philosophy

1. See below, ch. 16.

2. See, for instance, P. Deussen, *AGPh* I/1, 1f.; H. von Glasenapp, *Die Philosophie der Inder*. Stuttgart, third ed., 1974, 9.

3. See below, §13ff.

4. The most recent and comprehensive edition of the text, together with the extant commentaries, is by M.K. Jain. Calcutta, 1969 (Jñānapīṭha Mūrtidevī Jaina Granthamālā). The commentary by Maṇibhadra is also available in an edition by G. Dāmodara Śāstrī. Benares, 1957 (*ChSS*); Guṇaratna's commentary was first edited in its entirety by L. Suali, Calcutta, 1905–1914 (*Bibliotheca Indica*).

5. Cf. e.g., *NS* (with *NBh*) I,1, 26ff. (*tantra* in the sense of "system"); *NBh* on I,1,1 (ed. A. Thakur, p.2, 1.6: *tantrārtha*) uses *tantra* with reference to the *Nyāya* system, which is otherwise also called *nyāyaśāstra, nyāyavidyā*, etc. The word *tantra* has a special affinity with the Sāṃkhya system; cf. *Sāṃkhyakārikā* 70;72. The term *siddhadarśana* in *VS* IX,2,13 (ed. Jambuvijaya: IX, 28) and *YS* III,32 has nothing to do with the doxographic use of *darśana*.

6. Cf. *Ṣaḍdarśanasamuccaya*, v.1–2; Guṇaratna explains *saddarśana* as *sarvajña*, but also mentions another explanation, which takes *darśana* in the sense of *mata*. Maṇibhadra paraphrases: *śobhamānaṃ śāsanam*.

7. The chronology of Śaṅkara continues to be problematic. The widely accepted dates 788–820 are not well attested. On the other hand, there is no compelling evidence for the thesis that Śaṅkara was a predecessor or an older contemporary of Maṇḍana. The doxography *Sarvasiddhāntasaṃgraha*, which has been ascribed to Śaṅkara, is not authentic.

8. Cf. *Word-Index to the Brahma-Sūtra-Bhāṣya of Śaṅkara*, ed. T.M.P. Mahadevan. Madras, 1971–1974. See, eg., II,1,1; III,1,1: *kapilasya tantram*; II,1,3: *sāṃkhyasmṛti; yogasmṛti*.

9. On *BS* II,1,8; the Sūtras use *darśana* primarily in the sense of "scriptural evidence," i.e. mentioning by *śruti* (e.g., I,3,30: *darśanāt smṛteś ca*). The Vedānta is otherwise referred to as *vāda* (commentary on I,4,28), *śāstra* (I,1,4) or *siddhānta* (I,4,6).

10. On *BS* II,2,1. The expression *advaitadarśana* (as "non-dualistic view") is used repeatedly in Śaṅkara's commentary on Gauḍapāda's *Māṇḍūkyakārikā*, which is possibly his earliest contribution to Advaita Vedānta. In this work, the expressions *mithyādarśana* and *samyagdarśana* (cf. introduction to *kārikā* IV, 1) seem to reflect the Buddhist terms *micchādiṭṭhi* and *sammādiṭṭhi*. In a "doxographic" sense, *advaitadarśana* is used by Kamalaśīla, Pañjikā on *Tattvasaṃgraha*, v.328.

11. *Prasannapadā* on *Madhyamakakārikā* XV, 11 (ed. L. de La Vallée Poussin, p. 120).

12. Cf. *PB*, 177; Śrīdhara's *Nyāyakandalī* (ib., 179) emphasizes the soteriological meaning of *darśana* in *trayīdarśana*.

13. Cf. Nyanatiloka, *Buddhistisches Wörterbuch*. Konstanz, 1953, art. *diṭṭhi*. Also *The Discourse on the All-Embracing Net of Views*, trans. Bhikkhu Bodhi. Kandy, 1978 (for the *Brahmajālasutta* and its commentaries; this text, which epitomizes the Theravāda critique of "views," often uses the compound *diṭṭhiṭhāna*). Pali commentaries (e.g., the Kathāvatthu commentary) frequently use the term *laddhi*, "religious theory," "heresy," instead of *diṭṭhi*. Unlike *dṛṣṭi*, *darśana* has no pejorative connotation in Buddhism (cf., e.g., the term *darśanamārga*).

14. Cf. *NBh* on *NS* IV,1,14: *pravādukānāṃ dṛṣṭayaḥ*; Manu XII,95: *kudṛṣṭayaḥ* (Medhātithi paraphrases" *asattarkadarśanāni*). See also *Bhagavadgītā* XVI,9 and Śaṅkara's commentary on *Gītā* XVIII,17 (*laukikī/pāramārthikī dṛṣṭiḥ*). Compounds like *ātmadarśana*, *tattvadarśana*, etc. (cf., e.g., Manu VI,74; Sureśvara, *Naiṣkarmyasiddhi* II,103) may, indeed, have the meaning "vision," "realization." *Śivadṛṣṭi*, the title of Somānanda's systematization of Śaivism in Kashmir, seems to allude to the meanings "vision" as well as "philosophical system"; there are also compounds like *yogadṛṣṭi*. See also Śaṅkara on *Bṛhadāraṇyaka Upaniṣad* I,1,2; 2,1; 3,1 ("visualization", etc.).

15. Cf. *Mahābhārata* XII, 289, 9: *vratānāṃ dhāraṇaṃ tulyam, darśanaṃ na samaṃ tayoḥ* (referring to Sāṃkhya and Yoga; the preceding verses 6 and 7 use *mata*). XIII,148,22 has *darśana* in the plural; XII,289,5 uses *mokṣadarśana* in the sense of "theory of final liberation."

16. Cf. *Lokatattvanirṇaya* I,38 (ed. L. Suali, *Giornale della Società Asiatica Italiana* 18, 1905, 278): *pakṣapāto na me vīre, na dveṣaḥ kapilādiṣu/yuktimad vacanaṃ yasya, tasya kāryaḥ parigrahaḥ* (quoted by Guṇaratna and Maṇibhadra in their commentaries on *Ṣaḍdarśanasamuccaya*,v.44; by Guṇaratna also in his introduction; ed. M.K. Jain, 11). The concepts of "neutrality" (*mādhyasthya*) and "unbiased cognition" (*pakṣapātarahitā buddhiḥ*) appear in Guṇaratna's commentary on the first as well as the final verse of Haribhadra's work, both times in association with "reason" and "reflection" (*yukti; vicāra*). On the possibility of a Buddhist prototype for Haribhadra's verse, see L. de La Vallée Poussin, "Une stance jaina et bouddhique." *JA* X/17 (1911), 323–32. For other claims to *yukti*, see below, n. 94.

17. Cf. *Sūyagaḍanga* I,1,1,19; 2,24 (*kiriyāvāidarisaṇa*); see also W.B. Bollée, *Studien zum Sūyagaḍa*. Wiesbaden, 1976, 76ff. (78: *sakkadarisaṇa* for "Buddhism"). In addition to *vāda/vāya*, *samaya* is also commonly used.

18. Cf. Umāsvāti, *Tattvārthasūtra* I,1 (with autocommentary). For another juxtaposition of *jñāna* and *darśana* (corresponding to *sākāra-* and *anākāra-upayoga*) see N. Tatia, *Studies in Jaina Philosophy*. Benares, 1951, 70ff. The lost twelfth *aṅga* of the Jaina canon was called *Diṭṭhivāya* and contained debates about opposing "views."

19. See N. Tatia (see above, n.18), 22. On the "objectivity" of Haribhadra, see Sukhlal Sanghvi, *Samadarśī ācārya haribhadra*. Jodhpur, 1963. The attempt of Dalsukh Malvania to find the *anekāntavāda* in the original teachings of the Jina Mahāvīra seems to go too far; see his *Āgamayuga kā jainadarśana*. Agra, 1966, 51ff.

20. On the systematic function of *naya* in Jainism, specifically in the works of Siddhasena and Mallavādin, see D. Malvania (above, n.19), 293-320; on *naya* in Umāsvāti: B. Bhatt and Ch. Tripathi, "Tattvārtha Studies." *ALB* 38 (1974), 71ff.; on "perspectivism" as applied to Advaita Vedānta: H. Nakamura, "The Vedānta as Noticed in Medieval Jaina Literature." *Indological Studies in Honor of W.N. Brown*. New Haven, 1962, 186-194.

21. For an interesting juxtaposition of *naya* and *dṛṣṭi*, see the Buddhist *Laṅkāvatārasūtra*, ed. B. Nanjio, Kyoto, 1923, 264 (introduction to the *Sagāthaka* appendix): . . . *śṛṇu mahāyānanayaṃ citraṃ dṛṣṭijālavighātanam*.

22. *VP*, ed. W. Rau. Wiesbaden, 1977, II, 136.

23. *VP* III,9 (*kāla*), 62.

24. Cf. *VP* I,75; 110 (*darśanabhedo hi pravādeṣv anavasthitaḥ*). See also below, ch. 19, n.26 (on *dṛś-darśana* in the *Sarvasiddhāntasaṃgraha*).

25. Cf. *VP* III,1 (*jāti*), 103f.

26. Cf. *Mahābhāṣyaṭīkā*, ed. V. Swaminathan. Benares, 1965, 25; 36. See also 24: *etasmin darśane*; 29: *idaṃ darśanam*; 37: *keṣāṃcid darśanam*. See also the edition by K.V. Abhyankar and V.P. Limaye (under the title *Mahābhāṣyadīpikā*), *ABORI* 43 (1962), 20ff. Conversely, Mallavādin refers to the *bhartṛharyādidarśana*; cf. *Dvādaśāranayacakra*, ed. Jambuvijaya, vol.2. Bhavnagar, 1976, 594.

27. *VP* II,487; 489: see also *Vṛtti* on I,9 (the quote *sarvaṃ darśanam anyūnam* . . . and the expression *sarvadarśanodayapratyastamayayoni*). *Darśana* in the sense of "view," "doctrine" appears also in Vātsyāyana, *NBh* on III,2,34: . . . *iti kasyacid darśanam*.

28. See above, ch. 9; and below, ch. 16, §22; also, for instance, M. Hiriyanna, *Outlines of Indian Philosophy*. London, sixth ed., 18.

29. Cf. Vātsyāyana, *NBh* on I,1,9; for the Vaiśeṣika response, see, e.g., the introduction to Śrīdhara's *Nyāyakandalī*.

30. Cf. Uddyotakara, *NV* (ed. A. Thakur), 14: *sukhaduḥkhasādhanabhāvāt tu sarve 'rthās cetanaṃ prayojayanti*; Kumārila, *Tupṭīkā* on *MS* VI,3,2: *na hi phalam antareṇa puruṣaḥ pravartate; keṣucit sākṣāt keṣucit pāramparyeṇa*.

31. See, for instance, Dharmottara's introduction to his *Nyāyabinduṭīkā* (ed. P.Peterson, 1): *yasmāt samyagjñānapūrvikā sarvapuruṣārthasiddhiḥ* . . .

32. See above, ch. 9; and W. Jaeger "Über Ursprung und Kreislauf des philosophischen Lebensideals." *Sb. Preuss. Ak. Wiss.*, 1928, 390-421. F. Edgerton emphasizes that the Indians did not seek "abstract truth for its own sake," or "for the

pure joy of knowledge in itself" ("The Upaniṣads: What Do They See, and Why?" *JAOS* 49, 1929, 101f.). But when and how did the Europeans seek truth in this sense?

33. Cf. J. Habermas, *Knowledge and Human Interests*, trans. J.J. Shapiro. Boston, 1971, 301-317; especially 309. (German original: *Erkenntnis und Interesse*. Frankfurt, 1968. For the Appendix: *Merkur* 213, 1965, 1139-1153).

34. Cf. *Hist. Wb. Phil.*, art. "Erlösungswissen"; see also *Werturteilsstreit*. ed. H. Albert and E. Topitsch. Darmstadt, 1971.

35. See above, ch. 9, §15 (n.77).

36. Cf. W. Halbfass, "Karma, apūrva, and 'Natural' Causes." *Karma and Rebirth in Classical Indian Traditions*, ed. W.D. O'Flaherty. Berkeley, 1980, 268-302; E. Frauwallner, *Gesch. d. ind. Ph.* I, 91ff.

37. See above, n.29; also Dasgupta I, 282.

38. Cf. *Pramāṇavārttika* II (i.e., Pramāṇasiddhi), 33 (I,33 in the edition of Dvārikādāsa Śāstrī. Benares, 1968). See also above, n.13; for a comparison of the *Brahmajālasutta* with the work of Nāgārjuna, cf. N. Dutt, "The Brahmajāla Sutta." *IHQ* 8 (1932), 706-746.

39. Cf. e.g., Śaṅkara on *BS* I,1,4; *Upadeśasāhasrī* I,1; introduction to *Bṛhadāraṇyaka Upaniṣad* III,2 (attachment to the world as *sādhyasādhanalakṣaṇa*). According to these standards, even yogic meditation is a goal-oriented "mental activity" (*mānasī kriyā*).

40. Cf. *Māṇḍūkyakārikā* IV,56: *yāvad-dhetuphalāveśaḥ saṃsāras tāvad āyataḥ/ kṣīne hetuphalāveśe saṃsāro na-upapadyate*.

41. The Advaita Vedānta (or Uttaramīmāṃsā) has articulated such reflections in its critique of the ritualistic and "activistic" Pūrvamīmāṃsā school. On its part, the Pūrvamīmāṃsā itself has made subtle contributions to problems concerning the motivation for action as well as cognition; see, for instance, Maṇḍana's *Vidhiviveka* and *Bhāvanāviveka*.

42. "Zur Frühgeschichte der indischen Philosophie." *Sb. Preuss. Ak. Wiss.* 1911, 732-743 (also in: *Kl. Schr.* II, 547-558). Long before Jacobi, M. Müller observed that *ānvīkṣikī* is "one of the most common synonyms of Nyāya" ("eines der gewöhnlichsten Synonyme von Nyāya") and means "logic," cf. "Beiträge zur Kenntnis der indischen Philosophie I." *ZDMG* 6 (1852), 3, n. A. Stenzler, *Yājñavalkyas Gesetzbuch*, Breslau, 1849 (on I,310) also used the translation "Logik."

43. Cf. the translations by J.J. Meyer and R.P. Kangle; the first translator, R. Shamashastry, left *ānvīkṣikī* untranslated.

44. "Ānvīkṣikī und Ātmavidyā." *Indologica Pragensia* 1 (1929), 1-8; especially 8f.; cf. also W. Ruben, "Zur Frühgeschichte der indischen Philosophie." *Beiträge zur Literaturwissenschaft und Geistesgeschichte Indiens* (Festgabe H. Jacobi). Bonn, 1926, 346-357.

45. *Das Mahābhārata als Epos und Rechtsbuch*. Berlin, 1895, 225ff.

46. P. Hacker, "Ānvīkṣikī." *WZKSO* 2 (1958), 54-83 (also in: *Kl. Schr.*, 137-166). Cf. A.K. Warder, "The Description of Indian Philosophy." *JIPh* 1 (1970-1972), 4-12 (without reference to Jacobi or Hacker); cf., e.g., p. 7: ". . . it would seem correct to identify *ānvīkṣikī* as philosophy and more accurately as what is sometimes

called analytical philosophy."

47. P. Hacker, loc. cit., 58; 60.

48. Loc. cit., 81; on the other hand, the term *nyāya* was also adopted by other systems (such as Mīmāṃsā or Viśiṣṭādvaita) as a general term for correct and methodically disciplined thought and used as such in the titles of numerous works.

49. Loc. cit., 74, n.18.

50. *Arthaśāstra* I,1.

51. P. Hacker, loc. cit., 55.

52. Cf. Vātsyāyana, *NBh* on *NS* I,1,1; the expression *vidyoddeśa* ("enumeration of sciences") may refer to Kauṭilya. *NBh* on I,1,4 presents a *tantrayukti* which also appears in the final section of the *Arthaśāstra*.

53. Cf. *NBh* on I,1,1 (ed. A. Thakur, 3); *NV* (ed. Thakur), 14: *saṃśayādibhedānuvidhāyinī ānvīkṣikī*; *NBh* (ed. Thakur), 2: *adhyātmavidyāmātram iyaṃ syāt, yathā-upaniṣadaḥ*. The expression *ātmavid* appears in *Chāndogya Upaniṣad* VII,1,3; the classification of sciences in this section also mentions *vākovākya* (translated as "logic" by R.E. Hume, as "Dialektik" by P. Deussen).

54. P. Hacker, loc. cit., 65; 73.

55. Cf. P. Hacker, loc. cit., 71f.

56. The "four relevant matters" are "what is to be abandoned," "abandonment," "the means of abandonment," and "what has to be attained" (*heya, hāna, hānopāya, adhigantavya*). *Yogabhāṣya* II, 16 (*saṃsāra, saṃsārahetu, mokṣa, mokṣopāya*) reflects the "four noble truths" even more clearly.

57. Cf. *Nyāyabhūṣaṇa*, ed. Yogīndrānanda. Benares, 1968, 441ff. Cf. also *NBh* on IV,2,1; for the coordination of *arthapada* and *padārtha* in Udayana's *Pariśuddhi*, see *Nyāyadarśana*, ed. A. Thakur, vol. 1. Darbhanga, 1967, 103f.

58. Cf. Manu VII,43; also XII, 106; Kāmandaki, *Nītisāra* II,7; 11.

59. Cf. P. Hacker, loc. cit. (see above, n.46), 75f.; W. Halbfass, *Studies in Kumārila and Śaṅkara*, 53ff.

60. *Mahābhārata* XII,306,27; 33; XII, 203,20 classifies "various systems of logic" (*nyāyatantrāṇy anekāni*) as "orthodox" sciences. Madhva contrasts the *ānvīkṣikī parā* with the *ānvīkṣikī kutarkā*, cf. *Bhāgavatatātparyanirṇaya* on I,3,11.

61. *Mahābhārata* XII,59,33 gives the fourfold, II,149,31 the threefold list of sciences.

62. Cf. Jayanta, *NM*, 4.

63. See above, §15 (n.53); the commentator Viśvanātha explains in his *Vṛtti* (ed. D.S. Joshi. Poona, 1922, *ASS* 91, 10): *śravaṇād anu paścād īkṣā anvīkṣā*. "Inference" (*anumāna*) may also be explained in an analogous manner; cf., e.g., Madhva, *Anuvyākhyāna* III,3,139: *pratyakṣaśabdānusārād anumā . . .*

64. See above, §14. We may also mention the term *parīkṣaka* ("examiner," "judge") which is used in *NS* I,1,25 and in Maṇḍana's *Vibhramaviveka*, v.1. Both W. Ruben in his German version of *NS* and L. Schmithausen (*Maṇḍanamiśra's Vibhramavivekaḥ*. Vienna, 1965, 53) render this term as "philosopher" ("Philosoph").

65. Cf. Raghūttama, *Bhāṣyacandra* on *NS* I,1,29 (ND, ed. G. Jha, 133): *yogo yuktiḥ tarkaḥ pradhānatayā vidyate yeṣām te yogāḥ*; G. Jha explains in his own commentary

Khadyota that this refers to the Nyāya; cf. also Vācaspati, *Tātparyaṭīkā* on this passage.

66. Cf. Guṇaratna's commentary on Haribhadra's *Ṣaḍdarśanasamuccaya*, v. 13ff.; Guṇaratna observes that the Naiyāyikas are also called *yauga*, "followers of Yoga." The Nyāya is affiliated with the Śaivas, the Vaiśeṣika with the Pāśupatas (ed. M.K. Jain, Calcutta 1969, 76ff.).

67. Cf. Tucci, "Linee di una storia del materialismo Indiano." *Opera Minora* I, Rome 1971, 49-156 (originally published 1923-1929); Dasgupta III, 512-550.

68. Cf. *Mahābhārata* XII, 173, 45ff. (Indra speaking in the shape of a jackal): *aham āsaṃ paṇḍitako haituko vedanindakaḥ/ānvīkṣikīṃ tarkavidyām anurakto nirarthikām*).

69. Cf. *Rāmāyaṇa* II,94,32f. (. . . *buddhim ānvīkṣikīṃ prāpya nirarthaṃ pravadanti te*; this is quoted by Bhāruci in the oldest extant commentary on Manu XII, 106; Bhāruci also uses the terms *tarkābhāsa* and *nyāyābhāsa*).

70. Cf. *Dīghanikāya* II (*Brahmajālasutta*), 20 (*takkī hoti vīmaṅsī*).

71. Gautama XI (=II,2),3: *trayyām ānvīkṣikyāṃ vā-abhivinītaḥ*.

72. Cf. Manu IV,30: *Bhāgavatapurāṇa* XI,18,30.

73. Cf. R.C. Hazra, *Studies in the Upapurāṇas*, vol. 1. Calcutta, 1958, 332ff. (on *Bṛhannāradīyapurāṇa* 38, 46ff.).

74. Cf. Kṛṣṇamiśra, *Prabodhacandrodaya*, ed./trans. S.K. Nambiar, Delhi, 1971, 154: *tarkavidyābhayād anupraviṣṭā*; Vaiśeṣika, Nyāya and Sāṃkhya appear as "pupils" (*śiṣya*) of the *tarkavidyā* (loc. cit., 162).

75. Cf. Keśavamiśra, *Tarkabhāṣā*; Annaṃbhaṭṭa, *Tarkasaṃgraha*; this use is different from *tarka* as one of the sixteen "themes" (*padārtha*).

76. See Śaṅkara on *BS* II,1,6; and in general on Śaṅkara's treatment of "reason" and "revelation": W. Halbfass, *Studies in Kumārila and Śaṅkara*, 27-84. *Maitrī Upaniṣad* VII,8 uses the expression *vṛthātarka*, "frivolous reasoning."

77. See Śaṅkara on *Kaṭha Upaniṣad* I,2,9 (sc. *na-eṣā tarkeṇa matir āpaneyā*): *tārkiko hy anāgamajñaḥ svabuddhiparikalpitaṃ yatkiṃcid eva kalpayati*.

78. On *anvayavyatireka* in the philosophy of Śaṅkara and his successors, cf. W. Halbfass (see above, n.76), 54-67.

79. See Śaṅkara on *BS* II,1,11: *puruṣotprekṣāmātranibandhanās tarkā apratiṣṭhitā bhavanti*; the sūtra itself has the expression *tarkāpratiṣṭhāna*.

80. Cf. *VP* I,34: *yatnena-anumito 'py arthaḥ kuśalair anumātṛbhiḥ/abhiyuktatarair anyair anyathā-eva-upapādyate*. On *śuṣkatarka*, cf. II,484 (ed. W. Rau) and *Vṛtti* on I, 129/137 (ed. K.A. Subramania Iyer; in Rau's edition, the verse appears as I,153): "dry reasoning" as abstract analysis and calculation, "conforming to mere similarities and dissimilarities" (*sādharmyavaidharmyamātrānusārin*); see also *Vṛtti* on I,30 (on *puruṣatarka*, "human reasoning").

81. In his "Presidential Address" in the Philosophy and Religion Section, *PAIOC* 18 (1955), 105, R.D. Karmarkar quotes this statement as evidence for Śaṅkara's "rational" attitude, without noticing that it is an opposing view (*pūrvapakṣa*).

82. The focus on "refutation" (*khaṇḍana*) is indicated by the title of Śrīharṣa's great work *Khaṇḍanakhaṇḍakhādya*. Śaṅkara himself states that in its negative, reductive usage reason may be considered autonomous (*svatantra*), and not dependent on sacred texts (*vākyanirapekṣa*); see his commentary on *BS* II,2,1.

83. On the role of "prejudice" ("Vorurteil") and the "rehabilitation of authority and tradition," see H.-G. Gadamer *Truth and Method*. New York, 1985, 245ff. (German original: *Wahrheit und Methode*. Tübingen, 1960, 261ff.).

84. Cf. G. Oberhammer, "Die Überlieferungsautorität im Hinduismus." *Offenbarung, geistige Realität des Menschen*, ed. G. Oberhammer. Vienna, 1974, 41-92.

85. Cf. R. Garbe, *Die Sāṃkhya-Philosophie. Eine Darstellung des indischen Rationalismus*. Leipzig, 1894 (second ed.: 1917).

86. Cf. T. Vetter, *Erkenntnisprobleme bei Dharmakīrti*. Vienna, 1964, 32f. On the other hand, Kumārila claims that his own school does not rely on faith, but on arguments: *vayam aśraddadhānās tu, ye yuktīḥ prārthayāmahe*. This verse from his lost *Bṛhaṭṭīkā* is quoted by Śāntarakṣita, *Tattvasaṃgraha*, v. 3242 (see also 3600; 3609), and Ratnakīrti, *Sarvajñasiddhi*: cf. G. Bühnemann, *Der allwissende Buddha*. Vienna, 1980, 71.

87. See also Dasgupta III, 512-550; however, Dasgupta's statement that Indian philosophy kept "only a lip-loyalty" to the Veda (*Contemporary Indian Philosophy* I, 253) is inaccurate.

88. See Jayanta, *NM*, 4.

89. In his commentary on the *Mahābhārata*, Nīlakaṇṭha paraphrases *tārkika* by *prāśnika*; cf. J. Dahlmann, *Das Mahābhārata als Epos und Rechtsbuch*. Berlin, 1895, 224.

90. P. Hacker, loc. cit. (see above, n.46), 74, n. 18 (*Kl. Schr.*, 157).

91. P. Hacker, loc. cit., 7 (*Kl. Schr.*, 158).

92. See Medhātithi on Manu VII,43; Nārāyaṇa's interpretation is similar; cf. also Gautama XI,3; Yājñavalkya I,3;10.

93. Cf. Kullūka on Manu VII,43: *ānvīkṣikī* is explained as practically useful *tarkavidyā, ātmavidyā* as *brahmavidyā*. Most modern translators, including G. Bühler, basically follow this inaccurate interpretation.

94. See below, ch.19. Occasional invocations of *yukti*, "reason," do not change the basic picture; for such references to *yukti* see, for instance, *Yogavāsiṣṭha, Mumukṣuvyavahāraprakaraṇa* 18,3; Yāmuna, *Siddhitraya*, ed. Rāmamiśra Śāstrin, Benares, 1910 (*ChSS*), 88 (*vayam aśraddadhānāḥ smo ye yuktiṃ prārthayāmahe*); Madhva, *Anuvyākhyāna* I,1,6 (*yuktimūlatā*). Yāmuna uses the verse from Kumārila's *Bṛhaṭṭīkā* referred to in n.86.

95. *NM*, 4.

96. Cf. Yājñavalkya I,3; Jayanta, *NM*,4 (*nyāya* instead of *tarka*); see also O. Stein, "The Numeral 18." *Poona Orientalist* I (1936), 1-37; especially 6, n.4.

97. Cf. *Nītisāra* II,13: *trayī-idaṃ sarvam ucyate*.

98. Cf. *Kāvyamīmāṃsā*. Baroda, 1916 (second ed.: 1924; GOS), 4. The heterodox

systems appear as *pūrvapakṣa*.

99. P. Hacker (see above, n.46), 81 (*Kl. Schr.*, 164): "Es ist ein bezeichnender Zug der Hindukultur, dass sie zwar den Begriff der Philosophie kannte, aber kein Wort, das ihn ganz und ausschliesslich ausdrückte."

100. Loc. cit. 80 (*Kl. Schr.*, 163). Towards the end of his life, P. Hacker returned to the problems concerning *ānvīkṣikī* and the applicability of the term "philosophy" to Indian thought; cf. *Grundlagen indischer Dichtung und indischen Denkens*, ed. K. Rüping. Vienna, 1985, 39–62; this posthumous publication gives the text of Hacker's last lecture at the University of Münster (summer 1978).

101. See above, ch. 9; also ch. 10, §9.

16. The Adoption of the Concept of Philosophy in Modern Hinduism

1. See D.P. Sinha, *The Educational Policy of the East India Company in Bengal to 1854*. Calcutta, 1964, 299ff. (on the "Educational Despatch" of 1854, which initiated the foundation of English-language universities).

2. English works by S.N. Dasgupta, S. Radhakrishnan, U. Mishra and several other historians of Indian philosophy were translated into Hindi. Among the works on classical Indian philosophy, which include chapters on modern Indian thought, we may mention P.T. Raju, *The Philosophical Traditions of India*. London, 1971; K. Damodaran, *Indian Thought*. New York, 1967.

3. Other philosophical journals are entitled *Darshana International* (Moradabad) and *Ānvīkṣikī* (Benares; both in English). A Bengali Philosophical Association (Baṅgīya Darśana Pariṣad) was founded in 1941.

4. We may recall here the names of Gopīnātha Kavirāja, Udayavīra Śāstrī, Sukhalāla Saṅghavī (Sukhlal Sanghvi) and, in the nineteenth century, Phaṇibhūṣaṇa Tarkavāgīśa.

5. Cf. also Baladeva Upādhyāya, *Bhāratīya dharma aur darśana*. Benares, 1977; *Bauddhadarśanamīmāṃsā*, ib. 1978. On Indian historiography of philosophy in the first half of the twentieth century, see *The National Bibliography of Indian Literature*. 1091–1953, 4 vols. New Delhi, 1962–1974 (ed. Sahitya Akademi); on works in Hindi also: *Hindī-Sāhitya-sāriṇī or Hindi Bibliography*, ed. P. Narain and S.B. Nair, vol. 1. Hoshiarpur, 1971 (up to 1964).

6. Among Divānacanda's other works, cf. his more systematic *Tattvajñāna*. Lucknow, 1968.

7. Lucknow, n.d. (preface dated 1884 śaka, i.e. 1962); on the "nature of Indian philosophy" (*bhāratīya darśana kā svarūpa*) and the meaning of *darśana*, see 1ff.; the great majority of U. Miśra's (Mishra's) works are in English.

8. English trans.: *Indian Philosophy*. Ahmedabad, 1977. On the normative implications of *tattvajñana*, see V. Subramania Iyer, *The Philosophy of Truth or Tattvagnana*. Madras, 1955, 4ff. Among the dictionaries, we may mention: S. Bhaṭṭācārya and D.C. Bhaṭṭācārya, *Bhāratīya darśana koṣa*. Calcutta, 1978ff. (in

Bengali; vol.1: *Nyāya-Vaiśeṣika*).

9. London, fourth ed., 1966.

10. See, for instance, the following contributions: Y. Deshpande, "Are there Sensations?"; B.N. Ray, "G.E. Moore and the Autonomy of Ethics": P.K. Sen, "Variables and Quantifiers."

11. See also K.S. Murty's Hindi anthology on "contemporary Indian philosophy": *Samakālīna bhāratīya darśana*. Faridkot, 1962. More recently, Murty has published: *Indian Philosophy since 1498*. Waltair, 1982; *Philosophy in India: Tradition, Teaching and Research*. Delhi, 1985.

12. Cf. R.N. Upādhyāya, *Gāndhī-darśana*. Brahmanapuri, 1968; R. Sinha, *Gāndhī-darśana-mīmāṃsā*. Patna, 1973.

13. Cf. Y. Masih, *A Critical History of Modern Philosophy*. Patna, third ed., 1967 (Hindi version: Patna, 1972); A.K. Varmā, *Pāścātya darśana*. Patna, third ed., 1970 (in Hindi); T.C. Rāya, *Pāścattya darśaner itihāsa*. Calcutta, 1952 (3 vols., in Bengali). Several histories of philosophy by Western authors were translated into Hindi, for instance those by F. Thilly (*Pāścātya darśana kā itihāsa*. Allabad, 1954) and W. Durant (*Darśana kā kahānī*. Allahabad, 1963).

14. Also Aurobindo, R. Tagore and Dayānanda Sarasvatī did not want to be classified as "philosophers."

15. Cf. e.g, *Ānvīkṣikī* (Benares) 6/1(1973); this issue of the journal is devoted entirely to the topic "Future Course of Indian Philosophy."

16. Cf., e.g., *English Works*, ed. K. Nag and D. Burman. Calcutta, second ed., 1958, vol. 2, 63; 75. "Theology" is more significant with Rammohan than "philosophy."

17. *Lectures in India* I. London, 1901, 325f. (see above, ch. 13, n.37). See also *Keshub Chunder Sen in England*. Calcutta, 1980, 358.

18. *Complete Works* II, 387; I,502ff.

19. II, 72; I, 502ff.

20. I, 504; cf. II, 280.

21. I, 72 (*Karmayoga*, ch. 5).

22. IV, 374; Vivekananda adds that all fully developed religions contain these parts. See also II, 382.

23. VII, 36.

24. See *Contemporary Indian Philosophy*, ed. S. Radhakrishnan and J. Muirhead. London, fourth ed., 1966, 59. Cf. also Vivekananda VIII, 15: religion as "practical philosophy."

25. Abhedananda, loc. cit., 59; 57.

26. "The Value of Philosophical Thought." *Arya*, July 15, 1918, 764f.; quoted in *A Source Book in Indian Philosophy* (see below, n.64), 578.

27. See R.C. Trivedi, "Sri Aurobindo's Conception of Philosophy." *Proceedings of the Indian Philosophical Congress* 39/40 (1965/66), 111–123; especially 122.

28. Loc. cit., 122.

29. On B.N. Seal, see below, Appendix III.

30. *Contemporary Indian Philosophy* (see above, n.24), 315.

31. Cf. H. Haldar, *Neo-Hegelianism*. London, 1928.

32. *Contemporary Indian Philosophy*, 105. His presentation is entitled "The Concept of Philosophy."

33. See also N.V. Banerjee, *The Concept of Philosophy*. Calcutta, 1968, 9.

34. "The Concept of the Absolute." *Search for the Absolute in Neo-Vedānta*, ed. G.B. Burch. Honolulu, 1976, 175 (also in: K.C. Bhattacharya, *Studies in Philosophy*, 2 vols. Calcutta, 1956–1958).

35. *Contemporary Indian Philosophy* (see above, n.32), 116.

36. Loc. cit., 113.

37. "The Concept of the Absolute" (see above, n.34), 179, §10; instead of "freedom," Bhattacharya also presents "reality" as the correlate of volition.

38. *Comtemporary Indian Philosophy*, 123.

39. Cf. P. Schreiner, "Concepts of Philosophy: K.C. Bhattacharyya and G.R. Malkani." *WZKS* 21 (1977), 239–256; ib., 254f. (quoting *Philosophical Quarterly* 7, 404).

40. P. Schreiner, loc. cit., 248.

41. Cf. K.S. Murty, *Philosophy in India*. Delhi, 1985, 157ff. (originally presented between 1928 and 1930; published in: *Visva-Bharati Journal* 20, 1954, 103–114; not included in Bhattacharya's *Studies in Philosophy*. Calcutta, 1956–1958). On Bhattacharya's hermeneutical situation, see also J.L. Mehta, "The Problem of Philosophical Reconception in the Thought of K.C. Bhattacharya." *PEW* 243 (1974), 59–70 (also in: *India and the West*, 160–178).

42. P. Schreiner (see above, n. 39), 256.

43. *Contemporary Indian Philosophy*, 409f.

44. Loc. cit., 419.

45. "The Concept of Philosophy." *Philosophical Quarterly* (Amalner) 38 (1965/66), 75–82; ib., 82.

46. *The Concept of Philosophy*, ed. T.R.V. Murti. Benares, 1968, 48.

47. *Contemporary Indian Philosophy*, 458; cf. also 471: "Only a spiritual philosophy can serve as the basis of a world-culture."

48. *Alternative Standpoints in Philosophy*, 363.

49. *The Fundamentals of K.C. Bhattacharyya's Philosophy*. Calcutta, 1975.

50. "What is Philosophy?" *Proceedings of the Indian Philosophical Congress 31 (1956), 3*–16; ib., 9.

51. V. Subrahmanya Iyer in: *Contemporary Indian Philosophy*, 596; 617; 619.

52. Cf. the survey given by P. Schreiner (see above, n.39), 240ff.

53. Cf. e.g, S.C. Chatterjee, "The Basis of World Philosophy." *Proceedings of the Indian Philosophical Congress* 28 (1953), 3-21; id., "On Philosophical Synthesis."

PEW 10 (1960/61), 99-103. For critical comments, see G.R. Malkani, "Philosophical Synthesis." *Philosophical Quarterly* (Amalner) 35 (1962/63), 79-87.

54. N.G. Damle in: *Contemporary Indian Philosophy*, 179.

55. S. Chakravarti in: *Current Trends in Indian Philosophy*, ed. K.S. Murty and K.R. Rao. Waltair, 1972, 67.

56. T.M.P. Mahadevan, "Social, Ethical and Spiritual Values in Indian Philosophy." *The Indian Mind*, ed. Ch.A. Moore. Honolulu, 1967, 152.

57. P.T. Raju, *Introduction to Comparative Philosophy*. Carbondale, second ed., 1970, 6; and as quoted in: K. Damodaran, *Indian Thought*. New York, 1967, 490.

58. V.S. Krishna in: *Current Trends in Indian Philosophy* (see above n.55). 5.

59. *Indian Philosophy* I. London, seventh ed., 1962, 24.

60. *Contemporary Indian Philosophy*, 475.

61. *An Idealist View of Life*. London, fifth ed., 1957, 84.

62. *The Hindu View of Life*, 16.

63. *The Brahma Sūtra*. London, 1960, 180.

64. *A Source Book in Indian Philosophy*, ed. S. Radhakrishnan and Ch.A. Moore. Princeton, 1957, XXXI. Cf. also P.D. Shastri, *The Essentials of Eastern Philosophy*, New York, 1928, 39: "internationalism in politics" is based upon "internationalism in philosophy."

65. *The Brahma Sūtra*. 10.

66. See, for instance, S. Joshi, *The Message of Śaṅkara*. Allahabad, 1968, 161: "Radhakrishnan's conception of one world-philosophy ends in co-existence, equality, fellowship and brotherhood."

67. Cf. P. Schreiner, "The Indianness of Modern Indian Philosophy as a Historical and Philosophical Problem." *PEW* 28 (1978), 21-37 (on S. Radhakrishnan and B.K. Mallik). On the question of the "Indianness" of Indian philosophy, see also *Indian Philosophy: Past and Future*, ed. S.S. Rama Rao Pappu and R. Puligandla, Delhi, 1983, Part 1; and the thoughtful observations by J.N. Mohanty ("Indian Philosophy between Tradition and Modernity") in the same volume, 233-252; especially 233: "One who is asking 'What is Indian Philosophy? What is Indian about it?' has already situated himself outside of that tradition which we call 'Indian.' None of the philosophers who shaped that tradition, and with whose writings we are acquainted, ever asked such a question. They lived and thought within that tradition, which today we are, by the very questions we are asking, thematizing. In that very act of thematizing, a rupture has taken place."

68. *The Brahma Sūtra*, 20; Radhakrishnan adds somewhat casually: "The scholastic developments are also called *darśanas*."

69. *The Hindu View of Life*, 13.

70. *Indian Philosophy* I, London, seventh ed., 1962, 44; on p.43, Radhakrishnan also refers to the connotations "critical expositions, logical surveys, or systems."

71. Cf. *The Brahma Sūtra*, 111ff.

72. Already Vivekananda states: "Philosophy in Sanskrit means 'clear vision'. . ." (*Complete Works* VIII, 15). M. Hiriyanna's association of *darśana* with the meaning "philosophic opinion" (*Outlines of Indian Philosophy*. London, sixth ed., 1967, 182f.) is somewhat unusual among Indian authors.

73. P.S. Sastri, *Indian Idealism* I. Delhi, 1975, 220.

74. S.C. Chatterjee and D.M. Datta, *An Introduction to Indian Philosophy*. Calcutta, seventh ed., 1968, 2.

75. R. Chaudhuri, *Doctrine of Śrīkaṇṭha*. Calcutta, 1962, 102.

76. U. *Mishra, History of Indian Philosophy* I. Allahabad, 1957, 5 (referring to *Bṛhadāraṇyaka Upaniṣad* II,4,5; identical with IV,5,6).

77. C. Sharma, *A Critical Survey of Indian Philosophy*. Delhi, second ed., 1964, 13.

78. Y. Pandey, "The Future Course of Indian Philosophy." *Ānvīkṣikī* 6 (1973), 124–133; ib., 125.

79. P.N. Rao, "The Spirit of Indian Philosophy." *Philosophy, Religion and the Coming World Civilization. Essays in Honor of W.E. Hocking*, ed. L.S. Rouner. The Hague, 1966, 213–222; ib., 213.

80. "The philosopher or seer . . ." (G.R. Malkani in: *The Concept of Philosophy*, ed. T.R.V. Murti. Benares, 1968, 48).

81. Cf. e.g., *Bhāratīya darśana*, ed. N.K. Devarāja. Lucknow, 1975, 16 (on *anubhava*); D.S. Śāstrī, *Bhāratīya darśanaśāstra: Nyāya-vaiśeṣika*. Benares, 1953, 29f. (emphasizing the implication of "seeing," *dekhanā*, against *mīmāṃsā* and *philāsaphī*).

82. Cf. *Bhāratīya darśana*. Benares, seventh ed., 1966, 3f. The term *vicāraśāstra* already occurs in the doxography *Sarvamatasaṃgraha*, ed. T. Gaṇapati Śāstrī. Trivandrum, 1918, 4. See also S.B. Varmā, *Śrī aravinda vicāradarśana*. Delhi 1974.

83. Cf. Śaṅkara, on *BS* II,1,1ff.; see also K.S. Murty, *Revelation and Reason in Advaita Vedānta*. New York, 1959, 44ff.

84. See below, Appendix I.

85. The Mīmāṃsā teachers also reject the idea of "yogic perception" (*yogi-pratyakṣa*).

86. See below, Appendix I.

87. *Nirukta* II,11: *ṛṣir darśanāt* (referring to Aupamanyava). See also J. Gonda, *The Vision of the Vedic Poets*. The Hague, 1963, 18ff.; P.V. Kane, *History of Sanskrit Poetics*. Delhi, fourth ed., 221 (on *darśana* and poetry).

88. Cf. *Chandodarśanam* by Ṛṣi Daivarāta. With a comm. by Kāvyakaṇṭha Gaṇapatimuni, Bombay, 1968.

89. See below, Appendix I.

90. Cf. P.J. Marshall, 130.

91. Cf. *Vyacarana seu locupletissima samscrdamicae linguae institutio*. Rome, 1804, XVII; 227.

92. Cf. *Account of the Writings, Religion and Manners of the Hindoos* I. Serampore, 1811, 329ff.; also 329, n.: "Durshunu signifies the act of seeing. . . ."

93. Cf. *Miscellaneous Esssays* I, London 1837, 295; 329.

94. A. Bharati, *A Functional Analysis of Indian Thought and its Social Margins*. Benares, 1964, 105ff., suggests that Max Müller was responsible for the association between *darśana* and "philosophy"; this is obviously incorrect.

95. Cf. also *PW*: "Anschauungsweise," "Lehre," "Doktrin."

96. Here, we also find the terms *paramārthavidyā, śrutividyā, dharmavidyā*.

97. Reprint Gauhati, 1971.

98. Bombay, second ed., 1893; and several reprints.

99. Rammohan Roy and his immediate successors used the word *darśana* in the traditional sense. One of the most important Indian philosophical publications of its time appeared under the title *Tattvavidyā* (4 vols., Calcutta 1866-1869; in Bengali). Its author was Dvijendranātha Ṭhākura (Tagore; the eldest son of Debendranath).

100. Cf. *Racanāvalī* II, 217ff. The idea that philosophy in India was a "mere means" (*sādhanamātra*) has often been emphasized; cf., e.g., H.P. Sinha, *Bhāratīya darśana kī rūparekhā*. Calcutta, 1963, 4ff.

101. Cf. *Racanāvalī* II, 221,n.: *Comter "Positive Philosophy" nāmaka darśana kī rūparekhā*. Calcutta, 1963, 4ff.

102. Cf. S.S. Das, *Hindi Scientific Glossary*. Benares, 1906, XVIII. On philosophical terminology, cf. 243-359.

103. Nagpur, sixth ed., 1966; in 1944, Raghuvira began publishing special glossaries for scientific disciplines. Vīra Rājendra Ṛṣi, *Rūsīhindī śabdakośa (Russko-chindi slovar')*, New Delhi, 1957, gives only *darśanaśāstra*.

104. Ed. R.C. Pathak, Benares, eleventh ed., 1963; C. Bulcke, *English-Hindi Dictionary*, gives *tattvajñāna* together with *darśana*.

105. Among other works, S.N. Dasgupta's *History of Indian Philosophy* appeared in an Urdu translation.

106. In addition, compounds with *tattva* (*tattuva*) have been used.

107. Cf. G.K. Piovesana, *Contemporary Japanese Philosophical Thought*. New York, 1969, especially 1-17; also 249ff.; Th.R. Havens, *Nishi Amane*. Princeton, 1970.

108. Cf., e.g, *Hindī-viśvakośa*, vol.6. Benares, 1966, art. *darśana*. "Science" is usually rendered as *vijñāna*.

109. In addition, *pāramārthikaśāstra* appears in the sense of "metaphysics"; for "philosophy," Govinda Pillai uses *tattvaśāstra* and *tattvajñāna*.

110. In addition to its central term *tattvajñāna*, D.D. Vāḍekara's *Tattvajñāna mahākoṣa* (3 vols., Poona 1974) contains numerous Marathi equivalents for specific philosophical disciplines and methods, for instance *viśleṣaka tattvajñāna* ("analytical philosophy"), *rājakīya tattvajñāna* ("political philosophy"), *itihāsa-tattvajñāna* ("philosophy of history"), *dharma-tattvajñāna* ("philosophy of religion"), *vijñāna-tattvajñāna* ("philosophy of science"), *tāttvika anubhavasattāvāda* ("logical positivism"). *Philosophy in the Fifteen Modern Indian Languages*, ed. V.M. Bedekar, Poona, 1979, is based upon articles written for *Tattvajñāna mahākoṣa*.

111. Cf. *Comparative Studies in Vaishnavism and Christianity*. Calcutta, 1899, V; VIIff.

112. Loc. cit., 83; on Rammohan, cf. B.N. Seal, *Rammohan Roy - the Universal Man*. Calcutta, n.d. (ca. 1933).

113. See below, Appendix III. On Seal's last work, *The Quest Eternal*, London, 1936 (a work on the unity and universality of mankind), see D. Kopf, *The Brahmo Samaj and the Shaping of the Modern Indian Mind*. Princeton, 1979, 64ff. Kopf's statements on the *Comparative Studies in Vaishnavism and Christianity*, which he treats as if it were an unpublished manuscript, are unreliable and confusing.

114. Cf. e.g., P.T. Raju, *Thought and Reality*. London, 1937; R.K. Tripathi, *Spinoza in the Light of Vedānta*. Benares, 1957; and the symptomatic formula of S.L. Pandeya, *New Allahabad Philosophy (Navyam prayāgadarśanam)*. Allahabad, second ed., 1971, v.53: "Kant in the eyes of Śaṅkara and Śaṅkara in the eyes of Kant . . .—*śaṅkarābhimukhaḥ kāṇṭaḥ, kāṇṭābhimukhaḥ śaṅkaraḥ* . . ." Among the most recent additions to this genre, see, for instance, P. Parameswaran, *Marx and Vivekananda*. New Delhi, 1987.

115. S.N.L. Shrivastava, *Śaṅkara and Bradley*. Delhi, 1968, 246; 253f.

116. Cf. loc. cit., 82: "Śaṅkara's concept of the Ātman . . . fully meets Bradley's demands."

117. *The Chief Currents of Contemporary Philosophy*. Calcutta, 1950, 519.

118. "Modern Indian Philosophy: Its Needs and Its Social Role." *Proceedings of the Indian Philosophical Congress* 27 (1952), 3f.

119. K.M. Panikkar, *The Foundations of New India*. London, 1963, 135.

120. Cf. K.S. Murty, *Philosophy in India: Traditions, Teaching and Research*. Delhi, 1985, 148–156 (observations by Kalidas Bhattacharya and Suresh Chandra).

17. *Dharma* in the Self-Understanding of Traditional Hinduism

1. See, for instance, Maheśvarānandagiri, *Cāturvarṇyabhāratasamīkṣā* II, Bombay, 1968, 6: *santi dharmāḥ haindava-bauddha-kraistava-māhammadanāmabhir abhidhīyamānāḥ*.

2. See above, ch. 16, n.5; also, for instance, V. Gairolā, *Bhāratīya darśana*. Allahabad, 1962, 16ff.

3. Cf. "Glossary of Technical Terms" appended to the *Constitution of India*. New Delhi, 1950.

4. For details concerning these and other dictionaries, see above, ch. 16, §21ff.

5. P. Hacker, *Kl. Schr.*, 589.

6. S. Radhakrishnan, *Indian Philosophy* I. London, seventh ed., 1962, 52.

7. See above, ch. 11.

8. *Pāli dhamma, vornehmlich in der kanonischen Literatur*. Abh. Bayer. Ak. Wiss. 31/1. Munich, 1920. This was supplemented by J.R. Carter, *Dhamma: Western Academic and Sinhalese Buddhist Interpretations*. Tokyo, 1978.

9. See especially P. Hacker, "Dharma im Hinduismus." *ZMR* 49 (1965), 93-106 (*Kl. Schr.*, 496-509) *The Concept of Duty in South Asia*, ed. W.D. O'Flaherty and J.D.M. Derrett. New Delhi, 1978, contains contributions of uneven quality. G.H. Mees, *Dharma and Society*. The Hague, 1935 (reprint Delhi, 1980) and A.B. Creel, *Dharma in Hindu Ethics*, Calcutta, 1977, have to be used with caution.

10. G.J. Larson, "The trimūrti of dharma in Indian Thought: Paradox or Contradiction?" *PEW* 22 (1972), 145-153; ib., 146.

11. Gonda I, 289f. See also H. Zimmer, *Altindisches Leben*. Berlin, 1879. 180f.

12. Gonda I, 291.

13. Gonda I, 292: "Dharma, Karman und Saṃsāra bilden *einen* Komplex, *ein* weltanschauliches System."

14. F. Edgerton, "Dominant Ideas in the Formation of Indian Culture." *JAOS* 62 (1942), 151-156; ib., 151.

15. R. Lingat, *Les sources du droit dans le système traditionnel de l'Inde*. Paris, 1967, 17 (trans. J.D.M. Derrett, *The Classical Law of India*. Berkeley, 1973, 3:

Dharma is a concept difficult to define because it disowns—or transcends—distinctions that seem essential to us, and because it is based upon beliefs that are as strange to us as they are familiar to the Hindus. . . . The most general sense is provided by its root, *dhṛ*, which signifies the action of maintaining, sustaining, or supporting and which has produced *fre* in Latin (*fretus*, depending upon, daring to) and *fir* (*firmus*, strong in the physical and moral senses, whence solid, hard, durable). *Dharma* is what is firm and durable, what sustains and maintains, what hinders fainting and falling.—Applied to the universe, *dharma* signifies the eternal laws which maintain the world.).

16. R. Lingat, loc. cit., 18 (trans. J.D.M. Derrett, 3f.:

. . . the concept of *dharma* is widened: it envelops the moral world as much as the physical; and the norm of ritual becomes a norm of conduct . . . From there it is an easy step to the sense which *dharma* most frequently bears in our texts. This is the totality of duties which bears upon the individual according to his status (*varṇa*) and the stage of life (*āśrama*) at which he stands, the totality of rules to which he must conform his conduct if he does not want to 'fall' . . .).

17. P. Hacker (see above, n.9), 99f. (*Kl. Schr.*, 502f.).

18. P. Hacker, *Kl.Schr.*, 508f . . .

Als Ausdruck des Selbstbewusstseins des Aryatums ist dann der Dharmabegriff, mit manchen Anpassungen an fortgeschrittene Auffassungen, aber doch im Kern wenig verändert, durch die Zeiten erhalten geblieben. Er war, in all seiner Unbestimmtheit und in seinem Empirismus, das einzige, was die Vielgestaltigkeit des Hindutums irgendwie zusammenhielt.

19. "Der Dharmabegriff des Neuhinduismus," *ZMR* 42 (1958), 1-15 (*Kl.Schr.*, 510-524; ib., 511f.:

Dharma ist zunächst das *religiöse Gebot* oder die *religiöse Ordnung*. Diese umfasst aber nicht nur das Kultische und das Moralische, sondern darüber hinaus die gesamte Rechtsordnung sowie auch eine Fülle von herkömmlichen Sitten und Gebräuchen . . . Zweitens ist dharma auch die *Ordnung im Vollzug*. Alles der Dharma-Ordnung entsprechende Tun ist dharma. Drittens ist dharma auch die *Ordnung nach dem Vollzug*, d.h. das, was man auch 'gutes Karman' nennt. . .).

20. Already Ch. Wilkins uses many of these terms in his pioneering translation of the *Bhagavadgītā* (London, 1785). As the earliest attempt to translate *dharma* into a European language, ευσεβεια ("piety," "reverence towards gods or elders") appears in the Greek-Aramaic Aśoka inscription of Kandahar (third century B.C.).

21. Cf. Kane I, 1ff.; H. Grassmann, *Wörterbuch zum Rig-Veda*, Wiesbaden, third ed., 1965, 659f.; P. Horsch, "Vom Schöpfungsmythos zum Weltgesetz." *Asiatische Studien* 21 (1967), 31–61; ib., 36.

22. Cf. *Ṛgveda* I, 164,43; 50; X,90,16; also III,17,1.

23. Cf. *Chāndogya Upaniṣad* II,23,1; also *Taittirīya Upaniṣad* I,11,1: *satyaṃ vada, dharmaṃ cara.*

24. The phrases *dharman ṛtasya* and *ṛtasya dharman* (*Ṛgveda* IX,7,1; IX,110,4) do not support such attempts, since they presuppose the distinction between *ṛta* and its "upholding." The connection between *ṛta* and *dharman* and *satyadharman* in V,63,1 and 7 is more significant, though problematic as to its implications. H. Lüders, *Varuṇa* II: *Varuṇa und das Ṛta*, has only one explicit reference to the connection of *ṛta* and *dharma* (on *Bṛhadāraṇyaka Upaniṣad* I,4,14). A close connection or even identity has been postulated by many Neo-Hindus.

25. Cf. *Gītā* I,40; see also XVIII,66 (*sarvadharmān parityajya*); and Manu VII,98. Even the oldest known usages of *dharma* in conjunction with *varṇāśrama* are in the plural; cf. *Viṣṇusmṛti* I,4; also Yājñavalkya I,1.

26. S. Schayer, "Die Struktur der magischen Weltanschauung nach dem Atharva-Veda und den Brāhmaṇa-Texten." *Zeitschrift für Buddhismus* 6/2 (1925). 259–299; ib., 283.

27. Cf. Manu XII, 99: *bibharti sarvabhūtāni vedaśāstraṃ sanātanam*; also VIII,15; III,75ff.

28. Cf. *Über das Wesen der altindischen Rechtsschriften*. Leipzig, 1927, 1ff.

29. Cf. *Taittirīya Āraṇyaka*, ed. Bābāśāstrī Phaḍke, vol.2. Poona, 1898 (*ASS*), 895. the passage is also included in *Mahānārāyaṇa Upaniṣad* XX,14; XXI,2; XXII,1. See also J. Gonda, "Pratiṣṭhā." *Selected Studies*, vol.2. Leiden, 1975, 338–374.

30. Loc. cit. (ed. B. Phaḍke): *śrutismṛtipratipāditavāpīkūpataṭākādinirmāṇarūpo dharmo viśvasya jagataḥ sarvasya prāṇijātasya pratiṣṭhā. . .*; for similar statements, see 892 (Sāyaṇa on X,78).

31. See above, §5. The interpretation of *dharma, dhārayati, dhṛta* in *Śatapatha Brāhmaṇa* XIV,2,2.29f. also requires caution.

32. Cf. *Mahābhārata* VII,49,49f.; XII,10,10f.; the misleading French translation for which R. Lingat (see above, n.15), 17,n.2 gives the reference "Śāntip.,109.59" is obviously based upon XII, 110,11 (crit. ed.).

33. *Ṛgveda* VIII,41,10; cf. P. Horsch (see above, n.21), 32ff.

34. Cf. also *Atharvaveda* XII,1,17: *dhruvāṃ bhūmiṃ pṛthivīṃ dharmaṇā dhṛtām*; and P. Horsch, loc. cit., 36f.

35. Cf. P. Horsch, loc. cit., 38f.; and especially *Ṛgveda* II,13,7: *dharmaṇā . . . vy . . . adhārayaḥ*. In a remarkable passage, *Bṛhadāraṇyaka Upaniṣad* II,8,9 describes

the phenomena of this world as being "held apart" (*vidhṛta*) "under the rule of the imperishable" *(akṣarasya śāsane)*.

36. Cf. *Ṛgveda* I,164,50; X,90,16.

37. Cf. P. Horsch, loc. cit., 39f.

38. Cf. P. Horsch, loc. cit., 41f.

39. Cf. *Atharvaveda* XVIII,3,1; a peculiar passage is XII,1,45, which characterizes the earth as having various languages and laws or customs (*vivācas; nānādharman*); cf. also P. Horsch, loc. cit., 44f.; 49f.

40. *Mahābhārata* XII,110,11.

41. Cf. Manu II,75ff.; VIII,15.

42. Madhva on *Kaṭha Upaniṣad* (introduction).

43. *Dharma* is frequently associated with *svabhāvadhāraṇa* or *svalakṣaṇadhāraṇa*, "upholding one's own nature" or "character"; cf. e.g., Vasubandhu, *Abhidharmakośabhāṣya* I,2; Candrakīrti, *Prasannapadā* on *Madhyamakakārikā* XVII,1; see also O. Rosenberg, *Die Probleme der buddhistischen Philosophie*. Heidelberg, 1924, 80ff.

44. Cf. XIV,7,3,15 (= *Bṛhadāraṇyaka Upaniṣad* IV,5,14): *anucchittidharman*, "having the property of non-destruction" (or: "not being subject to the condition of being destroyed").

45. Cf. Maheśacandra Nyāyaratna, *Brief Notes on the Modern Nyāya System*. Calcutta, n.d. (in Sanskrit), 8: *dhriyate tiṣṭhati varttate yaḥ sa dharmaḥ*.

46. See, for instance, *MS* II,1,41; II,3,23; III,4,20; III,7,51; VIII,1,35; IX,1,26; IX,4,41; X,5,11; cf. F. X. Clooney, "The Concept of Dharma in the Mīmāṃsā Sūtras of Jaimini." *Prof. Kuppuswami Sastri Birth-Centenary Commemoration Volume*, part 2. Madras, 1985, 175–187.

47. Cf. H. Losch, *Rājadharma*. Bonn, 1959; M. Jauhari, *Politics and Ethics in Ancient India*. Benares, 1968, 42ff. See also F. Wilhelm, "The Concept of Dharma in Artha and Kāma Literature." *The Concept of Duty in South Asia* (see above, n.9), 66–79.

48. On "righteousness" and "correctness" ("Richtigkeit"), cf. J.J. Meyer, *Über das Wesen der altindischen Rechtsschriften*. Leipzig, 1927, 2ff.

49. Cf. Bhartṛhari, *VP* I,29ff. (with *Vṛtti*); Kumārila, *TV* on *MS* 1,3,25ff.; especially 27. G.J. Larson (see above, n.10) notices the analogy between *dharma* and linguistic correctness, but overlooks the specifically Indian implications of this relationship. In grammar as well as in *dharma*, specific rules and exceptions (*apavāda*) have a validity which is superior to that of the general rules (*utsarga*).

50. See below, §22f.; *VP* I, 158 (ed. W. Rau) characterizes grammar as "dealing with the knowledge of correctness" (*sādhutvajñānaviṣaya*), and in his own *Vṛtti* on this verse (= I,141/149 according to K.A. Subramania Iyer's edition), Bhartṛhari explicates the analogy between the traditions of *dharma* and grammar. Cf. also K.A. Subramania Iyer, "Bhartṛhari on Apabhraṃśa." *Vishveshvaranand Indological Journal* 2 (1964), 242–246.

51. Cf. Manu X, 81ff.

52. Cf. R. Lingat, "Dharma et temps." *JA* 249 (1961), 487–495; also *Les sources du droit* (see above, n.15), 211ff. (trans. J.D.M. Derrett, 189ff.; on "prohibitions proper to the kali age").

53. Cf. Manu I,118; VII,203; VIII,41; Vasiṣṭha I,17; see also A. Wezler, "Dharma und Deśadharma." *Regionale Tradition in Südasien*, ed. H. Kulke and D. Rothermund. Wiesbaden, 1985, 1-21.

54. Cf. Manu IX,66; *godharma* is used in the pejorative sense of "indecent sexual behavior" (cf. the Sanskrit dictionary of V.S. Apte).

55. Cf. N. Mironov, *Die Dharmaparīkṣā des Amitagati*. Leipzig, 1903; also A.N. Upadhye, "Hariṣena's Dharmaparīkṣā in Apabhraṃśa." *ABORI* 23 (2941), 592-608.

56. Ed./trans. S.K. Nambiar, Delhi, 1971, 72f.; 76 (*kīliso tumha dhammo*); 78; Jayanta, *NM*,243 uses the term *vedadharma*; see also Guṇaratna on Haribhadra, *Ṣaḍdarśanasamuccaya*, v.86.

57. Cf. *Mahābhārata* XII, 336; especially v.20: *dharma eṣa sanātanaḥ*.

58. See above, ch. 11, §28; for *kauladharma* etc., see *Kulārṇavatantra*. I,119; II,72; 89ff.; *Mahānirvāṇatantra*, XIV, 190ff. In 1639, Dāmodarasvāmin wrote a drama *Pākhaṇḍadharmanāṭaka* against the Vallabha sect in Gujarat. On the *mahārāṣṭradharma*, which was first articulated by Sarasvatī Gaṅgādhara around 1540, see S.G. Tulpule, *Classical Marāṭhī Literature*. Wiesbaden, 1979, 395; G.S. Sardesai, *Main Currents of Maratha History*. Bombay, second ed., 1949, 14ff.; and A. Wezler (see above, n.53), 17.

59. *Vāyupurāṇa*, ed. H.N. Apte. Poona, 1905 (*ASS*), CIV, 11-17, especially 16.

60. See above, §4.

61. Cf. Śaṅkara on *Bhagavadgītā* XVIII,66; Madhva explains *dharmatyāga* as *phalatyāga*.

62. Cf. J.A.B. van Buitenen, "Dharma and Mokṣa." *PEW* 7 (1956/57), 33–40; D.H.H. Ingalls, "Dharma and Mokṣa." Loc. cit., 41–48.

63. Cf. Śaṅkara's introduction to his *Gītā* commentary; cf. also Manu XII,88f.; Nāgārjuna, *Ratnāvalī* I,21; 24f. (*naiḥśreyasa dharma*, etc.); *VS* I,1,2.

64. Cf. Manu II,6; 12; Yājñavalkya I.1.1f.; *Mahābhārata* III,198,78 gives three sources (*veda, smṛti, śiṣṭācīrṇa*); cf. also XIII,129,5 (*trayo dharmāḥ sanātanāḥ*).

65. P. Hacker, *Kl. Schr.*, 501 (see above, n.9); see also Bhartṛhari, *VP* I,31 (on *dharma* and *lokaprasiddhatva*, "traditional recognition").

66. See above, §6 (n.17).

67. On the absence of "natural law" in traditional Hinduism, see M. Weber, *Gesammelte Aufsätze zur Religionssoziologie* II: *Hinduismus und Buddhismus*. Tübingen, fifth ed., 1972, 141ff.

68. "The Reexamination of Dharma in Hindu Ethics." *PEW* 25 (1975), 161-173; ib., 162.

69. Cf. Jayanta, *NM* 255: *saṃskāro nṛguṇaḥ sthāyī*; see also Kumārila, *ŚV* II,195f.

70. See above, §6. The precise meaning of *dharma* in VS I,1,1 has been debated by the commentators.

71. Cf. Uddyotakara, *NV* on *NS* I,1,7; Vyomaśiva, *Vyomavatī*. Benares, 1931 (*ChSS*), 639f. P. Hacker's observations on the "substantialism" in the Hindu notion of *dharma* have to be modified.

72. Cf. *PB*, 272: *tasya tu sādhanāni śrutismṛtivihitāni varṇāśramiṇāṃ sāmānyaviśeṣabhāvena-avasthitāni dravyaguṇakarmāṇi*. The Śaivite Praśastapāda sees the Lord (*īśvara*) as the ultimate source of the Vedic norms. See also Manu X,63: five rules for all castes; VI,92: ten rules for the *ārya*.

73. Cf. *MS* I,1,2; on the "rationality" and justifiability of the *vedamūlatva* principle, see Medātithi on Manu II,6 (ed. J.H. Dave, 163).

74. Cf. *TV*, 128: *vede 'pi hi bahūny eva dṛṣṭārthagandhaspṛṣṭāni vidhīyante iti na tāvatā vedamūlatvābhāvaḥ*; the basic principle is that the Veda teaches "what is inaccessible to other means of knowledge" (*ananyapramāṇavedya*; see, for instance, Medhātithi, loc. cit., 164).

75. See above, ch. 11, n.61.

76. Cf. W. Halbfass, "Karma, apūrva, and 'Natural' Causes." *Karma and Rebirth in Classical Indian Traditions*, ed. W.D. O'Flaherty. Berkeley, 1980, 268–302.

77. Cf. Rāmānujācārya, *Tantrarahasya*, ed. R. Shama Shastri. Baroda, second ed., 1956 (GOS), 57; 59.

78. Cf. *Vidhiviveka with Nyāyakaṇikā by Vācaspatimiśra*, ed. M.L. Goswami. Benares, 1978.

79. Cf. *TV*, 127 (on 1,3,7): *pratyakṣavedavihitadharmakriyayā hi labdhaśiṣṭatvavyapadeśāḥ*; Mādhava Sarasvatī, *Sarvadarśanakaumudī*, ed. K. Sāmbaśiva Śāstrī, Trivandrum, 1938, 3, simply defines the *śiṣṭa* as somebody "who admits the authority of the Veda" (*vedaprāmāṇyābhyupagantā śiṣṭaḥ*).

80. Jayanta is more liberal in his philosophical drama *Āgamaḍambara*.

81. Cf. Jayanta, *NM*, 243, on "recognition by the majority" (*mahājanaprasiddhi*); he notes that "the whole population follows mostly the Vedic dharma" (*vedadharmānuvārtī ca prāyeṇa sakalo janaḥ*).

82. Cf. Venkaṭanātha, *Nyāyapariśuddhi*, Benares, 1918 (*ChSS*: a Śrīvaiṣṇava work), *384*: . . . *bahujanaparigrahādimātrasya mahājanaparigrahatvena-avivakṣitatvāt*.

83. Cf. *TV*, 125 (on 1,3,7).

84. *TV*, 128f.; see above, §18.

85. Medhātithi on Manu II,6 (ed. J.H. Dave, 175f.).

86. Cf. *VP* I,5; *Vṛtti* on I,30; see also K.A. Subramania Iyer, *Bhartṛhari*. Poona, 1969, 95ff.

87. *The Nirukta of Yāska*, ed. with Durga's comm. by H.M. Bhadkamkar, vol. 1. Bombay, 1918, 146: *tad etat karmaṇaḥ phalavipariṇāmadarśanam aupacārikyā vṛttyā-uktaṃ sākṣātkṛtadharmāṇa iti; na hi dharmasya darśanam asti.*

88. Cf. Medhātithi on Manu II,6 (ed. J.H. Dave, 168).

89. Cf. *TV*, 127ff. (on 1,3,7); on the *dhārmika*: *ŚV* II (*codanā*), 192ff. According to Bhartṛhari, competence in the grammar of the Sanskrit language characterizes the *śiṣṭa*; cf. *Vṛtti* on *VP* I,29; this is also important for Kumārila; cf. his references to the linguistic deficiencies of the Buddhists, *TV*, 164, (on 1,3,12).

90. Cf. *TV*, 128: . . . *sa eva kevalo dharmaḥ, na-itaraḥ prāṇimātragaḥ*.

91. *ŚV* V/1 (*autpattika*), 7; also V/1, 1ff. (on *anugraha* and *pīḍā*); II (*codanā*), 243ff.; on the *saṃsāramocaka*, see W. Halbfass, *Studies in Kumārila and Śaṅkara*, 10–15; 23.

92. Cf. *TV*, 112 ff. (on 1,3,4); especially 114: on the Buddha's transgression of his caste duties (*svadharmātikrama*).

93. Cf. *Mahābhārata* I,11,12; III,198,69; XII,10,10f.; XIII,116,1-25; 117,37; in general also XII,237,18f; on the formula *ahiṃsālakṣaṇo dharmaḥ*, see XII,117,13; XIV,43,19. See also above, n.32; on the "orthodox" response, cf. W. Halbfass (see above, n.91), 1-26

94. Cf. *Mahābhārata* V,39,57; also *Vikramacarita* XIII,2 (*Vetālapañcaviṃśatikā* X,2): *śrūyatāṃ dharmasarvasvaṃ yad uktaṃ śāstrakoṭibhiḥ/paropakāraḥ puṇyāya, pāpāya parapīḍanam*. For further references, see L. Sternbach, "Similar Thoughts in the Mahābhārata, the Literature of 'Greater India' and in the Christian Gospels." *JAOS* 91 (1971), 438–442.

95. Cf. *Mahābhārata* III,149,28: *ācārasambhavo dharmaḥ*; XIII,107,9: *ācāralakṣaṇo dharmaḥ*; also XII,130,15; the *ācāra* which Manu I,108 presents as the "highest dharma" is strictly Vedic. The Mahābhārata also praises *ānṛśaṃsya*, "kindness," "compassion," as "highest dharma"; cf. XII,316,12; XIII,59,6. Cf. also Aśvaghoṣa, *Buddhacarita* IX,17: *sarveṣu bhūteṣu dayā hi dharmaḥ*..

96. See the nine commentaries on *Bhāgavatapurāṇa* I,1,2 which are compiled in the edition by Kṛṣṇaśaṅkara Śāstrī. Benares, 1965ff. Cf. specifically Vīrarāghava (p.75f.) on the distinction between the *sādhyadharma* and the *siddhadharma* (the fully "established dharma," i.e. the divine self). See also XI,12,1ff.

97. Cf. Gonda I, 291 ("Weil Fremde den Dharma nicht in Ehren halten. . ."). On the idea of an increasing distance from the dharmic center, and a corresponding dharmic "deficit," cf. Bhāruci and Medhātithi on Manu X,24ff.; 43ff.

98. Cf. W. Halbfass, *Zur Theorie der Kastenordnung*, 27.

99. See above, ch. 11, §7; 10ff.

100. Cf. *Mahābhārata* XII,181,10ff.

101. W.D. O'Flaherty's use of these terms is particularly incautious; cf., e.g., *The Origins of Evil in Hindu Mythology*. Berkeley, second ed., 1980; and her contribution in *The Concept of Duty in South Asia* (see above, n.9). *Svadharma* is not more "relative," but more specific than *sādhāraṇadharma*; and this does not contradict its "absoluteness." Moreover, O'Flaherty confuses the distinction between these two types of *dharma* with that between *pravṛtti-* and *nivṛttidharma*, or between *dharma* and the transcendence of *dharma*. Her textual references are often inaccurate or irrelevant.

102. Even such phenomena as a "dharma for thieves," or the ritual code of the Thags, still reflect the exemplary power of the "orthodox" *svadharma* scheme.

18. Reinterpretations of *Dharma* in Modern Hinduism

1. Cf. XIV,7,3,15 (*anucchittidharman*; see above, ch. 17, n.44; cf. Pali *uppādavayadhammin*, "subject to origination and decay"). A transition and overlap of the meanings "property" and "ritual norm" occurs in XI,5,7,1, which refers to the four *dharma* of the brahmin (*brāhmaṇya, pratirūpacaryā, yaśas, lokapakti*). Similar ambiguities can be found in several compounds with - *dharman*, e.g. *satyadharman*.

2. Vyāsa, *Yogabhāṣya* on *YS* III,15 defines *dharma* as "the potential of a substrate specified by a suitability" (*yogyatāvachinnā dharminaḥ śaktir eva dharmaḥ*), i.e., a capacity suitable for a specific purpose or function. Of course, no "ethical" conclusions are drawn.

3. See, for instance, Medhātithi on Manu I,85f. (*dharma* in the sense of *guṇa*).

4. Cf. Maheśacandra Nyāyaratna, *Brief Notes on the Modern Nyāya System*. Calcutta, n.d. (in Sanskrit), 8: *dhriyate tiṣṭhati varttate yaḥ sa dharmaḥ* This semantic duality (or ambiguity) is not used to develop the idea of reciprocity which is sometimes associated with *dharma* and which implies that it supports and protects those by whom it is supported and protected; see above, ch. 17, §11.

5. Cf. Candrakīrti, *Prasannapadā* on *Madhyamakakārikā* XVII,1: *dharmaśabdo 'yaṃ pravacane tridhā vyavasthāpitaḥ, svalakṣaṇadhāraṇārthena, kugatigamanavidhāraṇārthena, pañcagatikasaṃsāragamanavidhāraṇārthena*; see also above, ch. 17, n.43.

6. See above ch. 17, n.19; and R. Antoine, "A Pioneer of Neo-Hinduism. Bankim Chandra Chatterjee." *Indica. The Indian Historical Research Institute Silver Jub. Comm. Vol.* Bombay, 1953, 5-21.

7. P. Hacker, *Kl. Schr.*, 513.

8. P. Hacker, loc. cit.

9. *Śrīmadbhagavadgītā* (as quoted by P. Hacker, loc. cit., 515).

10. *Kl. Schr.*, 516; on *iuropīya hindu*, cf. *Dharmatattva* (*Racanāvalī* II), 596. For an early occurrence of the word *svadharman*, see Ṛgveda III,21,2.

11. Cf. XVIII,43: *karma svabhāvajam*; 45: *svabhāvaniyataṃ karma*; this applies also to *Bhāgavatapurāṇa* I,9,26 (*puruṣasvabhāvavihita*).

12. *Kl. Schr.*, 514 ("metaphysisch geronnene Tat").

13. Cf. *Vedāntasiddhāntasaṃgraha* 1,61 (ed. D.P. Śarmakavi, Benares, 1912ff., 12): *svocitakaṭakriyādi*.

14. Bhāskara's introduction emphasizes the special association between the *bhagavān dharmaḥ* and the Brahmins.

15. Cf. Rāmānuja on *Gītā* XVIII,66. On the transition from traditional to modern interpretations of the *Gītā*, see also G.J. Larson, "The Bhagavadgītā as Cross-Cultural Process." *Journal of the American Academy of Religion* 43 (1975),

651–669; for a collection of studies on modern interpretations, see *Modern Indian Interpreters of the Bhagavadgītā*, ed. R.N. Minor, Albany, 1986 (especially 34–43: A. Ray, "Bankim Chandra Chatterji's New Hinduism and the Bhagavadgītā.").

16. Cf. Srila Thakur Bhakti Vinode, *Jaiva Dharma*, ed. B.V. Tirtha Goswami Maharaj, trans. B.S. Nishkinchana Maharaj. Madras, 1975. Cf. the phrase "religion or the essential and natural characteristics of the individual souls" in the introduction by the editor. On Thakur Bhaktivinode (Bhaktivinoda Ṭhākura; originally Kedāranātha Datta) and his movement, cf. Th.J. Hopkins, "Hindu Sects in America: The Kṛṣṇa Consciousness Example." *Identity and Division in Cults and Sects in South Asia*, ed. P. Gaeffke and D. Utz. Philadelphia, 1984, 174–188.

17. *Vāmanapurāṇa*, ed. A.S. Gupta, trans. S.M. Mukhopadhyaya et al. Benares, 1968, XI, 13–29. In the translation, *dharma* appears as "righteousness," "religion," "characteristic quality" and "virtue;" cf. also *Bhāgavatapurāṇa* I,9,26ff.

18. Cf. R. Tagore, *The Religion of Man*. London, fifth ed., 1958, 154; 143ff. See also B. Kuppuswamy, "The Concept of svadharma in the Gītā." *Proceedings of the Indian Philosophical Congress* 39/40 (1965/66), 17–24.

19. *Religion and Society*. London, second ed., 1948, 130.

20. Loc. cit., 131; the British philosopher Th.H. Green (1836–1882), with whose work Radhakrishnan was familiar, used the phrase "fulfillment of the law of his being" (*Principles of Political Obligation*. London, 1955, 17).

21. *The Bhagavadgītā*. London, 1948, 364. Cf. P. Hacker, *Kl. Schr.*, 522.

22. *Religion and Society*, 107.

23. See above, ch. 17,§4.

24. A.B. Creel, "Dharma as an Ethical Category Relating to Freedom and Responsibility." *PEW* 22 (1972), 155–168; ib., 157.

25. J.M. Koller, "Dharma: An Expression of Universal Order." *PEW* 22 (1975), 133–144; ib., 131.

26. "The Real and the Apparent Man." *Selections from Swami Vivekananda*, ed. Gambhirananda. Calcutta, fourth ed., 1963, 157. See also S. Radhakrishnan, *The Bhagavadgītā*, commentary on I,1.

27. *The Hindu View of Life*, 70.

28. *Religion and Society*, 108, 114f.; 119.

29. Loc. cit., 107.

30. Cf. *The Dhammapada*. London, 1950, 32ff.

31. See above, ch. 13,§31 (n.125); cf. also S.K. De, *Bengali Literature in the Nineteenth Century (1757–1857)*. Calcutta, second ed., 1962, 609ff.

32. *Racanāvalī* II, 671f.; Bankim quotes from his own article *Dharmajijñāsā*.

33. *Racanāvalī* II, 672ff.; especially 673; on A. Comte, cf. 675.

34. In a note (loc. cit., 674), he explains that he did not add a Bengali translation since it would have been unintelligible to his readers.

35. *Letters on Hinduism* II; *Racanāvalī* III (= *Rachanavali, English Works*), 230.

36. Loc. cit., 234.

37. Ch. Wilkins used the translation "religion" repeatedly in his English *Bhagavadgītā* (London, 1785); cf. III, 35; XVIII,66; A.W. Schlegel's Latin version (Bonn, 1823) has "religio" in I,40; II,7;40; IX,3; XVIII,66; etc. Al-Bīrūnī's work on India (ed. E. Sachau, London, 1887, 64), in addition to *dīn*, also gives the Arabic term *ajr*, "merit," to describe the meaning of *dharma*.

38. Cf. B. Tiliander, *Christian and Hindu Terminology*. Uppsala, 1974, 66f.

39. Cf. loc. cit., 290ff.

40. Ed. J. Aelen, Nellore, 1931 ("*Satyawedasaarasangraham*").

41. Cf. *Vyacarana seu locupletissima samscrdamicae linguae institutio*. Rome, 1804, 199f.

42. Cf. B. Tiliander (see above, n.38), 58f.

43. In Bengali: 1801; in Sanskrit (first for the New Testament only): 1808; *nūtanadharmaniyama* appears in the third edition. Calcutta, 1886. A translation by T.C. Chakravarty (Calcutta, n.d.; ca. 1944) is entitled *Khrīṣṭopaniṣad*.

44. J.R. Ballantyne, loc. cit., 19ff.; 91ff.

45. See, for instance, *Hindī viśvakośa*. vol.6., Benares, 1966, art. *dharmapracāra*. *Dharma* is also used to translate the New Testament term δικαιοσυνη; cf. J.S.M. Hooper, *Greek New Testament Terms in Indian Languages*. Bangalore, 1957, 44f. For "sermon," Monier-Williams suggests *dharmaviṣayavākya* and *dharmopadeśa*; cf. the Buddhist expression *dhammadesanā*.

46. Cf. *The Autobiography of Maharshi Devendranath Tagore*, trans. S.N. Tagore and Indira Devi. London, 1914, ch. 29 (especially p.201).

47. See, for instance, Śrīśa Candra Vidyārṇava (i.e. S.C. Vasu; Anglicized Bose), *A Catechism of Hindu Dharma*. Allahabad, second ed., 1919 (*Sacred Books of the Hindus*, Extra Vol. 3); several reprints (New York, 1974; New Delhi, 1978). See below, §13, on Annie Besant.

48. Cf. P.R. Sen, *Western Influence in Bengali Literature*. Calcutta, 1932, 371.

49. Cf. *Mahānirvāṇatantra* I,22; IV, 74; XIV,190ff.; on *hinduharma*, see above, ch. 11, n.93f.

50. Cf. S.K. Sen, *Early Bengali Prose, Carey to Vidyāsāgar*. Calcutta, 1966, 141f.; 150. The followers of Rammohan's Brāhma Samāj called their "religion" *brāhmadharma*.

51. Cf. *Granthāvalī* VII, 15; cf. also *Mahānirvāṇatantra* III, 104.

52. Cf. M.M. Ali, *The Bengali Reaction to Christian Missionary Activities, 1833–1857*. Chittagong, 1965, 36f.; R.F. Young, *Resistant Hinduism*, Vienna, 1981, 26ff. (on two responses to Christianity in Marathi: *Śrīhindudharmasthāpana* by Morabhaṭṭa Dandekara and *Svadeśadharmābhimānī* by Nārāyaṇa Rāo).

53. Cf. Maheśvarānandagiri, *Cāturvarṇyabhāratasamīkṣā* II. Bombay 1968, 6f.: *ataś ca vaidika āryahindudharmo 'yam anādiḥ sanātanaś ca-ity ucyate*.

54. Cf. P.R. Sen, *Western Influence in Bengali Literature.* Calcutta, 1932, 370 (quoted from *Bhūdebcarita* III, 315).

55. P.R. Sen, loc. cit., 366.

56. Cf. *Mahābhārata* XII,96,13; 128,30; 131,2; XIII,44,32; 96,46; XIV,50,37; cf. also the suggestive use of the adverbial *sanatā* in *Ṛgveda* III,3,1: *dharmāṇi sanatā na dūduṣat.*

57. Cf. XII,336,20 (Nā*rāyaṇīya* section): *dharma eṣa sanātanaḥ*; XIV,94,31; see also Dhammapada 1,5: *esa dhamma sanantano.*

58. I,40; cf. I,43; also XIV,27; and *Mahābhārata* XII,54,39; *dharmān pṛṣṭaḥ sanātanān.*

59. Manu, I,118: *deśadharmāñ jātidharmāṅ kuladharmāṃś ca śāśvatān*; cf. also IX,325; VII,98; IX,64.

60. Cf. *Mahānirvāṇatantra* II, 104; VIII,35; XII,1; 127; cf. also VIII,133: *vṛttaṃ sanātanam.*

61. Ed. S.L. Katre, Ujjain, 1951, e.g. III,2: *dharmāḥ sanātanāḥ.*

62. See above, ch. 14,§17.

63. Bharati Krishna Tirtha, *Sanatana Dharma.* Bombay, 1964, 38.

64. See above, chapters 13–14; also P.R. Sen, *Western Influence in Bengali Literature.* Calcutta, 1932, 366ff.

65. *Annual Report of the Central Hindu College*, 1901,8; cf. *Sanātana-Dharma. An Advanced Text-Book of Hindu Religion and Ethics.* Madras, 1940, Xf. See also Sister Nivedita (i.e., Margaret Noble), *Religion and Dharma.* London, 1915.

66. F.O. Schrader, "Neues über die Bhagavadgītā." *Aus Indiens Kultur, Festgabe R. von Garbe*, Erlangen, 1927, 171–183, misrepresents this work.

67. Ed. by the Sri Bharat Dharma Mahamandal. Benares, n.d. (ca. 1920; *Hall of All Religions* I).

68. Trans. J. Abs, 144ff.; see also R. Krishnaswami Aiyar, *The Eternal Law.* Madras, 1965.

69. See for instance, S. Radhakrishnan, "Fragments of a Confession." *The Philosophy of S. Radhakrishnan*, ed. P.A. Schilpp. New York, 1952, 80; "this perennial wisdom, the eternal religion behind all religions, the *sanātana dharma.*"

70. A.K. Banerjee, *Discourses on Hindu Spiritual Culture.* Delhi, 1967,5.

71. *Religion and Society.* London, second ed., 1948, 102.

72. *An Essay on Hinduism.* London, 1911, 157. This is the more radical and programmatic continuation of *The History of Caste in India* I, Ithaca, N.Y., 1909, i.e. Ketkar's doctoral dissertation at Cornell University.

73. Loc. cit., 4.

74. Loc. cit., 155; see also 18; 60.

75. For literature on Ketkar, see below, Appendix III, n.14.

76. Cf. L.S. Joshi, *A Critique of Hinduism*, trans. G.D. Parikh. Bombay, 1948, 96f. The work was originally published in Marathi: *Hiṃdudharmācī samīkṣā*. Nagpur, 1940.

77. See above, ch. 13, §26ff. On *dharma* and ethics, see E.W. Hopkins, *Ethics of India*, New Haven, 1924, 90ff.; A.B. Creel, "The Reexamination of Dharma in Hindu Ethics." *PEW* 25 (1975), 161-173; id., *Dharma in Hindu Ethics*. Calcutta, 1977 (based exclusively upon materials in English). Contributions by Indian authors: S.K. Maitra, *The Ethics of the Hindus*, Calcutta, 1925; I.C. Sharma, *Ethical Philosophies of India*, London, 1965 (idealizing and apologetic).

78. Cf. *Racanāvalī* II, 268; on *ahiṃsā* and ethics among the followers of Svāminārāyaṇa (i.e. Sahajānanda, 1781-1831), cf. R.B. Williams, *A New Face of Hinduism: the Swaminarayan Religion*. Cambridge, 1984.

79. S. Radhakrishnan, *The Dhammapada*. London, 1950, 34.

80. Cf. S. Radhakrishnan, *Religion and Society*. London, second ed., 1948, 119: "Dharma is an elastic tissue which clothes the growing body"; see also S. Gopalan, *Hindu Social Philosophy*. New Delhi, 1979.

19. The Sanskrit Doxographies and the Structure of Hindu Traditionalism

1. Cf. M. Piantelli, *Śaṅkara e la rinascita del Brāhmanesimo*. Fossano, 1974, 217ff.

2. S.C. Chatterjee and D.M. Datta, *An Introduction to Indian Philosophy*. Calcutta, seventh ed., 1968, 9.

3. S.N. Dasgupta, *A History of Indian Philosophy* I. Cambridge, fourth ed., 1957, 64; see also 5f.

4. Cf. *Ph.d.W.* II, 366.

5. See, for instance, *Indiens Religion: Der Sanātana-Dharma*, trans. J. Abs. Bonn, 1923,2; Motilal Shastri, *Vedic Concept of Man and Universe*. Jaipur, n.d., 3.

6. *AGPh* I/1, 40.

7. Cf. *The Sarva-Darśana-Saṃgraha*, trans. E.B. Cowell and A.E. Gough. Benares, sixth ed., 1961 (originally published in installments, *The Pandit*, vol.9ff., 1874ff.). For an edition with a modern Sanskrit commentary, see below, n.18. The identity of the author has been debated for many years; see, for instance, R.R. Rao, "Identity of Vidyāraṇya and Mādhavācārya." *IHQ* 10 (1934), 802-810; A. Thakur, "Cannibhaṭṭa and the Authorship of the Sarvadarśanasaṃgraha." *ALB* 25 (1961), 524-538.

8. The most recent and comprehensive edition of the text with the available commentaries is by M.K. Jain. Calcutta, 1969 (Jñānapīṭha Mūrtidevī Jaina Granthamālā). For a partial Italian translation (with Guṇaratna's commentary) by L. Suali, see *Giornale della Società Asiatica Italiana* 17-20 (1904-1907); without commentaries, the text was edited and translated into English by K.S. Murty. Tenali, 1957.

9. Ed./trans. M. Raṅgācārya. Madras, 1909.

10. Cf. V. Varadachari, "Treatment of the Schools of Religion and Philosophy in the Maṇimekhalai." *Sri Venkateswara University Oriental Journal* (Tirupati) 14 (1971), 9–26 (on chapter 27 of this important Buddhist work in Tamil).

11. The European doctrines are coordinated with, and derived from, the Indian ones. There are manuscripts of several other doxographies, e.g. Harirāma, *Darśanasaṃgraha*. Another Jaina work with doxographic contents is: Jinadatta, *Vivekavilāsa*. Ahmedabad, 1898.

12. *Sarvamatasaṃgraha*, ed. Gaṇapati Śāstrī, 42f.; eight *pramāṇa* are ascribed to the Paurāṇika, i.e. the six "means of knowledge" accepted in classical Vedānta and, in addition, *sambhavā* and *aitihya* (cf. 14f.). According to the *Sarvasiddhāntasaṃgraha*, all doctrines culminate in the Vedānta (ib., v.99: *vedāntānta*); yet the final verses of the work refer to the *hiraṇyagarbhapakṣa* and the teachings of Kṛṣṇa.

13. A list of six philosophical systems appears already in the *Maṇimekhalai*; cf. V. Varadachari (see above, n.10), 15; see also H. von Glasenapp, *Die Philosophie der Inder*. Stuttgart, third ed., 1974, 140.

14. Haribhadra notes in the introduction to his *Lokāyata* section that for those who regard Nyāya and Vaiśeṣika as one system, there would only be five systems which are *āstika* (in the wider sense, i.e. recognizing the difference between *dharma* and *adharma* and the possibility of final liberation), and that therefore the *Lokāyata* system may be added to the list. The later commentator Maṇibhadra states: *darśanānāṃ ṣaṭsaṃkhyā jagati prasiddhā*; cf. *Ṣaḍdarśanasamuccaya*, ed. G. Dāmodara Śāstrī. Benares, 1957 (*ChSS*), 64.

15. Cf. *Sarvamatasaṃgraha*, 14; *Sarvadarśanakaumudī*, 4.

16. Cf. G. Jha, *Pūrva-Mīmāṃsā in Its Sources*. Benares, second ed., 1964, 1ff. (with unreliable chronological data).

17. Cf. *Sarvamatasaṃgraha*, 10f.; in the *Sarvadarśanasaṃgraha*, the systems of theistic Vedānta occupy a low rank in the vicinity of the heterodox systems.

18. Cf. Sāyaṇa-Mādhava, *Sarvadarśanasaṃgraha*, ed. with an original commentary in Sanskrit by V.S. Abhyankar, second ed. by K.V. Abhyankar. Poona, 1951, especially 84ff. Abhyankar begins with the division *nāstika-āstika*, then divides the *nāstika* into *ādhyakṣika* and *tārkika*, etc.

19. *Upodghāta*, v.2–25; on the fourteenfold list, see, for instance, Yājñavalkya 1,3; Kālidāsa, *Raghuvaṃśa* V,21; for older lists of "sciences" (*vidyā*), cf. *Chāndogya Upaniṣad* VII,1,2; 2,7; and P. Horsch, *Die vedische Gāthā- und Śloka-Literatur*. Bern, 1966, 17ff. Such lists appear also in Buddhism, in particular a fivefold list; for a curious enumeration of nineteen "sciences," see *Milindapañha*, ed. V. Trenckner, 3f. (including *visesikā*, i.e. Vaiśeṣika), and other philosophical systems).

20. *Sarvamatasaṃgraha*, 7.

21. Loc. cit., 11f.; also Mādhava Sarasvatī, *Sarvadarśanakaumudī*, 4.

22. There are several printed editions of the *Prasthānabheda* (for instance ed. Gurucaraṇa Tarkadarśanatīrtha. Calcutta, 1939); for a German translation, see P. Deussen, *AGPh* I/1, 4ff.

23. See above, ch. 15; cf. also Guṇaratna on Haribhadra, *Saḍdarśanasamuccaya*, v.1 (ed. M.K. Jain, Calcutta, 1969, 12ff.). On the relationship between the "opinions of others" (*parasamaya*) and the perspectivistic "viewpoints" (*naya*), see Siddhasena Divākara, *Sanmatitarka* III,47; the systematic culmination of Jaina perspectivism is found in Mallavādin's *Dvādaśāranayacakra* (with commentary by Siṃhasūri).

24. Ed. H.R. Kapadia. Baroda, 1940 (*GOS*; with useful, but somewhat apologetic introduction). Even Mallavādin's work ultimately refutes all one-sided, non-perspectivistic doctrines; cf. *Dvādaśāranayacakra*, ed. Jambuvijaya, vol.2, 503: *etena sarvo 'syādvādaḥ pratyuktaḥ.*

25. Cf. *Samayasāra* I,8 (which is reminiscent of Āryadeva, *Catuḥśataka* VIII, 19); see also S.M. Shaha, "Kundakunda's Concept of vyavahāra naya and niścaya naya." *ABORI* 56 (1975), 105–128

26. Cf. Upodghāta, v.1: *vādibhir darśanaiḥ sarvair dṛśyate yat tv anekadhā / vedāntavedyaṃ brahma-idam ekarūpam upāsmahe.*

27. Cf. W. Halbfass, *Studies in Kumārila and Śaṅkara*, 88f.; 92f. (referring to Saṅkara's and Vācaspati's commentaries on *BS* I,1,1); see also Gauḍapāda, *Kārikā* III, 18ff.

28. This *samanvaya* is the special topic of the first *adhyāya* of *BS*.

29. Cf. *Ṛgveda* I, 164,46; *ekaṃ sad viprā bahudhā vadanti*; among later adaptations, cf., e.g., Manu XII,123.

30. Cf. *Nyāyakusumāñjali* I,2 (prose section); *Ātmatattvaviveka*, ed. Ḍhuṇḍhirāja Śāstrī. Benares, 1940, 448ff.; especially 450.

31. Cf. V.V. Gokhale, "Masters of Buddhism Adore the Brahman through Non-Adoration." *IIJ* 5 (1961), 271–275; H. Nakamura, "The Vedāntic Chapter of Bhavya's Madhyamakahṛdaya." *ALB* 39 (1975), 300–329; but on the other hand, L. de La Vallée Pousin, "Madhyamaka." *Mélanges chinois et bouddhiques* 2 (1933), 115f.

32. Cf. *Aṇubhāṣya* on *BS* II,2,9; *yad śūnyavādinaḥ śūnyam / tad eva brahma māyinaḥ.*

33. Cf. *The Problem of Two Truths in Buddhism and Vedānta*, ed. M. Sprung. Dordrecht, 1973.

34. S.C. Chatterjee and D.M. Datta, *Introduction to Indian Philosophy*. Calcutta, seventh ed., 1968, 11. The reference to "natural aptitudes" reflects the Neo-Hindu reinterpretation of *adhikāra* (although even traditional authors did not always associate the concepts of *adhikāra/adhikārin* with the caste system; cf., e.g., Abhinavagupta, *Tantrāloka* XXXV,35).

35. *Sarvadarśanaikavākyatā* is the title of a manuscript (cf. *A Descriptive Catalogue of the Sanskrit Manuscripts in the Collection of the Asiatic Society*, XI, No. 8880); see also the expression *sarvaśāstraikavākyatā* in the commentary by

Jayaratha on Abhinavagupta, *Tantrāloka XXXV,1*. A modern *Sarvadarśanasamanvaya* in Sanskrit was published by Gopālaśāstrī Darśanakeśari. New Delhi, 1981.

36. Cf. Vijñānabhikṣu, *Sāṃkhyapravacanabhāṣya*, introduction (ed. R. Garbe. New Haven, 1895, 1ff.; 4f.).

37. On his numerous works, cf. N. Ramesan, *Sri Appayya Dikshita*. Hyderabad, 1972. In addition to his Vedānta works, he also wrote on Pūrvamīmāṃsā and poetics.

38. Cf. *Vedāntakalpalatikā* 1,4 (ed./trans. R.D. Karmarkar, Poona 1962,2); on the *Prasthānabheda*, see above, n.22.

39. Cf. Śaṅkara on *BS* II,2,18: *sa ca bahuprakāraḥ pratipattibhedād vineyabhedād vā*.

40. Cf. Bhāmatī on *BS* II,2,18; *ye tu prakṛṣṭamatayas, tebhyaḥ sākṣād eva śūnyatātattvam pratipādyate*; for the text of the *Bodhicittavivaraṇa* from which Vācaspati quotes in this section, see Chr. Lindtner, *Nagarjuniana*. Copenhagen, 1982, 180ff. See especially v.98f.

41. Cf. II,4,10; also IV,5,11.

42. Cf. XII,203,13ff.; 171ff.; see also Bhartṛhari, *Vṛtti* on *VP* I,5 (on the *vedāṅga*); Vātsyāyana, *NBh* on II,1,68 (on the status of the tradition of medicine, *āyurveda*); Jayanta, *NM*, 5: *ādisargāt prabhṛti vedavad imā vidyāḥ pravṛttāḥ*.

43. Cf. the commentaries by Śaṅkara, Bhāskara, Rāmānuja, Madhva, Nimbārka and Vallabha on *BS* II,2,42-45.

44. Cf. Madhva, *Mahābhāratatātparyanirṇaya* 1,30f. This agrees with claims made by the Purāṇas themselves; cf. the demarcation of "canonical" texts which Vidyāraṇya's *Sarvadarśanasaṃgraha* quotes from the *Skandapurāṇa* in its chapter on "Pūrṇaprajña" (i.e., Madhva). See also B.N.K. Sharma, *The Brahmasūtras and Their Principal Commentaries*, vol.1. Bombay, 1971, 2ff.; S. Siauve, *Les hierarchies spirituelles selon l'Anuvyākhyāna de Madhva*. Pondicherry, 1971, 35f. (v.90ff.).

45. Cf. G. Oberhammer, "Die Überlieferungsautorität im Hinduismus." *Offenbarung, geistige Realität des Menschen*, ed. G. Oberhammer. Vienna, 1974, 41-92. On Buddhist theories of tradition and hermeneutics, see É. Lamotte, "La critique d'interprétation dans le bouddhisme." *Annuaire de l'Institut de Philologie et d'Histoire Orientales et Slaves* 9 (1949), 341-361; E. Steinkellner, "Remarks on Tantristic Hermeneutics." *Proceedings of the Csoma de Körös Memorial Symposium*, ed. L. Ligeti. Budapest, 1978, 445-458.

46. Cf. Jayanta, NM, 239ff.; 245ff.; the expression *sarvāgamaprāmāṇya*, "validity of all traditions," which we find in this section, is also used by Jayaratha in his commentary on *Tantrāloka* XXXV,1.

47. Cf. *Āgamaḍambara*, ed. V. Raghavan and A. Thakur. Darbhanga, 1964, 96f. See also A. Wezler, "Zur Proklamation weltanschaulicher Toleranz bei dem indischen Philosophen Jayantabhaṭṭa." *Saeculum* 27 (1976), 329-348; especially 339ff. Cf. Manu XII,96 on "recentness" (*arvākkālikatā*); but also Medhātithi on Manu II,6 (ed. J.H. Dave, 273f.) on the question of how a text originating in our own time can later on be regarded as *smṛti*.

48. Cf. J. Abs, "Beiträge zur Kritik heterodoxer Philosophie-Systeme in der Purāṇa-Literatur." *Beiträge zur Literaturwissenschaft und Geistesgeschichte Indiens*, Festgabe H. Jacobi. Bonn, 1926, 386–396; W.D. O'Flaherty, "The Origin of Heresy in Hindu Mythology." *History of Religions* 10 (1971), 271–333; especially 306ff.

49. See above, ch.11.

50. See above, ch.15, especially §11.

51. See, for instance, the "hymn of creation," *Ṛgveda* X,129; for a linguistic analysis of *Ṛgvedic* questions, cf. A. Etter, *Die Fragesätze im Ṛgveda*. Berlin, 1985.

52. Cf. Śaṅkara on *BS* IV,1,3: *kasya punar ayam aprabodha iti cet, yas tvam pṛcchasi tasya ta iti vadāmaḥ*; on *Bhagavadgītā XIII,2: sā-avidyā kasya-iti, yasya dṛśyate tasya-eva . . . avidyā kasya dṛśyata iti praśno nirarthakaḥ*. The *Svātmanirūpaṇa*, which has been ascribed to Śaṅkara, characterizes questions concerning the essence and cause of things (v.93: *kim idam . . . amuṣya ko hetuḥ*) as *māyā*. Rhetorical questions, as well as questions which serve as dialectical devices, are, of course, common in later literature.

53. *NM*, 363.

54. *NM*, 1 (v.8f.); cf. Kamalaśīla on Śāntarakṣita, *Tattvasaṃgraha*, v.2: *vaktuṃ vastu na mādṛśā jaḍadhiyo 'pūrvaṃ kadācit kṣamāḥ* . . .

55. *NM*,5.

56. 363: *ātmīyā kācana nirdoṣā sādhvī kalpanā*.

57. Cf. E. Frauwallner, "Die Reihenfolge und Entstehung der Werke Dharmakīrtis." *Asiatica, Festschrift F. Weller*. Leipzig, 1954, 142–154, especially 150f. (also in: *Kl. Schr.*, 677–689; ib., 685f.). The verse *Pramāṇavārttika* IV,286, which Frauwallner quotes in his article, is found in the edition by R. Sāṅkṛtyāyana, but missing in other editions. For Abhinavagupta, see *Tantrāloka* XXXVII, 79ff. For further expressions of personal pride, independence and accomplishment, see, for instance, the concluding verses of Raghunātha's *Padārthatattvanirūpaṇa*, or the extreme self-glorification of Lakṣmīdhara in the final verses of his commentary on the *Saundaryalaharī*.

58. On the "new way" of the *Pratyabhijñā* system, cf. Utpaladeva, *Īśvarapratyabhijñākārikā* IV,2,1; *navyamīmāṃsaka* is used by Madhusūdana Sarasvatī, *Vedāntakalpalatikā* X (ed./trans. R.D. Karmarkar. Poona, 1962, 29).

59. See above, n.57; also, for instance, the conclusion of Śrīdhara's *Nyāyakandalī* or Vijñānabhikṣu's ambitious claim to restore the Sāṃkhya system which had been "consumed by the sun of time" (*kālārkabhakṣitaṃ sāṃkhyaśāstram*; cf. *Sāṃkhyapravacanabhāṣya*, introduction).

60. Cf. R. Suga, *Der Abschnitt über die Weltzeitalter im Brahmāṇḍa-,Kūrma-,Linga-,Matsya-,und Vāyupurāṇa*, Diss. Bonn, 1951; C. Dimmitt Church, "The Myth of the Four Yugas in the Sanskrit Purāṇas." *Purāṇa* 16 (1974), 5–25.

61. On *BS* I,3,33; this may imply a cautious criticism of Kumārila and his uncompromising argumentation against "yogic perception." At the same time, Śaṅkara is very reserved in his attitude towards Yogic accomplishments (*siddhi*).

62. Cf. Yāmuna, *Āgamaprāmāṇya*, section 86 (ed./trans. J.A.B. van Buitenen, Madras, 1971, 45; with quotes from the *Varāhapurāṇa*).

63. Cf. Jīva Gosvāmin, *Tattvasandarbha*, ed. S.N. Goswami (with commentary by Baladeva Vidyābhūṣaṇa). Calcutta, 1967, sections 22f.

64. Cf. A. Avalon (i.e. J. Woodroffe), *Śakti and Śākta*. Madras, sixth ed., 1965, 90: on the affiliation of *dharma* texts with different ages of the world, see *Parāśarasmṛti* I, 13ff.

65. Cf. *Kulārṇavatantra* II,85; 140: *vedātmakaṃ śāstraṃ viddhi kaulātmakam*; according to Hārīta (see Kullūka on Manu II,1), the *śruti* itself is twofold, i.e. Vedic and Tantric (*vaidikī tāntrikī ca*). For some useful references concerning the relationship between Tantra and Veda, see T. Goudriaan and S. Gupta, *Hindu Tantric and Śākta Literature*. Wiesbaden, 1981. Some authors of the *Śrīvidyā* tradition claimed a special affiliation with the Veda, e.g. Lakṣmīdhara in his commentary on the *Saundaryalaharī*, which contains many quotes from Vedic texts, including the *Ṛgveda* (on v.5), several *Upaniṣads*, and the entire *Taittirīya* corpus (see especially on v.11).

66. See above, §7ff.

67. See also *Muṇḍaka Upaniṣad* 1,4 on "higher" and lower knowledge (*parā* and *aparā vidyā*).

68. *Mahābhārata* XII,336,76 (quoted by Rāmānuja on *BS* II,2,42).

69. Cf. *Tattvasandarbha*, sections 26–28; the *Bhāgavata* itself has the status of the supreme *śruti* (*paramaśrutirūpatva*); references to the Vedas are only meant to explicate the *Purāṇa*, but not to validate it. Its superiority is illustrated with a quote from the *Nāradīyapurāṇa*: *vedārthād adhikaṃ manye purāṇārtham . . . vedāḥ pratiṣṭitāḥ sarve purāṇe*.

70. Cf. *Tattvasandarbha*, sections 15ff.; ed. S.N. Goswami, pp. 22; 26; 34ff; 38. On the "strengthening" of the Vedas by "Itihāsa and Purāṇa" see also *Mahābhārata* I,1,204.

71. *Mahānirvāṇatantra* XIV,180; for the metaphor, cf. *Mahābhārata* XII, 237,18f.

72. Cf. Vādirāja, *Yuktimallikā*, with commentary by Surottamatīrtha, ed. T.R. Krishnacharya. Bombay, 1903, I,v.8ff.

73. Cf. *Tattvasandarbha* (see above, n.63), section 15, p.21: *kvacid anitya-śravaṇaṃ tv āvirbhāvatirobhāvāpekṣayā*. For a study of the *Tattvasandarbha*, together with an edition and English translation, see S.M. Elkman, *Jīva Gosvāmin's Tattvasandarbha*. Delhi, 1986.

20. Epilogue

1. See above, ch. 13, §29.
2. Cf. *Kl. Schr.*, 386; 480.
3. *Kl. Schr.*, VIII.
4. *Kl. Schr.*, 482.

5. *Kl. Schr.*, 386; see also 599.

6. See below, Appendix II.

7. Cf. *Thirty-Four Conferences between the Danish Missionaries and the Malabarian Bramans...*, trans. J.T. Philipps, London, 1719, 14f.; H. Grafe, "Hindu Apologetics at the Beginning of the Protestant Missionary Era in India." *Indian Church History Review* 6 (1972), 43–69.

8. London, second ed., 1777, LXXIIIf.; this "Preliminary Discourse" is missing in the *Vivādārṇavasetu*, the Sanskrit text which the pandits compiled as basis for the Persian and English translations. The first edition of the *Code* was published in 1776.

9. See below, Appendix II, §6 (also above, ch. 4, n.50); the traditional concept of *adhikāra*, ritual and soteriological "qualification" or "mandate," provided a convenient device for Hindu apologetics; cf. R.F. Young, *Resistant Hinduism*. Vienna, 1981, 161ff. (specifically on Nīlakaṇṭha Sāstrī Gore).

10. Cf. P.R. Sen, *Western Influence in Bengali Literature*. Calcutta, 1932, 369f Cf. also Debendranath Tagore's universalistic description of the Brāhma Samāj, loc. cit., 366f.

11. *Complete Works* III, 251f.

12. The expression *pūrvabhūmi* is used by Sarvajñātman, *Saṃkṣepaśārīraka* II, 61; here, the *pariṇāmavāda* ("doctrine of evolution") appears as "preliminary stage" of the *vivartavāda* ("doctrine of illusory transformation").

13. Cf. S.H. Nasr, "Conditions for Meaningful Comparative Philosophy." *PEW* 22 (1961), 53–61; K.R. Stunkel, "The Meeting of East and West in Coomaraswamy and Radhakrishnan." *PEW* 23 (1973), 517–524.

14. D.N. Shastri, "Foreward" to: M.C. Bhartiya, *Causation in Indian Philosophy*. Ghaziabad, 1973, VI.

15. *Racanāvalī* III (= *Rachanavali, English Works*), 144.

16. See above, ch. 16, §26.

17. H. Bürkle, *Dialog mit dem Osten. Radhakrishnans neuhinduistische Botschaft im Lichte christlicher Weltsendung*. Stuttgart, 1965, 249.

18. Loc. cit., 44; see aslo 246f.

19. On the encounter between Christian and Hindu universalism, cf. R. Panikkar, *The Unknown Christ of Hinduism*. London, 1964. See also *Indische Beiträge zur Theologie der Gegenwart*, ed. H. Bürkle. Stuttgart, 1966; P. Wietzke, *Theologie im modernen Indien - Paul David Devanandan*. Bern, 1975. For some thoughtful observations on the "East-West dialogue" by an Indian Christian author, see Paulos Mar Gregorios (the Metropolitan of Delhi), *Truth Without Tradition?* Tirupati, 1978 (with references to H.-G. Gadamer).

20. E. Troeltsch, *Der Historismus und seine Probleme*. Tübingen, 1922 (reprint Aalen, 1961), 710.

21. Loc. cit., 711.

22. Loc. cit., 708.

23. Loc. cit., 713.

24. Loc. cit., 725.

25. Cf. M. Scheler, "Der Mensch im Weltalter des Ausgleichs." *Philosophische Weltanschauung*. Bonn, 1929 (quoted in: H. von Glasenapp, *Indienbild*, 133).

26. Cf. J.A. Hutchinson, *Living Options in Philosophy*. Honolulu, 1977, ch.1: "Toward Global Philosophy."

27. See above, ch.10, §6 (on H.-G. Gadamer).

28. See above, n.21.

29. The expression "dialogic situation" is borrowed from H.P. Alper's "Feature Book Review" of *Indien und Europe, PEW* 33 (1983), 189-196; ib., 189.

21. The Concept of Experience in the Encounter Between India and the West

1. See J.E. Biersdorf, *Hunger for Experience: Vital Religious Communities in America*. New York, 1975 (a book not dealing directly with India).

2. H. Cox, *Turning East*. New York, 1977, 132.

3. See S. Radhakrishnan, *The Hindu View of Life*. London, 1968 (originally 1927), 44 (quote from: W.R. Inge, *The Platonic Tradition in English Religious Thought*, 113).

4. J.M. Moore, *Theories of Religious Experience*. New York, 1938, VII.

5. *Experience and God*. New York, 1968, 21.

6. W. Kasper, *Glaube und Geschichte*. Mainz, 1970, 121ff. (quoted in: P. Neuner, *Religiöse Erfahrung und geschichtliche Offenbarung*. München, 1977, 353).

7. H.-G. Gadamer, *Wahrheit und Methode*. Tübingen, 1960, 329: "Der Begriff der Erfahrung scheint mir...zu den unaufgeklärtesten Begriffen zu gehören, die wir besitzen." Engl. transl.: *Truth and Method*. New York, 1985, 310. See also M. Oakeshott, *Experience and Its Modes*. Cambridge, 1933 (reprint New York, 1985), 9: "'Experience,' of all the words in the philosophic vocabulary, is the most difficult to manage."

8. On the history and implications of this word, see K. Sauerland, *Dilthey's Erlebnisbegriff*. Berlin, 1972.

9. *Oxford English Dictionary*, vol. III. Oxford, 1933, 430.

10. See above, ch. 17.

11. See above, ch. 15.

12. C. Sharma, *A Critical Survey of Indian Philosophy*. Delhi, 1964, 13. See also P.S. Sastri, *Indian Idealism I*. Delhi and Benares, 1975, 220: "Our philosophy is a philosophy of experience."

13. P. Hacker, "Aspects of Neo-Hinduism as Contrasted with Surviving Traditional Hinduism," *Kleine Schriften*, ed. L. Schmithausen. Wiesbaden, 1978, 599.

14. *An Idealist View of Life*. London, fifth edition, 1957, 84.

15. *The Hindu View of Life*, 16.

16. *The Brahma Sūtra*. London, 1960, 180.

17. *The Hindu View of Life*, 13.

18. *The Hindu View of Life*, 14ff.

19. "The Spirit in Man," in: *Contemporary Indian Philosophy*, ed. S. Radhakrishnan/J.N. Muirhead. London, fourth edition, 1966, 492.

20. See *An Idealist View of Life*, 14; also the introductory statements of most chapters in: *Recovery of Faith*. London, 1956.

21. *The Hindu View of Life*, 13; see also 16.

22. See W. Cremer, *Die universale Religion des Geistes*. Diss. München, 132f.

23. *The Principal Upanishads*. London, second edition, 1968, 103.

24. *The Hindu View of Life*, 15.

25. *The Brahma Sūtra*, 113f.

26. *Indian Philosophy, Vol. I*. London, 1932, 25; 32.

27. *The Hindu View of Life*, 15.

28. *The Hindu View of Life*, 27.

29. "The Spirit in Man" (in: *Contemporary Indian Philosophy*), 503.

30. *The Hindu View of Life*, 43f.

31. "Fragments of a Confession" in: *The Philosophy of S. Radhakrishnan*, ed. P.A. Schilpp. New York, 1952, 10.

32. M. Lederle, *Philosophical Trends in Modern Mahārāṣṭra*. Bombay, 1976, 395 (referring to the report by G.B. Burch in: *Aryan Path* 30/8, 1959, 345).

33. See A.O. Fort, *Turīya and the Catuṣpād Doctrine in Advaita Vedānta*. Diss. University of Pennsylvania, Philadelphia, 1982.

34. In both cases, we have also a large number of Western followers or admirers. As another incarnation of "experience" in modern Hinduism, we may mention the popular female saint Mā Ānanda Moyī (Ānandamayī).

35. See A. Bharati, *The Light at the Center*. Santa Barbara, 1976, 109. Bharati adds: "of all modern mystical literature Ramaṇa's words reflect the most direct uninterpreted zero-experience."

36. We should not forget that the young Ramaṇa attended two Christian schools in Madurai and acquired a good knowledge of the Bible.

37. On Aurobindo, see ch. 14. For a survey of Aurobindo's different "experiences," see R.N. Minor, "Sri Aurobindo and Experience: Yogic and Otherwise." *Religion in Modern India*, ed. R.D. Baird. New Delhi, 1981, 277–304.

38. S.H. Phillips, *Aurobindo's Philosophy of Brahman*. Leiden, 1986, 3. Also 92ff., on Aurobindo's "reports" on his experiences.

39. See S.H. Phillips, "Is Sri Aurobindo's Philosophy Vedānta?" *ALB* 48 (1984), 9 (referring to Aurobindo's introduction to his commentary on the *Īśā Upaniṣad*).

40. *The Life Divine* (Sri Aurobindo Birth Centenary Library, vol. 19) Pondicherry, 1970, 650f.

41. Dharmakīrti, *Pramāṇavārttika*, ed. Y. Miyasaka, Kyoto, 1971-1972 (*Acta Indologica* 2), I (Pramāṇasiddhi), 145. Many texts in the Pāli canon refer to personal realization and criticize Vedic traditionalism; see, for instance, the *Kassapasīhanāda, Kūṭadanta, Poṭṭhapāda* and *Tevijja Suttas* (all in *Dīghanikāya*).

42. We find this specifically among the *Gauḍīya Vaiṣṇavas* and the *Vallabhīyas*.

43. K.S. Murty, *Revelation and Reason in Advaita Vedānta*. Delhi, second edition, 1974, 254.

44. See W. Halbfass, *Studies in Kumārila and Śaṅkara*, ch.II: "Human Reason and Vedic Revelation in the Philosophy of Śaṅkara." One of the most concise and coherent presentations of Śaṅkara's basic ideas concerning knowledge, action and the authority of the Veda is found in his commentary on *BS* I, 1, 1–4 (*catuḥsūtrī*).

45. See W. Halbfass, *Studies in Kumārila and Śaṅkara*, ch.I: "Kumārila on Ahiṃsā and Dharma."

46. See above, ch. 17.

47. See *Upadeśasāhasrī* II, 2, 45; 73 (*duḥkham anubhavāmi*); II, 2, 88 (experiencing of the waking state, etc.).

48. See, for instance, *BSBh* IV, 1,2.

49. *BSBh* IV, 1,2; *Upadeśasāhasrī* I, 18, 201 says that *duḥkha* is a mere object, not belonging to the inner sphere of the self; see also the term *svasaṃvedyatva* in v. 200.

50. *Upadeśasāhasrī* I, 18, 202.

51. *BSBh* IV, 1,2: *eṣa vyāvṛttasarvasaṃsāradharmako 'nubhavātmako brahmasaṃjñakas tatpadārtho vedāntābhiyuktānāṃ prasiddhaḥ*. The frequency of *anubhava* and other derivatives of *anubhū* is most conspicious in *BSBh* IV, 1,2.

52. *Upadeśasāhasrī* I, 5, 5; see S. Mayeda, *A Thousand Teachings*. Tokyo, 1979, 115, n.5: "Ānandajñāna, Bodhanidhi and Rāmatīrtha take this '*anubhava*' (Pure Experience) as 'sākṣin'." Even in the *Pratyabhijñā* school, which seems to leave more room for "personal" experiences, *anubhava*, as coinciding with the divine presence of *prakāśa* ("light," "openness"), ultimately assumes an ontological, as well as soteriological meaning.

53. See *Upadeśasāhasrī* I, 12, 8f (*anubhava* as *mṛṣā*).

54. We may recall here the presence of the root *bhū*, "to be," in *anubhū*, a word which is also found in the meanings "to attain" and "be equal to" or "in accordance with," specifically in Vedic literature.

55. See W. Halbfass, *Studies in Kumārila and Śaṅkara*, 69; 84, n.202f.(specifically the reference to *BSBh* I, 1,4).

56. Even the term *svahṛdayapratyaya* in *BSBh* IV, 1, 15 does not refer to such "worldly" evidence.

57. S.H. Phillips, "Is Sri Aurobindo's Philosophy Vedānta?" *ALB* 48 (1984), 24. Similar questions have been asked about Nāgārjuna.

58. The notion of sacred texts as objective self-revelation of the absolute, and the correlation of levels of experience with stages of manifestation of the "word," is more explicit in the works of other thinkers, most notably Bhartṛhari and Abhinavagupta. On this issue, as well as on "yogic perception," "omniscience," etc., see the important article by G. Kaviraj, "The Doctrine of Pratibhā in Indian Philosophy," *Aspects of Indian Thought*. Burdwan, 1966, 1–44 (cf. specifically 16ff.).

59. See, for instance, *BSBh* IV, 1,3, which justifies the assumption of the ultimate irrelevance of the Veda by quoting *Bṛhadāraṇyaka Upaniṣad* IV, 3, 22 (*vedā avedāḥ*).

60. See above, n.26 (Radhakrishnan's claim that Advaitic monism is "based on the data of phychological observation").

61. *Pañcapādikā*, ed. Rāmaśāstrī Bhāgavatācārya, Benares, 1891 (Vizianagram Sanskrit Series), 10f.

62. *Pañcapādikā*, 24.

63. See *Pañcapādikā*, 19; P. Hacker, *Untersuchungen über Texte des frühen Advaitavāda*. 1: *Die Schüler Śaṅkaras*. Wiesbaden, 1951 (Abh. Ak. Wiss. Mainz, 1950), 133ff.; 146f.

64. See *Bṛhadāraṇyakopaniṣadbhāṣyavārttika* II, 4, 131f.; also S. Hino, *Sureśvara's Vārtika on Yājñavalkya Maitreyī Dialogue*. Delhi, 1982, 135f.; especially v. 132: *vicāryamāno 'nubhavo rūpyaśuktyanubhūtivat* . . . On the ontological and epistemological irreducibility of "self-experience" (*ātmānubhava*, etc.), see also *Sambandhavārttika*, v. 468ff. (ed./trans. T.M.P. Mahadevan. Madras, 1958, 243ff.).

65. See, for instance, Medhātithi on Manu II, 6 (beginning).

66. As an idealized fountainhead of certainty, the Veda plays a role which is, in a peculiar and interesting sense, comparable to that of the Cartesian Cogito.

67. See *Bhāmatī* on *Brahmasūtrabhāṣya* II, 1, 1(concluding portion).

68. See R.E. Gussner, "Śaṅkara's Crest Jewel of Discrimination: A Stylometric Approach to the Question of Authorship," *JIPh* 4 (1976/77), 265–278; specifically 272.

69. See also *Experience of Immortality. Engl. rendering of Jnaneswar's "Amritanubhava" with a commentary by R.S. Balseker*. Bombay, 1984; S.G. Tulpule, *Mysticism in Medieval India*, Wiesbaden, 1984, specifically 211–299: "Testimony of God-realisation." For "personal" statements among the Śaivite philosophers of "recognition" (*pratyabhijñā*), see, e.g., Utpaladeva, *Pratyabhijñākārikā* I,1; also his *Stotrāvalī*.

70. *Śrībhāṣya* on *BS* I, 1,3 (beginning; translation by G. Thibaut).

71. On *sphuṭatva*, see Ch. McDermott, "Yogic Direct Awareness as Means of Valid Cognition in Dharmakīrti and Rgyal-tshab," in: *Mahāyāna Buddhist Meditation*, ed. M. Kiyota. Honolulu, 1978, 151ff. (not always reliable.)

72. Candrakīrti, *Prasannapadā*, Introduction, ed. L. de La Vallée Poussin, Petersburg, 1903–1913 (Bibliotheca Buddhica), 58: . . . *anubhava eṣa mṛṣā, anubhavatvāt, taimirikadvicandrādyanubhavavad.*

73. See above, ch. 18.

74. See *NM*, 91: *idaṃ bhāti na bhāti-iti saṃvidvipratipattiṣu parapratyāyane puṃsāṃ śaraṇaṃ śapathoktayaḥ.*

75. See Vyāsa's *Yogabhāṣya* on *YS* I, 32; other authors like to invoke the "noble (immediate) awareness" (*bhagavatī saṃvit*).

76. See Bhīmācārya Jhaḷakīkar, *Nyāyakośa*. Bombay, second edition, 1893, article "anubhavaḥ"(23f).

77. See *Khaṇḍanakhaṇḍakhādya* with Ānandapūrṇa's *Khaṇḍanaphakkikāvibhañjana*, ed. S.L. Drāvida Śāstrī, Benares, 1904–1914 (ChSS), 252ff. Also Ph. Granoff, *Philosophy and Argument in Late Vedānta*. Dordrecht, 1978, 12ff.

78. P. Hacker, Aspects of Neo-Hinduism (see above, n.13), 601; Hacker quotes W. James, *The Varieties of Religious Experience*. London, 1952, 370.

79. However, Rammohan took great interest in the ideas of the *OM* and the "four states of awareness" (*catuṣpād*) which we find in the *Māṇḍūkya Upaniṣad*. Yet, among all the *Upaniṣads* which he translated, it was the *Māṇḍūkya* alone which he translated only into Bengali and not also into English. Perhaps he thought that its speculative "experiential" content was more suitable for Indian than for Western readers.

80. See above, ch.13, §7ff.

81. See *Ātmajīvanī*, ed. S.C. Cakravarttī. Calcutta, fourth edition, 1962, 124 (Engl. transl.: *The Autobiography of Maharshi Devendranath Tagore*, trans. Satyendranath Tagore and Indira Devi. London, 1914, 161).

82. *Ātmajīvanī*, 124 (*Autobiography*, 162); *parīkṣā* was suggested in Monier-Williams' *Dictionary, English and Sanskrit* (1851) as a Sanskrit equivalent for "experiment," and it is indeed used in this sense in several modern Indian languages.

83. See *Ātmajīvanī*, 124ff.(*Autobiography*, 161ff.).

84. See K.M. Sen, *Medieval Mysticism of India* (trans. from the Bengali by M.M. Ghosh; foreword by Rabindranath Tagore), London, 1936(reprint, New Delhi, 1974).

85. See A.K. Cakravarttī, *Maharṣi Devendranātha Ṭhākura*. Allahabad, 1916 (reprint Calcutta, 1971), 572ff. There is not much literature on Debendranath; Cakravarttī's Bengali biography is still the major reference work I thank Sagaree Korom-Sengupta for her helpful advice on this text.

86. The term *ātmapratyaya* occurs in *Māṇḍūkya Upaniṣad* VII as part of the compound *ekātmapratyayasāra*, which refers to the non-dual presence of absolute awareness. Debendranath's association of the term with "intuition," "self-evidence," etc., obviously amounts to a radical reinterpretation. Śaṅkara uses the term *ātmapratyaya* in his commentary on *Praśna Upaniṣad* V, 1 in the sense of "self-identification" (of the meditator with the object of meditation), i.e., in a sense which has no connection with Debendranath's usage.

87. The works of Th. Reid (1710–1796), the founder of the Scottish School, were edited by W. Hamilton, Edinburgh, 1846. On Debendranath's distinction between "criticized" and "uncriticized" self-evidence, cf. A.K. Cakravarttī, *Maharṣi Devendranātha Ṭhākura*, 572.

88. See A.K. Cakravarttī, *Maharṣi Devendranātha Ṭhākura*, 575.

89. See S.H. Phillips, "Is Sri Aurobindo's Philosophy Vedānta?" *ALB* 48 (1984), 10.

90. See above, ch. 13.

91. See M. Lederle, *Philosophical Trends in Modern Mahārāṣṭra*, Bombay, 1976, 195.

92. Cf. K.H. Potter, *Bibliography of Indian Philosophies*. Delhi, second ed., 1983. 500f.

93. See *Die Welt als Wille und Vorstellung* (The World as Will and Representation), II, ch. 48; in: *Sämtliche Werke*, ed. A. Hübscher, vol.3. Wiesbaden, 1949, 704.

94. Cf. "Fragments of a Confession," in: *The Philosophy of S. Radhakrishnan*, ed. P.A. Schilpp. New York, 1952, 7ff.

95. See F.H. Bradley, *Essays on Truth and Reality*. Oxford, 1914, ch.VI: "On our Knowledge of Immediate Experience;" cf. also T.S. Eliot, *Knowledge and Experience in the Philosophy of F.H. Bradley*. New York, 1964 (originally Diss. Harvard University).

96. S.N. Dasgupta, "Philosophy as Dependent Emergence," in: *Contemporary Indian Philosophy*, ed. S. Radhakrishnan/J.N. Muirhead, London, fourth edition, 1966, esp. 257: "The Absolute of Bradley, which he describes as 'Experience,' is no experience at all, as it is never felt or realized."

97. Cf., for instance, S.N.L. Shrivastava, *Śaṃkara and Bradley*. Delhi, 1968; esp., 164–182: "Immediate Experience."

98. Cf. also J. Watson, *The Interpretation of Religious Experience*. Glasgow, 1912; D.C. Macintosh, *Theology as an Empirical Science*. New York, 1919; J. McMurray, *The Structure of Religious Experience*. New Haven, 1936, 2: "What are the facts which have the same relation to religion that its data have to science?"

99. See F. von Hügel, "Experience and Transcendence," *Dublin Review* 138 (1906), 357–379; cf. also P. Neuner, *Religiöse Erfahrung und geschichtliche Offenbarung*. München, 1977, 310; 314ff.

100. For instance in his notes on *Bhagavadgītā* XVIII, 78.

101. See F. von Hügel, "Der Mystiker und die Kirche: aus Anlass des Sādhu," *Das Hochland* 22/1(1924), 320–330.

102. F. Heiler, *Sādhu Sundar Singh: Ein Apostel des Ostens und Westens*. München, 1924; fourth edition: 1926; abridged trans. by O. Wyon: New York, 1927 (132ff.: "Theologia Experimentalis").

103. R. Gordon Milburn, "Christian Vedantism," *The Indian Interpeter* (Madras) 7/4 (1913), 155.

104. See above, ch. 13, §19.

105. See Vivekananda I, 128ff.; on Yoga as empirical science; specifically 129: "Yet we know we must observe in order to have a real science. . . . The science of Raja-Yoga, in the first place, proposes to give us such a means of observing the internal states." In his work on Rāja Yoga (e.g., 125ff.), Vivekananda also refers to the role of experience in general, and to the possibility of re-experiencing the insights of the ancient religious teachers. The concept of experience is less conspicuous in his other works. On Radhakrishnan, see above, n.26.

106. P.D. Ouspensky, *Tertium Organum*. New York, 1981, 220. The work was first published in Russian in 1912, and in English translation in 1920.

107. J. Woodroffe (alias A. Avalon), *The World as Power* (1921), Madras, third edition, 1966, 4; see also F.S.C. Northrop, *The Meeting of East and West* (1946), New York, 1968, 365ff.; A.de Riencourt, *The Eye of Shiva*, New York, 1981, 90f.

108. Cf. J. Woodroffe (alias A. Avalon) and P.N. Mukhopādhyāya, *Mahāmāyā*. Madras, 1954, 73–83: "Pure Experience"; 84–96: "Perfect Experience."

109. "Maharishi Technology of the Unified Field" (1984; paper published by the "International Association for the Advancement of the Science of Creative Intelligence"), 1; 16.

110. F. Capra, *The Tao of Physics*, revised edition. New York, 1984, 5.

111. The Tao of Physics, 70.

112. The Tao of Physics, 297.

113. The Tao of Physics, 6.

114. See above, §2.

22. "Inclusivism" and "Tolerance" in the Encounter Between India and the West

1. Cf. *Inklusivismus. Eine indische Denkform*, ed. G. Oberhammer. Vienna 1983, 11–28; in addition to Hacker's posthumous article, this volume contains contributions by W. Halbfass, A. Wezler and G. Oberhammer. For biographical information on Hacker, cf. K. Rüping, "Paul Hacker (6.1.1913–18.3.1979)." *WZKS* 25 (1981), 5–16.

2. *Kl. Schr.*, VIII.

3. Cf. R.D. Baird, *Category Formation and the History of Religions*. The Hague, 1971, 151; for other recent discussions on syncretism, eclecticism and related notions, see R. Panikkar, "Some Notes on Syncretism and Eclecticism Related to the Growth of Human Consciousness." *Religious Syncretism in Antiquity. Essays in Conversation with Geo Widengren*, ed. B.A. Pearson, Missoula, 1975, 47–62; R.L. Taylor, "Proposition and Praxis: The Dilemma of Neo-Confucian Syncretism." *PEW* 32 (1982), 187–199.

4. "Religiöse Toleranz und Intoleranz im Hinduism." *Saeculum* 8 (1957), 167–179; also in: *Kl. Schr.*, 376–388; for a later reference to this article, see *Kl. Schr.*, VIII.

5. Cf. *Kl. Schr.*, 377ff.

6. Cf. *Kl. Schr.*, 386: "Die Praxis, das Fremde unterordnend dem Eigenen anzuschliessen, diese eigentümliche Mischung von doktrinärer Toleranz und Intoleranz, scheint eine dem indischen Geiste besonders gemässe Form der religiösen Selbstbehauptung und vielleicht auch der religiösen Werbung zu sein."

7. Cf. *Kl. Schr.*, 387f.

8. "Zur Geschichte und Beurteilung des Hinduismus." *OLZ* 59 (964), 231–245; also in: *Kl. Schr.*, 476–483 (especially 480f.).

9. Cf. *Kl. Schr.*, 482f.; for additional references, and in general for a more complete documentation of Hacker's statements on inclusivism, cf. my contribution in *Inklusivismus* (see above, n.1), especially 29–36; this appendix is based upon this contribution.

10. *Kl. Schr.*, 599f.

11. *Kl. Schr.*, 601.

12. Cf. *Grundlagen indischer Dichtung und indischen Denkens*, ed. K. Rüping. Vienna, 1985, 134f.

13. *Kl. Schr.*, 384: "die interessanteste Erscheinungsform der Duldsamkeit im Hinduismus"; see also 377, on "syncretism."

14. *Kl. Schr.*, 386.

15. Cf. *Kl. Schr.*, VIII.

16. *Inklusivismus*, (see above, n.1), 11.

17. *Inklusivismus*, 28.

18. J.W. Hauer, *Toleranz und Intoleranz in den nichtchristlichen Religionen*. Stuttgart, 1961, 101f.

19. Loc. cit., 90.

20. Cf. G. Mensching, *Tolerance and Truth in Religion*. University of Alabama, 1971, 69 (originally published as: *Toleranz und Wahrheit in der Religion*. Heidelberg, 1955; the translation was made by H.-J. Klimkeit in collaboration with the author and contains several additions).

21. "Toleranz und Fanatismus in Indien." *Jahrbuch der Schopenhauer-Gesellschaft* 41 (1960), 44–51; especially 51.

22. See, for instance, J. Gonda, *Viṣṇuism and Śivaism*. London, 1970, 94f.; R. Hummel, *Indische Mission und neue Frömmigkeit im Westen*. Stuttgart, 1980, 145; 149ff.; 170ff.; R.F. Young, *Resistant Hinduism*. Vienna, 1981, 143; 146ff.

23. See above, ch. 3, §11.

24. Cf. F. Bernier, *Voyages*. Amsterdam, 1699, vol.2, 138. The first edition of the work, which does not generally glorify India, was published in four parts with different titles (*Histoire de la dernière révolution* . . . etc.; Paris, 1671–1672).

25. Cf. H. von Glasenapp, *Kant und die Religionen des Ostens*. Kitzingen, 1954, 32.

26. Loc. cit., 33.

27. See above, ch. 5, §2.

28. *On the Gods of Greece, Italy, and India* (lecture delivered in 1786; first published in: *Asiatic Researches* I, 1789); cf. P.J. Marshall, 245.

29. Cf. P.J. Marshall, 27.

30. See above, ch. 12, §18.

31. Vivekananda, *Complete Works* III, 186ff.

32. Loc. cit., 512.

33. Loc. cit., 251; see also I, 119; and above, ch. 13.

34. G.N. Mallik, *The Philosophy of Vaiṣṇava Religion* I. Lahore 1927, 5; see also 376 (*Gauḍīya Vaiṣṇavism* and "universal religion").

35. *The Hindu View of Life*, 18.

36. Cf. H.P. Blavatsky, *Collected Writings*, vol. 10 (1888/89), Madras, 1964, 161: "It is perhaps necessary, first of all, to say that the assertion that 'Theosophy is not *a* Religion' by no means excludes the fact that 'Theosophy *is* Religion' itself."

37. See above, n.11; cf. also R.N. Minor, "S. Radhakrishnan on the Nature of Hindu 'Tolerance'." *Journal of the American Academy of Religion* 50 (1982), 275–290.

38. Cf., for instance, *Inklusivismus* (see above, n.1), 11f.; *Kl. Schr.*, VIII.

39. But see the thoughtful observations by A. Wezler, "Bemerkungen zum Inklusivismus-Begriff Paul Hackers," *Inklusivismus*, 61–91.

40. See in particular J. Locke's classical *Epistola de tolerantia*. Gouda, 1689 (trans. W. Popple: *A Letter Concerning Toleration*. London, 1689); in its introductory statements, the letter refers to the "*mutua inter Christianos tolerantia*" (ed. R. Klibansky/trans. J.W. Gough. Oxford, 1968, 58). Pioneering suggestions concerning tolerance were made by Nicolaus Cusanus (Nicholas of Cusa) in the fifteenth century; cf. B. Kuhn-Emmerich, *Die Toleranz bei Nikolaus von Cues*. Diss. Bonn, 1968.

41. See M. Freund, *Die Idee der Toleranz im England der Grossen Revolution*. Halle, 1927; H. Kamen, *The Rise of Toleration*. New York, 1967 (reprint 1971); P. King, *Toleration*. London, 1976; *Zur Geschichte der Toleranz und Religionsfreiheit*, ed. H. Lutz. Darmstadt, 1977.

42. *Religionsfreiheit und Toleranz im Altertum* (Rheinisch-Westfälische Ak. Wiss., Vorträge G 233), 16.

43. Cf. J.W. Hauer, *Toleranz und Intoleranz in den nichtchristlichen Religionen*. Stuttgart, 1961, 14.

44. *Cf. Kl. Schr.*, 378ff.; see also A. Wezler, "Zur Proklamation religiös-weltanschaulicher Toleranz bei dem indischen Philosophen Jayantabhaṭṭa." *Saeculum* 27 (1976), 329-347.

45. Cf. L. Dumont, *Homo hierarchicus*. Paris, 1966, 242ff. (English trans.: Chicago, 1980, 191f.).

46. *Cf. Kl. Schr.*, 599f.; also 386; 488; 791; *Inklusivismus*, 12.

47. *Cf. Kl. Schr.*, 529; see also 385f.

48. *Cf. Kl. Schr.*, 481; see also 385: "doctrinal tolerance" and "spiritual monism" ("*Geistmonismus*").

49. Cf. Śaṅkara on *BS* II,2,18; 32 (with Vācaspati's *Bhāmatī*) see also W. Halbfass, *Studies in Kumārila and Śaṅkara*, 90ff.

50. See above, ch. 19, §7f.; the *Sarvasiddhāntasaṃgraha*, which has been ascribed to Śaṅkara, is not authentic.

51. *Inklusivismus* (see above, n.1), 15; see also 12ff.

52. *Chāndogya Upaniṣad* VI,1,2 (following the translation by R.E. Hume); this is then illustrated by the metaphors of clay, etc. On this section and the meaning of *ādeśa*, see P. Thieme, "*ādeśa.*" *Mélanges d'Indianisme à la mémoire de L. Renou*, Paris, 1968, 715-725 (also in his *Kl. Schr.*, 259-267), especially 722f. and 718 (on the *Upaniṣadic* "substitutions," which do not postulate a complete identity between two elements, but only the possibility of "unilaterally" replacing one element with another which has a higher cognitive and soteriological validity. We cannot discuss here how these "substitutions" relate to Hacker's "inclusivism"; nor can we compare the procedure in *Chāndogya* VI with the way in which Thales and other Pre-Socratics "explained" the phenomena of our world by reducing them to water and other fundamental substances.

53. See above, ch. 19; cf. also B.K. Matilal, *The Central Philosophy of Jainism (Anekānta-Vāda)*. Ahmedabad, 1981, 18: "acceptance and inclusion" as characteristics of Jaina thought.

54. *Mahānirvāṇatantra* XIV, 180; *Mahābhārata* XII,237,18f.; see also XII,336,76, where Vedas, Āraṇyakas, Sāṃkhya and Yoga appear as complementary parts (*parasparāṅgāni*) within the higher unity of *Pāñcarātra*.

55. Cf. *Yogavārttika, Nāndiśloka* 4: *gāṅgādyāḥ sarito yadvad abder aṃśeṣu saṃsthitāḥ*.

56. Cf. *Inklusivismus*, 28.

57. See Apuleius, *Metamorphoses* VI, 3ff.; and above, ch. I, §7.

58. See, for instance, the hymn to Zeus by Cleanthes.

59. Cf. *Acta Apostolorum* 17, 23; in general, cf. E. Norden, *Agnostos theos*. Stuttgart, sixth ed., 1974 (first ed.: 1912).

60. See above, ch. 3, n.33.

61. See above, ch. 3, §6ff.; 11f.

62. Cf. *De docta ignorantia* II,12 (ed. R. Klibansky with German trans. by H.G. Senger, Hamburg, 1977,88): "*Intra maximum autem omnia includuntur, quoniam*

ipsum omnia ambit. Hinc in fide Christi Iesu omnis vera fides et in caritate Christi omnis caritas vera includitur . . ."

63. "Christentum und Toleranz. Toleranzfreundliche und toleranzfeindliche Aspekte der christlichen Tradition." *Christentum und Toleranz*. Loccum, 1977 (*Loccumer Protokolle* 7/77), 33–65; ib., 44.

64. Loc. cit., 51; for Buddhist perspectives on "tolerance," cf. Phra Khantipalo, *Tolerance: A Study from Buddhist Sources*. London, 1964.

65. H.A.R. Gibb, *Mohammedanism*. New York, 1962 (first ed.: 1949), 59f.

66. Cf. R. Nath, "On the Authenticity of the Allopaniṣad." *JOI* 26 (1976/77), 238–250.

67. Cf. A. Wezler (see above, n.39), 65ff.

68. See above, n.11; 36f.; also *Kl. Schr.*, 600f.

69. Cf. H.von Glasenapp, *Indienbild*, 163ff.

70. See above, ch. 3, §14f.

71. Cf. E. Sharpe, *Not to Destroy but to Fulfil*. Upsala, 1965, 11f.; H. Kraemer, *Religion and the Christian Faith*. Philadelphia, n.d. (first ed.: London, 1956), 401ff.; 374.

72. See above, ch. 19, §17.

73. Cf. *Kl. Schr.*, 385f.; 481; *Inklusivismus*, 15ff.

74. Cf. *Berl. Schr.*, 185; 190; 192; *Phänomenologie des Geistes*, ed. J. Hoffmeister. Hamburg, sixth ed., 1952, 18. See also above, ch. 6, on Hegel's attitude in general.

23. India and the Comparative Method

1. This appendix is based in part upon my article "India and the Comparative Method," *PEW* 35 (1985), 3–15.

2. See above, chapters 1; 2; 4.

3. See E. Rothacker, "Logik und Systematik der Geisteswissenschaften" (in: *Handbuch der Philosophie*). Munich, 1926, 91–106.

4. See above, ch. 5. Humboldt's *Plan einer vergleichenden Anthropologie* appeared in 1795.

5. *Chips from a German Workshop*, vol. 4. London, 1895, 343.

6. Cf. *Introduction to the Science of Religion*. London, 1873, 283–334.

7. Cf. *Oupnek'hat*. Strasbourg, 1801–1802, vol. 1, 711–724.

8. A new and revised edition of the work was published in 1822.

9. Cf. L. Geldsetzer, *Die Philosophie der Philosophiegeschichte im 19. Jahrhundert*. Meisenheim am Glan, 1968, 100.

10. Cf. *The Theological and Miscellaneous Works of Joseph Priestley*, ed. J.T. Rutt. London, 1817–1831, vol. 17, 132.

11. Cf. H. von Glasenapp, *Indienbild*, 163ff.

12. While there is also considerable interest in Japan (see, for example, the works of H. Nakamura and M. Saigusa), "comparative philosophy" plays a less conspicuous role in Europe. A Japanese "Society for the Comparative Study of Religions" (*Hikaku Shūkyō Kenkyū-kai*) was founded in 1896.

13. There are also numerous "comparisons" between traditional Indian philosophy and modern science; see, for example, H.C. Barthvāla, *Tattvavijñāna-bhāratīya tattvajñāna aur ādhunika vijñāna, tulanātmaka adhyayana*. New Delhi, 1977. *Upamāna* in the traditional sense of a "means of knowledge" (*pramāṇa*) which is accepted in somewhat different meanings in Nyāya and Mīmāṃsa and often translated as "comparison," has, of course, nothing to do with comparative research in the modern sense.

14. On Ketkar, see M. Lederle, *Philosophical Trends in Modern Mahārāṣṭra*. Bombay, 1976, 324ff.; also D.N. Gokhale, *Do. Ketakara: jñānakośakāra śrīdhara vyaṃkateśa ketakara yaṃce caritra*. Bombay, 1959, 34; in Marathi, the expression "comparative theology and philosophy" is rendered as *taulanika daivataśāstra aṇi tattvajñāna*.

15. See specifically the introduction, Vf. The subtitle of the work is: *With an Examination of the Mahabharata Legend about Narada's Pilgrimage to Svetadvipa and an Introduction on the Historico-Comparative Method.*

16. A reprint was published in 1958 (Delhi). B.K. Sarkar, an important Indian scholar who was inspired by Seal, also referred to the connection of the "comparative" sciences with Indian studies; cf. *Creative India*. Lahore, 1937, 121ff.

17. See above, chapters 8; 16.

18. *Ph. d. W.* I, 175; see also above, ch. 6.

19. G.W.F. Hegel, *Phänomenologie des Geistes*, ed. J. Hoffmeister. Hamburg, 1952, 19.

20. G.W.F. Hegel, *Wissenschaft der Logik*, vol. 2, ed. G. Lasson. Leipzig, 1951, 36f.

21. See above, chapters 7; 8.

22. See É. Durkheim, *La science sociale et l'action*, ed. J.-C. Filloux. Paris, 1970, 156f.

23. *La philosophie comparée* is dedicated to Lévy-Bruhl.

24. *La philosophie comparée*, 3.

25. *Comparative Philosophy*, 25 (*La philosophie comparée*, 7).

26. *La philosophie comparée*, 2.

27. *La philosophie comparée*, 11 (*Comparative Philosophy*, 29).

28. *La philosophie comparée*, 32ff. (*Comparative Philosophy*, 14ff).

29. *La philosophie comparée*, 32 (*Comparative Philosophy*, 50).

30. *La philosophie comparée*, 45 (*Comparative Philosophy*, 62).

31. *Histoire comparée des systèmes de philosophie*, vol. 1, second ed., Paris, 1822, 54 (quoting the letter of Leibniz to Remond, August 26, 1714: "*perennis quaedam*

philosophia"). For a "comparative history of philosophy" which tries to include Asia, see also A. Dempf, *Selbstkritik der Philosophie*. Vienna, 1947.

32. See G.H. Forbes, *Positivism in Bengal*. Calcutta, 1975.

33. Cf. *Hist. Wb. Phil.*, art. "Geisteswissenschaften."

34. See *Einleitung in die Geisteswissenschaften*, ed. B. Groethuysen. Stuttgart/Göttingen, 1962 (*Gesammelte Schriften*, vol. 1), 105ff.

35. See *Der Aufbau der geschichtlichen Welt in den Geisteswissenschaften*, ed. B. Groethuysen. Stuttgart/Göttingen, 1973 (*Gesammelte Schriften*, vol. 7), 99.

36. See "Über die vergleichende Psychologie" (1895/96). *Die geistige Welt* I, ed. G. Misch. Stuttgart/Göttingen, 1961 (*Gesammelte Schriften*, vol. 5), 241f.

37. Cf. *Briefwechsel zwischen W. Dilthey und dem Grafen P. Yorck v. Wartenburg*, 1877-1897. Halle, 1923, 193; 202.

38. Cf. P. Yorck v. Wartenburg, *Bewusstseinsstellung und Geschichte*, ed. I. Fetscher. Tübingen, 1956, 57ff.

39. Cf. R. Schwab, *The Oriental Renaissance*, 306.

40. W. Dilthey, "Das Wesen der Philosophie" (1907). *Die geistige Welt* I, ed. G. Misch. Stuttgart/Göttingen, 1961 (*Gesammelte Schriften* vol. 5), 380.

41. See, for instance, *Gesammelte Schriften*, vol. 5, 388f. (on Vedānta); 50 (criticism of P. Deussen for separating "Indian speculation" from the "religious process"); vol. 8, 208 (references to Vedānta); 215 (references to India and China).

42. Misch criticizes "historical positivism" and wants to regain the "unity of philosophy" as a "dynamic unity" (*Der Weg in die Philosophie*. Munich, second ed., 1950, 65;76).

43. Schlechta III, 639 (Colli/Montinari XIII, 167).

44. Cf. O. Spengler, *Der Untergang des Abendlandes*. Munich, 1969, 34; 69f.

45. See above, Appendix II.

46. P.T. Raju, *Introduction to Comparative Philosophy*. Carbondale, Ill., second ed., 1970, 3.

47. Cf. on this question R. Panikkar, "Aporias in the Comparative Philosophy of Religion." *Man and World* 13 (1980), 357-383; especially 357: "comparative philosophy" as "inherently self-contradictory."

24. In Lieu of a Summary and Conclusion: Europe, India, and the "Europeanization of the Earth"

1. This appendix is based upon a presentation prepared for a meeting held in the Papal Summer Residence at Castel Gandolfo (August 1987). It tries to provide a thematic thread through the chapters of *India and Europe*, and it borrows freely and often literally from the book itself.

2. See above, ch. 10, §8.

3. *India and the West*, 163 (as quoted above, ch. 14, §19).

4. See above, ch. 10, §8ff.

5. J.L. Mehta, *Martin Heidegger: The Way and the Vision*. Honolulu, 1976 (first ed.: Benares, 1967), 466.

Index

The index lists proper names, as well as a selection of important terms, from the text of the book. With the exception of important anonymous works, titles of works are usually not listed. Names and concepts from the notes (pp. 450–579) are indexed only if they are of special thematic relevance and go beyond the information provided by the text. Names which appear in bibliographical references have been omitted.

In general, the index tries to supplement the table of contents. Entries do not necessarily appear in the form in which they appear in the text. In a number of cases, variant spellings have been added in parentheses. Some terminological entries refer to exemplary usages only. Subheadings have been generally avoided. All references are page references. David Purpur deserves special recognition for his contribution to this index.